LA
CAPITAL

JONATHAN KANDELL

LA CAPITAL

THE BIOGRAPHY OF MEXICO CITY

AN OWL BOOK

HENRY HOLT AND COMPANY · NEW YORK

Published by Henry Holt and Company, Inc.,
115 West 18th Street, New York, New York 10011.
Published in Canada by Fitzhenry & Whiteside Limited,
195 Allstate Parkway, Markham, Ontario L3R 4T8.

Library of Congress Cataloging-in-Publication Data
Kandell, Jonathan.
La capital : the biography of Mexico City / Jonathan Kandell — 1st Owl bk. ed.
p. cm.
Includes bibliographical references.
ISBN 0-8050-1267-2 (pbk.)
1. Mexico City (Mexico)—History. I. Title.
F1386.3.K36 1989
972'.53—dc20 89-38908
CIP

Henry Holt books are available at special discounts
for bulk purchases for sales promotions, premiums,
fund-raising, or educational use. Special editions
or book excerpts can also be created to specification.

For details contact:

Special Sales Director
Henry Holt and Company, Inc.
115 West 18th Street
New York, New York 10011

First published in hardcover by Random House, Inc., in 1988
First Owl Book Edition—1990
Design by Debbie Glasserman
Printed in the United States of America
1   3   5   7   9   10   8   6   4   2

Grateful acknowledgment is made to the following for
permission to reprint previously published material:

Encounter Limited: Eight lines from a poem translated by
Robert Graves, which appeared in *Encounter #3*, December 1953.
Farrar, Straus & Giroux, Inc.: Excerpts from *The
Discovery and Conquest of Mexico* by Bernal Díaz del
Castillo, translated by A. P. Maudslay. Copyright © 1956 by
Farrar, Straus and Cudahy, now Farrar, Straus & Giroux,
Inc. Reprinted by permission of Farrar, Straus & Giroux,
Inc., and Routledge & Kegan Paul.
The University of California Press: Excerpts from "The
Letters of Don Carlos de Siguenza y Góngora to Admiral Pez
Recounting the Incidents of the Corn Riot in Mexico City,
June 8, 1692" from *Don Carlos de Siguenza y Góngora: A
Mexican Savant of the Seventeenth Century*, translated by
Irving A. Leonard, 1979.
Yale University Press, London: Excerpts from *Hernán
Cortés: Letters from Mexico*, translated by A. R. Pagen, 1986.

To my parents,
Jack and Sara

ACKNOWLEDGMENTS

I owe my greatest debt for this book to the staff and resources of the New York Public Library, where I spent most of four years taking advantage of the writing and research facilities of the Frederick Lewis Allen Memorial Room.

In Mexico City, Leonor Ortiz Monasterio, director of the Archivo General de la Nación, generously guided and advised me in best making use of the vast material contained in the archives. She was also invaluable in offering her own insights as a historian and directing me to other Mexican scholars. I wish also to express my gratitude to members of other academic centers in Mexico, particularly Gustavo Garza and Martha Schteingart at the Colegio de México, Hector Castillo Berthier at the Universidad Nacional Autónoma de México, and Enrique Florescano, director of the Instituto Nacional de Antropología e Historia. Among politicians and government officials, Carlos Hank González, the former mayor of Mexico City and governor of the state of Mexico, deserves singular mention. With grace, humor, and intelligence, he outlined the daunting tasks involved in governing the world's largest city.

When I first embarked on this project, Norman Gall, friend and journalist, urged me to broaden its scope as much as possible—and I am deeply grateful for that advice. In Paris, the late Fernand Braudel allotted me priceless hours to explain some very basic methods of historical research.

Several friends read chapters of the manuscript and offered valuable comment: thank you, Rudolph Rauch, Elio Gaspari, Philippe Bourgois, Oscar González. And finally, I had the very good fortune of working with a formidable editor, Robert Loomis, whose innumerable suggestions and criticism were invariably on target.

CONTENTS

LA
CAPITAL

PROLOGUE

The inspiration for this book has been my long relationship with Mexico City. As the son of American expatriates, I grew up there during the 1950s when it was still a city of very human proportions. I was raised in San Angel, then a semiurban, semirustic district on the southwestern edge of the metropolis. From my bedroom window every morning, my gaze easily encompassed the city landscape: the red-tiled roofs of Spanish colonial-style houses, the fields where cattle and sheep grazed amid corn patches, and beyond, in the crystal-clear horizon, the purple and dun-colored mountains dominated by the snow-crowned volcanoes of Popocatépetl and Iztaccíhuatl.

In those days, Mexico City displayed a gracefully simple geography that linked it to centuries past. The easily identifiable epicenter of the metropolis was the Plaza de la Constitución, better known as the Zócalo. Here, on top of the demolished palaces and temples of the ancient Aztec city, the Spanish conquistadores imposed a political-religious citadel of their own. On the north side of the giant plaza, almost straddling the foundations of the largest Aztec pyramid, they erected the hulking Cathedral with its twin towers. The rest of the Zócalo was bordered by the viceroy's (later the presidential) palace, the municipal council, and the balconied town houses of the colonial aristocracy. Stores and offices, in arcaded buildings only two or three stories high, lined the grid of narrow streets leading away from the Zócalo. Just southeast of the plaza lay the great wholesale marketplace, La Merced, with its mounds of grains, vegetables, fruits, and meats trucked in from the provinces.

The neighborhoods or barrios, including my own, replicated the same pattern on a smaller scale. The focal point of each barrio was a grassy, tree-shaded square, bounded by church, municipal buildings, and bulky, whitewashed, upper-class houses. A block away, the make-shift stands of an outdoor market, with their patchwork quilt of gray-and-white awnings, beckoned clients as they emerged from the banks, offices, and shops. These were middle-class neighborhoods of sturdy stone and brick homes, their front gardens and back patios enclosed and protected by high walls topped with barbed wire and jagged glass imbedded in cement. The sounds of these barrios were the barking of dogs behind those walls, the peeling of church bells, and the distinctive music of the various tradespeople: the arpeggio of the knife sharpener's harmonica; the tinkle of the ice-cream vendor's cart as it jolted over cobblestoned streets; the high note–low note of the nightwatchman's whistle.

The neat urban symmetry ended abruptly on the periphery of the middle-class neighborhoods. Beyond, berthed like blackened ships on a flat sea of dusty plains, were the factories, producing uncomplicated wares—steel, cement, glass, paper, textiles, beer, and processed foods. There were not many manufacturing plants in those days, and their gray smoke rose in isolated plumes that only accentuated the azure of the skies. And then on the outskirts of the city, beyond the factories, where asphalt roads shriveled into dirt streets without names, lived the poor.

On weekend hikes to the wooded hills, my friends and I passed their hovels. They were made from the unlikeliest debris: sticks and corn-stalks, adobe and cardboard, with roofs of corrugated tin, plastic sheets, and tarpaper weighted down by loose bricks and stones. Rows of liter-size oil cans sprouting herbs and flowers were the only decorative touch. The stench of human excrement wafted in the air. Goats, chickens, and pigs wandered between the shacks, and scavenged among the garbage heaped into ditches and down the steep sides of a ravine. Children lined up at communal faucets to collect water in paint buckets which they hoisted precariously on their tiny shoulders. Above the angry bark of mangy, mottled dogs, we could make out the constant patter of women slapping the corn dough into tortillas.

During the week, the men of the shantytown would cram into buses that listed heavily starboard under the weight of passengers clinging by one foot and hand to the vehicles' doors. Fares were passed by relays to the morose driver peering through a windshield that was almost completely obscured by lace curtains, religious statuary, and plastic skeletons dancing from the rear-view mirror. At each stop, the bodies would disentangle and then quickly entwine again as passengers descended and others squeezed aboard. The factories were the closest destinations, but most riders stayed on the bus for the duration—the downtown district. They were the messengers and sweepers for the business offices and stores, or the construction workers, or most likely, the porters. In those days when delivery vehicles were in short supply, swarms of small men trotted down the streets with almost unbearably heavy loads of bricks, textiles, and store merchandise. Their backs were bent to a parallel plane above the sidewalks, their faces fixed in a sweaty grimace, and their downcast eyes unable to search out more than a few feet ahead.

The women of the poor arrived downtown by midmorning. Some were ambulant vendors of candies, cakes, and wobbly colored gelatins. Others, with barefoot infants in tow, staked out street corners, wrapped their heads in black-gray shawls, and stretched out a hand to beg for coins. Even as children, we learned to stare past them, to filter out their wails, to walk around them as if they were fire hydrants or lampposts.

Cars were no novelty in Mexico City during the 1950s, but traffic was light enough so that middle-class people could make their way home for a three-hour lunch break. It was a practice rooted in the centuries'-old tradition of the siesta. The midafternoon heat supposedly required a refreshing nap after a leisurely lunch, the main meal of the day. My father, I recall, was already home from the office, halfway through his afternoon break, when the school bus deposited my brothers and me at our doorstep.

The poor timed their forays into the middle-class barrios at about four every afternoon, just as the long lunch break and siesta were ending. They rang the doorbell, and waited patiently behind the front garden gates for a maid or my mother to bring out the leftovers from the meal. From their straw baskets, the beggar women withdrew an assortment of containers: empty glass jars for the lukewarm leftover soup; tin cans for scraps of meat and lumpy rice; gingham cloths to wrap the half-stale buns and cold tortillas. They sat on the grassy sidewalks and shared the food silently with their kids, then packed what remained and headed back to their shanties.

I always heard the poor referred to as *"indios"* or *"inditos,"* even if many were *"mestizos"* (mixed bloods). *"Indio"* was almost inevitably a term of derision. *"Pareces indio"*—"You're like an Indian"—could mean you were acting uncouth, or being stupid, or had let the sun tan your skin to an undesirably ocher complexion. And yet at school and at home, we—the foreigners, the descendants of Europeans, or the lighter-skinned mestizos—were taught that this was their city and they were the great protagonists of its history.

Mexican history, which was a required course all through elementary school, essentially highlighted three great events: the fall of the Aztec empire to the Spanish conquistadores; the Independence wars that liberated the country from colonial rule and sent the Spaniards packing; and the Revolution of 1910–20, which was supposed to have been fought on behalf of the landless poor. We spent hours memorizing the tongue-twisting names of Aztec rulers: Motecuhzoma,* Cuitláhuac, and Cuauhtémoc. On visits to the Anthropological Museum, our teachers showed us plaster models of what Mexico City looked like before the Spanish Conquest—an Aztec Venice greater than any European city of that era.

I also encountered Mexican history almost every day outside the classroom. My brothers and I scavenged for ancient Indian arrowheads, artifacts, and small idols in the open meadows only a few blocks from home. Up the street, Diego Rivera, the painter and muralist, had his studio, where we were often invited to view his enormous canvases depicting scenes of Mexico City during the Revolution. Rivera would enthrall us with stories of Zapata's Indian peasant troops wandering through the neighborhood, knocking on doors to ask—broad sombrero in hand, Springfield rifle hidden under serape—for a taco and beans.

But it was hard to relate those Indians—Aztec warriors and artisans, revolutionaries and artist's models—to the ones I saw every day. In history, they were glorified. In life, they were simple survivors, the folkloric supporting cast of a city that claimed to be transforming itself into a modern metropolis without shedding its traditional charms.

When I left Mexico in the 1960s to study in the United States, it was still a manageable city. But urban sprawl was accelerating. The factories, once confined to the northern and southern periphery, now surrounded the metropolis on all sides. My parents moved to Ciudad Satélite, an American-style northwestern suburb which in a decade grew from nothing to a community of more than one million inhabitants—and then two million by the early 1980s. My old San Angel barrio was unrecognizable. Colonial houses were overwhelmed by apartment towers, cobblestone streets largely paved over, neighborhood

---

* The conquistadores referred to the Aztec king as "Montezuma," presumably because they could not properly pronounce his name. Various other spellings appear in historical texts. Throughout the book, I have used "Motecuhzoma" because it is the spelling most frequently used by Indian informants in the earliest Spanish missionary accounts of the Aztec era.

shops replaced by huge malls. The nearby grazing lands were covered with new residential complexes. Blue skies were a thing of the past as a heavy smog reduced the mountains to hazy gray silhouettes, if they were visible at all. The church bells, dog barks, and peddlers' music were drowned out by the constant roar of traffic along newly broadened avenues and the insistent honking of flustered drivers. The long lunch break and siesta back home were abandoned because traveling to and from work had become such a time-consuming odyssey.

I have returned to Mexico City many times since I moved away. Years ago, I stopped searching for physical traces of the barrios where I lived, played, and wandered through. No longer do I ask what happened to the house with the crenellated stone facade or the cypress with a trunk so thick that it took eight children linking outstretched arms to encircle. No use viewing the city in microcosm. I seem able to bring it into focus only through the widest angle lens.

For today, Mexico City is the largest urban center the world has ever known. It is a megalopolis of twenty million people, about six times the population of the city in my early childhood. In less than a generation, it will inexorably have more than thirty million inhabitants—four times as many people as live in New York. By what logic has it grown so huge in so short a space of time? And is it truly possible to conceive of a city capable of feeding, housing, transporting, and employing thirty million inhabitants by the dawn of the twenty-first century?

Sprawling across a 7,500-foot-high valley surrounded in every direction by even taller mountains, Mexico City is poorly endowed as the industrial and commercial hub of a nation. The closest seaports lie hundreds of miles away, at the end of curving, tobogganing mountain roads. Unable to supply its hydraulic needs, the city must pump hundreds of millions of gallons of water every day from distant, lower-lying terrains. Once used, the darkened waters—the "black waters," as the liquid industrial wastes and human sewage are known—must be pumped back out of the city because its valley has no natural drainage. Like water, the sources of energy lie far away from the capital, mostly in rich oil deposits on the eastern coasts of Mexico. The growth of industry and, especially, the huge crush of new inhabitants have wiped out much of the valley's farmland. So foodstuffs are trucked into the city by a perpetual caravan of vehicles chugging up the broad, winding highways from agrarian zones that are increasingly further removed from the capital.

Elsewhere in the world, cities in this century have grown mainly in vertical fashion, with office skyscrapers and high-rise apartments. In Mexico City, expansion has been mostly horizontal. For decades, the soft, watery foundation beneath the city and the constant danger of earthquakes discouraged construction of tall buildings. Breakthroughs in engineering technology have largely overcome these obstacles, and buildings of thirty stories and more are common enough. But the city continues its unchecked horizontal sprawl because the spectacular demographic explosion makes a mockery of government plans for low-income, high-rise housing projects. The elevated birthrate and rural migration translate into two thousand additional inhabitants a day—enough to populate a city the size of San Francisco every year. Some seven million people began life in the capital as squatters. They continue to invade vacant industrial parks, parched cornfields, public land, private land, anybody's land. Overnight, they set up their tents, then cardboard and tarpaper shacks, and eventually, more solid dwellings of wood and cinder block. Fusing into one another, the gray-and-white box-shaped houses run down the eroded mountainsides and carpet the arid plains. In the process, metropolitan Mexico City swells, doubling its surface area over the last three decades. And still the Mexican capital bursts past new boundaries, swallowing mountainous wasteland, grinding up meadows and farm plots, engulfing sleepy villages.

Size alone qualifies Mexico City as a compelling subject of study. Surely, we can find here a vision of what the twenty-first century has in store for the megacities emerging in the Third World. Since I am a journalist by training, I had initially assumed that this book would focus mostly on the present era. But in the end, my writing was shaped far more by my childhood curiosity about Mexican history. I have no regrets about surrendering to this impulse. I discovered a history that matches the city's monumentality. It is a tumultuous past that encompasses all the stages of urban development more clearly than any other community on earth. For Mexico City can trace its existence continuously from Paleolithic site to cradle of ancient civilization, and from colonial stronghold to contemporary megalopolis.

ONE

THE VALLEY
AND ITS FIRST
INHABITANTS

About fifty million years ago, Mexico had not yet assumed its familiar mountainous horn shape, tapering and curling at its southern reaches. Central Mexico was still submerged under a sea that linked the Atlantic and Pacific oceans. Dinosaurs reigned over the humid, tropical forests and plains that blanketed the land north and south of this broad, watery isthmus, while giant, armor-plated fish ruled the hot, turbulent sea and oceans. It was such an incomprehensively distant past that if we used a meter-stick to represent the full fifty million years, the birth of the earliest humanlike beings in the world would be marked four centimeters from the end of our measuring rod. The first traces of people in Mexico, itself, would merit a notch set only 1/20th of a centimeter from the very end of our stick—a measurement unit so small that we would need a magnifying glass to perceive it.

But it was in these prehistoric times fifty million years ago that a series of extremely slow, yet violent geological phenomena began to shape the destiny of what was to become the Valley of Mexico and of its future inhabitants. An era of extraordinary volcanic activity was unleashed throughout the world, moving continents apart, bringing other landmasses together, and shaking the depths of the oceans. Off the Pacific coast of Mexico, with an epicenter not far from the present location of Acapulco, the ocean floor collapsed into an undulating northwest-to-southeast trench a thousand miles long. The sinking of the ocean floor along this lengthy axis created enormous pressures within the earth's crust. To the east of the new Pacific trench, the basalt rock layer beneath the sea covering central Mexico began to rupture. Wherever the fractures appeared, hot, liquid rock seeped out.

As soon as it made contact with the sea, the molten basalt exploded, sending upward furious profusions of bubbles that vaporized when they reached the water's surface. There was no appearance of a mountainous landmass thrusting out of the sea. Instead, for millions of years, the thick clouds of steam intermittently hissing out of the water were the only signs of dramatic geological change deep beneath the surface.

Slowly, ever so slowly even in geological time, the liquid rock oozing out of the many fissures in the sea floor accumulated in hardened mounds, which eventually ruptured and burst. The cycle of explosion and accumulation repeated itself innumerable times until, about forty million years ago, the mounds building upon the sea floor raised themselves above the water's surface. And still the explosions continued. The sea across central Mexico gave way to a thick volcanic range that tapered out as it reached the Pacific and Caribbean coasts. At the very center of these volcanic formations, the land rose highest. Some peaks crested at over 12,000 feet, and between them were created basins and plateaus.

The highest and most extensive of these plateaus became the Valley of Mexico. It was shaped in several volcanic phases. The earliest phase seems to have occurred on the northern boundary of the valley, where the sides of heavily eroded, irregularly shaped hills contain lava deposits dating back more than thirty million years. Mountains then vaulted upward, enclosing the valley on its western and eastern peripheries. And lastly, a string of volcanoes towering above the other mountain ranges erupted to the south, completing the encirclement about two million years ago. The plateau that was thus created has a somewhat oval shape, extending 68 miles north to south, and about 50 miles east to west, with a total surface of about 2,700 square miles—roughly eight times the area of New York City's five boroughs.

Although the present contours of this plateau, the Valley of Mexico, were achieved so long ago, it would be a mistake to assume that they have been permanently set in geological time. Certainly, the Aztecs and the tribes that preceded them did not believe their valley had attained physical stability. Their religion was filled with prophecies that the world would be torn asunder by cataclysmic earthquakes. The Spanish conquistadores witnessed volcanic activity in the crater of Popocatépetl, today a serene, cone-shaped, snowy peak. In 1985, thousands of Mexico City residents perished and hundreds of buildings were destroyed by a giant quake. And dozens of times every year, the capital's inhabitants experience the stomach-churning sensation of smaller tremors that cause no damage but remind the populace that the earth beneath their feet is unsettlingly alive.

The Valley of Mexico does not have uniform characteristics. It is marked throughout by ancient mountains, standing singly or in clusters, that have been bent, folded, crumpled, and worn down into smaller hills by lava flows, glaciers, and erosion over millions of years. The valley's altitude varies between 6,800 and 7,900 feet. Volcanic activity, glaciation, and erosion have created an assortment of soils. Even the climate is not constant throughout the valley, with a low annual average rainfall of less than 20 inches in the arid northeastern plains to more than 31 inches in the foothills of the southwestern mountains. Scientists have identified nine ecological zones in the Valley of Mexico, which differ slightly or markedly from each other according to soil, altitude, temperature, and wetness.[1] And finally, the Valley of Mexico is technically not a valley at all. So effectively have the mountains sealed it off that natural drainage for its waters—a condition that defines valleys—does not exist. It would be more correct to call it a closed hydrographic basin. But through the ages, the name Valley of Mexico has stuck.

The lack of natural drainage and the multiplicity of ecological zones proved to be the two most significant phenomena in the valley's eventual emergence as a center of human settlement. The first led to the formation of a lake system fed by rain and underground springs whose waters were unable to escape from the basin. The second created a series of different habitats where a large variety of plant and animal life was able to flourish within a relatively small area.

The earliest traces of human beings in the New World appear thirty thousand years ago, much later than on any other continent. Humans had already existed over one million years in Africa, at least 500,000 years in Asia, and 300,000 years in Europe. More than 75,000 years ago, modern *Homo sapiens* replaced the Neanderthals and the other earlier human types who met extinction in the evolutionary process. So, the men and women who first arrived in the New World were undoubtedly *Homo sapiens*. They crossed from Siberia into the Americas over the Bering Strait, where a land bridge rose when the Ice Ages caused the northern ocean to shrink. The various physiognomies of Native American people today indicate that several different racial strains were represented in the waves of human migration that continued to cross the Bering Strait over some twenty thousand years, until the glaciers of the last Ice Age melted and separated Siberia from

North America. During different eras, the migrants were Mongoloids, Eurasians, and a copper-skinned race that no longer survives in the Old World. All these people had one thing in common: they were big-game hunters, searching for mammals that had trekked into the New World over the Bering Strait long before them. During their first twenty thousand years in the Americas, these inhabitants remained hunters and gatherers of wild plants as they fanned out southward in search of game. They lived in bands of twenty to fifty people, clashing with adversaries in an attempt to stake out their shifting hunting territories or to steal women to replenish their mating stock.

Groups of these nomads entered the Valley of Mexico at least fifteen thousand years ago, judging from the remains of a mammoth found in a northern section of the valley. The bones of this extinct, hairy, elephantlike brute showed the unmistakable scrape marks of stone implements, particularly near the joints, indicating the work of rather skilled butchers. The valley must have delighted its first human discoverers. Its climate was temperate, rarely dropping to freezing temperatures or reaching tropical heat, and a dense foliage on the mountainsides raised humidity above today's semiarid levels. The bottom of the valley was covered by extensive lakes—some saline, others fresh—which permanently solved the water problem for the inhabitants and drew hordes of animals to their shores. Besides the birds, fish, wild pigs, wolves, foxes, rabbits, and deer that are still found today elsewhere in Mexico in dwindling numbers, the prehistoric valley also harbored animal species that later would become extinct: mammoths, mastodons, giant sloths, cameloids, and a type of horse. And from the point of view of the early hunters, the beauty of it all was that the high mountains virtually trapped this abundant prey in the relatively small confines of the valley. No longer was it necessary to travel vast distances over mountains and dry plains with little certainty of even encountering elusive game. In the valley, the animals were there for the taking. An errant spear, a poorly aimed rock, an inept ambush no longer meant hunger. The beasts that scampered away did not get far. The hunters had only to stake out a corner of the lengthy lakesides and wait for the animals to come for water. The chief concern of the early inhabitants of the Valley of Mexico must have been protecting their oasis from other nomadic hunting bands who arrived wave after wave, inexorably drawn by the basin's riches.

Until ten thousand years ago, the hunting life prevailed not only in the Valley of Mexico but everywhere on earth. Then, a combination of climatological changes, overpredation of large game, and growing human populations began to disrupt the lives of prehistoric people throughout the world. With the end of the last Ice Age, many large mammals—mastodons, mammoths, giant ground sloths—disappeared. The receding glaciers and warmer weather created a different habitat that permitted new flora to replace the plants which were the staple of these animals' diets. Forests rose where grasslands had once proliferated. The large-bodied animals were also doomed by the proficiency of Paleolithic hunters, whose numbers appear to have increased sharply twelve to fifteen thousand years ago, just as the last Ice Age was melting away.

Conditions were created for a transition to a sedentary agricultural existence. This changeover took place at a far earlier date in the Old World than in the Americas, but nowhere did it occur quickly. It was neither stupidity nor lack of perception that accounted for the fact that prehistoric people were slow to take up farming. They had a keen enough sense of observation to have known that seeds sprouted into plants, some of them quite edible and nourishing. But Paleolithic people clung to their hunting existence as long as possible because where game was plentiful, a hunter's life was easier than farming. The hunt could be accomplished in two or three hours a day, about half the time required to work primitive agricultural plots, and with considerably less expenditure of energy.

Even when game dwindled, people took several millennia to evolve into full-fledged farmers. The earliest evidence of an intermediate era has been uncovered in southwestern Asia, around the hills of Turkey and Syria.[2] About twelve thousand years ago, small villages arose where inhabitants collected the grains of wild plants. Precursors of modern wheat, barley, and rye grew in large patches among these Middle Eastern hills and valleys. There must have been enough of these wild plants to enable the inhabitants to store grain in baskets or other containers for the long months between harvests. These primitive grain bins—too large and heavy to carry on nomadic hunting-and-gathering treks—helped spur permanent settlements. The other important basis of these early villages was the existence of herds of animals that were drawn to the wild grain patches. These animals were predecessors of domesticated livestock: sheep, goats, cattle, horses. At first, the inhabitants trapped and killed the animals when they strayed too close to the villages. Eventually, animals were tamed and bred. Wild grains were replaced with varieties deliberately selected, planted, and tended in true farming fashion.

It was at this point, around 8000 B.C. in the Middle East, that the world's real agricultural revolution finally occurred. It entailed the almost simultaneous domestication of plants and animals. Grain alone was not enough of an incentive to make people forsake their heavy reliance on meat, no matter how arduous the hunting life had become. The new herds made the transition to full-time farming more palatable. Although meat declined as a proportion of the diet, livestock was able to supply palatable quantities of animal protein. Livestock also served as draft animals in the fields, as beasts of burden, and sources of fertilizer. The agrarian life spread either through slow cultural diffusion or by independent discovery to Mesopotamia, the Nile Valley, northern India, and China.

The rise of urban civilization is inextricably linked to the establishment of a sedentary agricultural existence. Regular harvests made it possible for people to gather in ever larger communities. The storage of grain and the existence of livestock provided stable food supplies on a year-round basis. Agriculture, particularly after the advent of irrigation, freed large numbers of people from food production. The relatively egalitarian, nomadic hunting bands—in which only a few individuals stood apart as chieftains or shamans—were replaced by more socially stratified societies of political aristocrats, priests, warriors, merchants, artisans, construction workers, farmers, and shepherds. Several thousand years before the Christian era, true cities appeared in Mesopotamia and then Egypt, and later in India and China.

But what about the New World and the Valley of Mexico in particular? Why was the transition toward full-time agriculture here so different and so much slower than in the Old World? Why did urban civilization arise here thousands of years after cities were created in Asia, North Africa, and even Europe? The ultimate answers to these critical questions are bound up with the failure of prehistoric Americans to develop animal husbandry.

As in the Old World, the glaciers that receded northward across the Americas at the end of the Ice Age ten thousand years ago spelled the extinction of many large mammals. The biggest animals, including bison, moose, and bear, were able to survive only in the forests and plains far to the north of Mexico. In and around the Valley of Mexico, zealous hunting wiped out the horses, cameloids, and prehistoric oxen that might have served as domesticated livestock for future farmers. Perhaps these animals never existed here in as large numbers as in the Old World. Or perhaps they had long before evolved into species too wild to have been domesticated anyway. But the fact remains that their absence postponed the farming revolution in Mexico for many, many years.

The strains on hunting life were already in evidence around the Valley of Mexico about nine thousand years ago. At sites dating back to that era, the bones of small mammals, birds, and reptiles are far more abundant than larger species like deer, peccaries, and bison. The inhabitants undoubtedly had to shift from the pursuit of big game to the trapping of smaller animals. In the Tehuacán region southeast of the Valley of Mexico, sites that are between 6,500 and 8,000 years old indicate that wild game was not the only source of animal protein: charred human bones scraped of their flesh and skulls roasted apparently to cook the brains are found in ceremonial burials and in common refuse heaps.[3]

As in the Old World, the transition away from big-game hunting in Mexico was marked by an increased emphasis on the gathering of wild plants and fruit. Maize, that most essential of New World crops, was harvested as a wild grass, just as the pre-agricultural Middle Easterners had done with their primitive grain plants. Traces of the first domesticated varieties of maize have been found in the Tehuácan region and date back almost six thousand years—not much later than the appearance of true agriculture in parts of the Old World. By 3000 B.C., corn was being cultivated in the Valley of Mexico itself. But lacking domesticated livestock as a reliable source of meat, the ancient Mexicans continued to postpone the fateful choice between hunting and farming as long as possible. The few small villages that appeared were occupied only part of the year. Most inhabitants of the Valley of Mexico maintained a seminomadic existence: May through October was devoted to the planting and harvest; hunting was carried out during the dry season between November and February; wild plants and fruit were gathered between March and May; and fishing in the lakes took place throughout the year. What made this seminomadic life possible was the existence of the variety of ecological zones in and around the Valley of Mexico. A multiplicity of edible animals and plants flourished within an accessible radius.

But it must have been a precarious way of life. The inhabitants—whether temporarily ensconced in their villages or wandering through the valley—probably lived in groups of less than one hundred people just like their ancestors, the big-game hunters. They must have fought hard and often to exclude other bands from their valley. Population was sparse, probably less than five thousand people for the whole valley.

And it must have been kept down to this level by some form of infanticide: the smothering of newborn babes, the withholding of food to children in times of shortage, or neglect in periods of illness. In Mexico, as elsewhere in the world, dense population was possible only after the advent of intensive agriculture.

As recently as 1000 B.C., there were still less than ten thousand inhabitants in the Valley of Mexico. At that time, splendid civilizations had reached their peak or declined in Mesopotamia, the Nile Valley, India, and China. Their temples, palaces, marketplaces, dams, and irrigation canals dwarfed anything that had been built in the puny Mexican villages. The whole population of the Valley of Mexico could have been housed in a middle-sized town along the Tigris-Euphrates delta or the Indus River. And within the boundaries of what is now the modern nation of Mexico, there were fewer than 100,000 inhabitants. Most of them lived in environments that were less naturally endowed than the central valley. Mountains cover four fifths of the country. The highlands to the north are arid, often turning into desert. South of the central plateau, in the highlands of Oaxaca, the rainfall is more regular, though not plentiful. The lowlands of southern Mexico and along the country's eastern Gulf coast are humid and hot, but like most rain forests their soils do not remain fertile under continuous cultivation.

A thousand years before the birth of Christ, the inhabitants of the Old World civilizations would probably have been impressed with only one tribe in the whole of Mexico: the Olmecs, living along the Gulf coast. Little is known about these people whose culture flourished between 1200 and 800 B.C. and then suddenly disappeared. Their round-faced, voluptuous ceramic and stone figurines appear not only in their strongholds, but in the central highlands north and south of the Valley of Mexico, indicating that they traveled widely and had great cultural impact on other tribes. Architecturally, the Olmecs' greatest accomplishment was the series of temple centers they built in the jungles and coastal plains of Veracruz and Tabasco. The most notable of these sites was La Venta, where on a three-acre island rising out of a mangrove swamp, the Olmecs erected a 100-foot-high, cone-shaped temple surrounded by 50-ton stone slabs with elaborate animal designs and freestanding, 10-foot-tall stone heads with helmets and Negroid facial features. Until recently, La Venta was thought to be a center of worship, inhabited only by priests and their attendants. But further archaeological excavation has determined that it was indeed a community with thousands of inhabitants. Since the 1970s, other lost Olmec towns have been uncovered at San Lorenzo in the Gulf state of Veracruz and at Copalillo in the state of Guerrero near the Pacific. Thus, in founding the earliest civilization in the Americas, the Olmecs must have achieved an agricultural breakthrough that laid the basis of true urban communities.

The great ancient cities of the Old World all rose around mighty rivers: the Tigris-Euphrates, the Nile, the Indus, the Yellow, and the Yangtze. The rivers served to link communities by transporting people, commodities, and construction material. Dikes along these waterways were erected to reclaim the fertile soils of deltas and flood plains. And most important, irrigation canals branched out from the rivers to take advantage of their strong flow.

But in Mexico, the volcanic eras had created a mountainous terrain that blocked the course of rivers after short distances. Nowhere in Mexico can inland waterways be navigated for hundreds of miles. The rivers broaden and constrict, drop underground and resurface, only to plunge down impassable waterfalls and through boulder-strewn rapids. Over the ages, these snaking rivers have dug their way between mountains, carving out ravines and canyons with no significant deltas or flood plains. The ancient Mexicans could not readily guide these waters to their agricultural plots. Not even the extensive lakes in the Valley of Mexico were suited for irrigation. Their still waters lay at the lowest levels of the plateau, and pumping them against gravitational force to the slightly higher farm plots required a technology that the early Mexican agriculturalists did not possess.

Yet it is certain that the first permanent agricultural settlements in and around the Valley of Mexico sought to maximize the use of water, wherever possible taking advantage of gravity to wet their farm plots. They had to do so. Rainfall is almost entirely confined to the months of May through October, and even then, droughts occur with distressing frequency. Thus, early farm communities between 1100 and 500 B.C. were most numerous along the southern slopes of the valley where rainfall was highest. By clearing land on the hillsides and enclosing it in steplike terraces that prevented erosion, the agriculturalists could trap larger quantities of water dribbling down the mountain slopes.

A more significant breakthrough in water usage, however, took place at the other end of the valley, in the Teotihuacán area about twenty-five miles north of the present site of Mexico City.[4] There, the farmers who had been slashing, burning, clearing, and terracing the hillsides began to move down into the Teotihuacán plains to make use of the bubbling waters of underground springs. Single families or small groups acting together dug crude irrigation ditches to divert the spring waters into the fields. By this simple act, a permanent source of water for farming was secured for the first time in the Valley of Mexico. The momentous discovery lured other farmers to the valley floor. Steady harvests over the years encouraged a population boom. With more food available, more infants were allowed to live. A growth cycle was set in motion: more extensive irrigation led to greater food production; abundant crops could support greater numbers of people; the larger population demanded even bigger harvests; and to increase food output, more laborers were needed to build more irrigation projects. By the first century B.C., a moderate-size town existed at Teotihuacán, and two centuries later it probably had a population of twenty thousand people.

This true agricultural revolution, sustained by irrigation, soon spread elsewhere stimulating similar population booms. Southwest of Teotihuacán, within the Valley of Mexico, irrigated agriculture brought thousands of farmers together around Cuicuilco, and to the east in the Valley of Puebla, a large community arose around Cholula. But nowhere in Mexico was growth as spectacular as in Teotihuacán, where the New World's first city was exploding into being.

Around A.D. 500, Teotihuacán had a population of more than 100,000 people and sprawled over eight square miles, a larger area than imperial Rome. It was a religious and trade capital, drawing pilgrims and merchants from as far away as the Maya region in Yucatán and Guatemala, and Monte Albán in the Oaxacan highlands—the other two great civilization centers of that era. Closer to home, Teotihuacán dominated the Valley of Mexico by trade and through tribute exacted by its powerful armies.

What is remarkable about Teotihuacán is how closely its spatial development and social structure repeated the pattern of the first cities of the Old World. Between A.D. 100 and 200, Teotihuacán's most impressive building, the Pyramid of the Sun, was completed. Rising to a height of more than one hundred feet, it has a broad base that extends over an area as great as the Pyramid of Cheops in Egypt. But at some later date, after A.D. 200, the focus of religious activity shifted just south of the Sun Pyramid to an enormous walled enclosure of temples, palaces, and granaries. This was the classic citadel found in all the ancient capitals of the Old World. Here the ruling class of king, aristocrats, and priests created a sacred precinct, monopolizing political and religious powers, and dispensing grain to their subjects in time of famine. Adjoining the citadel was a huge marketplace, where the normal distribution of food and merchandise was carried out under the supervision of the authorities.

Around this political-religious-commercial center, along a grid of well-defined streets, arose more than four thousand stone and mudbrick buildings where the artisans, merchants, and warriors resided. These were one-floor structures, each consisting of several connecting rooms. To the narrow streets, they presented only a door and windowless walls, but on the other side, the rooms led to inner, sunlit, airy patios where residents could enjoy their privacy. Archaeological evidence indicates that these quarters immediately surrounding the citadel were associated with specific professions. Some neighborhoods had a heavy concentration of potters. Other districts were identified with weavers, animal-skin and featherworkers, and artisans of obsidian, the black volcanic glass used for tools and weapons. Teotihuacán controlled one of the largest obsidian quarries in central Mexico and apparently established an important commerce in the unworked and finished glass over a region extending hundreds of miles away.

On the outskirts of Teotihuacán, beyond the citadel and the merchant-artisan-warrior quarters, lived the farmers in far less imposing houses built of mudbrick, reeds, and cornstalks. They outnumbered the rest of the urban population by as much as three or four to one. Although they continued to tend their fields, they were forced to live within the city limits where they could be more easily brought under political control.

It bears repeating that the Teotihuacanos created a great city despite the total absence of some of the most essential ingredients associated with the rise of urban civilization in the Old World. They had no animals to plow their fields, to transport their people and goods, or to aid in their huge construction projects. Because there were no mules, donkeys, cattle, or horses, the Teotihuacanos did not bother to "invent" the wheel. Their mountainous terrain rendered even hand-pushed carts almost useless. They lacked the rivers of the Old World civilizations, rivers that made transportation and irrigation so much easier tasks. And for reasons that are harder to explain, they had no metal implements, even though they had enough metallurgical knowledge to work gold and copper into jewelry and ornaments.

The Teotihuacanos did, however, have one comparative advantage over the Old World civilizations: the possession of that miracle crop, maize. Wherever a sedentary agricultural existence was established on the globe, people tended to cultivate one major grain as their staple, relegating all other plants to minor roles. Uniformity meant efficiency.

Labor could be better organized around a single crop, whose cycle from seed to harvest did not vary much from field to field. Once the stage of subsistence agriculture gave way to regular surpluses, it was easier to collect tribute or carry out commerce in one dominant crop. Its grains had to be hardy enough to store over long periods for use in times of scarcity. The three great plants linked to the rise of ancient civilization—wheat, rice, and maize—all shared these attributes. And to this day, they occupy most of the world's cultivated land.

Wheat was the primary crop associated with the birth of agriculture in the Middle East, and later in Mediterranean Europe. Its main disadvantage was a low yield, the result of so many of its grains failing to sprout. Rice was certainly more productive, and could often be counted upon for two annual harvests. But it was a far more demanding crop in terms of labor and hydraulic requirements. After its grains sprouted, the seedlings had to be transplanted by hand to fields submerged in water throughout the growing season. Not only did rice farmers have to work longer hours in their plots than wheat cultivators; they also had to expend far more energy in the construction and maintenance of irrigation facilities to ensure copious water supplies.

Maize seemingly had all the advantages of wheat and rice, with none of their drawbacks. It was the "laziest" of the major grains. It grew quickly, and required a peasant's labor for perhaps only fifty days a year. Even in ancient times, its yields were bountiful, assuming water supplies were adequate. And in the event of drought or frost, the grain was edible before it ripened. Maize also could share its bed with other vegetables. In its shadow, the ancient Mexicans often planted squash, chili, and beans which could make up most of the protein deficit that resulted from the lack of meat. These plants also enriched the soil, enabling farmers to harvest corn on the same plot of land year after year. Wheat farmers, on the other hand, were forced to practice crop rotation, leaving land fallow every other year to prevent soil erosion.

While the Teotihuacanos were blessed by the availability of maize, the civilization they founded upon this humble grain proved to be every bit as despotic as the Old World cultures built on wheat or rice. No matter what the choice of crop, it was water and its management that determined the course of agricultural and urban development. In Mexico, as in the Old World, irrigation set into motion a process that transformed a tribal society into a centralized, autocratic state.[5] The first voluntary, small-scale family or communal projects that channeled Teotihuacán's underground springs toward farmland soon gave way to a stronger, more authoritarian leadership as irrigation works grew larger and employed greater numbers of laborers.

One can only guess how rulers extended their powers after they had achieved absolute control over laborers engaged in hydraulic projects. Perhaps the next step was to gain possession of crop surpluses by convincing subjects that the ruler should be entrusted with the community's granaries because only he could ensure the efficient distribution of food supplies in time of crisis. To strengthen his legitimacy, the chieftain elevated himself to kingship, and surrounded himself with ever more impressive secular and religious trappings. He became higher than other mortals, acting as an interlocutor between his people and the gods, sometimes gaining divine status himself. Everywhere in the ancient world, the agricultural and urban civilizations were governed by theocracies. Rulers achieved a monopoly of political and religious power that prevented the formation of rival, countervailing forces.

As Teotihuacán's population expanded, its society became more stratified. The ruler needed extensive bureaucracies—religious, political, economic, and military—to regulate the affairs of so many subjects. The elites were rewarded with status and by wealth, in the form of tribute collected from commoners and subjugated peoples. The commoners were ultimately held in check by fear and reverence of the ruler and his state, whose powers were boundless. The same authority that directed people to dig new irrigation works was used to harness thousands of laborers behind grandiose plans to build majestic palaces and temples, broad avenues, and streets. The same power to command was used to create large standing armies, as protection against enemies outside and within the city-state and as instruments of conquest.

At the peak of its efficiency, the city-state of Teotihuacán could ensure food supplies even for its lowliest subjects. We know this because the population tripled between 100 B.C. and A.D. 650. No form of encouragement or coercion could have caused such an increase if food was scarce. Faced with severe malnutrition or hunger, the commoners would have reverted back to the old practices of infanticide. But to say that the lowliest subjects received adequate food supplies does not mean they were well fed. Their diet was almost exclusively vegetarian: beans, chili, squash, other vegetables, and maize, above all maize, in the form of tortillas or in a watery porridge. As in any other ancient society—and many recent ones as well—meat was the prerogative of the wealthy. Virtually all the animal bones uncovered in Teotihuacán are found in the royal and priestly quarters, and in the refuse piles of the artisan, commercial, and warrior neighborhoods. Archaeological data indicates that the relatively sparse wild game accounted for less than 1 percent of the caloric intake of the Valley of Mexico's inhabitants—all of the inhabitants.[6] So even among people who ranked above the commoners, only a small minority would have had regular access to animal protein.

To some extent, cannibalism may have compensated for this meat shortage. Three miles west of Teotihuacán in its subject village of Maquixco, human bones, mandibles, and skull fragments have been found scattered through the kitchen refuse and even in cooking pots.[7] In Teotihuacán itself, the evidence is less conclusive. The presence of pyramids with platforms at their summits—like the religious structures used by the Aztecs centuries later to immolate uncounted thousands of victims—hints at large-scale human sacrifices. But the midden heaps that have been unearthed thus far within the city limits contain no human remains.

Teotihuacán could have survived without any meat at all. But it was vulnerable to water shortages. Water—the essential ingredient of agricultural and urban development—began to dwindle in the second half of the first millennium A.D. Perhaps a long era of repeated droughts—a frequent enough occurrence in Mexican history—lowered the flow of the underground springs around Teotihuacán. The intense slashing and burning of the hillside forests, either to recover more farmland or to obtain wood for construction, was also a contributing factor. Once denuded of their trees, the hills failed to absorb the rain runoff that partially fed the underground springs. As food production fell, a demographic decline began in Teotihuacán after A.D. 650. The peripheral areas of the city show signs of abandonment about this time. Building projects are less numerous, and far less spectacular in scale, reflecting a smaller labor force. Even the pottery is of a lesser quality.

Meanwhile, north of the Valley of Mexico, where the highlands had always been too arid for permanent agricultural settlements, lived a people who had never abandoned a seminomadic existence. They farmed only part of the year, and spent the rest of their time scavenging for small game and wild plants. They were far less numerous than the Teotihuacanos, and eyed the great city-state with fear and envy. Throughout Teotihuacán's long centuries of splendor, bands of these northerners often swooped into the rich agricultural valley to plunder harvests and small granaries, and then melted back into their moun-

tainous redoubts and deserts before Teotihuacán's armies could organize punitive expeditions. At the height of the city-state's power,
these northern jackals were no more than a frequent nuisance. Their
lands were too infertile for the Teotihuacanos to permanently conquer
and settle.

The relationship between the northern barbarians and Teotihuacán
had its parallels in the Old World. In ancient China, the Middle East,
and India, societies were divided between sedentary agriculturalists
under the aegis of city-states and mobile nomads who lived on herds
of domesticated animals. Most of the time, the nomads posed no fatal
threat. But eventually, a city-state weakened and a charismatic leader
emerged to unite the many small wandering bands into a powerful
invading force. Thus, the Mongol hordes of the inner Asian frontier-
lands several times devastated the sedentary agricultural empire of
ancient China, and the Aryan nomads of Persia and Afghanistan overwhelmed the rich farmlands of northern India.[8] Like the ancient
Chinese, who built their Great Wall to hold back the barbarians, the
Teotihuacanos essentially depended on a static defense line to deal
with their northern enemies. They conceded to them the pinprick,
hit-and-run raids, confident that these nomads could never breach the
massive walls of Teotihuacán or defeat its numerically superior armies.

But in the wake of droughts, Teotihuacán's military power and
population diminished, making the city more vulnerable. The morale
of the inhabitants, particularly the poorest subjects, must have declined
as food supplies grew scarcer. The king ruled both by force and moral
suasion. He was the keeper of the granaries, the great provider, the
divine agent who interceded with the gods of fertility, water, and
agriculture. But he could no longer deliver enough food. The gods
obviously no longer listened to him.

If the drought produced strains within the great city-state, its effects
must have been catastrophic elsewhere in the Valley of Mexico. Vassal
tribesmen were forced to contribute greater portions of their crops as
tribute to Teotihuacán. Those who escaped starvation reverted to a
seminomadic existence, harvesting what they could, hunting and trapping the scarce wild game, gathering any wild plants and fruit that
could be found.

By A.D. 700, the northern barbarians were showing temerity in their
attacks on the weakened city-state of Teotihuacán. Their raids on the
farmlands were more frequent, and carried out by larger numbers of
warriors. They gathered allies among the starving tribes further south
in the Valley of Mexico. And eventually they may have even won

support among disaffected subjects within the city-state. Around A.D. 750, the barbarian hordes and their allies could no longer be resisted. Teotihuacán was devastated by invasion. Much of the city's center, including the citadel, was looted and burned.

It was about this time that the two other great Mexican civilizations—the Oaxacans around Monte Albán and the Maya in Yucatán and Guatemala—also collapsed. Drought seems to have played a decisive role in the downfall of Monte Albán. In the case of the Maya, the debacle was caused by the slow erosion of the weak jungle soils under continuous cultivation by increasing numbers of inhabitants. The Teotihuacanos, Oaxacans, and Maya were civilizations that expanded to the point of ecological disaster. They carried intensive agriculture to its natural limit, just as their predecessors breached successive environmental barriers as they moved through the various stages of big-game hunting, nomadic scavenging, and part-time farming. So thoroughly did the Teotihuacanos destroy their environment that the center of their civilization failed to regain the population density of their era of splendor until modern times.

Archaeological evidence indicates that three centuries after the sacking of Teotihuacán, the population of the entire Valley of Mexico had dropped to about 150,000 people—100,000 inhabitants less than the golden age of Mexico's first city-state.[9] The effects of the great drought had long been overcome, and other dry periods of less severity had come and gone. The notion of irrigation, once discovered, was not forgotten, and was practiced wherever possible in the valley and its surrounding areas. But there was no great city-state capable of molding large labor forces that could erect and maintain colossal irrigation projects. And without works of this scale, harvests were not bountiful enough to encourage a return to the demographic levels of Teotihuacán's heyday.

During the three hundred years that followed the collapse of Teotihuacán, bands of northern nomads continued to enter the Valley of Mexico in successive waves. In the late tenth century, one of these tribes established itself just north of the valley in the Basin of Tula. Some of its members may have been descendants of the hordes who participated in the sacking of Teotihuacán. Others may have included distant offspring of the Teotihuacanos themselves. Whatever its true origins, the tribe came to be known as the Toltecs, meaning "Builders" in the Nahua language spoken by most of the inhabitants of the Valley of Mexico. In Tula, the Toltecs built a city-state clearly inspired by Teotihuacán's monumental architecture. The Toltecs also shared the

Teotihuacán passion for large-scale irrigation projects. And from Tula, they soon spread their hegemony over large portions of the Valley of Mexico. They even sent military expeditions as far as Yucatán, where the remnants of the Maya had created new villages and ceremonial sites away from their older, ecologically devastated centers.

The reign of the Toltecs was briefer than the Teotihuacanos, lasting about two hundred years. Ecology again seems to have played the key role in their demise. The legendary chronicles of the Toltecs, passed on by later tribes to the Spanish colonial historians, tell of severe crop failures around Tula after seasons of devastating frosts and droughts. In this weakened state, the Toltecs were defeated by one of the many nomadic hordes who were considered as barbaric as the Toltecs themselves had once been. The new intruders into central Mexico destroyed Tula around the middle of the twelfth century.

No tribe achieved a dominant position for long during the two centuries following the Toltec collapse. But agriculture continued to flourish in the Valley of Mexico and its inhabitants reached unprecedented numbers. Population would grow even more spectacularly beginning in the fifteenth century when another northern barbarian tribe, the Aztecs, succeeded in creating the most powerful Mexican city-state, one that expanded hydraulic agriculture, urban civilization, and state terror to new limits.

TWO

THE
CANNIBAL EMPIRE

The Aztecs were the last of the many barbarian tribes who drifted southward into the Valley of Mexico. They traced their tribal origin to a nebulous enclave called Aztlán located somewhere in northwest Mexico. Aztlán is described in the ancient Aztec annals as a complex of caves on the rim of a lake, where fish and wild game abounded:

> There they feasted on great numbers of ducks of all kinds, storks, sea crows and water hens. They enjoyed the melodic songs of the red-and-yellow-headed little birds. They gorged themselves on a variety of great and beautiful fish. They rested in the cool shade of the trees that grew on the water's edge. . . . But later, when they left this delectable land, everything turned against them. The underbrush bit at them, the stones scraped them, the fields were filled with burrs and spines . . . and were impassable, with no place to sit or rest.[1]

The description of Aztlán does not match any locale in the arid, mountainous terrain of northwestern Mexico, and archaeologists have long ago given up efforts to uncover it. But Eden has always been painted in idyllic terms, the better to convey the sense of Paradise Lost and the travails that followed. Just why the Aztecs fell from grace and departed from Aztlán is not revealed in their chronicles. Perhaps it was the depletion of hunting game. Maybe a more powerful tribe routed them—an event the Aztecs were not likely to record since their annals display acute embarrassment over any defeats.

In any case, after abandoning Aztlán, the Aztecs wandered for centuries in the wilderness, on a zigzag course that slowly moved them southward in search of a new promised land. They were guided, they said, by their chief deity, Huitzilopochtli, which means "Humming-bird-of-the-left." The significance of the "left" lay in the fact that the sun set in the west, and if one stood facing that sacred direction, the left hand pointed to the south, where the new Aztec homeland would presumably be found. But Huitzilopochtli was not originally an Aztec god. The Aztecs probably began to worship this deity only after having temporarily settled west of the Valley of Mexico, in Michoacán, where a tribe called the Tarascans had already placed the hummingbird in their own pantheon of deities. As had happened to them everywhere, the Aztecs were eventually expelled from Michoacán. They departed carrying an effigy of Huitzilopochtli in a portable, cagelike shrine made of clay. The deity was supposed to have whispered to their priests the likeliest location of game and edible plants. But whenever the Aztecs lingered too long in one place, Huitzilopochtli allegedly ordered them to continue their quest for the promised land, which they would rec-ognize as a lake with a small island where an eagle perched on a cactus plant was devouring a snake. This divinely appointed scene unfolded on a lake in the Valley of Mexico, and it was there that the Aztecs built their great city-state of Tenochtitlán, the precursor of Mexico City. This legendary version of the Aztec arrival in the Valley of Mexico is still taught as factual history to Mexican schoolchildren. And the central emblem on the Mexican flag is an eagle clasping a serpent in its beak and talons.

But divine guidance played a lesser role than the Aztecs would have us believe in their appearance in the Valley of Mexico. A closer approximation of the truth is that the Aztecs arrived at the lakes' edge in a hungry and savage state around the middle of the thirteenth century. They were scorned by the tribes who were already established in the valley. As one surviving account puts it: "And when the [Aztecs] arrived here after their long peregrinations, they were the very last to come into the valley, and nobody knew of them or welcomed them, and everywhere people asked who are these people and where do they come from, and they were turned away from every village."[2]

The Aztecs stumbled into the Valley of Mexico almost a hundred years after the fall of the Toltecs. The valley was living through an unsettling era of both political turmoil and economic prosperity. The land was partitioned among several powerful, warring tribes. It was a time of shifting alliances and constant treachery, with vassal groups seizing every opportunity to revolt against their masters. Each domi-nant tribe claimed to be the rightful heir to the Toltec legacy, in much the same fashion that the barbarian peoples who overthrew Rome disputed title to the Roman Empire.

Despite the political instability, breakthroughs in irrigation techniques had revolutionized agriculture in the Valley of Mexico, encouraging a remarkable demographic expansion and concentrating the population on the periphery of the lakes. The most important agrarian innovations were the small, artificial islands, called *chinampas*. Built on the freshwater lakes from layers of reed and mud, the chinampas were extremely fertile and could produce several harvests a year. In effect, the chinampas were an ingenious solution to a dilemma that had vexed the inhabitants of the Valley of Mexico for more than a millenium: since the low-lying lake waters could not be guided to the fertile land on slightly higher ground, then the land would be brought to the water.

As the new technique spread, economic power in the valley shifted away from the foothills with their underground springs to the lower terrain around the lakes. The lakes began to serve the same functions as rivers did for the ancient civilizations of the Old World. Boats connected the burgeoning lakeside communities and stoked a lively trade between the various tribes. For the first time, the inhabitants of the valley, who always lacked beasts of burden, could rely on another means of transporting goods besides the usual army of human pack carriers. With the growth of commerce, other industries—ceramics, weaving, jewelry, featherwork—also flourished.

The Aztecs must indeed have seemed a primitive people to the valley's tribes, anxious to deny their own nomadic, barbaric past. Nowhere in their travels had the Aztecs come across the wealth and sophistication they encountered here. The only commodity they could trade upon was their skill as fighters, a skill honed by their peripatetic hunting life and the constant skirmishes with tribes who had chased them away from temporary sanctuaries elsewhere in the country. And so the Aztecs offered themselves as mercenaries to the Tepanecas, the strongest tribe among the valley's lakeside inhabitants. The Tepanecas allowed the Aztecs to settle in what is now the Chapultepec district of Mexico City, and what was then a patch of wooded high ground located just west of the lakes.

It was around 1280 that the Aztecs wedged themselves into Chapultepec, and began the difficult transition from a hunting-gathering existence to a sedentary agricultural way of life. Chapultepec—the name translates as "Hill of Grasshoppers"—was infested with insects, but its sloping land was fertile and watered by underground springs. The newcomers paid tribute to their Tepanec masters in levies of wood, harvests of maize, and, above all, military service. The Aztecs were fierce fighters, and quickly gained a reputation for cruelty. They transformed Huitzilopochtli, their relatively benign hummingbird deity, into a god of battle, and regularly offered him sacrificial victims from the warriors they took prisoner. Human sacrifice and cannibalism were by no means considered loathsome by the other tribes in the valley. They simply objected to the fact that the Aztecs elevated these practices from occasional ritual to regular feasts.

Around the year 1300, the tribe of Culhuacán, who lived on the southern periphery of the lakes and emerged as the chief rival of the Tepanecas, sent an expedition into Chapultepec to subdue the hated Aztec mercenaries. Many Aztecs were slaughtered, and the defeated remnants of the tribe were herded back to Culhuacán as slaves. At first, the Culhuacán lords seemed intent on humiliating the Aztecs. They relegated them to menial tasks, as porters, messengers, servants, and fieldworkers in the chinampas. They were forced to live in a stark terrain strewn with boulders and jagged volcanic stones and infested with poisonous serpents. The Aztecs not only survived the ordeal, but staved off hunger with a diet of snakes.

Impressed by their hardiness, the Culhuacán lords decided to send the Aztecs into battle against a nearby rival tribe, the Xochimilcas. If the Aztecs triumphed, their masters promised to raise their status from slaves to mercenaries. The Aztecs crushed the Xochimilcas, and brought back hundreds of enemy ears as victory trophies. Though aghast at the barbaric methods of the Aztecs, the Culhuacán ruler, Coxcoxtli, released them from bondage. And when the Aztecs requested that one of his daughters marry their chieftain, Coxcoxtli again complied, hoping to maintain the loyalty of these brutal mercenaries.

But the Aztecs had secretly been nursing their grudge against the Culhuacán tribe. They had not forgotten the massacre dealt them at Chapultepec, their twenty-five years of servitude, or the long seasons of bare subsistence in that volcanic wasteland where only snakes thrived. When Coxcoxtli arrived at the crude, foul-smelling, and smoky Aztec temple to witness his daughter's wedding ceremony, he was greeted by a priest dressed in a freshly flayed human skin. Only after his eyes had grown accustomed to the darkness of the temple did Coxcoxtli scream and recoil in horror: it was his own daughter's skin draped around the priest. She had been sacrificed to one of the Aztec gods. Rather than risk being annihilated by the superior forces of Culhuacán, the Aztecs fled before Coxcoxtli could rally his army. They paddled across the lakes northward to a small uninhabited island a short distance from the western shores where their former Tepanec masters had their stronghold and could guarantee them protection from the irate Culhuacán tribe.

This was the island which the Aztec legends describe as the promised land of the eagle devouring the serpent. They named it Tenochtitlán, and their settlement there in 1325 is now considered the official founding date of Mexico City.

Tenochtitlán rose in the midst of Lake Texcoco, one of five interconnecting water bodies that spread south to north across the floor of the Valley of Mexico. Texcoco was the largest and most centrally placed of the lakes. Because of its location at the very bottom of the valley, it constantly received the nitrate soils washed down from the surrounding slopes by the rains, and its waters were too salty for human consumption or irrigation. But the Aztecs were more concerned with their island's strategic potential than the quality of the surrounding water. They wanted a natural barrier between themselves and the tribes on the mainland. And although the lake was brackish, it was by no means lifeless. It teemed with fish, frogs, turtles, an algae that could be dried and rolled to a cheeselike consistency, and billions of mosquito eggs that were skimmed off the lake's surface and beaten into a protein-rich paste. All of the lakes were a stopover for the countless numbers of birds migrating from the northern hemisphere. Ducks, geese, storks, and egrets were so abundant that they could be trapped by the dozen simply by setting up large nets between clumps of reeds. The island itself had enough fresh water in underground springs to satisfy the Aztecs' drinking and irrigation needs, at least for a few decades after their arrival.

Soon after settling in Tenochtitlán, the Aztecs had to somehow deal with the very cramped conditions of their small island. They put to use the chinampa techniques they had learned from their former Culhuacán masters. By building artificial isles, they were able to incorporate more land into Tenochtitlán and expand the inhabitable area. The lake was shallow, ranging in most places from three to nine feet deep. Still, the chinampas required enormous expenditure of time and labor. Timber and stone had to be brought over from the mainland, where they were purchased with the fish, birds, and other animals caught by the Aztecs in their lake. Once a wood and rock foundation had been laid at the bottom of a lake section adjoining Tenochtitlán, reed and mud were heaped on top until a solid strip of land was formed.

Not all the water was drained out of the chinampas. The lake was allowed to seep into the expanding island of Tenochtitlán along a series of ditches, so that a network of canals was created to facilitate transportation. The canals, filled with canoes and barges, alternated with dirt paths for pedestrians and pack carriers. A spider's web of irrigation channels was also built to guide the waters from the few underground springs to the maize and vegetable fields. A few decades after its settlement, Tenochtitlán was still a primitive, ramshackle community of mostly mud and wattle huts, but the land and hydraulic projects were shaping it into a city.

With this permanent changeover to a sedentary farming and fishing existence, the Aztecs had to remold their social structure. During their long odyssey in the wilderness, they divided themselves into family clans, called *calpulli*. The calpulli not only served as a relatively self-contained hunting-and-gathering group, but also was the basic political and social unit of the tribe. Each calpulli had its council of elders who maintained tribal laws, meted out justice, sanctioned marriages, presided over religious ceremonies, and elected a clan chieftain. The chieftains of the various clans in turn elected the tribal ruler, usually from among male members of the same family. This relatively egalitarian system functioned well in a nomadic society where women gathered wild plants, cooked, and stitched together garments, while the men hunted and fought rival tribes. But the simple social structure and autonomy of the calpulli were inadequate when the Aztecs undertook the larger-scaled, more disciplined group efforts required to build chinampas and irrigation projects.

Like the Teotihuacanos, the Toltecs, and other tribes, the Aztecs evolved toward a more authoritarian and stratified society. They began by dividing Tenochtitlán into four wards, each holding administrative power over several clans. Even this relatively mild movement toward more political centralization provoked intense dissent. Angered over their loss of autonomy, a number of clans broke away from the main tribe and paddled over to a nearby, uninhabited island, Tlatelolco, to form their own community. Eventually, the furious pace of landfill projects physically linked this island to Tenochtitlán, and Tlatelolco's independence was severely curtailed. Meanwhile, the calpulli or clan system continued to decline in significance. It survived mainly to denote neighborhoods, and as a system of holding a clan's farmlands in communal ownership. An individual family could work an agrarian plot and pass it on to its progeny. But ownership of the property legally rested with the whole clan or calpulli, in order to prevent the land from being purchased or transferred to an outside group.

In the fifty years after the founding of Tenochtitlán, political power ebbed away from the calpulli to the ward. But even the four-ward system was proving too weak to direct the Aztecs' ambitious construction plans for their island and too cumbersome to handle relations with neighboring tribes. The most powerful tribes in the Valley of Mexico were all governed by strong monarchies, and a more centralized rule seemed inevitable for the Aztecs as well.

To forestall the kind of internal rivalries that had led to the creation of a renegade community in Tlatelolco, the Aztec political chieftains from the four wards decided to select their king from the royalty of a neighboring tribe. Some thought was given to offering the throne to a member of the ruling family of the Tepanecas, the most dominant group in the valley. But the Aztecs were already paying tribute to the Tepanecas, and inviting a Tepaneca to rule them risked transforming Tenochtitlán into an abject vassal state. Instead, the Aztecs turned to Culhuacán. The choice may have seemed surprising. The Aztecs, after all, had fled to Tenochtitlán to escape the Culhuacán forces. But the ill feelings between the two tribes had long dissipated because of their common fears over the growing power of the Tepanecas. Commerce between Tenochtitlán and Culhuacán was flourishing, and there were numerous instances of intermarriage. Throughout the valley, the Culhuacán tribe also enjoyed great prestige because its members were reputed to be direct lineal descendants of the Toltecs, who were considered the fountain of civilization. After a careful genealogical investigation, the Aztec leaders selected a young Culhuacán nobleman, Acamapichtli, whose mother was Aztec, a circumstance that made the choice more palatable to the people of Tenochtitlán.

In 1375, Acamapichtli became the first Aztec monarch. His enthronement served as an excuse to radically reorganize Aztec society and politics. The leaders of the Aztec clans joined Acamapichtli's court as a new order of nobility with far more privileges and powers than the commoners. When Acamapichtli's wife proved barren, he was allowed as many mistresses as he desired. They were chosen from among the daughters of the court nobles, and the children sired by Acamapichtli from these unions became known as "*pipiltín*," or "sons-of-lords." The pipiltín and the older court aristocrats also claimed for themselves the right to their own harems among women selected from Aztec noble and commoner families or those taken in battle. Multiplying prodigiously over the next two generations, the pipiltín and their offspring monopolized the administrative, commercial, military, and religious bureaucracies in Tenochtitlán. They had their own military and religious schools. They built imposing stone villas and palaces with brigades of conscripted labor, and supported themselves by heavily taxing the harvests of the commoners. Over the years, the pipiltín always defended their aristocratic legitimacy by tracing their lineage—however tenuously—to Acamapichtli, and by extension to the revered Toltecs. By the beginning of the fifteenth century, almost nothing remained of the egalitarian calpulli or clan system that had served the Aztecs so well during their lengthy nomadic existence as hunters and gatherers. Tenochtitlán society had become as centralized and stratified as any in the Valley of Mexico. The single possibility for a commoner to escape his dreary lot as farmer or construction laborer and join the ranks of the pipiltín was by distinguishing himself in battle and capturing prisoners for sacrifice to Huitzilopochtli, the ever hungrier hummingbird god.

In the years following the establishment of the monarchy, the population of Tenochtitlán expanded greatly, not only among the sexually prolific pipiltín, but among commoners as well. A high birthrate was officially encouraged because the island-state's strength was linked to its growing citizenry. More laborers were required to extend and maintain the land reclamation and hydraulic projects. More warriors were needed to mount a credible defense against encroachments by the hostile tribes who surrounded the Aztecs on the mainland. But inevitably, Tenochtitlán began to reach its ecological limits. New cultivable land was scarce. Even more alarming, by the early 1400s the few underground springs that existed on the island were insufficient to meet the agricultural needs of the burgeoning population.

The closest available freshwater source lay just a few miles west across the lake, in the springs of Chapultepec, the woody hills on the mainland where the Aztecs had first settled when they arrived in the Valley of Mexico 150 years before. But Chapultepec was still firmly under Tepanec control. It took the Aztecs several decades of sycophantic diplomacy to convince the Tepanecas to cede them a small portion of Chapultepec's waters. The Aztecs increased their tribute of harvests and lake goods to the Tepanecas, and once again offered their services as mercenaries. They also agreed to have Acamapichtli's suc-

cessor wed a daughter of Tezozomoc, the Tepanec monarch. This
policy of extreme accommodation appeared to be successful when the
firstborn son of this marriage ascended the Aztec throne in 1414. His
name was Chimalpopoca, and he became a favorite grandson of the
powerful Tepanec king, Tezozomoc, who finally allowed the Aztecs
to build an aqueduct bringing Chapultepec's fresh waters over the lake
and into Tenochtitlán.

The era of goodwill ended abruptly when Tezozomoc died in 1428.
The new Tepanec monarch, Maxtla, was determined to impose his
rule over the Aztecs. He sent a squadron of warriors to Tenochtitlán
to murder Chimalpopoca, the Aztec king, while he was presiding over
a religious ceremony. Almost simultaneously, another band of Maxtla's
assassins killed the ruler of Tlatelolco, the other Aztec island-state.

In an attempt to extend Tepanec hegemony throughout the valley,
Maxtla demanded tribute from all tribes and schemed to replace their
leaders with his own agents. A diplomacy of appeasement was discredited everywhere. In Tenochtitlán, a faction of younger, more com-
bative pipiltín gained control of tribal politics and installed Itzcóatl, a
relative outsider, on the throne. Although he could claim to be descended from Acamapichtli, the first Aztec king, his mother was a
slave, the lowliest of many mistresses in the royal harem.

As soon as Itzcóatl was crowned, the Aztecs began secret negotiations
with other tribes in the valley for a war pact against the Tepanecas.
The Aztecs formed a so-called Triple Alliance with the city-state of
Texcoco, on the northeast side of the lake, and Tlacopán, a small
vassal state of the Tepanecas on the western mainland. Moving their
warriors across the lake into Tlacopán under the cover of darkness,
and simultaneously sending other columns to join with the Texcoco
soldiers for a thrust from the north side of the valley, the Aztecs and
their allies ambushed the Tepanecas at dawn. The surprise attack was
devastating. The Tepanec warriors were almost all slaughtered or taken
prisoner for sacrifice. Their capital was razed to the ground, and survived in later years only as a slave market. The Tepanec women were
forced into the harems of the Aztec aristocrats, and their children were
pressed into service as farm serfs and slave laborers for the construction
brigades. Maxtla, the Tepanec ruler, escaped from the battlefield, but
was eventually tracked down and killed.

With the victory over the Tepanecas, the great Aztec era dawns. It is
at this stage that the historical accounts, illustrated and written by the

Aztec scribes,* begin to offer a plethora of details about the nature of their society, religion, and leadership. It becomes possible for the first time to link individuals to the development of the unique city-state of Tenochtitlán and its expanding empire.

Among these individuals, none was more important than Tlacaelel, a nephew of King Itzcóatl. While still in his twenties, Tlacaelel rose to prominence as a leading Aztec general in the campaign against the Tepanecas. He himself never sat on the throne; but as chief adviser to a succession of monarchs, he unquestionably wielded more influence than anybody else in forging society, religion, and politics during the Aztecs' brilliant fifteenth century. When he died in 1496, at the incredible age of ninety-eight, Tlacaelel had shaped Tenochtitlán's destiny from behind the throne for almost seven decades.

As a boy, Tlacaelel attended a *calmecac*, one of the schools where adolescent pipiltín—sons-of-lords—were taught about their alleged Toltec ancestry and the ideas of empire thought to have been handed down by the Toltecs. Life in the calmecac was Spartan and monastic. The young nobles, barely out of childhood, were sequestered in the school compound away from their families and the rest of society. During the day, they dressed simply in loincloth and white-cotton mantle. Besides being instructed in religion, history, and political rule, those who were not destined for the priesthood were taught spear throwing, archery, and combat with an obsidian-studded club. Not an evening of uninterrupted sleep was permitted. The youths were awakened around midnight and told to pierce their earlobes and tongues with cactus thorns, as signs of penitence. And again, in the cold hours before dawn, they were forced to rise from their slumber and dip into the chilly waters of Lake Texcoco. Their basic diet consisted of tortillas and water, occasionally supplemented by morsels of human flesh from sacrificial victims. For human sacrifice was on the rise. Besides Huitzilopochtli, the hummingbird god, new deities were continuously being embraced by the Aztecs: Quetzalcóatl, the plumed serpent, whom the ancient Toltecs had worshipped as their god of civilization; Tlaloc, the deity of rain and water; Tezcatlipoca, lord of darkness and patron of young warriors; and numerous other deities representing fire, fertility, women, music, dance, flowers, gold, the Underworld. Most of these gods had to be honored by sacrifice. The

---

* Aztec writing combined ideograms, simple illustrations, and phoneticisms from their Nahua language. These "books" or annals served as learning aids for the nobles, who were required to memorize and recite historical accounts, hymns, and poems.

victims were mainly prisoners of war, but also slaves, young women, even children chosen from among the Aztecs themselves.

Just as the pantheon of deities was being expanded, so the history of the Aztecs was in the process of being rewritten during the early 1400s. Barely two generations had passed since Acamapichtli, the first Aztec king, had been enthroned. The Aztecs' supposed Toltec heritage was still a fresh invention. In the calmecac, young pipiltín like Tlacaelel were now taught that the Aztecs were not nearly as barbaric a tribe as they themselves had believed when they arrived in the Valley of Mexico. In their legendary birthplace of Aztlán, they allegedly had already known about agriculture. And according to the new calmecac mythology, their ties to the Toltecs were far stronger than had previously been imagined. In their odyssey toward the Valley of Mexico, they claimed to have spent many years in Tula, the seat of the Toltec empire, and to have been integrated into that glorified civilization before it was brought down by barbarians. This was a blatant distortion of history because the Aztecs were nowhere near Tula when it fell.

The young Tlacaelel was evidently fascinated by the power of human sacrifice and the creative rewriting of history which he encountered in the calmecac. Years afterward, he would manipulate both these practices with devastating political effect. But in the meantime, he and the other young pipiltín emerging from the calmecac were a rebellious, frustrated generation. Around them they could see none of the tribal greatness evoked by their priestly instructors. Tenochtitlán paid heavy tribute to the Tepanecas, and the Aztec king, Chimalpopoca, groveled before the mainland tribe. Even while Chimalpopoca was alive, Tlacaelel and his half brother, Motecuhzoma I,* were gathering ever stronger support from a militant faction of young pipiltín. When Chimalpopoca was assassinated, this more radical group overruled the older, conservative nobles and installed Itzcóatl as king. And Tlacaelel and Motecuhzoma I were immediately anointed the leading Aztec generals in the war against the Tepanecas.

In the Aztec annals, whose writings he oversaw, Tlacaelel emerges as the most uncompromising militarist in his tribe's ruling circle. As soon as the Tepanecas were slaughtered, he urged the Aztecs to strike at the Tepanec allies in Coyoacán, on the southwestern shores of Lake Texcoco. While the Aztecs justified their war against the Tepanecas as a struggle for self-preservation, the attack on Coyoacán was defended

---

* He is not to be confused with Motecuhzoma II, who reigned over the Aztecs at the time of the Spanish Conquest.

by Tlacaelel on shakier grounds of tribal honor. The Coyoacán people allegedly provoked war by stealing goods from Aztec women en route to market. When an Aztec peace delegation, led by Tlacaelel, arrived in Coyoacán, their hosts forced them to dress in women's clothing and perform a dance—an indignity that could only be rectified by an Aztec declaration of war against Coyoacán. But this official Aztec account sounds too contrived. The same excuses—the mistreatment of Aztec merchants and the dressing of Aztec warriors in women's garb—would be frequently invoked to justify Aztec incursions against other tribes in the years ahead. Meanwhile, Tlacaelel led the vengeful Aztec forces against Coyoacán, crushing that tribe almost as brutally as the Tepanecas. Again, the men were massacred or enslaved, the women turned into concubines, and the farmlands appropriated by the victors.

Tlacaelel viewed the war not only as an end to Tepanec power in the Valley of Mexico, but also as an opportunity to establish even firmer, authoritarian control by the Aztec pipiltín over their own tribe's commoners. In rewriting the history of the Tepanec campaign, Tlacaelel's scribes claimed that the Aztec internal debate over war or peace was not carried out between younger, militant pipiltín and their older, more cautious peers, but instead pitted the valorous nobility against the cowardly commoners. In one account handed down to us, King Itzcóatl with Tlacaelel at his side convoked the commoners to announce the war against the Tepanecas:

> [The commoners] cried out: "And if you do not emerge victorious, what will become of us?"
> The king responded: "If we [the pipiltín] fail, we will place ourselves in your hands, so that you may wreak vengeance by eating our flesh on broken and dirty pottery [that is, without ceremony]."
> They answered back: "Then we will do so, because you have sentenced yourselves. But if you do gain victory, we promise to serve you, to give you tribute, to be your serfs, to build your homes, to have our children serve you as their true lords, to carry your food and arms whenever you go off to war, and finally to offer ourselves and our possessions to you forever."[3]

The Aztec rulers had never before consulted the commoners, and it is far more likely that any discussion over whether or not to engage the Tepanec forces was confined to the Aztec nobility. But this highly suspect version of history, inspired by Tlacaelel, became a sort of social contract for the Aztecs. Thanks to their victory over the Tepanecas, the pipiltín now had the right to demand anything from the commoners. Later annals, also written under Tlacaelel's supervision, elevated the nobility to demigod status. They instructed commoners that the nobles who led them in war were "fathers and mothers of the sun . . . whose task it is to give food and drink to the sun and earth with the blood and flesh of their enemies. Their wealth is their shields and weapons, and they deserve the rich earrings and lip plugs, the tassels and bracelets, the yellow-leather thongs, the gold ornaments and beautiful feathers. All these things they merit because they are brave. . . . And they are held up as mothers and fathers, protectors of their people . . . like trees that give shadow to those beneath."[4]

Tlacaelel had distorted history to condemn his tribe's commoners to eternal servility. He now reinterpreted religion to justify the expanding empire of the Aztecs and their brutal treatment of conquered peoples. The key to the new religious orthodoxy was Huitzilopochtli, the hummingbird god. Initially, he had been a harmless deity—a tiny, beautiful bird who guided the Aztecs in their search for wild game and an eventual homeland. Once the Aztecs settled in the Valley of Mexico and became mercenaries, Huitzilopochtli metamorphosed into a god of battle. For a century, he remained only one of numerous gods worshipped by the Aztecs. But after the victories over the Tepanec and Coyoacán tribes, Huitzilopochtli was raised above all other deities. He became the lord of creation, the all-powerful sun god. He was chosen for this exalted role because he was the oldest of the Aztec gods, the one they could most comfortably claim as their own. His bloated stature was well suited to the Aztecs' new imperial notions. It became the divine duty of the Aztecs to force all peoples of the world to worship Huitzilopochtli.[5] A simple profession of faith was not enough. The conquered tribes would have to supply a constant stream of sacrificial victims, whose blood and flesh would nourish Huitzilopochtli, thus ensuring that the sun moved across the heavens every day. The Aztecs apparently felt it unnecessary to explain why the sun, which had shined brilliantly for ages, suddenly required their gruesome efforts to maintain its vitality.

The Xochimilcas were the first tribe to suffer the calamity of the Aztecs' new sun-god cult of Huitzilopochtli. Ensconced around Lake Xochimilco directly south of the Aztec capital of Tenochtitlán, the Xochimilcas were the most proficient farmers in all the valley. They had converted their freshwater lake into a maze of chinampas—those extremely fertile artificial isles. Their agricultural wealth alone marked the Xochimilcas as the likeliest next victims for the expanding Aztec empire. But the Aztec annals preferred to ascribe other, less self-interested motives for war. After the victory over the Tepanec and Coyoacán tribes, Tlacaelel prodded the Aztec king, Itzcóatl, to order the construction of a new pyramid-temple to Huitzilopochtli, a structure commensurate to the deity's grander status. A request was sent to the Xochimilcas for their aid in raising the new sanctuary. According to the Aztec annals, Itzcóatl and Tlacaelel informed the Xochimilcas in the humblest diplomatic language that they stood ready to "kiss your feet and hands . . . and appeal to your greatness and generosity . . . to permit us to take a bit of your stones and pine wood to build a temple to the god Huitzilopochtli."[6]

Whether or not such a polite message was conveyed to them, the Xochimilcas could decipher its true meaning. The Aztecs were asking for nothing less than the Xochimilcas' abeyance to Huitzilopochtli and vassalage to Tenochtitlán. Not surprisingly, the Aztec annals claim that the Xochimilcas replied in the rudest possible language. The annals then record what had become the ritual litany of complaints against an enemy who is about to be conquered: the Xochimilcas stole goods from innocent Aztec merchants and mistreated Aztec emissaries of peace. Their patience at an end, the Aztecs invaded Xochimilco. The battle was fierce, and the annals describe in gory detail the lopping off of enemy limbs, particularly by the ubiquitous Tlacaelel, who is portrayed awash in blood to his ankles. Thousands of Xochimilcas were slain or carried off for sacrifice, thousands of others were pressed into construction brigades, their women were bundled off to harems, and their lands were expropriated. In what passed for a peace treaty, the surviving Xochimilcas were allowed to plead eternal submission using language that was strikingly similar to the social contract imposed by the Aztec pipiltín on their commoners: "We will go and serve in your homes and furnish you labor for all your needs, and we will build your houses, and wherever you go we will carry your loads, and if you go to war, we will provide you with food and all the necessary weapons, supplies and soldiers. We will be your subjects forever."[7]

No sooner had Xochimilco been subjugated than the Aztecs turned their imperial gaze on Cuitláhuac, the small city-state on a swampy stretch of land partially separating Lake Xochimilco from the other great freshwater body, Lake Chalco. Recounting the events leading to hostilities, the Aztec annals affect their usual tone of sweet reasonableness: Could the Cuitláhuac lords bring "their mistresses, daughters and sisters to celebrate with their songs and dances a solemn festival for our god Huitzilopochtli"?[8] And again, the Aztecs are portrayed as the aggrieved party. Their request was spurned by the Cuitláhuac king, who replied to the Aztec messengers: "Are our daughters, sisters and cousins toys or whores for your god?"[9] Following the customary allegations that Aztec merchants were harassed, the inevitable war ensued, and the Cuitláhuac tribe was crushed.

This was the last major conquest carried out under Itzcóatl. The king died a few years later, in 1440. His twelve-year reign had seen the Aztecs burst their confinement on the island of Tenochtitlán and rapidly achieve hegemony over most of the Valley of Mexico, including four of its five lakes. Only the powerful Chalcas, who controlled the freshwater, southeastern lake of Chalco, remained independent. And eventually, they also would be subdued.

Tlacaelel was the likeliest candidate to succeed Itzcóatl. But the Supreme Council of the pipiltín, perhaps already troubled by Tlacaelel's domineering role, chose instead his half brother, Motecuhzoma I, as king. Intense negotiations must have been involved in this decision because Tlacaelel extracted enormous concessions for giving up his claim to the throne. He was appointed *cihuacóatl*—literally, "serpent-woman"—the post of chief adviser to the monarch, which existed in Toltec times but fell into disuse after the demise of that ancient empire. Besides resurrecting this forgotten office, Tlacaelel greatly expanded its functions. He became all powerful in ceremonial affairs, and the king's most important counselor on political and military matters. He placed himself higher than the Supreme Council, the group of pipiltín who were supposed to advise the ruler and choose his successor. From this point on, the Supreme Council was gradually emasculated. Mentioned less frequently in the Aztec annals, it eventually acted as a mere rubber stamp for decisions taken by Tlacaelel and the succession of monarchs he served and manipulated.

The annals make it clear that Motecuhzoma I consulted Tlacaelel at every turn. Whenever Motecuhzoma I wavered or inclined toward moderation, Tlacaelel responded forcefully, implacably. It was Tlacaelel who redefined for his half brother the rules of the monarchy: "You are obligated as king to constantly seek advantage for your household, court and domains, to enlarge and expand the throne and the empire."[10] In fact, if not officially, Tlacaelel became a sort of vice-monarch. He sat next to Motecuhzoma in court, and was the only one who addressed him as a peer and was allowed in the king's presence without removing his sandals. When the Aztecs went to war, it was Tlacaelel who organized military expeditions, named their commanders, and selected the heroes to be rewarded. If the king personally led a military campaign, Tlacaelel temporarily replaced him on the throne. A drawing that has survived from this period pictures Tlacaelel as a virtually identical twin of Motecuhzoma, standing directly behind the ruler. To further emphasize their closeness and nearly equal status, the chronicles begin to assert that the two half brothers were born on the same day, at exactly the same moment, to different mothers.

The first task undertaken by Motecuhzoma I and Tlacaelel after the death of Itzcóatl was to establish their tribe's supremacy over its allies. In theory, at least, the Aztec empire was still a Triple Alliance between the city-states of Tenochtitlán, Texcoco, and Tlacopán. All three tribes had joined in the surprise attack against the Tepanecas, and in the campaigns against Coyoacán and Xochimilco. Only in the battle against Cuitláhuac did the Aztecs act entirely without the aid of their allies. All three members of the Triple Alliance shared the spoils from these wars. Each of the allies also had a representative in the Supreme Councils of the other two tribes. But even when Itzcóatl was alive, it was obvious that the Aztecs were first among equals in the Triple Alliance. They took the lion's share of the tribute exacted from new vassal tribes, a proportion that would eventually grow to more than half of the total. Moreover, the new religious orthodoxy surrounding Huitzilopochtli was making Tlacopán and Texcoco increasingly uneasy. They were not pleased at the Aztec assertion that all peoples must accept Huitzilopochtli as supreme being, lord of creation, and sun god, and that the Aztecs were responsible for his continued wellbeing in the heavens. The Tlacopán and Texcoco tribes included Huitzilopochtli in their divine pantheon, but not as their most revered deity.

Tlacopán, the weaker of the two city-states, offered little resistance to Aztec claims of hegemony. Its rulers accepted whatever imperial tributes were allotted to them by Tenochtitlán. And their city-state dwindled in political significance to the point that it is barely mentioned in the Aztec chronicles after Itzcóatl's death.

But Texcoco posed a more complicated problem, particularly because of its king, Nezahualcóyotl, and his special ties to the Aztec royal family. Nezahualcóyotl was a cousin of Tlacaelel and Motecuhzoma I. His mother was an Aztec princess, sister of Itzcóatl, and his father was king of Texcoco. In his childhood, the Tepanecas conquered Texcoco, forcing Nezahualcóyotl and his father to flee the city to the eastern mountains. They were tracked down, and while Ne-zahualcóyotl hid behind a tree, he saw his father being slain by the Tepanecas.

For the next dozen years, Nezahualcóyotl constantly moved about the Valley of Mexico and beyond. He gained a reputation for cunning and became a master of disguise and subterfuge. At various times, the annals place him in Tenochtitlán seeking protection with his mother's relatives, or in Texcoco trying to rally his father's subjects, or even in the Tepanec capital where he arrived incognito to mock his pursuers before slipping away again. During his years as a fugitive, he learned a great deal about the engineering methods used by the tribes through-out central Mexico. He also became a poet, and his verses are the oldest handed down to us from the pre-Columbian era. In almost all respects he was so unlike his cousin Tlacaelel that the annals inevitably portrayed him as a foil to the Aztec strongman.

He joined Tlacaelel, Motecuhzoma I, and Itzcóatl in their secret plotting to end Tepanec rule over the valley, and raised an army in Texcoco to fight alongside the Aztecs. After the victory over the Tep-anecas, Nezahualcóyotl assumed the throne of Texcoco. He continued to offer his troops to the Aztecs in their campaigns against other tribes. But he resisted the growing cult of Huitzilopochtli, which the Aztecs were trying to impose on both foes and allies. In Texcoco, his own city-state, he fostered the worship of Quetzalcóatl—the plumed serpent god whom the ancient Toltecs deemed the creator of civilization. Pointedly, the annals remark that Quetzalcóatl had always opposed human sacrifice, and that Nezahualcóyotl prohibited the bloody cer-emony among his subjects. In effect, Nezahualcóyotl was denying the supremacy of Aztec religion and thus of Aztec sovereignty over Texcoco.

This show of autonomy was tolerated while his uncle, Itzcóatl, remained the Aztec ruler. And when Motecuhzoma I assumed the throne, Nezahualcóyotl pledged his loyalty in exchange for Texcoco's continued independence. According to the annals, Motecuhzoma was fully satisfied by this pact. But his half brother and chief adviser, Tlacaelel, strenuously objected:

"Let not the nations of the world think that we, out of fear and cowardice, have sought this accord. What will prevent other states everywhere from seeking a similar arrangement, and denying us ben-efits and authority? It seems to me that if we want to be considered the most powerful nation, the other states must hear that we have vanquished Texcoco."[11]

Tlacaelel then proposed an ingenious plan that would demonstrate Tenochtitlán's supremacy over Texcoco with a minimum of bloodshed. A phony battle would be staged between the Aztec and Texcocan warriors. Nezahualcóyotl would quickly surrender, announce the vassalage of his people, set fire to Texcoco's temple to Quetzalcóatl, and publicly embrace the cult of Huitzilopochtli. In return, Texcoco would continue to receive a portion of imperial tributes and maintain a measure of autonomy not accorded to other tribes in the valley. The fake war between Tenochtitlán and Texcoco was duly carried out, following all of Tlacaelel's conditions. Sacrificial victims for Huitzilopochtli were even handed over to the Aztecs. But Nezahualcóyotl knew he was in fact dealt a resounding defeat. His own considerable wiles were no match for Tlacaelel's cunning. And Nezahualcóyotl winced in real pain when he heard Tlacaelel, at the head of the "victorious" Aztec army, boisterously warn the Texcocans and their king: "Make certain your subjects do not rue what has been done and regret not having tested their valor and strength. And when we ask for your aid, let them dare not deny they are our servants."[12]

Henceforth, a division of duties was imposed by the Aztecs on their allies. Tlatelolco, the island just north of Tenochtitlán where a dissident Aztec faction had settled a century before, became the great commercial and market center; its merchants carried out trade with distant, still unconquered provinces, where they also served the Aztecs as spies. Tlacopán, on the western shores of Lake Texcoco directly across from Tenochtitlán, was charged with supervising the supply of food from the mainland to the Aztec capital. Texcoco, where Nezahualcóyotl would reign for almost forty years, emerged as the great cultural center of the Valley of Mexico, home to the best poets, musicians, artists, architects, and engineers.

To maintain their hegemony over the Valley of Mexico, the Aztecs now undertook a dramatic transformation of their city-state and its social structure. The successful wars had brought new farmlands, serfs, and slaves under Aztec rule. Great numbers of young Aztec men were freed from the requirements of agrarian and construction labor, and joined a rapidly expanding pool of potential soldiers. A new hierarchy of values in Tenochtitlán glorified the warrior above all social groups. "If you are faint-hearted or cowardly and don't dare go to war," the Aztec king warned his subjects, in an edict prepared by Tlacaelel, "then go till the earth and harvest corn."[13] A proliferating system of military schools recruited not only sons of pipiltín, but also young commoners, who viewed the warrior's life as their only chance for social mobility.

Because the military absorbed so many Aztec men, foreign workers and artisans began to account for a sizable portion of the population of Tenochtitlán. Here and there, the annals refer to whole neighborhoods being occupied by jewelry workers from Xochimilco, goldsmiths from the tribes in the mountains west of the Valley of Mexico, and weavers, potters, and featherworkers from provinces to the east and south. Far more numerous were the vassals brought into the city to work on construction projects. Initially, they were enlisted to raise temples to Huitzilopochtli and the other Aztec gods. But many, if not most, of these slave laborers remained in Tenochtitlán to build palaces and villas for the Aztec nobility, to improve and widen the canals and streets, to expand the island's surface by adding more chinampas to its edges, and to construct broad causeways linking the island-state to points west and south on the mainland.

By the 1450s, Tenochtitlán, with over seventy thousand inhabitants, had far outgrown all other cities in central Mexico. The focal point of the Aztec capital was the great ceremonial precinct with its pyramid to Huitzilopochtli. The pyramid-temple was rebuilt several times as the god rose in stature, but always on the same location where, according to legend, the Aztecs had first discovered an eagle devouring a serpent—the sacred sign that they had found their promised land. The ceremonial precinct also included dozens of temples to other gods and scores of residential buildings for their priestly attendants.

This large religious compound formed the northern boundary of Tenochtitlán's central plaza, a rectangular expanse measuring about 175 by 200 yards. On the east and west of the plaza were the palaces and the two-story villas of the most important dignitaries. The open space within the plaza served as the city's largest marketplace. It was crowded every day with thousands of merchants, artisans, and shoppers. A veritable inventory of ancient Mexico's produce, raw materials, and finished goods exchanged hands here: ornaments of gold, silver, copper, stones, bones, and feathers; waterfowl, turkeys, doves, parrots, hawks, and eagles; rabbits, dogs, deer, wild pigs; fish, turtles, frogs; maize, beans, chili, tomatoes, amaranth, onions, garlic, artichokes, and every sort of vegetable and fruit; honey and "octli," the fermented cactus juice; a huge assortment of cooked dishes ready to eat; medicinal herbs of all kinds; ceramics and common kitchenware, including jugs, pots, and plates; wild animal skins and textiles, in long bolts or cut into mantles, dresses, and robes; firewood and charcoal; lime, rock, and timber for construction.[14]

The goods arrived by boats on the canal that bordered the central plaza on its southern side, or by pack carriers trudging along the four broad avenues that converged on the marketplace from the cardinal directions. These same avenues marked off the four great wards that the Aztecs had created a century before. Mimicking the central plaza on a smaller scale, each of the wards had its own square, where a marketplace was bounded by a temple precinct and the villas of the local dignitaries. Finally, each ward embraced several neighborhoods, named after the old "calpulli" or clans, with small marketplaces and shrines of their own, as well as religious and military schools. Although the neighborhoods continued to be identified with specific calpulli, this was no more than a traditional formality because the rigid clan structure could not have survived the high birthrate, intermarriage, and heavy immigration into Tenochtitlán.

The gleaming, whitewashed stone villas and palaces, with their feathery banners fluttering atop parapets and towers, dominated the urban landscape. But most of Tenochtitlán's residents lived in modest mudbrick houses. Inhabited by the commoners, these homes were walled compounds of a dozen or more one- and two-room "apartments." Their facades on the streets were windowless, with a doorway as their only aperture. But in back, each dwelling unit opened into inner patios with vegetable and flower gardens and kitchen areas.[15] While the nobility made use of chairs, tables, and chests, the commoners had no furniture except for a matted bed elevated a few inches above the tamped-earth floor.

What gave Tenochtitlán an inestimable advantage over any other city in the New World was the spectacular transportation revolution achieved by the Aztecs in harnessing the full potential of the surrounding lake waters. Almost every street in the capital was paralleled by a canal, and all families owned at least one canoe. Through the use of barges and canoes, the Aztecs were largely able to compensate for the total absence of beasts of burden. Within Tenochtitlán, goods probably moved more efficiently than in European cities with their animal-drawn carts. Boats also connected the Aztec island-state directly to farms on the mainland and to the fertile chinampas of Xochimilco and Chalco to the south.

But rising demands for food and fresh water soon forced the Aztecs to radically alter their lake environment. The brackish waters of Lake Texcoco surrounding the capital were unfit for irrigation or human consumption. Lowest lying of the Valley of Mexico's five interconnecting lakes, Texcoco posed a frequent flood threat for Tenochtitlán in the rainy season when the other water bodies drained into it. A major catastrophe occurred in 1449, during the rule of Motecuhzoma I, when Lake Texcoco's "waters rose so high that the entire city was inundated and its inhabitants retreated to their canoes and rafts without knowing what to do."[16] Heavy rains and hail destroyed harvests and provoked widespread famine throughout the Valley of Mexico. With his own people occupied by military duties, Motecuhzoma I appealed for help to his cousin Nezahualcóyotl, the ruler of Texcoco, who was already renowned for engineering feats in his city-state.

The solution offered by Nezahualcóyotl was to build a giant dike that would control the levels of Lake Texcoco's waters and also decrease their salinity around Tenochtitlán enough to permit their use for irrigation. Nezahualcóyotl's dike, as it was called, was the largest and most sophisticated hydraulic project in pre-Columbian America. Tens of thousands of laborers from vassal tribes took almost a decade to complete the structure. It stretched nine miles along the eastern side of Tenochtitlán, virtually bisecting Lake Texcoco from a point on the mainland just north of the Aztec capital to a peninsula in the south. Huge logs were driven into the lake bottom forming two parallel rows sixty feet apart, and the space in between was filled in with boulders, gravel, and earth. This was no simple wall. All along its course, the dike was fitted with sluice gates that could be momentarily opened to permit the passage of boats. From now on, the portion of Lake Texcoco on the western side of Tenochtitlán was fed only by the fresh waters of Lake Xochimilco to the south when it overflowed during the rainy season. Gradually, the salinity of western Lake Texcoco decreased enough to make it suitable for irrigation purposes, and chinampas were built there to provide additional nearby food supplies for the capital.

The waters in and around Tenochtitlán were kept relatively unpolluted by strict prohibitions on the disposal of human wastes in the canals and lake. Some of the excrement was used in the curing of animal skins. Most of it—collected in outhouses by the water's edge and carried off by canoes—was applied to chinampas and fields as fertilizer. But the lake waters around Tenochtitlán were never fresh enough to drink, and the island's own underground springs and the old aqueduct from the western mainland were no longer sufficient to meet the needs of the growing population. Thus, no sooner had Nezahualcóyotl finished overseeing the construction of the dike than he was called upon again by Motecuhzoma I to manage the building of a second, larger aqueduct from Chapultepec to Tenochtitlán.

It became a project almost as complicated as the great dike. Two parallel ducts—each six feet in diameter and made of stone and wood—were built from Chapultepec's main underground spring to the Aztec capital three miles away. They were set high enough over the lake so as not to impede boat traffic. Only one of the ducts was in use at any time. The second functioned as a backup, carrying water when the other had to be cleaned or repaired.

The water was dispensed to Tenochtitlán's populace by two distinct methods. For commoners, the water was syphoned from the aqueduct into large jugs aboard canoes, and then apportioned to households all along the city's canals. But the nobility and high priests benefited from a remarkably advanced system of piped water. Shortly after reaching Tenochtitlán—just past the points where its waters were drawn off for the majority of the citizenry—the aqueduct was directed underground to the central plaza. There, it split off into a maze of clay pipes that reached the temples and residences of the ceremonial precinct and the palaces and villas of the great dignitaries. Additional plumbing guided the water into individual chambers and pools in these noble residences, and then drained it away into nearby canals.

By the mid-1400s, Tenochtitlán had become the glittering hub of an empire that provided the Aztecs with economic and military security. They could have emulated the more ancient Teotihuacanos and Toltecs, who limited their realms to the Valley of Mexico and carried out a lucrative trade with more distant tribes. There were no compelling economic or strategic reasons for the Aztecs to extend their conquests. They themselves claimed to be motivated by their commitment to impose the cult of Huitzilopochtli throughout the known world. But they had always reinterpreted religion and recast the gods to fit their new circumstances. And so, as their self-esteem swelled, the Aztecs embarked on an era of almost continuous warfare that confused their divine mission with visions of tribal grandeur.

Motecuhzoma I began the new cycle of conquest shortly after assuming the throne in 1440. Goaded by his half brother Tlacaelel, he ordered the building of a temple to Huitzilopochtli even larger than the one constructed during his predecessor's reign. Motecuhzoma decreed that all vassal peoples contribute laborers and material to the grand enterprise. He hesitated, however, to demand the participation of the Chalcas, the only major tribe in the Valley of Mexico not yet under Aztec rule. He had reason to vacillate, because the Chalcas were the fiercest and most numerous warriors the Aztecs had yet encountered. But Tlacaelel was insistent, and issued the strongest rebuke to an Aztec monarch found anywhere in the annals: "Oh powerful king, what are you saying? Is it possible you are not made of the stuff of our generation of [Aztecs]?" A contrite Motecuhzoma, "almost ashamed," replied: "My brother, you know what is best. Do as you wish."[17]

The war against the Chalcas was costly, lasting on and off for twenty years. In the beginning, Aztec forces were directly under Motecuhzoma's command, in keeping with Tlacaelel's novel creed that a new ruler should mark his enthronement by personally leading his people in war and splashing his feet with the blood of sacrificial victims. Motecuhzoma acquitted himself well in battle, and returning to Tenochtitlán, he executed the first batch of Chalca prisoners. In the already ritualized ceremony, a victim was led up the steps of the pyramid (still the old temple because the new structure was not yet completed). Reaching the platform at the summit, the prisoner was toppled onto his back on a large ceremonial stone set in front of Huitzilopochtli's statue. Four priests with long, blood-encrusted hair, wearing blood-soiled black robes, each held a leg or an arm, and a fifth priest secured the victim's neck with a rope. Then Motecuhzoma raised a heavy obsidian knife above his head, quickly rammed it into the victim's thorax, reached a hand into the gaping wound and wrenched the heart loose. The organ, still beating, was held aloft by the king and its blood was sprinkled in the air, in the general direction of the noontime sun, to fuel its course across the heavens. The heart was then jammed into the open mouth of Huitzilopochtli's statue, nourishing the god. The lifeless body of the Chalca warrior was removed, and another prisoner took his place on the ceremonial stone slab.[18] Motecuhzoma and Tlacaelel took turns dispatching the first few victims. The remainder were executed by the chief priests, relieving each other when fatigue set in.

As the war with the stubborn Chalcas continued, Tlacaelel devised more macabre methods of sacrifice. After one battle in which five hundred Chalca warriors were captured, he ordered that they be roasted alive. Whole groups of prisoners were lowered into a giant charcoal-burning brazier set in the ground in front of the great Huitzilopochtli idol. The charred victims, convulsing in pain, were pulled up from the brazier before they died, and their hearts were carved out.[19]

Yet the Chalcas would not surrender, and they dealt heavy losses to the Aztecs, even killing three brothers of Motecuhzoma and Tla-caelel. The Aztec ruler, saddened by the loss of his relatives, turned to Tlacaelel for solace. But he received no sympathy from Tlacaelel, who remarked that these deaths were "neither frightening nor admirable . . . after all, that is what war is about."[20]

Tlacaelel welcomed the conflict against the Chalcas as an opportunity to train Aztec youngsters year after year in the art of war. He enlisted boys as young as twelve years of age to carry supplies and weapons, to witness the ferocious battles around Chalco in the southeast of the Valley of Mexico, and to guard prisoners before they were marched back to Tenochtitlán for sacrifice. And despite the prolonged war against the Chalcas, the Aztecs extended their empire elsewhere. During the quarter-century reign of Motecuhzoma I, his forces conquered tribes eastward all the way to the Gulf of Mexico, southward through Morelos, Oaxaca, to the edge of the Maya lands in Yucatán and Chiapas, and westward to the Pacific Ocean.

To maintain power over these new domains, Tlacaelel created a political system aimed at making the rulers of the conquered tribes more beholden to the Aztecs than to their own people. He used the same social and religious elements that had served the Aztecs so well. The Aztec pipiltín or nobles had long defended their right to rule by tenuously tracing their bloodlines back to the ancient, revered Toltecs. And so, the lords of the conquered provinces were allowed to make the same preposterous claims if they wed daughters of the Aztec pipiltín. The male offspring of these marriages were eventually chosen by the Aztec monarch to become rulers of the vassal tribes.

Like their masters in Tenochtitlán, the lords of the subject provinces were entrusted with the sacred task of nourishing the sun god, Huitzilopochtli. They not only had to send back regular levies of sacrificial victims to the Aztec capital; they were also required to carry out sacrifices among their own people in the local temples that were built to honor the sun god. While the Aztec pipiltín largely confined their cannibalism to victims selected from other tribes, the provincial lords were forced to eat their own subjects. And to ensure that these gruesome practices were carried out, thousands of priests were sent from Tenochtitlán to villages and towns throughout the Aztec realm.[21]

The Huitzilopochtli cult and sacrifices to the other Aztec gods claimed ten to twenty thousand victims a year, most of them warriors from conquered tribes.[22] Immolations on such a vast scale greatly weakened the potential of a military revolt against the Aztecs by their vassals. The lords of newly subdued provinces were invited to Tenochtitlán so that they might be graphically initiated into the workings of the system. First, the Aztecs gave them mantles, robes, and jewelry as rewards for helping to keep their tribes submissive. Then, they were made to witness the butchering of their own warriors, as a warning against the consequences of rebellion. Some provincial rulers "were beside themselves with fear, on seeing the killing and sacrificing of so many of their men, and were left speechless in terror."[23] And "from then onwards, all their provinces and cities no longer rebelled or disputed the will of the [Aztecs]."[24]

But these claims on the efficacy of religious terror were exaggerated. There were numerous minor uprisings throughout the fifteenth century, and on some occasions the Aztecs were forced to reconquer whole tribes. The situation became especially serious during the first half of the 1450s when natural disasters struck central Mexico. Two successive harvests in the Valley of Mexico were partially devoured by grasshoppers, and frosts destroyed most of the remaining crops. One year, heavy snows and rains caused severe floods throughout the valley, and the two succeeding years witnessed a prolonged drought. There was famine almost everywhere in the Aztec domains, including Tenochtitlán. Starving people scavenged for roots and wild plants in the hills and mountains. Many Aztec commoners sold their children for maize from distant tribes unaffected by the crisis.[25] Facing hunger, vassal tribes refused to meet the growing Aztec demands for food tribute. Rebellion seemed imminent throughout the empire as the provincial lords, who had collaborated with the Aztecs in order to remain in power, struggled to control their subjects.

But Tlacaelel was able to cope with the challenge. If conflicts appeared inevitable, they would be battles that the Aztecs could manipulate. He resurrected the same stratagem of a phony war that he had used to bring Nezahualcóyotl and his Texcocans to heel. Before hostilities erupted, Tlacaelel and Motecuhzoma I secretly met with their provincial puppet rulers—the chieftains of the rebellious tribes—who informed them of the size and placement of their forces, thus ensuring victory for the Aztecs. Tlacaelel gave utmost priority to the taking of prisoners, and decreed that Aztec warriors who failed in this task risked losing their pipiltín status and falling back into the lowly ranks of commoners.[26]

These phony wars proved so successful that they were declared on an almost monthly schedule between the Aztecs and a half-dozen of their most troublesome vassal tribes. After each battle, the erstwhile enemy chieftains were secretly invited to Tenochtitlán to witness the sacrifice of their own warriors and eat their flesh in the banquets that followed. They observed the executions to Huitzilopochtli while hiding behind a screen of roses—and thus the staged struggles came to be known as "Flower Wars."[27] When the sacrificial ceremonies were over, the vassal chieftains, laden with gifts from their hosts, left Tenochtitlán as they arrived: under the cover of darkness and in disguise, so that neither their own subjects nor the Aztec warriors and commoners would suspect their complicity.

The Flower Wars effectively stifled the widespread unrest during the famine years of the 1450s, and they were periodically revived in the decades ahead, whenever a crisis loomed or real wars failed to provide the requisite number of sacrificial victims to Huitzilopochtli.

When Motecuhzoma I died in 1468, two years after the obstinate Chalcas were finally subdued, Tlacaelel turned down the monarchy. He was too old to fulfill the strenuous military obligations which he himself had hoisted upon whoever was to occupy the Aztec throne. But he was confident that he could control Tenochtitlán and its empire even more easily than he had while his prestigious half brother was alive. The new ruler, chosen by Tlacaelel, was Axayacatl, one of the numerous sons of Motecuhzoma I. He was young and vigorous enough to satisfy Tlacaelel's unending appetite for wars and sacrificial victims.

Axayacatl began his reign auspiciously by leading the Aztecs to victory over the Toluca tribe in the fertile highlands west of the Valley of Mexico. But he met disaster when he followed up this campaign with an invasion of the mighty Tarascans in Michoacán further to the west, the same tribe the Aztecs had encountered in their wandering through the wilderness many generations before. The Tarascans annihilated the Aztec columns in an ambush, and Axayacatl returned to Tenochtitlán with only a few hundred surviving warriors.

It was the worst defeat in the empire's history, and brought unrest to the very doorstep of the capital. In Tlatelolco, the island adjoining Tenochtitlán, which originally had been populated by a dissident Aztec faction and had grown into the commercial center of the empire, the ruling pipiltín sensed an opportunity to displace the aging Tlacaelel and his now discredited ruler Axayacatl. The Tlatelolco nobles conspired with vassal and allied states of the Aztecs, and called for an end to Tenochtitlán's hegemony. But in a fierce battle with Axayacatl's forces in 1473, the Tlatelolco warriors were routed and their leaders executed. The great marketplace and merchant bureaucracy of Tla-

telolco were allowed to continue their activities, but the semiauton-
omous status of the island ended, and it was placed under a regent
appointed by Tenochtitlán.

Axayacatl died in 1479, perhaps from old war wounds. Tlacaelel,
more politically powerful than ever despite his eighty-one years of age,
had little trouble manipulating the Supreme Council into appointing
Axayacatl's younger brother, Tizoc, to the throne. But Tizoc turned
out to be a calamitous choice. An incompetent military commander,
he failed to conquer new provinces and instead ordered expeditions
against tribes already under Aztec rule. In a tasteless display of vanity,
he commissioned sculptures of himself that bore an unmistakable
resemblance to paintings of Huitzilopochtli leading the Aztecs in battle. Tizoc was poisoned in 1484, on orders from Tlacaelel, who covered
up the sordid affair by orchestrating an enormous funeral for the king.

Tlacaelel knew his own life was nearing the end. He was the sole
surviving founder of the Aztec empire. He had directed the rewriting
of his people's history so thoroughly that only he could separate fact
from myth. Who else could remember the days when Tenochtitlán
was a miserable muddy island and the tribes throughout the Valley of
Mexico scoffed at Aztec claims to a noble past and future? Who else
could recall the times when Huitzilopochtli was just another tribal god
of battle? And what would prevent the Aztecs from slipping back into
ignominy? After all, what had become of the mighty Tepanecas, so
feared and powerful for one hundred fifty years? The last decade had
not been illustrious for the Aztecs. Axayacatl, for all his youthful energy
and valor, had been routed by the Tarascans, and had to stifle a
rebellion in Tlatelolco, a stone's throw from the capital, by people
who called themselves Aztecs. And Tizoc . . . Tizoc had been far
worse, a wretched bungler, who "spent most of his reign closeted in
his palace, without showing a speck of brilliance, but rather a lot of
cowardice."[28] Tlacaelel had often warned Aztec rulers that they must
never appear to be weak in the eyes of other provinces, "lest they hold
us in ridicule and contempt." Would he now live to see such a shameful thing come to pass?

Before he died, he wanted one last demonstration of Aztec greatness,
of his own greatness, really. A new temple-pyramid would be erected
to Huitzilopochtli, far more imposing than the others. The entire
empire would send forth armies of laborers for the monument. And
all the rulers of vassal tribes and even of unconquered provinces would
be convoked for the inauguration of the temple in a ceremony so
bloody that it would be remembered for generations.

But first a new Aztec king had to be enthroned. Tlacaelel was determined to make the right choice, for it would be his last. Again, he picked a son of Motecuhzoma I, this time a mere adolescent named Ahuizotl. There were murmurs of protest among the pipiltín that he was too young to reign. A few nobles couched their opposition with a cunning proposal: they demanded that Tlacaelel himself assume the throne, although they knew full well that he was too old to accept. Tlacaelel dismissed these maneuvers with brutal frankness:

"Have I not always judged and commanded? Have I not had the power to kill transgressors and pardon the innocent? Have I not made and unmade lords? Have I not written the laws . . . taken up the knife and sacrificed men . . . ? Why should you be concerned that my nephew Ahuizotl be king? I will always be at his side to crush any evil-doers. . . . So hold your tongues and do my bidding for I am already king and I will remain so until I die."[29]

The youthful Ahuizotl was crowned king. Three years later, in 1487, the colossal new temple to Huitzilopochtli was completed. At the platform on its summit, there were two dark sanctuaries—one for Huitzilopochtli and the other for the rain god Tlaloc—and in front of these chapels were placed four sacrificial slabs of stone. The four sides of the pyramid were carved with steps angled slightly downward so that the bodies of the immolated victims could roll easily to the foot of the temple where butchers would await to cart them away.

Four days were set aside for the ceremonies inaugurating the temple. Rulers and nobles of all the vassal provinces and enemy tribes were invited, and they were asked to bring their warriors and even commoners. An unprecedented mass of humanity converged on Tenochtitlán, "so that there was no space left in the streets, the plazas, the markets, the houses, which took on the appearance of an anthill with too many ants."[30] The numbers of prisoners for sacrifice were also far greater than on any other occasion—the sources estimate anywhere from twenty to eighty thousand men.[31] They were arranged in four long columns, stretching beyond the city's limits all the way up to the pyramid's summit in front of the four sacrificial slabs. A few thousand of the victims were prisoners from the most recent Aztec conquests; but the great majority were handed over to the Aztecs by their vassal rulers or captured in the Flower Wars. As usual, the nobles from the tributary provinces and enemy states were seated behind screens of roses, discreetly out of sight from the multitude. They feasted on corncakes, fruits, barbecued meats, beans, and any delicacies their hosts could conjure up. They drank copious drafts of cocoa. And they nibbled on hallucinogenic mushrooms to dull their senses during the bloody spectacle.[32]

At dawn, the ghastly celebration began. The kings of Texcoco and Tlacopán, the two other members of the old Triple Alliance, were invited to join Tlacaelel and Ahuizotl as chief executioners. Holding a heavy obsidian knife, each of the luminaries stood in front of a sacrificial stone slab. To the lugubrious beat of giant drums and the ear-splitting wail of conch shells, the four columns of prisoners began their death march. One after another, the victims were grasped by priests and slammed down on the stone slabs. Their hearts were ripped out, and their bodies kicked over the sides of the pyramid. Each prisoner was dispatched in a matter of seconds. Their screams were muffled by the booming drums. All struggle was useless. Nothing interrupted the steady movement of the human columns as one life after another was snuffed out. When the kings, splattered in blood, tired of the killing, they ceded their places to high priests, who in turn were eventually relieved by their juniors. For four days and nights, the massacre proceeded without respite. "The streams of human blood that ran down the temple's steps congealed into great, horrible clots. Many priests scurried around to scoop up this blood in urns and rushed to all the temples and chapels in the neighborhoods to smear their walls and roofs and idols. . . . The stench was so great throughout the city that the populace found it unbearable."[33] The dead were decapitated, and their heads placed on racks that would be covered with lime to shore up the walls of the pyramid. The bodies were dragged off to neighborhood temples to be dismembered and cooked. But on this occasion, the victims were so numerous that many headless corpses were simply thrown into Lake Texcoco.[34] "The butchery was so enormous and cruel that neither before nor afterwards was there anything like it."[35]

At the end of the four days, the noble guests were all given rich gifts by Ahuizotl: finely woven cloths, ceramics, jewelry, wild animal skins, gold necklaces and bracelets. But Tlacaelel remarked to Ahuizotl that long after these rulers forgot about their sumptuous presents, they would remember the slaughter: "Let our enemies go and tell their people what they have seen."[36]

Tlacaelel lived almost a decade longer, until 1496, but there is little mention of him in the annals following the hideous death feast to Huitzilopochtli. Since the annals were written under his direction, we must assume that he preferred it that way. Nothing would be allowed to overshadow what he considered his final great moment.

THREE

MOTECUHZOMA

Ahuizotl, the last monarch appointed by Tlacaelel, did not long survive his mentor's death. In 1500, a badly engineered dam, built on the southern mainland to service a new aqueduct for Tenochtitlán, collapsed sending an uncontrolled torrent of water into Lake Texcoco. A flash flood enveloped the Aztec capital. Thousands of residents drowned or were crushed by falling buildings. Ahuizotl was in his garden when the waters began to engulf him. Rushing for safety toward the roof of his palace, he slammed his head against a stone beam and was knocked unconscious. The king was rescued by his attendants, but he died three years later still in a coma.

With his death, the Supreme Council of Aztec nobles or pipiltín were finally able to appoint a monarch—a privilege that had been denied them for more than six decades by Tlacaelel. Perhaps for this reason, the annals describe the selection of the new ruler in great detail, and emphasize that the Supreme Council members took their task solemnly, with much speechmaking and consultation. A long list of potential candidates is mentioned by the chroniclers. But in the end, only one man was seriously considered: Motecuhzoma II, named after his grandfather, the great king.

In his youth, the second Motecuhzoma distinguished himself in battle as a leading general. At the time of his candidacy for the throne, he was a high priest of Huitzilopochtli, the terrible hummingbird god. This combination of military prowess and religious piety raised him above his rivals in the eyes of the Supreme Council. He often secluded himself in a dark chamber in Huitzilopochtli's pyramid to commune with the god, or retreated to the solitude of the mountains to write poetry. In fact, when the Supreme Council members announced his election as monarch, they had trouble locating him to convey the news and finally found him cloistered in his chapel, praying to Huitzilopochtli. At his coronation, the main speech was delivered by Nezahualpilli, the ruler of Texcoco, who lauded Motecuhzoma for his valor, knowledge, prudence, and spirituality, and asserted that Huitzilopochtli must have indeed loved the Aztecs "because he has given them the light to choose the man most suited to rule."[1] Upon hearing this homage, Motecuhzoma modestly lamented that "with so many noble and generous men in this kingdom, you have chosen me, the least worthy of all."[2]

The humility exhibited by Motecuhzoma II before and during his enthronement pleased the Aztec nobles and the rulers of the allied tribes, who had been treated shabbily by the monarchs of Tenochtitlán for so many decades. Here at last was a reasonable young man, who seemed so deferential to the elder pipiltín and so willing to seek their counsel. But these early impressions were to prove deceptive. Behind his piety and introversion, Motecuhzoma II secretly harbored an arrogance and ambition unmatched by any of his predecessors, including Tlacaelel.

Only a few days after becoming king, Motecuhzoma ordered the resignation of advisers held over from previous monarchies, and the removal of all the leading generals and vassal rulers. Officials who showed reluctance or hesitated to give up their posts were summarily executed or exiled.[3] To replace them, Motecuhzoma chose inexperienced sycophants because, as he explained, "those who have been in the service of some other great lord or king will question anything new I order, and will whisper behind my back and undermine me . . . and so I do not wish to have such people around me."[4]

Motecuhzoma was especially eager to root out any bureaucrats risen from the ranks of the commoners, whom he despised even if they had gained pipiltín status by heroism on the battlefields. On his prejudice against the commoners, the annals record the following exchange between the ruler and one of his senior counselors:

[Motecuhzoma]:   I have decided that all who serve me be lords or sons of lords and princes, and not only here in my household, but throughout my kingdom, because I am deeply offended that past rulers entrusted such posts to low-born people. So, I have decided to remove them from any royal posts, and thus ennoble my household and kingdom by cleansing them of such people.

[Counselor]: Great lord, wise and powerful as you are, you are entitled to do as you please, but it seems to me that this will not be thought of well because people will say that you are undoing things decreed by past kings, and you will alienate yourself from the poor, humble commoners, who will not even dare to look at you.

[Motecuhzoma]: That is precisely what I pretend. Let no commoner consider himself the equal of a lord nor dare to gaze upon his king. . . . After all, these are crude people, and as industrious as they might be, they smell of barbarity.[5]

Motecuhzoma then took the extraordinary step of elevating himself to a deity, something not even Tlacaelel had attempted. Because he considered himself divine, he decreed that any commoner who looked at him would be sentenced to death. "And so they worshipped him as a god, prostrating themselves on the ground until he passed by them."[6] This practice was so strictly enforced that many years later the Spanish missionary historian Fray Diego de Durán reported that his old Indian informants were unable to physically describe Motecuhzoma.

Purged of all descendants of commoners, the king's household staff consisted of hundreds of youthful pipiltín, sons of the greatest lords in Tenochtitlán and the Valley of Mexico. Never had such high-ranking nobles been required to provide their children as menial servants of a monarch, sweeping his palace floors, dressing and feeding him, attending to his every personal need. Like commoners, the youths were taught to prostrate themselves in the presence of Motecuhzoma. They had to learn a new, highly stilted form of speech to address their king, "speaking without stuttering, without excitement, neither too loudly nor too softly, and slowly and with much gravity. . . . And so they all wandered about mortified, and so modest, polite and obliging that they seemed like another breed of people."[7] Whenever these young nobles faltered in their tasks, Motecuhzoma would angrily demand "how in the house of god could they dare be so negligent, for he called his household 'the house of god,' and for any irreverence he meted out the punishment of death."[8]

Simple delusions of grandeur are not enough to explain Motecuhzoma's harsh arrogance. The purge of his household presaged a general reordering of Aztec society and imperial politics. And his elevation to divine status was part of a policy aimed at enabling him to make unprecedented demands on his subjects in an effort to confront serious problems in his realms. Beyond the Valley of Mexico, Aztec rule faced growing challenges from enemy and vassal tribes. Within the valley's confines, there is evidence of an ecological crisis as population began to outstrip natural resources.

By the early 1500s, Tenochtitlán had become the center of a vast connurbation in the Valley of Mexico. The island-state itself was densely populated with about 200,000 inhabitants, more than any European city of that epoch. The pace of urbanization well beyond Tenochtitlán's outskirts was almost as impressive. About 400,000 people lived on the lake bed, plains, and foothills within a radius of fifteen miles from the capital's epicenter. From the mountain peaks, Greater Tenochtitlán must have appeared like a single sprawling metropolis linked by a complex network of causeways and canals. The 2,700 square miles encompassing the whole Valley of Mexico was populated by as many as 1.2 million people, a figure all the more startling because it was not surpassed until the beginning of the twentieth century—an era of livestock and pack animals, trains and some motorized vehicles, rudimentary electrification and communications, and a health system that could at least cope with epidemic disease.[9]

To support this rapidly expanding population, the Aztecs had to raise the valley's agricultural output above the already high levels achieved during the previous century. They focused these efforts mainly on the chinampas of Xochimilco and Chalco, the freshwater lakes south of the capital which were the closest and most productive farming centers. Before they were conquered by the Aztecs, the Xochimilcas and Chalcas were able to enjoy a rather leisurely agrarian life. They attempted no more than one or two harvests a year on their fertile, artificial isles, consuming most of the crops and trading the surplus with nearby tribes. But the increasingly heavier food demands of Tenochtitlán put an end to this slow-paced existence. By the early 1500s, the two southern water bodies were covered by 25,000 acres of chinampas and looked more like swamps than lakes. Not only did the Xochimilca and Chalca farmers have to build more artificial isles, but they were also forced to raise their production per acre. Seeds were allowed to germinate in small beds on the mainland, and only the seedlings that sprouted were transplanted to the chinampas, thus maximizing yields. This technique of planting seeds separately from the maturing crops also ensured several harvests a year on a single chinampa plot.

An effort was also made to coax greater output from the more conventional agriculture practiced on the plains, away from the lakes. Even in the times of the ancient Teotihuacanos and Toltecs, the inhabitants of the Valley of Mexico had been able to achieve higher yields than Old World farmers by intercropping—that is, planting beans, squash, and chili beneath their maize stalks. This replenished the nitrogenous content of the soil and made it unnecessary to periodically leave fields fallow as the Europeans were forced to do. Under Aztec hegemony, the harvests on the plains were increased through a much greater use of human excrement for fertilizer and by a pronounced expansion of irrigation. Although the most spectacular hydraulic projects were carried out within the lakes, hundreds of smaller-scaled efforts were promoted throughout the valley to draw into the fields the waters of underground springs, streams, and rivers. The most notable of these feats took place north of the lake system where a major river, the Cuauhtitlán, was diverted off its course by dams and canals to irrigate a large farming zone.[10]

Finally, under the Aztecs there was extensive terracing of the hills and mountainsides surrounding the Valley of Mexico. Some highland cultivation of maize and other vegetables dated back to the first millennium A.D. and continued to be practiced in Aztec times. Stone terraces were built to hold the thin mountain soils in place and capture rainfall trickling down the slopes. But the Aztecs were more concerned that these zones be used for fruit trees, the cactus plants that produced their alcoholic beverages, and, above all, for timber reserves to meet their heavy construction and fuel demands. The extensive terracing also decreased the amount of nitrate soils that were being washed down by the rains into the lakes and spoiling their waters.

According to the annals, Motecuhzoma II was prepared to ruthlessly ensure that the largest possible harvests be gathered from all these agrarian zones in the Valley of Mexico, "Throughout the villages and provinces of his kingdom, planting was carried out by force," explained an Indian account cited by a Spanish colonial writer. "And there were inspectors to see that the lands were planted, and if not [the local ruler] was put in prison, which was worse than death. . . ."[11]

When harvests were bountiful, the Valley of Mexico was able to feed almost all its inhabitants. The chinampas alone provided between one half and two thirds of the food requirements of Tenochtitlán.[12] And most of the capital's remaining deficit was covered by surpluses in the plains. Usually no more than 10 to 15 percent of Tenochtitlán's food came from outside the valley, because beyond the reach of the lakes goods could be moved only on the backs of men, who themselves had to be fed along the way.

But pests and inclement weather often created a precarious balance between the supply and demand of food. And after Motecuhzoma ascended the throne, efforts were made to control overpopulation in the valley. Probably inspired by Tlacaelel's tactics in the previous century, the new monarch implemented this policy under the guise of religion. To satisfy the voracious appetite of the gods, Aztec commoners joined the conquered peoples as sacrificial victims.

The increase in child sacrifice was particularly appalling. Infanticide became most prevalent during food shortages because children, being unproductive, were the most expendable members of the tribe. Child sacrifices were carried out at the height of the dry season, during the first three months of the Aztecs' eighteen-month calendar year, when the rain god, Tlaloc, had to be honored. The children were purchased by Motecuhzoma's priestly agents from their mothers, who could not refuse these offers. Many of the infants were so young they were still being nursed. Somewhat older children were selected by arbitrary criteria, such as birthmarks or cowlicks, which were alleged to be divine signs. "And when [the priests] took the children to the places where they would be killed, if they cried and shed many tears, the onlookers became joyful because it was considered a sign that the rains would come soon," states one account.[13] But the joy was confined to the priests and their attendants. The same source mentions that wherever the processions of tiny victims passed, the commoners who saw them began to weep.

Even if the commoners were fortunate enough to escape this dragnet in their childhood, they had no assurance that they would not be sacrificed as adults. Their fate was quite literally in their stars. They were taught by the priests that they were born under one of twenty astrological signs. Four of these signs were especially unlucky, marking their bearers for death or enslavement.[14] Whenever slaves or sacrificial victims were in short supply, the priests fulfilled the new quotas by simply glancing through the birth records that were assiduously kept for all Aztecs.

According to the annals, it was under Motecuhzoma that Aztec commoners for the first time became victims of cannibalism by their own tribe. Cannibalism has long been a subject of intense controversy among scholars of ancient Mexico. A number of historians and anthropologists assert that the practice never went beyond occasional religious ritual.[15] They are especially wary of eyewitness accounts of Aztec cannibalism provided by the Spanish conquistadores, who were trying to morally justify their brutal subjugation of the natives by casting them in the most inhuman light. For the same reasons, these scholars question the evidence of widespread sacrifice and cannibalism that appears in the Indians' own written and oral annals. Most of this documentation was transcribed by sixteenth-century Spanish missionaries and Indian or mestizo converts who were anxious to discredit the religious practices of the Aztecs and other tribes. But the annals and the commentaries of the early colonial missionaries are the major fountains of our knowledge of Aztec civilization. Their descriptions of ritualized mass executions and the eating of human flesh ring as true as their accounts of warfare, monarchical successions, architectural and engineering accomplishments, and the details of everyday life. If these histories are not to be believed on the subject of sacrifice and cannibalism, then they probably should not be accepted on any matters.

At the other extreme are a few scholars who suggest that cannibalism was indeed widespread, that it was necessary to meet deficiencies in animal protein in the Aztec diet, and that the practice increased in times of food shortage.[16] But this is overstating the case. The scarcity of meat did not endanger human survival in central Mexico. Most people there, like everywhere in the world throughout history, maintained themselves on an almost entirely vegetarian regimen. The diet of Aztec commoners—maize, beans, chili, amaranth, and other vegetables—probably provided them with more calories, carbohydrates, and proteins than their counterparts in Asia, Africa, and Europe.

If we accept the accounts of large-scale cannibalism described in the annals and later chronicles, the most plausible explanation for the phenomenon is its link to social status. As anywhere in the premodern world, meat in ancient Mexico was a luxury, the exclusive prerogative of the advantaged classes. In the near absence of wild game and domesticated animals, cannibalism was not a taboo in Mexico even before the Aztecs. But in the fifteenth century, under the auspices of Tlacaelel, the consumption of human flesh became far more frequent, and was a powerful sign of privilege. It set the warriors, priests, and aristocrats apart from lowlier groups. They deserved human flesh because they were closer to the gods than the commoners were. It was through sacrifice and cannibalism that the gods—particularly Huitzilopochtli—remained vital and content. And the upper castes communed with the deities by sharing their holy food.

As a sign of their rising social status under Motecuhzoma II, merchants and artisans were also allowed to consume human flesh. Since they could not go into battle to capture enemy warriors, they were permitted to purchase slaves for sacrifice. Almost invariably their victims were not members of vassal or enemy tribes, but Aztec commoners, who had been reduced to slavery because they had fallen into debt or were born under an unlucky astrological sign. They were sold at the great slave market of Azcapozalco, a site on the mainland a few miles west of Tenochtitlán.

At Azcapozalco, the slave traders dressed up their wards—both men and women—as attractively as possible, with mantles and robes, garlands of flowers, and strings of precious stones. To better display their figures, the slaves were ordered to dance. The buyer haggled with the traders until a price of thirty or forty mantles per victim was agreed upon. Before the slaves were led away by their new master, the traders took care to remove the costumes and jewelry they were wearing and save them for another batch of slaves. The buyer housed the slaves until they were suitably fattened for sacrifice. Only the women were made to work, usually as weavers, taking advantage of their skills up until the day they were killed.[17]

Prisoners of war and vassals handed over as tribute, of course, continued to be the largest group of people to face ritual slaughter in Tenochtitlán. Following a major battle or Flower War, a single ceremony could claim thousands of victims. But now that merchants and artisans could stage their own bloody festivals, hardly a week went by without sacrifices and cannibalism in the Aztec capital and its vassal provinces. Merchants, artisans, and other professional groups each had a patron deity associated with their trade or craft, and some of these gods were important enough to be honored by sacrifice several times a year. The feasts that followed these religious ceremonies were an opportunity for the merchant or professional to flaunt his wealth. The host who served his guests the most sumptuous banquet of human flesh and other meat greatly enhanced his prestige.[18] As cannibalism spread to these newly privileged social classes, it spawned a culinary tradition with an assortment of recipes: human flesh stewed in corn, or squash, or chili.[19] The victim's thigh, considered the most delectable part, was frequently offered as a gift to Motecuhzoma or his provincial rulers.[20]

By claiming greater powers than any of his predecessors over the nobles and, especially, the commoners, Motecuhzoma II tightened his grip over Tenochtitlán. But beyond the Valley of Mexico, the Aztec empire was showing signs of unrest and fissure. The Huitzilopochtli cult— with its massive requirements of sacrificial victims—could terrorize tribes into submission, but also created a permanent potential for revolt. And the tribute demanded by the Aztecs was a constant source of complaint. A very partial listing of the levies collected from vassal tribes during a single year included 214,000 cloaks, 16,000 bales of cotton, 14,400 wooden beams, 28,800 bowls, 3,200 deerskins, 32,000 bundles of paper, 6,400 bunches of quetzal feathers, and 240 large gold discs.[21]

A rising spirit of rebellion took hold during the last three years of Ahuizotl's reign, when that king lay comatose between life and death. With Aztec leadership paralyzed, few military expeditions could be mounted against troublesome provinces. The more far-flung vassal tribes began refusing to send tribute or sacrificial victims to Tenochtitlán. They even dared to murder Aztec missionaries and merchants, and attack undermanned Aztec garrisons. Some of these rebellious peoples surrounded their cities with fortified walls and established reconnaissance networks that could alert them to the arrival of Aztec forces. No longer could the Aztecs count on simply intimidating their enemies into submission. Any war was costly in supplies and casualties. Thus the annals speak of expeditionary forces of unprecedented size during Motecuhzoma's reign, numbering 100,000, even a quarter million men. So large were his military requirements that he had to reach beyond his forces and those of his allies from the old Triple Alliance to recruit warriors from loyal, vassal tribes.

The first war under Motecuhzoma was launched in 1503 against Nopallán and Icpatepec, rebellious provinces located about four hundred miles southeast of the Aztec capital. Motecuhzoma's huge army included Aztecs, Texcocans, Tepanecas, Chalcas, Xochimilcas, and warriors "from all the other provinces."[22] They attacked the fortified rebel cities by night, scaling the walls and killing many of the defenders in their sleep, and then overwhelming the disorganized inhabitants. Aztec garrisons were installed in Nopallán and Icpatepec to ensure that tribute from these provinces resumed, and more than five thousand prisoners were marched back to Tenochtitlán for sacrifice.

The victory ceremonies were a throwback to the splendid horror of the Tlacaelel era. Motecuhzoma invited the lords of all his vassal states and the rulers of the traditional enemy provinces—the unconquered Tarascans from the west, and the Tlaxcalans, Huexotzincas, and Cholulans to the east. These enemy guests arrived and departed in disguise, "always moving about at night and by hidden passages so that they would not be seen or recognized" by Aztec warriors or commoners who would never understand why enemy rulers should be honored.[23]

Motecuhzoma was hoping to impress his guests the same way Tlacaelel did—by showing them the brilliance and might of Tenochtitlán, and the cruel death that opponents could expect on the sacrificial stone. All 5,100 prisoners were slain on the summit of Huitzilopochtli's pyramid, with the king himself dispatching the initial victims. The guests, inebriated with fermented cactus juice, witnessed the spectacle from their rose-screened balconies. They munched on the delicacies placed before them while they awaited the main course of human flesh. And at the end of the festivities, they received the customary gifts of jewelry, robes, and rich featherwork. But the intended effect of striking awe and fear in Aztec opponents no longer worked the way it had in Tlacaelel's day.

The victory celebrations for his first war had hardly ended when Motecuhzoma was forced to organize another military expedition, this time against the Xaltepec tribe, which was refusing to send either tribute or sacrificial victims. Xaltepec lay at the southeastern extreme of the Aztec empire about eight hundred miles away from Tenoch-titlán. The distance that Motecuhzoma's army had to cover was so great that careful planning was necessary to ensure that food and supplies could be collected from subject tribes all along the way. Though heavily outnumbered, the Xaltepec forces battled the Aztec army for several days before they were routed. To set an example against other vassal tribes that might be tempted to revolt, Mote-cuhzoma ordered the execution of every Xaltepec man and woman above the age of fifty, asserting that "these are the ones who commit treason and are the cause of rebellions and incite the younger people by always giving them bad advice."[24] But sporadic uprisings continued, especially on the Pacific and Gulf coasts where the tribes still hoped that the many miles separating them from the Aztec capital would discourage punitive expeditions.

Motecuhzoma was facing a far more serious challenge closer to his capital. Just east of the Valley of Mexico, tribes like the Tlaxcalans, Cholulans, and Huexotzincas, who had never been conquered by the Aztecs, sought to take advantage of the fact that Motecuhzoma's army was being stretched too thin in its efforts to quell revolts over his far-flung empire. For decades these enemy tribes had maintained their independence by agreeing to lose Flower Wars to the Aztecs. But now these staged battles became deadlier, verging on all-out conflicts.

When Motecuhzoma invited the Huexotzincas to meet a combined army of Aztecs and their Texcocan allies for a Flower War in 1508, rumors circulated throughout the Valley of Mexico that this was not to be any mock battle. Motecuhzoma appointed three of his own brothers as generals, and before going into combat, one of them, Tlacauepan, requested an audience with the Aztec king during which he expressed his premonition of impending disaster: "Powerful lord, I do not think I will ever see your face again. I charge you with the care of my wives and children."[25]

The battle was fierce and drawn out. Contrary to the rules established in previous Flower Wars, few prisoners were taken. Tlacauepan was surrounded by enemy soldiers, but instead of accepting their offer to die later on the sacrificial stone, he preferred to be killed fighting on the field. His two brothers were also slain. When a truce was declared, the Huexotzincas were exultant. Back in Tenochtitlán, there were no victory celebrations or sacrifices, and Motecuhzoma went into seclusion for days. His ally, the Texcocan king Nezahualpilli, whose forces suffered the greatest casualties including the death of his favorite son-in-law, accused Motecuhzoma of having knowingly sent Texcocan troops to certain defeat against a superior enemy army. And Nezahualpilli made his complaint public by composing what became a popular song denouncing Motecuhzoma for "treasons and deceits."[26]

Meanwhile, following Huexotzinco's impressive battle feats, the eastern tribes were eager to engage the Aztecs in more Flower Wars. The Cholulans, not even waiting for the traditional invitation from the Aztecs, took the initiative and challenged Motecuhzoma. Reluctantly, Texcoco and Tlacopán, the other old Triple Alliance states, agreed to send their armies to fight alongside the Aztec warriors. For Motecuhzoma and his allies, the outcome was a bloody stalemate at best. The death toll was heavy on both sides, and again few captives were taken for sacrifice. When the battered Aztec forces returned to Tenochtitlán, they were met by grieving widows, "their hair disheveled, wailing loudly and beating their breasts."[27] To restore his people's morale, Motecuhzoma ordered his armies to march against weak provinces that were rumored near revolt. These were easy victories, and the thousands of prisoners sacrificed back in Tenochtitlán helped bolster the Aztec ruler's self-confidence.

But the enemy tribes in the east did not allow him to celebrate for long. Again and again, he was forced to accept their challenges to Flower Wars. An exasperated Aztec monarch decided to intimidate these rivals by reviving the cruelest sacrificial methods used by Tlacaelel. After a successful Flower War against the Tlaxcalans, Motecuhzoma decreed that special ceremonies be held for an Aztec goddess, Toci, at her new shrine on a mountain overlooking Tenochtitlán. The

Tlaxcalan prisoners were divided into three groups. The first batch were quickly dispatched by the traditional method of cutting out their hearts. Other prisoners were roasted in a giant brazier. And the remaining victims were crucified and shot full of arrows. When word of these execution methods reached the eastern tribes, they were outraged at the breach of religious etiquette—a warrior was entitled to a swift death, not a slow, painful one. One night, the Huexotzincas, allies of the Tlaxcalans, staged a raid on the Aztec goddess's shrine and burned it to the ground. An enraged Motecuhzoma arrested his own priests serving the goddess. He accused them of negligence, perhaps even complicity, and ordered them starved to death in cages strewn with sharp, jagged glass.

In reprisal against the Huexotzincas, Motecuhzoma then challenged them to a Flower War. This time both sides took numerous captives on the battlefield. The Huexotzinca rulers accepted the invitation to Tenochtitlán for the traditional postwar ceremonies during which the newly rebuilt temple to the Aztec goddess was inaugurated. There they witnessed the excruciating immolation of their captured warriors: some of them were burned alive, others gutted, flayed, and their skins distributed to Aztec beggars to wear while they made their rounds through the city asking for alms. But instead of being cowed, the Huexotzincas plotted revenge. And when the Aztec lords agreed to visit Huexotzinco, in keeping with the etiquette of the Flower Wars, it was their turn to sit through an equally barbaric ceremony during which Aztec warriors were disemboweled, roasted alive, and strung up as targets for Huexotzinca archers.[28]

By 1509, the Aztec empire was in a state of constant turmoil. Motecuhzoma had failed to quell his enemies and his rebellious vassals. Although harvests did not fall to the famine levels of a few years before, they were not enough to ensure a comfortable level of food supplies in the Valley of Mexico, and the subject provinces were openly cheating in their tribute payments to the Aztecs. Motecuhzoma, who believed himself a deity, looked everywhere for divine signs of encouragement, and cursed the gods when they were not forthcoming. His rivals, knowing that his piety verged on superstition, interpreted every drought, every freak occurrence of nature, as an omen against his empire. Among the enemy tribes, Huitzilopochtli, the supreme Aztec deity and symbol of imperial power, was demoted in favor of Quetzalcóatl, the ancient Toltec god of civilization, who was viewed as a foe of Aztec sacrificial practices. According to legend, Quetzalcóatl was defeated by another god in Toltec times, but vowed to come back someday and reclaim his realms in central Mexico. Now, in Cholula, Quetzalcóatl's priests prophesied the god's return and the imminent fall of the Aztecs.[29]

The Quetzalcóatl cult gained secret adherents among Aztec vassals, allies, and even subjects, who were sickened by the endless wars and sacrifices. Texcoco, northeast of the Aztec capital across the lake, became a center for the worship of Quetzalcóatl. And its ruler, Nezahualpilli, openly preached the return of the god and an inevitable apocalypse for the Aztec empire.[30] Despite this treasonous attitude, the Texcocan king still enjoyed great prestige in Aztec eyes. Like his father, Nezahualcóyotl, he had overseen important construction projects in Tenochtitlán. He was a courageous warrior and a faithful ally on the battlefields even though he criticized Motecuhzoma's military strategy. He was also renowned as a necromancer who could divine the future. And as a revered old man, with only a few years left, he could dare speak about unpleasant matters to the Aztec ruler without fear of being put to death. Thus, upon hearing that Motecuhzoma was in a despairing mood over the discontent spreading across his realms, Nezahualpilli paid the Aztec king a visit and predicted impending doom for the empire:

> Oh powerful and great lord, as much as I would wish not to disturb your tranquility, I am obliged to tell you of a strange, wondrous event that by the will of the lords of the skies, the night, the day and the air will occur within your lifetime. Be forewarned that . . . in a very few years our cities will be laid to waste, that we and our children and our vassals will be annihilated. And of this have no doubt. . . . And I tell you more: that before many days there will be signs in the skies that foretell of what I say to you. And do not lose faith or become anxious about what will happen because it is impossible to evade. I am comforted only by the knowledge that I will not see these calamities and afflictions because my own days are counted. And because of this, before I die, I wish only to warn you as if you were my own dear son.[31]

We can assume that Nezahualpilli was not motivated by paternal affection for the Aztec ruler. He could see that he had left Motecuhzoma "very anguished and terrorized."[32] Before returning to Texcoco, Nezahualpilli further predicted that as evidence of all these dire future events the Aztecs would never again win a Flower War against the eastern enemy tribes. Determined to prove Nezahualpilli wrong, Motecuhzoma ordered his warriors into an ill-prepared Flower War against the Tlaxcalans. The Aztecs were routed and their generals were taken prisoner. In a rage, Motecuhzoma had his surviving officers demoted to commoners and made them go about barefoot in rough-hewn cloth mantles "like vile and lowly men."[33] But short of experienced commanders, he suspended this edict within weeks and sent his officers into battle against the Tlaxcalans once again. Although it was by no means a clear-cut triumph for the Aztecs, Motecuhzoma was at least consoled by the thought that the Tlaxcalans could not claim victory either.

During the months that followed, Motecuhzoma was heartened by a number of favorable developments. Taking advantage of discord among the eastern tribes, he played a brilliant diplomatic game of further dividing his foes by offering sanctuary and support to the Huexotzincas against the Tlaxcalans. The recent harvests had been abundant. No new uprisings by vassals were reported, and tribute had resumed normal levels. The empire was holding. Perhaps Nezahualpilli was wrong after all.

But then one night, a startling event unfolded. Aztec sentinels sighted a huge comet hurtling across the dark skies, "like a fiery fuse, like a flame, like the break of day, dripping through and piercing the heavens."[34] Could this have been one of the "signs in the skies" forecast by Nezahualpilli? Motecuhzoma questioned one after another the nightwatchmen who claimed to have witnessed the terrible happening. They all repeated the same version. Next, Motecuhzoma convoked his astrologers, magicians, and soothsayers, and asked them the meaning of the shooting star. When they were unable to explain its significance, the monarch ordered all of them jailed and starved to death for their incompetence. He called Nezahualpilli back to his court, and pleaded with him for more information. But Nezahualpilli merely recited his gloomy predictions again, almost word for word: death, destruction of the empire, apocalypse.

Motecuhzoma lapsed into a mournful soliloquy:

"Oh you who have created us, oh mighty gods who have the power to kill and give life, how can you allow, after so many kings and great lords, that it be my destiny to witness the destruction of Mexico, to witness the death of my wives and children, to see myself dispossessed of my kingdom and lands and vassals we have won in conquest . . . ? What shall I do? Where shall I hide?"[35]

And then the king exploded at his underlings. Those bungling, ignorant, inept astrologers and diviners—he would not permit them to live even a day longer. Starvation was too good for them. He ordered them strangled, their houses looted and burned to the ground, and their wives and children enslaved. He then commanded his aides to find other soothsayers, men who would not lie to him or plead ignorance. The new seers were appointed, and, understandably, they predicted only the disastrous events that Motecuhzoma was likely to accept as the truth. Any mysterious incident, no matter how inconsequential, was given the darkest interpretation. Pestilence, famine, war, death lurked in every sign.

The annals dutifully record some of these harbingers of catastrophe: a fire of unknown cause damaged Huitzilopochtli's temple; another temple was struck by lightning, even though there was little rain and no sound of thunder; a whirlpool roiled the placid waters of Lake Texcoco and flooded part of Tenochtitlán; Motecuhzoma's chief adviser sleepwalked at night screaming that "we must flee far away"; all manner of freaks and physically deformed people were marched into Motecuhzoma's court as if to prove to the king that the gods were populating his realm with monsters.[36]

With the passage of several months, Motecuhzoma began to blame his paralyzing gloom on Nezahualpilli. He concocted an elaborate plot to discredit the Texcocan ruler, bring his city-state under tighter Aztec control, and root out the Quetzalcóatl cult flourishing behind its ramparts. Motecuhzoma ordered Nezahualpilli to help him disprove his prediction that the Aztecs would not win another Flower War against the eastern tribes. Together, the Aztecs and Texcocans would challenge the Tlaxcalans. Suspicious of Motecuhzoma's motives, Nezahualpilli hesitated to comply. The Aztec monarch accused him of cowardice, and Aztec agents in Texcoco reminded its nobles and warriors that they had been absent from the battlefields in recent years. Probably pressured by his own commanders, Nezahualpilli reluctantly agreed to send a large force to fight alongside the Aztecs. But he was right to distrust Motecuhzoma. In secret negotiations with the Tlaxcalan rulers, the Aztec king informed them of the size and placement of Texcoco's army, and promised not to intervene in a battle between Texcoco and Tlaxcala.

The Texcocan forces set up their campsite in a deep ravine and waited for the opening of the Flower War the next morning. But during the night, they were ambushed by the Tlaxcalans. As he promised the Tlaxcalans, Motecuhzoma held back his warriors even though from his camp on a nearby hilltop he could hear the anguished screams for help from the Texcocans. "So great was the blood of the dead and wounded flowing through that ravine that it seemed like a river."[37]

Two of Nezahualpilli's sons were killed, along with most of the Texcocan commanders and many of their troops. The survivors were
marched back to Tlaxcala to be sacrificed.

With the Texcocan army shattered, Motecuhzoma now acted to
reduce his longtime ally to vassalage. The Huitzilopochtli cult was
again declared supreme in Texcoco. And the Aztec ruler ordered all
tribute owed Texcoco to be directed to Tenochtitlán. When Nezahualpilli protested this violation of the accords that had tied Aztecs
and Texcocans together ever since the Triple Alliance was created
almost a century before, Motecuhzoma replied contemptuously that
"times have changed . . . and now he was supreme lord of heaven
and earth."[38]

A broken man, Nezahualpilli shut himself in his palace. The humiliation was far worse than that suffered by his father, Nezahualcóyotl, who was outmaneuvered by Tlacaelel seven decades before.
The father had rebounded somewhat from defeat and claimed a measure of glory for Texcoco in the shadow of Tenochtitlán. But the son,
Nezahualpilli, lost everything to the Aztecs—his army, his provinces,
even the power to name his successor. He died in self-imposed seclusion in 1515, having ruled for forty-three years. He left behind a huge
harem and 145 children, some indication of the sexual profligacy
among the nobility. At least five of his sons vied for the monarchy of
Texcoco. But the kingmaker now sat on the throne of Tenochtitlán.
Motecuhzoma instructed the Texcocan Supreme Council of nobles
to pick Cacama as their new ruler. He was a son of Nezahualpilli,
but not his favorite. More important, he was a nephew and protégé
of Motecuhzoma. Cacama was bitterly opposed by his brother, Ixtlilxochitl, who staged an uprising that forced him to seek Motecuhzoma's
aid and protection. By threatening reprisals, the Aztec king ended
Ixtlilxochitl's brief revolt and installed Cacama on the throne of Texcoco. Although at the time the sibling rivalry appeared to be of no
lasting significance, only a few years later, with the arrival of the
Spaniards, Ixtlilxochitl's disgruntlement would have far greater
consequences.

With Nezahualpilli gone and Texcoco firmly in his grasp, Motecuhzoma's volatile mood swung toward euphoria. How could he have
doubted Huitzilopochtli, the hummingbird god who had raised the
Aztecs to such heights? Why did he, Motecuhzoma, ruler of the
greatest empire in the known world, succumb so easily to those auguries
claiming to portend catastrophe? As the king's new-found optimism
became public knowledge, his soothsayers gave a happier interpretation

to omens and brightened their forecasts. In atonement for his lapse in faith, Motecuhzoma ordered great levies of sacrificial victims from his vassal tribes, especially those rumored to be near rebellion. More than ever before, human flesh became a staple at banquets for the warriors, priests, nobles, and merchants. "And it is said of this king that not a day passed that he did not eat human flesh, for which purpose he had many slaves, and each day he had one of them slaughtered for him and his dinner guests to eat. . . ."[39] So numerous were these ritual killings that Motecuhzoma decided that Huitzilopochtli's temple needed a larger sacrificial stone. He ordered a search throughout the Valley of Mexico to uncover the greatest boulder for this purpose. It was found in Chalco on the southeast edge of the lakes. The huge rock was cut and chiseled into the appropriate round shape, and etched with elaborate religious symbols. But while being transported by rafts to Tenochtitlán, the stone broke loose from its bindings and sank to the bottom of the lake. And when Motecuhzoma commanded that it be retrieved, divers could not locate it in the muddy waters.

The incident toppled Motecuhzoma back into deep depression. This, he decided, was a divine omen he could not ignore. He convinced himself he would soon die, and ordered his likeness sculptured on a hillside of Chapultepec, next to a great carving that his grandfather, the first Motecuhzoma, had made of himself when he was near death. The sculpture was hastily completed, and the king, beholding it, uttered a tearful lament:

"Oh, if only our bodies were as durable in life and perpetual as this effigy on the hill which will last forever—who then would fear death? But I can see that I am to die and only this memory will be left of me."[40]

Attempting to shake his painful melancholia, Motecuhzoma gathered about him his closest advisers and shared with them his fears about Nezahualpilli's predictions on the end of his empire. "My brothers, how can I be consoled if I see myself encircled by so much anxiety and fear?"[41] His counselors tried to assure him that the gods looked upon him with favor, and they reminded him of his greatness and the splendor of his realms. But Motecuhzoma remained dispirited. He then convoked his jesters—hunchbacks and dwarfs—to entertain him, and when they failed to humor him, he pathetically confided in them his anguish and doubts. Close to insanity, the king told his deformed servants that it was his intention to flee, "to hide in some cave in the mountains where I will never be found." And he pleaded with his bewildered listeners to escape the city with him and keep him company in hiding. "The hunchbacks and dwarfs replied that he was their lord, that they would do whatever he commanded, that they would obey and go wherever he wished to send them."[42]

The urge to flee and hide subsided. Instead, Motecuhzoma assembled all the neighborhood political leaders of Tenochtitlán and demanded to know if any of them were having dreams about him or his empire. When the chieftains replied they had not, he ordered them to return to their neighborhoods and interrogate all elderly men and women about their dreams concerning his realm or himself. Naturally, in a population so large there would inevitably be some people who in their sleep conjured up the subjects that interested the king. The neighborhood chieftains returned with a small group of frightened old men and women, who told the king their nightmares: temples in flames, floods engulfing the imperial palace, mass flight from the city. They spoke freely because Motecuhzoma had promised not to harm them. But after listening to them, he broke his word and had them thrown into jail until they starved to death.

Next, he turned to his soothsayers and demanded that they also confess their nightmares. When they denied having dreamed of calamities, Motecuhzoma rebuked them as liars and ordered them incarcerated. They escaped their jails with the aid of accomplices who told the king that being sorcerers the prisoners simply made themselves vanish. The superstitious monarch could understand this. But he vented his rage on the soothsayers' families and properties: their wives and children were slaughtered, their homes toppled, all their belongings confiscated. And if ever the false seers were found, they were to be stoned to death and their bodies fed to the beasts in the imperial zoo.

Until now, Motecuhzoma had been grappling with symbols and signs, nightmares and psychotic fantasies. But in 1517, his fears and anxieties finally fastened onto a real event. A vessel larger than any known boat and with white wings fluttering above its deck was sighted off the coast of Yucatán. It carried pale-skinned, bearded strangers and fearful beasts larger than any other animal. The visitors had weapons that thundered and spit fire, and even though these alien beings were few, they defeated much larger forces of Indians before returning to their vessel and sailing away. The ship, we now know, was a Spanish vessel from Cuba, captained by Francisco Hernández de Córdova, and had among its crew Bernal Díaz del Castillo, who would later accompany Hernán Cortés and chronicle the conquest of Mexico. The boat was searching out new lands when a storm blew it toward Yucatán.

The Spaniards made several landings, first to explore and then simply to find fresh water and food. But wherever they went ashore, they were attacked by Indians. Almost all the 110 Spaniards were wounded, and possibly half of them were killed in the several battles before they finally secured their needed supplies and sailed back to Cuba. Captain Córdova himself died from his wounds shortly after reaching Cuba. But the crew brought back news of unknown lands inhabited by many natives living in well-constructed villages and towns. Other expeditions would follow.

The reports received by Motecuhzoma were sketchy and confusing because the sighting of the boat took place in the Maya lands, which were beyond the Aztec empire. But he alerted his vassals all along the Gulf coast to keep a permanent watch and inform him if the strangers reappeared. He had not long to wait. A year later, in 1518, four of the wondrously large vessels were seen off the coast of Tabasco and Veracruz. It was another Spanish exploratory expedition from Cuba, this time 240 men led by Juan de Grijalva. When one of the ships anchored at the mouth of the Papaloapan River in present-day Veracruz, word reached Motecuhzoma and he immediately sent two of his close aides to spy on the strangers.

From a treetop, the king's envoys observed the Spaniards for many hours, and then returned to Tenochtitlán, a two-hundred-mile journey that even at a forced pace must have taken several days. They described the vessel to Motecuhzoma as "a house on the water, from which emerge white men, white of face and hands, and with long, thick beards and robes of all colors."[43] As he listened, Motecuhzoma clamped a hand across his mouth to stifle uncontrolled moans of terror. Nezahualpilli's predictions were coming true. Surely, this was Quetzalcóatl, the ancient Toltec god, returning with his retinue to take possession of his domains as he had sworn he would. Regaining his composure, Motecuhzoma decided to seek proof that the strangers were indeed Quetzalcóatl and his followers. The king ordered his jewelers to fashion splendid bracelets, rings, and necklaces of gold and precious stones. And he commanded his vassal ruler on the Gulf coast to prepare a feast of birds, tortillas, vegetables, fruits, and chocolate for the bearded intruders. If the strangers accepted the jewelry, it would mean that Quetzalcóatl and his agents had come to reclaim the "gold and silver and precious stones that they left hidden in the mountains," just as the legends said they would. And if the strangers ate the food prepared for them, it would also be proof that Quetzalcóatl had returned because "he knows the food of this land."[44] Motecuhzoma told his aides to convey these offerings to the leader of the intruders, and if he turned out to be Quetzalcóatl:

"Tell him that I beseech him—that he do me this favor—that he allow me to die, and that, after I am dead, he come with all honor to reclaim his realm, since it is his and he left it in the safekeeping of my ancestors, and what I have is only borrowed. . . . And if by chance, he does not want the food offered to him, and prefers instead human flesh, let him eat you, for I vow to care for your wives and children and all your relatives."[45]

Naturally, the Spaniards furnished Motecuhzoma with the proof he needed that they were Quetzalcóatl and his agents. They were over-joyed at the rich jewelry, a treasure greater than they had hoped to find. And famished, they devoured the delicious food placed before them. Motecuhzoma's envoys delivered their king's plea that the Span-iards abandon the land and return after his death to take legitimate possession of the empire. But it was a dialogue of the deaf and dumb, for neither group understood the other's language. The Spaniards gave the Aztec emissaries some beaded necklaces and hard biscuits and salted bacon. And then both sides took leave of each other, the Span-iards sailing back to Cuba, the Aztecs returning to Tenochtitlán.

As soon as they reached the Aztec capital, the envoys went to Mo-tecuhzoma's palace where the king demanded from them every possible detail about the white strangers. He had a court artist paint a portrait of the intruders based on the descriptions given by his emissaries. Then he had the portrait circulated among sages and priests throughout the Valley of Mexico to discover if anyone recognized the painted figures. At first, nobody confessed any knowledge of the strangers. But word spread that Quetzalcóatl had returned, and there were many secret practitioners of his cult. Eventually, an old soothsayer from Xo-chimilco stepped forward and claimed that the figures in the portrait did indeed bear a likeness to Quetzalcóatl. After listening to the elderly seer, Motecuhzoma said he was at least consoled because he had asked Quetzalcóatl and his aides to depart "and they obeyed me and left, and perhaps they will not return."[46]

As months went by with no news about winged vessels along the coasts, Motecuhzoma convinced himself that he had made a lasting agreement with Quetzalcóatl. While the king lived, the empire was his. The time for self-pity was past. Perhaps he would be the last Aztec monarch, but he might still be as great as any before him. With renewed vigor, Motecuhzoma ordered any sign of revolt in his vassal provinces to be mercilessly crushed, and raised the sacrificial levies to all the gods, not only Huitzilopochtli. Throughout the Valley of Mexico, he purged provincial rulers and replaced them with members of his own family.

But in the following year, 1519, Motecuhzoma's hopes crumbled. His informants reported that ships bearing the white strangers had anchored briefly in Yucatán, and were sailing northward within sight of Aztec vassal states along the Gulf coast. It was the expedition led by Hernán Cortés, who knew about the treasure brought back to Cuba by Grijalva. This time the bearded strangers would stay until all of Nezahualpilli's terrible prophecies were fulfilled.

FOUR

THE SPANISH BACKGROUND

In his certainty that the disturbing intrusion of the white-skinned strangers heralded Quetzalcóatl's return, Motecuhzoma was relying entirely upon Aztec concepts of geography and religion. For the Aztecs, the universe was a flat surface of land surrounded by water and the heavens. The watery edge was visible to the east in the Caribbean and Gulf, and to the west in the Pacific. Manifestly, no human beings lived in these endless oceans which could only be inhabited by gods. Even on land, religious notions shaped geography beyond the borders of the Aztec empire, where firsthand knowledge of terrains and peoples was lacking. The mountainous deserts north of the Valley of Mexico, past the hunting-and-gathering grounds of the nomadic barbarians, were considered the Underworld of the dead. The south, beyond the Maya lands, was the domain of Huitzilopochtli, the hummingbird god. According to this cosmology, humanity existed only within the confines of the Aztec empire and those peripheral lands that the Aztecs sought to conquer or chose to ignore—a territorial space known as Cem Anahuac, the One World.

The One World was neither static nor permanent. The Aztecs believed that four eras preceded their own, and that each ended in a great natural cataclysm—fire, earthquake, flood, drought—linked to the triumph of one god or group of deities over another. Motecuhzoma and his subjects could point to the archaeological remains of the Toltec and Teotihuacán civilizations as evidence of past catastrophes. The Aztecs' meteoric rise to eminence, which they associated with the supremacy of Huitzilopochtli, was proof enough of rapid upheavals in the One World. And a deep pessimism imbued Aztec thinking on their own transience. History to them was cyclical. Adhering to their religious calendar, they prepared every fifty-two years for the sudden demise of their empire. On the final day of such a time cycle, all fires were extinguished everywhere in the Aztec realms, and priests led prayers through the night beseeching the gods to let the sun rise and grant their faithful followers another fifty-two years of life.[1]

But such fatalism was tempered by the belief that no matter what gods and tribes emerged from the ashes of a cataclysm, they would at least be familiar ones. Society, religion, and the routines of everyday life would never be altered beyond recognition. A newly conquering tribe would necessarily seek legitimacy by establishing its ties to the civilization and gods that came before. Had not the Aztecs sought to trace their lineage to the revered Toltecs, just as the Toltecs had claimed descent from the more ancient Teotihuacanos? It was painful enough for Motecuhzoma to acknowledge that the bearded strangers sailing their white pyramids into the Gulf were part of Quetzalcóatl's retinue come to reclaim the Toltec god's earthly domains. It meant that a historical cycle was over. A new, and yet familiar, era was about to begin. The impending upheaval would restore an old deity to preeminence and replace the Aztecs with another tribe. But how much more terrifying it would have been for Motecuhzoma to accept the harsher reality: the Spaniards were a race beyond the reach of the Aztecs' universe and the power of their gods; the Spaniards were a people with a conduct and ideology, a political and economic system, a technology and weaponry that would inevitably subjugate the tribes of Mexico, obliterate every aspect of their world view, and shatter their society more thoroughly than any previous catastrophe.

There were coherent reasons why Europeans, and particularly the Spaniards, waited until the turn of the sixteenth century to embark on their transoceanic voyages of discovery. The naval technology for travel on the open seas existed long before Columbus crossed the Atlantic in 1492. By the twelfth century, the famous center-line rudder, acclaimed as the technological innovation that ensured the success of the great maritime journeys, had already been invented. And more than a hundred years before ships were fitted with center-line rudders, the Vikings had sailed their long boats to North American shores. There is more truth than irony in the statement attributed to the great

Belgian historian Henri Pirenne: "America [when the Vikings reached it] was lost as soon as it was discovered, because Europe did not yet need it."[2]

Western Europe would have to undergo five more centuries of development and setbacks before it "needed" to discover the Americas again. Beginning in the eleventh century, the European economy and population entered a period of marked expansion. Technological breakthroughs like the horse collar, which replaced the yoke harness, and improved plows, which sliced the ground more efficiently than older implements, produced larger harvests that fed greater numbers of people. Forest, marsh, and heath were cleared by the growing peasantry, doubling, tripling, and even quadrupling the land brought under cultivation. After 1150, Europe advanced beyond "direct agricultural consumption"—that is, a self-sufficient rural existence—to an "indirect agricultural consumption" by which farm surpluses were marketed in urban communities.[3] This agrarian surplus both fed and was stimulated by the urban revival that began in Europe as early as the eleventh century. With the rebirth of towns and cities came the commercial revolution, spawning its own "technological" innovations like the expanded use of money, letters of credit, and accounting.

Two regional economies, weaving together scores of cities and towns, emerged in Europe by the 1200s. To the north, the ports and nearby inland cities of the Low Countries and the Baltic carried on a lively trade of wool, furs, textiles, wood, wax, salt, wine, and grain. To the south, the Italian city-states and to a lesser extent Catalonia dominated the Mediterranean trade of textiles, wine, grain, and the silks and spices of the Levant and East Asia. Up until the 1300s, the meeting points of these northern and southern European regional economies were the inland trade fairs, particularly the great markets of Champagne. But larger and more seaworthy vessels from Genoa and Venice undercut these inland fairs by navigating through the Strait of Gibraltar, around the Iberian peninsula, and directly into the North Sea harbors. A single one of these Italian merchant galleons—ranging up to 300 tons—could carry as many goods as fifty horse-drawn carts. And despite the greater nautical distance, the maritime trade offered fewer hardships than the journey through the Alps, along poorly delineated roads, and on small river barges.

By the mid-1300s, Western Europe was poised for more spectacular transoceanic voyages. The naval technology existed. An international commerce tied to a web of city-states was in place. With the Italians and Turks monopolizing the high-profit trade in spices, drugs, and silks from Asia, there was also a strong incentive for other Europeans to search out alternative maritime routes to the Far East.

But then, Europe suffered a setback of unprecedented proportions with the advent of the Black Death, a devastating epidemic of pulmonary plague beginning in the 1340s. The origins of the Plague have been traced to various locations of inner Asia—northern India, central Persia, western China, and the Mongolian steppes. It was spread by a bacillus carried by fleas that infested the *Rattus rattus*, or black rat. The rats infiltrated ships plying between Asian and European ports, and infected the crews. Among human carriers, the disease was transmitted by sneezing, coughing, even the simple act of breathing.

The Black Death struck in tidal waves during each of the last six decades of the fourteenth century, reducing Europe's inhabitants by one third or more. Towns and cities became charnelhouses as merchants, sailors, peddlers, and beggars traveling between communities quickly spread the disease. Many small villages were wiped out, literally erased forever from the map. Catalonia, the most economically vigorous region of medieval Spain and the only European rival to Italy's commercial supremacy in the Mediterranean, saw its population shrivel from a pre-Plague high point of 430,000 in 1365 to less than 300,000 by 1400. Even after a demographic recovery, it failed to regain its economic preeminence. Social and economic life was disrupted throughout Europe. The rich fled the cities and towns to their country estates. Trade and industry slowed as labor and consumption fell. The Plague rotted the foundations of feudal serfdom by reducing the peasant population so substantially that surviving rural workers could sell their services at a premium. Large swathes of the countryside were abandoned to shrubs and wild animals. Only the most fertile land—which required less work for greater yields—continued to be cultivated.

It took Europe one hundred years—until 1450—to recover its pre-Plague economic and population levels, and to rekindle an expansion of maritime trade. In subsequent centuries, death by epidemic disease would remain a permanent specter. But the Old World had achieved a measure of biological unity: the frequent contact between Europeans, Asians, and Africans ensured them of a partial immunity from death by plague, smallpox, measles, influenza, and a host of other illnesses. The Black Death cut short what might have been an early European attempt to venture into the unknown high seas. But when transoceanic voyages finally were launched, it was the capacity of the Europeans

to transmit diseases from which they were partly immune that proved
to be their deadliest weapon in the New World.[4]

In the mid-1400s, Spain seemed particularly disadvantaged to assume
leadership of what was soon to become the European discovery and
conquest of the Americas. It had shared in Europe's economic and
demographic recovery from the century-long ravages of the Plague.
But Spain was a jumble of feudal kingdoms, economically backward,
and still partially occupied by Moors on its Mediterranean shores.

Nowhere else in Europe, save Portugal, had the Moslems made
their presence felt as strongly as in Spain. In seven brief years during
the eighth century, the Moors conquered much of the country. But
it would take the Spaniards seven hundred years to fully recover these
lands. The Reconquista—the struggle of the Spanish Christians against
the Moorish occupation—was neither a continuous nor unified endeavor. The largest territorial gains of the Reconquista were achieved
during the 1200s. In the west and center of Spain, Christian forces
from the provinces of Castile and Leon pushed southward into the
Moslem domains of Andalusia, but failed to recapture the large enclave
of Granada. In eastern Spain, the Christians of Aragon and Catalonia
were more successful, and reconquered their provinces as well as the
strategic Balearic Islands off the Mediterranean coast.

But by 1270, the unity and momentum of the Reconquista sputtered.
Castile was racked by struggles for succession in its royal household,
and by dissent among the nobility over ownership of the vast lands
that had been wrested from the Moors. Meanwhile, Aragon and Catalonia, having recouped all of their territory, lost interest in Castile's
continuing confrontation with the Moslems, and shifted their attention
instead to the profitable commerce of the eastern Mediterranean. This
was, after all, the age of city-states. The image of a powerful, unified
Spain was less appealing to Barcelona, the preeminent Catalonian
port, than the wealthy status enjoyed by Italian city-states like Genoa
and Venice. Thus, the two hundred years following 1270 saw a prolonged stalemate between Christian Spain and Granada, the last redoubt of the Moors.

The impetus to resume the war on Granada came not in Spain,
but at the other end of the Mediterranean. In 1453, the Ottoman
Turks besieged and captured Constantinople from its Christian defenders. Fears of a resurgent Moslem empire under the Ottomans led
to papal appeals for a Christian European crusade against the infidels

throughout the Mediterranean. In Spain, the Castilian court organized military expeditions against Granada between 1455 and 1457. None achieved significant victories. But anti-Moorish sentiment among the Spanish populace remained strong when Isabella of Castile and Ferdinand of Aragon married in 1469, becoming heirs to the two major feudal kingdoms of Spain. It took a dozen more years for the monarchs to consolidate power over dissident aristocrats in their realms. Then, in 1482, they unleashed the final campaign against Granada, hoping, in the words of the historian J. H. Elliott, that "it would do more than anything else to rally the country behind its new rulers, and associate Crown and people in a heroic enterprise which would make the name of Spain ring through Christendom."[5] A decade later, in 1492, Granada was in Spanish hands, ending Moslem power on the Iberian peninsula.

Spain emerged from the long, arduous struggle against the Moors with considerably more political assets than the rest of Europe. It had a strong monarchy centered in Castile and a powerful military force with a crusading tradition. By enthusiastically taking up the papal challenge to the infidels, Isabella and Ferdinand also cemented a special relationship with the Church. The Spanish monarchs could count on political and ideological support from Rome both at home and abroad.

Along with the impressive assets that Spain acquired in its successful Reconquista, there were also considerable debits that were to plague the nation at home and in its future overseas empire. While glorifying the warrior, the Spaniards disdained agriculture and manual crafts, which were associated with the Moslem infidels. Through irrigation and intensive farming, the Moors and their subjects had coaxed plentiful harvests from their Mediterranean Spanish domains. Their textiles, handicrafts, and metallurgy—the equivalent of industry in a preindustrial society—surpassed in quality the output of Christian Spain. But "to the Christian crusader these practical activities and hard labor were suitable for the enemies of God and a befitting badge of servitude," wrote the historian Irving A. Leonard. "[The Spanish warrior] derived the benefits of the toil of the conquered as a legitimate reward for bringing them into the Christian fold; his position as a feudal lord was a mark of divine gratitude for his military prowess while the manual labor of his serfs was proper punishment for their allegiance to a false faith."[6] By the early 1500s, this neglect of farming and industry was making itself felt in Spain. There were serious crop failures that were only partially mitigated by imports of foreign grain. Spain soon fell behind other European countries in industrial production and competitiveness. This same prejudice against manual labor carried over into Spain's New World colonies, where Indians were expected to work the estates of the Spaniards. Homesteading was simply not considered a proper pursuit by most Spanish colonists. Nor did the Spaniards encourage manufacturing in their New World domains which, like Spain itself, were inundated with more competitive industrial products from other European countries.

Finance was yet another enterprise that elicited the contempt of Spaniards imbued with the warrior ethic. Just as the Moslems were linked to agriculture and craftsmanship, it was the other infidels, the Jews, who were most associated in the Spanish mind with money-lending, credit, and finance. The expulsion of at least three fourths of the 200,000 Jews from Spain beginning in 1492, the same year that the Reconquista triumphed, was motivated above all by the monarchy's desire to purge the country of its two unwanted religions—Mohammedism and Judaism. But the financial and commercial skills lost to the nation by this act had long-lasting consequences. "The gap left by the Jews was not easily filled," says one historian, "and many of them were replaced not by native [Spaniards], but by colonies of foreign immigrants—Flemings, Germans, Genoese—who would use their new opportunity to exploit rather than to enrich the resources of Spain. The effect of the expulsion was thus to weaken the economic foundations of the Spanish monarch at the very outset of its imperial career."[7]

The Reconquista was not the only long-term force that shaped Spain's institutions and outlook as the country neared its era of empire. Equally important was the growth of a maritime tradition that largely paralleled the progress of the wars against the Moors. The recovery of the spacious lands of Andalusia from the Moslems in the thirteenth century led to a rapid expansion of sheep farming. Much of the wool was exported to Flanders by ships based in northern Spanish ports, like Santander and San Sebastian. This naval trade with Northern Europe was Spain's first meaningful commercial contact with the world beyond its borders. To the south, on the Mediterranean side of the country, Seville developed into Spain's most important port, eventually overtaking plague-stricken Barcelona in the exchange of Spanish wool and wine for Asian spices and silks handled by Italian middlemen. By the 1470s, during the early reign of Isabella and Ferdinand, the Spaniards, like other Europeans, were anxious to discover alternative routes to the spices and silks of the Orient that would circumvent the eastern

Mediterranean which was firmly under the control of the Ottoman Turks and the merchants of the Italian city-states.

Historians have debated at length on the significance of the international trade in luxuries like spices, pepper, drugs, and silks in stimulating Europe's thrust overseas and its New World discoveries. Although used in great quantities to preserve and flavor the food of a wealthy elite, spices accounted for only a small portion of the total bulk and value of Europe's commerce. Certainly, the luxury trade could not approach the volume of grain, wool, and common textiles that were sold across national borders. But the extremely high profits of the long-distance trade in spices and other luxuries played a key role in the development of capitalism, particularly in the accumulation of great capital. "[A] kilo of pepper, worth one or two grammes of silver at the point of production in the Indies, would fetch 10 or 14 grammes in Alexandria, 14 to 18 in Venice, and 20 to 30 in the consumer countries of Europe," wrote the French historian Fernand Braudel. "Long-distance trade . . . made super-profits; it was after all based on the price differences between two markets very far apart, with supply and demand in complete ignorance of each other and brought into contact only by the activities of the middleman."[8]

The problem for Europe was that the Asian suppliers of such luxuries were interested primarily in gold and silver as payment. Whether panned as gold dust in the Sudan and North Africa, or mined from silver lodes in Germany and Hungary, these precious metals were constantly draining away from Europe to India, China, and the East Indies. Thus, Europe's (and Spain's) quest for alternative routes to the Asian luxury trade coincided with a frantic search for new sources of gold and silver.

Spain's maritime interests were also stimulated by an intense rivalry with neighboring Portugal. Although both countries had shared the experience of a lengthy Moslem occupation, Portugal succeeded in recovering its territories from the Moors two centuries before the Reconquista triumphed in Spain. At times, Portugal joined the Spanish forces in their offensives against the Moors ensconced in Andalusia. But, just as often, Portuguese rulers laid claim to the lands and thrones of Castile and Leon in Spain. Isabella, who gained the throne of Castile in 1474, was particularly bitter at the Portuguese royal household for attempting to prevent her marriage to Ferdinand of Aragon and for supporting her niece as heiress to the Castilian Crown.

The altercations between Spain and Portugal soon found an outlet overseas, in the pursuit of precious metals and a new passage to the

Indies. Both countries had a geographic advantage over the rest of Europe because their territory thrust furthest out into the Atlantic. With the Spaniards still fighting the Moors in Granada, the Portuguese were first to venture beyond Europe, establishing enclaves and trading posts on the western coasts of Africa during the 1480s. The Portuguese strategy was to explore the African shores to their southernmost point in the belief that eventually an eastern passageway to India would be found—a feat finally achieved by the four-ship expedition led by Vasco de Gama in 1498.

The cautious naval strategy of the Portuguese was understandable. The compass and center-line rudder notwithstanding, the late 1400s were still an era when shipping was active mainly within sight of land. It was not only a matter of fear of the unknown in the open seas. Sailing close to shore was a protection against the elements, an opportunity to buy and sell and exchange goods between ultimate destinations, and, of course, a chance for sailors to drink and revel with native women.

The Portuguese did not altogether eschew exploration westward into the Atlantic. By 1445, they had colonized the previously uninhabited islands of Madeira and the Azores, respectively 535 and 740 miles off the coast of Portugal. The islands supplied the mother country with considerable wheat harvests, and their sugar, exported to Europe, became an important source of revenue.

It was in the Atlantic that the Spaniards chose to contest Portugal's overseas ventures. Using as an excuse Portugal's unwarranted meddling in the Castilian succession, Isabella and Ferdinand sent an expedition in 1478 to occupy the Canary Islands, located sixty miles west of Africa and already claimed by the Portuguese. A year later, a treaty between the Castilian and Portuguese royal households ceded the Canaries to Isabella and Ferdinand, giving Spain its first overseas territory in exchange for recognition of Portugal's claims over the Azores, Madeira, and its West African possessions. The Canaries were soon to become an invaluable way station and resupply center for Spanish ships en route to the New World.

Isabella and Ferdinand did not immediately follow up their seizure of the Canaries with other maritime expeditions. They were too preoccupied with the reconquest of Granada to consider financing vessels and sailors for ocean voyages of uncertain success. Thus, when an obscure Genoese ship captain, Christopher Columbus, first presented himself at the Spanish court in 1486 with the rather unorthodox notion that the shortest route to Asia lay west across the Atlantic, he was flatly turned down. Two years earlier, Columbus had approached the Portuguese Crown with the same proposal. But Portugal had already committed itself to the strategy of finding a passage to Asia by sailing around Africa. Columbus tried without success to find sponsors in France and England, before attempting once again to interest the Spaniards in 1492. The moment was now propitious. This was the same year that Granada fell to the crusading Spanish forces, and the Crown was anxious to reduce Portugal's substantial lead in the race to the Asian Indies.

It is not altogether surprising that Isabella and Ferdinand entrusted an overseas expedition to a foreigner from Genoa. The Genoese were recognized as more expert navigators than the Spaniards. Columbus himself had the experience of commanding a Portuguese ship on voyages to Guinea. After considerable negotiations, the Spanish monarchs agreed to finance Columbus and meet his steep demands: that he be given the hereditary title of Grand Admiral and one tenth of the commercial profits from any lands he discovered.

In August 1492, Columbus set sail on what proved to be the momentous voyage of the era. He departed from the small Spanish Mediterranean port of Palos with a crew of eighty-eight men aboard three caravels. The first stop was the Canary Islands, where the vessels were resupplied with food, water, and wood. Then, after thirty-three days in the Atlantic, land was sighted—the Bahaman island of Watling, or San Salvador—and Columbus led his crew ashore. It was the morning of October 12, 1492, subsequently celebrated as the date of the European discovery of the Americas.

Before returning to Spain, Columbus discovered several other minor Caribbean islands as well as Cuba and Hispaniola (present-day Haiti and the Dominican Republic), where he established a fort after one of his vessels ran aground. In three other voyages undertaken between 1493 and 1504 at royal expense, Columbus sighted or landed in Jamaica, Puerto Rico, Honduras, and South America along the Venezuelan coast.

But Columbus himself did not believe that he had unveiled a New World. Until his death in 1506, he was convinced that the Caribbean lands he had claimed for Spain were part of an archipelago lying off the coast of Asia and that further exploration would undoubtedly reveal a passage to the riches of the East Indies. His royal sponsors, Isabella and Ferdinand, basically shared this view, at least for a few years. Ironically, it was the rival Portuguese who were the first to realize that Columbus had in fact discovered a New World. Fortunately for the

Spaniards, Portugal did not think these territories would prove rewarding. The native population of the Caribbean Islands seemed primitive and the natural resources meager. By the Treaty of Tordesillas
in 1494, the Portuguese happily acknowledged Spanish claims to the
New World lands, and agreed to abide by a north-south demarcation
line across the Atlantic that was to give Spain possession of all the
Americas except Brazil, which fell into the region ceded to the Portuguese. In Lisbon, the Treaty of Tordesillas was considered a resounding diplomatic victory because it also confirmed Portugal's
uncontested right to pursue the route eastward to the Orient, around
the Horn of Africa—a route that still seemed more promising to the
Portuguese than Spain's search for a western passage to Asia.

Spain viewed its new Caribbean possessions in much the same way
the Portuguese looked upon their African coastal enclaves—as supply
centers and staging points for further expeditions in the direction of
Asia. This necessarily involved colonization. Already on his second
voyage in 1493, Columbus had been ordered by the Spanish monarchs
to transport twelve hundred settlers to Hispaniola before continuing
his explorations. The colonial model drew its inspiration from the
Reconquista and the occupation of the Canary Islands a few years
before. As in Granada and the Canaries, the conquering Spaniards
were rewarded with land grants and infidels as forced laborers—in this
case, the peaceful Tainos of Hispaniola. This system—the virtual enslavement of the native inhabitants and the appropriation of their
lands—was known as *repartimiento*, and was later extended throughout
Spain's New World domains with the same disastrous impact on the
Indians everywhere.

The Tainos, a tribe that subsisted on fishing, the gathering of wild
plants, and the tilling of garden plots, were turned into plantation
workers and gold miners. Resistance was punished by implacable terror. The Spaniards "spared neither children nor the aged nor pregnant
women nor women in childbed, who were disemboweled and dismembered as if they were sheep in a slaughter house," wrote Bartolomé
de las Casas, a Spanish priest who witnessed the early colonization of
the Americas. "They made bets on who among them could slice a
man in half, or decapitate him or gut him with a single sword-stroke
or pike-thrust. They took infants from their mothers' breasts, swung
them by the legs and shattered their heads against boulders."[9]

The Tainos who lived through the horrors of the conquest did not
long survive Spanish occupation. Within a few years, their numbers

declined drastically and later dwindled to complete extinction. The Spaniards—even the handful of priests who defended the Tainos—claimed that the Indians perished because they did not have the stamina for ordinary, regimented labor after a supposedly languid, primitive life of fishing and food gathering. In fact, it was European-borne diseases that annihilated most of the tribe. But the Spaniards could not comprehend how measles, influenza, smallpox—common illnesses which most Europeans survived—could have such a devastating effect on these natives. It was easier to believe that these people were simply unfit for physical labor, that it was work which induced fatal sickness in them.[10]

The first wave of Spanish settlement in Hispaniola under Columbus was followed by twenty-five hundred new colonists a decade later. They brought with them great herds of cattle and pigs, which roamed wild in the forests and in the former tribal lands that were abandoned as the Indians died off. With its agriculture and livestock, Hispaniola became a base for further exploration in the Caribbean. And the dwindling of the island's Indian population provided an incentive for further voyages of discovery: unless the Spaniards found new native laborers elsewhere, they would have been forced to work their estates and mines with their own hands.

By the time Columbus died in 1506, the Caribbean was attracting a different breed of Spaniard. Columbus had identified himself with the European tradition of maritime commerce. He had embarked on his expeditions to discover a new route to the spice and silk markets of Asia, a hope which he never relinquished. But the Spaniards who came after him into the Caribbean were no longer fired by the dream of a western passage to Asia. Repeated explorations had failed to discover this route, and though it still might exist, there were plenty of new territories at hand to enrich Spanish adventurers who could gain possession of Indian laborers and estates.

The men now sailing from Spain across the Atlantic were the progeny of the Reconquista—its crusading military tradition, its enmity toward infidels, its strong allegiance to Church and Crown. But most of these Spaniards were born too late to have participated in the last wars against the Moors, and thus failed to enrich themselves with the Reconquista's spoils. Among them were the younger sons of the aristocracy, cheated out of their inheritance by the laws of primogeniture. They included "hidalgos"—minor nobility whose titles masked their straitened circumstances. And some were commoners who had fought as mercenaries in Spain's campaigns in Italy (1495–97 and 1501–4) and were still seeking to parlay their military skills into fortune and higher social status.

With the great crusade against Moorish rule a generation behind them, these adventurers looked elsewhere for inspiration. They found it in the new popular literature, particularly the so-called Romances of Chivalry that were taking hold throughout Europe. These romances were often medieval versions of ancient Greek myths such as the treasure-hoarding Amazons, the Seven Enchanted Cities, the Golden Fleece, the Fountain of Youth, and the River of Silver. Spain, at the beginning of the 1500s, had a vast audience for these accounts of strange, opulent, infidel kingdoms in distant places, waiting to be pillaged by Christian knights courageous and determined enough to find them. In his great novel *Don Quixote*, Cervantes would later satirize the chivalrous state of mind induced by these popular tales. But monarchs, aristocrats, clergymen, adventurers, and foot soldiers, if they were literate, devoured and believed these Romances of Chivalry. When the New World was discovered, it seemed to confirm the myths. Where else could those enchanted kingdoms exist if not across the Atlantic? Young Spaniards, wrote a historian, "were convinced that by participation in overseas enterprises they would see and experience . . . the wonders, the riches and the adventures so seductively depicted in the pages of the popular books."[11]

And yet, after reaching the Caribbean, they were still restless, these men who would soon be known as conquistadores. A bureaucratic sinecure or a sizable estate in Hispaniola, Jamaica, or Cuba was not enough to satisfy their longings for greater adventure and treasure. They were also politically unruly. Their profession of fidelity to the Spanish Crown was tempered by the fact that the monarchs lived across the ocean. Royal commands took many weeks to reach the Caribbean, and were always subject to varied interpretations. Worse still, the death of Isabella in 1504 had created a crisis of authority. She intended her grandson, Charles of Ghent, to eventually succeed her, but he was still a boy living outside Spain and ignorant of the Spanish language. In the meantime, Isabella's widower, Ferdinand, held power. But he was Aragonese, not Castilian like most of the New World settlers, and even in Spain, he was being challenged by subjects who claimed he favored his native Aragon. In the New World, the Crown's authority was diluted among royal agents and the governors of islands where Spanish settlers were most numerous. Rivalry was intense among these officials, who vied with each other to patronize new expeditions of discovery and conquest. And in this conspiratorial atmosphere, the future conquistadores carefully gauged their own interests in backing one official against another. Everybody was for Church and Crown. But it took an honest, plainspoken man like Bernál Díaz del Castillo to slice through the cant and put motives in perspective: "We came here to serve God and the king, and also to get rich." Díaz del Castillo knew the hearts of his peers. He was companion and chronicler of Hernán Cortés, the greatest conquistador of them all.

Cortés was born in 1485 in the small town of Medellín, part of the landlocked, windswept, and almost treeless province of Extremadura, birthplace of hundreds of other Spaniards who became conquistadores. Located north of Andalusia, it was among the poorest and most isolated regions of Castile. The Extremadura's mountains and dusty plains, creased by valleys that drew their pale green from meandering streams, were better suited for shepherding than agriculture. But the sheep flocks required few people to tend them, fewer still to own them. In the mid-1400s, many of the province's men sought their fortune in war, as mercenaries against the Moors in the south or against the Castilian monarchy to the north. Cortés's father, Martín Cortés de Monroy, an hidalgo or minor nobleman of modest means, had chosen the latter course. He led a small cavalry band that sided with Extremaduran aristocrats who unsuccessfully resisted the efforts of Isabella and Ferdinand to impose their authority over the provincial nobility. The father buried his grudge against the monarchs when they showed mercy to most of the defeated rebels. He seems to have wished for his son a life of peaceful service to the Crown, and sent Hernán at the age of fourteen to the University of Salamanca to study law.

With the Reconquista accomplished, the monarchy was recruiting thousands of young hidalgos to staff a growing bureaucracy aimed at tightening royal authority throughout the country and improving the collection of taxes. A law degree from Salamanca could guarantee a secure post in government. But security was of little concern to a teenage hidalgo like Cortés, living in a Spain that had suddenly become Europe's most ebullient country. The Castilian monarchs were turning their gaze abroad. They launched military expeditions to press their claims of sovereignty in southern Italy, gateway to the riches of the eastern Mediterranean. And across the Atlantic, their admiral, Columbus, was discovering new lands with each voyage. Such adventures tugged far more powerfully at a young student's imagination than the prospect of becoming a notary or minor bureaucrat in Spain.

After two years at Salamanca, Cortés quit the university. It had not been entirely wasted time. He learned enough Latin, composition, and law to give his later writings and speeches an aura of sophistication, authority, and intellectual rigor. In his years of glory, he would leave his admirers with the mistaken impression that he was a university graduate, fluent in Latin and expert in the law. Salamanca also exposed him to youths of greater social and economic standing. Unlike other hidalgos, he would never be awed by aristocrats. He moved easily in their company, mimicked their social graces, and was determined someday to join their ranks.

Cortés returned home to Medellín at sixteen years of age. Though disappointed at his decision to drop out of university, his parents agreed to support his plan to travel to the New World. His father wrote to a fellow Extremaduran, Nicolás de Ovando, who was about to lead a large group of Spanish settlers to the Caribbean island of Hispaniola, and Ovando invited the young Cortés to sign up for the expedition. But while waiting in Seville for the fleet to depart, Cortés became involved with a young woman. One night, he scaled the walls of her family's house in an attempt to reach her bedroom; he slipped and fell to the ground, breaking a leg. The injury kept him bedridden for months, and Ovando's fleet sailed without him in 1502. For two years, Cortés lingered in the port of Seville, working as a notary while he decided whether to join the Spanish armies in Italy or wait for another opportunity to sail to the Caribbean.

In 1504, Cortés made his choice. With money advanced to him by his father, he bought passage aboard a merchant ship headed for Hispaniola. The ship, part of a five-vessel convoy, followed what had now become the traditional Atlantic route mapped out by Columbus: stopping in the Canaries for resupply and repair; then catching a trade wind south of the islands, which, with luck, blew all the way to the Caribbean.

Not yet twenty years of age, Cortés stepped ashore in Hispaniola. He sought out his fellow Extremaduran, Ovando, who after leading the earlier convoy of settlers had become governor of the island. Ovando granted Cortés a moderate-sized estate and Indian laborers, and made him a notary public in the colonial government. For seven years, Cortés led the life of a young gentleman-farmer and bureaucrat in Hispaniola, confining his adventures to womanizing and duels. The swordplay left his face marked by scars that were not fully concealed by his brown beard. He was a physically impressive opponent: though only of average height, he had powerful shoulders, a barrel chest, and glowering eyes. The opposite sex probably found him attractive. Not that it really mattered, because most of the women on the island were Indians who were there for the taking—by rape or intimidation.

By the age of twenty-five, Cortés could have smugly reflected that he was a far richer man than he would have been if he had remained in Spain as a university-educated bureaucrat. But soon after reaching Hispaniola, he had confided to a friend that "neither in this island nor in any other of this New World do I wish or mean to stay for so long."[12] As soon as he fulfilled the usual five-year residency requirement for settlers in Hispaniola, he volunteered in 1509 to join an expedition to establish an enclave on the Central American coast. Misfortune with women again prevented him from setting sail. He withdrew from the enterprise apparently because of a painful flare-up of venereal disease.[13] But two years later, in 1511, he participated in the conquest and settlement of Cuba.

The Spaniards were no less brutal to the Cuban natives than they had been to the Hispaniola inhabitants. Fray Bartolomé de las Casas, who accompanied the expedition to Cuba, chronicled the torture and slaughter of Indians who surrendered or even welcomed the invaders. Las Casas summed up the terror by recounting the fate of the Indian chieftain Hatuey. Captured by the Spaniards and about to be incinerated at the stake, Hatuey was urged by a Franciscan friar to convert to Christianity in order to achieve salvation in Heaven rather than eternal suffering in Hell. The Indian asked the friar if all Christians went to Heaven. When told that was indeed the case, he answered that he preferred Hell, "so as not to be where they were and thus not have to see such cruel people."[14]

No account exists directly linking Cortés to the atrocities in Cuba. His chief concern was to ingratiate himself with the leader of the expedition, Diego Velázquez, who emerged as governor of Cuba and made Cortés his personal secretary. Velázquez, a corpulent and ill-tempered aristocrat, had the absolute power to decide how the spoils of Cuba would be distributed. He was the rising political figure of the Caribbean, and would soon have the authority to launch new expeditions of discovery and conquest. At first, Cortés succeeded well enough in gaining the governor's favor. He received from Velázquez a substantially larger estate than he had in Hispaniola and a generous allotment of Indian laborers. Cortés became an important cattle and sheep rancher, and owner of profitable gold mines.

But his relationship with the mercurial Velázquez soon turned stormy. The conflict seems to have had a romantic strain. Cortés seduced a noblewoman, Catalina Suárez, who had recently come to the Indies from Spain, and then refused to marry her. Velázquez, who himself was a suitor of another Suárez sister, ordered the imprisonment of Cortés. Friends arranged his escape from jail, and he fled to the sanctuary of a church. Cortés received a pardon from Velázquez only after swearing loyalty to the governor and agreeing to wed the Suárez woman. It was a miserable marriage. She had to endure the humiliation of a parade of mistresses and their offspring, whom Cortés openly flaunted.

It was during Cortés's residence in Cuba that Velázquez commissioned the first two exploratory expeditions to the shores of Mexico. In 1517, the ship captained by Hernández de Córdova was blown off its course and landed in Yucatán. A year later, Grijalva's vessels reached the Tabasco and Veracruz coasts, and returned to Cuba with Motecuhzoma's precious gifts. Cortés did not volunteer as a member of these expeditions. He was by now less impetuous, more cunning, older, and more prosperous. If he were to sail to unknown lands, it would be only as a commander, with a greater share of the booty.

Even before the discovery of Mexico, Cortés had groomed himself for the eventual command of a colonial enterprise. He had done everything in his power to regain Velázquez's friendship and trust: carrying out with alacrity any task entrusted him by the governor, offering political advice, joining campaigns against pockets of Indian resistance in Cuba. Cortés even enlisted Velázquez as godfather in the baptism of an illegitimate child of one of his Indian mistresses. The governor rewarded his exemplary conduct by appointing him mayor of Santiago, one of the more important settlements in Cuba. It was the first opportunity for Cortés to exercise leadership on his own, and he proved to be a skilled politician, dispensing favors and weaving a network of friends and allies at all levels of Cuban colonial society.

Cortés avidly sought out all possible information from the Córdova and Grijalva expeditions. He interviewed members of the crews on the nature of the Indians they had encountered and the coasts they had explored. He knew all about the gold and jewelry brought back by the Grijalva ship that sailed into Santiago, where he was mayor. Cortés had no doubts that the next expedition to Mexico would uncover even greater treasures, and now he resolved to secure leadership of such an enterprise. He entered into a secret accord with Velázquez's two closest aides. They would convince the governor to appoint Cortés captain-general of the next expedition, and in return, Cortés would divide with them his share of any booty.

Velázquez, who had a reputation for being somewhat miserly, was swayed by Cortés's offer to finance much of the enterprise from his own funds and borrowings. In the next few months, Cortés assembled a fleet of seven ships and recruited about three hundred and fifty men as soldiers and crew. He purchased guns, powder, crossbows, food supplies, and articles for barter. He also took care to dress the part of an illustrious captain-general, who could command the respect of followers. "He wore a plume of feathers with a medal, and a gold chain, and a velvet cloak trimmed with knots of gold, and in fact he looked like a gallant and courageous Captain," noted one of his recruits, who was suitably impressed.[15]

Even after gaining the governor's backing for the expedition to Mexico, Cortés tried to spend as much time as possible in the company of Velázquez, assuring him of his loyalty. Cortés knew that his many rivals in Cuba were attempting to get his command revoked. They warned Velázquez that Cortés would betray him and appropriate most of the glory and spoils if the expedition proved successful. Velázquez had good reason to fear Cortés or any other commander. The Indies favored the adventurer with initiative and daring. Velázquez himself had risen to prominence by ignoring the commands of his superior, the governor of Hispaniola, and imposing his own authority on Cuba, the island he had conquered. What was to prevent Cortés from declaring himself master of the new lands and then successfully appealing to the Spanish Crown to appoint him governor? Velázquez may have briefly considered personally heading the expedition to Mexico. But what a risk it would have been. In Cuba, he was governor and a man of wealth and social prominence. He could lose all with no certainty that the new domains would prove more rewarding. The alternative was to try to keep Cortés in harness, even across the wide Caribbean. Velázquez forced Cortés to accept under his command a number of men who were clearly the governor's spies. He drafted instructions for Cortés that deliberately left ambiguous whether the purpose of the expedition was to trade or to conquer and settle. And what if Mexico turned out to be as opulent as the fabled kingdoms described in the Romances of Chivalry? Surely, Cortés would be unable to subdue the heathen lands with such a modest army at his disposal. He would have

to return to Cuba for reinforcements, and give Velázquez the opportunity to decide on what course of action to pursue next.

But still, Velázquez remained deeply suspicious of Cortés. And as
preparations for the voyage neared completion, Cortés himself feared
that the wavering governor would change his mind and abort the
mission. He resolved to keep his departure date a secret from Velázquez. Late one evening, he suddenly ordered his men to board the
ships and prepare to cast off. Velázquez rushed to the pier in time to
see the vessels set sail into the darkness. Aware that Cortés intended
to stop briefly in Trinidad, another Cuban port, for more men and
supplies, Velázquez sent word overland to the Trinidad authorities to
capture him. But Trinidad held a small garrison which would have
been no match for Cortés's army of conquistadores eager to press on
with the voyage. Thus the expeditionary force anchored in Trinidad
and then in Havana, without incident, picking up additional soldiers,
vessels, and supplies.

On February 10, 1519, the thirty-three-year-old Cortés sailed from
Cuba to Mexico with a fleet that had grown to ten ships and some
650 men. With the perspective of history, this remarkable expedition
has come to be viewed as the logical culmination of two key events
that occurred twenty-seven years before, in 1492: the triumph of the
Reconquista in Spain, bringing the entire country under a Catholic
monarchy anxious to extend its temporal power and crusading religion
over infidels abroad; and the discovery by Columbus of a New World
to serve as an arena for Spain's imperial pretensions. But those who
participated in the expedition commanded by Cortés saw it as a very
private venture, born of the courage, greed, and cunning of men for
whom God and Crown seemed distant indeed. Many years later, Bernál
Díaz del Castillo, who told the story best, would gloat that the conquest
of Mexico was accomplished "by our own efforts without His Majesty
knowing anything about it."[16]

FIVE

CONQUEST

Even to its participants, the Cortés expedition must have seemed an act of sheer bravado. Cortés justified his mission in terms of his loyalty to Church and Crown, but he had no royal or papal sanction to conquer and settle Mexico. He and his men faced charges of treason if they attempted to return to Cuba, and they could expect to be pursued to Mexico by a punitive expedition acting on Velázquez's orders. Moreover, Cortés had not elaborated any grand strategy to conquer Mexico. For all his diligence in gathering information, he knew little about that landmass. The Spaniards who had traveled there before him— and many of them were now members of his expedition—had not ventured beyond Mexico's Gulf coast, and were ignorant of the nature of the Aztec empire. Arrayed against all these risks and uncertainties were the gold and jewelry that the Indians had given to Grijalva—and the hope that these presents were only a tiny portion of a vast treasure.

Cortés's immediate plan was to follow the same route as the Grijalva expedition, reaching Yucatán and then making his way along the Gulf coast to the Veracruz region where Motecuhzoma's emissaries had dispensed their valuable gifts. Yucatán was the first destination because Cortés, during his many conversations back in Cuba with the men who accompanied Grijalva and Hernández de Córdova, was intrigued by reports that the Yucatán Indians had greeted the Spaniards with cries of "Castilan, Castilan!" Astute as he was, Cortés suspected the Indians meant "Castilian," and that perhaps a few Spaniards had shipwrecked on these shores and found refuge with the natives.

Among Cortés's crew was a Yucatán Indian who had been taken prisoner during the Hernández de Córdova expedition and brought back to Cuba. Christened as Melchorejo and taught a rudimentary Spanish, he served the conquistadores as an interpreter. Through him, Cortés queried the Yucatán tribes on the whereabouts of any Spaniards on the peninsula. Eventually, they informed Cortés that two ship-wrecked Spaniards were indeed living among the Indians. One of them had been elevated to a tribal chieftain. Married to an Indian woman who bore him several children, he had no desire to rejoin his fellow Spaniards. The other, Jerónimo de Aguilar, became a valuable inter-preter for the Spaniards in their dealings with the natives, particularly after Melchorejo fled his Spanish captors at the first opportunity.

From Yucatán, the fleet followed the sweeping curve of the Gulf coast as it dipped southwest and then rose north. After a violent storm, the Spaniards landed on the shores of Tabasco, where they were at-tacked by Indians. Though far more numerous than the conquista-dores, the natives were routed by Spanish artillery and cavalry. During peace negotiations with the defeated tribe, Cortés experimented with the shrewd, psychological techniques he would later use even more effectively in his dealings with the Aztecs. Playing on the Indians' terror of Spanish arms, he pretended that the artillery and horses had a life and will of their own. Cortés warned the assembled Tabasco chieftains that the cannon were still angry because of the Indian attacks, and at that very moment, a hidden artillery piece roared its displeasure, sending a cannon ball exploding into the nearby hills and causing the Indians to drop to their knees in terror. Cortés then ordered a stallion to be brought forth. A mare in heat had been placed behind the chieftains, out of their view. When the stallion caught her scent, he reared up and neighed in excitement. The frightened Tabasco natives now capitulated unconditionally. They supplied the Spaniards with food and gold ornaments, and they turned over to them twenty women. The Indians quickly agreed to abandon their idols, and embraced the image of the Virgin Mary and a wooden cross placed in a newly constructed altar in their main village. They also declared themselves vassals of the Spanish monarch, Charles V.

Among the Tabasco women given to the conquistadores was an Indian christened Marina, who became one of Cortés's most trusted counselors, and later, his mistress. But her great value to Cortés at the moment was as an interpreter. She was born into an Aztec vassal tribe, and in her childhood was sold as a slave to the Tabasco Indians. She spoke both the Nahua language of the Aztecs and the Maya dialect of her Tabasco masters. A communication link was now created that would operate smoothly in the months ahead: Marina translated Nahua into the Maya understood by Aguilar, who in turn informed Cortés in Spanish. Cortés had added a key weapon to his arsenal. Through Marina and Aguilar, he discovered far more about his Indian adversaries than they knew about the Spaniards. Already Marina had made him aware of the existence of the Aztec empire, its capital of Tenochtitlán and its system of subject provinces. Departing from Tabasco, Cortés continued to follow Grijalva's route west and north along the Gulf coast, in hopes of encountering the Aztec gift bearers who greeted his predecessor's expedition.

Meanwhile, through his spies, Motecuhzoma had been aware of the return of the strange vessels from the moment they reached the Yucatán peninsula. He knew also how easily the bearded intruders defeated the Tabasco tribes. From the fleet's progress, he could guess that the ships were making their way to the same landing point where his messengers had met them a year earlier. The Aztec king had no doubt that his realm was being visited again by the god Quetzalcóatl, or his agents. He ordered that gifts be prepared for the strangers, even more sumptuous presents than before: turquoise serpent masks, gold disks, jade necklaces, crowns, and robes of resplendent feathers. He told his envoys to carry the offerings as quickly as possible to the rendezvous point on the Veracruz coast, where he presumed Quetzalcóatl and his retinue would disembark. "And when you see the god," the Aztec monarch instructed them, "tell him: your vassal Motecuhzoma has sent us and here is what he gives you because you have returned home."[1]

On Holy Thursday, April 21, 1519, the Spanish fleet anchored off the shores of Veracruz. Almost immediately, Motecuhzoma's envoys paddled their canoes to the vessels and were waved aboard Cortés's flagship. They prostrated themselves before Cortés, and by their very first words let him know that he was considered a deity: "Hear us, o god, your vassal Motecuhzoma bids you welcome."[2] The emissaries then adorned him with the richly embroidered robes and jewelry they brought as gifts. The other Spaniards were dazzled by the ceremony. Cortés, however, remained impassive. He sensed that in this initial encounter with the Aztecs he had to impress them with his power and unpredictability.

As soon as Motecuhzoma's envoys finished dressing him, Cortés coldly inquired if these were their only offerings of welcome. When they answered in dismay that these were in fact all the gifts they bore, Cortés ordered them bound in irons and gave a signal that large cannon be fired into the sea. The emissaries fainted at the roar of the gun.

They were revived with cups of wine, which made them giddy. In this drunken state, they were handed swords and spears by Cortés, who challenged them to a duel that would take place the following morning on shore. The Indians were aghast as they paddled back to land. How could they accept personal combat against a god? The next day, Good Friday, the Spaniards disembarked. The duel apparently was forgotten. Instead, Cortés staged a devastating display of his weaponry. Rounds of artillery were fired into the forest and hills. Cavalrymen galloped their horses through the surf. Fierce mastiffs, straining at their leashes, were held within a few feet of the terrorized Indian envoys. Then, after treating them to another dizzying bout of wine and strange European food, Cortés told the emissaries that "I and my companions suffer from a disease of the heart which can be cured only by gold."[3] The Indians were now allowed to depart. They hurried back to Tenochtitlán, barely stopping to rest or eat during the two-hundred-mile journey. Although they reached the Aztec capital late at night, they were summoned immediately by Motecuhzoma, who had been experiencing insomnia and complete loss of appetite ever since the Spanish ships appeared at the rendezvous point.

The exhausted envoys blurted out a description of the supernatural intruders and their infernal armaments:

> A weapon of fire that roars like thunder causing one to faint and turn deaf. And a thing like a ball of stone comes out of its entrails, spitting sparks and smoke, smelling of sulfur. . . . And if the stone strikes a mountain, the mountain splits open. And if it strikes a tree, it shatters the tree into splinters as if the tree had exploded from within. Their costumes are made of metal. They cover their heads with metal. Their swords and spears and shields and arrows are made of metal. And their deer [horses] carry them on their backs wherever they wish to go, holding them as high as the roof of a house. They cover their bodies completely so that only their faces are visible. Their faces are white as lime. They have yellow hair, though some have black. Their beards are long and also sometimes yellow. Some have curly hair. . . . And their dogs are enormous, with flat ears, great tongues that hang, with eyes that seem on fire . . . with hollow bellies and long, narrow flanks. They are savage, like demons, always bounding about.[4]

Awestruck by these accounts, Motecuhzoma was uncertain about how to deal with the intruders. He did not even consider attacking them, convinced as he was that his warriors would be useless against supernatural beings. His only thought was to delay their advance on

Tenochtitlán and try to placate them with more gifts, especially the gold they valued so highly. And so, Motecuhzoma sent a large delegation bearing more treasure and food for the Spaniards. Leading the embassy were priests and sorcerers who would attempt by means of magic to subdue the bearded strangers. But the spells were so pathetically ineffective that the Spaniards mistook the chants and gestures of the priests and sorcerers for ceremonial rituals of welcome. The strangers were far more impressed by the gifts: "A wheel like a sun, as big as a cartwheel, with many sorts of pictures on it, the whole of fine gold . . . another wheel . . . of greater size made of silver of great brilliancy in imitation of the moon . . . twenty golden ducks, beautifully worked and very natural looking . . . and many articles of gold worked in the shape of tigers and lions and monkeys. . . ."[5]

The only moment of tension occurred when the banquet was served. Since they believed the Spaniards to be gods or divine agents, the Aztec priests sacrificed several slaves and sprinkled their blood on the food. The Spaniards howled in disgust and spat on the ground until the dishes were replaced by uncontaminated food.

All these events were reported back to Motecuhzoma along with the disturbing news that the strangers had asked to travel to Tenochtitlán and meet the king. The envoys, on previous orders from their ruler, turned down the request to visit the capital. But the strangers continued to question them about Motecuhzoma, his appearance, his age, his character. "And when Motecuhzoma heard how they asked about him, how they wished to see him face to face, he felt anguish in his heart. He wanted only to flee, to hide from these gods."[6]

By now, the presence of the foreigners on Mexican soil was common knowledge. In Tenochtitlán, "despair reigned among [the inhabitants]. People met to discuss. There was weeping and lamenting. People walked about downcast and greeted each other with tears. They tried to console each other and their children."[7] Motecuhzoma convoked his nobles and sought their counsel. Some argued that the foreigners were not gods, but men from an unknown land, who like any mortals could be defeated in battle. Others, more inclined to accept the divinity of the intruders, urged the king to receive them in Tenochtitlán. In the end, Motecuhzoma leaned toward the advice of his brother, Cuitláhuac, who said it was folly to "bring into your household those who would throw you out of it."[8] Motecuhzoma ordered that the Spaniards be quarantined. Neither the Aztecs nor their vassal tribes were to make contact with the strangers, nor feed them nor aid them in any way. Then perhaps they would board their ships and sail away.

At first, the quarantine seemed to have the intended demoralizing effect on the Spaniards. Their swampy beachhead swarmed with mosquitoes, and more than thirty men, who had been wounded in the skirmishes against the Tabasco Indians, died of fever and gangrene. Deprived of food, some Spaniards, especially agents of Velázquez, the governor of Cuba, urged a mutiny against Cortés. He quashed the incipient rebellion by sharing out the treasures he had received from Motecuhzoma. With the approval of his men, Cortés then ordered the building of a settlement on the beach enclave, and named it Veracruz—the True Cross.

The food crisis ended when emissaries from the Totonacs, a nearby vassal tribe of the Aztecs, violated Motecuhzoma's decree and invited the Spaniards into their villages. Leaving a small contingent behind in Veracruz, Cortés and his men marched north along the Gulf coast toward Cempoala, the main Totonac town. They passed through lush fields of corn, manioc, and cacao. A thick jungle of mangrove, cedar, and mahogany trees blanketed the hot plains west of the Indian plantations, and a few miles further inland the forests gave way to a chain of mountains. In every village the Spaniards saw evidence of the Aztec cult of sacrifice, with altars smeared in blood and littered with the mutilated remains of victims. Díaz del Castillo, chronicler of the expedition, observed that "as many readers will be tired of hearing of the great number of Indian men and women whom we found sacrificed in all the towns and roads we passed, I shall go on with my story without stopping to say any more about them."[9] And yet, again and again, he was drawn by morbid fascination into detailed accounts of ritual killings and the eating of human flesh. He knew that many of his companions had participated in the wanton murder and torture of the Indians in Cuba and Hispaniola, but like other Spaniards who witnessed the conquest of Mexico, he considered cannibalism an unspeakable evil, far greater than any atrocities committed by his fellow Christians.

The Spaniards ended their march in a fortified town where the Totonac chieftains had gathered to meet them. The Totonacs expressed hatred of their Aztec overlords and asked Cortés to become their ally and protector. "Besides relating the way that they had been brought into subjection," wrote Díaz del Castillo, "they told us that every year many of their sons and daughters were demanded of them for sacrifice, and others for service in the houses and plantations of their conquerors; and they made other complaints which were so numerous that I do not remember them all . . ."[10]

For Cortés, the Totonac account was a revelation. He became aware for the first time that dissatisfaction and the potential for rebellion against the Aztecs ran deep among their vassal tribes. He could now begin to devise a sophisticated strategy to deal with Motecuhzoma. He would build alliances with vassal tribes without openly declaring his enmity toward the Aztecs.

Even while Cortés was negotiating with the Totonac chieftains, he had an opportunity to test this strategy. A delegation of Motecuhzoma's tax collectors arrived in the village, interrupting the talks between the Spaniards and Totonacs. In the presence of Cortés, the five Aztec emissaries upbraided the frightened Totonac chieftains for dealing with the Spaniards. As punishment, they demanded that the Totonacs turn over to them twenty men and women for sacrifice. Cortés, who had been listening through his interpreters, angrily ordered the Aztecs to be taken prisoner. "When [the Totonac chieftains] heard this, they were thunderstruck at such daring. What!—to order the messengers of the great [Motecuhzoma] to be maltreated?"[11]

But Cortés had calculated on precisely this reaction from his hosts. He would make them accomplices in an act of such insolence against Motecuhzoma that they would be compelled to accept the protection and leadership of the conquistadores. Not only did Cortés have the haughty Aztec envoys bound and jailed, but he even had one of them flogged for protesting. The excited Totonac chieftains sent messengers throughout their provinces to spread word of the incident, and it quickly stirred the latent spirit of rebellion among the Totonacs against their Aztec conquerors. There was no need for Cortés to negotiate laboriously for an alliance between Spaniards and Totonacs. Within days after his brusque handling of Motecuhzoma's agents, he could count on the allegiance of twenty Totonac towns.

Now, Cortés acted to assuage Motecuhzoma, or at least confuse him. He secretly released the Aztec tax collectors, told them that he had saved them from certain death at the hands of the Totonacs, and sent them back to Tenochtitlán bearing a message of friendship for the Aztec monarch. Motecuhzoma was bewildered. Through his envoys, he upbraided Cortés for fomenting treason among his vassals and encouraging them not to pay tribute. Cortés told Motecuhzoma that he had no choice because the monarch had forbidden food supplies to the Spaniards, who now had to exact from the Totonacs the tribute that normally would be turned over to the Aztecs.

Motecuhzoma responded the way Cortés hoped he would. The Aztec monarch vowed to subdue the rebellious Totonacs, but he set no date for the promised retribution. He seemed far more concerned that Cortés and his retinue still intended to journey to Tenochtitlán, and again sent gifts of gold and fine cloth to persuade the Spaniards to remain on the coast. The Totonacs considered Motecuhzoma's gifts as further evidence that the mighty Aztec ruler feared Cortés, and they were even more willing to throw their support behind the Spaniards.

The stalemate with Motecuhzoma suited Cortés. He needed time to consolidate his position before marching inland toward the Valley of Mexico. During the next four months, he sought to expand his alliance with local tribes and impose more discipline over his unruly conquistadores.

Cortés became aware that their chieftains were trying to enlist him in their grudges against neighboring tribes. At one point, the Spaniards were almost duped into attacking an Indian community that the Totonacs had falsely accused of being an Aztec garrison. Cortés prodded the rival tribes to enter into peace pacts, arguing that only through unity could they hope to overcome their common enemy, the Aztecs.

Hatred of the Aztecs was not the only means by which Cortés sought to increase his Indian following. He also wanted to convert the tribes to Christianity as quickly as possible. Like his fellow conquistadores, Cortés was a militant Christian, totally intolerant of other faiths. He reacted with physical revulsion to the idol worship and sacrificial ceremonies of the Indians. The expedition's three priests counseled more patience and discretion in the efforts to proselytize among the Indians so that they would more clearly understand and freely accept Church teachings. But Cortés was not really concerned with the spiritual welfare of the Indians. He linked political loyalty to religion. Just as the Aztecs imposed their Huitzilopochtli cult on their vassal tribes, Cortés demanded that his Indian followers embrace Christianity before their alliance with the Spaniards could be complete. He believed their conversion had to involve a dramatic break with their heathen past.

Cortés assembled the Totonacs and denounced their religious practices. He threatened to abandon them to the Aztecs. And then, to the tribe's dismay, he ordered fifty of his soldiers to scale the Indian altars and cast down their idols, which shattered into fragments as they rolled to the bottom of the temples' steps. When the Indian warriors attempted to attack the Spaniards, Cortés and his men held their chiefs and priests as hostages. They were not released until the tribe agreed to rid their temples of idols and replace them with images of the Virgin Mary.

Cortés used these same methods of brinkmanship to strengthen his leadership over his conquistadores. Convoking his soldiers, he explained that he had decided to write to the Spanish monarch, Charles V to render him an account of the expedition's progress and request him to appoint Cortés as his governor in Mexico. He asked his men to turn over the gold they had received in Mexico to the Spanish king to help assure he would grant Cortés's demands. In return, he promised them future treasure, which they were more likely to keep if their expedition received the approval of the Crown. Soon a ship, carrying the letter and the treasure, set sail for Spain. This was a remarkable feat of manipulation by Cortés. He had convinced his followers that royal approval for their expedition of conquest and his own ambition to become governor of Mexico were inseparable issues— and that it was in their own interests to bribe Charles V to ensure his backing for these ventures.

Cortés's ranks included agents of Velázquez, the governor of Cuba. A dozen of them now plotted to seize a ship and sail back to Cuba to inform Velázquez of the promising discoveries in Mexico and of Cortés's initiative to the Crown. But on the night the boat was to depart, one of the conspirators confessed the plan to Cortés, who immediately ordered his soldiers to apprehend the others. Two of the conspirators were hanged, another was condemned to lose his feet, and the rest were whipped. With his men still numbed by the harshness of these reprisals, Cortés ordered them to strip the remaining nine vessels in his fleet of their armaments, supplies, and all useful material, and then had the ships burned. There would be no turning back for the Spaniards. With this dramatic gesture, Cortés committed his conquistadores to his cause as firmly as he rallied the Totonacs behind him by seizing Motecuhzoma's tax collectors and dashing their idols to pieces.

On August 16, 1519, Cortés's forces began the journey westward to the Valley of Mexico, leaving behind one hundred fifty soldiers to man the fortified base camp built in Veracruz. The expedition inland included some four hundred conquistadores, two hundred Totonac bearers, and forty chieftains, who acted as guides and informants. The plan was to reach the province of Tlaxcala, whose tribe had emerged in recent years as a formidable enemy of the Aztecs, and to negotiate an alliance before proceeding to Tenochtitlán. The two-week journey to Tlaxcala was arduous. From the tropical coast of Veracruz, the Spaniards climbed the steep mountain trail that rose above 10,000 feet as it wound past the snow-capped volcano of Orizaba (17,365 feet). Battered by frigid winds and hail, the conquistadores descended 3,000 feet through salt lakes, sand, and volcanic ash to the plateau of Tlaxcala. "As we had come from the coast, which is very hot, and had nothing with which to cover ourselves, only our armor, we suffered from the frost," wrote Díaz del Castillo. "There was nothing to eat, and the cold was intense."[12]

The highland plains of Tlaxcala, 7,000 feet above sea level, were somewhat warmer, but uncomfortably wet because it was the height of the rainy season. The Totonacs led the Spaniards through lands inhabited mainly by tribes who were hostile to Aztec rule. Before entering Indian villages, the conquistadores sent ahead their Totonac allies to vaunt the supernatural power of Spanish weapons. Cortés then promised the Indians protection against the Aztecs and an end to tribute. But he was met by skepticism from these tribes, who believed the Spaniards were no match for Motecuhzoma's armies. The Indians lodged and fed the conquistadores with reluctance, and were glad to be rid of them as quickly as possible.

At the end of August, the Spaniards entered the province of Tlaxcala. His Totonac guides had assured Cortés that he would be well received by the Tlaxcalans because they were mortal enemies of the Aztecs. But, in fact, the Tlaxcalans were deeply suspicious of the Spaniards. They had heard that Motecuhzoma had sent valuable gifts to Cortés and had refrained from mounting any attacks on the conquistadores even though they were marching toward the Aztec capital. For the Tlaxcalans, it seemed evident that the Spaniards were on friendly terms with the Aztecs, perhaps even their secret allies. Before the conquistadores had an opportunity to explain themselves, they were attacked by Tlaxcala's sixty thousand warriors.

"How they began to charge us!" wrote Díaz del Castillo. "What a hail of stones sped from their slings . . . ! [Their] javelins lay like corn on the threshing floor; all of them barbed and fire-hardened . . . would pierce any armor and . . . reach the vitals where there is no protection; the men with swords and shields and other arms larger than swords . . . and lances, how they pressed on us and with what valor and what mighty shouts and yells they charged upon us!"[13]

The Cortés expedition might well have ended in a massacre of the conquistadores on the wet Tlaxcalan fields. They were spared only because of the poor military tactics of the Tlaxcalans, who massed their warriors in dense formations that were especially vulnerable to Spanish artillery. "The enemy was so numerous and so crowded one on another that the shots wrought havoc among them," according to Díaz del Castillo.[14] But Cortés feared that it was only a matter of time before the Tlaxcalans revised their tactics and overpowered the small

Spanish forces. By using several captured warriors as envoys, he managed to convey his peaceful intentions to the Tlaxcalan leaders. Impressed by his troops' firepower, they were willing to consider negotiations with these awesome strangers. Only one Tlaxcalan chieftain continued to counsel war, but his considerably reduced forces were soon subdued by the Spaniards, bringing an end to the hostilities.

The conquistadores then accompanied the Tlaxcalans back to their capital. It was by far the most impressive example of urban civilization that the Spaniards had yet encountered in the Americas. "The city is much larger than Granada and very much stronger, with as good buildings and many more people . . . and very much better supplied with the produce of the land, namely bread and fowl and game and fresh-water fish and vegetables and other things they eat which are very good," wrote Cortés. Turning his gaze to the rest of the province, he marveled at the "many beautiful valleys and plains, all cultivated and harvested, leaving no place untilled."[15]

The news of the Spanish victories over the Tlaxcalans was another setback for Motecuhzoma, who had hoped that his enemies would stop the conquistadores' advance on Tenochtitlán. He was even more perturbed that Cortés and his men were being lodged in the Tlaxcalan capital. That could only mean that the white intruders and the Tlaxcalans were negotiating an alliance against the Aztecs. Again, Motecuhzoma sent messengers bearing more treasure for the Spaniards. Through his spies in Veracruz, the Aztec ruler was aware that Cortés demanded his Indian allies become vassals of the Spanish monarch. And so, Motecuhzoma instructed his envoys to inform Cortés that he also was willing to declare himself a vassal of Charles V, and to pay him annual tribute. But Motecuhzoma still insisted that the Spaniards not come to Tenochtitlán.

Cortés asked the Aztec envoys to give him time to formulate a response. He had no reason to trust Motecuhzoma, who had been attempting by any means short of an attack to get the Spaniards to quit the country. And if the Spaniards sailed away, there was nothing to prevent Motecuhzoma from reneging on his agreement to become a vassal and tributary of the Spanish Crown. Even more important, however, Cortés wanted to be governor of these realms and coveted the Aztec riches for himself and his conquistadores. He was determined to reach Tenochtitlán and fulfill these ambitions, either through guile or outright conquest. It was best to continue his strategy of wooing vassal and enemy tribes of the Aztecs while assuring Motecuhzoma that the Spaniards had no hostile intents toward his empire. Thus,

Cortés used Motecuhzoma's latest proposals as leverage to negotiate a treaty with the Tlaxcalans. Like Motecuhzoma, the Tlaxcalan chieftains also agreed to become vassals of Charles V. But they were temporarily allowed to keep their idolatrous religious practices—a pragmatic concession by Cortés to Tlaxcalan resistance to Christian conversion. In return, the Spaniards would lead the Tlaxcalans in an alliance ultimately aimed at overthrowing Aztec rule.

Cortés then informed Motecuhzoma's envoys that he had concluded a peace accord with Tlaxcala, although he did not tell them that it was a pact directed against the Aztecs. He continued to value Motecuhzoma's friendship, he said, and still hoped to resume his journey to Tenochtitlán to meet the monarch.

Motecuhzoma was not deceived by Cortés's assurances. The Spanish pact with the Tlaxcalans was a threat that he could not ignore, and at last, he prepared for an armed confrontation with the strangers, whether or not they were gods. But instead of meeting them in open battle, he attempted to lure the Spaniards into an ambush. Motecuhzoma sent yet another embassy to Cortés with more gold, and this time, invited him to Tenochtitlán. The Aztec envoys were to guide the Spaniards to their capital by a route that would take them through Cholula, a city that had recently fallen under Motecuhzoma's control. The Cholulans would attack the Spaniards, and the Aztecs, hidden outside the city, would join the assault.

The Tlaxcalans warned the Spaniards to expect only treachery from the Cholulans and Motecuhzoma. But Cortés was confident that he could deal with any attack short of an all-out war with the Aztecs. If he smothered a threat in Cholula, it would enhance his aura of invincibility and gain him more Indian allies before he entered Tenochtitlán.

Accompanied by six thousand Tlaxcalan warriors, the Spaniards made the one-day march south from Tlaxcala to Cholula. The conquistadores were welcomed by the Cholulan chieftains, who invited them into the city. The Cholulans insisted, however, that the Tlaxcalans remain camped beyond the city limits because of their enmity and distrust of the tribe. Cortés agreed to this demand, but as soon as he and his men were lodged in a large walled compound near the center of the city, they turned it into a fortress and maintained themselves ready for battle. At first, the precautions seemed unnecessary. The Cholulan chieftains treated Cortés with respect, listened attentively to his explanations about the purpose of his expedition, and supplied the Spaniards with as much food as they desired. Cortés toured the city and found it even more impressive than Tlaxcala. "The city . . . is more beautiful to look at than any in Spain, for it is very well proportioned and has many towers," he wrote. "I counted more than 430 towers, and they were all temples. From here to the coast I have seen no city so fit for Spaniards to live in, for it has water and some common lands suitable for raising cattle, which none of those we saw previously had. . . ."[16]

But within days, the hospitality of the Cholulans waned. "They fed us worse, and the lords and principal persons of the city came only rarely to see and speak with me," wrote Cortés.[17] And then, evidence of the suspected treachery by the Cholulans was uncovered by Marina, the Indian interpreter who had served Cortés so well during the march inland. She learned from an old Cholulan woman that some twenty thousand Aztec warriors had gathered a short distance from the city, and would strike as soon as the Cholulans attacked the Spaniards. Cortés ordered his men to seize and interrogate a Cholulan priest, who confirmed the story. Cortés then asked the Cholulan chieftains to meet with him in the Spanish quarters. As soon as the Indian leaders, accompanied by several thousand of their warriors, assembled in the walled compound, Cortés denounced their duplicity and commanded his Spaniards to slaughter them. At the same time, his Tlaxcalan allies fought their way into the city. The Aztec troops, camped a few miles away, were not even aware of the battle until it was over, and made no move to aid their Cholulan vassals.

The massacre of the Cholulans was horrendous. Cortés estimated that his conquistadores—using their artillery, firearms, cavalry charges, swords, and spears—killed more than three thousand warriors trapped inside the Spanish compound. But the Cholulans suffered even greater losses at the hands of their Tlaxcalan enemies, who cut down every man, woman, and child they came across. "The Tlaxcalans went about the city . . . plundering," wrote Díaz del Castillo, "and the next day more companies from the Tlaxcalan towns arrived, and did great damage, for they were very hostile to the people of Cholula, and when we saw this, both Cortés and the captains and the soldiers, on account of the compassion that we had felt, restrained the Tlaxcalans from doing further damage. . . ."[18]

The news of the Spanish victory in Cholula jolted the Aztec leaders and subjects. "The common people were terrified . . . they could do nothing but shiver with fright. It was as if the earth trembled beneath them."[19] Motecuhzoma cloistered himself for two days in the temple of Huitzilopochtli seeking divine inspiration from the hummingbird god on how to deal with these supernatural beings who seemed prescient about his every move. But it was Cortés who cunningly manipulated Motecuhzoma into the next course of action. In a message to the Aztec ruler, he laid blame for the recent battle entirely on the Cholulans, and claimed that not for a moment did he believe their assertions that they were following Motecuhzoma's will. Cortés also instructed his envoys to tell the Aztec ruler that "as we look upon him as our great friend and wish to see and speak to him, we are setting out at once for his city to give him a more complete account of what Our Lord the King has commanded us to do."[20]

Motecuhzoma was relieved that Cortés had exonerated him of blame. He even professed to be shocked by the Cholulan accusations of his complicity. And to signal his continuing friendship, he sent Cortés several high-ranking Aztec chieftains, laden with the usual gifts of gold and jewelry, to lead the Spaniards on the final stretch of their journey to Tenochtitlán. This was the reaction that Cortés had hoped for. He wanted no more battles on his way to Tenochtitlán. And although he told Motecuhzoma that he was "setting out at once" for the Aztec capital, he in fact intended to stall a bit longer and recruit more Indian allies.

After two more weeks in Cholula, Cortés felt he was ready for the seventy-five-mile march to Tenochtitlán. His conquistadores, numbering less than four hundred men, were now backed by twenty thousand Indian allies—Totonacs, Tlaxcalans, and assorted other tribes. From Cholula, the huge Spanish and Indian army proceeded northwestward through the high pass between Popocatépetl and Iztaccíhuatl, the majestic snow-cropped volcanoes overlooking the Valley of Mexico. Like a giant magnet drawing innumerable metal shards, the slow-moving column accumulated defectors from Aztec rule. In every village and town, nobles and commoners besieged the Spaniards with "great complaints about [Motecuhzoma] and his tax-gatherers, who robbed them of all they possessed, and carried off their wives and daughters, and made the men work as though they were slaves, and made them carry pine timber and stone and firewood and maize either in their canoes or over land, and many other services such as planting cornfields, and they took their lands for the service of the idols."[21]

At the southeastern ridge of the Valley of Mexico, the conquistadores stopped to behold Tenochtitlán and its satellite communities shimmering on the lakes like the magical provinces foretold by Amadis of Gaul and the other Romances of Chivalry. "And when we saw so many cities and villages built in the water and other great towns on dry land and that straight and level causeway going towards [Tenoch-titlán], we were amazed and said it was like the enchantments they tell of in the legend of Amadis, on account of the great towers and [temples] and buildings rising from the water, and all built of masonry," wrote Díaz del Castillo. "And some of our soldiers asked whether the things that we saw were not a dream."[22]

On November 8, 1519—almost three months after they began their inland march, almost seven months after they disembarked on the Veracruz shores—the Spaniards reached the causeway leading into the Aztec capital. They were greeted there by thousands of nobles, richly attired in feather headdresses, flowing robes, and pendulous jewelry. The Aztec lords took turns kneeling and kissing the ground in front of Cortés, who loomed imperiously high above them on horseback. The ceremony of abeyance lasted almost an hour before word came that Motecuhzoma was approaching, and only then did Cortés deign to dismount.

The Aztec king was held aloft on a litter. When he got down to walk, his attendants swept the ground before him and shaded him with a canopy of green feathers embroidered with gold, silver, pearls, and jade. He was "about forty years old, of good height and well propor-tioned, slender and spare of flesh, not very swarthy," wrote Díaz del Castillo. "He did not wear his hair long, but so as just to cover his ears, [and] his scanty black beard was well shaped and thin. His face was somewhat long, but cheerful, and he had good eyes and showed in his appearance and manner both tenderness and, when necessary, gravity."[23] He wore a sumptuous mantle and feather headgear, but what really distinguished him from the other nobles, who were bare-foot, were his sandals with soles of gold and straps inlaid with jewels.

It was evident to the Spaniards that Motecuhzoma was exalted by his subjects as a god. The warriors dared not look at him, and even the nobles did not gaze directly into his face. Yet in this very first encounter with the Aztec ruler, Cortés was intent upon demonstrating that he was at least equal in status to his host. He brazenly stared at Motecuhzoma, and attempted to embrace him—a gesture that was quickly prevented by the king's aides. Cortés was allowed, however, to place his necklace of glass stones around Motecuhzoma's collar. After the king and the Spaniard exchanged speeches of greeting, Mo-tecuhzoma led the huge entourage into Tenochtitlán.

As they traversed the broad southern causeway over the blue lake waters, the Spaniards marveled at the white city rising against a back-drop of green mountains. Every building—from modest adobe houses to the stone villas and palaces—was plastered with lime. Trees bordered the cobbled streets and canals. Thousands of Aztecs peered through the flowers and shrubbery of their rooftops at the bearded strangers marching below.

Motecuhzoma lodged Cortés and his Spaniards in the palace that had been built for his father, King Axayacatl, and then left them to enjoy a banquet and rest after their journey. As soon as Motecuhzoma withdrew, Cortés ordered that guards and artillery be deployed around the palace, turning it into an armed stronghold. From its parapets, he could see the base camp of his numerous Indian allies beyond the city walls and the placid lake.

After the Spaniards had eaten, Motecuhzoma rejoined Cortés, who placed at his side the interpreters, Marina and Aguilar. The Aztec king recounted to Cortés the legend of the return of the Toltec god, Quetzalcóatl:

> We have always held that those who descended from [Quetzalcóatl] would come and conquer this land and take us as their vassals. So because of the place from which you claim to come, namely from where the sun rises, and the things you tell us of the great lord or king who sent you here, we believe and are certain that he is our natural lord, especially as you say that he has known of us for some time. So be assured that we shall obey you and hold you as our lord in place of that great sovereign of whom you speak. . . . And in all the land that lies in my domain, you may command as you will, for you shall be obeyed, and all that we own is for you to dispose of as you choose.[24]

Motecuhzoma's capitulation seemed complete. He even pleaded with Cortés not to pay heed to the exaggerations voiced about him and his city by enemy tribes:

"I . . . know that they have told you the walls of my houses are made of gold, and that the floor mats in my rooms and other things in my household are likewise of gold, and that I was, and claimed to be, a god; and many other things besides. The houses as you see are of stone and lime and clay."

Then, removing his mantle and pinching the skin of his arms and chest, Motecuhzoma implored Cortés: "See that I am of flesh and blood like you and all other men, and I am mortal and substantial. See how they have lied to you. It is true that I have some pieces of gold left to me by my ancestors; anything I might have shall be given to you whenever you ask."[25]

How easy their triumph over the great Aztec empire seemed to Cortés and his conquistadores! They had lost no more than fifty men in their march to Tenochtitlán. And a day after their arrival in the opulent capital, the powerful Motecuhzoma had renounced his divinity, declared himself a vassal of the Spanish king, and offered his realms to the Spaniards.

An elated Cortés took what he assumed would be the last step to ensure his power over Mexico. He explained the Christian religion to Motecuhzoma. He urged the Aztec ruler to renounce his satanic idols, sacrifices, and cannibalism, and replace them with the cross and image of the Virgin Mary. But here, the conquistador encountered unbudging resistance from Motecuhzoma, who told him that "throughout all time we have worshipped our own gods, and thought they were good, as no doubt yours are, so do not trouble to speak to us any more about them at present."[26] And later, Motecuhzoma repeatedly warned Cortés that his priests, nobles, even the commoners would never tolerate the desecration of their idols.

It was not simple fanaticism that accounted for Cortés's insistence on the swift religious conversion of the Aztecs. Ever since the Reconquista of southern Spain from Moslem rule, the Spaniards had associated the triumph of their government, their civilization, with the evangelization of infidels. Their hold over the Caribbean Indians was not complete until they had been Christianized. Cortés's experience with the Totonacs had proved to him the effectiveness of this course. His power over the Totonacs was total only after he had forced them to worship the Virgin Mary. True, he had permitted the Tlaxcalans to continue their religious practices, but that was a temporary political expedient which he soon intended to correct. The Aztecs were another matter, however. If he allowed them to perpetuate their cult of Huitzilopochtli and the other deities, he believed that sooner or later a resistance movement would coalesce behind new Indian leaders who could claim to be defending these false gods and their people against Spanish rule.

There were nobles and priests who were far more reluctant than Motecuhzoma to accept Spanish sovereignty. From his very first day in Tenochtitlán, Cortés saw in the faces of the Aztec king's entourage men who could not hide their dismay at Motecuhzoma's gestures of complete surrender. Cortés decided upon a dual strategy. He would use Motecuhzoma's authority to impose Spanish will over the Aztecs and if need be, to protect the Spaniards against the possibility of an uprising. At the same time, Cortés determined to inform himself more about Aztec religious practices and overcome resistance to Christian conversion.

Cortés asked Motecuhzoma to show him Huitzilopochtli's temple. The monarch agreed to meet Cortés at the top of the great pyramid the following day. In the morning, Cortés and some of his conquistadores were guided around Tenochtitlán and its adjoining island-city, Tlatelolco. They were astonished at the wealth and size of an urban civilization that was superior in many ways to anything they had encountered in Europe. With its 200,000 inhabitants, Tenochtitlán was several times more populous than any city in Spain. The great marketplace of Tlatelolco was "twice as big as that of Salamanca," wrote Cortés, "with arcades all around, where more than sixty thousand people come each day to buy and sell, and where every kind of merchandise produced in these lands is found."[27] And the city was so clean and orderly, with streets swept of all debris and whole blocks reserved for specific trades and professions. With their intricate network of canals and avenues, the inhabitants appeared none the worse for the lack of wheeled carts and beasts of burden. There were palaces and villas more splendid than the residences of Spanish aristocrats. The towers of the largest temples rose higher than the Cathedral of Seville. Intoxicated by the smells, sights, and sounds of the Aztec capital, Cortés and his entourage entered the great religious precinct and scaled the 114 steps of Huitzilopochtli's pyramid for their rendezvous at the summit with Motecuhzoma. And at that moment, their euphoria vanished.

Two slabs of stone in front of Huitzilopochtli's chapel were bathed with blood from victims who had been freshly sacrificed by Motecuhzoma to appease the hummingbird god for the unprecedented invitation of foreigners to his temple. Inside the dark chapel, the walls "were so splashed and encrusted with blood that they were black, the floor was the same and the whole place stank [so] vilely . . . that in the slaughter houses of Spain there is not such another stench," recalled Díaz del Castillo. On his altar, Huitzilopochtli stood twice the height of a man, with "a very broad face and monstrous and terrible eyes, and the whole of his body covered with precious stones, and gold and pearls . . . and girdled by great snakes made of gold and precious stones, and in one hand he [held] a bow and in the other some arrows."[28] His hollow mouth, dripping blood, had been stuffed with the hearts of the recent victims.

Cortés could not contain his feelings of repugnance. He told Motecuhzoma that his idols were "not gods, but evil things that are called devils,"[29] and he asked the king to set aside and cleanse part of Huit-zilopochtli's chapel for an altar to the Virgin Mary. Motecuhzoma and his priests, standing guard at his side, angrily refused the sugges-tion. Not wishing to provoke them further, Cortés excused himself and descended the pyramid with his conquistadores, leaving Mote-cuhzoma behind to try to appease Huitzilopochtli with prayers for the insults uttered by the Spaniard. The conquistadores spent the rest of the day touring the great religious precinct. In every temple, they found the same bloody remains of sacrifice. In the priests' quarters, human flesh was being boiled in large pots. And in the open court, an enormous rack held uncounted thousands of human skulls.

The Spaniards decided to build their own altar to the Virgin Mary in their quarters in Axayacatl's palace. Searching out a suitable corner for the altar, they discovered what appeared to be a walled-off entrance to a hidden chamber. When they knocked through the wall, they found a room full of riches—so much gold and jewelry, wrote Díaz del Castillo, that "I took it for certain that there could not be another such store of wealth in the whole world."[30] The Spaniards had stum-bled upon the treasure of Axayacatl, which his son, Motecuhzoma, had stored to honor his memory.

But even the possession of these riches could not diminish the apprehension that the Spaniards' position in Tenochtitlán was becom-ing precarious. In the week that had passed since their triumphant welcome, they noticed a coldness in their Indian hosts, particularly after the incident at Huitzilopochtli's temple. They began to feel more like prisoners than masters of the great city. They wondered if Mo-tecuhzoma had invited them into Tenochtitlán to lull them into an ambush. What could they do against his great armies if they decided to attack? And how could their Indian allies, camped outside the city on the other side of the lake, come to their aid if the Aztecs raised the drawbridges? Many conquistadores argued that Motecuhzoma should be seized as a hostage to guarantee their security. Cortés agreed, but told them to wait for the right moment to act.

The excuse was provided almost immediately. The following day, Tlaxcalan messengers brought Cortés news of an Aztec attack against the Spanish garrison in Veracruz, on the Gulf coast. Seven conquis-tadores had been killed, and Cortés's Totonac allies, fearing that the Spaniards had lost their power, were refusing to provision the garrison. The Tlaxcalan messengers also reported that the Aztec attack was made on Motecuhzoma's orders. Accompanied by several of his soldiers, Cortés confronted Motecuhzoma in his palace. He accused the Aztec king of perfidy, and then several conquistadores, drawing their swords, took him prisoner. Motecuhzoma pleaded that his son and two daughters be taken as hostages in his place. "What will my chieftains say if they see me taken off as a prisoner?" asked the king, afraid that he would lose the throne if his nobles suspected he had allowed himself to become an instrument of the Spaniards.[31] But Cortés was adamant. He ordered Motecuhzoma to accompany him to the Spanish quarters, and to deceive the Aztec guards by telling them that Huitzilopochtli, the hummingbird god, had commanded him to live temporarily with the Spaniards. The bewildered Aztec guards allowed Motecuhzoma and the conquistadores to walk out of the imperial court.

Once they arrived at Axayacatl's palace, Cortés commanded Motecuhzoma to send for the Aztec chieftains who led the attack on the Spaniards in Veracruz. While waiting for the chieftains, the Spaniards permitted Motecuhzoma to carry out a semblance of normal activity— even his harem moved into the Spanish quarters to keep him company. He met there with his closest counselors, and even received ambassadors bringing him tribute from his distant vassal provinces. Motecuhzoma seemed as concerned as the Spaniards to maintain the fiction that he was still an all-powerful monarch, because he feared a rebellion if the truth of his imprisonment became known.

The Aztec chieftains summoned from Veracruz finally arrived at the Spanish compound after two weeks. They were led by Quauhpopoca, lord of Coyoacán, the province on the southern rim of the lake surrounding Tenochtitlán. Interrogated by the conquistadores, Quauhpopoca confessed that he had attacked the Spanish garrison on orders from Motecuhzoma. Quauhpopoca, his son, and fifteen of their captains were then burned alive in front of the palace by the conquistadores, as an example of the brutal punishment in store for any Aztecs who dared to raise their weapons against the Spaniards.

Now that he had direct evidence of Motecuhzoma's treachery, Cortés placed the king in chains. He also decided to break the already emotionally unbalanced monarch by using psychological techniques more associated with the modern era. He let Motecuhzoma writhe for several days in anger, fear, and self-pity before releasing him from his humiliating bonds.

"Cortés himself took off the fetters, and he spoke such loving words to him," wrote Díaz del Castillo.

> Cortés told him that he . . . regarded him as a brother, but much more, and that, as he was already Lord and King of so many towns and

provinces, if it were possible he would make him Lord of many more countries as time went on . . . and he told him that if he now wished to go to his Palace, that he would give him leave to go . . . and while Cortés was saying it the tears apparently sprang to [Motecuhzoma's] eyes. He answered with great courtesy, that he thanked him for it . . . and that now at present it was better for him to stay there a prisoner. . . . When he heard this reply, Cortés threw his arms round him and embraced him and said: "It is not in vain Señor Montezuma that I care for you as I care for myself."[32]

The once proud Aztec ruler had been reduced to a pathetic figure. He denounced Huitzilopochtli and the other gods for having abandoned him, and accepted instruction in the Christian faith of his captors. He lost all interest in maintaining any pretense of being a monarch, and declined to carry out his usual administrative tasks. Instead, Motecuhzoma preferred to pass the days gambling away gold pellets in games with Cortés and other Spaniards, not even protesting when he was cheated. He became an avid informer for the Spaniards, an active ally of the conquistadores against his own people. He wanted only the approval of his jailers. "He knew each one of us and even knew our names and our characters and he was so kind that to all of us he gave jewels and to some mantles, and handsome Indian women," wrote Díaz del Castillo.[33]

Despite Motecuhzoma's assertions to his nobles that he was not a prisoner, word of his predicament soon spread through Tenochtitlán. A rebellion against the monarch and the Spaniards began to coalesce around Motecuhzoma's brother, Cuitláhuac, and nephew, Cacama. It was Motecuhzoma himself who warned Cortés of the plot. At the conquistador's suggestion, Motecuhzoma then invited Cacama, Cuitláhuac, and a dozen other leading conspirators to meet him in the Spanish quarters. There, they were taken prisoner by the Spaniards, chained, and thrown into dungeons.

Emboldened, Cortés decided that the time had come to confront Huitzilopochtli, the hummingbird god, whose cult posed the most sustained threat to the conquistadores. The Aztec priesthood was preaching to the populace that the deity had forsaken Motecuhzoma and was angered by the continued presence of the Spaniards. With a squadron of his men, Cortés climbed the god's pyramid, shoved aside the priests protecting the altar at the summit, and attacked Huitzilopochtli's grotesque stone effigy with iron bars. Hearing the commotion, Motecuhzoma rushed to the scene and begged Cortés to relent. An

agreement was reached whereby the Aztecs would be allowed to remove
Huitzilopochtli and the other idols to safety, and in their place a cross
and altar to the Virgin Mary would be installed on top of the pyramid.
But Cortés was mistaken in believing that the Aztecs would resign
themselves to the overthrow of their religion as easily as the Totonacs
did in Veracruz. In the weeks ahead, the Aztec priests preached that
Huitzilopochtli had ordered his people to destroy the Spaniards for
their desecration of his temple.

Just as the potential for an Aztec rebellion against the Spaniards was
cresting in Tenochtitlán, Cortés received the worst possible news from
Veracruz: a fleet of nineteen ships had anchored off the Gulf coast,
and landed 1400 soldiers under the command of Pánfilo de Narváez,
who had been sent by the Cuban governor, Velázquez, to capture
Cortés and take charge of his mission in Mexico.

The dilemma seemed beyond solution even for a man as enormously
resourceful as Cortés. To remain with his conquistadores in Tenochtitlán was folly. It would give Narváez time to consolidate his hold
over Cortés's Indian allies and prepare for a march inland. As the
Aztecs became aware that Cortés was the target of a Spanish punitive
expedition, they would almost certainly rise up against his conquistador
garrison. And even if he could control such a rebellion, what hopes
would he have of holding off Narváez? Narváez's army would lay siege
to Tenochtitlán against a smaller conquistador garrison that faced the
additional threat of a hostile Aztec force within the city's walls.

To abandon Tenochtitlán and attack the Narváez forces before they
had a chance to organize themselves seemed equally risky to Cortés.
As soon as he left the city, he could expect a militant Aztec faction
to overthrow Motecuhzoma and declare war against the Spanish invaders. To retake Tenochtitlán by force would be a long, arduous,
and costly enterprise that Cortés hoped to avoid if at all possible.

In the end, Cortés sought a middle course between the alternatives
of remaining in the Aztec capital and rushing to Veracruz to face the
Spanish punitive expedition. Judging that Narváez posed a greater
danger than a possible Indian uprising in Tenochtitlán, he decided to
leave a rump garrison in the Aztec capital and march back with most
of his conquistadores to Veracruz where he would attempt to subdue
Narváez's army through guile and force. It was a plan that had little
chance of succeeding. But Cortés was a man who drew confidence
from situations of despair. His feats over the last year—the escape from
Cuba, the long-distance jousting with Motecuhzoma, the battles
against far superior Indian forces, the kidnapping of the Aztec mon-

arch—proved to him that audacity and unpredictability were the only choices when faced with great odds. If he now did the expected or surrendered the initiative to his adversaries, then all his accomplishments would be forgotten; all his hopes for treasure, fame, and colonial leadership would be shattered.

Cortés placed his lieutenant, Pedro de Alvarado, in charge of about one hundred forty soldiers in Tenochtitlán, and led the rest of his conquistadores—some two hundred men—to Veracruz. Even before reaching the Gulf coast, Cortés sent ahead a priest and several soldiers to sabotage Narváez. The priest appealed to Narváez's lieutenants by proclaiming Cortés's great spiritual values and religious efforts to convert the Indians. Cortés's soldiers were even more effective: they showed Narváez's men some of the Aztec treasures and promised them riches beyond their imagination. Narváez's troops were corruptible; they were soldiers of fortune like the conquistadores who followed Cortés. The notion of risking their lives to punish him in order to satisfy a personal vendetta by Velázquez seemed senseless to them—all the more so, when they found out that Cortés already claimed control of the Aztec capital and was prepared to share its wealth with them.

By the time Cortés and his main force arrived in Veracruz, diplomacy and bribery had severely undermined the Narváez expedition. During the night, Cortés's men, aided by defectors, stole much of Narváez's arsenal, and then launched their attack while their opponents slept. It was a quick victory. Only a few hundred out of the original 1400-man punitive army put up any resistance. Narváez was wounded and taken prisoner, and his soldiers quickly swore loyalty to Cortés. The events in Veracruz could not have turned out better. Cortés had virtually quadrupled his conquistador force, and added scores of cannon and hundreds of horses to his arsenal.

In Tenochtitlán, however, the Spaniards he left behind were considerably less adept than Cortés at handling a crisis situation. Alvarado, the garrison commander, was a firebrand with none of Cortés's flair for inspired maneuvering. When thousands of Aztec nobles gathered in the great religious precinct of their city for a ceremony honoring one of their gods, Alvarado feared that the assembly was the beginning of the rumored uprising against the Spaniards. And perhaps it was. But Alvarado's reaction only hastened such an eventuality. Leading his men and a large contingent of their Tlaxcalan allies, Alvarado had the gates of the religious precinct sealed off, and then ordered an attack on the Aztec nobles, who were virtually unarmed. Most of the highest-ranking Aztec aristocrats were hacked, speared, and bludgeoned to death. When word of the outrage spread among the city's inhabitants, they exploded against the Spaniards. Alvarado and his men were besieged in their palace by thousands of warriors and commoners, who stormed the walls of the Spanish quarters for six successive days and nights. Alvarado dragged Motecuhzoma to the ramparts of the palace and forced him to beg his people to withdraw. He was shouted down and stoned by the attackers, who were led by his nephew, Cuauhtémoc, the most militant anti-Spaniard among the surviving Aztec lords. The Aztecs halted their offensive only after being apprised that Cortés was returning to Tenochtitlán with an enlarged army of 1300 Spaniards and several thousand Indian allies. Cuauhtémoc reasoned that his warriors had a better chance of annihilating the Spaniards if they could be lured into the capital, where their cavalry and artillery were less effective than in the open fields.

Eager to save Alvarado and his garrison, Cortés fell into the trap. His forces encountered no resistance as they made their way through the eerily empty streets. But soon after they entered Axayacatl's palace and rejoined Alvarado, the Aztecs resumed their siege. "Little availed our cannon, or our muskets, crossbows and lances, or the thrusts we gave them, or our good fighting," wrote Díaz del Castillo, "for although we killed and wounded many of them, yet they managed to reach us by pushing forward over the points of our swords and lances, and closing up, their squadrons never desisted from their brave attack, nor could we push them away from us."[34]

Once again, the Spaniards dragged Motecuhzoma to the palace roof. And again he was greeted by jeers and rocks. On Motecuhzoma's advice, Cortés freed Cuitláhuac, the king's brother, after extracting a promise from him to act as a peacemaker. But the very next day, Cuitláhuac was seen leading the Aztec charge against the palace.

The battles continued without respite for several days and nights. Those Spaniards who were not manning the ramparts frantically tried to extinguish the fires set by flaming arrows. Food and water supplies ran out. Finally, in an act of total desperation, Cortés ordered his conquistadores and Indian allies to attempt a breakout from Tenochtitlán in the darkness before dawn. But the column was discovered as it left the palace, and the Aztecs launched an assault from all directions. The conquistadores managed to slash their way to the western edge of the city, and then across the causeway to the mainland on the other side of the lake.

It was Cortés's first defeat—and a stunning one. Almost one thousand Spaniards and a much greater number of their Indian allies perished in the siege and especially in the flight from Tenochtitlán, which has come to be known as the *Noche Triste*, or the Night of Sorrow. Virtually all the treasure was lost on the way out of the city. As Cortés, his surviving 440 conquistadores, and the remnants of their Indian troops circled south along the mainland beyond the lakes' edge and then fled back toward Tlaxcala, they could hear the deep, ominous beat of the huge drum atop Huitzilopochtli's pyramid, announcing that the shrine to the Virgin Mary had been displaced by the triumphant hummingbird god and that Spanish prisoners—perhaps a dozen in all—were being sacrificed to his pleasure.

Motecuhzoma also was a casualty of the struggle, and two differing accounts of his death have been handed down. The less credible one is the Spanish version, propagated by Cortés and Díaz del Castillo, who asserted that the pathetic monarch was stoned to death by his people when he last attempted to pacify them from the palace ramparts. But according to Indian sources, the Aztecs found the corpses of Motecuhzoma, Cacama, and the other imprisoned nobles still chained in their dungeons, their bodies slashed open by Spanish daggers.

The Aztecs made only one serious attempt to overtake the battered Spaniards, engaging them on the plains southeast of Tenochtitlán in a battle which neither side could claim as a victory. After that, the Aztecs decided to regroup and organize their army and vassal forces for a final war against the Spaniards. The Aztec chieftains preferred to draw the Spaniards again toward Tenochtitlán where the lakes would reduce the effectiveness of their artillery and cavalry. And then, if the Spaniards laid siege to the capital, Aztec vassal forces would attack them from the rear while the Aztec warriors rushed them in a pincer move.

But at this point, the Aztecs encountered the most powerful weapon in the Spanish arsenal, a weapon which the conquistadores themselves were unaware they possessed. Tenochtitlán, far from being a secure fortress, harbored the deadly germs of smallpox left behind by the fleeing Spaniards.

Smallpox was accepted by the Spaniards as an inevitable condition of their lives, a rite of passage into adulthood. In preindustrial Europe, it was the most widespread of all diseases, infecting ninety-five out of every hundred inhabitants.[35] It was rare indeed to find a European whose face did not display the ugly pockmarks of the illness. So prevalent was the disfigurement that men and women fortunate enough to avoid it were singled out for their beauty on that basis alone. But exposure over many centuries had made the Europeans partially immune to death by smallpox. In Spain during the 1500s, the disease killed one out of every seven of its victims, most of them infants and the infirm.

Introduced by the Spaniards into the New World, smallpox proved far more virulent than in Europe. The Caribbean Indians were the first to suffer its consequences. With no history of exposure, no partial immunity developed over generations, they usually died within days after contracting the disease. Referring to the smallpox epidemic that ravaged the island of Hispaniola in 1518, Father Las Casas wrote that only a thousand Tainos survived, a mortality rate close to 90 percent in a population that had already been afflicted by measles and influenza—other common European illnesses for which no native immunity existed.

According to Díaz del Castillo, it was an African sailor in the Narváez expedition who first brought smallpox to Mexico. Though ill, the sailor joined Cortés's forces after Narváez had been subdued. He then marched back with the conquistadores to Tenochtitlán where the Alvarado garrison was under siege. In those few days before the Spaniards made their costly escape, the disease had time to claim its first known Aztec victim and carrier. He was Cuitláhuac, Motecuhzoma's brother, who after being released by the conquistadores was crowned king of the Aztecs and took charge of their siege against the Spanish-held palace. Stricken by smallpox, Cuitláhuac died shortly after the Spaniards fled Tenochtitlán, and his nephew, Cuauhtémoc, succeeded him. As the Aztecs prepared for their final encounter with the Spaniards, their populace was scourged by smallpox.

"It began to spread," relates an Aztec account, "striking everywhere in the city and killing many of the people. Sores erupted on their faces, breasts, bellies. They had so many painful sores over their bodies that they could not move, not even turn over in their litters, and if someone tried to move them, they screamed in agony. This pestilence killed untold numbers of people, many of them dying because there was nobody to feed them, so they starved. Those who survived had holes in their faces, or were left blinded."[36]

Even as they were being enfeebled by the horrible epidemic inside their city walls, the Aztecs also found that their strength was rapidly ebbing beyond the confines of Tenochtitlán. The bitter legacy of tribute, war, sacrifice, and cannibalism had alienated their vassals and other potential allies. Cuauhtémoc sent his envoys to appeal for aid from the powerful Tarascans of Michoacán, the province west of the

Valley of Mexico, which had never been conquered by the Aztecs. But the Tarascan king had them put to death and dispatched a message to Cuauhtémoc rejecting any alliance and gloating at the Aztecs' predicament: "What would I gain by sending men to [Tenochtitlán], for we are always at war when we approach each other, and there is rancor between us. . . . Let the strangers kill the [Aztecs]."[37]

At least the Tarascans would remain neutral in the war against the Spaniards. Far worse for the Aztecs was the news that their most powerful vassal province, Texcoco, just across the lake on its northeast shore, had joined the Spanish cause. This startling betrayal was a direct consequence of recent Aztec imperial policy. Motecuhzoma had humiliated Nezahualpilli, the Texcocan king, and ended Texcoco's relatively independent status as an ally of the Aztecs by installing a puppet ruler, Cacama, on that province's throne. But Cacama was found dead alongside Motecuhzoma in the Spanish dungeon. And now Cacama's brother and rival, Ixtlilxochitl, had gained power in Texcoco and secretly negotiated a pact with Cortés.

While disease and political disarray racked the Aztecs, Cortés and his conquistadores spent five months in Tlaxcala recovering from their wounds and assembling an army of twenty thousand Tlaxcalans, Totonacs, and other Indian tribes. The day after Christmas, 1520, Cortés launched his offensive against the Aztecs by marching his columns to Texcoco, where he was welcomed as a savior and offered additional warriors for his army. Then the Spaniards swept southward along the periphery of the lakes to attack the rich agricultural provinces of Chalco and Xochimilco that supplied the Aztecs with the bulk of their food. Cortés's strategy became apparent: he would not repeat the mistake of being lured into Tenochtitlán; instead, he would isolate the Aztecs from their vassals and starve the capital into submission, or weaken its defenders in case an assault proved necessary.

Aware of these intentions, the Aztecs rushed their warriors to Chalco to reinforce their vassals against the Spanish advance. But illness again worked in Cortés's favor. The diseased Aztecs spread smallpox among the Chalcas, whose ruler succumbed to the epidemic. The debilitated remnants of the Chalco army defected to the Spanish side. And when Cuauhtémoc attempted to recover control of Chalco, his warriors were routed by the Spaniards and their Indian allies. Cortés held the periphery of the lakes in a vast semicircle from northeast to south. He now directed his forces to complete the encirclement of Tenochtitlán by occupying the mainland on the western shores of the lake. This was accomplished by May 1521, and enabled the Spaniards to cut the Chapultepec aqueducts supplying fresh water to the Aztec capital.

Then, using small warboats called brigantines, constructed with Indian labor in Tlaxcala and transported by thousands of Indian bearers overland, the Spaniards bombarded Tenochtitlán from the lake. The conquistadores, led by their cavalry, also charged across the causeways and breached the city's defenses at several points. Wrote Díaz del Castillo:

> The [brigantines] vanquished the canoes which were wont to attack us from the water, and so we had an opportunity to capture several bridges and barricades, and while we were fighting, so numerous were the stones from the slings and the javelins and arrows that they shot at us that although the soldiers were well protected by armour they were all injured and wounded, and not until night parted us did we cease contending and fighting. . . . Whenever we left a bridge or barricade unguarded after having captured it with much labour, the enemy would retake and deepen it that same night, and construct stronger defences. . . ."[38]

But slowly, the Aztecs were forced to withdraw from Tenochtitlán and retreat into the adjoining island-city of Tlatelolco. Cuauhtémoc's last hope was that the conquistadores would once again be trapped in Tenochtitlán. He had negotiated secretly with his vassals in Toluca, a province northwest of the capital, to send their huge army in a rearguard attack against the Spaniards after they had entered Tenochtitlán. But Cortés's spies informed him of the plan, and he defeated the Tolucan forces in an ambush before they even reached the lakeside. The siege now entered its final, most brutal stage. According to a surviving Aztec account:

> The people were tormented by hunger, and many starved to death. There was no fresh water to drink, only stagnant water and the brine of the lake, and many people died of dysentery. The only food was lizards, swallows, corncobs and the salt grasses of the lake. The people also ate water lilies . . . and chewed on deerhides and pieces of leather. . . . They ate the bitterest weeds and even dirt. Nothing can compare with the horrors of that siege and the agonies of the starving. We were so weakened by hunger that, little by little, the enemy forced us to retreat. Little by little, they forced us to the wall.[39]

On August 13, 1521, the Spaniards captured Cuauhtémoc and Aztec resistance collapsed, ending the two-and-a-half-month siege of the capital. But days later, the Tlaxcalans and other Indian allies of Cortés continued to rampage through the streets in search of their hated enemies, torturing, maiming, and slaughtering any Aztec man, woman, and child they came across. "The cruelty of our allies was so great that on no account would they spare a life in spite of our reproofs and example," wrote Díaz del Castillo.[40]

When the Spaniards finally imposed a semblance of peace, no more than a third of Tenochtitlán's 200,000 inhabitants were still alive. Huitzilopochtli's blood-encrusted altar on top of the largest pyramid was in flames, and thick columns of smoke billowed from temples and houses all across the city. A heavy downpour extinguished the fires, but flooded the canals and turned the streets into quagmires. Palaces, villas, shrines were wrecked and looted. Idols lay shattered in the broad courtyards. The stench of rotting corpses was so great that Cortés and his conquistadores abandoned Tenochtitlán for the fresher air of Coyoacán, the neighboring province to the south, where they would plot a new era for the Valley of Mexico and its fallen capital.

"Our cities will be destroyed and laid to waste . . . we and our children will die, and our vassals will be decimated," Nezahualpilli had forewarned Motecuhzoma only a few years before. And now all of his predictions had come to pass.

We can speculate whether the outcome might have been different under an Aztec ruler with a more stable psyche than Motecuhzoma's, or one less a prisoner of his tribe's religious mythology. Surely, Tlacaelel, who forged religion to match political and military strategy, would not have been paralyzed into inaction and surrender by the inexplicable appearance of the bearded foreigners. The Maya, a much weaker tribe than the Aztecs, had forced the first Spaniards to land on Mexican soil back onto their ships. The powerful Aztecs, under a more decisive king than Motecuhzoma, could certainly have repelled any Spanish party disembarking on the shores of their vassal provinces on the Gulf coast. But this would have been a short-lived victory. The Mexican coastline along the Gulf is so lengthy that the Spaniards would eventually have established a permanent base camp where they could consolidate their forces before confronting the Aztec armies. The dissension in the Aztec empire, the fear and hatred of Aztec rule among vassal tribes, in time would have gained allies for the Spaniards. European armor, artillery, and cavalry would have imposed themselves. And, most important, the terrifying biological warfare unleashed by European diseases would have inevitably melted Indian resistance, as it did everywhere in the Americas.

SIX

BIRTH
OF THE
SPANISH CITY

For months, the Spaniards debated whether or not to rebuild Te-nochtitlán as their colonial capital. There were good reasons to abandon the Aztec city. It was in shambles and the population was only a fraction of its pre-Conquest levels. Neither its location nor its design offered the same advantages to the Spaniards as to the Aztecs. Lacking beasts of burden, the Aztecs, of course, had used the lakes and an intricate canal system to move their goods and people. But the Spaniards, with their horses, oxen, and wheeled carts, had a transportation method of their own, one that was better suited for dry land than a water-logged island. During the siege of Tenochtitlán, the aqueduct supplying fresh water from the western mainland was cut, and the huge dike built by Nezahualcóyotl sixty years before to hold back Lake Texcoco's waters was severely damaged. Now, the city faced the threat of flooding by the briny lake while its surviving inhabitants were unable to obtain enough fresh water to drink. And finally, the military virtues of the Aztec capital had proved illusory: under the well-executed siege by the Spaniards and their Indian allies, the supposedly impregnable island-fortress became a charnelhouse for its occupants.

Some Spaniards urged that a new city be created on dry land west of Tenochtitlán, or in Texcoco, across the lake to the northeast. A few conquistadores favored Veracruz, on the Gulf coast, because it offered immediate access to the seas that led to the Caribbean Islands and to Spain. But Veracruz, surrounded by tropical swamps, was disease-ridden, and it was distant from the richest, most populous domains in and around the Valley of Mexico.

In spite of the objections raised by his followers, Cortés found a compelling argument to rebuild Tenochtitlán. The Aztec capital was the hub of an empire that efficiently funneled the wealth of vassals into the coffers of a ruling elite. Cortés wanted the Indian tribes to understand that the imperial system would be maintained with Tenochtitlán as the seat of power. Only instead of the Aztecs, the Spaniards would rule from the island-capital and receive the tribute that had previously flowed into Motecuhzoma's treasury. Pagan temples would give way to Christian churches, and the Aztec palaces would be altered or replaced by Spanish dwellings.

But before Cortés was able to organize the rebuilding of Tenochtitlán, he had to cope with the mounting impatience of his Spaniards, who were less interested in future tribute than in the immediate spoils of war. At every stage of the arduous Conquest, Cortés had paid for their loyalty with promises of great wealth. And now, the Spanish survivors of battle were eager to collect their due.

They could hardly contain their euphoria and greed at a ribald victory celebration organized by Cortés at his temporary base camp in Coyoacán, just a few miles southwest of the shattered Aztec capital. After news of the Conquest had reached Cuba, a supply ship from that island arrived in Veracruz, and Cortés had commandeered its cargo of pigs and wine to enliven the festivities. Reeling from their first taste of alcohol in many months, conquistadores clambered on top of tables and boasted of their riches. The cavalrymen vowed they would henceforth buy only gold saddles for their horses. The crossbowmen bragged they would fashion their arrows in gold. And then the Spaniards rushed out of the Coyoacán camp to rape the Aztec women who had been captured in the final battle.[1]

But the celebratory mood vanished the next day, and Cortés, faced with the clamor of his men for booty, led them across the causeway from Coyoácan to Tenochtitlán where the promised treasure would be assembled and divided up. The Spaniards gathered together in one of the few palaces that was still left standing. In the building's largest hall, the surviving Aztec chieftains, including Cuauhtémoc, were publicly interrogated by Cortés on the whereabouts of the riches that had been abandoned by the conquistadores during their flight from Tenochtitlán on the Night of Sorrow. Cuauhtémoc ordered his subjects to bring gold and jewels, which soon piled high in the middle of the palace room, lighting up the eyes of the Spaniards. But when the booty was counted, it was far less than the treasure the Spaniards had lost during their escape from the Aztec siege. Cuauhtémoc and his Aztecs claimed they had dumped much of the gold into the lake shortly before the fall of Tenochtitlán, and now could not find it. They also accused Cortés's Indian allies of having stolen some of the treasure. After Cortés took his one-fifth share of the spoils, and set aside the same amount for the Spanish monarch, the remainder was distributed to his men. Each cavalryman received the equivalent of 80 pesos, and each foot soldier 50 or 60 pesos—a pittance, an outrage for men who had suffered every ordeal![2]

The Spaniards returned to their base camp in a foul, rebellious temper. The white walls of the Coyoacán villa where Cortés had ensconced himself were defaced with graffiti: "Not conquerors, but conquered by Cortés," and, "Not content with his captain's share, he takes a royal share as well." Cortés responded by covering the graffiti with his own: "White walls, paper of fools."[3] But wit could not defuse the anger of his men, incensed by rumors that Cortés had conspired with Cuauhtémoc to hide the bulk of the Aztec fortune. How else to explain the leniency being displayed by Cortés toward the captured Indian monarch? The conquistadores demanded that the Aztec leader be forced to confess the whereabouts of the missing gold, and Cortés allowed them to place Cuauhtémoc's feet to a fire. But the torture achieved little. Only a few more gold and copper objects were uncovered. If nothing else, the unsavory episode finally convinced the Spaniards they had overestimated the booty at hand. Now, they were willing once again to look to Cortés for leadership, and back his plans to rebuild Tenochtitlán into a Spanish capital that would draw tribute from the former Aztec vassal tribes.

Cortés reasoned that Mexico could easily be adapted to *encomienda* and *repartimiento*—the basic economic institutions put into place after the reconquest of Moorish lands in Spain and the settlement of the Caribbean Islands. Encomienda empowered the Spaniards to collect tribute from conquered lands and communities, without actually granting them ownership of these properties which remained in native hands. Repartimiento was the use of forced native labor for agricultural and construction tasks demanded by the Spaniards. Encomienda and repartimiento were viewed as rewards for bringing heathen lands and peoples under the Crown, and supposedly obligated the conquistadores to ensure the spiritual and material well-being of their native tributaries and workers.

To implement the system of encomienda and repartimiento, Cortés had only to decipher Motecuhzoma's tribute rolls. These illustrated documents provided details on the quantity, quality, and origin of goods and services turned over to the late Aztec monarch by his vassals.[4]

According to Díaz del Castillo, Motecuhzoma's tribute books also guided the Spaniards to the provinces that rendered the greatest output of precious metals.[5] Expeditions were sent out to these locations, and resulted in the discovery of important silver and gold mines.

Within six months after the defeat of the Aztec empire, Cortés had distributed much of the Indian domains as encomiendas. Not surprisingly, he claimed for himself the largest tributary zones by far— enormous expanses of Indian lands and communities around Tenochtitlán and extending into the distant south. Only a minority of the conquistadores received what they considered satisfactory encomiendas. Some of them, including Díaz del Castillo, who complained that Cortés mainly rewarded his cronies, later set out from Tenochtitlán to conquer and settle Indian lands as far south as Guatemala. And a few disgruntled conquistadores, like Martín López, builder of the brigantines that played such a crucial role in the final siege of Tenochtitlán, eventually filed lawsuits against Cortés for a greater share of the spoils of conquest.

Despite its defects, the encomienda tribute system was capable of sustaining a colonial capital, and Cortés now turned his attention to rebuilding Tenochtitlán. In early 1522, he ordered the former Aztec king, Cuauhtémoc, still hobbling from the burns inflicted during his torture, to direct his tribe in the reconstruction efforts. First, the rubble of shattered buildings was dumped into the canals to create more paths and streets for Spanish cavalry and foot soldiers. Then, the Chapultepec aqueduct was repaired, restoring the flow of fresh water into the city. The center of Tenochtitlán—including the citadel of the Aztec ruling class and its adjoining religious precinct—was set aside as an exclusive preserve for the conquistadores. The symbolism of Spanish replacing Aztec sovereignty appealed to Cortés. And there were practical reasons as well: the toppled Indian palaces, temples, and pyramids became convenient quarries for Spanish churches, government buildings, and residences. One other area marked off for Spanish houses was the broad avenue leading west from the city center to the Tacuba causeway connecting with the mainland. Indians were cleared from both sides of this route, which had been used by the Spaniards during their flight from the city on the Night of Sorrow, and could presumably serve the same purpose again in case of an Indian uprising. The rest of Tenochtitlán remained for the time being a city of Indians, living in the same four large wards that had been mapped out by Aztec planners a century before.

A number of historians have suggested that Cortés was inspired by

Italian Renaissance notions of urban design in his reconstruction of Tenochtitlán. It is true that the colonial capital bore no trace of the narrow, winding streets and claustrophobic fortress walls of Spanish medieval cities. But Cortés took advantage of what the Aztecs already had put in place, including a grid pattern of streets and canals, flat-roofed villas and palaces blanketed with flowers and greenery, and neighborhoods dominated by municipal and religious buildings clustered around open squares.

The Spanish quarter repeated the pattern already established in the Caribbean islands. Its focal point was the central plaza—later called the Zócalo—surrounded by the administrative palace, the *cabildo* or municipal council, the cathedral, and the townhouses of the conquistadores. The Spaniards were deeded housing plots that ranged from about half an acre for foot soldiers to almost three acres for cavalrymen. Cortés chose for himself a residence ten times as large as any other Spaniard's: the former palace of Axayacatl, where he and his men had been lodged by Motecuhzoma when they first arrived in Tenochtitlán. A huge, rectangular two-story structure, it was intended to serve both as Cortés's living quarters and as the seat of his government—in other words, a royal palace in everything but name. All these early Spanish buildings doubled as fortresses, with thick stone facades, massive wood doors, turreted roofs, and narrowly slit windows for archers and gunners. Houses bordering canals had drawbridges, which could be quickly raised if the Indians ever attacked.

All these precautions were unnecessary. The Aztecs were reduced to docile obedience. Massacred in the recent siege, scourged by disease, weakened by malnutrition, they still devoted themselves to the building of the Spanish city from the ashes of the Aztec capital. Fray Toribio de Benavente Motolinía, an early Spanish missionary, likened the Indians' travails in the reconstruction of Tenochtitlán to a biblical epic:

> More people worked in building the great city . . . than upon the Temple of Jerusalem in Solomon's time. . . . The crowds of people who labored at the projects or carried materials, tribute and food to the construction sites were so thick that one could hardly squeeze through the broad streets and avenues. So many of them died crushed by beams, or slipping from great heights, or buried under the rubble of ancient buildings. The Indians themselves were responsible for finding the construction material, the masons and carpenters, and if they failed to bring enough food, they went hungry. They carried everything on their backs. They dragged stones and beams with ropes . . . four hundred men at

a time, singing and shouting, with voices that never ceased night and day, for such was the great fervor with which they erected the city in those early years.[6]

These enormous construction brigades were the earliest examples in Mexico of repartimiento, the forced-labor system that the Spaniards traditionally imposed on infidels. But the Indians undoubtedly identified repartimiento with Aztec practices. The labor crews continued to be organized in much the same way as they had been in pre-Conquest times. Tribal chieftains led their people—from Texcoco, Coyoacán, Xochimilco, Chalco, and dozens of other nearby cities and towns—into the island-capital to work on specific construction tasks, as part of their tribute obligations. Only instead of building Aztec pyramids and palaces, they were now erecting Spanish churches and fortified townhouses and blocklike government quarters.

A remarkable manuscript, written by the Aztecs in their Nahua language, offers some insight into the mentality and internal organization of the Indian laborers engaged in these construction efforts.[7] The document deals with the building of the town hall of Tlatelolco, the island community adjoining Tenochtitlán. Although it dates to 1581—sixty years after the Conquest—there is no reason to doubt that it describes practices that survived from the Aztec era into Spanish colonial times. The manuscript begins with a speech by the Indian governor of Tlatelolco to his assembled neighborhood chieftains and their labor forces. The Spaniards required native communities to provide town halls for the use of local Indian government officials and to host Spanish dignitaries. Tlatelolco's Indian governor was proposing to his people a major reconstruction of a municipal building left over from the Aztec period. The renovated town hall would have two wings—a nineteen-room structure held up by thick stone columns to accommodate visiting Spanish bureaucrats, and a less ostentatious twelve-chamber building reserved for the Indian officials.

Some of the funds for the town hall, explained the Indian governor to his subjects, were part of the inheritance left to the community "by our great King Cuauhtémoc." But the remainder of the cost would have to be financed "by our farmers and orchard-keepers . . . and by all of you here assembled." The project, said the governor, would have to be of such quality that "we will not feel humiliated before the Spaniards," and he warned his neighborhood chieftains that if their workers fell behind schedule, "very great punishment awaits you." The chieftains vowed to the governor that his wishes would be carried out:

"We, your children, will do it, we will labor, for surely this is the legacy of our [ancient] kings. And for this reason [the town hall] will not be lost nor left unfinished, even though they have died and been swept away by God. . . ."

The Indians then divided themselves into twenty brigades, each drawn from a different neighborhood of Tlatelolco and assigned a specific construction task. Chanting to the beat of drums, they embarked on the project. The manuscript ends with a rollcall of the neighborhood chieftains, who listed the date on which each brigade completed its portion of the town hall.

What is striking about the Tlatelolco document is the evidence it offers of Indian will to maintain a sense of dignity and continuity with their lost heritage even under Spanish rule. All the Tlatelolco Indians who assembled before their governor were aware that the construction of their town hall had been ordered by the Spanish colonial authorities. But they preferred to view their chore as a legacy from their pre-Conquest monarchs. They chose to carry it out by organizing themselves just as they had in Aztec times. And they strove to produce a structure whose quality would in no way be considered inferior to Spanish buildings. The style of the manuscript—a kind of contract between the community and its leader—is far more reminiscent of an ancient Indian annal than of a colonial Spanish bureaucratic document. Unfortunately for the Indians, the vast majority of their construction tasks in Mexico City could not be disguised as anything but Spanish projects—ordered and supervised by Spanish civil and ecclesiastical authorities, mainly for the benefit of Spaniards.

So furious was the pace of Tenochtitlán's reconstruction that only three years after the fall of the Aztec capital, Cortés bragged that the city "looks very beautiful" and "will be the most noble and populous in the known world, and will have the finest buildings."[8] Warfare and disease had reduced the capital's Indian population by two thirds, to perhaps seventy thousand people, and most of them were refugees squatting on the city's outskirts. But Cortés claimed that by 1524 there were "some thirty thousand people living in the city, and the markets and commerce are organized as before. I have given them such liberties and exemptions that the population grows each day. . . ."[9]

It was about this time that Cortés and the other Spaniards started commonly referring to Tenochtitlán as Mexico City. *Mexico* means the place of the Mexicas, one of several other names for the Aztecs. It is likely that the Spaniards decided to call their colonial capital Mexico City because they had such difficulty pronouncing Tenochtitlán. Cortés, who mangled all Indian names, mistakenly referred to the Aztec capital as "Temixtitan" throughout his writings. Even before he completed the conquest of the Aztecs, he had decided to rename their empire "New Spain" because of "the similarity between this land and that of Spain, in its fertility and great size . . . and many other things."[10]

Cortés had carried out the Conquest and then energetically imposed his vision of a colonial capital without a shred of royal authority. Shortly after disembarking on Mexico's Gulf coast in 1519, he had written his monarch, Charles V, requesting permission to claim and govern the new land for the Spanish Crown. But more than three years went by before Cortés finally received a reply from Charles, congratulating the conquistador for his extraordinary exploits and naming him captain-general and governor of the colony. The long delay was a result of court intrigues against Cortés and the complexities of the Spanish monarchy under Charles.

Charles V had risen to the throne in 1516, after the deaths of his Spanish grandparents, Isabella and Ferdinand. From his father, Charles also inherited the Habsburg realms in central Europe and the Low Countries, and the mantle of Holy Roman Emperor, making him the greatest secular defender of Christendom. At nineteen years of age—almost all of them spent in Flanders—Charles was suddenly heir to more awesome powers and responsibilities than any other monarch in Europe. But in the eyes of many of his Spanish subjects, he was a foreigner whose ties abroad were more a drain than a benefit to Spain's own welfare. Even his physical appearance and style worked against him. He was an awkward adolescent with a comically elongated jaw, and he uttered his broken phrases of Spanish in an execrable Flemish accent. At the Castilian court, Charles surrounded himself with his more worldly, Renaissance entourage of Flemish advisers, to whom he felt a far greater affinity than to the dour Spanish nobility, still steeped in medieval values. Nationalist sentiment against Charles and his Flemish courtiers erupted in civil war, the so-called Revolt of the Comuneros, in 1520–21. The antiroyalist uprising was initially encouraged by Spanish nobles. But they soon sided with Charles and repressed the rebellion when it swelled into an antiaristocratic movement of radicalized peasants and urban commoners.[11]

Once the Revolt of the Comuneros was crushed, Charles set about his multiple imperial tasks in the manner his Spanish nationalist critics had most feared. He traveled frequently through his realms in the Lowlands and central Europe, spending all but sixteen years of his four-decade reign (1516–56) outside of Spain. Like his predecessor, Ferdinand, the young king committed Spain to confrontation with France over possession of Italian territories and, more importantly, with the Ottoman Turks over control of the Mediterranean. Even as Charles defended Christendom against the Turkish Moslems, he faced a religious schism in his northern European domains with the rise of Luther and his Reformation. Across the Atlantic, his Spanish subjects were conquering, settling, and evangelizing a New World. And in Spain itself, he had to inspire and cajole his subjects for the manpower and finances to uphold all these far-flung imperial designs.

In short, Charles was vastly overextended. To govern with any sort of effectiveness, he needed a system that could centralize political power in the Crown and yet enable decisions to be made during his prolonged absences abroad. His instruments of rule were a number of high-level bureaucratic councils, each entrusted with administering a part of the empire and formulating policies that could be offered to the monarch for his approval or rejection. It was the Council of the Indies, under the powerful Bishop Juan Rodríguez de Fonseca, that served this role for the New World. The twin pillars of the Council's policy were to ensure that the American colonies eventually became profitable enough to provide much needed revenues for the Crown, and to bring the pagan natives into the Christian fold, in keeping with the papal bull of 1493 that granted Spain sovereignty over most of the New World.

Because of the unruly character of the conquistadores and the distance that separated Spain from its American possessions, the Council of the Indies tried to impose an orderly chain of command on any new ventures of conquest and settlement. For this reason alone, it was quite natural for Bishop Fonseca, who headed the Council, to favor Diego de Velázquez, the governor of Cuba, over an unfettered adventurer like Cortés. Fonseca and Velázquez were also friends and political allies. Cortés was well aware of this situation when he launched his expedition to Mexico in 1519. His only hope was to appeal directly to Charles, over the head of the Council of the Indies. And so, Cortés addressed his letters from Mexico to the monarch, and sent Charles the shipments of Indian treasure in a blatant attempt to circumvent Fonseca.

But Fonseca's agents intercepted the first consignments of Aztec treasure. Only after strenuous efforts by Cortés's father and friends in

Spain did Charles become fully aware of the conquistador's feats in subduing a land more populous and richer than any other of his imperial domains. Even then, the monarch tempered his joy with distrust of this daring, independent warrior. The Revolt of the Comuneros had not yet been quelled, and Cortés's insubordination—no matter how extraordinarily beneficial it might prove to the Crown— smacked of the same spirit of rebellion against royal authority that ignited the civil war in Spain. Fonseca, Velázquez, and their allies argued that Cortés intended to create his own fiefdom in Mexico. Had he not audaciously named it "New Spain"? Charles did not give full credence to these warnings. He had no intention of punishing Cortés or removing him from Mexico. He was greatly impressed by the conqueror's courage and deeply indebted to him for his achievements. Still, a balance had to be struck. Cortés would be rewarded. Yet royal control would be imposed on New Spain—slowly, steadily, surely— over the next few years. And Charles would be the ultimate arbiter in this process.

The first hint of a conflict between monarch and conquistador appeared in the same royal letter of 1522 naming Cortés captain-general and governor. Charles objected to the encomienda system that Cortés had unilaterally established in the colony. Not only would it recreate the feudalism that the Crown had long tried to uproot in Spain, but it was associated with the harshest exploitation of the Caribbean natives, whose population was nearing extinction.

In a brazen display of effrontery, Cortés refused to dismantle the encomiendas, claiming that the monarch was too distant to know what measures were appropriate for the new colony. He wrote back to Charles that the encomiendas would ensure more royal revenues, offer spiritual and material protection to the Indians, and that they were necessary to stave off a rebellion by conquistadores who were already disappointed by their meager shares of booty.[12] Charles temporarily rescinded his prohibition against the encomiendas, but he was determined to end this feudal tributary system eventually and divert its benefits toward the Crown. The monarch also took note of Cortés's insubordination, and continued to whittle away the conquistador's powers.

Cortés never fully grasped the Crown's aims and tactics. He felt he had earned the right to exercise his own judgment in handling New Spain's affairs without incurring any stigma of insubordination. With no instructions, manpower, or financial support from the Crown, he and his small band of conquistadores had accepted every conceivable risk and physical hardship in sailing the seas, plunging across tropical swamps and plains, and climbing through cold mountain passes. With shrewd diplomacy, Cortés had wooed Aztec vassal and enemy tribes to his side, and forged them into an army which defeated the mighty Aztecs after a long, brutal campaign. And he claimed to have done it all for his monarch. Surely, his demands for fortune and power to govern the new empire on Charles's behalf were not too lofty.

But Cortés, who had demonstrated such military and diplomatic brilliance during the Conquest, soon proved considerably less adroit in managing his personal and political problems as leader of the new colony. Not the least of these problems was his marriage. In the summer of 1522, his wife Catalina Suárez arrived unexpectedly in Veracruz on a ship from Havana carrying some of her relatives and other Spanish women. Years before, Cortés had been forced to wed her to gain a pardon from his old enemy, Velázquez, the Cuban governor who was wooing her sister. Except to supply his wife with Indian servants and the most fashionable Spanish garments, Cortés had virtually ignored her when they lived together in Cuba, and made no attempt to conceal his numerous extramarital affairs. In Mexico, he had all but forgotten about his wife. He had several Indian mistresses, most notably his close counselor and interpreter during the Conquest, Marina, who bore him a child. Díaz del Castillo described Cortés as being "greatly depressed" by the news of Catalina Suárez's arrival in New Spain, although he did say that Cortés organized welcoming committees for his wife and her entourage along their two-week overland journey from Veracruz to Mexico City.[13]

Since Cortés had not yet moved into his sumptuously renovated palace in Mexico City, he installed his wife in his Coyoacán villa. The couple quarreled frequently, as Cortés continued to flaunt his mistresses. At a banquet held in their Coyoacán residence three months after her arrival, they argued violently before their guests. Catalina left the table in tears over a stinging insult from her husband—something to the effect that he had lost all physical desire for her. Later that evening after the guests had departed, Cortés joined her in their chamber. He emerged from the room a few hours afterward to announce to the maids that his wife was dead. "A necklace of golden beads she was wearing was broken and there were some dark spots on her neck," wrote a biographer of Cortés, citing court testimony.[14] Cortés claimed that his wife, who suffered from asthma during her sojourn in Mexico City, had died of her illness. But his adversaries and even many of his friends remained convinced that he had strangled her. He was plagued by this accusation the rest of his life, and had to fight off charges brought against him in court by his wife's relatives. The episode would be wielded with devastating effect by his political enemies, who repeatedly brought it up in their communications with the Spanish monarch.

Charles might have been inclined to dismiss the sordid affair as an aberration or personal tragedy, except that guile and timely misfortune seemed to be a pattern in Cortés's conduct. Earlier in 1522, for example, Cortés had used considerable deceit in ridding himself of Cristóbal de Tapia, the first of several Crown agents sent to Mexico to contest the conquistador's political authority. Tapia, a bureaucrat from the Spanish Caribbean colony in Hispaniola, arrived at Veracruz with a royal decree authorizing him to take over the government of New Spain. Through informants, Cortés discovered that the decree was actually issued by his enemy, Bishop Fonseca, the head of the Council of the Indies, which oversaw New World affairs on the monarch's behalf. Cortés not only declined to meet Tapia, but made veiled threats against him, and finally bribed him to return to Hispaniola. He later explained to Charles that New Spain was still militarily unstable despite the Conquest, and that widespread Indian rebellions might have somehow erupted if he had turned over the new colonial government to Tapia. "Thus, as Tapia had no experience of the land or its people," wrote Cortés, "his presence would have caused great harm if God had not remedied it."[15] Whatever Charles thought of the Tapia mission, he would hardly conclude that divine intervention had aborted it.

A year later, in 1523, Francisco de Garay arrived on the Gulf coast with a fleet of ships, four hundred soldiers, and a royal decree empowering him to conquer and govern lands along the littoral north of Veracruz. Cortés had no intention of permitting a rival conquistador to diminish his glory. He dispatched his lieutenants to dissuade Garay by the same method used against Tapia. When Garay proved stubborn, his men were bribed into rebellion. Stripped of his army and dignity, the would-be conquistador made his way to Mexico City, where Cortés magnanimously offered him lodging, guided tours of the capital, and a round of banquets. But Garay, by constantly bemoaning his fate, irked Cortés. Following a gloomy Christmas dinner hosted by Cortés, Garay retired to his chamber complaining of intense pains and high fever. Three days later, he was dead. Cortés informed Charles that Garay "fell ill of grief, and of this sickness passed from this life."[16] Other reports reaching the monarch suggested that Garay died of pneumonia. But Charles must surely have wondered if there was any truth to the rumors being spread by Cortés's enemies that Garay had been poisoned by the conquistador.

Faced with a host of opponents both abroad and in the colony, Cortés sought new friends and allies in New Spain, chief among them the Franciscan missionaries. Shortly after the fall of the Aztec empire, Cortés had written to Charles urging the monarch to send missionaries to convert the Indians. A stalwart Christian, Cortés had always linked sovereignty and religion. He could not bear to rule over pagans. But his request also had a political motive. He specified that the monarch should select devout friars as missionaries rather than bishops. "Because if we have bishops and other dignitaries," he wrote, "they will only follow the customs which, for our sins, they pursue these days, of squandering the goods of the Church on pomp and ceremony, and other vices, and leaving entailed estates to their sons or kinsmen."[17] Perhaps Cortés had in mind bishops like his enemy Fonseca. No doubt also, Cortés felt that lowly clergymen were less likely to contest his colonial powers than the princes of the Church. Still, it took considerable audacity to remind the monarch that Church prelates abandoned their chastity vows and sought wealth, power, and social status. These were the same charges that Luther was making against the Church.

But Charles accepted Cortés's suggestion, and the first important group of missionaries to arrive in New Spain were a dozen humble but zealous Franciscan friars. Known as "The Twelve"—in obvious allusion to the original apostles—they disembarked in Veracruz in 1524, and insisted on walking barefoot the entire two hundred miles to Mexico City. On the outskirts of the capital, Cortés rode out to meet them, followed by a huge cortege of bewildered Indians and their chieftains. Cortés was still considered a conquering deity by the Indians, and they were greatly impressed when he dismounted his horse, knelt down, and kissed the hands and tattered robes of these strange Spaniards. Almost every Franciscan chronicler of these years extols this episode as a powerful symbol for the Indians of Cortés's allegiance to the Church and as an incident that made the native chieftains and their subjects more receptive to conversion.

For the Church, the discovery and conquest of Mexico, with its millions of pagan natives, represented a religious opportunity that could be compared only to the earliest Christian era. Here was the rich harvest of souls that surely presaged the Second Coming of Christ. If the natives of the Americas—and perhaps later, the peoples of Asia and Africa—could be converted, then the world was ready for the

Resurrection. The spiritual fervor among the more mystical clergymen mirrored the materialistic excitement that drove the conquistadores onward. Just as the conquerors looked to their Romances of Chivalry for guidance, the priests plumbed their Bibles to explain the new lands and peoples suddenly revealed to them. Missionary writings of the 1500s are filled with references to the Indians as one of the ten lost tribes of Israel. "The popularity of the Jewish-Indian myth in the New World was due partly to the fact that it provided a kind of explanation for the origin of American man," writes John L. Phelan, a historian of the early Spanish colonial era. "But . . . the real source of appeal for the spread of this curious legend can be found only in the apocalyptical mood of the Age of Discovery. If the Indians were in reality the lost tribes, such a discovery would be convincing evidence that the world would soon end."[18]

For many priests who shared this messianic vision, Hernán Cortés was a sixteenth-century Moses. "The dominion of the Devil over the pagan Aztecs corresponded to the power of the Pharaoh over the Jews," adds Phelan. "The idolatrous rituals and human sacrifices of the Aztecs represented the slavery of the Jews in Egypt. The Promised Land to which Cortés led the Indians was, of course, the Church."[19]

As much as they exalted Cortés's religious role, the early Spanish missionaries had more pragmatic reasons for offering their loyalty to the conquistador. He supported their conviction that priests should be the only Spaniards allowed to live in Indian communities, so that the natives would be less exposed to "the diverse vices and sins" of their conquerors. Cortés also allowed the clergy to share the Indian tribute of the encomienda system and the forced native labor of the repartimiento, both of which were essential in the building of churches and the maintenance of parishes. As a result, many of the clergy joined Cortés in his defense of encomiendas, even when Charles expressed his opposition.

Still, there were limits to any political alliance between Cortés and the clergy. The Church in Mexico was directly dependent on the goodwill of the Spanish Crown, which had been granted by the Pope the right to appoint or remove any clergy in the New World. Thus, there was no question of an open conflict in the colony between Church and monarch.

In spite of his powerful allies in the Church and secular society, Cortés's political fortunes took a sudden turn for the worse in 1524, and the conquistador had nobody but himself to blame. He sent one of his captains, Cristóbal de Olíd, on an expedition to conquer and settle Honduras, a land reputed to be rich in gold. Olíd, who felt he had been insufficiently rewarded for his role in the Conquest of Mexico, sailed with his small army to Cuba, where he made an agreement with Cortés's old nemesis, Governor Velázquez, to share any wealth that might be uncovered in Honduras. By the time Cortés learned of the betrayal some months later, Olíd had taken control of Honduras. Cortés ordered his cousin, Francisco de las Casas, to head a punitive expedition against Olíd. After an initial setback, Las Casas was able to capture and execute Olíd. But Cortés, having heard nothing from his cousin for several months, decided to personally lead an army to Honduras. Because this expeditionary force was so large, the journey was taken overland instead of by ship. Cortés left his colonial government in the hands of several royal treasury officials, and began the thousand-mile march in late 1524 accompanied by a few hundred Spaniards and thousands of Indians, including Cuauhtémoc, the last Aztec king.

It was a hideous trek through rugged mountains and dense jungles, and half the army perished from heat prostration, fever, and starvation. Dispirited and unnerved, Cortés turned his ire against the hapless Cuauhtémoc, when the Spanish soldiers fanned rumors of an impending mutiny by the Indian troops. After a hasty trial, Cortés ordered the execution of Cuauhtémoc. The hanging of the Aztec leader was to brand Cortés as an unredeemable tyrant for future generations of Mexicans. It was also during the Honduras expedition that Cortés rid himself of his longtime Indian mistress and interpreter, Marina, marrying her off to one of his lieutenants. The image of Marina, abandoned once she had played out her usefulness and charms, was to become yet another powerful symbol of Cortés's perfidy in the minds of contemporary Mexicans.

Cortés's haggard army finally reached Honduras after eighteen months, only to discover that the mission had been unnecessary since the country was already under the rule of loyal forces. It took Cortés several more months to complete the return voyage—this time, mainly by ship—to Mexico.

His absence of almost two years had proved disastrous both for the colony and his own political standing with the Crown. The royal treasury agents he had left behind to govern had stolen tribute intended for Charles and turned over encomiendas to their henchmen. They had even had Cortés officially declared dead. When Cortés reappeared in Mexico City, his followers rose against the interim government, imprisoned its leaders, and installed the conquistador once again as governor. But news of the chaotic situation in the country had already reached the Spanish court, and a process was set in motion that was soon to remove every vestige of political power from Cortés.

The Honduras expedition was an act of folly by Cortés, an abdication of his responsibilities at a crucial period in the development of the colony and its capital. There is a strong temptation to believe that Cortés had tired of the political intrigues against him in Mexico City and become bored with his administrative burdens. Two months before setting out to Honduras, he had written a letter to Charles expressing the desire to organize other missions of discovery and conquest not only in Mexico, but across the Pacific Ocean.[20] There is evidence here of a still restless conquistador, yearning for more military action and chafing over the bureaucratic tasks that confront him. The ill-fated Honduras expedition defies logic unless viewed from this perspective.

Within days after Cortés returned from Honduras, he received news that a ship had landed in Veracruz carrying Luís Ponce de León, a royal agent appointed to investigate the conquistador's conduct of New Spain's affairs. This time Cortés was facing an official whose mission had been ordered by Charles himself instead of the Council of the Indies, and so Cortés greeted him with considerably more courtesy and openness than he had displayed toward earlier envoys. But almost as soon as the inquest of Cortés began, Ponce de León fell ill, apparently of typhus, and died a few days later. Cortés's enemies accused him of yet another murder, despite the fact that thirty other members of Ponce de León's entourage also were fatally stricken with the same symptoms. On his deathbed, Ponce de León handed over his command to his deputy, Marcos de Aguilar, an elderly man who treated his advanced case of syphilis with a standard remedy of the day—"by sucking the milk of a woman's breast."[21] And soon, Aguilar also was dead.

Charles might not have believed most of the lurid tales of murder attributed to Cortés, but people who obstructed the conquistador's path did have a way of dying: Catalina Suárez, Francisco de Garay, Ponce de León, Marcos de Aguilar. Whether or not Cortés was innocent probably mattered less to the Spanish monarch than the fact that the scandals had politically weakened the conqueror in New Spain.

The moment was opportune for Charles to end Cortés's stewardship over the colony. It would be done with such grace and generosity that even Cortés would at first fail to perceive the monarch's true intent. Thus, Charles sent Cortés a letter inviting him back to Spain on the next available ship so that he might be properly honored for his great accomplishments. And in 1528, after an absence of almost a quarter century, Cortés returned to his homeland.

He stayed in Spain for two years. Charles ensured that his welcome was triumphant. He fêted the conquistador on several occasions at the court. He named Cortés Marquess of the Valley of Oaxaca, and granted him encomiendas over Indian lands extending from the outskirts of Mexico City hundreds of miles south into Oaxaca. By bestowing a noble title on Cortés, the monarch also enabled him to marry Juana de Zúñiga, daughter of one of the highest-ranking Spanish aristocrats. But Cortés was given no political post in New Spain. And in 1530, he returned to the land he conquered as a private citizen—extremely wealthy and famous, yet stripped of all power.

Even while Cortés was in Spain, Charles had already named a judicial and administrative council, called the First Audiencia, to take over rule in the colony. Led by Nuño de Guzmán, an old adversary of Cortés, the new government installed itself in Mexico City in 1528. By all historical accounts, the brief two-year reign of the First Audiencia was the most despotic and corrupt period of colonial government in New Spain. Guzmán ordered the enslavement of large numbers of Indians and a heavy increase in the tribute and forced labor required from them. Spaniards who still supported Cortés were imprisoned or executed, and their properties and encomiendas were turned over to Guzmán's allies. For himself, Guzmán had appropriated Cortés's palace in Mexico City, and the tribute from the conquistador's encomiendas. When Cortés returned to Mexico from Spain in 1530, the First Audiencia prohibited him from entering the capital, and so he settled in Texcoco, across the lake from the city he had conquered and rebuilt.

Guzmán surrounded himself with *letrados*, or lawyer-bureaucrats. During the last two generations, the letrados had become an important social and political phenomenon in Spain and its overseas empire. Usually from minor noble families, they had come out of universities with legal degrees that gained them easy entry into the burgeoning royal bureaucracy at home and abroad. The Spanish high nobility, with its strong military values, had nothing but contempt for these petty officials. In the words of one lofty military aristocrat writing in sixteenth-century Spain: "The Catholic Kings put the management of justice and public affairs in the hands of the letrados, men of middling condition, neither very high nor very low born, offending neither the one nor the other, and whose profession was the study of law. . . .

Jealous of other men's offices, they are always ready to encroach on the competence of the military authorities. . . . This manner of governing has spread throughout Christendom and stands today at the pinnacle of its power and authority."[22]

Cortés certainly shared these sentiments. Since adolescence, he had known the letrados well. He came from the same modest social background and even considered joining their ranks. But he quit his law studies at the University of Salamanca, and chose instead to seek his fortune and glory in New World conquests. As a triumphant conquistador, he adopted the military aristocrats' disdain for the letrados. Shortly after the fall of the Aztec empire, he wrote to Charles begging the monarch not to send letrados to the new colony.[23]

In Spain, under the watchful eyes of the royal authorities, the letrado was known as a cautious, relatively scrupulous, if annoying, official. But in the New World, he was sorely tempted by corruption. All around him, he could see in the conquistadores the example of men who survived and often prospered by daring to be predatory. Diego Delgadillo was one of the many letrados who succumbed to these temptations. He was a member of the First Audiencia headed by Nuño de Guzmán, and his letters leave no doubt that he came to Mexico City to profit from his political office.

Writing to a Sevillian merchant-friend in 1529, shortly after taking up his administrative post in the colonial capital, Delgadillo boasted: "You may believe that since I have exposed myself so to fortune and strange lands, I will eat mud or do whatever is necessary to obtain my purpose."[24] Delgadillo went on to say that he had entered the slave trade, gold mining, agriculture, and commerce, and had placed his brother, cousin, and friends in lucrative provincial government posts and enterprises, whose profits he expected to share: "I know you will be glad that I do things for my relatives and friends. I do beg you to tell me if there is any way I can serve you here; you well know I will do it most willingly."[25] Delgadillo concluded his letter by pointing out to his Sevillian merchant-friend that Spanish women were at a premium among the conquistadores in Mexico City, many of them bachelors willing to pay commissions on their prospective wives' dowries. "So if you are to send any merchandise, let it be women, which is the best business in this country. . . ."[26]

The only serious opposition that Guzmán, Delgadillo, and the First Audiencia encountered in their greedy machinations came from the Franciscan clergy, especially Juan de Zumárraga, who had been appointed by Charles to head the diocese of Mexico. As bishop, Zumárraga also held the ambiguous title of "Protector of the Indians." While he could not directly aid Cortés or his followers, Zumárraga was able to contest the Audiencia's brutal treatment of the Indians. The bishop ordered his clergy to preach openly against Guzmán, Delgadillo, and their henchmen. When one of the priests was dragged from his pulpit by thugs acting on Delgadillo's orders, Bishop Zumárraga excommunicated the Audiencia members and placed Mexico City under interdict, banning all church services for several weeks. The Audiencia imposed strict censorship on all correspondence to Spain, but Zumárraga managed to smuggle out a letter to Charles detailing the government's reign of terror. The monarch eventually ordered the suspension of the Audiencia and the arrest of its members. Delgadillo, the buoyant letterwriter, died in prison back in Spain. But Guzmán escaped from Mexico City, and led an army of adventurers into western Mexico, where for several years he continued to brutalize the Indians and enrich himself from their tribute.

Cortés was allowed back into Mexico City. Yet in spite of strong support from his Franciscan allies and other colonists, he was kept on the margins of the political arena. Charles appointed a Second Audiencia to rule Mexico, this time led by a bishop with considerable administrative experience and untainted by corruption. Mexico City regained its political calm. Indian tribute, though still unbearably high for most native communities, was decreased somewhat. Properties that had been stolen by the First Audiencia were restituted to their Spanish owners. Cortés emerged as the wealthiest colonist, perhaps even as the richest Spaniard in the world with the exception of Charles. Besides the tribute he received from at least 23,000 Indian families on his widespread encomiendas, he profited greatly from his sugar mills, mines, and livestock. He chose to spend much of his time in Cuernavaca, where he built a palace for himself and his second wife, but he still hoped he would be called back to Mexico City, perhaps to fill the rumored post of viceroy.

Charles did in fact appoint a viceroy in 1535 to replace the Second Audiencia which had ruled the colony for five years. But the monarch never gave a thought to offering the post to Cortés. The man he selected, Antonio de Mendoza, perfectly embodied Charles's desire for a figure of great stature, administrative talent, and loyalty. Mendoza was from a wealthy Castilian noble family whose record of military service against the Moors was impressive. He claimed descent from the Cid, the almost mythical warrior-chieftain who fought against the Moslem invaders in the Middle Ages. Mendoza's father was captain-general of the Christian forces that captured Granada in 1492, ending the Reconquista against Moorish occupation of Spanish soil. His uncle was cardinal of Seville. Mendoza himself had fought on the monarch's side in the Revolt of the Comuneros. And his wife was a favorite lady-in-waiting to the queen. With no relatives or personal stake in Mexico, aloof as he was to the factional struggles there, and utterly dependent on the Crown, he "could be trusted to place imperial concerns before his own."[27]

In Mendoza, Cortés met his diplomatic match. The viceroy brushed aside the conquistador's wily attempts to rebuild his political alliances among his former followers or to regain entry into government. He kept Cortés off balance by constantly investigating the levels of Indian tribute and labor from his encomiendas. He ignored the conquistador's suggestions on the management of the colony's political and economic affairs. Mendoza did pay homage of sorts to Cortés by inviting him to take the leading role in the rich pageant staged annually in the central plaza of Mexico City to reenact the conquest of the Aztec capital. But even then, Cortés might have suspected that he was exposing himself to ridicule as he shouted and brandished his sword, bobbed between parchment-and-wood models of his famous brigantines, and bowed to the applause and drunken praises of the festive audience.[28] After five years of vice-regal government, Cortés had had enough. In 1540, he set sail back to Spain, never again to see the empire he had conquered.

Cortés died seven years later. In keeping with his wishes, his remains were eventually brought back to Mexico and, after several temporary resting places, were installed in the chapel of the Hospitál de Jesús in Mexico City. In 1823, a conservative Mexican historian hid Cortés's bones because he feared they would be desecrated by nationalists in the wake of the Independence wars against Spain. The bones were rediscovered 122 years later, in 1945, and returned to the chapel in the Hospitál de Jesús. A small bust of Cortés installed in the Hospitál in 1981 and another statue in a Cuernavaca hotel are the only public monuments to Cortés in all of Mexico. No streets bear his name, and no date has been set aside to commemorate him.

With the demise of Cortés, the struggle for the spoils of conquest tilted irreversibly in the Crown's favor. But even before Cortés passed from the scene, a significant influx of Spanish immigrants was blurring the once clearly drawn political lines between conquistadores and royal agents. Within five years after the fall of the Aztec empire, the European population of New Spain had swelled to several thousand people, as the conquistadores were joined by merchants, adventurers, bureaucrats, and their families. These latecomers were resented by the conquistadores, who viewed them as undeserving competitors for the colony's spoils. Díaz del Castillo, for example, often railed against Spaniards who received lands, titles, and Indian tribute and labor without having earned these rewards in battle. [29]

Almost all the new Spanish immigrants gravitated to Mexico City, ostensibly because by concentrating their numbers they achieved a sense of security against the far larger Indian population. But there were other, more enduring reasons that drew them to the capital. The Spaniards were by preference urban dwellers. Most of them had no wish to settle in the hinterlands as farmers or ranchers. They despised manual labor, and dreamed of a life of leisure surrounded by Indian retainers. "The Spaniards," wrote Jerónimo de Mendieta, an early missionary, "even the most lowly and impoverished among them, want to be lords and live that way, and not serve anybody, but rather be served upon." [30] Though commoners in their majority, they pretended to be "hidalgos," or minor aristocrats. While crossing the Atlantic from Spain to Mexico, they often added a preposition before their last names to give themselves a petty noble air. [31] Like the wine that accompanied them in their ships' holds, they seemed to improve over distance and time. If they could not have a rural estate or a mine, they would settle for a secure, easy bureaucratic niche or a profitable commercial monopoly in Mexico City, the great source of sinecures. Even those who were fortunate enough to receive the native tribute of distant encomiendas continued to reside in the capital, rarely visiting the Indian communities and lands that sustained them.

But most of the new settlers who installed themselves in Mexico City soon discovered that wealth and leisure were not easily acquired. They were forced to survive as artisans and petty merchants, hucksters and quacks, vagrants and parasites. Burdened by more mundane preoccupations, they were aloof to the great political and economic struggles between conquistadores and Crown agents. And their stories surface not in the lofty correspondence between the colonial authorities and the Spanish monarch, but rather in the Inquisition records, criminal court cases, and municipal council archives of Mexico City.

There is, for example, the case of Juan Franco, a jeweler, who was brought to trial by Church officials in 1536 on charges of sorcery and superstition. [32] Aided by Beatríz, his Indian mistress, Franco supplemented his income by claiming to divine the profitability of mines and to foretell which Spaniards would be receiving land grants from the colonial government. The leading witness against him was his wife. Embittered by his longstanding concubinage with the Indian woman, she testified that Franco, a convert from Judaism, had lapsed back to his old religion; that he associated with other secret Jews; that he talked with the devil; and that he performed his divining ceremonies by examining the entrails of chickens. Franco was given a light sentence—a penitential appearance in church and a 10 gold peso fine—perhaps because his inquisitor, Bishop Zumárraga, suspected that his wife's accusations against him were aggravated by jealousy.

There were other Spanish immigrants who managed to survive by preying on the superstitious nature of their neighbors. Pedro Ruíz Calderón, a priest, was the most notorious of these characters in early Mexico City.[33] An astrologer, hypnotist, and practitioner of the occult arts, he claimed to have descended into Hell to obtain the devil's signature on one of the many books in his extensive library. His clients included noteworthy conquistadores, allegedly even Cortés, who consulted him on the whereabouts of the Aztec treasure lost during the Conquest. According to his Inquisition trial records, Ruíz Calderón traveled widely in the Middle East, Italy, France, and central Europe to learn magic and alchemy before arriving in New Spain. He even claimed to have a papal license to practice his occult arts. Found guilty on charges of necromancy by the Inquisition in 1540, he was fortunate enough to suffer only exile back to Spain.

Cristóbal Méndez, a medical doctor, was yet another early colonist who profited from the gullibility of the more prominent and wealthy residents of Mexico City.[34] He made a considerable income by convincing his patients to wear his medallions around the neck as a cure for kidney disease and other ailments. Dr. Méndez claimed to manufacture the charms from gold and silver provided by his patients. But using only a portion of the precious metals for his amulets, which were mostly alloys of copper and iron, he pocketed the bulk of the gold and silver. He was brought to trial by the Inquisition in 1538 for sorcery rather than fraud. The outcome of his case is not known since the final trial records have not survived.

Latecomers like Franco, Ruíz Calderón, and Méndez could only scavenge for the crumbs of the Conquest's booty. But even real conquistadores struggled for years to obtain modest shares of the spoils.

Martín López was fairly typical of these disappointed warriors whose desperate quest for greater rewards led them to side with every political faction in the colonial capital at one time or another.[35] López had joined the Cortés expedition in Cuba in 1519, and lent funds to the great conqueror for the enterprise. In Mexico, he distinguished himself in battle, and oversaw the construction of the thirteen brigantines that laid naval siege to Tenochtitlán. For his contributions to the Conquest, López received only a half share in Indian tribute from a small encomienda located about forty miles north of Mexico City, which yielded him an annual income of less than 100 pesos—a paltry sum even in the sixteenth century. López soon shifted his political allegiance from Cortés to the Crown agents who were the conqueror's enemies. In 1528, he began a long and unsuccessful court suit against Cortés for 8,000 gold pesos which he claimed were owed to him for his role in the Conquest. The following year he became a supporter of Nuño de Guzmán, the brutal president of the First Audiencia who replaced Cortés at the helm of the colonial government. And when Guzmán was removed in 1530, López joined him in his marauding expeditions against the Indians of western Mexico.

López eventually returned to Mexico City, where he spent the last four decades of his life dabbling in ranching, commerce, and urban real estate, and repeatedly petitioning the colonial authorities and the Spanish court for financial recognition of his services during the Conquest. He was constantly in debt. Four of his five daughters remained unmarried because he had no suitable dowries for them. And three of his five sons became clergymen, apparently so as not to divide the small family inheritance.

There were, of course, hundreds of other Spaniards in Mexico City far worse off than Martín López. Lacking the status of conquistadores or the cleverness of petty merchants and charlatans, these men drifted on the fringes of Spanish colonial society as bodyguards for wealthier settlers or as thieves and vagabonds. Many of them had already been vagrants in Spain. They cluttered the roads, stopping to beg at every town until they reached Seville, where they joined the crews and passengers bound for the New World. Columbus expressed disgust at the rabble aboard his ships, and once wrote: "I take my oath that numbers of men have gone to the Indies who did not deserve water of God or man."[36] Writing from Mexico City, Cortés was already complaining to Charles in 1524 that "it is notorious that most of the Spaniards who come here are the lowest sort of people, laden with vices and sins."[37]

But even vagabonds felt they deserved a share of the Conquest's booty, if only because of the pale color of their skin. In Mexico City

and its rural outskirts, they barged into the Indian communities to
demand "tribute" or temporary sustenance.[38] And the Indians, fearful
of any Spaniard, usually complied. For the Indians constituted the
economic base of all segments of Spanish colonial society. Without
them there would have been no spoils.

SEVEN

THE INDIANS UNDER SPANISH RULE

For the Spaniards of Mexico City, the decades following the fall of the Aztec empire were a struggle for the spoils of conquest. For the Indians, these years were a struggle for survival. In the aftermath of the Conquest, they died in total numbers and proportions unmatched by any other people in history—including the victims of twentieth-century genocide.

There were between twelve and twenty-five million Indians in Mexico before the arrival of the Spaniards, according to estimates based on tribute rolls, archaeological evidence, and eyewitness accounts by early Spanish settlers.[1] Yet only about 1.2 million Indians were alive a hundred years after the Conquest—a fatality rate of at least 90 percent.

Most deaths were linked to European epidemics, transmitted to native communities with no capacity to resist these diseases. But even though the Spaniards were unwitting agents of fatal illness, the essential truth is that the near annihilation of the Indians, in Mexico and elsewhere in the New World, was a direct consequence of European colonial rule. Had there been no contact with the Spaniards, a much larger Indian population would exist today. Moreover, Spanish land policies, tribute, and labor requirements thoroughly disrupted Indian agriculture and contributed to famines that often set the stage for deadly epidemics. Only by dying in such grotesque numbers did the Indians in their own pathetic way significantly shape the outcome of the struggle over the spoils of conquest among the various Spanish factions. The steep decline in the native population forced the Spaniards to compete for the dwindling reservoir of Indian tribute and labor, and for ownership of the huge tracts of land that lay abandoned as the Indians succumbed to disease.

The Aztecs and other tribes of the Valley of Mexico were especially vulnerable to epidemics for a number of reasons. This was the zone of densest population and urbanization, spreading communicable diseases with the speed of a chemical reaction. Besides devastating Tenochtitlán's inhabitants by smallpox, famine, and war, the Spanish siege disrupted their freshwater supplies and agricultural production for many months. After the Conquest, Mexico City became the focal point of Spanish settlement, drawing immigrants who brought new, fatal diseases from Europe.

The Indians of the capital and its outlying regions suffered through nineteen major epidemics in the century following the Spanish victory.[2] In 1531–32, measles and typhus struck with the same deadly force as the smallpox brought by the conquistadores a decade before. Another outbreak of smallpox occurred in 1538. Between 1545 and 1548, a form of plague, called "*cocoliztli*" by the Indians, became the greatest killer of all, wiping out one third of the surviving native population throughout the country. Like many European diseases, it produced symptoms among the Indians—profuse bleeding in the nose and eyes—that had rarely been seen in the Old World. Two years later, the Indians of Mexico City had their first contact with the mumps, a relatively benign disease in Europe, but fatal to many thousands of natives. The plague returned in 1559. A combination of pleurisy, measles, and smallpox scourged the Valley of Mexico in 1563–64. Then, just as the Indian population was stabilizing itself, a plague epidemic, as terrible as the first one, again killed off one third of the country's natives between 1576 and 1581. The century ended with several smaller epidemics of plague, pneumonia, influenza, measles, and diarrhea. The Indian population of the Valley of Mexico began to edge upward after 1650, but by then there were only about seventy thousand natives, compared to 1.2 million inhabitants in the valley before the Conquest.

Although relatively few Spaniards succumbed to the Old World epidemics, there was one native American disease—syphilis—that spread among Europeans as rapidly as their microbes had overcome the Indians. There is no mention of a disease with syphilis's symptoms in European literature prior to the New World discoveries. The remains of ancient Greeks, Romans, Egyptians, and Asians show none of the bone lesions left by the illness in its last stages. On the other hand, such evidence has been uncovered in a few pre-Columbian grave sites. Syphilis appears to have been brought back to Spain in 1493 by sailors on Columbus's first expedition. Many more European contacts with the disease were made in Mexico. In the first few decades of the 1500s, syphilis spread so quickly throughout the Old World that neighboring countries accused each other of originating it. In Italy, it was known as the French disease; the French called it the disease of Naples; Middle Easterners named it the European pustules; and the Japanese referred to it as the Portuguese disease.[3]

Just as Old World illnesses took on new, deadly symptoms among the Indians, syphilis proved far more disfiguring and fatal for Europeans than it was for American natives with their long history of exposure to the disease. Only a short time after infection, rashes and ulcers spread into the mouth and throat, across the face and over the whole body. The victim soon suffered extreme fevers and skeletal pains, and, quite often, early death. The Indians of Mexico needed about one hundred years to develop a partial resistance to European diseases. And likewise, it was only after a century in the Old World that syphilis took on the slower progressing symptoms and fatality rates which are associated with the untreated disease today.

In Europe during the 1500s, syphilis spared no social class. It ravaged kings and popes, peasants and town dwellers, soldiers and generals. A familiar sight was the court noble masking the venereal pustules on his face with a silk patch. Henry VIII died of the disease. Cesar Borgia declined to give audiences because he was disfigured by the red spots and pimples of syphilis. And Pope Julius II allegedly refused to allow his foot to be kissed by the faithful because it was covered with syphilitic sores.[4]

But as fearsome as syphilis was in the Old World, there was no wholesale annihilation of communities, no alteration of the entire social structure, as occurred in Mexico and throughout the Americas in the wake of European epidemics. Syphilis was a small price to pay in exchange for the smallpox, plague, measles, influenza, typhus, and malaria that the Spaniards inflicted upon the Indians.

Epidemic disease was the most dramatic element of what one recent historian has called the greatest biological revolution in the Americas since the end of the Ice Age more than ten thousand years ago.[5] Besides spreading their fatal microbes, the Spaniards invaded Mexico with Old World plants and animals that rapidly transformed the native landscape. European vegetables, grains, and fruit trees were sown wherever Spaniards settled. But most of the Old World plants that made their way to Mexico and the rest of the Americas were not food staples.

They included grasses, weeds, and wild flowers, whose seeds were inadvertently transported across the Atlantic in the baggage, cargo, and livestock of the immigrants. Many of these European plants were heartier than the native varieties, and proliferated across the New World to such an extent that one can easily find whole meadows today without a single species of plant from the pre-Columbian era.[6]

European plants and livestock were certainly no boon to the Mexican natives in the first decades that followed the Conquest. Their fields were infested by Old World weeds and grasses. And Spanish cattle were an even graver threat, invading Indian plots, destroying their crops, and eroding their soils.

Cattle were first brought to Mexico in 1521, while the Conquest was still in progress. Their slaughter was initially forbidden in order to build up a breeding stock and allow their use for hauling carts. But a decade later, cattle herds abounded, especially in the Valley of Mexico. A sure sign of their great numbers was the 75 percent drop in beef prices in Mexico City between 1532 and 1538.[7] Father Alonso Ponce, a Franciscan priest who traveled throughout the colony in the late 1500s, remarked that livestock "have so multiplied that it seems they are native to the country, so full are the fields of them. They reproduce as in Castile, only more easily, because the land is temperate and there are no wolves or other animals to destroy them. . . . [And they are bred] at less cost and with less labor [than in Spain]."[8]

In the 1530s, Charles V decreed that cattle in Mexico would be allowed to graze on anybody's land after it had been harvested. This was a traditional practice going back to the Middle Ages in Spain, where it was intended to aid the rural poor who had little grazing land of their own. But in Mexico, colonial laws prohibited the natives from owning or slaughtering cattle, presumably because there was not enough beef for Spaniards. And yet, many Spanish cattlemen allowed their livestock to graze on Indian lands before they were harvested. So, instead of eating beef, the Indians were in effect "eaten" by the cattle.

Early colonial court records are filled with Indian suits protesting the ravaging of their lands by cattle. There were numerous instances of irate Indians slaying livestock that encroached on their fields, which only led to harsh reprisals. Some historians have suggested that the picturesque cactus fences seen today throughout the Mexican countryside are a legacy from the colonial era when Indians sought to protect their agricultural plots from marauding Spanish cattle.[9] But helpless despair was a more common reaction, according to Franciscan missionaries, who reported that many Indians fled into the mountains upon witnessing the invasion of their land by cattle.[10]

Some enlightened colonial officials realized the threat posed to the native population by the uncontrolled growth of herds. When Viceroy Mendoza retired in 1550, he warned his successor, Luís de Velasco: "Your lordship must understand that if cattle are allowed, the Indians will be destroyed."[11] Velasco tried hard to prevent the anarchical movement of cattle and sheep across unharvested Indian lands; but by the mid-1560s, after his tenure ended, droves were again invading native plots and leaving their villages desolate.[12]

Even the most determined viceroy was not strong enough to hold off the Mesta, or cattlemen's association. The Mesta had its roots in medieval Spain. Formed in Mexico City in the 1530s to promote the growth of herds, it quickly became one of the most powerful pressure groups in the early colony. Mesta members dominated the Mexico City municipal council, and used it to grant themselves grazing lands around the capital, despite royal decrees strictly limiting the acquisition of Indian properties. In an attempt to compromise with the Mesta, the viceroys agreed to recognize many of the cattlemen's land claims if they would keep their livestock at least half a league away from Indian plots. But it was impossible to enforce this restriction for long, as the herds multiplied and wandered out of control.

Because they could offer their fellow Spaniards abundant and cheap supplies of beef, the cattlemen enjoyed great support among the settlers. By the 1550s, beef in Mexico City was only one eighth the price in Spain. Immigrants who considered meat a luxury back in the mother country were able to indulge themselves daily. "Without a profession or trade, even without working, a white man could always see to his food and creature comfort in New Spain," wrote a historian of the colonial era. "Low prices made it all the easier for the rich to keep open house and support their numerous retainers."[13]

Meanwhile, the devastation caused by livestock on native lands resulted in a growing shortage of Indian food staples, particularly maize. And this scarcity was reflected in an eightfold rise in corn prices between 1545 and 1555.[14] Malnutrition and famine became widespread among Indian communities, making them all the more vulnerable to Spanish epidemic disease. From microbes to plants and animals, the European biological invasion of Mexico was striking the Indians on many fronts.

The chronicles of the missionaries in the 1500s trace the startling decline of the once numerous Indian population in the face of this biological onslaught. The early religious accounts reveled in the multitude of pagan converts to Christianity. Bishop Zumárraga proudly wrote his superiors in Spain that the Franciscans alone had baptized more than a million Indians by 1524. Father Motolinía claimed that about five million natives had been converted by 1536.[15] There were so many Indians, said Motolinía, that the priests "were often unable to raise the pitcher with which they baptized because their arms were so weary."[16] The "open chapel," a form of ecclesiastical architecture peculiar to Mexico, was invented to cope with the huge crowds of new faithful because, as Motolinía noted, "the people do not fit into the churches."[17] The main feature of this novel religious structure was a large walled courtyard with an enormous cross in its center facing a chapel, so that the outdoor Indian congregation could witness the celebration of Mass.[18]

But by the end of the century, the open chapels were unnecessary, and traditional churches easily accommodated the dwindling native congregations. The same missionaries who cited the remarkable numbers of native baptisms gave testimony of equally dramatic statistics of Indian deaths. Father Bernardino de Sahagún personally buried more than ten thousand Indians of the Tlatelolco district in Mexico City. Father Ponce, the itinerant Franciscan missionary, asserted that in the province of Texcoco across the lake from Mexico City the Indian population plummeted from sixty thousand at the time of the Conquest to eighteen thousand "a few years later."[19]

"They died in heaps like bedbugs," wrote Motolinía, describing the pandemics that scourged the Indians in Mexico City. "And many starved to death because everybody was struck down at the same time, and there was no one to care for the sick or to prepare their food. In many neighborhoods, whole families were wiped out. The stench was so terrible and the dead so numerous that they could not be buried, and so, houses were toppled upon the corpses and became their tombs."[20]

The canals of Mexico City and its surrounding lake filled with corpses. The fields around the capital were littered with Indians who dropped dead at work, according to Jerónimo López, a former conquistador and holder of an encomienda near Mexico City. Writing to the Spanish monarch in 1545, in the midst of the first great plague epidemic, López asserted that 400,000 Indians had died "within ten leagues" of the capital.[21] But it was the victims themselves who left some of the more moving testimonies of the diseases that slaughtered them. One account, handed down by the Maya to their descendants, speaks for Indians everywhere in Mexico and the Americas: "Great was the stench of the dead. After our fathers and grandparents succumbed, half of the people fled to the fields. The dogs and vultures devoured the bodies. The mortality was terrible. . . . So it was that we became orphans, oh my sons! So we became when we were young. All of us were thus. We were born to die."[22]

The fact that the Spaniards seemed almost invulnerable to disease astounded and demoralized the Indians. During the Conquest, they had already considered the Spaniards as deities or divine agents. How else to explain their mighty weapons, infernal horses, superior military tactics, and the winged vessels that carried them across the seas where no human beings were believed to have ventured? The Spanish god evidently was invincible, and the Indians regarded their own gods "as mute or dead," in the words of Father Diego de Durán, a chronicler of the Conquest. For the Indians, the epidemics that followed the fall of the Aztec empire were a sign of the continuing impotence of their deities, in contrast to the miraculous protection that the Spaniards enjoyed from their god.

The early missionaries shared this belief. Fathers Sahagún, Motolinía, and Zumárraga all wrote about the diseases afflicting the Indians as a form of divine retribution for their pagan rituals, human sacrifices, and cannibalism. By linking epidemics to divine will, they were able to convince the natives to acquiesce completely to Spanish secular authority and to seek both physical and spiritual salvation in the Spanish Church. The rapid conversion of so many Indians is a measure of the effectiveness of this campaign. Indians readily joined Spanish priests in toppling pyramids and temples, in denouncing secret practitioners of paganism, and in uprooting hidden idols. Nowhere else outside of the Americas were Europeans as successful in gaining Christian converts. Perhaps this was because Asians and Africans who fell under European domination had long before developed as much immunity to epidemic diseases as their colonial rulers. They would not be fooled into believing that divine retribution in the form of mortal disease awaited them if they refused baptism.

As the Mexican Indians continued to succumb to epidemics even decades after the Conquest, the Spanish clergy was faced with an insoluble riddle: If the spread of Christian faith was supposed to arrest fatal disease, why were the Indians, almost all of them now converts, dying in greater numbers than ever? Some priests sought the answer in secular explanations. Motolinía, for example, was certain that the Indian habit of bathing daily—anathema to Europeans at the time—

was making the natives especially susceptible to illness.[23] By discouraging baths, the Spaniards soon brought Indian hygiene down to European levels. And, of course, epidemics became even more rampant. Many priests and colonial government officials linked labor practices to the high death rate—an explanation that had already been offered in the Caribbean where the Indians reached extinction. It is true that the Spaniards were often cruel taskmasters in Mexico. Work in construction, mining, and agriculture was extremely arduous, involving long hours and little food. But epidemic disease was the paramount cause of Indian fatalities, even for those who died at their work posts.

By the end of the 1500s, some clergymen claimed to see the hand of both God and Spaniard in the annihilation of the natives. Father Jerónimo de Mendieta, a Franciscan missionary, wrote that God, in striking down the Indians by disease, was actually punishing the Spaniards for their harsh labor practices by depriving them of native workers! "Doubtless our God is filling the thrones of heaven with Indians as the end of the world approaches," added Mendieta.[24]

Interestingly, the New England Puritans, who arrived in the Americas a century after the Spaniards, also sought religious explanations for the fatal diseases that struck down so many Indians. But in contrast to the Spanish priests, the early English settlers were inclined to believe that God, by smiting the Indians, was favoring the whites. "In sweeping away great multitudes of the natives . . . [God intended to] make room for us here," wrote John Winthrop, an English colonist who described a smallpox epidemic among the Indians of Massachusetts in 1633. "God hath thereby cleared our title to this place."[25]

Most of the Spanish settlers in Mexico did not dwell on the religious or philosophical significance of the fatal epidemics afflicting the Indians. Their concerns were more practical. From the colony's beginnings, the Spaniards had counted on native labor and tribute. But with the disappearance of millions of Indians, the livelihood of the colonists was endangered. Settlers, Crown agents, and clergymen had to compete fiercely for the shrinking numbers of Indians workers and their dwindling supply of tribute.

As part of the tribute required from them, Indians were forced to labor without pay for weeks or months at a time. They became *tamemes* or bearers, carrying loads in Mexico City and throughout the country. Some of the more humane priests and colonial officials decried the bitter lot of the tamemes, who, often underfed, collapsed under their agonizing loads. In 1531, the president of the Second Audiencia, in charge of colonial government, wrote Charles V to denounce the cruel treatment of bearers and to suggest that they be replaced by donkeys— "burdens should be carried by beasts and not men," he said.[26] But even after pack animals became abundant in the colony, the tamemes were considered indispensable by most colonial authorities and settlers. In a letter written to the Spanish monarch in 1553, Viceroy Velasco insisted that Mexico City would starve if Indian carriers were prohibited:

"Carts and pack animals are not sufficient, and they have more than they can do [anyway] to provide wood and charcoal, because the Indians have been relieved of bringing it in, which they consider a great bother. [But] provisioning of this city with wheat and maize— as well as the other cities in the country—cannot be done unless it be done with Indians. . . . As personal services are removed, the necessity becomes as great as that suffered by a city besieged."[27]

Velasco also defended the use of unpaid, involuntary Indian labor in the silver mines, which had become the greatest source of royal revenue from Mexico by the 1540s. "Let your Majesty not be persuaded that the mines can be worked without [the forced labor of] the Indians," he wrote. "The royal treasury as well as private citizens will suffer a great loss, because there is no mine so rich that it can stand being worked by wage-earners, for it will cost twice as much as it produces."[28]

The problem was that every colonial faction could plead the utter necessity of forced Indian labor, especially as the number of able-bodied natives dropped precipitously because of epidemic disease. Settlers complained that Indian workers on their agricultural estates were being drafted by the colonial authorities for construction projects in Mexico City. A number of government officials became notorious for selling the rights to Indian labor to the highest bidders.

Although clergymen often raised their voices against these abuses, they themselves freely used unpaid natives to erect the scores of churches, hospitals, monasteries, and convents that dotted the capital and the countryside. The missionary accounts of the first few decades after the Conquest tend to gloss over the fact that Indians were not remunerated for these ecclesiastical building tasks, and emphasize instead the great fervor of these construction brigades of new converts. But if these early labor hordes were indeed enthusiastic volunteers, their descendants showed considerably less eagerness. In 1556, no less an authority than the archbishop of Mexico, Fray Alonso de Montúfar, castigated his clergymen for abusing Indian laborers:

The excessive costs and expenditures and personal services, and the sumptuous and superfluous works being erected by the religious in the Indian villages at the Indians' expense, should be remedied. With respect to the monasteries, in some places they are so grandiose that, although they are designed to accommodate no more than two or three friars, they would more than suffice for Valladolid [the Spanish royal court]. . . . It is nothing for a religious to begin a new work costing ten or twelve thousand ducats . . . and bring Indians to work on it in gangs of five hundred, six hundred, or a thousand, from a distance of four, six or twelve leagues, without paying them any wages or even giving them a crust of bread. . . .[29]

Quite aside from temporary, unpaid, forced labor, there was widespread use of permanent Indian slaves in the early colonial years. Slavery was imposed as a punishment on Indians who allegedly rose up in revolt. In reality, there were few instances of native rebellion under Spanish rule, and thus theoretically little opportunity to enslave Indians. The most serious Indian uprising of the colonial era occurred in the north, where the Chichimeca tribes battled fiercely before being subdued by the Spaniards in the so-called Mixton War during the early 1540s. But where revolts did not exist, the Spaniards simply invented them in order to justify Indian slavery.

In 1535, for example, a Crown agent, Vasco de Quiroga, wrote to the Council of the Indies describing a consignment of Indians slaves— men, women, and children, some of them infants less than a year old—who had supposedly rebelled against the Spaniards in a province northwest of Mexico City and had been herded into the capital for sale. When Quiroga asked the slaveowners what crime the Indians had committed, he was told that they were captured in "caves in the mountains where they had hidden in flight from the Spaniards." According to Quiroga, these Indians were branded on the face with the initials of the owner, and the process was repeated every time they were sold. "There are some who bear three or four initials," he observed, "so that a man's face, which was created in the image of God, has become a piece of paper in this country. . . ."[30]

In the 1540s, the Spanish Crown formally abolished Indian slavery in Mexico and its other New World possessions, but the practice continued under the guise of punishment for crimes. Slavery was defended as a humane alternative to the more gory penalties of Spanish law, including strangling, torture, mutilation, severe whipping, or the frequently fatal stints on the royal galleys. Criminals became an ex-

cellent source of slave recruitment because of the huge rise in delinquency as social order broke down among the Indians during the
colonial era. But it was just as easy for unscrupulous Spaniards to
falsely charge Indians with heinous crimes as it was to accuse them
of rebellion.

No matter what means were used to recruit Indian workers, the
continuing mortality rate among the natives required other sources of
labor. Thus, in the decades following the Conquest, an ever greater
number of black slaves were imported into Mexico from the Caribbean
colonies or directly from Africa. The first blacks arrived with the conquistadores. But they were considered a luxury. Indians were so populous at the time that they could be had for nothing, and were
responsible for providing their own food, shelter, and clothing. Blacks,
on the other hand, were sold at high prices, often reflecting the cost
of transporting them overseas, and they had to be supplied with their
basic necessities. The steep decline of the Indian population, however,
soon overcame any Spanish reservations over the price of black slaves.
By the end of the 1500s, more than sixty thousand blacks had entered
Mexico, a figure that actually surpassed Spanish immigration.[31] In
1553, a worried Viceroy Velasco was writing to the Spanish monarch
that there were too many blacks in the colony, creating a potential
threat of revolt: "Let Your Majesty command that so many licenses
to import slaves not be granted, because . . . they could become so
numerous as to plunge the land into confusion."[32]

Velasco perhaps had in mind a well-publicized incident that occurred under his predecessor, Viceroy Mendoza, in 1536. Mendoza
claimed to have uncovered a far-fetched plot by black slaves to revolt
and drive the Spaniards out of Mexico City with the aid of the Indians.
The suspected ringleaders were seized, and after being tortured into
confession, they were publicly drawn and quartered in the main plaza
of the capital.

There were, however, numerous defenders of black slavery, chief
among them some of the priests who decried forced Indian labor. Fray
Bartolomé de las Casas, whose writings contain the strongest denunciations of Spanish brutality toward the Indians, was one of the earliest
advocates of black slavery as an alternative to forced Indian labor. Like
other priests, he argued that blacks were constitutionally more fit for
heavy labor than the New World natives and more resistant to diseases.
Clergymen joined other colonists in owning, buying, and selling black
slaves. The Cathedral of Mexico City, for example, partially defrayed
its expenses by selling black slaves in the provinces during the late

1500s.[33] The Jesuits used black slaves to help run their numerous ranches, plantations, and mills. One of their institutions of higher learning just outside Mexico City, the College of St. Peter and St. Paul, bought more than five hundred slaves in the course of the 1600s, and listed them in their account books as "items."[34]

Even with the growth of black slavery, most labor in colonial Mexico continued to be done by the Indians. But the Spaniards tended to belittle the burdens placed on the natives, and throughout the 1500s, many colonists believed that the Indians were lazier and less hard-working than they had been under Aztec rule. A letter written to Charles V in 1545 by the former conquistador Jerónimo López summarized this view. López extolled the harsh policies of Motecuhzoma that had extracted maximum productivity from the Indians. By contrast, he wrote, "now all of them are vagabonds and idlers . . . and they do not work or sow their fields beyond their own needs."[35] These sorts of letters, petitions, and speechmaking by the Spanish colonists were intended to scuttle efforts by some reform-minded government officials and priests to abolish or curtail forced Indian labor.

But the accusations of Indian laziness lose credibility when one considers the enormous accomplishments of native labor in the construction field alone. In the first eight decades of Spanish rule, the quantity of structures built by forced Indian labor far exceeded the total volume of construction during the entire Aztec era.[36] The Mexican landscape was transformed by churches, government palaces, private villas and townhouses, and irrigation projects. And all this was undertaken by an Indian population so ravaged by epidemics that its numbers fell to only a fraction of its pre-Conquest total.

The same excesses that marked the use of Indian labor also prevailed in the collection of tribute from the natives. Since few Indians had money, most tribute consisted of portions of the harvest, wood, stone, lime, woven goods, pottery, jewelry, and precious metals. The fearful toll of disease should have logically led to smaller tribute collections commensurate with the reduced size of the Indian population. But throughout the 1500s, levies grew increasingly onerous for the surviving Indians because of wholesale frauds committed by their Spanish overlords. According to Alonso de Zorita, a Crown official in Mexico City between 1555 and 1565, the Spaniards who held encomiendas regularly overstated the number of able-bodied Indians in their domains in order to maintain high tribute levels. "The practice has arisen of collecting tribute from cripples, blind and maimed persons, and other wretches who cannot work and even lack food," wrote Zorita.

"And they collect from minors and single young women without means of support."[37]

Clergymen also used questionable methods to extract payments from their Indian wards. Despite Church prohibitions on the collection of fees for sacraments, it was common for priests to charge the Indians for weddings, burials, baptisms, Masses for the dead, and occasionally even confessions. In many Indian parishes, alms or charitable contributions became compulsory.[38] Priests often colluded with the local Indian chieftains, called caciques, to steal community funds. Archbishop Montúfar described this practice in a letter written from Mexico City in 1556:

> In one monastery we found a hundred and twenty Indians serving as cantors, without counting the sacristans and acolytes and players [of musical instruments] . . . and since all the cost of such works and the rich and superfluous ornaments is met by assessing these poor people, the caciques or headmen, who are supposed to take a hundred ducats from the community strongbox, take a thousand for themselves. No one knows this better than the friars, who have told me that the caciques and headmen want the friars to ask them for money, so that with this pretext they can make an assessment for themselves.[39]

The killing off of the Indians by epidemic disease eventually did force the Spanish colonists to accept lower levels of native tribute and labor. But from the Spanish vantage point, the high Indian mortality rate had at least one important, beneficial consequence: the appropriation of huge expanses of fertile land that became vacant as the natives died.

In the immediate aftermath of the Conquest, the Spaniards had little interest in owning land in Mexico. The encomienda system enabled them to collect revenues from Indian communities without taking possession of their properties. Even livestock owners limited their acquisition of land as long as they were permitted to graze their animals on Indian fields. Yet, by the end of the 1500s, more than half of the agricultural land in the Valley of Mexico had moved from Indian to Spanish ownership.[40]

As entire Indian communities succumbed to disease, their properties came under the administration of the colonial government. Since the Crown wanted to curtail the feudal encomienda system, it often paid off former encomienda holders by granting them abandoned Indian properties. Spaniards also acquired land as a consequence of tribute.

To pay levies, Indians went into debt and were forced to sell their plots, bit by bit, until their descendants were left without property. Even the clergy participated in the land grabs unleashed by the massive deaths of Indians. The most common way for a parish to accrue Indian property was through native wills and testaments that left tracts of land to the clergy on condition that Masses be perenially recited for the deceased benefactors. The Church received much larger individual blocks of land from faithful Spaniards. But it was through the slow accumulation of many small Indian properties that the Church eventually became the largest corporate landowner in Mexico.[41]

There was yet another important method by which Indian estates fell into Spanish hands, namely, the *congregación*. The term implies the forcible relocation of scattered Indian families into new, larger communities. The congregación was championed by all colonial factions. Priests viewed it as an efficient way to tend to their Indian flocks who survived the epidemics but lived in greatly reduced numbers and in small, isolated villages. Crown officials argued that the congregación would make for more economically viable Indian communities. Other colonists asserted that it would be easier to collect tribute and labor if the Indians were brought together in denser numbers. But it was the Mexico City municipal council or cabildo that was most forthright in stating the implications that the congregación concept held for Spanish landowning ambitions. On several occasions, the cabildo suggested that native farmlands around the capital be given to the colonists and that the Indians receive new, less fertile properties around congregaciónes located further away from Mexico City.[42]

Mortal illness . . . forced labor . . . unbearable tribute . . . dispossession of the lands that provided their main livelihood. The tragedies suffered by the Indians were of such magnitude that the Spaniards felt the need to create a philosophical underpinning, a set of moral attitudes, to justify their exploitation of the natives.

The colonial era in Mexico began with a serious debate among Spaniards over whether Indians were people or perhaps some subhuman species. The latter viewpoint was best expressed by Gonzalo Fernández de Oviedo y Valdés, a royal chronicler of the early 1500s who portrayed the Indians as "—naturally lazy and vicious, melancholic, cowardly, and in general a lying, shiftless people. Their marriages are not sacrament but sacrilege. They are idolatrous, libidinous, and commit sodomy. Their chief desire is to eat, drink, worship heathen idols, and commit bestial obscenities. What could one expect from a people whose skulls are so thick and hard that the Spaniards had to take care in fighting not to strike on the head lest their swords be blunted?"[43]

A final solution to the Indians was at hand, predicted Oviedo. "God is going to destroy them soon," he wrote. "Who can deny that the use of gunpowder against pagans is the burning of incense to Our Lord?"[44]

This sort of racist doggerel was widespread enough to provoke a rebuttal from the Pope, who in 1537 asserted "that the Indians are truly men, and that they are not only capable of understanding the Catholic faith but, according to our information, they desire exceedingly to receive it."[45]

Eventually, the colonists in Mexico grudgingly accepted that the Indians were human beings, but continued to consider them inferior to whites in religion, social mores, and intellect. The Spaniards had an obligation to raise the Indians to European levels of civilization, but this was balanced by Spanish rights to exploit the natives while they were still wallowing in inferiority. A few idealistic Spaniards, like Fray Bartolomé de las Casas, maintained that there was nothing inferior about the Indians except for their ignorance of Christianity, and that once they had been converted, the natives should be allowed to carry on with their existence free of Spanish exploitation. But this was not an argument that gained a hearing in the Spanish court or among the colonists.

Around the mid-1500s, it became fashionable among Spaniards to consider the Indians as children. The first viceroy, Mendoza, explained to his successor in 1550 that the Indians "should be treated as sons and loved and punished in that spirit." He said he always granted them audiences and that, "although they lied to him often, it did not annoy him, since he never acted until he verified their statements, nor had he punished them for misstatements, lest they cease coming to him with their troubles and childish stories."[46] The missionaries were especially prone to view the Indians as minors who needed adult guidance and protection for an indefinite duration. "All these Indians are like nestlings whose wings have not yet grown enough to allow them to fly by themselves," wrote the Augustinian priest Fray Pedro Juárez de Escobar to the Spanish monarch in 1579. "They still need to have their parents lovingly provide their food and nourishment, so they will not suffer from hunger and die. They must always, so long as they live, have near at hand their encouragement and presence, their aid and their support. . . . The religious, as Your Majesty should know, are their true fathers and mothers. . . ."[47]

The enthusiasm with which the colonists embraced the notion of

Indians as children is understandable. After all, children did not enjoy the same rights as adults. They needed permanent supervision. Their protests were not to be taken seriously. They were to be manipulated, ordered about, and, when necessary, punished. With the excuse that the natives were not yet *"gente de razón"*—"people of reason," like the whites—the Spaniards were able to postpone for many years the entry of Indians into economic activities that placed them in competition with Europeans. For decades after the Conquest, the Spaniards imposed strict limitations on Indian ownership of cattle, sheep, and horses. Spanish guilds in Mexico City excluded Indian craftsmen because their skills and products were deemed inferior to the Spaniards' own. And when Indians were admitted into guilds in the second half of the 1500s, their numbers were restricted and their status was often fixed at the apprenticeship level.[48]

If the Indians were ever to be raised above childhood, they needed a lengthy tutelage that only the Church could provide. Segregation of the Indians from the vice-ridden, abusive Spanish settlers became the ideal. Thus, priests were usually the only Spaniards allowed to live and freely mingle with the natives in the Indian neighborhoods of Mexico City and provincial communities. The forced relocation of natives to new villages through the congregación system spawned experiments in utopic Indian Christian villages under missionary guidance.

Religion was, of course, the main thrust of missionary tutelage over the Indians. By the 1550s, virtually all natives had been baptized, but it was a sacrament administered without preliminary instruction. The clergy's main educational efforts were directed at Indian children rather than adults. Children of Indian commoners were taught the catechism at church every morning after Mass. But the sons of the Indian aristocrats were treated differently in recognition of their status as future leaders of their communities. They were sequestered from their parents and placed as boarders in convent schools for years of intensive religious training.[49]

A wide chasm opened between the older generation of Indians clinging to their traditional beliefs and the younger natives inculcated with a missionary zeal. Indian youths led Spanish priests to the hidden sanctuaries where idols were worshipped. They were encouraged by the clergy to inform against their peers and older Indians who failed to regularly attend Mass or marry in the Christian faith—violations that were often punished by whippings. In the worst instances, Indian children testified against their parents when they were brought to trial by the Inquisition on charges of idolatry or other religious deviations.[50]

The stamping out of idolatry was an obsession of the clergy. Even at the height of Christian conversion during the 1530s, missionaries expressed dismay at the pockets of pagan resistance. The natives placed their sacred figurines in the corners of their huts or imbedded them between their walls. They hid them in caves, on hilltops, in forests, or on secluded shores of the lakes. Under the cover of darkness, they gathered in ceremonies, burning incense, offering flowers, and sacrificing small animals to the old gods. According to Father Motolinía, Indians in Mexico City and its surrounding communities also concealed their idols behind and beneath Christian altars. They worshipped these deities while unsuspecting priests led them in prayers to Christ and the Virgin Mary.[51]

Because they feared this unholy mixture of paganism and Christianity, the missionaries discouraged the Indians from believing in miraculous apparitions. Too often the natives reported sighting the figures of Christ or the Virgin at locations where Indian deities had once been honored. The most important such case occurred in 1531 when a recently baptized Indian, Juan Diego, claimed to have beheld a dark-skinned apparition of the Virgin Mary at the site of a former chapel of an Aztec goddess on the northern outskirts of Mexico City. This was the beginning of the cult of the Virgin of Guadalupe which became immensely popular among the Indians. In an exceptional decision, the Church hierarchy gave its blessing to Juan Diego's vision, but the cult remained controversial for many clergymen and white colonists who viewed it as a dangerously independent native reaction to Spanish Christianity.

The clergy's desire to maintain control over their Indian converts was nowhere more evident than in the Church prohibition against the ordaining of native priests. All sorts of reasons were advanced by the missionaries to justify their opposition to Indian clergymen. Indians allegedly lacked the authority of white priests in the eyes of their brethren. They were supposedly incapable of understanding Christian doctrine in depth, and thus prone to spread heresies.[52]

This low opinion of Indian intellect was belied by the experiences of the College of Santiago Tlatelolco in Mexico City, where, under the guidance of progressive clergymen, elite Indian youths were trained in Latin, theology, and philosophy. But the college, founded in 1536, closed its doors four decades later because many Spaniards—clergy and laymen—were aghast at this attempt to "overeducate" the natives. That inveterate letterwriter and former conquistador Jerónimo López sent missives to Charles V in 1541 and 1545 denouncing the college as yet another example of the perverse efforts of certain priests to encourage a growing insolence among the Indians. Latin, asserted López, "was of no use to [the Indians] except to enable them to recognize which priests were idiots when they were saying Mass and performing the divine offices." In fact, López added, "reading and writing are harmful as the Devil" for the Indians.[53]

If all this seems to cast the clergy in too harsh a light, it is because they failed so utterly in their stated purpose of protecting the Indians and tutoring them until they could deal with Spanish society on an equal footing with their conquerors. Their efforts to seclude the natives from non-Indians were a sham. Though living in their own neighborhoods or villages, the Indians were still drafted to work for Spanish construction, mining, and agricultural enterprises. Spanish, black, and mulatto vagabonds, bandits, and ranch hands intruded on Indian communities to cheat, pillage, and rob the natives, and seduce or rape their women. The growing incidence of mestizo—mixed blood—children was proof enough that the contact between races was frequent.

The priests were the chief agents of the hispanization of the Indians, a process which was supposed to lift them out of paganism and childishness. It was, however, only a partial hispanization—of religion, language, social mores, acceptance of secular authority—that made the Indians more tractable to Spanish rule. Nobody could have stanched the epidemics that killed off most of the Indians. But there was a convergence of attitudes and interests among all white colonial factions—settlers, Crown officials, clergy—to ensure that the surviving natives remained docile in the face of Spanish demands for labor, tribute, and land.

The colonial era in Mexico began with optimism on the part of the Spanish Crown and clergy that the welfare of Spaniards and Indians could be reconciled. The 1500s ended with a frank admission by the colonial authorities that this goal was impossible because, as one viceroy asserted, "The two Republics of Spaniards and Indians which form this colony are so repugnant to each other . . . that it seems that the preservation of the former always means the oppression and destruction of the latter."[54]

Not all Indians were anonymous, passive, impotent victims of Spanish rule. But the history of the first colonial century—written almost exclusively by Spaniards—offers little evidence of how individual natives tried to react or adapt to the brutal society imposed on them. It is particularly difficult to reconstruct the lives of Indian commoners. Fragments of their stories emerge in Inquisition cases, and civil and criminal court records. But rarely is there enough material to resurrect them as three-dimensional human beings. The accounts of some Indian nobles are more complete. Among these native aristocrats, two stand out as diametrical opposites in their dealings with Spanish rule. Carlos of Texcoco, the cacique or chieftain of the town and province located just northeast across the lake from Mexico City, was offered every opportunity to reach a position of eminence within Indian colonial society. Yet he rejected Spanish political and spiritual blandishments. Juan de Gúzman, the cacique of Coyoacán, a southern suburb of the colonial capital (and in modern times, a residential neighborhood of Mexico City), was far more accommodating to the Spaniards, and achieved the sort of political and economic success that was rare among Indians.

Carlos of Texcoco was a man of impeccable Indian pedigree and Spanish Christian upbringing. His grandfather was Nezahualcóyotl, poet-king of Texcoco and architect of the grandiose hydraulic projects that transformed the Valley of Mexico in the pre-Christian era. His father, Nezahualpilli, was also king, and prophet of the Aztec demise. While still a child, Carlos became a protégé of Hernán Cortés and was raised in the conqueror's Mexico City palace. He was a student at the College of Santiago Tlatelolco, where the most promising sons of Indian nobles were taught theology and philosophy. Upon the death of his brother, Carlos left the school and became cacique— chieftain—of Texcoco, and the owner of various houses and rural properties in that province.

Texcoco was considered a stronghold of pro-Spanish and Christian sentiment. After allying themselves to the conquistadores during the siege of Tenochtitlán, the Texcocans contributed large labor brigades to rebuild the Aztec capital into the Spanish colonial city. The Texcocan nobles were avid converts to Christianity, leading their subjects to baptism and church marriages, and sending their sons to missionary schools. But a minority of the province's natives remained secret practitioners of the pre-Conquest cults. The Spanish clergy was especially fearful that the numbers of these clandestine pagans might swell if the Indians became convinced that Christianity was failing to protect them from the ravages of disease, drought, and famine. Throughout the

Valley of Mexico, the Church organized frequent religious processions drawing multitudes of natives to pray for bountiful harvests and relief from illness.

It was on just such an occasion that Carlos of Texcoco first came to the attention of the Spanish religious authorities. Early in June 1539, he paid a visit to his sister and brother-in-law, the cacique of Chiconautla, a village neighboring Texcoco. Carlos arrived in the midst of a religious procession led by the father provincial. The Indians, including the local nobles, were dressed in penitential robes and were flagellating themselves with strands of cactus fiber in supplication for rain and an end to plague. According to witnesses, Carlos viewed the ceremony with ill-disguised contempt. Later, he met with his brother-in-law Alonso, and the other Chiconautla nobles, and ridiculed their Christian beliefs and dogged faith in the Spanish missionaries.

"Woe to you," said Carlos to his brother-in-law, the cacique. "Where are you leading these Indians, and what do you think you are doing? You want to make them believe what these priests are preaching. Well, you have been fooled. The friars are worthless. That which they call the things of God are nothing. We already have what our ancestors have written. You forget that my father and grandfather were great prophets, and they said many things about the past and future, and never said anything of this."[55]

Alonso and the other Chiconautla nobles were shocked. Even the most ardent pagans among them pretended to accept the new Church dogma. The Inquisition had harshly punished nonbelievers for attitudes far less strident than those being voiced by Carlos.

"How can you say such things?" demanded Alonso. "These are things of God and they are sacred. The Father Provincial has indoctrinated us and preached to us. He is our father and has raised us from childhood. Do you really believe that it is a sin to obey the viceroy and bishop?"[56]

But Carlos would retract nothing. He reminded Alonso and the others that he was not speaking out of ignorance. Had he not been raised in missionary schools, attended church regularly, and even enrolled in the College of Santiago Tlatelolco? His religious education, he said, had taught him nothing but disdain for the Christians. Why, the priests could not even agree among themselves on how to worship their God. Were there not Franciscans, Dominicans, and Augustinians, each with their own garb and rituals and doctrine? Carlos laughed at the religious plays and pageants staged by the priests to spread their teachings. He dismissed the liturgy as nonsense. "Pater noster, Ave Maria, Credo, Salve Regina," he chanted, making them sound like childish ditties. He advised Alonso and the others not to teach the Indian commoners what the friars preached. "And if the viceroy, the bishop or the Father Provincial tells you something, keep it to yourselves, say nothing to anybody," added Carlos.[57]

Alonso beseeched him again to hold his tongue. But it was too late. A few days afterward, one of Carlos's listeners, an Indian named Francisco, reported the harangue to the father provincial. Carlos was arrested and imprisoned in Mexico City on June 22, 1539. The wheels of the Inquisition were set in motion.

The case drew the hierarchy of the Spanish colonial Church. Bishop Juan de Zumárraga presided over the trial. Father Bernardino de Sahagún, soon to be renowned as the greatest missionary historian of Aztec civilization, served as chief translator. Idolaters were common enough, but no previous Inquisition case had involved an Indian of Carlos's stature.

Zumárraga seemed especially perturbed by this incident. The bishop was already a figure of controversy among many Spanish colonists for what they considered his overly benevolent attitude toward the Indians. In 1529–30, Zumárraga had almost singlehandedly toppled the colonial government of Nuño de Guzmán, whom he denounced for brutal treatment of the Indian population. A year later, the bishop championed the cult of the Virgin of Guadalupe, which many colonists, including priests, feared as a manifestation of Indian independence from orthodox Spanish Christianity. Zumárraga was also one of the founders of the College of Santiago Tlatelolco. The school was under attack by Spaniards who felt that it was creating a potentially dangerous Indian elite. The fact that Carlos, cacique of Texcoco, now accused of idolatry, had attended the school would only add to its notoriety.

For the bishop, Carlos had betrayed the most progressive, pro-Indian elements in the Church. And by prosecuting the Texcocan cacique, Zumárraga could prove to his Spanish critics that he would not tolerate even a hint of rebellion from his Indian flock. Thus the bishop investigated every lead in the case against Carlos, calling dozens of witnesses, searching all of the cacique's properties, delving into his personal affairs and sexual conduct.

A search of Carlos's main residence uncovered nothing. But in a house deeded to him by his uncle, the Inquisition officers found two Christian altars and behind them, imbedded between the walls, a number of idols. Some of these stone figurines were identified as

Quetzalcóatl, the plumed serpent, a favorite deity of pre-Christian Texcoco; Tlaloc, the rain god; and Xipe, the flayed one, who used to be honored with human skins. Witnesses asserted that Carlos frequented this house, but no one claimed to have actually seen him worship the idols or offer sacrifices to them.

The discovery of these idols unleashed a frenzied hunt for more native religious altars and chapels. The priests ordered the Indians to spread out through Texcoco and its surrounding hills and woods, and to bring back any idols. Every roadside cross was dug up, and beneath many of them were found the stone figurines, and sometimes sacrificial knives still stained with animal blood. When Zumárraga asked the nobles how these practices could have continued without their knowledge, he was told that important Indians were implicated and they would not hesitate to carry out reprisals against informers. One Indian witness, Hernando de Chávez, who led a search brigade that uncovered and destroyed a large idol of Tlaloc, the rain god, told Zumárraga that Indians from Mexico City and elsewhere in the valley were furious because they believed the rains would now surely never come.

But it was difficult for Zumárraga to link Carlos to these discoveries of widespread paganism or to establish a clear-cut case of idolatry against him. His story that he was not aware of the existence of the idols hidden in the walls was plausible. He insisted that his uncle had built the house with its concealed idols before it became part of Carlos's estate.

Zumárraga then shifted his investigation to aspects of the cacique's personal life, and the case soon took a more promising direction, one that would severely impugn Carlos's character. According to several witnesses, Carlos had a longstanding affair with his niece, Inéz, who bore him two daughters. Such an incestuous relationship was hardly unusual in pre-Conquest society, especially among the nobility. But, of course, it was repugnant and sinful under Christian law. Both Inéz and Carlos confessed their illicit affair and admitted they knew it was against the Christian teachings which they had publicly embraced. Carlos's wife, María, testified she was aware of the relationship. She said her marriage was initially a happy one, but that for reasons she could not fathom, her husband lost sexual interest in her after two years.[58] At one point, Carlos brought Inéz to live at their home. According to María, the lovers spent most of their time in a back room, from which Inéz would occasionally emerge to order her aunt to prepare their food.[59]

Other witnesses testified that within weeks of his brother's death,

Carlos tried to force himself upon the widow. She had cloistered herself in her house with her servants, in keeping with traditional Indian practices of bereavement. Carlos paid her visits several times, but she refused to see him and told her servants to bar his way. When the servants asked why he persisted, Carlos claimed that by ancient Indian law he had a right and obligation to bring his brother's widow into his household. His sister-in-law testified that on some nights, Carlos prowled outside her home and howled like an animal in an attempt to frighten her. Late one evening he snuck into her residence, but was discovered and thrown out by the servants.[60]

Carlos's sister, also called María, told the Inquisition court that he encouraged her husband, Alonso, the cacique of Chiconautla, to practice polygamy as he did. According to María, Carlos said to her: "If your husband wishes two or three wives, do not protest. Follow the way of our fathers and mothers." And when María upbraided him, he called her a "nocone"—a whore's daughter—reducing her to tears.[61]

The list of family members arrayed against Carlos even included his eleven-year-old son Antonio. Asked if he had been brought up as a Christian, Antonio answered that his father prohibited him from attending church. Thus, he knew nothing of Christian doctrine. He could not say the Pater Noster, the Credo, or the Ave Maria. He did not even know how to genuflect.[62]

By this stage of the trial, the Inquisition officers were able to portray Carlos as morally depraved. He practiced and preached incest, polygamy, lechery, and possibly idolatry. He rejected his Christian upbringing and disparaged the true religion among recent Indian converts. Here was a loathsome human being, capable of even worse crimes. And now, Zumárraga pressed ahead with the most serious remaining charge against Carlos: incitement to rebellion against Spanish civil and ecclesiastical rule.

Francisco, the Indian who initially denounced Carlos to the Church authorities, was asked to amplify his testimony against the cacique. He recalled in more detail Carlos's statements to the effect that the Indians should ignore the directives of the Spanish government and Church. According to Francisco, the cacique lashed out at Spanish rule in the following terms:

"Who are these people who undo us and perturb us, who climb on our backs and subjugate us . . . ? These are our lands, our treasures, our possessions, and this province is ours alone. And if someone wants to do or say otherwise, we should mock him. Oh my brothers, I am full of anger and resentment . . . ! Who are these people to come here and order us about and pretend to teach us and repress us? They are not of our tribe or of our blood, and yet they claim to be our equals. . . . Well, here we stand and there should be nobody to ridicule us. . . ."63

Francisco's testimony was substantiated by other witnesses, including Alonso, Carlos's brother-in-law. When Carlos was brought before his Inquisitors, he denied all the accusations against him, except the charge of incest. He asserted he was a devout Christian. And he alleged that his accusers were plotting against him because they resented the tribute and labor he imposed on them in his official capacity as cacique of Texcoco.

Zumárraga was determined not to show any mercy to Carlos. But because the cacique was an important Indian noble, the bishop felt compelled to send the entire transcript of the case to Viceroy Mendoza and the ranking colonial judges for their approval before passing sentence. When they offered no objections, Zumárraga declared Carlos a "dogmatizing heretic" and sentenced him to death at the hands of the civil authorities.

Two days later, on November 30, 1539, Carlos was brought to the Plaza Mayor of Mexico City, where an enormous crowd of Indians and Spaniards had been convoked. The cacique was clad in the San-benito, the yellow sackcloth robe of a penitent. On his head, he wore the *coroza*, a mock crown symbolizing infamy, and he carried in his hands a large candle. He was led to the scaffold, where he heard his sentence read loudly to the audience after a brief sermon by Zumárraga. Carlos sought to save himself at the last moment by admitting his guilt and urging the assembled Indians to wholeheartedly embrace the Christian faith. But his repentance came too late. He was strangled slowly by a garrote, and his lifeless body was set aflame.

The execution of Carlos aroused great consternation in the Spanish court. The Inquisitor General in Spain wrote a letter reprimanding Zumárraga on the grounds that Indians were only recent converts to Christianity and thus vulnerable to pagan lapses. There were other cases of Indian heretics tried by the Inquisition in Mexico City in the years that followed. None were punished as harshly as Carlos. But among the Spanish colonists, the execution of Carlos continued to be applauded. What galled them most about the cacique was the fact that he was an Indian who, after thoroughly acquainting himself with the social and religious values of his conquerors, still held them in contempt as inferior to the ways of his ancestors.

Juan de Guzmán, the cacique of Coyoacán, knew Carlos of Texcoco. He married Carlos's niece, Mencia, and through her, he owned valuable properties in Texcoco. If Guzmán witnessed Carlos's death—which was probable since the Spanish authorities ordered all Indian chieftains and many commoners in the Mexico City area to attend the execution—he surely would have reflected on the different paths his relative and he had chosen under the new regime.

Guzmán emerges from this early colonial era as a troubling, complex figure. During much of his forty-four-year reign as cacique of Coyoacán, he seemed to be a rank opportunist, eager to ingratiate himself with the Spanish authorities, greedy enough to increase his wealth by cheating his Indian subjects, and obsessed with the trappings of social status and political prestige. But late in his life he shifted course dramatically, and used his considerable powers to defend his community against intrusions by the Spaniards.

To begin to understand Guzmán's enigmatic nature, we must return to the early days of the Conquest. In 1520, during the Spaniards' first visit to Tenochtitlán, Cortés took Motecuhzoma as hostage, using as an excuse an ambush secretly ordered by the Aztec king against a Spanish garrison near Veracruz. That attack was carried out by Quauhpopoca, ruler of Coyoacán and father of a youth called Ixtolinque, who would later be baptized as Juan de Guzmán. Cortés ordered Quauhpopoca to be burned alive as a warning against any Indians who would dare attack the Spaniards.

After the Conquest, Cortés appointed Quauhpopoca's son, now bearing the Christian name of Juan de Guzmán, as cacique of Coyoacán. This was in keeping with Cortés's strategy of maintaining the Aztec system of vassal chieftains in order to facilitate Spanish rule and tribute collection. Because Coyoacán was part of the huge encomienda that Cortés had granted himself, Guzmán was also a personal retainer, tribute collector, and labor overseer of the conquistador. He would necessarily have a closer relationship and more frequent contact with Cortés than almost any other Indian chieftain.

So, in effect, Juan de Guzmán owed his position as cacique to Cortés, the man who had murdered his father. Guzmán apparently wrestled with this moral dilemma, and he left behind evidence of how he justified in his own mind his loyalty to Cortés. In a letter written to the Spanish monarch, Guzmán practiced a bit of revisionist history concerning the events surrounding the death of his father, Quauhpopoca. According to Guzmán, his father, far from attacking the Spaniards during the Conquest, had actually saved them on several occasions from Aztec ambushes. Quauhpopoca—asserted Guzmán—

was framed by Motecuhzoma, and died at the pyre protecting the treacherous Aztec ruler.[64]

Guzmán, in fact, displayed more hatred of the fallen Aztecs than he did of the conquering Spaniards. In a petition he once wrote to Viceroy Mendoza, he reconstructed his genealogy omitting almost any Aztec relatives.[65] He claimed to be descended from the ruling house of the Tepanecas, the tribe that was virtually annihilated by the Aztecs during their sudden rise to power in 1428. Guzmán's implication was clear: his family was part of a vassal people harshly repressed and betrayed by the Aztecs; he and his relatives not only harbored no resentment against the Spaniards, but welcomed their conquest over the Aztec tyrants.

Guzmán went to great lengths in proving his trustworthiness to Cortés and the Spanish Crown. According to royal decrees issued to him in recognition of his accomplishments, Guzmán was credited in the immediate aftermath of the conquest of Tenochtitlán with having helped the Spaniards subdue "many Indians . . . who had hidden in the mountains, and he brought them into the service of our Lord, the King"—no doubt as slaves, the usual fate that awaited natives who persisted in rebellion. The same royal decrees also lauded Guzmán for saving the life of Cortés during an ambush by a large Indian force on the road between Mexico City and Cuernavaca. Guzmán was said to have rushed the attackers and killed their chieftain "with two arrow shots," causing the others to flee.[66] How easy it would have been for Guzmán to have avenged his father's death on that occasion. He had only to run away, leaving Cortés and his small escort to face the ambushers. But by then, Guzmán was committed to upholding the new colonial order and extracting every possible benefit from Spanish rule.

And those benefits were far from paltry. Guzmán acquired title to 23 sizable plots of land in Coyoacán and its vicinity.[67] As part of her dowry, his wife brought 31 properties of her own to the marriage. Between them the Guzmáns had 460 personal retainers from a dozen towns and villages in the Valley of Mexico. As regular tribute from his Coyoacán subjects, Guzmán received: 300 bushels of wheat and 400 bushels of maize every year; 700 chiles and 400 tomatoes a week; 2 chickens a day; 3 cords of wood and 3 loads of livestock fodder daily; 4 to 10 household servants paid for by his community; 10 Indian masons and carpenters at his constant disposal; and communal labor to work four fields whose harvest was reserved for his personal use.[68]

Besides this regular tribute, Guzmán had the opportunity to profit from overseeing the collection of Coyoacán's tribute to the Cortés family. According to information provided by Guzmán to Spanish officials investigating tribute in Coyoacán, his subjects paid yearly to the Cortés family: 1,386 gold pesos, 139,780 cacao beans (still used as currency by the Indians in the early colonial period), 3,834 chickens, 1,264 bushels of maize, and 447 mantles.[69] Guzmán admitted that the Cortés family demanded only two thirds of this tribute, and that he and his subchieftains deducted for themselves the remaining one third. Guzmán asserted that this "commission" was needed to cover expenses involved in tribute collection and in the staging of community festivals.[70] But in fact, Guzmán, like other caciques, was exaggerating to his subjects the amount of tribute required by the Spaniards, and then pocketing the excess. The Spaniards were well aware of this practice, but chose to ignore it as long as caciques continued to deliver a satisfactory amount of native tribute and labor.

Yet another source of income for Guzmán was his control over the Coyoacán marketplace or *tianguis*. The tianguis was one of the few Indian economic redoubts that the colonial authorities left entirely in the hands of the caciques, mainly because the Spaniards had little use for the simple, cheap goods traded by the natives in these markets.[71] Indian merchants and peddlars paid "taxes" to Guzmán for the right to sell their wares at the tianguis.

Guzmán also was among the earliest caciques to acquire Spanish livestock, and he obtained special permission from the colonial authorities to exceed the strict limits placed on Indian herds. Eventually, he owned over three thousand sheep, their wool providing him with still more revenues.

When all these various forms of tribute, graft, and taxes are added up, it appears that Juan de Guzmán was richer than many Spaniards, even some of those who were granted encomiendas. His two-story palace was built in the style of the most sumptuous Spanish residences of Mexico City.[72]

But besides wealth, Guzmán sought prestige, both in the eyes of his Spanish overlords and of his Indian subjects. It was a game that native elites played wherever European colonists established themselves in the world, and Juan de Guzmán was an early master of its intricate rules. These involved accepting a certain degree of hispanization in order to gain trust and a measure of authority from the Spaniards. At the same time, Guzmán had to uphold the native social mores and political traditions that had ensured leadership for his family over the Coyoacán Indians for generations.

Thus, Guzmán successfully petitioned the Spanish monarch for decrees confirming his status as cacique and title to his numerous properties. And he also convinced Charles V to grant him a noble coat of arms: one half showed a sphere with a hand clutching a cross, and in Latin the inscription, "I believe in God and Country"; the other half depicted a white tower rising from a golden field. On formal occasions when he visited or received colonial officials, Guzmán dressed himself in aristocratic Spanish costumes bearing his coat of arms, and exercised his right to carry a sword—an unusual privilege for an Indian.[73]

Guzmán perceived that his status as hereditary cacique would not be enough to ensure his political power over Coyoacán. When the Spaniards began establishing Indian cabildos, or municipal councils, to govern local native communities, Guzmán petitioned the viceroy for a cabildo in Coyoacán and got himself appointed as its governor. He asked that police be assigned in his community, another new symbol of Spanish-style authority.[74]

Guzmán also avidly embraced the religion of his conquerors. He was baptized, married by church ceremony, and he sent his sons to missionary schools. He sought a close relationship with priests, who were usually the sole Spaniards to reside in the Indian communities during the early colonial period and could be powerful political allies for any cacique. Guzmán welcomed the establishment of a Dominican monastery in Coyoacán, and he even petitioned the viceroy—unsuccessfully—to allow tithes to be collected among his subjects for the building of the structure.[75] It is possible that the cacique hoped to make "commissions" on church tithes as he did on tribute.

By the early 1550s—after a quarter century as ruler of Coyoacán—Juan de Guzmán was so confident of the backing of Spanish civil and ecclesiastical authorities that he tried to bully the neighboring Indian communities. He claimed lands for Coyoacán in Xochimilco to the south. He pressed for water rights in Cuauhximalpán to the west.[76] He had a particularly acid exchange with the cacique of Huitzilopochco, the neighboring community to the east, over lands which Guzmán asserted belonged to Coyoacán before the Conquest. In a somewhat ironical letter responding to Guzmán's claims, the Huitzilopochco cacique noted: "Those who have these lands own them and were born on them, and so we would like to know how it is that everything is yours and nothing ours. . . ."[77]

It was at this pinnacle of his prestige and power that Guzmán began to demonstrate an unexpected willingness to confront Spanish authority in the interests of his Indian subjects. His newly "militant" attitude probably reflected a growing malaise in his community. The epidemics had reduced Coyoacán's population to about fifteen thousand by 1550, a decline of almost one half since the Conquest. Indian commoners devoted one out of every four work days for unpaid labor to the Spaniards, and still had to deliver tribute at levels that remained constant despite the toll of disease. Coyoacán's natives complained that they had no time or manpower left to tend their fields.

Famine, disease, physical exhaustion, and unrest in Coyoacán set the stage for Guzmán's next course of action. In 1551, the cacique and his subjects filed a lawsuit in Mexico City against the Cortés family over lands, houses, payments for services, and materials. Guzmán protested that besides onerous tribute and tributary labor obligations, his subjects were required to help build the Cortés palace in Mexico City. The structure was so enormous and elaborate that the Coyoacán Indians—sometimes as many as 320 at a time—worked on it for twenty-seven years, from 1524 to 1551. Not only were they not paid for this labor, but they had to supply free-of-charge the stone, wood, and lime used in their construction tasks. Moreover, Guzmán and his Indians alleged that Cortés had stolen from them more than four hundred acres and the houses on this land, which were then rented back to the natives at a cost of 2,500 bushels of wheat annually for the last twenty-eight years.[78]

Cortés was long dead by the time this legal action was taken. His son and heir, Martín Cortés, was living in Spain. But the suit still caused a sensation in Mexico City. Never had a Spanish family as prominent as the Cortéses been brought to court by Indians. Even more remarkable, Guzmán and his subjects won their suit. The colonial authorities ordered the return of the contested properties to Guzmán, and put an end to the labor obligations of two hundred Coyoacán Indians who had to travel daily to Mexico City for service in the Cortés palace. The colonial officials also lowered the tribute requirements for Guzmán's subjects.[79]

Emboldened by this outcome, Guzmán asked the Spanish authorities two years later, in 1553, to investigate the Dominican friars in his community. Guzmán asserted that two hundred of his subjects were forced to labor daily without pay for the clergy in Coyoacán. Some of the Indians worked full time on the construction of the Dominican monastery; others labored to provide food, maintenance, and personal services for the priests. But most of the workers were engaged in tasks aimed at raising revenues in Mexico City for the

Coyoacán clergy. They chopped wood and sold it in the capital for the benefit of the monastery. They were hired out by the Coyoacán vicar, Fray Tomás de la Corte, to Spaniards in the city. On one occasion, Fray Tomás pocketed the 30 gold pesos he was paid for providing these Indian laborers to a Spanish house builder for a year. The priest claimed the money was used to buy oxen for his monastery.[80]

Guzmán produced witnesses among his subjects who stated that they were never paid for any of this work, and labored involuntarily, "out of fear of the friars who compel them and punish them with jail and whippings."[81] But the colonial authorities declined to rule against the Dominicans, and in effect chastised Guzmán for bringing a suit against the clergy by reducing the amount of tribute and labor that his subjects owed him.[82]

Guzmán's conflict with the local friars also hurt him politically. A year later, in 1554, the colonial authorities removed him as governor of Coyoacán, although he was allowed to keep his hereditary post of cacique. Guzmán had no doubts that the Dominicans were behind this move, and he stated so in an angry petition to the Spanish monarch. He complained to Charles V that the priests in Coyoacán and elsewhere were seeking to remove caciques from the governorships and replace them with "villainous commoners in the employ of the Church."[83]

Guzmán was close to the truth. By the mid-1550s, the colonial authorities, in collusion with the local clergy, had decided to reduce the powers of the caciques. The colonial system had evolved to the point that there was less need to depend on hereditary vassal rulers to help the Spaniards rule and collect tribute. A cacique was no longer automatically entitled to be governor of his community and preside over its cabildo, or municipal council. And often, Spanish officials in Mexico City asked local priests to suggest suitable candidates to replace caciques as governors. The Church recruited these candidates from the Indian petty aristocrats and commoners, known as *mandones*, who were the local clergy's eyes and ears, ensuring that all natives attended religious ceremonies, led Christian lives, and regularly made "voluntary" contributions to the parish coffers. These *mandones* were the "villainous commoners" whom Guzmán attacked in his petition to the Spanish monarch.

Some years later, however, Juan de Guzmán smoothed over his rift with the local clergy and with their support he regained the governor's post in Coyoacán. Shortly before his death in 1569, he donated land to build a chapel and pay for Masses to be recited in perpetuity for his soul. His widow and his son and heir did the same before they died.

On balance, Guzmán hardly qualifies as a heroic figure—a status accorded by modern Mexicans to the martyred Carlos of Texcoco. For most of his tenure as cacique, Guzmán was motivated purely by self-interest. But toward the end of his career, he proved to be one of the few Indian chieftains able to reduce the tributary and labor burdens placed on his subjects. He was also far more resourceful than his heirs in defending his position and his community against the excesses and encroachments of Spanish colonial rule.

Juan de Guzmán's genealogical line can be traced up to the nineteenth century. But the decline of the House of Guzmán began soon after his death. His son, Juan the Younger, was also cacique and briefly governor. He was unable to prevent the Cortés family, angered by the successful suit against them, from seizing back lands in Coyoacán. The son incurred far more expenses than his father in running his household and properties because new Spanish regulations required caciques to pay their laborers. Juan the Younger also had to sell some of his lands to meet his tribute obligations.

Juan the Younger died during one of the many epidemics after only four years as cacique. His will in 1573 lists numerous debts with provisions to repay them, mainly by turning over more family properties to Spaniards.[84] Because his eldest son, Felípe, was six years old, his two uncles temporarily took turns as cacique of Coyoacán. But both died in the great plague epidemic of 1576.[85] Meanwhile, some of Juan the Younger's choicest lands were being stolen by a Spaniard, who had been assigned by the colonial authorities to administer the dead cacique's estate while his children were still minors.[86] When Felípe Guzmán at last came of age, the powers and wealth of caciques had shriveled. The colonial government had rescinded the rights of chieftains to collect taxes from Indian markets or tianguis. The salary Felípe earned during a brief tenure as governor was his largest source of income, and when he was removed from that office by vice-regal order in 1594, he was forced to sell more of his family's lands to Spaniards.[87] Perhaps Felípe's sole distinction was the fact that he was the last full-blooded Indian to be cacique of Coyoacán. His successors would all be offspring of intermarriage with Spaniards who were moving into the community to claim lands.

EIGHT

CITY
OF SILVER

In spite of the death of so many Indians, Mexico City became a thriving urban center for many of its white inhabitants in the second half of the sixteenth century. A bonanza of silver was uncovered in the arid provinces north of the capital, and by the 1550s, New Spain emerged as the world's greatest source of that precious metal. The silver funneled into Mexico City, where it was minted into coins or packed in bars for shipment to Spain. Drawn by this seemingly inexhaustible torrent of silver, immigrants from the mother country flocked to the colonial capital. The Spanish enclave in the city burst its boundaries, pushing the surviving Indians further toward the urban periphery. With almost sixty thousand inhabitants of all races, the capital was ten times more populous than any other community in New Spain. It was in fact the only real city in the entire colony.

A glowing description of Mexico City written in 1554 by one of its Spanish residents, Francisco Cervantes de Salazar, reflects the ebullience and pride of the upper-class settlers, and their conviction that life in the colonial capital could be every bit as sumptuous and cosmopolitan as in Seville and Madrid.[1] The central square or Plaza Mayor remained the focus of the Spanish quarter. Its huge, open space served as the city's main market just as it had in Aztec times. Indian and Spanish merchants hawked their wares and foodstuffs from makeshift wooden stands, and their shouting could be heard blocks away.

The Aztec palace which Cortés had rebuilt for himself was now occupied by the viceroy and royal judges. Clearly the most impressive structure on the plaza, its balconies were framed by marble arches and held up by numerous round and smooth stone columns. The ground floor of the palace was turned over to the city's most expensive shops, stocked with European luxuries bought in Seville with silver revenues. "One could justly affirm that there flows together here whatever is well known in the whole world," remarked Cervantes de Salazar.[2]

The corridors of the palace were thronged by Indian and Spanish litigants awaiting entry into the Royal Tribunal. In that large courtroom, four judges sat around the viceroy on an elevated platform. Their bench was draped in silk woven with strands of gold, while the viceroy's seat was cushioned with plush velvet. Below the judges and viceroy, on either side of the courtroom, sat the lawyers, notaries, interpreters, and clerks. The remainder of the chairs were reserved for the nobility and the city councilors, in accordance with their office and rank. Behind them, a wooden grille divided the courtroom, separating the commoners—Indians, mestizos, poorer Spaniards—from the notables, judges, and jurists.

The Royal Tribunal was probably the most active government institution in the capital. Even in the mother country, the Spaniards were prone to frequent litigation, but in Mexico City the Indians surpassed them in a passion for lawsuits. Most of their legal actions concerned property disputes with Spaniards and among themselves. They were encouraged to enter into lawsuits by Spanish attorneys and notaries who took large portions of settlements as part of their fees. Clergymen and government officials often lamented the passion of the Indians for endless litigation which left them impoverished.

Addressing the Spanish monarch, Alonso de Zorita, who served as a royal judge in Mexico City between 1556 and 1566, attacked the legal profession with a vehemence that echoes the complaints sometimes voiced in modern times:

"Had these people not been allowed to engage in their senseless lawsuits, they would not have ruined each other. . . . This would have avoided many offenses to Our Lord: false swearing, hatreds, enmities, ruin of towns and provinces. . . . The very parties to a suit will speak the truth if they are not induced to act to the contrary by outsiders among them, by lawyers, or by others of that kind."[3]

The cabildo or municipal council was also located on the Plaza Mayor. Though officially responsible for the administration of the city, it was often forced to abide by the decisions of the far more powerful viceroy, and acted more as a forum through which the wealthier white settlers could express their criticism of the Crown's handling of colonial affairs. Adjoining the cabildo was the Royal Treasury, where the huge shipments of silver from the northern mines were minted.

Of all the major buildings bordering the Plaza Mayor, the least noteworthy was the squat, grayish Cathedral, which would be replaced by an enormous Baroque structure in the following century. The old Cathedral was apparently a source of embarrassment to the nobler residents of the capital, for as Cervantes de Salazar remarked: "It is deplorable in a city of such renown, whose equal I do not know, with so many wealthy citizens, that there has been erected here for all to behold a church so small, so humble, and so lacking in adornment."[4]

Cervantes de Salazar greatly admired the university, however, where he was a lecturer in Greek and Latin. Built in 1553 on the Plaza Mayor, it was the first to be established in the New World, and was a royal and ecclesiastical institution modeled after the great University of Salamanca. Its faculty, drawn from the colonial bureaucracy and Church, was reputed to approach the quality of the staffs in Spain's leading universities. But like the rest of his colleagues, Cervantes de Salazar complained that the professors' income was far too meager to cope with the inflation brought on by the silver boom. "When one considers their zeal in teaching and the high prices in this province, their salaries are quite low," he asserted. "The things you buy in Spain for a copper coin, three pence or four pence, you will not find on sale here even for two silver coins, [or] I should say, three."[5]

During its first decades, the university largely limited its enrollment to white males—Spaniards and their Mexican-born offspring, called creoles. The students, wearing long cloaks, with square caps pulled down to their ears, scurried about the halls under the glare of the beadle or warden, clad in an ankle-length robe and supporting a large silver mace on his shoulder. The curriculum emphasized Greek, Latin, rhetoric, philosophy, and theology. Student debates on religion and metaphysics could grow so heated that Cervantes de Salazar compared them to gladiatorial matches: "Some rush at the throat and force their opponents to a retraction; others attempt the same thing without success. Some attack with a leaden sword which is soon blunted because they are beginners who have never entered combat, or because they are not yet keen enough in ability."[6]

The bustle of the Plaza Mayor spilled over to the adjoining blocks. One entire street was exclusively set aside for the houses and shops of the recently arrived Spanish artisans: carpenters, blacksmiths, locksmiths, weavers, stonecutters, jewelers, tailors, armorers, cutlers, candlemakers, lathe turners. Tacuba Avenue, leading from the Plaza Mayor to the old Aztec causeway that connected the island-city to the western mainland, was still dominated by the massive, fortresslike residences built by the original conquistadores and now occupied by their progeny, some of them fortunate enough to have inherited titles along with wealth. The austere facades of these villas were brightened somewhat by newly installed stone mosaics and brilliant coats of arms carved over their lintels. The nearby street of Santo Domingo was favored by the new merchant, mining, and landed elite. With aristocratic pretensions of their own, they placed slaves dressed in livery as guards in front of their residences. On several holidays, the colonial nobles—whether sons of conquistadores or newly wealthy settlers—donned burnished armor and gathered an entourage of pages to participate in recreations of medieval jousting tournaments. They sent their wives and daughters to church in sedan chairs, surrounded by their ladies-in-waiting.

At the end of the street rose the monastery of Santo Domingo, far larger than the Cathedral on the Plaza Mayor. Like many other churches, Santo Domingo was erected on the site of a former Indian temple. This not only satisfied the Spanish desire to impose the Christian faith upon the ruins of native paganism, but also served the practical purpose of connecting the churches to the underground water distribution network built by the Aztecs for their palaces and temples. Subterranean pipes brought fresh water from the Chapultepec aqueduct to Santo Domingo and other churches, government buildings, and large, private residences. Visitors from the mother country constantly remarked that nothing like this existed in Europe.

Because it was Cervantes de Salazar's intention to extol the splendor of Mexico City's Spanish community, he paid little attention to the Indians who still constituted the majority of the urban population. Their shabby, low-slung residences, made of adobe, wood, and cornstalks, were "mingled together and grouped without order," and were dwarfed by "the proud and lofty buildings of the Spaniards, which . . . stand out with their towering turrets and churches."[7] While Spaniards on horseback or in carriages now controlled the broad avenues, the Indians continued to take advantage of the many canals that crisscrossed the capital. Their canoes, laden with native produce and handicrafts, glided toward Tlatelolco, the main Indian market. Here, the only reminder of Spanish authority was the scaffold with its fork-shaped gallows at the entrance of the marketplace. Cervantes de Salazar dismissed most of Tlatelolco's bounty as "cheap and of very little worth": chiles, beans, guavas, sweet potatoes, water chestnuts, prickly pears, and a myriad other native fruits and vegetables that did not yet appeal to European palates. He was repelled by the Indian

vendors, who protected themselves from cold and rashes by smearing
their bodies with a dark, viscous turpentine ointment, "so that they
are made blacker than the Ethiopians."[8] But the Tlatelolco market did
draw a number of Spaniards seeking remedies for diseases that their
own doctors could not cure. Here they could find herbs and roots that
reputedly relieved fever, head colds, ulcers, and diarrhea. The Spaniards were especially eager to buy any Indian antidote that purported
to cure syphilis. The disease had become so rife among the white
community that a hospital was built in 1541 to deal exclusively with
its victims.

The silver that buoyed the Spanish community of Mexico City came
from the great deposits discovered in the 1540s in Zacatecas, a province
of dry, barren plateaus some 350 miles northwest of Mexico City. The
Zacatecas miners were in the mold of the conquistadores of a generation before. They were soldiers of fortune who arrived in New Spain
too late to share in the spoils of conquest. There were no more encomiendas—mandates of Indian labor and tribute—left for them in
the Valley of Mexico, or around the other established centers of Spanish settlement in Puebla to the southeast, Oaxaca to the south, and
Querétaro and Guadalajara to the northwest. So the new adventurers
journeyed further north beyond the pale of pre-Columbian Indian
civilization, searching for their mythical El Dorado in desert lands
where the unconquered nomadic tribes, known loosely as Chichimecas, still clung to a primitive life of hunting and wild-plant
gathering.
    Silver-bearing stones obtained in barter with the Chichimecas led
the Spaniards to the rich deposits of Zacatecas. At first, high-grade
ores were mined close to the surface. But by the 1550s, the Spaniards
and their Indian workers had to dig shafts hundreds of feet underground, and the ores they retrieved were of much lower quality and
not easily smelted. Profits soared again after 1557 with the introduction
of a newly discovered European technique that amalgated mercury to
the silver ore and then separated the precious metal from its impurities.
For the next three hundred years, this technique remained crucial to
silver processing in Mexico.
    Before the first trickle of silver from the New World in 1500, there
were an estimated 20,000 tons of the precious metal circulating in
Europe. By 1650, this total was almost doubled by American treasure
flowing into Europe through Spain.[9] And Mexico accounted for two

thirds of these silver shipments between 1541 and 1575, after which the mines of Peru surpassed Mexican output.[10]

The town of Zacatecas—bearing the same name as its province— grew from a string of ramshackle base camps into the second-largest urban center of Mexico by the early 1600s, with a population of 1,500 Spaniards and 5,000 Indian and black laborers. With five churches, two-story residences in its center, and thriving shops and markets, Zacatecas was a substantial provincial town.[11]

Yet, Zacatecas could not challenge the economic and political supremacy of Mexico City, which absorbed a far greater proportion of silver revenues than the mining districts ever did. The unfertile province never achieved the self-sufficiency of Spanish settlements in central Mexico. Zacatecas had to import wheat, corn, livestock, wood, and equipment from communities hundreds of miles to the south, and the cost of all these items was several times higher than at their point of origin. Indian laborers for the mines had to be recruited from the Valley of Mexico and its surrounding areas because the local Chichimecas were too few and unruly.

Most mine owners were able to keep only a small percentage of their silver output. A fifth of all silver produced in the colony was immediately set aside for the Spanish Crown and shipped across the Atlantic. Most of the remaining bullion was collected by Mexico City merchants as repayment for loans and supplies extended to the miners.

The merchants invested or loaned their silver earnings throughout the colony—in mining, agriculture, stockbreeding, textile mills, and sugar refining. But none of these ventures was as profitable as importing luxury goods from Europe and Asia. The two ports that served as exclusive centers of this overseas trade were Veracruz on the Gulf-Atlantic coast of Mexico and Acapulco on the Pacific side. For much of the year, both communities languished in tropical torpor, rife with malaria, sparsely populated, and almost bereft of food supplies. But when the fleets arrived, caravans of Mexico City merchants descended on the two ports accompanied by heavily guarded mule trains bearing food and silver.

The fleet from Seville—numbering sixty to one hundred vessels— anchored at Veracruz every summer after a transatlantic voyage of two months. It brought to Mexico such luxuries as wine, olive oil, fine garments, cutlery, glassware, ceramics, weapons, furniture, and paper. The goods were exchanged for silver at a fair which lasted twenty to thirty days. The ships remained at Veracruz throughout the winter waiting for the favorable weather and trade winds that would blow them back across the Atlantic. The silver was carried to Spain on armed galleons which also served as escorts for the merchant vessels. Security and efficiency dictated the once-a-year schedule of the transatlantic fleet. Only a large, powerfully defended convoy could ward off attacks by British, French, and Dutch pirates. By limiting the transatlantic trade to a single, annual fleet, the Spanish Crown also felt it could better control pilferage of bullion imports and evasion of its levies on exports bound for Mexico.[12]

The Pacific trade—by which Chinese luxuries were bought with Mexican silver—involved only two vessels, known as the Manila Galleons, each making one round-trip a year between Acapulco and the Philippines. China was closed to direct trade with foreigners, but allowed its merchants to exchange mainland goods in other Asian ports. As the capital of the Spanish colony closest to China, Manila became the staging point for transpacific commerce. Chinese junks arrived at Manila with their cargoes of silk, velvets, damasks, satins, pearls, and spices. In exchange, they received bullion, and in such quantities that Mexican silver coins became standard currency along the Chinese coasts and Asian rimlands.

The Manila Galleons sailed between 1565 and 1815, enduring longer than any other ship line in the world. In the words of the leading historian of the trade: "No other regular navigation has been so trying and dangerous as this, for in its two hundred and fifty years the sea claimed dozens of ships and thousands of men and many millions in treasure."[13] A galleon, usually between 500 and 700 tons, navigated alone because the risks of inclement weather, rough seas, and insufficient food and fresh water were considered too great for a fleet or armed escort. The same reasons discouraged pirate attacks of the frequency encountered by Spanish vessels in the Atlantic.

The eastward passage across the Pacific was especially arduous, taking an average of seven months. The galleon set sail from Manila in June on a northeast course until reaching the latitude of Japan. It then caught a wind that took it within sight of California, and from there the ship coasted southeast to Acapulco. A noted world traveler, Giovanni Francesco Gemelli Careri, recorded the terrors of this route in a log he kept during a voyage made at the end of the 1600s. "We all watch'd day and night, the Danger was so great," he wrote, describing a typhoon encountered a month after leaving Manila. "The Waves broke upon the Galleon, and beat terribly upon its sides. There was no Standing or Sitting in a place, but we were tossed from side to side."[14] As the journey passed beyond the half-year mark, the crew and passengers faced death by thirst, starvation, and illness. "There are two dangerous Diseases in this Voyage," stated Gemelli Careri, "Berben [beri-beri] which swells the Body and makes the Patient die talking. The other . . . makes all the Mouth sore, putrefies the Gums, and makes the Teeth drop out. . . . This is no other than the sea-scurvy." The ship swarmed with vermin, "so swift that they in a short time not only run over Cabbins, beds, and the very dishes the Men eat on, but insensibly fasten upon the Body."[15] When at last the weakened survivors sighted the California coast, with its promise of food and fresh water, they "embraced one another with tears of joy" and chanted a Te Deum in thanksgiving.[16]

The arrival of the Manila Galleon in Acapulco caused the same resurgence in the soporific port as the anchoring of the Atlantic fleet in Veracruz. The merchants, with their great entourages and convoys of mules from Mexico City, set up camp on the cooler mountain heights overlooking the harbor. They stayed only until their silver had been exchanged for the Asian luxuries at a fair held under the tight surveillance of Spanish customs and tax officials. Once the fair closed, the Manila Galleon, laden with its silver cargo, set sail westward. This was usually a far easier voyage than the route eastward because the more favorable trade winds could blow the vessels to Manila in three months.

The silver had the potential to thrust Mexico, and especially its colonial capital, into center stage of the world's economy. It produced unprecedented quantities of silver that became currency around the globe, attaining a status not unlike the British pound and the American dollar in later centuries. The Mexico City merchants stood at the crossroads of a trade network that spanned the Atlantic and Pacific Oceans. Their profits were huge. They exercised a complete monopoly over the distribution of Asian and European goods within New Spain, and they could hold on to their luxury caches until scarcity bred feverish demand.

But silver did not lay the foundations of a stronger, multifaceted economy in Mexico. The Spanish Crown did not allow the creation of industries in the colony that might compete with the luxury goods its ships carried across the Atlantic. Nor did the monarchy encourage the development of a Mexican economy that could complement that of Spain.

There were other reasons that maintained the paramount role of silver in the Mexican economy. In the premodern era, long-distance commerce favored the exchange of expensive luxuries and commodities—goods that brought great profits for their relatively compact bulk. Ships were in tight supply because of a shortage of timber. By the late 1500s, deforestation in Spain had advanced so far that the country had to turn to the Northern European forests for the oak commonly used in ships' hulls and the pine for boat decks.[17] The Seville merchants also constantly complained of the scarcity of seamen and qualified officers to man their growing fleets.[18] And there were the risks, time, and costs involved in transatlantic journeys. All these factors made silver Mexico's export commodity par excellence. From the 1550s onward, bullion accounted for two thirds to nine tenths of the total value of Mexican goods shipped to Spain every year.

Thus, silver drained out of the colony: by the Crown in the form of taxes; by payment for imported foreign luxuries; and by the emigration of Spanish colonials and their fortunes back to the mother country. The return of these new rich was a frequent enough phenomenon to become the source of derisive humor in Spanish plays and novels of the late 1500s and early 1600s. As Miguel Cervantes remarked in one of his novellas, *El celoso extremeño* (published in 1613, a few years after *Don Quixote*), the New World was still considered "the refuge and protection of all the desperadoes of Spain, the church of rebels and sanctuary of murderers."[19] He then goes on to tell the story of one of these former ruffians who, after gaining wealth in the colonies, settles down in Spain cloaked in new-found respectability.

The eventual impact of all this New World silver on Spain was enormous, but not necessarily beneficial. Overestimating his revenues from bullion, Charles V carried out expensive imperial policies that led to the bankruptcy of the Spanish state in 1557. His son and successor, Philip II, was able to reflate Spain's foreign policy as the receipts of Mexican and Peruvian silver multiplied tenfold by the 1590s. In fact, Philip's initiatives abroad surpassed those of his ambitious father. During his reign, Spain involved itself in almost continuous military actions, underwritten by New World bullion: the suppression in 1566 of the Calvinist revolt in the Netherlands, a Spanish colony; the war against the Ottoman Turks in the Mediterranean, reaching its climax with the great naval victory of Lepanto in 1571; the 1580 annexation of Portugal and its overseas colonies in Brazil, Africa, and the Far East; and the protracted conflicts with Britain in the English Channel, the Bay of Biscay, and the Atlantic, culminating in the disastrous defeat of Spain's Great Armada in 1588. But not even the silver wealth of the Mexican and Peruvian mines could cover the costs of Spain's aggressive foreign policy, and in the end, Philip was no more successful than Charles in avoiding bankruptcy.

If the silver bonanza, by encouraging an overly ambitious imperialism, proved a mixed blessing for Spain's foreign affairs, its effects within the country were more clear-cut—and decidedly negative. The massive inflow of New World bullion was linked to a 400 percent rise of prices in Spain between 1500 and 1600.[20] This inflation caused Spain's incipient industry to lose its competitive edge and decline. Repeating the pattern of its silver-rich Mexican colony, Spain used its precious metal reserves to purchase foreign manufactures and luxuries. Foreign goods increasingly made their way into the transatlantic trade between Spain and its New World possessions. Although decrees issued by Philip II restricted the colonial trade to Spanish nationals, foreigners circumvented these laws by depositing their goods in Seville where Spanish vessels would take them to Mexico to be exchanged for silver. By the end of the century, the fleets bound for the New World carried almost nothing but foreign-manufactured products: textiles from Flanders and France; woolen goods from England; ceramics and glassware from Italy; refined copper from Hungary; mercury pellets from Idria (in present-day Yugoslavia).[21]

Foreign bankers—first the Germans in Antwerp and then the Genoese—also played a preponderant role in financing Spain's colonial trade and its expensive foreign policy. Because bullion from the New World arrived in Seville only once a year, the Spanish king and merchants needed foreign loans to tide them over between the sailings of the silver fleets. Both Charles and Philip had to regularly transfer sums of money over the huge, imperial chessboard they had created in Europe, and they paid high interest rates to their foreign bankers to accomplish this task. The reliance of the Spanish Crown on the Genoese financiers was so complete that when, in 1575, Philip quarreled with them and decided to do without their services which he claimed were too expensive, the Genoese blocked payments to Philip's army in Antwerp. The unpaid Spanish troops mutinied and looted Antwerp in 1576, forcing the king to give in to the demands of his Genoese creditors. And this at a time when Philip II was considered the most powerful monarch in the world.

There were a few perceptive Spaniards who realized that their country was not the ultimate beneficiary of the torrent of New World silver, and that the bullion was in fact exerting great strains on the Spanish economy. During the 1550s, Martín de Azpilcueta, a writer on monetary affairs at the University of Salamanca, pointed out that "in times when money was scarcer, saleable goods and labour were given for much less than after the discovery of the Indies, which flooded the country with gold and silver."[22] But such analyses were not heeded by Philip II. He had no intention of tampering with an economic system that enabled him to finance his far-flung imperial enterprises.

In Mexico, this royal policy translated into an almost single-minded obsession to increase silver production. Raising the output of the mines became the foremost preoccupation of the viceroys—the main yardstick to measure their success or failure in the Crown's eyes. A silver aristocracy of miners, merchants, and their bureaucratic collaborators rose to the pinnacle of colonial society, much to the resentment of the surviving conquistadores and their progeny. The bitterness of this conquistador class would lead to the first attempt in Mexico to gain independence from Spain. Fittingly, the key figure in the secessionist plot was Martín Cortés, son of the conqueror of Mexico.

Martín Cortés was everything his father was not. He started out in far better economic and social circumstances. His father was the most renowned Spaniard of the era, and perhaps the richest, save the king. His mother, Juana de Zúñiga, the conqueror's second wife, was a member of one of Spain's noblest families. Born in Mexico, Martín Cortés left the colony at eight years of age, accompanying his parents in 1540 back to the mother country, where he was raised as a Spanish lord. The youthful Martín had none of the restless energy, ambition, or desire for military glory that spurred his father. In place of courage, diplomatic genius, and a talent for leadership, Martín faced the world with a straightforward arrogance that he claimed as his birthright.

He befriended Prince Philip, the heir to the Spanish throne. And when Philip became monarch, Martín accompanied him on an expedition to Flanders where he saw his only battle action. He was also at Philip's side when the ruler journeyed to London in 1554 to wed Mary Tudor. (The marriage joined the crowns of Spain and England, but after Mary died childless in 1558, the two countries again drifted toward enmity.) Martín was able to gain the trust and backing of the Spanish throne that had always eluded his heroic father. Hernán Cortés had spent the last seven years of his life attempting to hold together his vast estates in Mexico, which were being whittled away by envious Crown officials. But it took only a simple plea by the young Martín to King Philip to put an end to these challenges to the Cortés properties. By the stroke of a pen, Philip commanded that all the estates and

Indian tributaries granted to Hernán Cortés in recognition of his conquests be passed on to his son. With his fortune thus assured, Martín
Cortés set sail for Mexico in 1562.

In Mexico, the conquistador class was fast becoming the most disaffected colonial faction. Most of the conquerors and their sons were
inept businessmen and entrepreneurs. Clinging to medieval prejudices
against finance and commerce, they bridled over the success of those
miners, merchants, and bureaucrats who seemed to effortlessly mul-
tiply their wealth. The ideal of the conquistador class remained a feudal
inheritance of land and vassals won through war. Only a minority of
them had achieved this goal by being granted encomiendas that provided them with Indian tribute and labor. And even these fortunate
few were being threatened by Philip II's plans to reclaim the encomiendas for the Crown.

Although Martín Cortés was unaware of it, before his arrival in
Mexico he was already being hailed by these dissatisfied colonists as
their standardbearer against the monarchy. For them, his chief attributes were his status as son of the conqueror of Mexico and his ownership of the colony's largest encomienda. No sooner had Martín
stepped ashore in Veracruz than he encountered raucous welcoming
parties. Celebrations were staged throughout his journey to the capital,
as he followed the same route taken by his father during the Conquest.
Three hundred horsemen—nobles in armor covered with silk—led the
way into Mexico City, with two thousand shouting admirers in tow.
Women leaned from their second-story balconies to catch a glimpse
of the marquis. Though ill with gout, Viceroy Luís de Velasco rose
from his bed to meet the young Cortés at the doors of the palace that
his father, the great conqueror, had built.

Even after the celebrations ended, the free-spending marquis in-
jected a spirit of revelry into upper-class society by introducing recent
fads from Madrid. There was the *bríndis,* a long series of toasts requiring all male guests at a dinner party to drink themselves into a
stupor—the first one to collapse had to foot the wine bill. Masquerades
gained great popularity. Nobles disguised themselves and rode through
the streets at night to serenade women under their balconies, or even
barged into the homes of the detested silver merchants and miners to
accost their daughters.[23] With Martín Cortés's encouragement, events
of leisure multiplied: horse races, medieval jousting, prolonged hunts
at encomiendas throughout the Valley of Mexico, and balls and banquets back in the city.

But the marquis was not appreciated by all Spaniards. According to one of his contemporaries, Juan Suárez de Peralta, he was so haughty that he addressed even nobles and clergymen with the familiar language reserved for servants and other social inferiors.[24] When Martín rode through the capital, he insisted that any Spaniard he encountered in the streets pay him the exaggerated courtesy of joining his entourage until he reached his destination. Anyone failing to fall into rank could expect insults or a whipping from the marquis's henchmen. It did not take long for Martín Cortés to contest Viceroy Velasco's claim as the foremost Spaniard in Mexico. The occasion was the arrival of Jerónimo de Valderrama, one of the emissaries periodically sent by the Crown to investigate and report back on colonial affairs. Instead of joining the viceroy's delegation to welcome the Crown official, Martín rode ahead with his own party to greet Valderrama at the city limits. Viceroy Velasco, already irked by this breach of etiquette, turned livid when Valderrama accepted Martín's invitation to stay at the Cortés residence instead of the vice-regal palace.

Under Cortés's influence, Valderrama wrote back to King Philip championing the cause of the encomienda holders, and urging that the system be maintained and that Indian tribute requirements be raised. He even advocated that Velasco—despite his reputation as an excellent colonial administrator—be removed from office. But Velasco died in 1564 before Valderrama's report reached the monarch.

Velasco's death created a sudden vacuum in political authority that encouraged the more radical antimonarchical elements in the conquistador class to plot against the Crown. Rumors swept the colony that the next viceroy sent from Spain would bring with him a decree ending the encomienda system. There were numerous secret reunions among the sons of the conquistadores. They swore that before relinquishing their encomiendas, "they would surrender their lives rather than lose what their fathers had won for them and leave their own children in poverty," wrote Suárez de Peralta, who knew some of the participants in these clandestine meetings. "And since the devil found the door open for him to have his way, there was always someone to say: 'Body of God! We are like chickens; if the king wants to take the food from our mouths and the roof from over our heads, then let us snatch away his realm here and give it to the marquis, for it is his, and his father and our own won it by their efforts. . . .' "[25]

The chief figures among the plotters were the Avila brothers, Alonso and Gil González, whose father had distinguished himself during the Conquest as a lieutenant of Hernán Cortés. It was Alonso de Avila who was chosen by the conspirators to convey to Martín Cortés their offer to crown him king of Mexico. Martín told Alonso that he wanted more details of the proposed rebellion and assurances that it had widespread support. But according to Suárez de Peralta, his heart was not in the revolt and he doubted it could succeed. He did not discourage the conspirators from looking to him as their leader, wrote Suárez de Peralta, yet at the same time, he wanted to leave himself the option of "rallying to the king and rendering him a great service" by denouncing the planned revolt.[26] Whatever Martín Cortés's real motives were, his indecision caused the conspiracy to drag through the whole second half of 1565.

Early the following year, Martín gave his approval to a plan calling for a revolt during a masquerade party in Mexico City. At the stroke of a bell in the Cathedral's tower, a squad of masked plotters would seek out and kill the leading colonial government officials in their homes. Rebels were then to march into the provinces to capture the port of Veracruz, the silver mines of Zacatecas, and other Spanish communities. Meanwhile, Martín Cortés would be proclaimed king of New Spain. The conspiracy was not outlandish. There were few royal soldiers stationed in Mexico because the colonial authorities depended on the encomienda holders to raise troops among their followers in times of crisis. And many encomienda holders were no longer prepared to fight for the Crown.

But Cortés wavered and forced the uprising to be postponed several times. As months went by, many conspirators doubted his resolve and lost interest, causing the plot to be abandoned altogether. The matter should have ended at this point, except for the remorse of a few of the participants. A former conspirator gave details of the abortive revolt to the royal judges who were administering the colony in the temporary absence of a viceroy. And a priest—in contravention of his vows—passed on to the authorities the confession of another plotter. In July 1566, the royal judges placed the Avila brothers, considered the chief conspirators, under arrest. They were convicted and beheaded three months later. Martín Cortés was arrested at the same time as the Avilas, but his well-known friendship with King Philip saved his life. A new viceroy, Gastón de Peralta, arrived in Mexico a few months later. Learning of the abandoned conspiracy and its aftermath, he thought it best to send Cortés back to Spain and allow Philip himself to decide his fate. The affair should have had no further repercussions, but some colonial officials who were angered at the new viceroy's leniency sent dispatches to the Spanish court asserting that the danger of a rebellion still existed.

These reports shook Philip profoundly. Fearing the loss of the silver mines that were financing his empire, he dispatched his most ruthless judge, Alonso de Muñóz, to Mexico and empowered him to deal with the situation as he saw fit. Muñóz behaved like a true despot. Although he arrived in Mexico in October 1567—a full year after the revolt was defused and the Avilas executed—he unleashed a reign of terror. Hundreds of Spanish settlers were arrested and tortured, and scores were beheaded, even those who had first informed the colonial authorities of the plot.

The excesses of Muñóz were eventually reported back to Philip. But the lengthy time involved in transatlantic travel and communication had given Muñóz six months to carry out his butchery before a royal decree ordering an end to his commission arrived in Mexico City. Muñóz himself was brought back to Spain under guard and thrown into prison, where he died.

Martín Cortés was able to evade harsh punishment, thanks again to his old friendship with the king. He spent a brief period under house arrest in Madrid, and agreed never to return to Mexico. He then resumed his aristocratic lifestyle in Spain with the exorbitant income from his colonial estates.

In Mexico City, the conquistador class withered. The encomiendas continued to revert to the Crown or were allowed to lapse as their Indian tributaries died off. Some of the conquistadores' progeny made the successful transition to landholding. But silver—and the miners, merchants, and bureaucrats who raked in its profits—had become the uncontested source of wealth, power, and status in Mexico.

NINE

THE FORGOTTEN
CENTURY

By comparison to the age of conquest and treasure that came before, the seventeenth century in Mexico is often disparaged by historians. It has been called "Mexico's forgotten century," an era of "few exciting events, few great names," when "undistinguished bureaucrats in church and state were slowly molding public life into a suffocating routine, and corruption, nepotism, and time-serving make the records of the day dismal reading."[1] Colonial politics was marked by constant bickering and personal antagonisms between a succession of viceroys and archbishops. The buoyant economy of the last decades of the 1500s—stoked by the great silver discoveries—either slowed down or perhaps even suffered through a "century of depression" in the 1600s.[2]

And yet, at a profounder level, the seventeenth century was filled with drama. It proved to be the crucible for many of the ecological, social, and political dilemmas that continue to confound Mexico City in modern times. The colony's landscape was being radically altered, particularly in the Valley of Mexico, where the degradation of the natural environment threatened the very existence of the capital. The most racially complex society the world had ever known was being forged, especially in Mexico City. Recent immigrants from the mother country and those Spaniards born in the colony vied with each other for power, wealth, and status. Their struggles occasionally swept up the poor and once even toppled a viceroy. Only their common fears of being overwhelmed by the non-European majority finally led the Spanish colonists to set aside their internecine quarrels. The clergy added its own discordant notes. Having successfully stamped out native paganism, the Church battled the devil in his other guises: haughty colonial administrators who failed to heed the political guidance of the high clergy; secret practitioners of heretical faiths; and women, in general, because even those who were not proven sinners were deemed potential temptresses.

Rapid ecological change is the bottom layer of the era's turbulent history. Hernán Cortés in his correspondence with the Spanish monarch described a land so densely inhabited that "not a palm's length" separated cultivated plots. Yet a hundred years later, Spanish travelers in provincial Mexico were most impressed by the starkness of the landscape, fallow and sparsely populated by the dying tribes. Journeyers guided themselves by astrolabes, as if they were sailing on the open seas. The huge bullock carts that transported bullion and supplies took three months and more to traverse the mountainous wastelands between Mexico City and the northernmost silver mines. Crossing the Atlantic was a shorter voyage, and less lonely. A seventeenth-century priest, Domingo Lázaro de Arregui, who meandered through the colony's hinterlands, remarked: "There is so much uninhabited space in these realms that I doubt whether Europe's entire population could fill them; not only do they have no known boundaries, but all is empty."[3]

Father Arregui was partially mistaken. The lands did have roughly known boundaries and they were not completely void. They belonged to the cattle barons, whose great estates, called haciendas, were the remarkable phenomenon of the age. The haciendas—supplying meat to the mines and cities—were a product of the ecological onslaught which the Spaniards unleashed on Mexico. The livestock chased away the relatively few Indians who survived the epidemics. Abandoned native agricultural plots were merged with infertile drier lands. And soon the haciendas, with their cattle and sheep roaming over great expanses, became the only economically feasible rural enterprises in much of the interior.

The haciendas were far less labor-intensive than crop raising, but they still had to compete with other Spanish colonists, the Church, and the government for able-bodied workers among the reduced native population. A significant number of Indians may have flocked to the haciendas to escape the heavy tribute requirement in their communities, or the backbreaking construction tasks in the capital. But once having joined an hacienda, they became peons, and were tied to the estate by a debt system under which they never managed to pay back the owner the money he advanced to them. The hacienda owners themselves lived for the most part in the cities, especially the capital.

They found their estates too isolated and lonely for comfort, and often left bailiffs in charge of hacienda operations.

The ecology of Mexico City and its surrounding valley was being transformed as dramatically as the haciendas were changing the rural landscape. Bernal Díaz del Castillo, the conquistador and writer, was astonished by the destruction of the natural environment when he briefly returned to the valley some forty years after the Spanish invasion and settlement. "I was never tired of looking at the diversity of the trees, and noting the scent which each one had, and the paths full of roses and flowers, and the many fruit groves," he wrote. "Of all these wonders that I then beheld, today all is overthrown and lost, nothing left standing."[4]

The Spaniards required far more wood than the Aztecs, and rapidly carried out the deforestation of the Valley of Mexico. Because Mexico City rose on soft, porous land reclaimed from Lake Texcoco, buildings had to be set on a foundation of wood pilings. As many as twenty-five thousand trees were cut down annually from the surrounding mountains for this purpose alone.[5] The wood pilings soon rotted and sank, and had to be constantly replaced. By the late 1500s, Father Alonso Ponce remarked that some of the largest ecclesiastical and government buildings were sinking.[6] In 1625, another priest, the English-born Thomas Gage, observed huge wood pilings being placed under the Augustinian convent of Mexico City for the third time.[7]

Large amounts of wood were also used as scaffolding, and for walls, roofs, and doors. Enormous amounts were consumed as charcoal. But much of the timber was simply burned away from mountain slopes to create grazing land. Thus exposed, the soil eroded, and the seasonal rains washed it downhill into the lakes at the bottom of the valley. The lakes were not deep even in Aztec times, but the steady accumulation of soil made them still shallower and reduced their periphery. By the early 1600s, the lake system had shrunk by one third, and large swampy or dusty expanses (depending on the season) separated Lake Texcoco and Mexico City from the smaller northern and southern water bodies.

The Aztecs had labored hard to control the lake system, using it for irrigation, transport, and fishing, yet building and maintaining extensive dikes to contain the waters in times of heavy rains. The Spaniards, who preferred to move about on dry land, would have been happy to see the lakes disappear altogether. As soon as the Conquest ended, they began filling in the waterways that crisscrossed Mexico City, and a hundred years later only a few major canals existed in the capital.

They allowed the dikes to fall into disrepair. In any case, there were no longer enough Indian laborers available to regularly maintain such huge hydraulic projects. Moreover, many of the colonists probably shared the view expressed early in the 1600s by the Franciscan missionary Father Juan de Torquemada, that the shrinking of the lakes was a sign of divine goodwill toward the Spaniards: "Just as the waters of the Deluge (which God sent to punish mankind) gradually diminished as a divine gesture of peace and mercy to the world, thus He wished to give a similar sign by allowing the waters to recede after having punished these idolatrous people [the Aztecs]. . . ."[8]

But faith in divine providence was being tested by periodic floods of increasing gravity. It was a situation that bewildered the Spaniards: the more the lakes receded, the more vulnerable the capital seemed to inundation. The problem was that waters from the rains—concentrated during the wet season between May and September—could no longer be contained by the shallower, smaller lakes, or drained off by the fewer canals that cut across the city. There were a half dozen serious floods between 1555 and 1604. And when the capital was heavily damaged by yet another inundation in 1607, the vice-regal government embarked on the costliest construction project undertaken during the first century of colonial rule: the Desagüe General, or the drainage of the Valley of Mexico.

Enrico Martínez, one of the most talented, multifaceted individuals living in the colony, directed the project. Born in the 1550s in Hamburg, of a German Protestant family, he traveled to Seville as a teenager and converted to Catholicism. Soon afterward, he moved to Paris where he received a mathematics degree from the university. He lived briefly in Poland before returning to Spain, where he worked as an engineer, architect, printer, and cartographer in Seville, Toledo, and the royal court in Madrid. In 1589, he sailed to Mexico and became a protégé of the viceroy. Martínez was employed by the Inquisition as an interpreter for cases involving allegedly heretical foreigners— French, Germans, Flemings, Dutch—who had illegally entered the colony and established themselves in commerce. He appropriated the printing machinery sequestered from a Dutch prisoner of the Inquisition, and opened a publishing house in Mexico City, eventually printing over fifty works on religious, technical, and Indian subjects. But Martínez's most important post was as royal cosmographer, responsible for interpreting astronomical phenomena, settling geographical questions in the colony, and offering advice on engineering projects.

Martínez was one of the few colonists to perceive that the floods afflicting Mexico City were caused by the damage wrought by the Spaniards on the surrounding landscape. Deforestation and erosion of the valley's mountains were depositing so much soil into Lake Texcoco, he wrote, that "the lake's bottom will soon be at an equal level with the city" and pose a constant threat of inundation.[9]

He understood that the Valley of Mexico was in fact not a true valley with natural drainage, but rather a sealed basin in which waters from rains and springs collected in the low-lying lake system. As a solution to the flood threats, he proposed the construction of an outlet for excess water, thus draining the valley for the first time in its history. This involved boring an eight-mile-long canal—half open trench and half tunnel—that would carry floodwater northwest of the city and into the Tula River, which flowed eastward to the Gulf of Mexico two hundred miles away.

Under Martínez's guidance, sixty thousand Indian laborers completed the project in ten months—by September 1608—at a cost estimated at 17 percent of the entire annual revenues that the Spanish Crown was receiving from its New World silver.[10] The desagüe or drainage canal would have been considered a remarkable engineering feat anywhere in the seventeenth-century world. During a sojourn in Mexico two hundred years later, the renowned scientist Alexander von Humboldt pronounced it "an hydraulic operation which in our time, even in Europe, would claim the admiration of engineers."[11]

Martínez had conceived the canal as the first part of a construction program that eventually would draw off waters directly from Lake Texcoco. But the expense and labor involved in the plan met such fierce resistance from the colonists that Martínez was unable to proceed with the enlargement of the drainage system, or even ensure its maintenance. "It is impossible to find hardly anyone who speaks well of the drainage," he lamented. "The common people hate it because of [taxes] . . . and so do the landowners and all those interested in the service of the Indians who work it."[12] By 1623, all maintenance work on the project had ceased. Debris and cave-ins blocked portions of the canal's trench and tunnel, finally rendering the system useless.

Disaster struck in 1629. An unusually wet summer had left the valley floor soggy, swollen the rivers and streams, and brought Lake Texcoco's waters to the level of the city's ramparts. Then, on September 21, a torrential rain lashed the capital and its surrounding mountains continuously for more than thirty-six hours. Virtually the entire city was under six feet of water. The Indian neighborhoods, with their low-slung adobe and cornstalk dwellings, were washed away. The Spaniards sought refuge in the upper stories of their houses. The only relatively dry zone in the capital was the Plaza Mayor and its surrounding government buildings and Cathedral. It became known as the "isle of curs" for the thousands of hungry dogs huddled there to escape the waters. Describing the inundation, a priest compared Mexico City to a sinking vessel: "Her houses and churches, though of stone, looked more like ships than buildings which rested on the earth. They seemed to be floating upon the water, and as with waterlogged boats, which need to pump incessantly, in the houses and churches the pumping went on day and night."[13]

Unlike other floods, the waters did not recede even after the rains stopped. The city remained submerged for five years, until 1634! The causeways leading out of the capital were toppled, cutting off food supplies. All but four hundred of the estimated eight thousand Spanish residents fled to communities on the mainland. As many as thirty thousand Indians perished by drowning, famine, or epidemics of typhoid, pneumonia, and plague. The remaining inhabitants squatted in the upper floors of buildings abandoned by the Spaniards, or lived on rafts and giant canoes, some of them fifty feet and longer. Priests held Mass from the belfries of churches, shouting down prayers to the faithful congregated in boats.

A serious question arose over whether or not to abandon Mexico City and construct a new capital on the western shores of Lake Texcoco. The archbishop, Francisco de Manso y Zúñiga, argued that most of the surviving buildings were so severely damaged that the cost of reconstruction and of future investments in flood control would exceed the expense of founding a new city on drier ground. King Philip IV agreed and in 1631 suggested that the colonial authorities begin surveying other sites for the capital. But in the end, the viceroy, the Marqués de Cerralvo, was swayed by property owners who bitterly resisted the prospect of losing their urban real estate, conservatively appraised at 50 million pesos[14]—more than twice the value of all New World silver exports to Spain in the previous five years.[15] An emergency council convoked by Viceroy Cerralvo voted to maintain the city in place, and informed the king that labor shortages and construction costs made unfeasible the transfer of the capital elsewhere.

The colonial authorities undertook a series of relief measures for the beleaguered city. Raised, wooden sidewalks were built throughout the Spanish quarters. The viceroy ordered thousands of canoes to be made available from the surrounding provinces. Emergency shipments of food arrived by boat. Priests regularly visited the worst-struck Indian neighborhoods, caring as best they could for the ill and hungry.

But there were also numerous instances of discord and opportunism. Initially, the flood unleashed a search for scapegoats. Popular discontent centered on the Jesuits, who were in charge of water control during the two years preceding the inundation. Clandestine pamphlets, possibly circulated by rival missionary orders, alleged that the Jesuits had deliberately perforated the dike system to raise Lake Texcoco's level and divert its waters to their plantations and haciendas. Resentment next focused on Viceroy Cerralvo. He, in turn, tried to deflect the criticism by ordering the imprisonment of Enrico Martínez because his costly drainage project had failed. Martínez was released shortly afterward and placed in charge of the efforts to stem the inundation. Aging and sick, he died in 1632, while the city was still under its watery siege.

But the flood was eventually beaten back by following Martínez's long-ignored advice to broaden and maintain the drainage canal and strengthen the existing dike system. By 1633, water levels in the city dropped below three feet, enabling inhabitants to wade across the streets instead of depending solely on canoes. And in 1634, evaporation and a series of minor earth tremors drew off the remaining water.

The devastating floods of the early 1600s forced the Spaniards to recognize and confront the slow but irreversible impact of their presence on the ecology of the Valley of Mexico. Their way of life was inimical to an island-city whose well-being depended on the preservation of mountain forests and the constant use of plentiful labor to rebuild and maintain intricate water-control projects. The Spaniards felt at ease only with firm ground under their feet; with salt flats rather than lakes in the horizon. In the aftermath of the Great Flood of 1629–34, they committed themselves to expand the drainage works begun by Enrico Martínez and to gradually dry up the entire lake system. They would not be satisfied until Mexico City ceased to be an island—a process that would take another hundred years.

The seventeenth century also dramatically exposed the complex, volatile, multiracial society that was taking shape in Mexico under Spanish rule. The Spaniards had begun their colonial regime with the simplistic notion that they could preside over two separate "republics," Spanish and Indian. The importation of black slaves added a third distinct racial element. And the inevitable sexual mingling of the three groups created a kaleidoscopic caste system which must have bewildered even the seventeenth-century colonists. The offspring of a white and Indian was called "mestizo"; "mulatto," if the parents were white and black; "zambo," if the mother and father were Indian and black; "morisco," when parents were white and mulatto; and "castizo," in the case of mestizo and Spanish progenitors.

The caste system was not merely descriptive. It was also used to determine the privileges and obligations of the colony's inhabitants, such as tribute assessments, the right to enter professions, eligibility for military service, and the bearing of arms. By virtue of their white-ness—which placed them at the top of the racial hierarchy—the Span-iards were of course entitled to the greatest social, political, and economic prerogatives. But what complicated this racial panorama was a growing tendency among Spanish immigrants, known as "gachu-pínes," to view themselves as "more white" and thus more deserving of privileges than creoles, as the Spaniards born in the New World were called. The creoles defended themselves against these claims by the gachupínes, and because the ensuing struggle could not always be contained within the parameters of the Spanish community, colonial politics were unstable during much of the seventeenth century.

Any discussion of race necessarily begins with the Indians. Although they maintained their majority everywhere in Mexico, including the capital, their social fabric was severely frayed. In Aztec times, there were nine distinct tribes in the Valley of Mexico. But the combination of fatal epidemics and Spanish colonial policies greatly weakened tribal identities. Many surviving Indians left their villages to seek employ-ment in haciendas, mines, or the cities. The "congregaciones"—which forcibly relocated scattered Indian families into new, larger commu-nities—brought together natives with no regard to their tribal origins. A deliberate Spanish policy to reduce the power and status of the caciques or Indian chieftains further undermined the cohesiveness of native groups. As social structures and mores broke down, there were inevitable increases in Indian criminality and drunkenness.

The social deterioration of the Indians was most evident in the Mexico City area, whose large and powerful Spanish community ex-erted constant pressures on the natives. In Coyoacán, the southwestern suburb of the capital (and nowadays a neighborhood of the city), the Indian clan once ably led by Juan de Guzmán, the cacique appointed by Cortés, had fallen on hard times. Stripped of their political powers and their wealth, the Guzmáns married off their daughters to Spaniards in the early 1600s. Such arrangements seemed to be the only way for them to preserve a modicum of their former social status. And by marrying into the clan, the Spaniards gained control of what remained of the Guzmán lands in Coyoacán.

For all its troubles, the aristocratic Guzmán clan still fared better than the Indian commoners of Coyoacán. By the mid-seventeenth century, their numbers had fallen to about seven thousand—from a pre-Conquest high of thirty thousand inhabitants, and fifteen thousand at the apex of Juan de Guzmán's reign in the 1550s. The posthumous wills of Indian commoners testify almost invariably to their general destitution. They bequeath their heirs a few pesos, windowless adobe huts, mats for bedding, kitchen pottery, old clothes, hoes and axes, and the barest of furniture—a stool, occasionally a table or wooden chest. If land is mentioned, it is a small plot, no more than a few acres.

Commercial agriculture in Coyoacán and throughout the colony was falling increasingly under Spanish control. This was even the case for maize, the Indian food staple. In 1630, a Spanish municipal councilman from Mexico City remarked that fifty years earlier the capital received its entire maize provisions from Indian farmers, but that now the city was being supplied by "wealthy Spaniards" while the Indians had been reduced to subsistence agriculture.[16] Most Indian peasants of Coyoacán had become sharecroppers or peons for the expanding Spanish haciendas. Although colonial laws existed to prevent the wholesale transfer of Indian lands to Spaniards, the hacienda owners managed to circumvent these regulations by building up their estates in piecemeal fashion. One Coyoacán hacienda, for example, was made up of tiny plots purchased for 2, 4, 8, 11, or 14 pesos, and received the official approval of the viceroy in 1641.[17] In most cases, land was sold by the Indians to pay their tribute debts to the colonial authorities. Little wonder, then, that government officials often waived the laws against the alienation of Indian properties.

Land was the main attraction for the earliest Spaniards who moved into Coyoacán. But the 1629–34 flood in Mexico City brought other kinds of Spanish settlers into the community, among them textile manufacturers. With its flocks of sheep, ample water supply from underground springs, and close location to the capital, Coyoacán offered ideal conditions for "obrajes," as the textile workshops were called. An obraje employed and housed within its walls a labor force of twenty to one hundred people, whose functions were divided between washing, carding, dyeing, spinning, and weaving of wool. The employees included free Indians, teenage apprentices, black or mulatto slaves, and convicts of every racial caste.

There has been some scholarly debate over whether or not the obrajes were any harsher on their employees than the mines, haciendas, or construction projects. At its worse, an obraje could certainly be gruesome, as evidenced by a 1660 investigation made by a colonial judge of a Coyoacán workshop owned by the Spaniard, Melchor Díaz de Posadas.[18]

The judge, Andrés Sanchez del Campo, and his entourage arrived at the obraje unannounced, and ordered Posadas to hand over all the keys to the workshop's chambers. As soon as the judge entered the first workroom and began his inquiries, he was treated to a litany of desperate complaints from many of the ninety-six employees. Lázaro de Lara, a mestizo, stood naked before the judge, explaining that he had been given no clothes. According to Lara, he was apprenticed to the obraje by his father six months before, but had received no pay. He begged the judge to release him from his bondage. Beníto de la Cruz, a slave, asserted that he was not allowed to leave the obraje even to visit his wife and daughter. Juan de San Francisco, an Indian sentenced to eight years for murder, claimed that he received a hundred whip lashes whenever he failed to meet his work quota. He asked the judge that he be transferred to another obraje, anywhere. Nicolás de Acevedo, a mulatto slave, said that he too was regularly beaten and that he was hungry—it was after midday, and he claimed he had still not been fed his breakfast. Jerónimo de Vergara, a mulatto slave, asserted that he had never been allowed to cohabit with his wife to the day she died. Several teenagers, who were apprenticed to the obraje because their parents considered them uncontrollable, said they were never permitted to step outside the workshop. Several Indian women reported that they were beaten because they refused to work in the owner's house where they feared they would be sexually assaulted.

The climax of the investigation at the Posadas obraje was the testimony by several laborers who had witnessed the fatal beating of a young mulatto by the owner's son and his henchmen. The judge ordered the obraje owner to release many of the workers who had claimed to be imprisoned or punished without justification. But the official records of the investigation make no mention of any punitive measures against Melchor Díaz de Posadas or his son.

It is difficult to determine whether the Posadas obraje was a cruel aberration or a fairly common example of conditions in colonial textile workshops. In the four other Coyoacán obrajes, workers made virtually no complaints. Their near unanimity might indicate, however, that they had been intimidated by their employers, who were already forewarned of the judge's presence in Coyoacán. Investigations of obrajes elsewhere in Mexico rarely seem to have had the element of surprise that Judge Sanchez del Campo achieved in his visit to the Posadas workshop. But throughout the colonial era, the usual reaction of outsiders stumbling upon an obraje was dismay at the appalling work conditions. Alexander von Humboldt, who visited obrajes in 1803 during his sojourn in Mexico, wrote that "every workshop . . . resembles a dark prison."[19]

The obrajes, with their racially mixed labor force, provide the most graphic evidence of the seventeenth-century influx of different castes into what had once been an Indian stronghold in Coyoacán. The Indians could do little to protest the increasing presence of Spaniards. But occasionally, they reacted with violence to the arrival of blacks and mestizos, as occurred in 1630 during the Great Flood which brought many refugees from Mexico City into Coyoacán. When a young priest, Estéban de Ríofrío, tried to conduct services for these destitute outsiders at the Dominican church, an angry mob of Coyoacán Indians interrupted the Mass, beat up the priest, dispersed the congregation, and then demolished the altar.[20]

But the outsiders remained in Coyoacán, gradually increasing their numbers and pulling assimilated Indians into their ranks. Disorderly, rootless groups of castes and Indians milled about the marketplace, drawn especially to the new *pulquerías*—taverns which served pulque, the fermented cactus juice. Alcoholism had existed in pre-Conquest times. The Aztec annals mention strict prohibitions against public drunkenness, indicating that pulque was certainly not limited to ceremonial use. But colonial sources are unanimous in noting the huge increase in native alcoholism under Spanish rule.

Spaniards tended to associate Indian drunkenness with native barbarism. Clergymen were appalled by lapses into idol worship that sometimes accompanied drunken revelries by Indians, and by occasional displays of hostility to Christianity by intoxicated natives who urinated on roadside crucifixes.[21] Social contact with the castes was often cited as a reason for increased Indian alcoholism. A few humanitarian colonists suggested that the breakdown of Indian society and the miserable lives of most natives might also be cause for blame. "If we should see a Spaniard living like an Indian who does not get drunk . . . we would take him for a saint," remarked Bishop Juan de

Palafox in a pastoral letter to his parish priests in the mid-seventeenth century.[22]

But any inclination by the colonial authorities to restrict pulque was more than balanced by their heavy dependence on tax revenues from the sale of the beverage to finance public works, especially the costly drainage projects. So great were these alcohol taxes that they eventually equaled one half of Crown revenues from the colony's silver mines![23]

A marked rise in Indian criminality coincided with increasing alcoholism in the 1600s. A great proportion of armed attacks occurred in or near the pulquerías, and alcohol was linked to most of the reported cases of homicide and assault and battery.[24] Toward the end of the seventeenth century, a priest in one Mexico City parish asserted that during his long tenure he found forty or more drunken, seriously wounded Indians in the local hospital almost every night.[25] A seventeenth-century magistrate's blotter tied about half the criminal cases in Coyoacán to alcohol—illegal sales of pulque, knifings, disorderly behavior. Other crimes mentioned are prostitution and concubinage, in much higher incidence than occurred in Coyoacán during the previous century when social cohesion was greater.[26]

While the Indians reached their nadir in the first half of the seventeenth century, black immigration climbed to its high point. By 1650, there were over 150,000 blacks and mulattoes in Mexico.[27] The importation of slaves was facilitated by Spain's annexation of Portugal between 1580 and 1640. The Portuguese were the great slave merchants of that era because of their African colonies. Even by the vile standards of their trade, Portuguese ship captains were notorious. They measured their human cargo in tons, and routinely understated the number of their slave passengers by 15 percent or more to avoid paying import licenses for the blacks who were expected to die during the transatlantic crossing. Since male slaves were in greatest demand in the colony, they outnumbered black women immigrants by three to one.[28]

The position of blacks in the colony's racial hierarchy was ambiguous. Their price, which quintupled to 500 pesos over the first century of Spanish rule, made it uneconomical for the colonists to use them for simple agricultural and construction tasks that could be entrusted to Indians. Often, blacks were skilled workers or foremen for Indian labor gangs. Black slaves also became status symbols in colonial households. At the turn of the seventeenth century, a Mexico City councilman asserted that in "each house belonging to each honorable citizen, there are eight and ten and twelve Negro slaves."[29] Traveling through the capital in 1625, the English-born priest Thomas Gage remarked that Spanish nobles enjoyed walking about the streets with their entourages of "blackamoor slaves, some a dozen, some half a dozen, waiting on them, in brave and gallant liveries, heavy with gold and silver lace, with silk stockings on their black legs, and roses on their feet, and swords by their sides."[30] Because the Spanish colonists preferred living in cities, especially the capital, a greater proportion of slaves were settled in urban areas than in the countryside—in contrast to black experience in Brazil or the North American colonies.

Their price, work roles, and occasional ability to gain freedom sometimes placed the blacks a rung above the Indians in the colony's social order. But in other ways, the Spaniards demonstrated more contempt for them than for the natives. There were almost no defenders of the blacks among the colonists. Colonial authorities peppered their writings with racist views toward blacks as "people of little shame and trust," a "vicious people," "naturally arrogant."[31] Juan Francisco Montemayor y Cuenca, a royal judge in seventeenth-century Mexico City, claimed that the blacks were accustomed "to treat the Indians as their slaves, while they themselves enjoy more leisure and comfort than anyone else."[32] Priests asserted that the Africans showed much less aptitude for Christianity than the Indians.[33]

Prejudice and contempt bred fear of blacks among the colonists. In the early 1600s, rumors of a black conspiracy swept Mexico City. They were fed in part by a rebellion led by Yanga, a runaway slave, whose followers terrorized travelers on the Mexico City–Veracruz road, fought Spanish troops to a standstill, and finally succeeded in negotiating their freedom with the authorities. Back in the capital, the fatal beating of a black woman by her master set off a riot in 1611 among blacks and mulattoes, who stoned the vice-regal palace and the Inquisition offices. The following year, the white residents of the city were still so unnerved that a nighttime stampede by hogs that escaped their pens was mistaken as an assault launched by runaway slaves. The next day, twenty-nine black men and seven black women were rounded up and accused of a conspiracy to establish an African kingdom in the colony. Under torture, they "confessed" the plot, which allegedly called for the slaughter of every white colonist. All thirty-six suspects were hanged at the gallows in a public square to the cheers of a large multitude. Their severed heads were displayed on pikes for more than a week. The executions were followed by laws prohibiting any blacks to own or bear arms, and banning them from the streets from sunset to dawn.

The low esteem or fear in which the colonists held the black race did not deter them from exhibiting a sexual fascination for black and mulatto women. According to Father Gage, "many Spaniards even of the better sort . . . disdain their wives for them." Parading through the streets and parks of Mexico City, mulatta prostitutes and mistresses flaunted the jewelry and dresses given to them by their white lovers. The spectacle was recorded by Gage with a relish bordering on voyeurism:

> Their clothing is a petticoat of silk or cloth, with many silver or golden laces, with a very broad blue ribbon of some light color with long silver or golden tags hanging down before the whole length of their petticoat to the ground, and the like behind. Their waistcoats are made like bodices, with skirts, laced likewise with gold or silver, and a girdle about their body of great price stuck with pearls and knots of gold. . . . Their sleeves are broad and open at the end, of Holland or fine China linen, wrought some with colored silks, some with silk and gold, some with silk and silver, hanging down almost unto the ground. The locks of their heads are covered with some wrought coif, and over it another of network of silk bound with a silver or gold ribbon which crosseth the upper part of their forehead, and hath commonly worked out in letters some light and foolish love posy. Their bare, black, and tawny breasts are covered with bobs hanging from their chains of pearls. . . . Most of these are or have been slaves, though love hath set them loose, at liberty to enslave souls to sin and Satan.[34]

The colonial authorities passed decrees forbidding black women to wear silks, jewelry, and sexually provocative clothing. But blacks and mulattas continued to cast a spell—literally—over Spanish men. Seventeenth-century Inquisition archives are filled with cases of black women accused of practicing witchcraft and spreading love potions.[35]

Joseph Batista de Cos, a Seville-born cacao merchant in seventeenth-century Mexico City, claimed to be a victim of this sort of sorcery. He had a mulatta mistress, named Juana, who was the slave of a nobleman. Joseph was so taken by her that he offered to buy her freedom. But Juana wanted matrimony as well. When the merchant rejected the notion of marriage, Juana spurned him. Shortly afterward, Joseph began suffering from insomnia and impotence. He was certain that Juana, through his cook, had been slipping a potion into his mealtime drinks. When his repeated attempts at sexual intercourse with other women failed, he swore to kill Juana, whose master saved her life by interning her in a convent. In a fury, Joseph then denounced the mulatta to the Inquisition as a sorceress.[36]

The Inquisition—so diligent in ferreting out the biographic details of its victims—is the best source on the lives of ordinary blacks. Among the more appealing characters to fall into the grasp of the Inquisitors was a runaway slave, Diego de la Cruz, who tried to manipulate the ecclesiastical authorities into declaring him a free man. His story reads like a picaresque tale of black survival in Mexico during the mid-1600s.[37]

Diego was born in Texcoco, nowadays a northeast suburb of the capital. His mother saved enough from her poultry business to buy freedom for herself and her children—all except Diego, whom she left in bondage because he was mischievous and disrespectful to her. His first master, Juan de Gorostiaga, a cacao merchant, hired him out to a tavern keeper. But Diego was repeatedly caught drinking the tavern's wine and gambling away some of the proceeds. Gorostiaga, who was forced to reimburse the tavern keeper, soon grew exasperated and decided to rid himself of Diego. To ensure that he would not be sold outside the Mexico City region, Diego, at his mother's urging, married one of her friends, an older, free mulatta. By his own admission, Diego never lived with her. But in keeping with colonial laws that forbade the separation of a slave from a free spouse, Gorostiaga agreed to sell Diego to someone nearby. His new master was Pedro Belarde, an official with the judicial courts, and he made Diego his coachman. Diego was often too intoxicated to drive the coach horses in a straight line. He would also run away for days at a stretch, although he took care never to remain a fugitive long enough to incur the heavier penalties—death or castration—spelled out by the slave laws. He was sold yet again, this time to a priest, Father Bartolomé de Balfermoso, who owned an obraje (textile workshop) in Mexico City where he placed the twenty-two-year-old slave as a wool carder.

At first, Diego sought to ingratiate himself with his new master. Whenever he caught sight of Father Balfermoso, he sank to his knees, wrapped a rosary around his neck, and prayed loudly. Impressed by Diego's piety, the priest sent him to church every Sunday and holy day, and agreed to hear his confession. But Diego disliked the obraje even more than his previous jobs. Before long, he was slipping out of the closely guarded workshop, only to be brought back in a drunken stupor. Father Balfermoso had him whipped. During one of these

beatings, Diego threatened to renounce his Christian faith. As the
lashes fell across his back, he cursed the Virgin Mary and invoked
the devil until the shocked priest suspended the punishment. From
the incident, Diego discovered that he could use blasphemy to his
advantage. He began to tell his fellow workers in the obraje that he
was possessed by Satan, and they became so frightened of him that
they prevailed on Father Balfermoso to isolate Diego in a room of his
own. The next time that Diego escaped from the obraje, Father Balfermoso informed the Inquisition that his slave was a blaspheming
heretic, and he was soon arrested.

During the weeks that Diego languished in the jails of the Holy
Office awaiting a hearing, he conceived an elaborate tale which he
hoped would gain him freedom from slavery. He would claim to be
not only a blasphemer but also a secret practitioner of Judaism, thus
bringing himself to the attention of the highest Inquisitors. Then, he
would try to convince them that he had falsely accused himself and
that he was a true Christian who only sought an end to a miserable
life in bondage.

Diego was incarcerated at a time when the Inquisition's campaign
against Jews in Mexico reached a hysterical pitch. The Jews, many of
them Portuguese who had publicly embraced Christianity while secretly continuing to practice their old faith, had sailed to the colony
after 1580 when Portugal was annexed by Spain. In Mexico, their
commercial accomplishments made them targets of economic jealousy. The successful revolt by the Portuguese against Spanish rule in
1640 also brought them under suspicion as potential traitors and sab-
oteurs. More than two hundred Jews in the colony were tried by the
Inquisition, mainly between 1642 and 1646, as believers in a heretical
faith. In 1649, thirteen Jews—seven men and six women—were
burned at the stake in Mexico City. The antiheretical ceremony, called
auto-da-fé (public act of faith), was the grandest ever held outside of
Spain. It drew enormous crowds into the Plaza del Volador, a large
public square, according to a priest, Father Gregorio de Guijo, who
described the occasion in great detail in his diary.[38]

The ceremony began on the afternoon of April 10, 1649, with a
procession of the entire aristocracy of the city, led by three nobles
bearing the standard of the Inquisition. Behind the laymen came a
large contingent of friars, dressed in black or white robes and chanting
hymns. The procession ended at a scaffold erected in the plaza, where
the friars remained overnight in vigilant prayer.

Before dawn the next day, thousands of Spaniards, Indians, blacks, and mestizos had already pressed around the scaffold. At six in the morning, troops escorted the Jews into the plaza. Besides the thirteen who were to be executed, there were twenty-seven others whose punishment was reduced to prison sentences. Indian bearers also carried into the square the effigies of sixty-six Jewish men and women who had died either in the Inquisition jails or from natural causes, or had escaped arrest. Behind the prisoners and the effigies, a large column of clergy and government officials paraded around the plaza in their most elegant attire. The highest officials—including the Inquisitors, the bishops, the city councilmen, the viceroy, and their closest aides— seated themselves in the balcony of a convent overlooking the scaffold. The thirteen Jews marked for death were briefly taken to a nearby courthouse to hear their sentences, and were then brought back to the plaza for execution. Twelve of them were garroted after yielding to the crowd's exhortations to repent and die as Christians. Their lifeless bodies were then burned at the stake along with the effigies of the Jews who had escaped the auto-da-fé. Only one of the victims, Tomás Treviño de Sobremonte, refused to repent or renounce his Jewish faith, and was burned alive. He was a leader of the Jewish community and its merchants, and like the other prisoners, he had seen his fortune confiscated by the Inquisition. As the flames seared his body, he shouted out: "Throw on more wood—after all, I'm paying for it!"[39]

In his diary, Father Guijo leaves no doubt that the auto-da-fé was an immensely popular mass spectacle. The cheering crowds lingered in the plaza through the night watching the huge fire around the stake until its flames died down the next day. It is quite probable that Diego de la Cruz, the wayward slave, was among the spectators. This was just the sort of religious event which his master, Father Balfermoso, would have allowed him to attend.

The 1649 auto-da-fé was still fresh on the Inquisitors' minds when Diego was brought before them a year later. Already accused of blasphemy, Diego denounced himself as "an observer of the law of Moses."[40] Under questioning from the Inquisitors, he told an intriguing story which, as they discovered only later, turned out to be a total fabrication.

According to Diego, on a Sunday, his day of rest from the obraje, he met up with a black free man, Pascual de Rosas, who was a friend of his. Pascual suggested that they begin a business of buying and selling clothing. With Pascual contributing 50 pesos, and Diego claiming to have put up 200 pesos, the two friends bought a consignment of clothes and a stand. Pascual convinced Diego that they could magically increase their merchandise by believing in the law of Moses, for "that was the reason why the Portuguese [Jews] had so much money."[41]

A week later, Diego fled from Father Balfermoso's obraje for the last time. As part of his alleged conversion to Judaism, Diego fasted that day with Pascual. They spent the afternoon together in the Alameda, Mexico City's most elegant park, watching the aristocrats gossip with their wives and friends while seductive mulattas sauntered by. As evening fell, Diego and Pascual wandered through the tavern district where they were joined by some black and mulatto friends with guitars and harps. They strolled along the streets singing and bantering until Diego, hungry from his fast, said he could bear it no longer and suggested they find someplace to eat. According to Diego, they went to an inn, where a mulatta girlfriend served them chicken and wine. Diego stayed at the hostel with the mulatta. But some days later, he said, he began to rue his decision to observe Jewish law. He went to Texcoco, his hometown, and confessed his sins to a priest there. The priest told him he did not have the power to absolve him, and instead turned him over to the Inquisition authorities, who had already issued a warrant for his detention on charges of blasphemy filed by his master.

At first, the Inquisitors took Diego's story seriously. But as the interrogation proceeded day after day, it became apparent that there was not one shred of truth in his confessions. No person by the name of Pascual de Rosas could be found in the city. Diego appeared to be entirely ignorant of the Jewish religion. His assertions that he had 200 pesos to start a clothing business—a sum nearly equal to half the price of a slave—seemed unbelievable to the Inquisitors.

Finally, Diego admitted that everything was a lie. His only intention, he asserted, was to gain access to the Holy Office, which alone had the power to grant him his freedom. He was a fervent Christian, he told his Inquisitors. But he could no longer bear his heavy workload in Father Balfermoso's obraje. He claimed he was beaten whenever he failed to fulfill his production quota, and that at the end of the workday he was practically "dead of fatigue and hunger."[42] Besides, he said, Father Balfermoso had reneged on his promises to treat him kindly and allow him to spend one night every two weeks with his wife in Texcoco.

The Inquisitors were evidently embarrassed by falling so easily for Diego's ruse. They made him swear, upon penalty of two hundred lashes and excommunication, to keep secret the entire Inquisition proceedings against him. They then summoned Father Balfermoso, and ordered him to reimburse the Holy Office 24 pesos for the court, prison, and food expenses wasted on Diego. They told the priest not to punish Diego since he had already spent weeks in the Holy Office jail, and to allow him to cohabit with his wife in Texcoco. The Inquisitors also advised Father Balfermoso to sell his troublesome slave as quickly as possible. There is no record of whether or not Diego eventually gained his freedom. But the Inquisitors noted that Father Balfermoso readily complied with their orders and advice.

The social and racial hierarchy of the 1600s ascended through the Indian and black communities to the various castes—the offspring of miscegenation between natives, Africans, and Spaniards. The castes were the fastest-growing racial element in Mexico. By 1650, they accounted for more than 20 percent of the inhabitants, ranking them behind the Indians as the second most populous community in the colony.[43]

Race mixing began almost as soon as the conquistadores set foot on the Mexican Gulf coast. In preparing his invasion of the Aztec capital, Cortés fashioned alliances with Indian tribes by marrying off some of his lieutenants to the daughters of native chieftains. Following the Conquest, there were a few marriages between Spaniards and daughters of the highest Aztec nobility, and a great many extramarital relationships between Spanish men and Indian women. Ostensibly, the lack of Spanish women in the new colony encouraged the white settlers to find solace with the natives. But even after the arrival of women from Europe, the Spaniards continued to seek out Indian mistresses. In the early colonial era, the mixed-blood children of these free unions were shunned by both Spaniards and Indians. "Roaming in packs like wolves, they did whatever they had to do in order to survive," wrote one historian.[44] Colonial authorities encouraged Spanish settlers to take them on as apprentices. Other mestizo children were isolated in church-run orphanages and schools. Indian chieftains sold them as slaves to other tribes.

But as fatal diseases scourged the native community, unmarried or widowed Indian women sought out Spanish men in the hopes that by such liaisons they and their mestizo children would receive some protection and sustenance. There were also many cases of Indian women associating with black slaves, who survived the epidemics at a higher rate than native men and usually had more economically secure positions in colonial society. The blacks turned to the natives not only because relatively few African women were brought to the colony, but also because their children by Indian wives and mistresses stood a better chance of gaining freedom from slavery.

Spanish attitudes toward mestizos oscillated between ambiguity and outright prejudice. At one extreme was the opinion offered by Gonzalo Gómez de Cervantes, a historian and colonial official in Mexico City, who wrote to the Spanish monarch in 1599 that "We are surrounded by enemies who outnumber us; the danger is great because Indians, Negroes, mulattoes, mestizos are present in much greater numbers than we who have to serve Your Majesty and defend the realm."[45] Throughout the 1600s, the colonists were still debating whether or not the offspring of Spanish and Indian parents deserved to be ranked as *gente de razón*—people of reason—like Europeans. Juan de Solorzano y Pereira, a seventeenth-century Spanish writer on colonial matters, conceded that mestizos had been uplifted by their Spanish blood, but that their illegitimate birth made them unfit for political or religious office.[46] None of the missionary orders admitted them into their ranks. Some of the colonial guilds, particularly the more prestigious trades such as armorers and swordmakers, prohibited mestizos from rising above the journeyman level.[47]

There was less ambiguity in Spanish attitudes toward the union of blacks and Indians. The children of such race mixing were thought to combine the worst defects and vices of both parents. Church officials feared that the black "would reinforce the Indian's attachment to paganism and perhaps even infect him with the infidelity of Islam"— the religion of some of the Africans before they were enslaved.[48] Throughout the seventeenth century, the colonial authorities attempted to limit the mixing of blacks and Indians, though with little success. In 1607, 1626, 1632, and 1654, viceroys decreed that any black found in an Indian neighborhood would be subject to a penalty of one hundred lashes.[49]

Despite the prejudices against them, the mestizos did have an opportunity to climb above Indians and blacks in the colony's social and economic hierarchy. Their whiter complexion and knowledge of Spanish society made some of them more acceptable to the European community. Parents of mestizos often sought to preserve these perceived advantages by preventing their children from marrying "beneath their race." A typical seventeenth-century case reaching the ecclesiastical courts of Mexico City involved a mestizo, Andrés Rodríguez. He tried for several years to persuade his mother not to impede his marriage to an Indian woman, Ana María, who had already borne him two children in the interval. The Church court dismissed the mother's objection to Ana María's allegedly lower status as an Indian and allowed the marriage to proceed.[50] In a similar case in 1641, a mulatto, Cristóbal de la Cruz, successfully appealed to an ecclesiastical court to allow him to marry a mestiza, whose father had locked her up in a convent because he objected to her suitor on racial grounds.[51]

Occasionally, mestizos did gain remarkable social and economic success. The Pimentel and Ixtlilxochítl families, descended on their Indian side from the royal household of Texcoco, had achieved high standing in Mexico City society by the seventeenth century. They became active in the Manila silk and silver trade, and were owners of textile workshops and haciendas. There were instances of mestizos from humbler family backgrounds who used their connections with Indians and Spaniards to become merchants for the two communities. These mestizos were unable to gain access to the luxury trade where profits were greatest. But they often emerged as muleteers and middlemen in the commerce of grain, cacao, and wool.

More frequently, however, the mestizos were poor and rootless. In seventeenth-century Mexico City, they were common laborers and vagrants. They gathered in the pulquerías or taverns where they socialized with blacks, mulattoes, and lower-class Spaniards. Their numbers were augmented by Indians who attempted to pass as mestizos in order to escape tribute payments. This huge underclass of castes came to be viewed with contempt and alarm by the white colonists. They seemed a drunken, shiftless lot of knaves and rogues, indolent and scornful of work, prone to riot and plunder in times of crisis. As the seventeenth century unfolded, the colonial authorities often expressed fear that social divisions between the castes were tending to disappear and that these unruly people might someday lead the Indians in a rebellion against Spanish authority.

The Spaniards' obsession with race insinuated itself into their own community, poisoning its political and social life. Because they were born in the mother country, the gachupínes asserted they were racially superior to the creoles, their brethren born in the New World. And such claims became the basis of gachupín monopoly of the colony's highest political and ecclesiastical posts.

This concern with racial purity had its roots in Spain as much as in the New World. The long centuries of Moorish and Jewish presence in the Iberian peninsula had spawned the doctrine of *"limpieza de sangre"* (purity of blood). Beginning about 1550, Spaniards applying for civil or Church office were required to hold legal certificates demonstrating that their family lines were free of any Moorish or Jewish blood. Professional investigators traveled around the country to interview witnesses and examine the pedigrees of candidates for bureaucratic or ecclesiastical posts. Since a family's reputation could be ruined by a single informant, there were frequent instances of blackmail and elaborate attempts at deception. People applying for government jobs or the priesthood changed their names, falsified their ancestries, and avoided marrying into families that might have had Moorish or Jewish blood in their past.[52]

The purity of blood concept traveled easily across the Atlantic to the New World. The Mexican Inquisition files are replete with hundreds of *limpieza de sangre* certificates that attest to the importance of racial purity in colonial society and politics.[53] Many seventeenth-century creoles, who had cut their family roots in the mother country, were less able to trace their genealogies than the more recently arrived gachupínes. Moreover, there was a growing inclination among the gachupínes to accuse the creoles of racial degeneration because of their contact with natives, blacks, and castes, or simply because of the allegedly ill effects of the climate and land of the colonies on their breeding over generations. Some Spanish writers of the sixteenth and seventeenth centuries asserted that the creoles had become more dark-skinned, barbarous, lazy, and stupid than recent immigrants from Spain, and thus were unfit for high political or religious posts. Juan de Mañozca, the archbishop of Mexico between 1643 and 1650, went so far as to remark that "although the creoles do not have Indian blood in them, they have been weaned on the milk of Indian women, and are therefore, like the Indians, children of fear."[54] Carlos de Sigüenza y Góngora, a creole who was the greatest savant of seventeenth-century Mexico, was reacting to this sort of prejudice when he observed caustically that "in some parts of Europe . . . through being more remote, they think that not only the original Indian inhabitants of these countries [of the New World] but also those of us who were by chance born in them of Spanish parents walk on two legs by divine dispensation. . . ."[55]

Using the alleged racial inferiority of the creoles as a convenient artifice, the small minority of gachupínes had themselves appointed as royal judges, chief aides to the viceroy, provincial magistrates, and leaders of the missionary orders. By virtue of his Spanish birth and perhaps a minor aristocratic title, a gachupín could condescendingly offer to marry the daughter of a wealthy creole, thus elevating her to the ranks of the racially pure.

The superior pretensions of the gachupínes were especially galling to many creoles because Spain in the 1600s was clearly not the world power it had been the century before. The defeat of the Great Armada by the English in 1588 marked the beginning of Spain's decline in Europe. Spanish forces were repeatedly humbled by the French, Dutch, and Germans in a series of conflicts linked to the Thirty Years' War that devastated Europe between 1618 and 1648. The British, French, and Dutch were staking out their own colonies in the New World, thus ending the monopoly accorded to the Iberians by the pope in the late fifteenth century. And in the Caribbean, Dutch and British pirates were carrying out deadly attacks on Spanish silver fleets. Within Spain, meanwhile, there was a permanent economic crisis. The New World silver, rather than infusing capital into Spanish industry and commerce, was squandered to pay royal debts incurred at home and abroad.

Just how badly Mexico was affected by Spain's deterioration has been the subject of intense debate among historians. The more traditional view is that the decline of transatlantic trade and the dwindling of the native labor force signaled a century of depression in Mexico. Recently, however, some historians have suggested that the colony was forced to become more economically self-sufficient, increasing its own manufactures, circulating more of its silver bullion domestically rather than exporting it to Spain, and carrying out a lucrative, illegal trade with the Philippines and Peru.

Contemporary descriptions of seventeenth-century Mexico City do provide anecdotal evidence that the colonial upper class continued to enjoy a prosperity that was envied in Spain. Thomas Gage, the English priest who visited Mexico City in 1625, was astounded by the thousands of horse-drawn carriages, "which do exceed in cost the best of the Court of Madrid and other parts of Christendom, for they spare no silver, nor gold, nor precious stones, nor cloth of gold, nor the best silks from China to enrich them." He was also dazzled by the sartorial splendor of the colonial aristocracy: "Both men and women are excessive in their apparel, using more silks than stuffs and cloth. . . . A hat-band and rose made of diamonds in a gentleman's hat is common, and a hat-band of pearls is ordinary in a tradesman."[56]

Notwithstanding the economic dislocations caused by the acute labor shortage and the devastation of the floods in the colonial capital,

Mexico in the first half of the seventeenth century must have seemed to upper-class creoles more prosperous and less turbulent than the mother country. How else to explain the continuing arrival of Spanish emigrants in greater numbers than in the sixteenth century? How else to account for the greater financial demands being placed by the Crown on its colony? The creoles were being called upon to pay higher royal taxes to meet the burdens of Spanish involvement in European wars, to finance a Caribbean fleet that would protect transatlantic commerce from pirates, and to rebuild flood-damaged Mexico City and construct vast drainage projects.

Yet another indication of Spain's decadence in the eyes of the creoles was the enormous increase in the sale of bureaucratic colonial posts during the century as a desperate measure to raise revenues for the Crown. Royal judges, provincial governors, treasury officials, even lower magistrates bought their way into their posts. To purchase a colonial office, an aspirant often borrowed heavily, and then repaid this debt by taking bribes, collecting illegal·fees, and embezzling royal revenues.

Given the pervasiveness of office buying and the corruption that inevitably accompanied it, the assertions by the gachupínes that creoles were not racially pure enough to merit high colonial posts must have struck many settlers as absurd and cynical. The dishonesty of the gachupín bureaucrats in seventeenth-century Mexico City was open and recognized by all. Landeras de Velasco, a royal official sent to the colonial capital in 1607–09 to investigate administrative affairs, was so appalled by the corruption that he prophesied paralysis and ruin. "And when I hear it said that the present scheme to drain Lake Texcoco is designed to save Mexico City," he remarked, "I reply that no drainage scheme in the world is adequate, unless it be of avarice, extortion, and immoral government, to preserve this city. . . ."[57]

It would be a mistake to view the creoles as helpless victims of venal, Spanish-born bureaucrats. Whenever possible, creoles bought colonial offices for themselves. They acted as office brokers for gachupínes. Through bribes, creole merchants were able to secure monopolies for the import of luxury goods. They colluded with the highest colonial bureaucrats to hoard food supplies and sell them in times of scarcity at prices higher than those fixed by official regulations. With payoffs to well-placed bureaucrats, the creoles smuggled enormous quantities of silver to the Orient in exchange for the luxuries brought by the Manila Galleons. In politics, creoles could press their views in the municipal councils, where they usually held a majority. But to gain even more influence and leverage in colonial affairs, the creoles had to look elsewhere for political allies, and they found them in the highest ranks of the Church.

In seventeenth-century Mexico, the Church could be described as an expanding army in search of a mission. The ranks of the clergy swelled until, by the end of the 1600s, there were more than 2,000 priests and 1,500 nuns among the capital's 100,000 inhabitants. Administering to the needs of the reduced Indian population was not enough to occupy the large numbers of priests. Increasingly, the Church turned its efforts to improving the spiritual and moral standards of the white colonists. Clergymen exercised a virtual monopoly over education. The Church censored all literature and art deemed to be heretical or vulgar. And the Inquisition avidly pursued persons suspected of being secret practitioners of Judaism, Protestantism, or Mohammedism. Clergymen also seemed far more preoccupied than in the sixteenth century with sexual repression.

In fact, the hierarchy of the Church in Mexico City became decidedly misogynist, reserving for women the same missionary zeal that had once been directed at stamping out Indian paganism. Francisco Aguiar y Seixas, archbishop of Mexico between 1682 and 1698, was as much renowned for his aversion to women as for his generous alms giving to the poor and downtrodden. His sermons were often violent diatribes against the inherent evils and defects of womankind. He prohibited women on pain of excommunication from entering his palace, and warned their husbands never to appear before him in the company of their spouses. He tried to avoid paying ceremonial visits to the viceroy out of fear that the vicereine might be present. He urged his priests to shun female suppliants, and if religious obligations compelled them to meet women, that they never look upon their faces. The archbishop's obsessions also extended to game cocks, which he ordered to be slaughtered wherever they were found, and to all plays and novels, which he sought to prohibit. But these were minor distractions compared to his loathing of females.

The archbishop's predecessor had established a shelter to confine prostitutes. Aguiar y Seixas, however, conceived a much more ambitious facility that would also imprison young women whose poverty might tempt them into harlotry; women who had been jilted or who wished to escape romantic entanglements; women whose parents thought them too flighty or vain; and females of every sort, since the archbishop blamed them all as the principal cause of perdition.

Aguiar y Seixas's attitude and conduct was by no means considered aberrant by the Church and civil society of the era. He found willing accomplices among the clergy, most notably three energetic priests, Domingo Pérez de Barcia, Pedro de Arellano y Sosa, and Juan de la Pedroza.[58] Barcia and Sosa entered the priesthood in repentance for youths misspent in adventure and violence. Barcia was born in Spain, and came to Mexico in search of fortune. He was prone to uncontrollable tantrums, and on one occasion, during a hunt, he inexplicably shot his companion in the face. The man survived the wound. But Barcia, horrified by his own unprovoked malevolence, decided to dedicate himself to a life of religion. Sosa was born in the Mexican silver center of Taxco. Sosa's conversion to the priesthood followed a life of gambling in the mining camps, where he was several times involved in knife fights. It was not only their unstable, violent backgrounds that drew Barcia and Sosa together after they entered the Church. As clergymen, they both experienced spiritual trances during which they claimed to be able to descend into Hell and rise to Heaven, and to levitate themselves while conducting Mass.

Pedroza, the third key figure in the archbishop's antiwomen brigade, was a different sort. He demonstrated his religious vocation at a very early age. As a child, he pretended to baptize and confess his friends, and assembled them to listen to his sermons. In his seminary, he irritated his peers with his austerity and saintly behavior. As a young priest, his strikingly good looks and charismatic personality attracted many women to his pulpit and confession box, much to the annoyance of his fellow clergymen.

Archbishop Aguiar y Seixas entrusted to these three priests the task of creating a new, enlarged women's shelter and populating it with as many inmates as they could find. Father Barcia discovered the perfect facilities in a group of interconnected villas on the outskirts of Mexico City donated by an army captain who sought to make amends for a life of debauchery. At first, Barcia, Sosa, and Pedroza used their pulpits to urge women to move into the new shelter, called Belén or Bethlehem. But the church, they soon realized, was an unlikely place to ensnare the devil's agents. And so, the three priests began to undertake nightly forays in search of women. They removed their religious garb, donned laymen's clothing, and visited the taverns, gambling houses, theaters, and brothels. Cornering women singly or in groups, the clergymen warned them of the inferno that awaited them in the afterlife and enticed them to Belén with promises of food and lodging. Once ensconced behind the walls of the shelter, few women regained their freedom.

This quest for converts was not without mishaps and danger. Father Sosa was drawn into an alleyway by three prostitutes who seemed willing to hear him vaunt the merits of Belén. But instead they embraced him, covered his face with kisses, and stroked his loins in an effort to seduce him. Sosa freed himself from their caresses and fled back to Belén, where he recounted the incident as a struggle against Satan himself, in female disguise. Father Pedroza also miraculously escaped from a similar peril. Invited to hear the confession of a beautiful woman who was alleged to be on her deathbed, Pedroza entered her chamber, heard the door slam shut behind him, and was astounded to see the woman standing naked before him pleading for his embrace. Pedroza valiantly fought her off and ran from the house. There were times when the three priests were stalked by men who were furious because their girlfriends and mistresses were sequestered in the Belén shelter. One irate lover tried to gun down Pedroza in church. But the weapon jammed and the would-be assassin fled.

It was Barcia, as the warden of Belén, who was said to have suffered the brunt of Satan's anger. Realizing they were his prisoners, the women in Belén refused to listen to Barcia's sermons or invitations to confess. They spat on the priest, hurled insults at him, and on occasion managed to surround and beat him. The priest ordered them to be whipped and deprived of food. But a spirit of rebellion soon spread among most of the several hundred women inmates. A few women lapsed into insanity. Others stripped off their clothing in defiance. At least one inmate committed suicide by slashing her throat.

Barcia steadfastly maintained that his wards were possessed by the devil, and he felt that his attempts at exorcism were vindicated when a calm descended on the Belén shelter for several weeks. But then, Barcia himself was gripped by a demonic fit. He frothed at the mouth and rolled on the floor in painful convulsions, howling like a dog and beating himself. He was under the delusion that women were attacking him. His assistants tried to keep his behavior a secret. But Barcia's psychotic episodes recurred, and finally came to the attention of his benefactor, Archbishop Aguiar y Seixas. Disgusted by Barcia's outrageous conduct, the archbishop wanted to have him locked up in Mexico City's insane asylum. He relented when Father Pedroza convinced him that Barcia was in fact being punished by the devil, who was angered by the priest's success in exorcising Belén's women inmates.

Barcia was transferred to a retirement home for clergymen and prohibited from proselytizing among women. But his breakdowns became more frequent. He was treated much the same way he had once dealt with his rebellious female wards—deprived of food, beaten, and prayed over—and he reacted toward his tormentors in similar fashion— spitting at the priests, insulting them, punching at them, and finally, in desperation, attempting suicide. He threw himself from the window of his upper-floor chamber, but survived the fall. He spent the remainder of his days slipping in and out of his psychotic state.

The Church weathered the Barcia scandal and resumed its anti-women's crusade. The Belén shelter continued to function and expand its population under the guidance of Barcia's colleagues, Sosa and Pedroza. And other able clergymen stepped up the misogynist campaign. Father José Vidal, for example, was so obsessed with chastity that he denounced the sacrament of marriage as repugnant.[59] Father José Montaño preached that beautiful women had ugly souls.[60] Father Salvador Rodríguez de la Fuente lobbied hard to have a mural painted behind his pulpit evoking a vision he once had of a prostitute tortured in Hell: the woman's robes and hair were on fire; flames shot out of her mouth, nose, eyes, and ears; serpents coiled around her neck, arms, and legs; and scorpions and spiders covered her body. The ecclesiastical authorities mercifully denied the priest's request.[61]

Given the virulence of seventeenth-century misogyny, it is surprising that one of the great personalities of the era turned out to be a woman, and even more startling that she should choose the cloisters of religious life to flaunt her talents in front of men who had dedicated themselves to proving the innate inferiority and evil of females. Her name, the one she adopted after becoming a nun, was Sister Juana Inés de la Cruz. She was renowned as the best Spanish-language poet of the seventeenth century.

She was born a bastard in 1651 on the outskirts of Mexico City in a tiny village located between the snow-capped volcanoes of Popocatépetl and Iztaccíhuatl. She learned to read at the age of three. When she was eight years old, she was sent to the capital to live with relatives—creoles like herself—and further her education. Her precocious talents in literature and music, and her preadolescent beauty brought her to the attention of the vicereine, who invited her to reside in the viceroy's palace as her companion and lady-in-waiting. Juana quickly became a court favorite, dashing off verses on command and discoursing with university scholars on the latest books and ideas to arrive in the colony.

Marriage and religious seclusion were the only options for respectable women in New Spain. Juana pronounced herself totally disinterested in matrimony, perhaps because, as some of her poems later indicated, she was more erotically inclined toward women. At age fifteen, she made her choice, and entered a Carmelite convent. Besides her deep religious vocation, she hoped the cloister would allow her the time and solitude to write poetry and indulge her voracious appetite for books on science, philosophy, metaphysics, history, and literature.

Juana was encouraged to become a nun by the viceroy's confessor, Father Antonio Núñez de Miranda, a Jesuit Inquisitor. Miranda was a woman hater, as he intimated in the rules of personal conduct which he wrote to guide himself: "With all women I must show great caution, and not let them touch me, nor kiss my hand, nor should I look upon their faces or robes . . . nor seek friendship or correspondence with them. And I must close the door on all familiarity with women and be prepared to flee heaven and earth from them no matter how saintly they seem."[62]

Miranda was troubled that Juana had become the focus of the vice-regal court's attention. Her talents could only inspire other young women to entertain literary and intellectual pretensions. Miranda urged Juana to abandon these worldly pursuits and dedicate herself entirely to the perfection of her soul. The Carmelite convent he selected for her was known as one of the most severe religious institutions in the colony. But with the cold, the meager food, the sleep constantly interrupted by prayer services and ritualistic self-flagellation, Juana soon fell ill, and much to Miranda's displeasure, she was transferred to a less rigorous Jeronymite convent. The priest was also appalled to discover that even behind the convent walls, Juana was still able to reach out for the favors of the vice-regal court. She was frequently visited by her benefactress, the vicereine, who brought her books and encouraged her to continue writing poetry.

Juana's verses could be intensely mystical, religious elegies composed in the ornate and abstruse style of the Baroque era. But many of her poems were lyrical evocations of unrequited, worldly love. In the stanza of one sonnet, she wrote:

Who thankless flees me, I with love pursue;
Who loving follows me, I thankless flee:

> To him who spurns my love I bend the knee,
> His love who seeks me, cold I bid him rue.[63]

Repeating the same theme in another sonnet, she lamented:

> That Fabio does not love me, when I adore him
> Is an unequaled grief, and hurts my will;
> But that Sylvio loves me, though I abhor him
> Is no less penance, if a lesser ill.[64]

The subject of Juana's most passionate and erotic verses, however, was the vicereine, who came to see her regularly at the convent. She compared the vicereine's body to the stars in the firmament, her fingers to "alabaster dates," her voice to the notes of a flute. "It matters not that you can escape my arms and breast," she wrote, "if I can imprison you in my fantasy."[65] When the vicereine and her husband ended their stay in the colony and returned to Spain, Juana implored her benefactress:

> Listen to me with your eyes
> Since your ears are so distant,
> Listen to my pen as it moans without anger:
> And since my harsh voice cannot reach you,
> Listen to me though you are deaf, since my laments are mute.[66]

With the aid of the vicereine, Juana's poetry was circulated throughout the colony and published in Spain. Her popular following was enormous, much to the dismay of the Church. The powerful bishop of Puebla, Manuel Fernández de Santa Cruz, condemned her verses as profane. Her spiritual guide, Father Miranda, broke off all contact and refused to hear her confessions.

Juana at first defended herself against ecclesiastical critics through her verse:

> Why, oh world, do you persecute me?
> In what have I offended . . . ?
> I esteem not beauty, for, when past,
> It is the spoils of age's cruelty;
> Nor faithless riches carefully amassed . . .[67]

With great courage, she openly mused whether the campaign against her was motivated more by her sex than her nun's habits. Her poetry took on distinctly feminist overtones at a time when the Church campaign to imprison wayward women in the Belén shelter was reaching its climax:

> Which has the greater sin when burned
> by the same lawless fever:
> She who is amorously deceived,
> or he, the sly deceiver?
> Or which deserves the sterner blame,
> though each will be a sinner:
> She who becomes a whore for pay,
> Or he who pays to win her?[68]

Worse still in the eyes of her clerical enemies, Juana became the first woman in the colony to dare address herself to theological issues. Turning to prose, she wrote that knowledge of the sciences could only help strengthen religious faith. She criticized religious writing as too opaque, too encumbered by obscure citations.

The reaction of the ecclesiastical authorities was not long in coming. In an open letter to Juana, the bishop of Puebla wrote: "What a shame that such a rich mind as yours does not strive to penetrate what is in Heaven, and instead soils itself in inconsequential worldly matters; better not to stoop so low, for hell lies not much farther."[69] Other clergymen accused Juana of heresy. After the vicereine had returned to Spain, Juana never again had a secular friend or protector of her stature. Now, with the pressure of the Church hierarchy rising against her, she was rarely visited by outsiders. And within the convent, her peers and superiors shunned her. In 1694 she finally capitulated, and begged her old spiritual guide and enemy, Father Miranda, to take her confession. Using her own blood as ink, she reaffirmed her vows as a nun, and signed, "I, Sister Juana Inés de la Cruz, the worst in the world." Her impressive library of secular and theological literature was removed from her cell. She "gave herself to excessive acts of penance, self-flagellation, and mortification of the flesh," wrote one of her biographers, as if she were a novice in the most rigorous convent of the capital.[70] There seems little doubt that she was seeking death. It occurred a year later, in 1695, at the age of forty-three during a cholera or typhoid epidemic that swept through Mexico City. Rather than flee to the outskirts, Juana insisted on staying at her convent to tend to the nuns who were stricken by the disease and soon fell victim herself.

The Church's involvement in every aspect of colonial life inevitably
drew it into politics. Its political conduct, however, was not always
skillful or high-minded. Priests were as susceptible as laymen to the
prejudices that divided gachupínes and creoles. And to further their
political ambitions, ecclesiastical leaders were willing to stir the passions of the mob against the civil authorities.

Underlying the Church's erratic political behavior was the fact that
the priesthood rarely spoke with one voice. In the decades after the
Conquest, a strong rivalry developed between the principal missionary
orders—the Franciscans, Dominicans, Augustinians, and Jesuits—
over the control of Indian communities and influence in colonial
government. In the late 1500s, a further broad division surfaced in
the Church with the growth of the "secular clergy"—priests who were
organizationally tied to the bishops instead of the missionary orders.
While the chief preoccupation of the missionaries—also called the
"regular clergy"—was to convert the Indians and isolate them from
Spanish society, the secular priests were more identified with parishes
inhabited by whites, castes, and assimilated Indians. As a result, the
secular clergy tended to sympathize with the interests of the settlers,
and recruited many of its priests from creole society. The regular clergy,
on the other hand, drew heavily on Spanish-born or gachupín priests,
particularly to fill its leadership posts, because creoles were alleged to
be too biased in favor of the settlers to uphold Indian interests.

In the 1600s, the conflict between regular and secular clergy was
aggravated by the racial dispute that was dividing gachupínes and
creoles. During his journey through Mexico in 1625, Father Gage
repeatedly pointed out that feuding between clergymen was so intense
that they segregated themselves into creole and gachupín parishes.
Spanish-born regular clergymen asserted that creoles lacked the faith,
discipline, and mental capacity necessary for high ecclesiastical or
political office. This prejudice against creoles was especially acute
among the Jesuits, who had become the most powerful of the regular
clergy. In a notable incident in 1618, a leading Jesuit of Mexico City,
Father Gómez, used a sermon to lash out at the viceroy's decision to
sell some prestigious bureaucratic posts to creoles. According to
Gómez, the creoles "were incompetent to run anything, even a hen-
pen, let alone a district governorship or municipality."[71] His audience
included many creoles, who bellowed in protest, unsheathed their
swords, and withdrew from the sermon in a fury. The creoles prevailed

on the secular clergy to pressure the archbishop into punishing Gómez, who was strongly defended by the Jesuit hierarchy. Eventually, the firebrand priest was exiled from Mexico City for several months.

The Gómez incident underscored the ability of the creoles to ally themselves with the secular clergy, including bishops and even the archbishop, against gachupín elements in the Church and colonial government. In fact, most of the seventeenth century was marked by constant political tensions between Church prelates—backed by the secular clergy and creoles—and the viceroy, supported by the Spanish-born settlers and regular clergy. Between 1620 and 1670, a half-dozen viceroys lost control of the colony in these disputes.[72]

The most violent of these conflicts was one that pitted the archbishop, Juan Pérez de la Serna, against the viceroy, the Marqués de Gelves. Gelves arrived in Mexico in 1621 with a royal mandate to increase colonial revenues for the Crown and to suppress corruption. As soon as he disembarked in Veracruz, he was determined to convince his colonial subjects that austere times were ahead. He snubbed the gala receptions held in his honor by the creoles of Puebla and Mexico City, calling these festive welcomes traditionally accorded to a new viceroy a waste of money. Gelves immediately raised taxes and con-fiscated large caches of contraband goods in the ports of Acapulco and Veracruz. He also moved swiftly against widespread food racketeering, dominated by creole merchants who, in collusion with government officials, were hoarding grain and selling it at exorbitant prices. Among the most prominent racketeers arrested by Gelves was a certain Melchor Pérez de Varáez, who sought refuge in a Dominican convent when a court sentenced him to pay a huge fine.

Reeling from this offensive by the viceroy, the creole community appealed to Archbishop Serna. A natural antagonism already existed between Serna and Gelves. The archbishop exercised immense influence in colonial politics under the previous viceroy, a man who displayed little taste for power and welcomed the prelate's advice and aid. But Gelves had no intention of sharing his authority with Serna, and in fact, seemed anxious to demonstrate that the archbishop would no longer enjoy special political privileges. The confrontation came over the apparently innocuous issue of a private slaughterhouse operating in the archbishop's palace in clear contravention to a colonial law that placed all meat supplies under royal license. When Gelves ordered the archbishop to close down the slaughterhouse, Serna became his openly declared enemy.

Serna retaliated against the viceroy in a similarly petty-minded fashion. When the food racketeer, Varáez, fled to the Dominican convent, Viceroy Gelves had the building surrounded by military guards. Archbishop Serna declared this act to be a violation of the principle of Church sanctuary, and ordered the viceroy to remove the guards. When Gelves refused, the archbishop stunned the capital by excommunicating the viceroy and his guards. And when Gelves appealed to other ecclesiastical authorities, the archbishop placed all of Mexico City under an interdict—indefinitely suspending all church services and sacraments.

The viceroy was able to secure the support of the hierarchy of the Franciscans, Dominicans, and Augustinians to lift the excommunication and the interdict. But Archbishop Serna countered by leading a large crowd of his followers—creoles, secular clergy, Indians, and castes—to the court of the royal judges in what the archbishop claimed was a humble plea for justice. Undoubtedly the prelate knew the judges were loyal to the viceroy. But Serna was intent on bringing the conflict to a climax. The judges not only turned down his appeal; they placed him under arrest and ordered him to abandon the colony and set sail for Spain.

Under escort, Archbishop Serna left the capital, but traveled only twenty miles northeast to Teotihuacán where he sought sanctuary in the local church and refused to continue his journey to the port of Veracruz. Back in Mexico City, secular priests and creoles organized protests in favor of the archbishop, who from his refuge again issued an interdict on the capital. The royal judges buckled under the pressure of the growing demonstrations and rescinded their decree banishing Serna. In a final gesture to reassert his authority, Viceroy Gelves arrested the royal judges and insisted that the archbishop's banishment would be upheld.

But the viceroy miscalculated the strength of the popular movement against him. His crackdown on food racketeering failed to endear him to the city's poorer inhabitants because it coincided with bad harvests that resulted in severe grain shortages—a situation for which the viceroy was unjustly blamed by his creole enemies. Gelves had also carried out an overly zealous campaign against banditry and petty crime. According to the peripatetic Father Gage, who was in Mexico City in 1625, "since the Conquest . . . there had never been so many thieves and malefactors hanged up as in [Gelves's] time."[73] But the viceroy's wide dragnet against delinquents undoubtedly ensnared many innocent victims.

The poorer elements in Mexico City were already supporting the archbishop and the creoles. The viceroy's arrest of the royal judges was the spark that caused the crisis to flare into a full-scale insurrection on January 15, 1624. Led by secular priests, a mob of creoles, Indians, blacks, mulattoes, and mestizos burst into the Plaza Mayor and chanted: "Long live the Church and the king! Death to bad government! Death to the excommunicated heretic! Hang the viceroy!"[74] The mob easily overpowered the few soldiers guarding the vice-regal palace and then set it afire. Viceroy Gelves escaped in disguise and sought refuge in the nearby Franciscan convent.

The royal judges were released from arrest, and Varáez, now an unlikely hero, was triumphantly carried out of his haven in the Dominican convent. Archbishop Serna was escorted back to Mexico City by an entourage that swelled along every mile of the road from Teotihuacán. By the time he reached the capital, all church bells were ringing and the insurrection had turned into a festival.

Viceroy Gelves remained a virtual prisoner in the Franciscan convent for many months, until his successor arrived from Spain to arrange his release and voyage back to the mother country. Archbishop Serna's victory was shortlived, however. He soon returned to Spain where he was treated coldly by the king, demoted to bishop, and forbidden ever to visit Mexico again.

Although the 1624 revolt lasted only a day and resulted in less than a score of deaths, it marked the first time that a viceroy had been deposed in the New World by a popular uprising. In the decades that followed, the creoles did not have to seek the support of the Indians, blacks, and castes to pressure the colonial government. Instead, they continued to effectively use their alliance with the secular clergy and their prelates to confront a succession of viceroys.

Creole influence in colonial affairs during the seventeenth century probably reached its zenith when Juan de Palafox, the bishop of Puebla and a strong favorite of the creoles, became interim viceroy in 1642. He appointed creoles to a number of bureaucratic and military posts that had previously been reserved for the gachupínes. He handed lucrative shipbuilding and maintenance contracts to creole merchants, and did little to impede their overseas commerce—legitimate or contraband. And he pleased the creoles by awarding to the secular clergy control over numerous Indian parishes which had been under the protection of the missionary orders. This had the practical effect of making the Indian laborers of those communities available to the creoles.

As the seventeenth century drew to a close, colonial politics was dominated by the growing rift between creoles and gachupínes. But the two factions of the Spanish community in Mexico City were pushed into a hasty reconciliation by a popular insurrection, the so-called Tumult of 1692, which was to prove far more violent and uncontrolled than the revolt of 1624.

What is perhaps most fascinating about the Tumult of 1692 is the way it wove together the various major historical forces at work in seventeenth-century Mexico City. The deteriorating ecology that made the capital so vulnerable to floods and famine created the setting for the crisis. The protagonists were the dispossessed mass of rootless Indians, blacks, mulattoes, and mestizos whose potential for social unrest had been growing over the previous decades. And at the summit of colonial society, the longstanding conflicts between creoles and gachupínes had eroded public respect for political authority.

Carlos de Sigüenza y Góngora, the remarkable seventeenth-century Mexican scholar, wrote a detailed eyewitness report of the upheaval.[75] His account begins in early June 1691, when Mexico City was celebrating the recent marriage in Madrid of the Spanish king, Charles II. The city's streets were jammed with revelers led by floats financed by the guilds. Masquerade balls lit up the palaces and villas so that "the successive nights of rejoicing were mistaken for days." There were bullfights, followed by banquets and the free distribution of food to the populace. Even the magistrates were in a generous mood, handing down lenient sentences and releasing all but the most serious offenders from the jails. "How joyous the common people were! How pleased the upper classes!" remarked Sigüenza y Góngora. "And how true are the Scriptures when they say that laughter is mingled with tears and that sorrow follows upon the greatest joys!"[76]

On June 9, 1691, a tempest of hail and water exploded over the Valley of Mexico, putting an abrupt end to the festivities. Ravines and dry streambeds quickly overflowed. The deforested mountains and hills could absorb little of the copious rain. The water swept away everything in its path, "exempting neither the Indian houses which were frail nor the stouter homes of the Spaniards which were scattered about on the hills and valleys."[77] The western suburbs of Mexico City were engulfed, and the capital was soon inundated when its canals failed to contain the excessive water. Over the next few weeks the downpours were so numerous and powerful that Lake Texcoco, which had shrunk after decades of drainage and was normally shallow at this time of year, expanded almost to its pre-Conquest dimensions. All roads and cause-ways leading out of the city were impassable. Canoes and larger vessels "were sailing where formerly pack trains had traveled."[78]

But unlike the Great Flood sixty years before, the capital no longer had a surfeit of boats. Charcoal, fruit, vegetables, grain, and meat were soon in short supply. Archbishop Aguiar y Seixas, the stern misogynist, displayed his more charitable side, and supervised the distribution of food relief, blankets, and clothing to the afflicted poorer neighborhoods. The viceroy, the Conde de Galve, quickly organized Indian brigades to build embankments around the capital, clear debris from the canals, and dig new drainage ditches.

These efforts prevented the disaster from reaching the proportions of the 1629–34 deluge. But the populace remained extremely jittery. When an eclipse briefly blackened the skies over the capital on the morning of August 23, 1691, "the Indian women and children, aban-doning their stalls where they sold fruits, vegetables, and other small wares . . . went shrieking and flying at full speed to get inside the Cathedral," wrote Sigüenza y Góngora. Being an avid astronomer, he himself was ecstatic: "I stood with my quadrant and telescope gazing upon the sun, exceedingly happy and thanking God repeatedly for having granted me the privilege of beholding what only happens very rarely in one given place and about which there are so few observations in the books."[79]

But the Indians, blacks, mestizos, and many Spaniards as well re-mained convinced that the eclipse foretold terrible times ahead. In the months that followed, the heavy rains destroyed large portions of the grain harvests. Cattle and sheep failed to fatten or starved because their pastures were flooded. Much of the surviving crops were afflicted by blight. As the shortages became more acute, wheat prices doubled and maize prices rose even higher. Viceroy Galve moved vigorously against farmers and merchants suspected of food hoarding, and managed to force them to deposit most of their harvests in the *alhóndiga*, the government granary in Mexico City.

But shortages continued into 1692, and the threat of famine sparked the usual fears in the Spanish community of an impending Indian revolt. According to a Franciscan priest, the Indians were planning to burn down the churches, rape the nuns, and massacre all the Span-iards.[80] Sigüenza y Góngora himself believed these rumors. As evi-dence, he wrote that he had personally found small clay figurines while supervising flood control projects in the city. "All [of the figurines] represented Spaniards and all were either pierced by knives and lances formed of the same clay or had signs of blood on their throats as if they had been gashed," he asserted.[81]

By the beginning of June 1692, frenzied crowds of Indian women were assembling every day in front of the alhóndiga to purchase the dwindling supplies of maize. On June 7, the throng was so unruly that guards at the public granary had to drive them back with whips and staves. An Indian woman was fatally beaten by an official, and her body was carried in protest by the other women to the palace of Archbishop Aguiar y Seixas. The prelate, who avoided females alive or dead, refused to meet the crowd and sent an aide to urge them to return to their homes. Instead, the protestors, still carrying the corpse, marched to the viceroy's palace. There, they were dispersed by the militia.

During the night, the pulque taverns filled with disgruntled Indians, blacks, mestizos, and vagrant Spaniards who called for large-scale demonstrations against the viceroy to demand more grain supplies. In the afternoon of Sunday, June 8, throngs of protestors began to gather in the Plaza Mayor in front of the vice-regal palace. Viceroy Galve, a devout Christian who attended Mass twice on Sundays, was at the nearby San Francisco Church—a happenstance that probably saved his life. The mob turned ugly, ransacking the merchants' booths in the plaza and stoning the vice-regal palace. It was at this point that Sigüenza y Góngora, at home leisurely perusing his books, became a witness to the upheaval:

"Although I had heard part of the noise on the street, it did not occur to me—since ordinarily on account of the habitual drunkenness of the Indians we are continually disturbed by uproars—to open the glass partitions of the window of my study to see what it was about until a man servant came in almost choking with excitement and shouted to me, 'Sir, a riot!' "

Half-dressed, the scholar ran down to the street and was swept up by a tidal wave of protestors as they swarmed into the plaza. "The number of people was so exceedingly great, not only of the Indians but of all castes," he wrote. "The shouts and howling were so raucous, and so thick was the storm of stones which poured on the Palace that the noise which the missiles made on the doors and windows exceeded that of more than a hundred drums of war."[82]

Sigüenza y Góngora immediately understood the racial overtones of the tumult. He observed that Spaniards, at first rushing with drawn swords to the aid of the palace guards, stopped short of the plaza and withdrew in fright. Meanwhile, blacks and mestizos joined the Indians and shouted: "Down with the Spaniards who are eating our corn!"

In the previous revolt, of 1624, secular priests had first exhorted and led the mob, and then managed to disperse it. But this time the clergy had no influence over the rioters. The archbishop and his entourage, including Sigüenza y Góngora, tried to drive their coaches into the plaza and draw the mob's attention with a huge, upraised crucifix. They turned back quickly, however, after being greeted by a volley of stones.

The mob crashed through the entrance of the palace and set the building afire. The flames swept through the Oriental rugs, the silk-brocaded furniture, and the heavy velvet curtains. Other rioters burned down the nearby buildings of the municipal council, the public granary, and the jail after releasing the prisoners. The mob then began systematically looting the luxury shops along the plaza and its adjoining streets. As soon as a store was ransacked, it was set aflame. The clergy tried once again to calm the rioters. Priests approached the plaza in procession, holding aloft images of Christ and the Virgin Mary and chanting church litanies. But they were routed by a hail of rocks and fireballs.

Merchants and aristocrats, both creoles and gachupínes, gathered at the San Francisco Church to offer their services to the viceroy. Since the small standing army was unable to control the mob, the viceroy asked his followers to form a militia. Armed with muskets and carbines, the merchant and aristocrat brigades charged into the Plaza Mayor and killed scores of rioters. But according to Sigüenza y Góngora, the upheaval was waning already because the looters had more goods than they could carry into the night. When dawn broke, the fires were still burning. Property damage was assessed at 3 million pesos—almost five times the amount that the colonial treasury received that year in silver taxes.

As a consequence of the Tumult, the viceroy's first measure was to ban the sale of pulque. The Spaniards almost unanimously blamed alcohol as the cause of the upheaval. But the prohibition lasted only a few weeks: taxes on pulque were too important a source of government revenues.

The viceroy also decided to move the Indians from the city's center and segregate them in their own neighborhoods as Cortés had done after the Conquest. According to Viceroy Galve, many Indians lurked in the darkest corners of the central district "with the object of hiding

themselves and coming out to commit grave crimes."[83] A report prepared by the clergy also recommended that the Indians be pushed back
into their neighborhoods because their contact with blacks and castes
had allegedly made them more aggressive.[84]

Sigüenza y Góngora himself was a strong advocate of these policies
and was appointed by the viceroy to draw up boundaries for the Indian
community. But assigning new places of residence to the natives was
no easy task. There were numerous complaints resulting from disputes
over land titles, dispossessions of property, and discontent among the
Indians chased out of the central district. The new segregation program
broke down within a few years. Stores, workshops, and households
pleaded for exemptions that would allow their Indian employees to
reside with them. Indian peddlers and vagrants milled about the city
center, sleeping in the alleyways and eventually building their shacks
off the main avenues.

Of more lasting consequence was the fear that the Tumult of 1692
instilled in the Spanish community. Creole and gachupín tensions
would continue to simmer in the century ahead. But both factions
agreed that they would have to stand together against any threat posed
by the multiracial majority of Indians, blacks, and castes.

TEN

THE BOURBON ERA

As the eighteenth century began, Mexico City's white colonists had far less to fear from internal disorders than from the pitiful deterioration of their mother country. Spain's economy was in total disarray. Its navy was reduced to twenty ships, and the army counted only twenty thousand soldiers. The country clung to its vast American possessions through the indulgence of the stronger European nations, who treated Spain as a mere channel for silver from its colonies.

The bullion paid for Spain's ever-mounting debts and for the merchandise which Britain, France, Holland, and Italy exported to the New World. As soon as the Spanish galleons laden with Mexican and Peruvian riches anchored in Cádiz—which had replaced Seville as Spain's chief Mediterranean port—foreign ships converged on the fleet to claim its silver.

Notwithstanding the benefits they received from this commercial arrangement, the European powers were tempted to dismember Spain's overseas empire because of the political incompetence of the Spanish Crown. The royal Habsburg household that had ruled Spain for two centuries and presided over the conquest of the New World was reaching an ignominious end with the inept Charles II. Sickly and emotionally unstable—he attempted to hang himself with his bedclothes—Charles somehow lingered on the throne for thirty-five years. He failed to father a child despite two marriages, and shortly before his death in 1700, his aides induced him to appoint as his successor Philip of Anjou, a grandson of the French Bourbon monarch, Louis XIV.

Anxious to prevent French domination of Spain and its empire, the English declared war on Louis and his grandson, who was crowned

Philip V in Madrid. The so-called War of the Spanish Succession lasted until 1713. The Treaty of Utrecht which ended the hostilities ensured England that Spain's American possessions would not fall under French rule and that the English would be permitted to continue their trade with the Spanish colonies. But the treaty did allow Philip and his Bourbon successors to remain on the Spanish throne.

Under the Bourbons, a new era of reform and revitalization began in Spain and its New World domains. Heavily influenced by French concepts, the Spanish Crown increasingly centralized political rule, achieved a more efficient government administration, dramatically raised royal revenues, and curtailed the power of the Church. Though implemented cautiously at first, these reforms gained momentum in the second half of the 1700s during the long reign of Charles III, one of the ablest monarchs in Spanish history.

In Mexico, the Bourbon era restored the faith of the white colonists in Spain's ability to manage itself and its empire. Nevertheless, it was evident on both sides of the Atlantic that Spain had become more economically dependent on Mexico than the colony was on Spain. A small, Mexico City-based elite with remarkable entrepreneurial talents grew enormously wealthy, dominated the colony's economy, and over-came every effort by the Crown to limit their powers. Most of these entrepreneurs were born in the mother country or were sons of recent immigrants to Mexico. They began their careers as merchants in the high-risk overseas and inland trade, then diversified into the even more speculative silver mines, and finally invested the bulk of their earnings into agriculture, a somewhat less profitable, but more secure enterprise.

What distinguished them from rich colonists of the previous two centuries were the much greater size of their fortunes, the diversity and sophistication of their business transactions, and the splendor of their urban lifestyle. In the late 1700s, Mexico City was the largest community in the Americas, with over 130,000 inhabitants and an architectural inventory that included 150 ecclesiastical buildings, a dozen hospitals, an Academy of Art, the most advanced school of mining, and one of the great universities of the world. Many of these structures were built or expanded with contributions from the wealthy. But the elite families of Mexico City saved their most generous im-pulses for their own residences. They tore down the villas built by the conquistadores and an earlier merchant class, and used their stones to erect Baroque and neoclassical-style mansions that survive to this day as the main legacy of domestic architecture from the colonial period.

Commerce was a natural starting point in the accumulation of wealth and social honors by this new elite. In Mexico, they encountered few of the medieval prejudices that aristocrats in Spain still attached to trade and finance. Already in the 1660s, a viceroy had remarked that "in these provinces every gentleman is a merchant and every merchant a gentleman."[1] Commerce thus attracted some of the ablest upper-class creoles and their newly immigrated gachupín (Spanish-born) relatives.

By the early 1700s, the astute commercial elite in Mexico City had clearly gained the upper hand over Spain's own merchants in overseas trade. With the decline of the royal navy, there were fewer ships available to carry goods across the Atlantic to Veracruz, and transport costs rose steeply for the Spanish traders. Once the goods disembarked in Veracruz, the Spaniards, who were not permitted to do business further inland, had to sell their wares to the Mexico City merchants. The Mexicans bided their time, well aware that the costs incurred by the Spaniards to keep their ships in harbor and pay storage bills on the docks would eventually force them to lower their prices.[2] Spanish merchants also faced keen competition from English, French, and Dutch traders who smuggled their goods into other Mexican ports on the Gulf coast. The end result was the same: further leverage for the Mexico City businessmen in their dealings with Spanish merchants engaged in legal trade at Veracruz.

The Mexican merchants held an even stronger whip hand over the Manila trade on the Pacific coast. No longer were they content to sit patiently in the foothills of Acapulco and negotiate prices for the Oriental fineries brought over by the Manila Galleons. Instead, they sent their agents to the Philippines to purchase consignments for the galleons, thus cutting out Spanish merchants from the profitable trade. And when the Spanish government passed regulations in the 1720s and 1730s forbidding such direct trading connections, the Mexicans deftly circumvented these obstacles by setting up dummy commercial firms in Manila. In 1776, Charles III was informed by one of his officials in the Indies that the Mexico City merchants had become the true masters of the Manila trade, and were "reputed to be the most fortunate and lucrative of all those that are known in Europe and America."[3]

Unhappy that colonial trade had fallen under the domination of foreigners and Mexico City merchants, the Spanish Crown created in the second half of the 1700s a freer commercial system by opening new ports in Spain and lowering the tariffs on transatlantic merchandise. The Crown also attempted to end the monopoly that the Mexico

City businessmen exercised over the colony's internal and overseas trade by establishing new, rival merchant guilds in Veracruz and Guadalajara. These reforms, extended throughout Spanish America, greatly profited the monarchy and resulted in a quadrupling of colonial trade between 1778 and 1788.[4] But they did nothing to threaten the preeminence of Mexico City's merchants in the colonial economy. With far more financial resources than the newly created Veracruz and Guadalajara merchant guilds, the Mexico City traders were able to snatch away cargoes from ships arriving on the Gulf coast. And they sent their agents directly to Spain to purchase goods for shipment to Mexico.[5]

The import of luxuries from abroad was extremely profitable, but in total value it could not compare to the revenues from trade within the colony—a sector also thoroughly dominated by Mexico City's entrepreneurs. These big merchants owned wholesale warehouses and retail shops in the colonial capital to distribute foreign and local goods. In the provinces, they sometimes entered into partnerships with local retailers. More often, they controlled provincial shopkeepers by extending them credit to purchase wholesale goods and by agreeing to be paid back in barter when currency was scarce.[6] The Mexico City merchants also advanced money to farmers against future production at a fixed price. In this way they were able to corner the market for valuable export commodities like sugar and cochineal dye.[7] There was an element of risk in such arrangements, but more so for the farmer than the rich merchant: prices could rise after the contract was signed, thus providing the Mexico City trader with a windfall of profits; and if prices declined, the merchant was usually wealthy enough to withhold sale of the commodities until an upturn occurred.

Whether dealing with foreign or internal trade, the aim of the Mexico City merchants was to rise above the ordinary forces of supply and demand. They attempted to maximize profits by securing exclusive contracts rather than purchasing and selling on the open market. Their chief instrument was their access to silver currency—for use as cash or to obtain and give credit.

Beginning in the sixteenth century when the first silver veins were struck, Mexico City merchants had been able to claim most of the precious metal output as repayment for loans and supplies extended to the miners. By the 1700s, however, the miners could no longer keep pace with the increasing silver demands of the commercial elite. The miners were so burdened by royal taxes on mercury—used to refine silver—that they concentrated only on high-grade ores. Miners also complained that they were at the mercy of the Mexico City merchants for their credit needs. And as their mine shafts sank deeper, their labor costs increased and water seeping underground flooded their galleys, in many cases forcing them to abandon their operations entirely. Given all these obstacles and expenses, there was little incentive for miners to search out and exploit new silver veins.

Anxious to increase its colonial revenues, Spain sought to stimulate a mining renaissance. Under Bourbon rule, taxes on mercury were steadily reduced. The Crown organized Mexican miners into a guild with its own courts and the power to exercise jurisdiction over mining litigation. Silver banks were created to offer miners alternative sources of credit and more financial independence from the powerful Mexico City merchants. Mining in the Bourbon era also benefited from technical innovations: gunpowder became more readily available for underground blasting; horse-and-mule hoists were used to haul ore to the surface, instead of the inefficient squads of workers who clambered up rows of ladders with loads of 150 pounds or more tied to their backs; and the animal-powered hoists also helped miners in their endless battle to remove water from shafts and galleys.

Aided by these reforms, silver output rose dramatically, from 3.25 million pesos in 1700 to 13.5 million pesos in 1750, and to 27 million pesos by 1804.[8] Toward the end of the colonial era, Mexico accounted for two thirds of the silver produced in the Spanish empire and half of the world's supplies.

But the greatest beneficiaries of this bonanza were the Mexico City merchants, who transformed themselves from creditors to investors in silver mines. The great mining families of the late Bourbon era in Mexico—the Reglas, Fagoagas, Bassocos—all had patriarchs who began their entrepreneurial careers as merchants before becoming silver magnates. There were several paths that took merchants into mining. Pedro Romero de Terreros, a Spanish immigrant who later acquired the title of the first Count de Regla, married into a merchant family, made a fortune in commerce, and then became the financial backer and partner of an experienced miner in a silver operation that produced about 20 million pesos between 1738 and 1781.[9] Agustín de Septién, a successful merchant born in Spain, entered mining through marriage—his wife was a creole silver heiress.[10] The Fagoagas found that their long involvement with miners through commerce and banking led them to make huge investments in mines of their own. In a more conservative, risk-sharing approach, seventeen Mexico City merchants, headed by Antonio de Bassoco, invested jointly in a company in 1788 that purchased, drained, and developed eight silver mines.[11]

Merchants not only had the capital to take advantage of new mining opportunities created by the Bourbon reforms and the increasing demand for silver bullion; they also had the finances to weather the tremendous losses that operating a mine could entail. A mine's productivity tended to follow an established pattern: a first seam was exhausted and the underground galley became flooded; a new operator made heavy investments to exploit a deeper deposit; and eventually, the mine was abandoned as the costs of excavation and drainage surpassed the silver yields.

"Money rapidly gained [in silver mining] is as rapidly spent," observed Alexander von Humboldt, the German-born scientist who traveled through Mexico in the early 1800s. "The rich proprietors of mines lavish immense sums . . . in new undertakings in the most remote provinces. In a country where the works are conducted on such an extravagant scale . . . a rash project may absorb in a few years all that was gained in working the richest seams."[12]

Fagoaga and Bassoco invested over 1 million pesos in a Zacatecas mining operation between 1786 and 1804 before reporting significant profits.[13] They had such enormous capital that they were able to wait until this venture gained them huge returns. But there were other magnates who tied up their wealth exclusively in mines and lost nearly all. The Count del Valle de Oploca, who made fortunes from mines in Bolivia and Mexico in the early 1700s, left only a modest inheritance for his widow, and their son died in poverty. Another once wealthy miner, the Count de la Laguna, had to relinquish his noble title in 1781 because he was unable to pay the taxes required to maintain it. As many as four out of every five investors in silver mining failed to recover their money.[14]

Having made fortunes in commerce and mining, Mexican entrepreneurs tended to invest in great rural estates. For many years, historians believed that this flow of wealth into land was motivated less by economic reasons than by a yearning for the social status which a vast hacienda bestowed upon its owner.[15] But more recent research indicates that investments in haciendas were a shrewd means by which elite merchants and miners preserved and enhanced their fortunes.[16] The great landed estates served a useful role in the inheritance squabbles that inevitably arose when a patriarch died, leaving numerous progeny. The haciendas could be far more easily partitioned among his heirs than mines or commercial firms. Rural property was also the most consistently accepted collateral for credit in Mexico, and even the wealthiest merchant-miners needed business loans for their great enterprises. Moreover, while returns from agriculture could be unstable and low for most farmers, this was not the case for the big hacienda owners, who regularly recorded annual profits of 6 to 9 percent.[17]

The Mexico City elite's strategy in agriculture was much the same as in commerce: to control market forces instead of being at their mercy. Not only did the great landowners invest in the whole range of livestock and crops; they also spread their holdings over a variety of geographical zones—thus guaranteeing that at least part of their estates would earn profits no matter what market and weather conditions prevailed. In the region surrounding Mexico City, for example, seventeen families controlled half the agricultural land.[18] A drought in the valley of Toluca to the west of the capital could be compensated by good harvests on other properties held by the same landowner in Chalco or Cuernavaca to the south.

Timing was a key calculation in profit taking by the great hacienda owners, and was linked to deplorable episodes of exploitation of the hungry poor in Mexico City. Maize and wheat were planted in May, at the beginning of the rainy season that normally extended to September, and the crops were harvested in November. Grain prices were lowest between November and March because small and medium-sized farmers, having exhausted their cash and credit, hastened to sell their produce. But the great landowners, with ample financial reserves, could afford to withhold their supplies from the market and benefit from price rises of 20 percent or more in the months of food scarcity between June and the next harvest.[19]

The private correspondence of hacienda families has yielded detailed admissions of market manipulation. For example, María Josefa de Velasco y Ovando, who managed her family hacienda, gave the following instructions to the estate's bailiff after the maize harvest of 1800: "About the current drop in the price of grain, it is to be expected at this time, as the small farmers sell quickly to take care of their pressing needs; but as we have no such needs, we will not sell now. Better, we shall buy as much maize as we can and sell it for profit in the future."[20]

Such economic self-interest did not prevent María Josefa and the other great agriculturalists from striking a charitable public pose. They participated in the invocation to the Virgin Mary traditionally held at the beginning of food scarcities. And when grain prices finally reached their pinnacle, María Josefa instructed her bailiff to sell the produce because, as she piously noted, to continue withholding it would "prejudice the lives of the poor, for whom maize is the sole support of life."[21]

The big hacienda owners could never have succeeded in manipulating the grain market without the collusion of many colonial officials, including some of the viceroy's trusted aides. Government regulations specified that most maize had to be sold through the public granary, the alhóndiga, at official prices. But only a small portion of the maize entering Mexico City reached consumers this way. In 1795, for example, the municipal records indicate that the alhóndiga handled only 102,000 bushels out of the 240,000 bushels sold in the capital. By bribing inspectors, the hacienda owners disguised most of their harvests as Indian crops or as payment of Church tithes—thus exempting them from taxes and sale to the public granary.[22]

The estate owners were not content simply to harvest and deliver their grains to market. From production to processing to distribution, they sought to control agrarian supplies, eliminating middlemen and extracting the highest possible profits. Some of the biggest farmers owned flour mills. An installation belonging to the González Calderón family, for example, processed a third of the wheat sold in Mexico City.[23]

The concentration of economic power was even more evident in meat supplies. Five great livestockmen—all of them members of the merchant-mining elite—operated the only slaughterhouses in Mexico City.[24] For reasons of hygiene, cattle and sheep were supposed to arrive in the capital on the hoof and be butchered there. But powerful livestock owners who lost animals on the trail were often allowed to sell the already dead animals, much to the dismay of some city officials.

"The introduction of 'dead' meat in this capital . . . has brought on many epidemic diseases," wrote one high official in 1788. "This [meat] is supposedly distributed or sold as dog food. But in a population so large, disorderly and poverty-stricken, it is not at all unusual [for people] to consume this food even if it costs them their lives. . . ."[25]

Pulque—fermented cactus juice—was yet another agricultural commodity firmly under the control of the big landowners. A native alcoholic beverage, its production remained in Indian hands for some decades after the Conquest, if only because cactus was grown on arid lands which at first did not attract Spanish settlers. But as consumption of pulque rose spectacularly among the Indians and other poor, the wealthy whites moved swiftly to monopolize the trade. The fact that cactus was unaffected by the frequent droughts made pulque all the more appealing to hacienda owners as a predictable source of huge profits. By the 1790s, two aristocratic families, the Jalas and Reglas, who were united by marriage, supplied about half of the pulque consumed in Mexico City, with a few other landowners providing the rest.[26] To further extract profits from the trade, most of the big pulque producers owned taverns in the capital, and had exclusive arrangements with innkeepers who agreed to buy the beverage only from them.

In all these ways, agriculture became a safe means for the Mexico City elite to perpetuate the wealth they had gained in more speculative, higher-yielding ventures such as commerce and mining. For most rich Mexicans, the acquisition of vast rural estates did not mean a withdrawal from trade and silver operations. They sought to diversify their investments in all three fields because colonial history had taught them that at one time or another every economic sector experienced cyclical booms and depressions. The extent to which they succeeded in protecting their immense wealth from these cycles elevated them to the highest ranks of capitalism anywhere in the preindustrial world.

The fortunes made by the richest Mexicans of the Bourbon era stunned even foreigners accustomed to the upper-class milieu of the Old World. The German-born scientist and writer Humboldt asserted that in terms of wealth and business acumen, the Mexican elite had nothing to envy from Europeans. And among the Spanish American colonies, he observed, only Mexico had produced true millionaires.[27]

Toward the end of the eighteenth century, there were about one hundred families in Mexico City with assets of over 1 million pesos or close to this amount (the peso being roughly equal to the American dollar of the day). Only a dozen families elsewhere in the colony had this kind of money.[28] Mexico City was the most obvious location for a businessman whose interests in commerce, mining, and agriculture were spread across the breadth of the colony. It was by far the strongest internal market for commercial and agricultural goods. Only in the capital could wealthy Mexicans effectively exert influence on the government bureaucracy. And then, of course, there were more flighty considerations: even individuals whose fortunes were entirely linked to a single, distant province felt compelled by social ambition to set up residence in Mexico City. There was, for example, Ignacio de Obregón, a millionaire miner and hacienda owner from the northern town of León, whose decision late in life to move to the capital provoked the following condemnation from one of his provincial cronies:

"I do not doubt that Obregón will [join high society], and that is the only benefit he has got from living in Mexico City and neglecting his business. What a pity . . . and what blindness to strive to ruin oneself by this mania for cutting a figure, which, well considered, is despicable. How much better it would be to live in León and there be the first. That crowd of empty-headed flatterers [in Mexico City] just rush to fleece the fools from the north."[29]

The concentration of wealthy families physically transformed Mexico City, or at least the central district where they resided. Humboldt described the capital as "undoubtedly one of the finest cities ever built by Europeans in either hemisphere." With the exception of St. Petersburg, Berlin, and parts of London, he added, "there does not exist a city of the same extent which can be compared . . . for the uniform level of the ground on which it stands, for the regularity and breadth of the streets, and the extent of the public places." He found mansions, public buildings, and monuments "of very beautiful structure" that "would adorn the principal places of Paris or London." And all this in a natural setting that "brings to mind the most beautiful lakes and mountains of Switzerland."[30]

The architecture of the principal public buildings and private residences displayed a variety of styles: the austere, fortresslike structures of the early post-Conquest era; the ornate curls and detailed sculpture identified with the Baroque era of the late 1600s and early decades of the 1700s; and, toward the end of the eighteenth century, the clean, straight lines and symmetry of neoclassical design.

At times, a single building blended more than one architectural style. This was the case of the Cathedral. Once a source of embarrassment because of its modest dimensions, it was rebuilt into the largest church in the New World. The remodeled structure was begun in a Baroque style, and completed in the early 1800s with a neoclassical design. Manuel Tolsá, the famed Spanish-born architect and sculptor who directed the final stages of the Cathedral's construction, was determined to impose a neoclassic face on the city. The centerpiece of his efforts was the school of mining, built like an Italian palace with massive staircases, monumental stone columns, and vaulted ceilings. It cost three times its original budget, but Tolsá was able to pry loose the required funds from the vice-regal government and the entrepreneurial elite who shared his vision of a new grandeur for the colonial capital.

The donations of the wealthy helped build schools, churches, and hospitals, yet these were minor outlays compared to the sums they lavished on their own houses. The greatest mansions were constructed at a cost of 100,000 to 300,000 pesos, in a colony where an annual income of 300 pesos was considered a "decent living."[31] The facades of these residences were covered with Chinese tiles, or the porous, pink *tezontle* stones so prized by the Aztecs, or thick granite chiseled in smooth swirls. Over monumental doors of oak studded with metal spikes, cherubs held up the families' coats of arms. Inner patios were decorated with fountains of mermaids and figures from Greek and Roman antiquity.

Huge retinues lived in these palatial homes. When the widow of a miner who lost most of his fortune complained that she was reduced to living "simply" with only a slave and seven servants, she no doubt elicited considerable sympathy in her social circle.[32] In the nearby Yermo household, for example, twenty-five servants attended to the needs of the seventeen family members. The Fagoaga mansion employed twenty-six servants for the ten family members. The Count de Heras had eighteen servants to care for his wife, two children, and himself.[33]

Ostentation marked all aspects of the elite's social life. They ate on Chinese porcelain, and rode about the city in imported coaches. Jewelry, clothing, and furniture cost them as much as the construction of their mansions: when the second Count of Regla married in 1780, his wife brought a dowry of her personal effects valued at more than 130,000 pesos.[34]

The leading families were a nobility in name as well as lifestyle. By the end of the Bourbon era, the Spanish Crown had bestowed more than fifty titles on wealthy subjects of the colony, all but seven of them residents of the capital. For the Crown, the granting of aristocratic honors was an effective means of raising needed revenues from the richest Mexicans. A count or marquis was required to pay annual taxes for the privilege of his title, and was expected to make additional, voluntary contributions to help defray the colony's administrative and defense expenditures. Perhaps the most outstanding example of such private outlays was a 2.5 million-peso gift of two warships to the royal navy by the Count of Regla.[35] Other aristocrats opened their coffers to recruit militia and to ensure the provision of grain and meat to Mexico City in certain emergencies.

Humboldt remarked that wealthy Mexicans wasted fortunes to quench their thirst for titles. But besides being an affectation, nobility offered at least one real economic advantage to its holder. It was often a prerequisite for an "entail"—a royal dispensation which allowed a family to pass on half of its fortune intact to a single heir instead of fragmenting it among siblings.

The same pragmatism that underlay this quest for noble titles marked almost every facet of the lives of the Mexico City elite. To accrue and protect their enormous wealth, they were prepared to manipulate all the forces that impinged on their private world. Economic calculation was at least as important as sentimentality in the patriarchical structure of their families, in the selection of their spouses, and in the clannishness that drew cousins and nephews from Spain to the New World. Their close ties to the Church had a financial logic that often exceeded religious fervor. In politics, they were less concerned with achieving high office than in rallying the bureaucracy behind their economic goals.

Patriarchy was the best means available for a wealthy family to control its wide-ranging businesses. This was an era when enterprises— no matter how large—were family concerns. Siblings and in-laws might head up individual enterprises, but only one member—the patriarch, and after him, usually his eldest son—could be trusted to oversee all the family's economic affairs and extinguish internal rivalries. The patriarch's role was not unlike that of a board chairman presiding over a highly diversified modern corporation.

The problem with a family business, however, was how to ensure that younger men of talent and ambition were available to maintain the vitality and growth of the multiple enterprises. The Mexican aristocracy spawned its fair share of dull, lazy progeny. A patriarch could always arrange to have his daughter wed a son of one of the hundred or so other elite families of Mexico City. But such marriages, while uniting parts of two great fortunes, did not necessarily provide the patriarch with a son-in-law of noteworthy business acumen. Frequently, a family head reached across the Atlantic to Spain for a suitable candidate to run the most complicated of his enterprises, the trading house which controlled overseas and colonial commercial operations. The candidate, invariably a nephew of the patriarch, or the son of one of his cousins, might begin his employment in Mexico City as a low-level clerk. If he displayed talent and a capacity for long working hours, he was slowly promoted to director of the trading house. He then married the patriarch's daughter, making him heir to the family merchant operations and to at least some of the mines and agricultural estates.

Examples of young, driven Spanish immigrants snatching up creole heiresses were commonplace in elite Mexican marriages. The Fagoagas, Bassocos, Reglas, and many other leading families began their rise to fortune in this way—and continued the pattern by marrying off their daughters and granddaughters to relatives who emigrated from Spain. The phenomenon gave rise to the stereotype of the aggressive gachupín shouldering aside his less-motivated creole cousin. The historian Lucas Alamán, who lived through the transition from colony to independent nation, contrasted the hardworking gachupínes—"a species of men who did not exist in Spain itself and will never exist again in America"[36]—with the "generally idle and careless" creoles.[37]

Although there were isolated cases of friction between the Spanish newcomers and their Mexican-born cousins, the Mexico City elite was generally aloof to the centuries-old creole-gachupín rivalry that still marked the rest of white colonial society. Rich creole families were powerful enough to absorb their entrepreneurial Spanish relatives. They welcomed them not only for their economic contributions, but because the gachupínes added luster to a family's pretensions of racial purity, always an elite concern in the colonial era.

The tensions that surfaced in these clans were more often associated with their overbearing patriarchical structure. When the head of a family lived too long—as was the case of the Conde de Jala, a great merchant and pulque producer—his eldest son never escaped an existence of wealthy dependence.[38] The anointment of a new patriarch could also cause considerable bitterness among family members. For example, the second Count de Regla took control of his clan upon his father's death in 1781, and ruled his siblings' affairs like a despot for more than two decades. When his younger brother, the Marquis de San Cristóbal, attempted to wed for reasons of love rather than economic and social gain, the marriage was blocked by the count. The marquis then tried to gain his independence by relinquishing his noble title and settling in Paris, where he became a physician. But his autonomy was always limited by the fact that he continued to live on an allowance doled out by his older brother.[39]

The Count de Regla was just as authoritarian toward his four sisters. The eldest achieved freedom of sorts by settling permanently on her estates north of Mexico City, but at the cost of renouncing the glittering social life of the capital. The count may well have discouraged two of his other sisters from marrying in order to keep their properties under his control. And he bullied his youngest sister into wedding a much older man, a Mexico City judge who could help protect the patriarch's economic interests.[40] But as the count himself discovered, his authority was more rooted in economic power than in his position as family patriarch. When a series of disastrous investments in mining edged him toward bankruptcy, he was forced to turn over management of the family's business affairs to his wife, who had brought into their marriage her own considerable fortune and a noble title.[41]

This was not the only instance of a woman taking the reins of an aristocratic clan. When the patriarch of the Santiagos, one of the oldest noble families in Mexico, died in 1793, the family enterprises fell under the control of two unmarried sisters. The eldest sister, who inherited the title of Countess de Santiago, resided in Mexico City, and allowed her sibling, María Josefa Velasco y Ovando, to manage the family's lucrative agricultural estates west of the capital. María Josefa was as tough as any hacienda owner in matters of grain hoarding and price gouging. And she brooked no disrespect from the neighboring estate holders, all of them men. For example, when Gabriel de Yermo, a wealthy merchant and hacienda owner, wrote a letter imperiously demanding the right to herd his cattle across her lands as the shortest route to the Mexico City stockyards, María Josefa twice rebuffed him before granting her permission at an expensive fee. She had never previously charged the other hacienda owners for the same privilege, but they had showed her more deference than Yermo did.[42]

María Josefa saw her powers ebb soon after her sister, the Countess de Santiago, died in 1802, leaving her noble title and estates to a third sibling, Ana María. The new countess was married to Ignacio Gómez de Cervantes, scion of another aristocratic family, who had no intention of allowing María Josefa to dispute his claims over his wife's estates. The once indomitable María Josefa was forced to surrender the haciendas she had managed so well, and moved to a smaller, less lucrative Santiago property northeast of Mexico City.[43]

But Gómez de Cervantes did not long enjoy his patriarchy over the Santiago fortunes. Shortly after his wife died, his two sons—claimants to the Santiago titles and properties—sued him in 1812 for control of their inheritances. The courts ruled in their favor and reduced the father's holdings back to his own inheritance, proving once again that the patriarchic ideal so strongly embraced by the Mexico City elite was more a function of economic power than family affection.[44]

Beyond family, the Church was closest to the hearts of the elite, although here too affection was tempered by economic self-interest. At first glance, the spiritual fervor and charity displayed by the wealthy toward the Church appear more extravagant than in any other period of Mexican history. José de la Borda, a mining magnate, invested half a million pesos in the construction of the Santa Prisca Church in Taxco, one of the greatest eighteenth-century architectural masterpieces in the world. The Count de Bassoco, a multimillionaire merchant, contributed 300,000 pesos to the building of Our Lady of Loreto in Mexico City. Scores of less renowned churches, chapels, and nunneries were erected with the help of donations from the elite, who in wills and testaments left additional money and properties to the clergy.

But the bulk of the elite's contributions to the Church was in the form of so-called pious works and chantries. An estate owner would designate part of his property—usually an hacienda—as a "pious work," contributing up to a third of its income to the Church coffers. In return, this gave the owner the right to pass on the property to a single heir, rather than having it partitioned among numerous progeny. The pious work thus served the same function as an entail—by which the Crown allowed a patriarch to will one half of his estate to a single heir of his choosing—but was far easier to arrange. A "chantry" permitted a wealthy family to ensure the financial welfare of relatives who had not benefited from pious works or entails. It involved the contribution of a fund to the Church—usually several thousand pesos, but often more—supposedly to pay for perennial Masses for the repose of the dead donor's soul. Since a Mass cost only a peso or two, the administrator of the chantry—a family member named by the donor—could live comfortably on the annual interest of the fund.

The huge capital from testaments, pious works, and chantries transformed the Church into the most important source of credit in Mexico. And this was perhaps the greatest economic benefit that the elite derived from its religious generosity. Merchants, miners, and hacienda owners regularly applied to the Church for loans. Even the wealthiest families—the Fagoagas, Reglas, and Bassocos—borrowed from the pious funds they created. Church loans in fact were available to any businessman large or small. By the early 1800s, credit advanced by the Church accounted for two thirds of the total invested capital in the colony.[45]

While the Church's economic power soared in the eighteenth century, its spiritual and political strength was ebbing. Enlightenment ideas with strong elements of anticlericalism were filtering into Spain and its colonies from France. Charles III, the Spanish monarch between 1759 and 1788, believed that the capital and lands which the Church had been allowed to accumulate over the centuries were to blame for Spain's economic decadence. His agents in Mexico, particularly the powerful royal inspector, José de Galvez, were deeply suspicious that the Church might become an obstacle to Bourbon attempts to increase royal authority and revenues in the colony. By the late

1700s, this attitude of distrust toward the Church had seeped into the reports of the colonial bureaucracy, as the following memorandum to Madrid made evident:

"Some people revere the clergy with religious enthusiasm, and this is the greater part of the [Indian] population. Others follow them out of a foolish adulation. Still others try to reap advantages from their wealth and power. . . . Indeed, it can be said that Ecclesiastics are the sole arbiters of the people and their customs. They can turn them without much difficulty toward good or evil."[46]

Although this assessment was probably true for the poor majority of Indians and mestizos, the Church's prestige was somewhat more tarnished among the whiter elements of the community. As one recent historian has observed, colonial officials in the 1700s "were known to scoff at the threats of ecclesiastical officials and it was said of some royal bureaucrats, that if they had not been excommunicated at least once by the local priests they were not adequately serving the Crown."[47]

Perhaps no other agency of the Church had suffered a greater loss of prestige than the once terrifying Inquisition or Holy Office, which by the mid-1700s expended its energies meting out mild punishments for offenses ranging from heresy and sorcery to sodomy and possession of prohibited literature. Attempts by the Inquisition to regain its authority simply backfired. In one celebrated incident during the 1760s, the Holy Office summoned the viceroy the Marquis de Croix to answer charges that he had publicly insulted the Church agency. The viceroy appeared at the Holy Office building accompanied by an artillery battery, and after a brief interview with the shaken Grand Inquisitor, he received assurances that the charges against him would be quickly dismissed.[48]

In an effort to weaken the colonial Church, the Crown openly played on divisions within the clergy. In the 1600s, royal officials had sought their chief religious allies among the "regular clergy"—those belonging to the missionary orders—who were believed to be more loyal than the so-called secular clergy—priests who were organizationally tied to the bishops. But a century later, in the Bourbon era, it was the regular clergy—and their great wealth and properties—that became the target of royal officials, who turned to the secular clergy for support. At the behest of Charles III, secular priests submitted reports claiming widespread disorderly and immoral conduct among the missionary orders, including violent crimes, gambling, drunkenness, abandonment of chastity, and extortion of the poor.

The charges were undoubtedly exaggerated, but for a variety of reasons standards of discipline had deteriorated among both the regular and secular clergy. The missionary fervor of the early colonial era had declined following the conversion of the native population. Large numbers of men were entering the clergy simply as a means of social advancement, or to earn a livelihood, or to receive the benefits of a chantry donated to the Church by their families (becoming a priest was a requirement for the beneficiary of a chantry). Folklore and popular literature were filled with anecdotes about wayward priests whose religious calling never prevented them from having commercial ventures or mistresses and children. In a best-selling novel of the late Bourbon period, a friend explains to the protagonist the worldly pleasures of joining the clergy:

"Look here: a priest is well received everywhere; everyone venerates and respects him even if he is a fool. They overlook his defects. No one dares to censure or contradict him. He has a place at the best ball, at the best gambling table, and he is appreciated even in the ladies' boudoirs. And lastly, he never lacks a peso, even if he has to recite a Mass badly and at breakneck pace. So study for the priesthood and don't be a boob."[49]

Dissensions among the clergy further damaged the Church's reputation. All the religious orders were torn by the old conflict between creole and gachupín priests over leadership in their parishes. During the 1700s, clashes between armed clerics sometimes spilled into the streets of Mexico City and required the intervention of royal troops.

The rivalries between the religious orders and the deteriorating public image of the priesthood made it easier for the Crown to strike against those elements of the Church that it considered threatening. The single most dramatic action undertaken against the Church in the entire colonial era was the decision by Charles III in 1767 to expel the powerful Jesuit order from his realms in Spain and overseas. The monarch claimed that the Jesuits were plotting against him, but the vast economic holdings of the order were surely a tempting prize.

In Mexico, the expulsion of the Jesuits set off riots among poorer segments of the populace in some provincial cities. Galvez, the Crown's inspector, led an army against the rioters, and quelled the revolts by executing 158 people and imprisoning 674 others after hasty trials. The Church hierarchy declared its support of the Jesuit expulsion. The Mexican entrepreneurial elite, who had contributed so generously to the Jesuits and had reaped so many economic benefits from them in return, did nothing to protest their expulsion. In fact, the aristocrats were the greatest beneficiaries of the expropriation of Jesuit wealth. Only they had the capital to buy the order's numerous agricultural estates that were now put up for sale by the Crown. The Count de Regla, for example, acquired twenty of the 119 ex-Jesuit haciendas—the largest single purchase of land in colonial history—at a fraction of their assessed value.[50]

The Church was by no means the only target of the Bourbon monarchy's strategy to eliminate potential rivals to its authority. Charles III and Galvez, his most powerful aide in the Indies, were determined to reduce what they saw as the pernicious influence of creoles in colonial administration. During the first half of the 1700s, creoles had managed to overcome royal prejudices against them and entered the civil and ecclesiastic bureaucracies at all levels apart from the posts of viceroy and archbishop. For Galvez, such a continuous infiltration undermined Spanish interests because, as he explained, the creoles were too encumbered by "the ties of family and faction in the New World to provide . . . impartial government."[51] The replacement of creoles by a new wave of military officers and bureaucrats from Spain posed a threat to the Mexican elite because it was their relatives and allies who were being pushed out of colonial posts.

Of even more concern to the aristocrats was Galvez's campaign against corruption in Mexico. He intended to sweep aside the network of provincial governors, magistrates, and lesser officials who augmented their low salaries with bribes, embezzlement of tributes, and illegal commissions often paid by the big merchants, miners, and hacienda owners to facilitate business transactions. Turning to France for political inspiration, Galvez proposed to replace this bloated, venal bureaucracy with a leaner provincial administration headed by eleven intendants and their subdelegates.

But despite their initial apprehension, the Mexican aristocrats made these Bourbon political changes work in their favor—much the same way they had done with previous reforms aimed at limiting their role in silver mining and overseas trade. The intendants and subdelegates soon realized that they needed the help of the Mexico City elite. The performance of any provincial administrator was measured by his success in delivering Indian tributes to the central treasury in Mexico City. Bad harvests, native recalcitrance, and transportation problems often meant a reduction in tribute totals, and left a blot on an official's record. The big merchants could dispel these anxieties by offering to advance an intendant or subdelegate the money he owed to the central treasury. In return, the official agreed to give the merchants exclusive trading rights in his district. In this way, for example, the Mexico City elite was able to gain control of virtually the entire lucrative trade in cochineal dye in Oaxaca.[52] By the end of the 1700s, many intendants and subdelegates—displaying the same venality as the bureaucrats they replaced—had become provincial business partners of the Mexico City elite.

The creole aristocrats were just as successful at foiling attempts to reduce their political influence in the capital. Despite the increase in gachupínes in the colonial government, there were still a number of elite creoles who managed to obtain appointments as royal judges and other ranking bureaucratic posts. Wealthy families cemented their ties with the colonial administration by marrying off their daughters to high officials, who dreamed of inheriting landed patrimonies after retiring from government service.

The growth of a colonial army offered yet another avenue for the advancement of elite creole influence. As late as 1758, there were only three thousand regular troops stationed in Mexico. But the increasingly powerful British garrisons in North America aroused Spanish fears of an invasion of Mexico, and led to an expansion of the colony's army and militia. The successful independence revolts in the English colonies as well as in Haiti convinced the Bourbons that their Mexican forces should be enlarged even more to cope with the possible threat of an insurrection. By 1810, there were twenty-three thousand troops in Mexico, most of them militias rather than regular army soldiers. The Bourbons would have preferred to recruit Spanish troops and officers exclusively, but the expense involved in transporting them across the Atlantic and supporting them in Mexico was onerous. By the late 1700s, the Crown was openly selling military commissions to wealthy creoles. For the Mexican elite, a commission in the militia or army became a sign of status. Aristocrats dressed in their resplendent uniforms for balls and formal gatherings. They also enjoyed the right to trial by their military peers rather than in the royal courts. By the late colonial period, military officers had surpassed middle-ranking clergymen and government bureaucrats in prestige.

As the eighteenth century neared its end, the Mexico City elite had accomplished many of the goals that eluded the conquistadores. They gained spectacular riches, and preserved them for their offspring. In title and lifestyle, they recreated a European aristocracy in the New World. Their influence was felt in every colonial sphere. And they were far more adept than the conquistadores and earlier colonial elites in evading the Crown's attempts to limit their power and wealth. Perhaps their most unexpected success was their ability to convince an initially suspicious Bourbon monarchy that a community of interest bound the fortunes of the Mexico City elite and the Spanish Crown.

The creole aristocracy rode the crest of an economic boom that was distributed in a grossly inequitable fashion. Nowhere was this disparity more evident than in Mexico City. Though mesmerized by the wealth of the capital's upper class, Humboldt was also appalled by the contrast between a small elite and a destitute majority—a gap which he asserted was greater than anywhere else in the Spanish empire. "The streets of Mexico swarm with from twenty to thirty thousand wretches, of whom the greatest number pass the night [without shelter], and stretch themselves out to the sun during the day with nothing but a flannel covering," he noted.[53]

An itinerant Spanish priest, Francisco de Ajofrín, who visited the capital in 1763 some forty years before Humboldt, had already made the same observations:

"In spite of so much wealth in Mexico . . . the poor people, so bloated in numbers and so ragged, disfigure and spoil all, arousing fear in those who are newly arrived from Europe. For if we counted all the miserable of Spain, we would not find among them as many naked people as there are in Mexico City. . . . Of every one hundred people you come across, only one is fully clothed and wears shoes. . . . Thus, in this city, one sees two diametrically opposed extremes: great wealth and maximum poverty."[54]

The capital was "whiter" than ever before. At the end of the 1700s, almost half of its 130,000 inhabitants were of European descent, a quarter recognizably Indian, and the rest mestizo and mulatto. By contrast, in the colony as a whole, less than 20 percent were whites and 60 percent were Indians, with mixed bloods accounting for the remainder. The number of blacks was negligible because the importation of African slaves had virtually ceased, and their offspring had been absorbed into the castes.

But race was no longer a sure yardstick of economic class in Mexico City, where 85 percent of the population was mired in poverty.[55] According to the Count of Revillagigedo, viceroy from 1746 to 1755, the capital's poor had become "a monster of as many species as there are castes, and including as well many Spaniards demeaned by poverty and laziness . . . vile customs, ignorance and irremediable vices."[56] Shared misery, however, did not take the edge off racism. Light-skinned mulattoes and mestizos flocked to the courts with petitions requesting that they be officially reclassified as Spaniards, in the hope, however remote, that "whiteness" would change their economic and social circumstances. "A white who rides barefooted on horseback thinks he belongs to the nobility of the country," wrote Humboldt. "And when [he] disputes with one of the titled lords of the country, he is frequently heard to say, 'Do you think me not so white as yourself?' "[57] Such cheek was unimaginable from an Indian or caste.

Whether white, Indian, or mixed blood, most of the poor lived far removed from the tree-lined boulevards, graceful public buildings, and lavish mansions of the central district. Their stick, straw, and adobe shacks were clustered in muddy alleys, and surrounded by rubbish, manure heaps, and puddles. Potable water was a rare commodity, with only twenty-eight public fountains for the entire city.[58] A permanent stench shrouded the poor neighborhoods. The foul odors emanated from everywhere: the nearby slaughterhouses and the many pens where hogs were fattened; the canals brimming with garbage and human wastes; the empty lots where "honeybucket" men deposited night soil; the cemeteries where the ground was too soggy and shallow to bury corpses properly.[59]

The plight of the poor elicited little sympathy from affluent Mexicans, who complained constantly of their filth, drunkenness, gambling, criminal behavior, shiftlessness, and beggary. Writing in 1788 to a friend who was about to assume a high municipal post, a royal judge counseled that any attempt to uplift these miserable people was hopeless because "they subsist thinking only of the here and now, even though they have nothing to eat; and they are without feelings of shame because if they had any they would not walk about naked. . . ."[60]

According to Hipólito Villarroel, a wealthy resident and chief prosecutor in the capital who wrote a treatise in 1787 on the ills afflicting the colony, the poor had transformed Mexico City into "a refuge of vicious and wayward beggars, a brothel of infamy and dissolution, a cave of rogues, a hell for gentlemen, a purgatory for men of good will."[61] He proposed that all persons without employment be banished to the provinces and that a wall be built around the city to prevent them from slipping back in.[62]

The affluent failed to see the obvious connection between the economic boom they were enjoying and the demographic explosion among the poor. In the preindustrial world, the link between population and economic activity was inextricable. When people increased in numbers, production and commerce also rose. And in Bourbon Mexico, the population was rising dramatically, from an estimated

3,336,000 inhabitants in 1742 to over 6.1 million in 1810.[63] The single most important factor in this surge was the development of at least a partial immunity to European diseases among the Indians. Fatal epidemics continued to affect the Indians more adversely than any other colonial sector, but never again in the hideous proportions of the first century of Spanish rule. By the end of the colonial era, the Indian community had tripled to 3.67 million people from its low point in 1650,[64] creating a larger and cheaper labor pool that revitalized mining, agriculture, and commerce, but also depressed wages and expanded the ranks of the unemployed.

The haciendas were among the chief beneficiaries of the population boom. Estate owners reduced the number of their peons because it was cheaper to keep only a small permanent staff and rely on the nearby Indian villages for temporary workers. Once the harvests and livestock roundups were completed, the haciendas dismissed most of their Indian employees. Some drifted back to their villages, but many others, unable to survive there, moved to Mexico City.

The rural immigrants often first sought jobs at the huge tobacco factory, a monopoly owned by the Crown and the largest employer of labor in the city with eight thousand workers.[65] Others joined craftshops where they served for years as apprentices with little chance of advancement; enrolled in construction crews; labored as water carriers; or swelled the household staffs of the wealthy. But with the unemployment rate in the capital hovering around one third of the economically active population,[66] many of the poor became criminals and beggars. There were so many beggars competing for alms that only the more resourceful could make a living by pretending to be blind, crippled, or mutilated.[67]

To have employment was no guarantee of survival in Bourbon Mexico City. Wages lagged far behind the price of corn, the staple of the poor. Between 1721 and 1814, maize prices doubled, while working-class income rose by no more than 50 percent.[68] By the end of the colonial era, laborers needed half of their income to purchase corn.[69] But these statistics, which point to a hand-to-mouth existence in normal periods, barely hint at the truly harrowing experiences of the city's poor during years of bad harvests and famine.

Weather-induced food crises scourged central Mexico in roughly ten-year cycles throughout the 1700s. At such times, the big hacienda owners who hoarded their grain could count on prices rising from 100 to 400 percent.[70] The worst of these crises followed a frost in August 1785 that destroyed most crops around the Valley of Mexico. By early

1786, the capital and its countryside were gripped by famine, and maize prices soared to unprecedented levels. Throughout the colony that year, an estimated 300,000 people died from hunger and disease.[71]

This time, the hoarding of grain and enormous profit taking by hacienda owners aroused the ire of the highest government and Church officials. The viceroy sent patrols to the estates to search for hidden grain supplies. At the height of the 1786 famine, the doors of Mexico City's churches were plastered with an edict from the bishops:

> Our hearts are pierced by grief and shame at the sight of the clandestine iniquities that are being committed in the sale and purchase of maize and other grains and food, placing the poor in a deplorable state of hunger. Oh, how many wealthy disciples of avarice have been revealed by this calamity! . . . In the name of God and the Holy Gospel, we must unburden our conscience and tell them that they will certainly find the Gates of Heaven barred and will hear from the mouth of Jesus Christ himself this . . . terrible sentence: "I was hungry and you refused me food, so be damned by eternal fire."[72]

The effects of the crisis were made even more devastating by a pneumonia epidemic that began a year before the shortages and lasted until 1787. Priests in Mexico City complained that there was no room left in their churchyard cemeteries to bury the victims. The San Andrés Hospital, one of the largest in the capital, reported hundreds of pneumonia fatalities among its patients every week.[73]

Epidemics almost invariably accompanied famines in Bourbon Mexico City. Besides the catastrophe of 1784–87, disease and hunger jointly ravaged the capital's inhabitants during six other crises between 1736 and 1813, claiming altogether more than 120,000 lives.[74] Spanish physicians mocked the Indians' reliance on superstition and folk remedies, but offered far-fetched cures of their own. One leading doctor asserted that a smallpox epidemic in 1779 was being spread by an "infection of the air," and suggested that it be countered by setting bonfires in the streets, firing cannons, and ringing church bells.[75] Citing Spanish physicians, newspaper articles proposed the following remedy during the 1784–87 outbreak of pneumonia: "In the present epidemic of pleuritic pains which currently attacks this city, not a single patient has died who has been treated with this method. At the first instant of pain . . . [apply] a poultice prepared from a cup of bran, a small amount of horse manure, half a handful of camomile . . . a pinch of salt, and a pitcher of white wine (if not available one can use vinegar or human urine), all stirred, well mixed and boiled. . . ."[76]

So distrusting were the Indians of Spanish medicine that they sought to conceal the corpses of relatives killed by epidemics out of fear that surviving family members would be quarantined in hospitals from which they would never emerge alive. Their anxieties were well founded: in the 1761–62 epidemic of typhus and smallpox, only two thousand out of nine thousand patients survived at the Hospital Real de Indios, where "a temporary wooden annex was erected . . . not without a certain logic . . . in the cemetery."[77]

In earlier colonial times, the Spaniards had attributed the disproportionate number of Indian victims of epidemics to divine retribution for their pagan ways. In eighteenth-century Mexico City, the conventional wisdom was that the Indians and other poor had mainly themselves to blame for their fatal illnesses. This, at any rate, was the reasoning of the Protomedicato, the leading physicians' tribunal for the colony. "Here you see, Your Excellency," wrote the tribunal to the viceroy in 1785, "the cause of ruin among the poor people: their vices in eating and [drinking] intoxicating beverages; their nudity during unreasonable and intemperate weather; their use of popular medicines which some [folk healer] prescribes. . . . In large part the epidemics which are propagated in this capital result . . . [from such abuses]."[78]

It is easy to dismiss as callous the assertions by the affluent that the poor were responsible for the malnutrition that made them so vulnerable to disease. The issue of alcoholism, however, is more complex. The huge increase in drunkenness among the Indians following the Conquest has sometimes been explained as an escape from depression and moral collapse under a harsh alien rule. Drink has also often been viewed as the refuge of society's poor from boredom and despair. But accounts of everyday life in Mexico City during the Bourbon era depict an impoverished people more prone to alcoholism than almost anywhere else in the world.

In the early 1800s, Humboldt had observed the night police using carts to collect drunkards stretched out in the streets. "These Indians, who are treated like dead bodies, are carried to the principal guardhouse," he wrote. "In the morning an iron ring is put around their ankles, and they are made to clean the streets for three days. On letting them go on the fourth day, they are sure to find several of them in the course of the week."[79]

Drunks splayed themselves across the steps of the churches. They stumbled into the canals at night, and their bloated corpses were retrieved from the fetid waters the following morning. Road construction workers were said to be so inebriated that the cobblestone streets they built or repaired were too bumpy for horse-drawn carriages and wagons.[80]

Statistical estimates bear out these anecdotes. The annual consumption of pulque reached an astounding 187 gallons for every adult resident of Mexico City in the late colonial period! Approximately 13 percent of the drinking-age population was intoxicated every day—and that proportion rose steeply during religious festivals. There was one tavern for every fifty-six people over fifteen years of age.[81]

Some pulque taverns were no more than circuslike tents, their canvas tops held up by poles and ropes, and without chairs so that patrons would consume their drink quickly and move on. Other taverns were cavernous wood and adobe buildings that accommodated six hundred or more people at long tables bordered by benches. They opened as early as six in the morning to serve workers en route to the tobacco factory and the craftshops.[82] Back rooms and corners with drawn curtains were made available for gamblers or prostitutes and their clients. Fights broke out regularly and the floors were piled with broken drinking vessels.[83]

"Every pulque tavern is a forge of prostitution, robbery, homicide, violent quarrels and all the other crimes that provide business for the courts," fulminated Villarroel, the chief prosecutor, in his 1787 treatise on the afflictions of Mexico City. "They are theaters where men and women are transformed into abominable, hellish furies. . . . Here lies the cause of the appalling nudity and voluntary misery of so many unhappy men who leave their wives and children to starve by squandering [in drink] what they have earned. . . ."[84]

This was not mere hyperbole. Drinking may have consumed close to half a laborer's weekly salary. To support their alcoholism, residents sold their clothing, tools, and household effects. Occasional searches conducted by the city authorities uncovered huge caches of pawned goods in the taverns.

Alcohol was linked to almost half of the city's crimes.[85] Drunks were frequently murdered as soon as they emerged from the taverns, and their corpses were stripped of clothes and any gambling earnings. Fearing they would be raped by drunken revelers, few women ventured into the streets after dark. Burglaries, larceny, and muggings were regularly committed by men still reeling from pulque but hoping to recover the money they spent on drink before returning home.

Clerics and outraged citizens complained that the burgeoning number of unlicensed taverns were responsible for much of the increase in criminal activity. But the authorities rarely responded because tax revenues from alcohol sales were a major source of royal income, and pulque production was monopolized by a small group of elite hacienda owners with powerful influence in the colonial government. And even when municipal officials ordered a sweep against illegal taverns, they were frequently ignored by policemen, who were bribed by pulque dealers or secretly owned shares in the taverns. The poor themselves resisted any efforts to curtail their alcohol supply. According to the folklore of the day, pulque aided in the performance of strenuous physical tasks, and was a cure for an assortment of ailments. Its defenders may have been closer to the mark when they suggested that at the very least pulque was less polluted than the drinking water available to the poor.

While excessive drinking was a constant factor in lawlessness in the city, crime rates tended to mushroom during periods of high corn prices and famine. As agricultural commodities became scarcer and more expensive, a whole range of related industries contracted or shut down because of the lack of raw materials or falling purchases by poor consumers. Workers dismissed from their jobs turned to petty thefts. The agrarian crises also brought thousands of unemployed rural migrants, who accounted for almost 40 percent of all arrests made in the capital during the late colonial era.[86]

By the 1790s, the courts were trying ten thousand criminal offenders a year, a tenfold increase from two decades before.[87] In general, the justice system displayed a leniency founded on economic considerations. Because it was too expensive to house and feed large numbers of criminals, judges sought to defray the costs of justice by fining offenders instead of imprisoning them. Additional revenues were collected by expanding the use of convict labor for public works, and in textile factories, bakeries, and butcher shops.

The increased arrests of criminals did not mollify critics, who were particularly bitter in their denunciations of police corruption and incompetence. In fact, three out of every five night policemen were arrested in 1798, most of them on charges of abandoning their posts, drinking, and sleeping on duty.[88] According to a royal judge, the problem was that many "decent people"—meaning whites—refused to join the police forces because there were too many mulattoes and other castes in their ranks.[89] At times the police forces were so depleted by arrests that the army was used to help out on night patrols through the city streets. Soldiers were also made responsible for traffic control in the central district, and stood guard at the Alameda Park ensuring that beggars and thieves would not trouble the more affluent citizens.

When the army began its expansion in the 1760s, the colonial government made an effort to keep its ranks as white as possible. The early colonial prohibition against Indians bearing arms excluded them from recruitment, and no more than one third of any militia unit was supposed to be of mixed race. But some officials believed even this figure was too high. According to Antonio Bucareli, viceroy from 1771 to 1779, mestizos and mulattoes did not make suitable soldiers, and because so few whites could be recruited, "a useful, regulated militia is not possible in this kingdom."[90]

But the image of the armed forces was so bad among the poor—no matter what their race—that by the end of the colonial period the military's personnel requirements could only be met by drafting illegal immigrants, vagabonds, and petty criminals. Many people shunned government censuses out of fear that the information would be used by military recruiters. According to a colonial official, "wives described themselves as widows, mothers neglected to list their sons, sisters left off their brothers, and some families simply disappeared, hiding from house to house or moving into districts of the city that had already been counted."[91]

Poor pay, food, and health facilities impeded recruitment. Draftees lived in special dread of being sent to the Veracruz garrison, where yellow fever killed up to one third of the soldiers every year. Even by the low medical standards of the era, patient care was atrocious for military men anywhere in the colony. Soldiers who fell ill often preferred to be sent to jail on charges of shirking their military duty rather than being interned in an army hospital.

Bobbing on the surface of this sea of poverty was the fragile middle class of late colonial Mexico City. It included small and medium-sized merchants, shopkeepers, bureaucrats, priests, academics, doctors, other professionals, and master artisans—only about 15 percent of the capital's population. With few exceptions, they were of European descent. For if whiteness was no sure passport from pauperdom, it was at the very least a prerequisite for anyone wishing to join the ranks of the "gente decente"—the respectable people.

An annual income above 500 pesos was enough to place a family on the bottom fringes of respectability. This was still a quantum leap away from the four hundred or so families with fortunes of 100,000 pesos who might aspire someday to become members of the capital's elite. The middle class in fact was far more likely to sink into poverty than to rise toward affluence.

Perhaps the clearest evidence of the tenuousness of middle-class life can be found in the housing statistics of the late colonial period. Only slightly more than 1 percent of Mexico City's middle-class families owned their homes, while the rest rented their quarters from wealthy real estate holders or the Church, the greatest landlord in the capital.[92] There were few distinctly middle-class neighborhoods. The tenants of a single building could include bureaucrats, tailors, factory workers, and beggars. Even those shopkeepers and master artisans who owned their homes set aside part of their properties for their businesses and allowed apprentices to sleep on the premises—either in the shops themselves or in cramped quarters on the roof. In general, the middle class could not afford the luxury of living apart from the poor.

The prototype of the middle-class resident was the small merchant. According to a 1790 census of Mexico City, there were 1,502 people who fell into this category, by virtue of owning shops, permanent stands, or peddling wares at homes and places of employment.[93] The most typical retail establishment was the *pulpería*, or general store, selling food items, liquor, rough cloth, tools, and other dry goods. Because the customers were poor, payment was mainly in the form of copper or wood tokens issued by the shopkeeper himself, or pawned goods.

The modest income of this sort of commercial establishment made it extremely unlikely that the proprietor would ever amass enough capital to invest in the more lucrative wholesale business, or to present himself or his children as marriage partners for upper-class families. But smaller merchants expressed their social aspirations in other ways. They affected the honorific title of "don," previously reserved for upper-class men. Like the wealthy traders, they invited their cousins and nephews from Spain to join their businesses as clerks. When the militia expanded in the late colonial period and an officer's epaulettes became a mark of status among the elite, many shopkeepers hastened to purchase low-level commissions. "Sometimes these militia officers are to be seen in full uniform, and decorated with the royal order of Charles III, gravely sitting in their shops, and entering into the most trifling detail in the sale of their goods," noted Humboldt with considerable amusement.[94] The petty merchants also emulated the wealthy elite in purchasing rural properties. These were much smaller and less productive than the haciendas. Not only did they fail to give the owner a seigneurial aura, but they often were a painful drain on his finances.

The most detailed and complete portrait of the late Bourbon middle class of Mexico City was etched by José Joaquín Fernández de Lizardi in his *Periquillo Sarniento*. The literary masterpiece of the colonial era, it was a social essay masquerading as picaresque fiction. The target of Lizardi's pen was the petty bourgeoisie, its foibles, pretensions, and the short distance that separated its members from the poor majority they so abhorred. The novel follows the protagonist, nicknamed "Periquillo Sarniento" ("Itching Parrot") by his schoolmates, from his early childhood in a moderately comfortable household through a youth of dissipation that tumbles him into the lowest rungs of colonial society.

Periquillo's parents represented the two extremes of middle-class mentality. His father, Manuel Sarmiento, a hardworking but modest businessman, wished to guide his son toward the security of a trade. His mother, whose distant relatives included a few nobles, displayed the old Spanish aristocratic prejudice against manual labor:

> "My son in a trade?" Periquillo recalled his mother upbrading his father. "God forbid! What will people say if they see the son of Don Manuel Sarmiento apprenticed as a tailor, painter, silversmith or some such thing?"
>
> "What can they say?" his father retorted. "That Don Manuel Sarmiento is a decent man, but poor, and not having a fortune to leave his son, he wishes to give him an honest, useful livelihood without burdening this country with yet another lazy lout. And that means learning a trade. That is what people will say, and nothing more."[95]

But the mother won out, and Periquillo enrolled in a college to become a priest after a school chum convinced him that it was the easiest of professions as long as one did not take seriously theological strictures and vows of celibacy. Periquillo soon flunked his courses, but resolved to join a monastery as a novice monk. He lasted only six months, unable to withstand the rigors of menial labor, nights interrupted by prayer services, and the denial of secular pleasures. Using his father's death as an excuse, he quit the monastery. He embarked on a spree of partying, drinking, gambling, and whoring until he exhausted the small savings his father had left for his mother. When she died, Periquillo was enticed by a friend into a career of gambling.

Mexico City in the late Bourbon era was a gambler's paradise. There were legal and illicit gambling houses everywhere—in taverns, private homes, military clubs, even in church-run buildings. Beggars and artisans, lawyers and priests, miners and merchants were gripped by the fever. Inheritances and dowries were gambled away on cards, checkers, dice, and cockfights. Employees stole from their bosses to cover their bets, and apprentices abandoned their trades to join friends in card games in the streets. Time and again, viceroys decreed limits on bets and curfews on gambling halls. Police staged raids on illegal betting parlors. But patrons were often warned beforehand by informers or by policemen who were paid commissions by the parlor owners. No one took these occasional dragnets too seriously, for it was common knowledge that the production of playing cards was a royal monopoly, one which brought the Crown sizable revenues.[96]

From his friend, Periquillo learned that it was possible to join a card game without a cent of his own. The tables were so crowded and unruly that he was able to scoop up a handful of coins, claim them as his own, and bet them on the next game. A lucky streak was soon followed by days of constant losses, forcing Periquillo to sell his clothes and bed down wherever night overtook him. After getting caught cheating, he was beaten so severely that he was hospitalized. The ward was filthy, with inedible gruel, medicines that spoiled before they could be administered, and orderlies who stole the meager belongings of patients as soon as they died. Periquillo survived his injuries and medical care. Back in the streets, his reputation as a cheat made him a pariah in the gambling halls. A bungled attempt at burglary landed him in prison. His fall from middle-class life was now complete. Without a penny to bribe his jailers for accommodations with Spanish prisoners, Periquillo had to share a cell with the dregs of society— mulatto, mestizo, and Indian convicts.

Emerging from prison, Periquillo hired himself out to a succession of middle-class professionals, most of them as unprincipled as his former cellmates: a notary who saved his clients from jail by sending innocent Indians to serve their sentences; a barber who supplemented his income by bleeding customers with leeches; a pharmacist who peddled concoctions of egg yolk, peppermint, parsley, and scorpion oil. From a physician who employed him, Periquillo stole medicines, instruments, and books, fled the city, and settled in a provincial town where he posed as a doctor. Despite arousing the suspicions of the local priest, he had little trouble gaining the confidence of the inhabitants by spouting nonsensical Latin medical phrases, doling out quack potions, and bleeding patients when nothing else worked. His ratio of cures to fatalities was no worse than that of any qualified physician of the era. It was the advent of a plague that proved his undoing. None of his patients survived, and he was forced to flee.

Periquillo's further adventures shuttled him between the middle class and the lower depths. He served as an assistant to a venal bureaucrat. He became a grave robber. He joined a brotherhood of beggars. He clerked for an enterprising army colonel and traveled with him to Manila. Returning to Mexico, he fell in again with thieves.

The madcap odyssey ended when Periquillo underwent a religious and moral conversion. A friend, who had experienced a similar rebirth, secured him a job as administrator of a large rural estate. Periquillo married happily, had children, and after an incurable illness he died a repentant sinner and respected citizen.

The *Periquillo Sarniento* was a huge success from the moment it was published in 1816. Its many readers apparently shared Lizardi's vision of an urban colonial society in which fraud, bribery, and all other unscrupulous means were used by a beleaguered middle class to attain a modicum of wealth and preserve its social status. Honest labor offered little security in a city where professions were over-crowded, apprenticeships led no place, and personal connections alone assured advancement. This was a middle class that did not waste its time dreaming of the stratospheric society of the merchant-mining-agrarian elite. Not to slip down the precipice of poverty was ambition enough.

ELEVEN

INDEPENDENCE

At the turn of the nineteenth century, few observers would have pre-dicted that Spanish rule in Mexico was nearing its end. The prosperity of the Mexico City–based elite was at its apogee. The vast majority of the colony's six million inhabitants were undeniably poverty-stricken, but that had always been the case. It was true that Spain was militarily weak in Mexico, with a colonial army of no more than twenty-three thousand men in the early 1800s, and only a fraction of them Spanish regulars. But allegiance to the Crown depended less on coercion than on the ingrained obedience of colonial subjects, and the racial divisions between whites, Indians, and castes which hampered any opposition movement against the mother country.

Yet, in 1821, exactly three hundred years after Cortés conquered the Aztecs, Mexico gained independence. Its revolt was part of the uprisings that swept Spain's New World colonies from California to the southern tip of South America between 1808 and 1825, leaving only Cuba and Puerto Rico under Bourbon control. The Mexican struggle was the most violent of these revolutions because its indepen-dence was achieved in two phases: initially, creoles and Spaniards based in Mexico City and other urban centers banded together to suppress a widespread rebellion by Indians and mestizos in the coun-tryside; only after this threat had been quelled did the creoles throw off Spanish rule.

Creole discontent with Spain had been mounting throughout the New World since the death of Charles III in 1788. His successor, Charles

IV, had none of his father's reformist zeal, and virtually abdicated power to his wife's lover, a young guardsman named Manuel Godoy, who governed Spain as first minister during most of 1793 to 1808. Impetuous, corrupt, lacking political experience and talent, Godoy launched the country on a disastrous course in foreign affairs. Spain declared war on the French Republic in 1793, allegedly to avenge the execution of Louis XVI. The defeat of Spanish forces brought the country under French political influence, and placed Spain on the side of France in the Napoleonic Wars against Britain and its allies.

The spectacle of a cuckold king allowing an incompetent guardsman to mismanage the Spanish empire severely damaged the Crown's prestige in its colonies. The financial demands imposed on the New World domains to support Godoy's costly foreign ventures exacerbated sentiment against the mother country. Spain's need for revenues from Mexico seemed insatiable, rising to more than 20 million pesos a year by the early 1800s, about seven times the annual levies of a century before. To this burden of taxes, the Crown added a tight squeeze on credit by decreeing the expropriation of the colonial Church's wealth in late 1804 to help pay for the war effort against Britain.

Under this so-called Consolidation of Ecclesiastical Funds, the Church was required to turn over to the Royal Treasury all of the loans and properties it had accumulated from testaments, pious works, and chantries. The Crown intended to sell off the ecclesiastical lands and speed up collection of loans extended by the Church to the colonists. The Church had been by far the most important source of loans and investment capital in the colony, and was a lenient creditor, willing to roll over debts until they could be paid off by borrowers. But the Crown showed no such leniency to the thousands of debtors it inherited from the Church. Within three years after decreeing the Consolidation, Spain repatriated more than one fourth of the estimated 44 million pesos it had expropriated from ecclesiastical holdings.[1]

The Mexican elite was forced to turn over huge sums to meet its Church debts, now in the hands of the Crown. The Fagoagas, for example, had to pay 60,000 pesos. Gabriel de Yermo, a wealthy merchant and agriculturalist, owed 400,000 pesos, and the Marquis de Aguayo, the greatest hacienda owner in the colony, had to surrender more than 450,000 pesos.[2]

The very rich, of course, could survive these financial outlays. But for the less wealthy, the Consolidation decree often meant bankruptcy because the only way to meet their debts was to sell their estates, or allow them to be seized and auctioned by the royal authorities. So many haciendas and farms were suddenly placed on the market that the value of real estate declined by half.[3] A prominent bishop, Manuel Abad y Queipo, warned that as many as ten thousand hacienda owners would lose their properties if the Consolidation decree was fully implemented. And the Mexico City municipal council asserted that if mine owners were forced to repay their loans, the lack of operating capital would cause a 75 percent drop in silver production.[4]

According to Lucas Alamán, the historian who lived through this agitated period, the Consolidation decree became the bitterest grievance of the creoles against the Crown. "By causing the ruin of property-owners," he wrote, "it awakened in them the desire for emancipation."[5] And their anger was heightened when they discovered that the bulk of their money was turned over by Godoy, the Spanish first minister, to Napoleon in 1806.

It was events in Spain, however, that brought the colony closer to rebellion. In 1808, French troops invaded the mother country. Charles IV abdicated in favor of his son, Ferdinand VII, and he in turn was taken prisoner and forced to relinquish the Spanish Crown to Joseph Bonaparte, brother of Napoleon. Revolts against the French occupation army erupted in Spain, and several Spanish cities set up juntas claiming to govern the country until the invaders could be expelled and Ferdinand restored to the throne.

Throughout Spanish America, white colonists debated over who rightfully ruled the mother country and whether the viceroys were still legitimately empowered to govern while Spain was under French occupation. In Mexico City, the creoles urged the viceroy, José de Iturrigaray, to convoke a junta, led by the capital's municipal council which they controlled, to help direct the colony's affairs in Ferdinand's name. A power struggle surfaced when this course of action was opposed by the gachupínes, the Spanish-born Mexicans. Despite their small numbers—there were only fifteen thousand of them in all of Mexico—the gachupínes exercised far more political influence than the million creoles because the Crown had always considered them more loyal subjects by virtue of their Spanish birth. The gachupínes were convinced that a junta under the domination of Mexico City's municipal council would transfer power to the creoles and become a first step toward independence from Spain. They advocated instead that the colony make no political changes in its government and recognize a junta of patriotic Spaniards in Seville until Ferdinand was restored to the throne.

Out of personal ambition, Viceroy Iturrigaray leaned toward the creoles in this struggle. The viceroy was known to have diverted 72,000 pesos from the funds collected by the Consolidation decree, and had amassed a fortune of more than 2 million pesos in graft.[6] He believed that French occupation of Spain would be lengthy and that, in the meantime, Mexico would probably move toward independence. He intended to save himself and his booty by striking a deal with the creoles that would allow him to remain in power and perhaps emerge as the ruler of an independent Mexico. As a first step, he declared that his colonial government would not recognize either the French-occupied regime in Spain or any of the Spanish juntas claiming to rule the mother country in Ferdinand's name. And he further curried favor with the creoles by suspending the infamous Consolidation decree.

Fearing that the viceroy was about to form a government that would rule the colony jointly with the creoles, Gabriel de Yermo, a wealthy gachupín, led a band of three hundred clerks, merchants, and militiamen in a palace coup against Iturrigaray on September 16, 1808. The viceroy and his family were arrested, and a number of creoles suspected of advocating independence were jailed. Pedro de Garibay, an octogenarian army officer backed by the gachupínes, was named acting viceroy. He pledged Mexico's allegiance to a Spanish junta in Seville, which claimed to represent the occupied mother country in Ferdinand's absence. Garibay dispersed creole militias to the provinces, and garrisoned the capital with regular army troops. In an attempt to assuage the creole merchant and agricultural community—and gachupín businessmen as well—he rescinded or reduced taxes on meat, alcoholic beverages, and other goods.

Until this point, the struggle over Mexico's political destiny had taken place within the boundaries of the capital, more precisely within the narrow confines of elite white society, between affluent creoles and gachupínes. But with the success of the Yermo coup, some creole advocates of autonomy or independence shifted their activities to the provinces and sought a wider political following among Indians and castes. The most important focal point of these conspiracies was the mining and agricultural region about one hundred miles north of Mexico City known as the Bajío.

The Indians and castes of the Bajío had a reputation for militancy. Many of them were mineworkers and muleteers, with few ties to the more conservative, isolated life of Indian agricultural communities. The area had been the scene of violent revolts to protest the expulsion of the Jesuits in 1767. Between 1808 and 1810, the Bajío seemed to be nearing another explosion after a succession of bad harvests that sent corn prices soaring. Unable to feed the mules and horses which powered hoists and ore-crushers, many mines shut down, swelling the ranks of the jobless. By mid-1810, provincial officials were warning the viceroy that famine and unemployment were making the population vulnerable to creole conspirators. The government acted quickly to abort several plots, but failed to uncover in time the most important of these conspiracies. It was led by a priest, Miguel Hidalgo, who would go down in history as the father of Mexican Independence.

It was not so surprising that a clergyman emerged at the helm of the revolt against Spanish rule. At least four hundred priests have been identified as active participants in the Independence movement, almost all of them creoles in the bottom ranks of the Church.[7] The growing hostility displayed by the Crown toward the Church throughout the Bourbon era had especially rankled the lower clergy. Many of them had suffered economic hardships as a result of the Consolidation decree, which bankrupted their families' small haciendas and jeopardized the chantries that supplemented their tiny church incomes. These creole priests were increasingly alienated from their own hierarchy because the choicest parish and bureaucratic assignments seemed to be reserved for gachupínes. Literate and often intellectually inclined, the lower clergy devoured the tracts of radical political literature from American and French revolutionaries that were smuggled into the colony and circulated clandestinely in dog-eared volumes. While they chafed at their inability to influence the ecclesiastical and government authorities or the white colonists, the power of these priests in their small provincial parishes was uncontested. For the Indian, mestizo, and mulatto faithful, they were religious guides, arbiters of social conduct, political brokers, family counselors, and educators. So strong was the hold of the lower clergy over the peasantry that they could dictate the political allegiance of entire villages.

Miguel Hidalgo shared many of the attributes that marked the rebellious lower clergymen. He was born in 1753 to a moderately well-to-do creole family with some Indian blood in its ancestry. His father was an hacienda overseer, and eventually bought a small estate of his own. Hidalgo spent his early youth working in haciendas and learned a smattering of Indian dialects from his contact with the peasants. He appears to have chosen the priesthood as a path to social advancement, for his interests remained largely secular throughout his life. He distinguished himself as an innovative, charismatic scholar and educator during twelve years of theological and humanistic studies. In 1790, he was appointed rector of San Nicolás Obispo College in Valladolid (now Morelia, in the state of Michoacán, west of Mexico City), and his income was enough to enable him to purchase three modest haciendas and a small, unproductive mine.

For a priest, Hidalgo did not lead an exemplary personal life. He had affairs with women, and fathered at least three children. He was also an inveterate gambler, and there is some evidence that he may have embezzled college funds to cover his card debts.[8] Perhaps for this reason, he resigned as rector after only two years, and accepted the far less prestigious and rewarding post of curate in the small town of Colima. A year later, he was appointed parish priest of another small community, San Felípe, where he remained for a decade. His house became a social and cultural oasis for the provincial town. European plays and concerts and native dances were staged in his living room and patio. Books, some of them officially banned by the authorities, were read and discussed. And a certain amount of gambling and drinking also took place. Considering Mexico's rigid social hierarchy, the Hidalgo household was also unusual for the mixed guest list of creoles, Indians, and castes, men and women. The priest met at least two of his mistresses during the course of cultural activities at his house.[9]

In 1803, Hidalgo was made curate of Dolores, east of Guanajuato. With fifteen thousand inhabitants, this was a more substantial parish than the previous ones and awakened his desire to make a greater social impact. He dedicated himself to an ambitious industrialization program for Dolores, including ceramics, silkworm cultures, beehives, tanning, carpentry, harness making, blacksmithing, weaving, and vineyards. His religious activities were largely confined to early morning Mass.

There are a few tantalizing indications that as Hidalgo passed fifty years of age he was a restless, somewhat frustrated man who secretly opposed the colonial regime. Early in the 1800s, he was investigated by the Inquisition on charges that in several conversations with other priests he had questioned Church doctrine, even the infallibility of the papacy, and had attacked monarchs as despots and tyrants.[10] His sympathy for Indians and castes went further than the usual spiritual concerns expected of priests. He relished social contacts with them. And the industrialization program he launched in Dolores was avowedly aimed at reducing their dependence on Spanish and other foreign imports.

Hidalgo almost certainly nursed personal resentments against the colonial regime. A man of his scholarship, talents, and energies may well have expected more social and economic rewards. Perhaps, had he been a gachupín, he would have been appointed a bishop. As it was, after leaving the rectory of San Nicolás Obispo College, he never again occupied a post of comparable prestige and remuneration. His generosity to his parishioners—and his propensity to gamble—kept him in financial straits throughout most of his life. But he could also blame the Crown for some of his monetary problems: as a result of the Consolidation decree of 1804, Crown officials sequestered the one small hacienda he still possessed, and rented it out until they recovered the 7,000 pesos he owed on his mortgage. Hidalgo did not regain control of the property until 1810.[11]

By 1808, following the French invasion of Spain and the gachupín coup in Mexico City, Hidalgo began meeting with other creole plotters in Guanajuato and Querétaro, the two main cities of the Bajío. He was already fifty-five years old, truly elderly in an era when most people were dead by their forties. And his contemporaries portrayed him as an aged man, with round shoulders, a dark but sallowing complexion, a drooping bald head fringed with white hair. Only his lively green eyes hinted at vigor.[12] Yet among his fellow conspirators he was certainly the most radical, placing his faith on a peasant uprising that would end gachupín political influence in the colony. His chief collaborator, Ignacio de Allende, a forty-year-old militia captain from an affluent creole hacienda family, was more distrustful of the armed potential of the Indians and castes, and favored wooing creole militias over to the antigachupín cause.

During most of 1810, Hidalgo met repeatedly with his peasant following in the countryside. He ordered artisans to make spears, slings, and machetes to be distributed to Indians and castes for an uprising that was supposed to take place in Querétaro on October 2. But the conspiracy was discovered by the colonial authorities, and Hidalgo, fearing that he was about to be arrested, raised the cry for revolt in Dolores on September 16.

The insurrection for Mexican Independence had begun. Within days, the small band of Hidalgo followers mushroomed into a horde of Indians and castes. Hidalgo at first disguised his call for independence by asserting that he backed the restoration of Ferdinand VII to the Spanish throne, and wished only to overthrow the gachupín government that had taken power by the Yermo coup in Mexico City. This was merely a tactic to gain creole support, and he abandoned it when large numbers of white colonists failed to rally to his cause. But the speed with which his revolt gathered force convinced Hidalgo that he had correctly assessed the revolutionary potential of the rural poor. Marching through a succession of small towns, the priest rallied twenty-five thousand followers in less than a week. They sacked and looted Spanish properties and killed a number of Spaniards along the way.

Hidalgo's appeal to the rebels was threefold: the gachupínes would be chased out of Mexico; all tribute would be abolished; and the cult of the Virgin of Guadalupe would reign supreme. The Virgin of Guadalupe was a powerful symbol among Indians and mestizos. The cult began in the 1530s when an Indian claimed to have witnessed the apparition of the Virgin Mary on the outskirts of Mexico City, and despite opposition from white colonists, it gained the following of the majority of poor Mexicans. The Independence uprising has often been described as the war of the two virgins: the Guadalupe cult of the insurgents against the Virgin de los Remedios embraced by white colonists, especially in Mexico City.

Advancing behind banners of the Virgin of Guadalupe, Hidalgo's horde arrived on September 28, 1810, at Guanajuato, where the first great battle and massacre of the insurrection was to occur. With 66,000 inhabitants, Guanajuato was the second-largest city in Mexico. It had become the most important mining center, with a strong merchant, banking, and agricultural community dominated by gachupínes who had married creole heiresses.

Located in a canyon surrounded by hills, Guanajuato was difficult to defend, and had only a small militia garrison to face Hidalgo's huge army. The royal intendant, Juan Antonio Riaño, who governed the city and its province, had a reputation as an able, fair-minded administrator, but he was no military genius. Instead of leading a retreat from the city, Riaño chose to cloister his militia, the leading white families, and himself in the massive, fortresslike public granary of Guanajuato, the Alhóndiga de Granaditas, and gamble that the rebels could be held off until the gachupín or royalist government in Mexico City sent reinforcements.

It was a catastrophic blunder. The spectacle of the elite white community seeking only its own safety and hoarding all weapons, food, and treasure in the granary infuriated Guanajuato's other inhabitants. Many of them rallied to the rebels pouring down from the hills. Unleashing a barrage of stones, Hidalgo's followers routed the militia from the ramparts of the granary. In less than five hours, the horde of Indians and castes battered into the Alhóndiga and slaughtered some three hundred creoles and gachupínes, including Riaño.

According to the historian Alamán, who witnessed the attack and its aftermath, "those who surrendered were vainly begging for mercy from their victors, pleading on their knees for their lives." A few militiamen managed to escape by stripping off their uniforms and joining the mob. Inside the Alhóndiga, there were nude cadavers everywhere, "half buried under corn and money that had been scattered about, and all was dripping with blood. The looters fought over the booty even killing each other."[13] Throughout the night, rebels pillaged the houses and shops owned by whites. The main plaza and streets were strewn with furniture fragments, the discarded remnants from the shelves of the stores, and broken liquor jugs. Indians, who by law were forbidden to wear European costumes, danced around bonfires dressed in the pettycoats, capes, embroidered uniforms, and top hats they had looted from the homes of the wealthy. Whites who had not barricaded themselves in the granary were hunted down by the insurgents. Allende, Hidalgo's chief lieutenant, galloped through the rebel ranks, even hacking away at his own men with a saber, in an effort to rescue some gachupínes and creoles. Hidalgo allowed two days to go by before ordering an end to the pillaging, but the havoc ceased only after the mobs had exhausted themselves.

Guanajuato was to be a Pyrrhic victory for Hidalgo. Any chance of gaining creole support for his revolution was shattered. Here was the centuries-old nightmare of the white colonists finally come to life: Indians and castes had exploded in a racial revolt against their Spanish conquerors. Overnight, a huge coalition formed against Hidalgo's insurrectionists. Landowners, merchants, miners, artisans, most clergymen, all those who felt threatened by the dark-skinned insurgents, joined together to suppress their revolt. The struggle between creoles and gachupínes was temporarily set aside. With few exceptions, the creoles—even those who had campaigned for autonomy—united behind the royalist cause. The contrast between the American Independence war and the first stage of the Mexican insurgency is startling. The English used their own troops and German mercenaries to battle the revolutionaries. The Spaniards depended almost entirely on Mexican-born soldiers and militias to combat the insurgents—less than 5 percent of the royalist army was Spaniard.[14] Only a few months after the Guanajuato massacre, the leading royalist general, Felix Calleja, candidly asserted that Spain was holding on to Mexico thanks to the backlash that the Hidalgo revolt had provoked by its excesses: "Natives and even the Europeans themselves are convinced of the advantages which would result from an independent government; and if the absurd insurrection of Hidalgo had been built upon this base, I should think it would have suffered very little opposition."[15]

But the ease with which Hidalgo had conquered Guanajuato made the priest euphoric. Independence for the colony would be achieved in a matter of weeks, he predicted. His still-growing army quickly occupied Valladolid—the city where he had studied and risen to college rector before resigning under a cloud. With the west now secured, Hidalgo advanced toward Mexico City with an unwieldy mass that had swelled to eighty thousand people—the largest army assembled in Mexico since the Aztec era.

Only twenty-five hundred royalist government troops blocked the insurgents' entry into the capital. But these were disciplined soldiers ably commanded and backed by artillery. On October 30, 1810, the armies clashed at Monte de las Cruces, a mountainous pass on the city's western outskirts. The battle lasted most of the day, and at nightfall, the royalist troops, after losing almost half their forces, retreated toward the capital. But they had killed about two thousand rebels, wounded many thousands more, and caused even larger numbers to desert. The following day, Hidalgo led his depleted force a few more miles toward the city, and then, after meeting continued royalist resistance, abandoned his offensive and began to withdraw.

Hidalgo himself later explained that the Battle of Las Cruces had exhausted his army's ammunition. But there were also other reasons that led to his retreat. For the first time, his movement was failing to gain new adherents. The Indians and castes in the Valley of Mexico were not joining his uprising. Moreover, Hidalgo and his lieutenants had made no provisions for food and water for their huge force of rebels. Lacking any military training or battlefield leadership, many of his followers were demoralized by the artillery and musket fire they had encountered. And in the north, a royalist army under the command of General Calleja had already taken Querétaro from the insurgents and was advancing toward Mexico City.

Whatever the reasons, the retreat from the outskirts of the capital was the turning point of Hidalgo's revolt. After Las Cruces, the rebels suffered an almost uninterrupted string of defeats in skirmishes and major battles. As he fled with his forces from the royalist troops, Hidalgo no longer even attempted to restrain his followers' murderous hatred of Europeans—whether gachupín or creole. In a telling incident in early November, a rebel leader informed Hidalgo: "Most excellent Señor, the Indians are very much out of control. On passing through the village of San Felípe, I found three Europeans and a creole torn to pieces, all of whom [had] safe-conduct papers from Your Excellency, and [the Indians] would not permit the priest to bury them. If these excesses are not punished . . . there will be no one to contain them."

But Hidalgo said he had no intention of castigating the Indians because "we have no other arms but theirs with which to defend ourselves, and if we begin to punish them, we shall not find them when we need them."[16] Increasingly, his rhetoric took on shrill antigachupín overtones. In a speech delivered in Guadalajara in late 1810, he denounced the Spaniards as "Catholics only by political expediency, for their real god is money. . . . Can such unnatural men who have broken the closest bonds of blood . . . abandoning their fathers, brothers, wives, even their own children be capable of any human feelings?"[17]

Bishop Abad y Queipo estimated that two thousand gachupínes were slaughtered in the Hidalgo revolt,[18] and probably even more creoles were killed by Indians and castes who made no distinction between whites. But royalist forces retaliated with greater atrocities. Whenever a town or city was recaptured by the royalists, they executed suspected rebel sympathizers in numbers that often exceeded gachupín and creole victims. The reprisals were much worse in the countryside, where royalist troops burned down villages and massacred entire families. Of the hundreds of thousands of fatalities during the long independence struggle, most were Indians and castes accused of rebel loyalties.

Hidalgo did not live to see the worst of the revolution's devastation. He was captured along with his chief collaborator, Allende, while fleeing from royalist troops in northern Mexico on March 21, 1811, barely six months after beginning his revolt in Dolores. In a confession whose authenticity has long been challenged by Mexican nationalists, Hidalgo abjured his revolt in the following terms:

"Be my witnesses all ye who have shared the excesses into which I have plunged blind and ungrateful! I have offended the Almighty, the Sovereign, Europeans and American-born. . . . I desire and beg that my death . . . be a convincing plea for the instant cessation of the insurrection."[19]

The priest was first brought to trial by the Inquisition, which condemned him as a heretic and ordered him defrocked. He was then convicted of sedition by a royalist court convoked in Chihuahua where he was being held a prisoner. On July 30, 1811, he was shot and decapitated. The heads of Hidalgo, Allende, and two other revolutionary leaders were transported to Guanajuato, and hung for a decade in metal cages on the corners of the same granary that had been stormed by the Indian and caste mobs.

With Hidalgo's death, the nature of the insurgency changed. No longer did the royalist government face disorderly hordes gaining size and force like cyclones sweeping through the countryside. Instead, there were guerrilla bands that only occasionally came together in regiment size to engage government troops in battle. The leader of this phase, which eventually proved more threatening to the royalists than the chaotic Hidalgo revolt, was another priest, José María Morelos.

Morelos came from an even humbler family background than Hidalgo. His father was a mestizo carpenter who was reclassified as white after repeatedly petitioning the courts. Morelos himself never claimed to be a pure-blooded creole. He was short and heavyset, with dark brown skin, thick lips, and a face and hands scarred by the accidents of physical labor. He was born in Valladolid in 1765. As a youth, he worked at his uncle's hacienda, and then became a muleteer on the famed "China Road," transporting to Mexico City the Oriental fineries unloaded by the Manila Galleons at Acapulco. He was twenty-five when he began to study for priesthood, first at San Nicolás Obispo College where Hidalgo was rector, and then at the Royal University in Mexico City. For sixteen years, he petitioned the courts for a chantry—a church fund—endowed by one of his deceased relatives. But it was awarded to a succession of other family members, perhaps because their complexion was whiter than his. Despite his sterling university credentials, he could obtain nothing better than a parish in a shabby small community of Michoacán, in the malaria-infested subtropical zone inland from the Pacific coast known as the *tierra caliente* or "hot country." From 1793 to 1810, he was a village priest, earning a monthly salary of about 24 pesos, which he later supplemented with the income from a small hacienda bought with money he inherited.[20]

There is not the scantiest evidence of Morelos's involvement in political controversy during these seventeen years spent in rural parishes. His correspondence with his ecclesiastical superiors mentions only his complaints about lazy, drunken peasants who declined to contribute to his small clerical fees, or his attempts to reassign the more distant members of his flock to a more accessible parish. There are records also that Morelos had illegitimate children by at least three different women.

And yet this anonymous, provincial, lackluster existence ended suddenly at age forty-five as soon as Morelos received news of the revolt led by Hidalgo. Perhaps he remembered the older priest's magnetism during the days when Hidalgo was rector at San Nicolás Obispo College. Or perhaps Hidalgo's decision to abruptly abandon a dissatisfying life as a lowly clergyman struck a common chord. Morelos made his way to Valladolid in October 1810 shortly after the insurrectionists occupied the city, and offered his services as a chaplain to Hidalgo. The rebel leader suggested instead that Morelos accept a military commission and form an insurgent force to conquer the Pacific coast, including Acapulco. Within three weeks after returning to his parish, Morelos had gathered an army of more than two thousand Indians and castes, and was laying siege to Acapulco.

From the beginning, Morelos rejected Hidalgo's faith in a huge, undisciplined horde, and instead became an advocate of guerrilla tactics. He split his two thousand well-drilled irregulars into small units that could strike quickly, harass royalist troops, disrupt highway traffic, or come together as battalions to attack larger garrisons.

Not only was he a more effective military leader than Hidalgo, he also had a better grasp of politics and economics. By November 1810, Morelos proclaimed a revolutionary program that called for independence and the abolition of the caste system, slavery, and tribute. He would later champion the distribution of land to peasants. In areas under the influence of his guerrillas, royal taxes continued to be collected, but were diverted to the revolutionary cause. He issued copper coins to be used as currency and redeemable at face value in gold or silver if the insurgency triumphed. And he even created a mail network in the zone he controlled.[21]

Initially, Morelos also made an effort to enlist creole support, promising to safeguard the property of white Mexicans and to grant them high civil and military posts if they rallied to his side. In a communiqué he released in 1811, he made an appeal to the creoles that stood in remarkable contrast to Hidalgo's virulent statements of a year before:

"The whites are the principal representatives of the kingdom, and they were the first to take up arms in defense of the Indians and other castes. . . . Therefore the whites ought to be the object of our gratitude and not of the hatred which some people are stirring up against them. . . . It is not our system to proceed against the rich, much less against the rich creoles. Let no one dare to attack their property, no matter how rich they are."[22]

But it was already too late to convert the creoles to the revolutionary cause. The cycle of massacres which began with the storming of the Guanajuato granary had escalated on both sides. And by 1814, Morelos himself, responding to royalist atrocities, was ordering the execution of all prisoners and the devastation of haciendas and villages loyal to the Mexico City government. Through guerrilla tactics, Morelos was able to harass the government for five years. But in 1815, while moving his units eastward in an attempt to cut the road between Mexico City and Veracruz, he was captured and executed on the outskirts of the capital. The insurgency would last for six more years, but at a much lower level of hostilities, with small rebel bands operating in isolated regions of the colony.

From the moment that the rural insurrection of Indians and castes erupted, Mexico City became the center of royalist reaction. A majority of creoles continued to resent Spanish rule, but their first priority was to crush the insurgency, which they viewed as a threat to all white colonists—creole and gachupín alike. And they were willing to rally around a strong, decisive viceroy with bona fide credentials from Spain.

In Spain, the junta opposing the French occupation fled Napoleon's forces from Seville to Cádiz in 1810, and renamed itself the Regency. Creoles and gachupínes in Mexico City agreed to recognize the Regency as the sovereign power in Spain, and accepted a new viceroy appointed by the Cádiz government to rule the colony. He was Francisco Javier Venegas, a determined official with considerable military and political experience.

Venegas arrived in Mexico City only two days before the Hidalgo revolt began, and quickly organized a broadly based front against the insurrection. Royalist propaganda churned out thousands of pamphlets asserting that atrocities were being indiscriminately committed by Hidalgo's forces against Indians and castes as well as whites. The Church was also enlisted in the royalist cause. The archbishop announced the excommunication of Hidalgo and his lieutenants, and clergymen were dispatched throughout the capital and its outskirts to portray the insurgent revolt as a satanic maelstrom. So sudden and rapid was Hidalgo's advance on Mexico City that he had no time for a propaganda campaign of his own aimed at the Indians and castes in the Valley of Mexico. The only news of the revolt that reached residents of the capital and its suburbs were the royalist pronouncements. At the very least, Venegas's propaganda succeeded in securing the neutrality of the lower classes as the rebel army approached Mexico City. Peasants either fled the insurgents or confined themselves to their villages, rejecting Hidalgo's pleas for their support.

The blunting of the insurgent attack by the small royalist army at the Battle of Las Cruces was seized upon by the viceroy and Church hierarchy as a divine omen. The Virgin de los Remedios—whose effigy was carried by the conquistadores in their battles against the Aztecs— became Mexico City's symbol of resistance to the Hidalgo forces and their Guadalupe cult. Nuns in the capital decorated the statue of the "royalist" Virgin with a general's baton and placed a sable in the hands of the infant Jesus at her side. A day after the clash at Las Cruces, the statue of armed mother and child was paraded through Mexico City and hailed as the protector of the royalist troops. On the first anniversary of the battle, a ranking clergyman in the capital exalted the Virgin de los Remedios with Homeric oratory:

"Mary blinded the innumerable bandits who lusting after the opulent riches of Mexico City hurled themselves recklessly on the few bayonets that opposed them. . . . It was Mary who blew bullets, spears and rocks off course. . . . It was Mary who personally took charge as general of the army, inspiring the leaders . . . giving courage to the faint-hearted, making our columns unbreechable, directing and sustaining our fire. . . ."[23]

Although the capital escaped the military devastation of the countryside and other cities, it remained under great strains. By 1811, the population rose by more than a quarter as refugees poured in from the provinces. Agricultural production fell in the war-torn countryside and rebel bands waylaid convoys en route to Mexico City, resulting in serious food shortages. The great merchant-landowners, displaying their usual opportunism, tried to salvage their haciendas and harvests by paying revolutionary "taxes" to the rebels. And in the city, they sold their produce on the black market, evading price controls and official distribution channels set up by the viceroy.

The combined effects of the rural insurrection and tax evasion reduced Mexico City's public revenues by two thirds, with disastrous consequences for urban services.[24] Garbage removal and street cleaning ceased. Sewage ditches and canals clogged, and then overflowed during the rainy season, flooding the capital. Packs of hungry dogs roamed the streets, invading homes and gardens, attacking livestock and people, even digging up corpses in the cemeteries. Neighborhood vigilante bands joined with policemen to slaughter the wild mongrels with guns, swords, staves, and spears.[25]

By 1813, famine, flooding, and filth had set the stage for another of the cyclical epidemics. Mysterious fevers—possibly typhus—afflicted half of the inhabitants. More than 20,000 people died, and an equal number fled the city in terror of disease, cutting down the population to about 124,000 by the end of the year.[26]

As usual, it was the poor who bore the brunt of famine and disease. But the attitude of the creoles and gachupínes was more sympathetic than during previous epidemics. There were few, if any, comments this time by the white elite blaming the slovenly habits and vices of the poor for their fatal illnesses. The fear that disease and hunger might turn the lower class toward the rural insurgents encouraged a more benevolent attitude. Dr. Luis José Montaña, a leading physician, appealed to upper-class humanitarianism by evoking the specter of a popular revolt. "Although the lower class, because of its apathy and for other reasons, views with equanimity the disturbances in the kingdom, or feels that these are only passing disorders, it is extremely sensitive to to its own problems and disasters," he wrote in a report to the city authorities recommending that charitable societies be established to aid the poor.[27] With the city virtually bankrupt, wealthy citizens and the Church responded by distributing food, medicine, and blankets in the slums. But the 1813 fevers became the most calamitous epidemic to sweep the capital in the nineteenth century.

Mexico City's poor were also burdened by the rising demands of military conscription. It was no longer possible to evade the draft by temporarily changing domiciles, or lying to the census takers as many residents had done during peacetime. Royalist officials barged into huts late at night or in the hours before dawn, and apprehended young men until conscription quotas were met. Exemptions from military service were often ignored, as letters addressed to the viceroy by destitute families clearly indicate. Juliana Zamudio, for example, wrote the viceroy that although one of her sons was already killed in battle, her other boy had not been allowed to return home to support her and her daughters. Ana María Hernández, a widow, complained that her son was taken by the army despite the fact that he was the only source of income for the family. And María Rita Camacho, who lost three of her four sons in the war, begged that the surviving boy be sent home. He had been sentenced to military service for refusing to marry an Indian woman he had seduced, and he remained in the army because his family's parish priest informed the viceroy that he was morally unworthy of clemency for his sexual transgression.[28]

In spite of all these vicissitudes, Mexico City's poor displayed steadfast loyalty to the government. The authorities, in fact, had more reason to complain about a small contingent of affluent creole radicals who were willing to betray their own social class to aid the rebel cause. Perhaps the most dismaying case encountered by the royalist government involved Leona Vicario, a young creole woman of impeccable social standing, who passed on intelligence to the insurgents for several years.

Her mother was a creole from northern Mexico, and her father was a gachupín who amassed a considerable fortune in commerce within a few years after settling in the capital. Leona, born in 1789, was their only child. When they died during her adolescence, she moved into the household of her uncle, Agustín Pomposo, a successful lawyer. There was almost nothing unconventional about her early life. She was somewhat of a spendthrift, and probably would have wasted her inheritance within a few years if her uncle had not limited her expenses. Surrounded by five or six personal servants, she spent her day like other upper-class creole women: most of the morning was occupied by dressing and makeup, followed by a long stroll with chaperons through the Alameda Park, and leisurely forays into the luxury shops under the arcades of the Plaza Mayor; after lunch at home, she had her siesta until sundown; then, after another time-consuming change of clothes and cosmetic applications, she was chaperoned to the theater or a ball, returning home close to midnight. Only her educational background set her apart from her friends. In the early 1800s, Mexico City supported only six schools with a total of 759 students for the 8,763 girls between the ages of eight and sixteen.[29] Even wealthy young women rarely learned more than rudimentary reading and writing. But Leona, instructed by private tutors, became an avid reader of politics, philosophy, and science while still a teenager.

Robustly handsome, with a broad forehead and large, luminous black eyes, she did not lack suitors. Before her nineteenth birthday, she became engaged to Octaviano de Obregón, son of the millionaire miner and merchant, Ignacio de Obregón. The elder Obregón had moved from his northern province to Mexico City in hopes of conquering the capital's high society. Despite earning the contempt of some of his peers for his late-blooming social ambitions, he succeeded beyond his expectations. He became a confidant of Viceroy Iturrigaray, reportedly by contributing generous bribes to that venal official, and was present so often at the palace that he was rumored to be the vicereine's lover. His close relations to the viceroy proved to be his undoing. When Iturrigaray was deposed in 1808 by gachupín plotters,

Ignacio de Obregón had to flee for his life. He broke a leg while jumping from the balcony of his mansion to escape the gachupín militias who had come to arrest him, and he hobbled back to his provincial home where he died a few months later. His son Octaviano, also fearing arrest, fled the colony to Spain, leaving behind his fiancée, Leona.

The whole affair awoke in Leona a strong resentment of the gachupínes and Spanish rule, and led to some violent quarrels with her uncle and protector, Pomposo, who was a diehard royalist. When news of Hidalgo's revolt first reached the capital, she stood on her balcony and shouted out, "Long live my brothers the insurgents!" until Pomposo dragged her back indoors.[30] She soon found a like-minded spirit in her uncle's law firm, Andrés Quintana Roo, a young lawyer, poet, and patriot. They fell in love, but when Quintana Roo asked Pomposo to annul her engagement to Octaviano de Obregón, her uncle refused. Quintana Roo then left Mexico City and joined the rural insurgent movement in Oaxaca under Morelos.

Leona assured her uncle that her ardor for Quintana Roo and the revolution had cooled. But she had in fact become an active conspirator for the rebel cause—writing voluminous letters to the insurgent leaders on political and military developments in Mexico City, using her inheritance to purchase arms for the rural guerrillas, and recruiting upper-class creole youths for the rebel armies. She may have taken a perverse delight in convincing her uncle's son to run off to join the insurgents. Pomposo never suspected her role, nor did he know about her other conspiratorial activities. He had become one of the leading propagandists for the royalist cause, and his own thoughts on his son's defection were perhaps revealed in a passage of a pamphlet he wrote to extol a woman who had denounced her rebel husband to the police: "May she be justly rewarded, for she deserves the gratitude of us all."[31]

It was Pomposo's reputation as a rabid monarchist that kept Leona above the suspicions of the authorities. His home was a meeting place for vice-regal officials and royalist officers, who were charmed by his attractive niece and spoke freely in her presence about their war efforts.

Her true sympathies were finally discovered in 1813 when rebel couriers were arrested with a packet of her letters. Warned in time by a rebel agent, Leona fled to a small village west of the capital. Pomposo tracked her down and convinced her to return to Mexico City with assurances that the authorities would not prosecute her. But once she gave herself up, Pomposo had her incarcerated in the Belén women's shelter and notified the viceroy. Belén was the notorious center established by the Church in the late 1600s to exorcise women who were believed to be possessed by demons. And Pomposo had no doubt that his niece was a satanic agent. Repeatedly interrogated by the royal justices, Leona refused to reveal anything about her conspiratorial role or the insurgent leaders. A few days before she was about to be brought to trial—and almost certain execution—she was rescued by a rebel band that broke into Belén. After hiding in a Mexico City slum for several weeks, she disguised herself as a muleteer and fled to Oaxaca, where she joined Quintana Roo. They were married and survived clandestinely for several years until they were granted amnesty near the end of the war.

While most creoles were shocked by Leona Vicario's radicalism, they did favor milder versions of autonomy from Spanish rule even at the height of the rural insurrection. They had an opportunity to demonstrate their feelings when the Regency in Cádiz, which claimed to govern Spain in spite of the French occupation, called for newly elected municipal councils in the colonies that would share power with the viceroys. In Mexico City, elections were held in 1812 and produced an overwhelming victory for the creoles. Not a single gachupín candidate was elected. Viceroy Venegas annulled the results, claiming widespread irregularities in the voting. Calleja, the royalist general who succeeded him as viceroy in 1813, was just as high-handed as Venegas but more politically astute. While allowing the new municipal council monopolized by creoles to be convoked, Calleja simply ignored any of its initiatives that interfered with his rule. The viceroy was confident that the creoles would do little more than protest, as long as the war against the rural insurgents remained their priority.

Both creoles and gachupínes were excited by dramatic news of the expulsion of the French occupation army from Spain in late 1813. Ferdinand was released by Napoleon and returned to Spain to claim the Crown in March 1814. By concealing his political beliefs during his long French captivity, Ferdinand had gathered the support of virtually all factions in Spain and its colonies (excepting, of course, the insurgents). During his absence, the liberal-minded Regency and Cortes (parliament) had doggedly resisted the French occupation from their refuge in Cádiz and had promulgated a liberal constitution which curtailed the powers of the Spanish monarchy. Despite this action, the Regency and Cortes claimed to be loyal to Ferdinand, and he himself did not raise any objections to the new constitution while he remained a prisoner of Napoleon. But as soon as he returned to Spain and took the throne, Ferdinand revealed himself an unrepentant absolutist. He annulled the liberal constitution and dissolved the Regency and the Cortes.

In Mexico City, Calleja and his gachupín supporters were delighted by this conservative turn of events in the mother country. The viceroy had tolerated the elected municipal council as a necessary evil imposed on him by misguided liberals in Spain. Now, with the backing of King Ferdinand, he removed all the autonomy-minded members of the Mexico City municipal council and replaced them with more compliant, conservative creoles and gachupínes. Calleja also arrested hundreds of creoles who had advocated autonomy too fervently. The viceroy met little resistance from creole dissidents. Like the liberals in Spain, they had gambled that they could advance their aims by wholeheartedly backing Ferdinand's return to the Spanish throne. Now that he had restored an authoritarian monarchy both at home and in the colonies, they had no alternative but to comply or be declared in open rebellion.

By 1816, the royalist cause in Mexico was triumphant. Hidalgo and Morelos were dead. The rural insurgency was essentially crushed. His mission accomplished to near perfection, Calleja stepped down as viceroy and set sail for Spain. But perceptive as ever, he warned his successors in a farewell letter that neither victory in the battlefields of the countryside nor in the political intrigues of Mexico City could justify a complacent attitude. There would always be, he asserted, "a predisposition of the colonies to emerge from dependence on [Spain] should an opportunity arise."[32]

Ironically, Spain itself created the opportunity for Mexican Independence that the former viceroy had feared. On January 1, 1820, an expeditionary force which Calleja was organizing in Spain against rebels in the South American colonies mutinied, and its leaders formed a junta that proclaimed the restoration of the liberal constitution. The junta again sharply limited Ferdinand's power, and restricted the Church's right to own property. The Spanish parliament then decreed a series of reforms for Mexico and the other colonies: extension of suffrage to everyone except Indians and castes, an end to the most oppressive labor laws, and the abolition of the entails by which wealthy colonists had protected their estates for their heirs.

Though no doubt aimed at preserving Spain's empire by creating a more enlightened basis for colonial rule, the new regime's actions backfired disastrously. In Mexico, the creole elite and Church hierarchy were appalled by the measures. They had sided with the royalist cause precisely because they wished to safeguard their economic and social privileges from the lower-class insurgents. For more than three decades, their faith had been severely challenged by the unpredictable shifts in Spain: the incompetence of Charles IV and his first minister, Godoy; the Consolidation decree and the increasing tax burden; the Napoleonic invasion; the liberal Regency and parliament in Cádiz; the return of absolutism with the accession of Ferdinand to the throne; and finally, a swing back to even more radical liberalism and a constitutional monarchy.

Through all this turbulence in the mother country, the creoles viewed themselves as the real saviors of the colony. It was they who had maintained social order. It was not a Spanish expeditionary force, but rather a Mexican army staffed mainly by creole officers that had fought Hidalgo's hordes and Morelos's guerrillas. And now, Spain was repudiating the creoles' aristocratic rights. The liberal Spanish regime was inadvertently pushing them to embrace independence in order to preserve their privileges. They only needed a leader—and they soon found him in Agustín de Iturbide, a creole military officer and landowner with strong ties to the Church hierarchy.

Iturbide was born in Valladolid in 1783. His mother was a creole and his gachupín father was an hacienda owner, with a fortune of more than 100,000 pesos. As a youth, Iturbide became an officer in the militia, the new vehicle of social advancement for status-conscious creoles. During the insurgency, he participated in more than forty military engagements, including key battles against Hidalgo and Morelos. After rebels ransacked his father's hacienda, Iturbide became notorious for executing rebel prisoners—butchering one hundred fifty insurgents seized during one battle in 1812, and several hundred more in another confrontation a year later. It was said that upon capturing a rebel priest whom he had known as a boy, Iturbide chatted amiably with him over a cup of chocolate and then casually informed him that he would be shot within two hours.[33]

By 1813, Iturbide's military exploits had earned him a promotion to colonel and command of the army in Guanajuato. But Iturbide complained that he was still not receiving the advancement and honors he deserved, and felt that he was being slighted because he was a creole. His resentment grew when he was forced to resign his command in Guanajuato in 1816 after numerous denunciations from the local citizenry that he was failing to prevent both his own troops and rebel bands from looting and burning haciendas and other properties. He himself was accused of having amassed a personal fortune through nebulous commercial operations.

Iturbide spent the next four years in Mexico City. Handsome, elegant, and charming, he was extremely popular with the creole elite, especially the women, and became notorious for his extramarital relationships and free-spending habits. He was said to have falsely accused his wife of infidelity and incarcerated her in a convent so that he could pursue his affair with an aristocratic creole beauty. According to the historian Alamán, who knew him well, Iturbide "surrendered without restraint to the dissipations of the capital. . . . He spent in lavish fashion the fortune he had made in [Guanajuato], and soon found himself in severe financial straits. . . ."[34] Another acquaintance asserted that the colonel had "squandered all [his] ill-gotten riches . . . and was reduced to such a decadent condition that he was miraculously transformed from a sanguinary royalist into an ardent patriot."[35] Iturbide's growing disillusionment with the royalist cause may also have been the result of his failure to receive complete official exoneration of the charges against him in Guanajuato, despite his strenuous attempts to clear his name.

Iturbide began to fraternize with creole advocates of independence. He claimed that he did not object to the insurgents' cause, only to their impolitic strategy. To succeed, he asserted, the Independence movement would have to broaden its base. He went about explaining his separatist notions to wealthy creoles, to clergymen who were alienated by the attack made on the Church by the liberal Spanish regime in 1820, and especially, to creole military officers with whom he still enjoyed extensive contacts. Iturbide must have been circumspect enough not to arouse the suspicions of the royalist government, because in 1820 he was recalled to active duty and appointed commander of the military district stretching from Taxco to Acapulco, the only region where rebel activity remained significant. Iturbide's orders were to crush the insurgents, led by Vicente Guerrero, a survivor from the Morelos movement, or to make them accept a general pardon, in keeping with Spain's new policy to promote reconciliation with rebels everywhere in the New World.

Iturbide now put into effect a devious political stratagem aimed at forging an Independence movement in the provinces without the knowledge of the royalist government in Mexico City. Instead of simply offering Guerrero an amnesty, he suggested that the rebel leader join forces with him and promote the independence of Mexico. Iturbide sent confidential letters to military commanders in garrisons throughout central Mexico urging them to back his independence project. And he corresponded with key clergymen, arguing that separatism from Spain was the best way to ensure the economic survival of the Church in Mexico. Meanwhile, he lulled the viceroy by informing him that Guerrero would soon lay down his arms and accept a pardon. The viceroy, not suspecting any duplicity, communicated his satisfaction and asked only that Guerrero be made to agree to a public oath of loyalty to Spain.

In February 1821, Guerrero met Iturbide at the village of Iguala, and signed the independence proposal put forth by the royalist commander. Known as the Plan of Iguala, its most important articles were the following:

- Mexico would be an independent nation.
- Roman Catholicism would be the religion of the country.
- No distinctions would be made between Mexicans and those inhabitants born in Spain.
- The caste system and slavery—already a dwindling institution—would be abolished.
- The government would be a constitutional monarchy under Ferdinand VII. If he or another member of his family declined to come to Mexico to take up the throne, then the Crown would be offered to another European royal household. In the meantime, Mexico would be governed by a junta headed by the viceroy.

This last article was a ploy aimed at gathering support for the Independence movement even from the most conservative creoles, who could not imagine living under a political system that was not a monarchy. In reality, nobody in Mexico believed that Ferdinand or any member of his family would forsake Spain to live and rule in the New World. Nor was it likely that the Crown of Mexico would be offered to other European royalty. The alternative then would be that an independent Mexico would chose its own leader.

The viceroy, Juan Ruíz de Apodaca, was staggered by the news of the Iguala Plan, and immediately denounced Iturbide as a "perfidious and ungrateful commander."[36] But faced with conflicting advice from his officers, the viceroy hesitated for many weeks before raising an expeditionary force against Iturbide. The delay allowed Iturbide to maintain the initiative.

He was prescient enough to realize that the last eleven years of insurrection had created an ambitious new elite in the colony—the creole military officers. The army and militia in Mexico had grown spectacularly, from less than thirty thousand troops in 1810 on the eve of the insurgency to more than eighty-five thousand by 1821. For the most part, they were commanded by creoles who, like himself, were dissatisfied with the rewards they had received from Spain for their services. Because the rebels conducted a highly mobile guerrilla war, the royalist forces had been decentralized into several regional armies whose commanders had great leeway both politically and militarily. While this proved to be an excellent strategy to crush insurgent threats, it also gave the regional commanders a taste for political power, a certain aloofness to vice-regal guidance, and an opportunity to enrich themselves in local commerce. For all his other failings, Iturbide instinctively understood the mentality of his fellow commanders. If he could win them over, he could then march on Mexico City with an army far larger than the garrison defending the capital.

Advancing through the provinces northwest of Mexico City, Iturbide's small force of a few thousand men gathered adherents with a speed reminiscent of Hidalgo's snowballing movement—except these men were disciplined, experienced soldiers. Virtually without firing a shot, Iturbide took control of the garrisons in Valladolid, Guadalajara, and Querétaro, bringing more than twenty-five thousand troops under his command. And not only soldiers responded to his call for independence. Clergymen, hacienda owners, merchants, even peasants, mineworkers, and artisans made voluntary contributions to sustain his army. In Guanajuato, from the ramparts of their convents, nuns tossed coins and rosaries to deserters from the royalist army, hailing them as champions of the Church.

In July 1821, as Iturbide was preparing to advance on Mexico City, Viceroy Apodaca turned over power to a hard-line royalist officer, Marshal Francisco Novella. Almost at the same time, General Juan O'Donojú, a hero of the war against the French, arrived in the port of Veracruz with orders from Spain to take military and political control of Mexico. Iturbide postponed his plan to besiege Mexico City, and decided instead to deal first with O'Donojú. Iturbide's forces encircled Veracruz, and forced O'Donojú into negotiations. Convinced that Spain's position in the colony was hopeless, he agreed to sign a treaty recognizing Mexico's independence and endorsing the main provisions of the Iguala Plan.

Back in Mexico City, Marshal Novella's position now became untenable: Spain's own emissary had granted independence to the colony. On September 7, he accepted an armistice with Iturbide. And on

September 27, Iturbide took control of Mexico City. The outpouring for the man acclaimed as Mexico's liberator was tumultuous. From the balcony of the vice-regal palace, with O'Donojú at his side, Iturbide reviewed sixteen thousand troops parading through the Plaza Mayor as salvos of artillery and rockets exploded in the sky. Then, making his way to the Cathedral for a Te Deum, the liberator was showered with roses from the rooftops.

To govern Mexico, Iturbide created a junta of thirty-eight men, including the most notable members of the Mexico City creole elite, and was himself appointed president. In theory, at least, the possibility still remained that Ferdinand VII or some other member of the royal household might arrive to assume the throne of Mexico, in keeping with the Plan of Iguala. But predictably, the Spanish regime repudiated the treaty signed between Iturbide and O'Donojú as soon as it received a copy of the document in early 1822.

Iturbide, as devious as ever, now went through the motions of convoking a constitutional congress to determine the newly indepen-dent nation's form of government. But when this legislature proved to be insufficiently docile, especially by suggesting that Iturbide's power base, the army, be sharply reduced, the liberator threatened to resign. On May 18, 1822, in what appears to have been a well-orchestrated coup, troops rushed through the streets of the capital proclaiming Iturbide as emperor. The cry was taken up by merchants, artisans, and beggars—some of them hired, others genuinely aghast at the prospect of Iturbide's resignation. Like Julius Caesar, whose story was familiar to the theater-loving creoles, Iturbide at first rejected the Crown. But then, as he later wrote, he feared to "insult the populace" and decided to "make this fresh sacrifice for the public good."[37] More than a mob was needed to legitimize this monarchy. And so, the following day, the Congress was convened. With most of his opponents absent—and in fact, lacking a quorum—the legislature swiftly voted to install Itur-bide as Agustín I, first emperor of the new Mexican nation.

Mexico had emerged from eleven years of revolt with a throne in Mexico City instead of Madrid. The Independence movement became a counterrevolution by the most conservative white elements in co-lonial society—first, against rural Indian and mestizo insurgents, and then, once they had been defeated, against the mother country, which had fallen into the hands of liberals no longer willing to uphold the privileges of the creole elite and the Church hierarchy.

Iturbide and his creole supporters did not envision a society radically different from the colonial model they had overthrown. Whiteness of skin remained as exalted as it had been under Spanish rule. The dominance of Mexico City over the provinces was uncontested. The capital would be the seat of a strong central government and the court-in-residence of the aristocratic creoles, who hoped to reflate their far-flung mining-commercial-agrarian enterprises to the prosperous levels of the Bourbon era.

TWELVE

A NATION
BETRAYED

In the decades that followed Independence, soaring expectations gave way to utter disillusionment about the economic, social, and political prospects of the new nation. Only ten months after his enthronement, Iturbide was forced to abdicate by his military rivals and flee abroad. Returning from exile less than two years later, in 1824, he was executed, and an era of uninterrupted army coups began. Mexico suffered three foreign invasions, the most serious during the Mexican-American War which resulted in the occupation of the capital and the loss of one half of the nation's territory to the United States. Sharp economic decline accompanied political instability. At the outset of Independence, almost everyone was confident that mining, agricultural, and commercial wealth would swell now that the country was no longer forced to support a decadent Spain. Instead, it would take a half century to match the income levels achieved in late colonial times. The poor experienced greater misery. The old creole aristocracy yielded to a more brutish elite. The Church maintained its spiritual supremacy, but was unable to arrest its economic and political decay. And in Mexico City, social disparities were greater than before.

Approaching Mexico City from the eastern route taken by the conquistadores, travelers glimpsed the distant capital with the same wonder experienced by Cortés and his chronicler, Díaz del Castillo. The city and its valley were enveloped in a purple and green belt of serrated mountains. To the south, higher than the other peaks, rose the two snow-covered volcanoes: Popocatépetl, shaped in a perfect cone, and

Iztaccíhuatl, like a nymph in slumber. Ducks and geese skimmed the lakes past fishermen casting their nets upon the placid waters. In place of the whitewashed Aztec temples and pyramids, there were scores of churches with domes of gold and blue tiling, spires, and belfries. The flowered terraces of houses formed a chessboard pattern broken by the great plazas with their sprawling outdoor markets.

The splendor faded, however, as the travelers' coach drew closer. Centuries of deforestation had left the mountainsides corrugated and barren, as if their vegetation had been scraped away with a dull knife. The receding lake waters exposed flat, arid plains and melancholy patches of marshland. The city was guarded at its every entrance by blocklike customs houses which brought traffic to a standstill. Mule-drawn carts and burros staggering under their loads clogged the road for hundreds of yards as they waited for permission to enter the capital. Within the walls of the customs houses, inspectors stumbled and poked through piles of boxes, barrels, and sacks while peasants, muleteers, merchants, and foreign visitors frantically waved their documents and clamored for the attention of morose petty bureaucrats.[1]

After a delay of several hours or more, the travelers' coach escaped into narrow, dusty streets lined by mudbrick huts with mounds of rubbish piled against their walls. Dogs ripped apart an animal carcass on the roadside. "The people were mere walking bundles of dirty rags—with oblique eyes, distorted limbs, bound-up heads, and offensive sores," wrote a first-time visitor from Britain. "They appeared to be of mixed descent, and of different shades of colour; but all looked sickly or ill-formed."[2] Only after a mile or so from the eastern outskirts did streets and buildings gain a semblance of cleanliness and solidity. Most travelers, exhausted by their journey and the customs inspection, repaired to an inn and waited until the following day to explore the city.

In the decades following Independence, about 200,000 people lived in Mexico City. The streets retained the grid pattern of colonial days over an urban zone that now sprawled roughly two miles north to south and three miles east to west. The focal point of the capital was still the great Plaza Mayor. Officially renamed Plaza de la Constitución, it was popularly known as the Zócalo after an imposing equestrian statue of Charles IV was removed in the 1820s leaving only the pedestal (zócalo) in place. The Zócalo remained the ceremonial and political center, just as it had been in the Aztec era and Spanish colonial times. The Cathedral, an enormous structure of Baroque, churrigueresque, and neoclassical styles, loomed over the northern side of the plaza. On the east, the former vice-regal palace was now the Palacio Na-

cional, housing the presidency, the Congress, and the federal bureaucracy. The municipal council assembled in a building on the south
side of the Zócalo. Throughout the colonial era, the council members
had been hamstrung by the viceroy in exercising power over city affairs,
and they continued to be shackled after Independence because the
capital was declared part of a Federal District under the direct control
of the nation's president. On its western side, the Zócalo was dominated
by the Monte de Piedad, the state-run pawnbrokerage, catering to all
social classes. The rest of the plaza was bounded by important public
buildings like the mint, the jail, and the courts. Luxury shops were
installed under arcades in the southwest corner.

The city awoke every morning on its periphery, hours before the
Zócalo came to life. At dawn, the neighborhoods clustered around
the great plaza were shaken from their slumber by the bells of cows
trooping from the suburbs to the many small public squares where
milk was sold fresh from the udder.[3] Among the earliest risers were
middle-class youngsters from the rural outskirts. En route to the downtown schools, they galloped their horses at breakneck speed, leaping
over fences, stampeding peddlers and servants, and occasionally las-
soing terrified pedestrians.[4]

By 8:00 A.M., the streets filled with at least thirty different types of
peddlers, each with a distinct musical cry.[5] The *carbonero*, selling
charcoal for stoves, was the first to be heard, singing out "*Carbó siu*"
("Charcoal, sir") in the clipped accent of the Otomí Indians, who
specialized in the trade. He was soon drowned out by a cacophony of
voices offering a banquet of "little fat cakes steaming from the oven,"
"chestnuts hot and roasted," curd cakes, maize cakes, "good salt beef,"
bananas, mangos, oranges, pomegranates, "coconut delight," cheese
and honey pastry, and "ducks, oh my soul, hot ducks."[6] Street vending
demanded great stamina, and often the skills of a juggler. The larder
lofted a pyramid of butter in a huge bucket on his head. The fishmonger
groaned under the weight of a tub-sized straw basket strapped to his
back. A sherbet peddler balanced a container of chipped ice on his
head, while holding a box of plates and spoons and a jug of syrup in
either hand. Fruit vendors carried their full day's offerings in their
head baskets, and so did the bread sellers. The most spectacular peddling act belonged to the *cabeceros*, who appeared to be ambulatory
restaurateurs. It took two of them to carry about a table holding the
severed heads of calves, goats, and sheep, along with a portable oven.
From their fingers and wrists hung containers of burning charcoal,
sauces and condiments, and pulque.[7]

Besides food vendors, there were dry goods peddlers of all sorts. Those selling clothes were agents of merchants who hoped to reach clients living far from their shops and stalls. Ambulatory mercers, representing a variety of artisans, carried in their baskets needles, files, thimbles, scissors, thread spools, hairpins, earrings, lace, clay toys and children's games, cheap editions of verses and short stories, and even catechism books.[8]

So congested were the streets with vendors and makeshift stalls that porters were a more efficient means of moving goods than animal-drawn vehicles. With the aid of tumplines strung across their foreheads, these human beasts of burden transported construction material, household goods, and bolts of cloth as heavy as 300 pounds. In the rainy season, they were hired to carry the wealthy across puddles, and were often accused of "deliberately splashing their clients or raising the skirts of ladies to indecent heights."[9]

The most essential of the street porters was the water carrier, or *aguador*. A majority of residents depended on public fountains serviced by two great aqueducts linked to mountain springs west of the city. Laboring fifteen hours a day, the aguador carried water to neighborhoods far removed from the fountains. A huge earthenware jug pressed against his back and a smaller one hung from his forehead by a tumpline. He was renowned as "the purveyor of local gossip, deliverer of love letters, and walking domestic employment agency." He was also called upon to dispose of unwanted pets, which he drowned in the public fountains.[10]

By midmorning, the Zócalo itself became the most congested zone in the capital. The vendors gathered here in greatest numbers. Its southwest side was occupied by dozens of stalls known as the Parián market. Once famous as an emporium of imported clothes and luxury goods for the wealthy, it was sacked by a mob in 1828 during the height of anti-Spanish fervor that followed Independence. In later years, the Parián merchants offered cheaper, locally produced goods. Next to their stalls, scribes sat under large parasols and tendered their services to illiterates who needed help with bureaucratic documents, letters to friends and family, or epistles of love.

The main vegetable and meat market was located off the southeast corner of the Zócalo in the Plaza del Volador, where the Inquisition had publicly executed its victims two centuries before. The alleys of the Volador market were slippery from animal entrails, rotten fruit, vegetable remains, shattered eggs, and a thick layer of mud that covered the cobblestones. Strings of sausages danced above greasy counters.

Flies buzzed around mounds of butter, pork rinds, tripe, and limp
fish. Shoppers were buffeted, elbowed, and shoved as they squeezed
from one stall to another. The putrid, rancid smells were suffocating,
and the harangue of the vendors was ear-splitting.[11] But because of its
cheap prices, the Volador market was favored by every class.

For the wealthy, who had servants to purchase household necessities,
midmorning was a time to enjoy the Alameda Park, just a few blocks
west of the Zócalo. Small cataracts of sunlight filtered through its leafy
canopy. The fragrance of flowers, the chirping of crickets, and the
warble of birds added to the park's serenity. The Alameda was a place
to be seen by one's peers. The men paraded about on their horses.
The women never descended from their coaches. "As to walking, it
is considered wholly unfashionable, immoral, and vulgar," wrote
Fanny Calderón de la Barca, wife of Spain's first envoy to independent
Mexico. "After all, everybody has feet, but only ladies have carriages,
and a mixture of aristocracy and laziness prevents the Mexican dames
from ever profaning the soles of their feet by contact with their mother
earth."[12]

The heavily guarded Alameda was a refuge for the wealthy from the
hordes of beggars. Poverty was endemic during colonial times, but the
economic stagnation of the Independence era multiplied the numbers
of poor. Every foreign visitor commented on the underclass of ragged,
whining paupers known as *"léperos."* Brantz Meyer, an American
diplomat in Mexico between 1841 and 1842, claimed the expression
came from "leper," and he asserted that such people were shunned as
if they actually suffered from the malady:

> Blacken a man in the sun; let his hair grow long and tangled, or
> become filled with vermin; let him plod about the streets in all kinds
> of dirt for years, and never know the use of brush, or towel, or water
> even, except in storms; let him put on a pair of leather breeches at
> twenty, and wear them until forty, without change or ablution; and,
> over all, place a torn and blackened hat, and a tattered blanket begrimed
> with abominations; let him have wild eyes, and shining teeth, and
> features pinched by famine into sharpness; breasts bared and browned,
> if female, with two or three miniatures of the same species trotting after
> her, and another certainly strapped to her back: combine all these in
> your imagination, and you have a recipe for a Mexican lépero.[13]

The persistent manner in which the léperos begged for alms intimidated the wealthy. Vagrants blocked the entrance of the Cathedral as

if collecting tolls, and inside, they wandered through the aisles during Mass demanding more coins. According to one European observer, the affluent were so haunted by the léperos that "most of the principal families here have small chapels in their houses, and have engaged the services of a padre to say Mass for them at home."[14]

But even behind the walls of their mansions, they could not always evade the alms seekers. While writing a letter in her library, Mrs. Calderón de la Barca was startled by the sight of a lépero groaning and thrusting a mutilated hand through the window bars. She ignored his pleas, but he was soon joined by a whole crowd: "There come more of them! A paralytic woman mounted on the back of a man with a long beard. A sturdy-looking fellow . . . is holding up a deformed foot, which I verily believe is merely fastened back in some extraordinary way. What groans! What rags! What a chorus of whining! This concourse is probably owing to our having sent them some money yesterday. I try to take no notice, and write on as if I were deaf. I must walk out of the room, without looking behind me, and send the porter to disperse them."[15]

R. H. Mason, the British traveler, described how a lépero on the street could be as eloquent with his maledictions as in his entreaties:

> "For the love of the Holy Virgin," he beseeches you, "take pity upon me! By the groans and wounds of a dying Saviour, have compassion upon my agonies! Have you a mother? By that mother's love, and for the sake of our Holy Mother above, regard me with pity! Have you a wife? By your dear remembrances of her, relieve my misery! Have you children? For their sakes, and for that of the Blessed Infant himself, hear me, and bestow your charity! And I will pray that all the blessings both on earth and in heaven may be your portion forever!"
>
> You pass on without proffering the anticipated alms; the fellow's brow lowers, and his face darkens as he turns away cursing: "May all the fiends of the bottomless pit seize upon you! May your wife and children be torn from your arms, and perish miserably before your eyes! May your flesh rot and wither upon your bones from day to day! And may your remains lie unburied for ever and ever!"[16]

The affluent and the middle class assumed that all léperos were professional beggars and criminals, a social group apart from the laboring poor. In fact, vagrancy and crime were structured into lower-class life in Mexico City.[17] Whenever he could, the lépero became a porter, stonemason, street paver, peddler, or any other unskilled laborer. But there were fewer jobs in the decades of economic depression that followed Independence. Those who had employment fought hard to keep newcomers out of their ranks, especially the recent immigrants from the countryside. Thus, the water carriers manhandled anyone caught practicing their trade without their permission, and beseeched clients to shun these intruders whose water they claimed was drawn from polluted founts. The porters were just as harsh with uninvited competitors. The scarcity of jobs made apprenticeships lengthier than in late colonial times. An eight-year-old boy could remain an apprentice until the age of sixteen, earning only his room and board. Even afterwards, he had no assurance of a permanent job or craft, and often joined the ranks of the léperos.

Unemployment and beggary were not the only measures of acute poverty in Mexico City. Between 1800 and 1845, per capita income dropped by more than a third.[18] Unable to afford Church ceremonies, most couples bore their children out of wedlock. They had secret burial places because legal cemeteries could easily consume their life savings.[19]

Housing conditions had also worsened. Besides the twenty thousand or more people described by Humboldt in the early 1800s as living on the streets, there were thousands more who squatted in the roofless shells of buildings destroyed by earthquakes and fires. The majority of the poor were crammed into dank one- or two-story buildings known as *vecindades*. Once inhabited by wealthier residents, many of the vecindades were now owned by the Church, which had inherited them in wills or through defaults on loans. The Church was by far the largest urban real estate owner, but it barely profited from these holdings because many destitute tenants were unable to pay the low rents. Religious agencies in turn made no effort to maintain the dilapidated buildings. Entire families huddled together in a single room, and slept shoulder to shoulder. The crowding, the dirt, the poor ventilation turned the vecindades into deathtraps during epidemics. Guillermo Prieto, a memoirist of the era, described his visit to one of these slum buildings in 1833 after all of its inhabitants had been wiped out by cholera: "I still remember entering the house which must have had thirty rooms, all of them empty, with doors that flapped in the wind, furniture and dishes abandoned . . . a frightening loneliness and silence as if death had suddenly been made custodian of the building."[20]

What few public services existed for the poor in the late colonial period declined or disappeared altogether after Independence. The collection of garbage and human waste virtually ceased in the lower-class zones. The refuse piled against the vecindades and huts, and eventually accumulated in huge mounds in the plazas and streets, blocking traffic and enveloping neighborhoods in a permanent stench. [21] During the colonial era, hospitals were under Church administration and were already infamous for their atrocious conditions. But following Independence, a number of these hospitals were taken over by the municipal government and became veritable charnelhouses. The lack of public funds forced the closing of some establishments. Others were so cramped that patients suffering from contagious and noncontagious diseases were placed side by side, and often in the same bed. Worst of all was the insane asylum, from which "no patient has left cured, and all have abandoned the little sanity that they once possessed," according to an 1848 report by the city's medical association. [22]

Private charity offered little relief to the lower class. Some wealthy women did contribute their time and money to support the city's orphanage, but callousness and hypocrisy were the general rule. Mrs. Calderón de la Barca recalled a ball staged at the municipal theater in 1840 by society ladies, ostensibly for the benefit of the poor: "Such was the original dirtiness and bad condition of the theatre that to make it decent these ladies unfortunately expended all the proceeds of the ball."[23] The only mention of the poor made at the affair came in the usual laments about the difficulty in finding trustworthy servants and complaints about the government's failure to control vagrancy and crime.

In fact, the government ferociously hounded léperos and other vagrants. A Tribunal for Vagrants was created in 1828 to fill the large draft requirements of the army. People caught openly begging were not the only targets. In August 1841, for example, the tribunal took less than twenty-four hours to convict and sentence to military service five hundred men who were deemed vagrants solely because they had been arrested in pulque taverns. [24] Waddy Thompson, an American diplomat in Mexico City, asserted that almost every day "droves of these miserable and more than half naked wretched are . . . seen chained together and marching through the streets to the barracks, where they are scoured and then dressed in uniform. . . ."[25] Unable to support their families on their negligible military incomes, most of them deserted at the first opportunity.

The authorities were even less successful in controlling the rise of criminal activity. Unidentified murder victims were displayed every day on the front steps of the capital's main prison. "It is almost impossible to take your morning walk to the adjoining fields, without seeing one, and frequently two corpses stretched bleeding on the stones," wrote a foreign envoy who witnessed this gruesome spectacle. "These are the victims of some sudden quarrel, or unknown murder during the night; and all who miss a friend, a parent or a brother, resort to these iron bars to seek the lost one. It is painful to behold the scenes to which this melancholy assemblage frequently give rise, and hear the wails of sorrow that break from the homeless orphan, whose parent lies murdered on the stones of the dead-house."[26]

Mrs. Calderón de la Barca described a murder that occurred one evening beneath her balcony, in full view of her guests who were drinking coffee. A group of poor people were bantering and laughing until a dispute erupted and they came to blows. "Suddenly," she wrote, "a man darted out from amongst the others, and tried to escape by clambering over a low wall. . . . Instantly, and quite coolly, another man followed him, drew his knife, and stabbed him in the back. The man fell backwards in a groan, upon which a woman of the party, probably the murderer's wife, drew out her knife and gave the wounded man three or four stabs to the heart to finish him—the others, meanwhile, neither speaking nor interfering, but looking on with folded arms and their usual placid smile of indifference."

When a squad of soldiers miraculously appeared on scene, the murderers tried to escape into Mrs. Calderón's house, but were arrested before they could enter. "As this is an everyday occurrence," she noted, "it excited no sensation whatever" among her guests.[27]

Robbery was a far more common crime. Most of it took place in the poor vecindades when their occupants left for the day. Street vendors burglarized unguarded residences. Outside the customs houses at the entrances of the city, thieves lassoed and robbed visitors and merchants, whom they knew were likely to be carrying large sums of money.[28] Other criminals prowled the state-run pawnbrokerage, the cavernous Monte de Piedad building on the Zócalo, where they robbed people of their heirlooms and then pawned the objects as their own. R. H. Mason, the British traveler, witnessed a crowd apprehending one of these thieves:

"He is surrounded by an indignant mob, grasping his limbs, and pushing him before them, struggling and protesting, to the doorway. Encouraged by his recent success, he has been plying his vocation upon the persons of several visitors in different parts of the building, and has been taken in the act: a small box of jewels, a watch, and an embroidered sash, have been found upon him; yet he persists in asserting his innocence."

Dragged outside the building, the thief was almost rescued by a group of léperos. A brawl ensued leaving several bystanders injured, until finally a police squad was able to restore order and arrest the robber.[29]

There were only twenty-five municipal policemen and a few dozen market guards in the capital. A paramilitary public security force of three hundred fifty men was also available, but it rarely cooperated with the regular police and often refused to carry out patrols.[30] After sundown, protection was largely entrusted to unarmed *serenos*, or nightwatchmen, who scraped a living from the gratuities of neighborhood residents. The cries of a victim occasionally attracted a half-dozen serenos, who ran toward the criminal attempting to scare or subdue him with their shouts and shrill whistles. But serenos were notorious for falling into drunken slumber on the sidewalks or doorways, and thus gained a reputation for "sleeping at home during the day and in the street at night."[31]

For the rich of Mexico City, the poor evoked troublesome images of vagrancy, crime, filth, and disease. But there was one sector of the lower class—the unassimilated Indians—who rose at least briefly in their estimation. With Independence came a romanticization of the nation's Indian heritage among creoles. Some of them openly bragged of Indian blood in their ancestry. A new nationalism exalted the Aztecs and denigrated the conquistadores. Legislation banned legal distinctions based on race. Newspapers and government publications ceased identifying individuals as Indians, castes, or whites.

There were forty thousand Indians in Mexico City, a fifth of the population. While foreign visitors, like Mrs. Calderón de la Barca, believed that "real" Indians existed only in the provinces, long-time residents of the city knew better. Manuel Payno, the novelist, described a large Indian neighborhood on the capital's northern perimeter.[32] It was an agglomeration of mud and stick huts that resembled beavers' lodges, he wrote. From the roadside, the village looked abandoned, except for mangy dogs lying in the dirt alleys, burros pulling away mouthfuls of weeds from the mud walls of the houses, and a few Indian women weaving cloth on their doorsteps. The men and children had left before dawn with their nets and spears to fish for frogs in Lake Texcoco, or to skim the water reeds for mosquito eggs that were beaten, dried, and confectioned into small cakes, and later offered for sale as delicacies in the capital's markets. Others hired themselves out as day laborers in nearby haciendas.

Indian men and boys also earned a living in the large garbage dump, known as La Viña, just a few blocks from the Zócalo. Every morning at eight, mule-drawn carts with jingling bells began circulating through the city center to collect refuse from house servants. By eleven, the overloaded wagons creaked toward La Viña to dump the garbage on mounds that had grown to the size of small hills. Armed with sticks and metal rods, Indian scavengers quickly poked through the newly arrived refuse for rags, old shoes, chipped plates, pieces of iron, even occasional silverware or bits of jewelry. Other Indians stood guard preventing beggars and dogs from interfering. When the search was over, booty was offered to the beggars who paid a few pennies for tattered hats, pants, or coats. And then the dogs were allowed to claim the bones and food scraps.[33]

In an effort to bring the Indians into the political mainstream, the municipality decreed an end to the old colonial system of segregating them into their own communities led by caciques or chieftains. The city authorities also ordered the caciques to equitably divide among their followers the community chests and communal properties they controlled.

But the Indians resisted these and other initiatives as unwelcome intrusions. They loudly objected when the government tried to abolish the annual pitched battles between Indians residing in the Tlatelolco quarter and those living in neighborhoods closer to the central district— a tradition harking back to the wars between the Aztecs of Tlatelolco and Tenochtitlán. They agreed only not to use firearms, and to confine their skirmishes to stone throwing.

Indian communities that had survived for more than three centuries were still wary of any whites settling in their midst. In 1827, for example, a schoolteacher sent by the municipality to a village on the southern edge of the capital complained that the Indians there were trying to expel her. The Indians feared that being a single woman, she might attempt to marry a resident and inherit his land.[34]

Not only were Indians seeking to protect what remained of their properties, but also—taking advantage of lip service by whites against the injustices committed during the colonial era—they made legal efforts to claim lands lost under Spanish rule. Thus, in 1846, the Indians of Tlatelolco sued to recover the Hacienda de Aragón, a property of several thousand acres near the capital, which they asserted was theirs by virtue of once having belonged to Cuauhtémoc, the last Aztec king.[35] The case dragged through the judiciary system for fifty years without being resolved. In the 1840s, in a northern suburb of Mexico City, another Indian community claimed that one of their families was descended from Motecuhzoma II, emperor of the Aztecs at the time of the Conquest. Their lawsuit demanding a portion of properties that once belonged to the Indian ruler was thrown out of court. But the incident supplied the plot for the best-known novel of the post-Independence era, Manuel Payno's *Los bandidos de Río Frío.*

This sort of Indian militance was mild by comparison to what was happening elsewhere in the country. In the northernmost provinces, the Comanches and other tribes were raiding white and mestizo settlements and ambushing wagons on isolated roads. Much worse was the so-called Caste War, an uprising by the Maya in Yucatán in 1847–48 that spread to Oaxaca, and roused fears of a possible revolt among Indian tribes on the outskirts of Mexico City itself.

By 1850, the creoles had abandoned their romantic notions about the precolonial era. Political pamphlets spoke of the Indians as people "without interest or affections." Their failure to rise up against the Yankee invaders in the 1846–48 Mexican-American War was held as proof of their lack of nationalism. They were alleged to have "seen the North American army enter [Mexico City] with the same apathy they used to show when the Spanish armies dominated the country."[36]

And more than three centuries after the Conquest, the Indians' Christian faith was still questioned by the creoles. The conservative newspaper *El Universal* asserted that if religions other than Roman Catholicism were tolerated in Mexico, "the Indians will return to their ancient idols and perhaps to human sacrifices, and the government will have no right to prevent this since the spilling of blood is part of their rituals."[37]

Prejudice against Indians reached petty extremes. When Mrs. Calderón de la Barca let it be known that she intended to wear a formal Indian costume to a fancy ball, the Mexican president and his cabinet called at her residence. "In solemn array they came, and what do you think was the purport of their visit?" she wrote in a letter. "To inform us that all Mexico was in a state of shock at the idea of my going in a Poblana dress, and to adjure me, by all that was most alarming, to discard the idea! They assured us that all Poblanas were 'femmes de rien.' "[38] She obliged the Mexican president and attended the ball in a more conventional European gown. But for weeks afterward she had to suffer anonymous insults for even having entertained the notion of attiring herself as an Indian.

Among the more dramatic changes precipitated by Independence was the decline in the wealth, power, and status of the old Mexico City elite. The great merchants, miners, and landholders had backed Iturbide's revolt against the mother country because the liberal regime in Spain was no longer willing to protect their aristocratic privileges. But by 1826, the upper-class creoles themselves supported the abolition of their noble titles and the entails which had preserved their estates for their heirs.

It was not any newfound sense of egalitarianism that led them to make these concessions. Many elite creoles felt threatened by a wave of nationalism and hatred of things Spanish that was sweeping Mexico in the wake of Independence. Spain's continued refusal to recognize the freedom of its former colony and its rupture of trade relations sparked apprehensions that it was planning an invasion. (The expected attack came in 1829, but was easily repulsed.) Because of the close ties that Mexican aristocrats maintained with the mother country, they became obvious targets of nationalist sentiment. Many of them were either born in Spain or had Spanish parents, cousins, and nephews. Their noble titles and privileges, granted by the Spanish monarchy, made them all the more suspect. And despite renouncing their claims to nobility, many members of the elite were forced into exile by laws passed in 1827 and 1829 that expelled Spaniards from Mexico.

The bleak economic panorama also helped convince the Mexican upper class to surrender its aristocratic privileges. Strapped for capital and facing steep taxes, the nobles no longer saw any advantage in the entail system. There was little sense in preserving an estate for one's heirs if bankruptcy loomed as an immediate danger. By giving up entails, the elite was able to mortgage or sell portions of estates to meet pressing financial needs.

During the late colonial era, the wealthiest Mexicans had diversified their investments into mining, commerce, and agriculture in order to protect their fortunes from cyclical disasters in any one economic sector. But the Independence wars had devastated all economic sectors. Mining output fell to less than a quarter. Agricultural and industrial production declined by one third. The luxury trade with Europe and the Far East was in disarray. Internal commerce lagged because of the dearth of currency and credit.

The depression in mining was especially catastrophic because Mexico's politicians and entrepreneurs had counted on silver production to rekindle the economy and exceed the profits of the colonial era now that Spain no longer collected its royal levies. But many mines had been heavily damaged by sabotage and fires during the insurrection. A longer-lasting and costlier problem was the drainage of shafts and galleys that had flooded after years of abandonment. More serious still was the shortage of mercury—crucial for the refining process—caused by Spain's refusal to supply its former colony with new shipments. According to H. G. Ward, a British diplomat and mining expert who resided in Mexico between 1825 and 1827, all these problems were exacerbated by "the want of confidence and the constant risk to which capitals were exposed."[39]

By creating a shortage in silver currency, the decline in mining output had a direct impact on the elite's investments in commerce and industry. In 1809, 26 million pesos were minted; in 1821, the total had dropped to less than 6 million pesos.[40] Not only were insufficient quantities of bullion reaching the mints, but hard currency was disappearing at an alarming rate as capital fled the country. Much of it left with the rich Spaniards who were expelled. But even those who stayed in Mexico considered it prudent to send the bulk of their fortunes abroad.

To compensate for the dearth of hard, silver currency, the government minted copper coins, which unfortunately could be counterfeited with ease. A European who visited the mint in Mexico City in 1841 reported seeing a large hall crammed with counterfeiting machines that had been uncovered in police raids: "I was assured by the directors, while wondering at the number of machines for false coining which had been collected, that there are twice that number now in full force in Mexico—but that they belong to such distinguished personages the government is afraid to interfere with them!"[41]

Counterfeiting caused the real value of the government-issued copper coins to plunge by 75 percent. The poor, who were paid in the worthless currency, were turned away by shopkeepers when they tried to purchase goods. The rich were also affected, at least to the extent that they abided by government regulations requiring up to one quarter of all business transactions to be conducted in copper money.[42]

Many wealthy creoles claimed the Independence wars had left their rural properties in ruins. The Marquis of Jaral, one of the largest livestock owners, asserted that his haciendas endured losses in excess of 650,000 pesos between 1810 and 1817. The Count of Jala said his great pulque estates suffered irreparable damage because they were occupied by rebel forces during the insurrection and the cactus plants became unproductive after being left untended for years. A large number of haciendas were plundered by insurgents and royalists. Hacienda mansions and other buildings were stripped of their beams by peasants who used the material to enhance their own homes and village churches.[43] But the prolonged setbacks to the big landowners resulted from the lack of capital and credit in the aftermath of the insurrection. Unable to secure enough loans or generate substantial profits, many large haciendas were advertised for sale or auction during the 1820s and 1830s in the *Gazeta de México*, the leading newspaper.[44]

In Mexico City during the early Independence era, a significant number of aristocratic families lived under reduced circumstances behind a facade of splendor. Mrs. Calderón de la Barca discovered traces of this sort of genteel poverty in a visit to the mansion of an ex-countess in 1839:

> She has a magnificent house of immense size, with suites of large rooms. . . . But although there are cabinets inlaid with gold, fine paintings, and hundreds of rich and curious things, our European eyes are struck with the usual numerous inconsistencies here in dress, servants, etc.—in all of which there is a want of keeping very remarkable. . . . We passed through numbers of rooms, beautifully painted, and found her [and her daughter, Paulita] . . . in a little ill-furnished miserable room, with two candles—the countess with an old rebozo and a pair of diamond earrings, Paulita bundled up in shawls and fur . . . everything looking poor, dirty, and uncomfortable.[45]

Nor was this an exceptional case. For according to Mrs. Calderón, almost all the aristocratic mansions she encountered showed signs of disrepair, "making these residences appear something of a crossbreed between a palace and a barn—the splendour of the one, the discomfort of the other."[46]

Even some creoles whom she assumed to be enormously wealthy were in fact close to economic collapse. She described Francisco José Fagoaga, son of the leading miner-merchant-landowner of the late colonial period, as "a man of great taste and a thorough gentleman, and . . . his house, which is one of the handsomest in Mexico, possesses that ornament so rare in this country—well-chosen paintings."[47] Yet that same year, 1841, Fagoaga went into bankruptcy and sold everything, including his art collection, to meet his obligations.[48]

To be sure, there were many old creole families who emerged from the colonial period with large portions of their wealth intact, and remained fixtures in high society. But they had to share the limelight with an upstart elite of military officers.

Wealthy Mexicans of the late colonial era had joined the militia as officers, but for them this was mainly a social honor, not a full-time calling. Less affluent creoles, however, took a military career far more seriously. It was their only opportunity for social advancement and, as they later discovered, for personal enrichment. They emerged from the insurrection against Spain as national heroes, with political strength by virtue of their command over regional garrisons, and with wealth based on contraband, looting, and embezzlement of tax revenues. Neither their power nor their illicit financial activities were curtailed in the decades following Independence. Mexico maintained a bloated army of eighty thousand men that absorbed up to 80 percent of public expenditures.[49] Regional commanders were able to demand hefty shares of the budget for themselves and their officers in exchange for temporary loyalty to the rapid succession of governments.

The career of General Manuel Barrera was typical of the new military class. He was a modest tailor during the late colonial period. He wooed the daughter of a wealthy family, but they rejected his marriage proposal. He then arranged to become a guard officer in the viceroy's palace. With his newly elevated status, he overcame the objections of his sweetheart and her parents. Using her dowry, he opened a larger tailoring business, which reaped a windfall when he received a government contract for the supply of officers' uniforms. His wife died, leaving him a fortune, and he soon remarried—this time to an attractive seamstress. He left no known battlefield record during the insurrection, but he emerged after Independence as a captain, and soon rose to general. His high rank enabled him to become a great smuggler of foreign luxury goods, a counterfeiter, and owner of gambling and prostitution houses.

By the 1830s, General Barrera was living in the finest mansion in Mexico City, which he bought along with its paintings, furniture, and silverware from the Marquis de Apartado, scion of the Fagoaga merchant-mining clan, who had fled to Europe. Located a block behind the Cathedral, this gray stone palace rose three stories and was crowned by a balustrade. Over its massive oak doors was the blank oval shield from which the Fagoaga coat of arms had been removed—an alteration made on all aristocratic mansions after the creoles surrendered their noble titles.

In his pleasure outings through the streets of Mexico City, General Barrera traveled with an entourage of at least three carriages, all with the same crimson and gold livery and drawn by white horses. "Is it the President?" Mrs. Calderón de la Barca remarked with sarcasm upon witnessing the procession. "Certainly not; it is too ostentatious. Were it in Europe, it might be royalty, but even royalty goes in simpler guise when it condescends to mingle in the amusements of its subjects." In the first carriage rode the general and his wife, wearing a velvet turban with twists of large pearls and puffing incongruously on a large cigar. She was no longer pretty, commented the Spanish diplomat's wife, "but her jewels are superb, and worth—it would be dangerous to calculate too nearly."

At the side of the carriage, an elderly relative rode his white steed. His gold-embroidered uniform gave him the air of a bullfighter. His whip had a large diamond set in the handle, and his saddle was covered with velvet and embossed in massive gold. The two coaches that followed behind the general and his wife were occupied by the children and servants. The avenues, Mrs. Calderón noticed, were lined with waifs and beggars gazing in wonder as the convoy rolled by. "How he and his have risen from nothing, making their fortune by the most highhanded smuggling—how their fortune is now colossal, while their meanness is indescribable," she wrote. "This is only one of the thousands of instances of corruption that are bringing disgrace and ruin upon this unfortunate country."[50]

Mrs. Calderón's judgment reflected the prejudices of the old creoles who viewed the military officers as parvenus, and generally declined to associate with them in politics, business enterprises, or social gatherings. But General Barrera certainly had his admirers. When he took ill and appeared near death, the great Cathedral bells tolled for him. Military officers in formal dress and monks bearing torches held a grieving procession through the streets, and two bands struck up martial music and religious hymns. Barrera miraculously recovered, and the ceremonies had to be repeated when he finally died a few years later.

The newly rich military class, their families and associates gave society in Mexico City a vulgar edge. With no confidence in their own taste for fashion, the women entrusted their wardrobes to second-rate French designers who overcharged them for dresses that Europeans considered farcical. "The French modistes who come here, and who are in fact the very scum of the earth, persuade them into all sorts of follies," wrote Mrs. Calderón. "Their gowns have a hunchy, loaded look, all velvet or satin. . . . The dresses, compared with the actual fashion, are made excessively, incredibly short, and sticking out all round at the bottom like hoops—so that when they stoop! Caramba!" An aversion to large feet—again fostered by the French modistes— encouraged upper-class women to wear shoes several sizes too small.

Dancing was an ordeal, and walking "a mixture of tottering and waddling."[51]

Jewelry was displayed to excess. At the many social gatherings she attended, Mrs. Calderón marveled that all the women wore diamonds and pearls—"old and young and middle-aged, including little children. . . . I did not see one without earrings, necklace, and brooch." She added that the diamonds, though superb, were frequently ill set, while rubies and emeralds were scorned as "trash."[52]

Upper-class men were just as poorly counseled by their French tailors, who foisted upon them expensive clothes that would find no customers in Europe: cashmere pants embroidered with branches, flowers, and dolls, as if the garments had been cut from a carpet; velvet waistcoats daubed cherry, sea green, or Prussian blue; and ties as large as towels. Garters were worn so tight that they snapped when a man sat down or crossed his legs.[53]

There were less affluent men who sought to imitate these garish tastes. The dandy or fop, known as the *catrín*, spent what little money he had to purchase a velvet overcoat, a top hat, boots with heavy buckles, an expensive gold watch and chain, and a small cane. Besides these, his entire wardrobe consisted of a pair of shirts, two trousers, two jackets, and two white handkerchiefs. "The catrín," wrote a novelist of the era, "is an undefinable paradox, for he is a gentleman without honor, rich without income, poor without hunger, in love without a lady, valiant without an enemy, sage without reading, Christian without religion. . . ."[54] But the catrín fooled nobody, and was barred from the social circle of the new upper class.

The discomfort of dress was matched by the strain in speech, as the newly rich labored to affect a formal tone suitable to their elevated status. R. H. Mason recorded the following conversation in the 1840s between the hostess of an evening party and one of her guests:

"Honoured madam, I feel most happy in offering myself, without novelty, to your service! I hope you are excellently well!"

"At your disposal, Colonel," was the reply, "as are also my husband and my house."

"Madam," continued the officer, "your most humble, dutiful servant!"

"Sir, I am rejoiced!"

"Madam, I have the supreme honour to kiss your feet!" (advancing a step, and bowing).

"Sir, I have the honour to kiss your hand!"

"Madam, I have pleasure in being your servant, and that of this honourable company."

"Colonel, we are all at your service!"

And finally, hostess and guest broke away from each other in relief.[55]

A European living in Mexico City in 1840 wondered how upper-class women spent their time. "They do not read—they do not write," she observed. "For the most part they do not play . . . nor do they lounge in the shops of a morning, or promenade in the streets—nor do they ride on horseback. What they do not do is clear, but what do they do?"[56] Some of the old creole families did send their daughters to Europe to be educated. But the newly rich thought this a waste of time. They removed their daughters from local schools by age ten, fearful that even in preadolescence they might attract sexual attention. When Mrs. Calderón innocently inquired if a lady's daughter went to school, the mother was shocked at the suggestion: "Good heavens! She is near eleven years old."[57]

Men and women of the new elite frequented the theater, but gave the impression of doing so because it was the kind of activity that upper-class people were expected to pursue. Their boredom was undisguised, and the actors responded with wooden performances. Spectators chattered away while plays were in progress, and never ceased smoking their cigars: "The whole pit smoked, the galleries smoked, the boxes smoked, the prompter smoked—a long stream of curling smoke ascending from his box. . . . And more than all, the ladies smoked. . . . Il ne manquait but that the actors should smoke—which they did, men and women in the side-scenes most devoutly."[58]

In seeking to enhance their social credentials, the newly rich could be just as maladroit in the countryside as they were in the capital. They purchased haciendas at depressed prices from the old creoles, and fancied themselves gentlemen-farmers, maintaining their residences in Mexico City. Iturbide led the way for the military elite by acquiring a choice estate in Chalco, the breadbasket southeast of the capital. General Antonio López de Santa Anna bought properties on the road to Veracruz. Even Vicente Guerrero, beloved in Mexican history as a populist and stalwart follower of Morelos, could not resist the lure of the haciendas.

But the new landed elite did not have the abilities of the great colonial entrepreneurs to coax profits from their estates. The case of Vicente Guerrero was fairly typical.[59] Even while he rose to prominence as the last great insurgent leader during the Independence wars, he formed a lucrative mule-transport operation for contraband trade between Acapulco and Taxco. After Independence, he leased several haciendas between those two towns. And when he became president in the 1820s, he rented a former Jesuit estate in Chalco which had been taken over by the government. Guerrero also bought storage facilities and a lakeshore landing (farm produce from Chalco was transported to Mexico City by barges) and a bakery in the capital. Using his presidential power, he avoided paying rent for the Chalco hacienda. But even with all these advantages, he left his widow saddled with a huge debt of 63,511 pesos on the Chalco estate. Guerrero's son-in-law then took over the hacienda, but was never able to make any profits and gave up the lease nine years later, in 1840.

The Guerrero family and other new landholders in Chalco blamed their troubles on poor climate, which reduced their harvests. But in the colonial era, the old creoles had welcomed weather-induced crises as opportunities for great profit taking. They always seemed to have hidden stockpiles of grain ready to be released when smaller farmers had exhausted their supplies and food prices in the capital were peaking. The Guerreros and their neighbors also faced labor difficulties that their predecessors had almost never experienced. Well aware that the new hacienda owners were vulnerable, the Indians in the Chalco region were able to demand better wages and work conditions, and always gave priority to their own village crops. In the 1830s, estate owners often complained about the insolence of the Indian laborers.

The hacienda masters of the early Independence era differed from the old creoles in yet another important respect: they were at the mercy of creditors in Mexico City who advanced them money on condition that they agree months before harvest to deliver produce at low prices.[60]

The creditors of the hacienda owners were entrepreneurs who rose to economic eminence in the decades following Independence. While the older creole families could barely stomach the military caste, these younger businessmen willingly associated with the uncouth colonels and generals. They fronted for the officers in legal and unlawful transactions, and sometimes put them on their payroll. They extended loans to the chronically deficit-ridden governments, and in return were awarded lucrative shares of state monopolies. Their fortunes were made above all in commerce and speculation. In an era when credit and capital were scarce, they acted as bankers of the most predatory kind— lending out money at usurious rates and quickly foreclosing on clients

who were unable to pay. Their investments in productive enterprises—
mining, agriculture, textile manufacturing—were secondary, often taking the form of shares in a venture in return for loans.

The paragon of the new entrepreneur was Manuel Escandón.[61] He
was born in Veracruz of a Spanish immigrant father and creole mother,
whose family had haciendas and links with military officers. The father
died, leaving the teen-aged Manuel to administer an inheritance of
about 120,000 pesos—not a large sum for a family that included his
mother and eleven brothers and sisters. But by the early 1830s, when
Escandón was barely twenty years old, he had become a close business
associate of another Veracruz native, General Santa Anna, the most
powerful politician and military officer of the era. Other business
opportunities opened for Escandón in 1833 when his brother married
Lina Fagoaga, an heiress to the old creole merchant-mining family.
Manuel convinced his brother to hand over his wife's dowry, despite
her bitter objections. He then used the money to purchase Mexico's
only stagecoach line.

Escandón's special genius was to pioneer ways to profit from the
extreme financial weakness of the government, which could not afford
to deliver even essential public services. Through his friendship with
Santa Anna during the general's first presidency, Escandón negotiated
a 20,000-peso-a-year contract in 1835 to use his stagecoach line for
mail delivery throughout Mexico. He was also granted by Santa Anna
a fifteen-year contract to repair roads leading north and south of Mexico
City, and was allowed to gain huge profits by charging tolls and customs
duties on all traffic. Established families like the Fagoagas and Bassocos
protested vehemently against this monopoly, to no avail.

Escandón's meteoric rise had barely begun. With the government
desperately seeking to raise 1 million pesos, he joined a group of
businessmen who lent the money in exchange for a 50 percent stake
in several state-owned silver mines. Under the terms of the twelve-
year contract, Escandón and his partners earned sums many times
greater than their loan. In a similar and much more lucrative deal in
1839, the government ceded its tobacco monopoly for more than fifteen
years to several private companies partly controlled by Escandón in
return for a series of loans. The contract allowed Escandón and his
associates to set production quotas for tobacco farmers, manage the
tobacco factories, hire road inspectors to guard against contraband,
and use government troops to suppress illegal tobacco growers and
smugglers. By trading a portion of his shares in the companies running
the tobacco monopoly, Escandón then bought some of the largest

textile mills in Mexico. He received permission from the government to lift its protectionist barriers and allow him to buy low-priced cotton from the United States, thus giving him an important advantage over competitors in textile manufacturing.

In the 1840s, Escandón and his associates used their loans to the government to gain complete control of Mexico's ports—building and managing new docks, warehouses, and offices in exchange for a large share of customs duties. The arrangement permitted Escandón to dominate contraband. One of his favorite ploys was to smuggle into the country English cloth, send it to his mills, and then sell it as Mexican-made textile.

Not even the 1846–48 Mexican-American War could disrupt Escandón's business empire. When American troops invaded Mexico, he arranged to have his properties and those of other leading Mexican entrepreneurs placed under British protection by providing investors from London with false bills of sale for the properties. And when Mexico emerged bankrupt from the war, Escandón, who was sent by his government to London to negotiate with the country's creditors there, attempted to arrange better terms for his own company debts than for those of the Mexican government. Escandón shrugged off the resulting scandal, and was soon embroiled in a larger one.

In 1853, Santa Anna sold what is today the southern strip of Arizona—known as the Gadsden Purchase—to the United States for $10 million. Coming only five years after the United States had forced Mexico to cede one half of its territory (today, the American Southwest and California), the transaction caused an outrage in the Mexican legislature and public opinion. The controversy heated up even more when it was discovered that Escandón and Santa Anna had embezzled the entire $10 million. The scandal led to Santa Anna's overthrow and exile in 1855, and Escandón also had to flee abroad. Commenting on the affair, a French diplomat in Mexico City wrote to his foreign ministry that "it is impossible to imagine in Europe the degree of corruption that reigns here in public finances."[62]

But Escandón soon returned from exile and became richer than ever. Though considered a conservative because of his ties to Santa Anna, he was too opportunistic to wear any political label for long. During subsequent years, he was identified with liberal Mexican politicians, who valued his entrepreneurial skills as much as their conservatives enemies had.

In their exploitation of the government's financial weakness, their indifference to political factions, their efforts to gain monopolies in their business sectors, and their appetite for profit, Escandón and his colleagues evoke comparison to the American robber barons of the post-Civil War era. But at the very least, the Carnegies, Rockefellers, Fricks, and Morgans presided over the transformation of a mercantile-agrarian nation into an expanding industrial society. The legacy of the Mexican entrepreneurs in the decades following Independence was far less impressive. In 1860, Mexican national income was still below the level achieved in the waning years of the colonial era.[63] As protagonists in their country's economy, Escandón and the other large entrepreneurs shared considerable blame for this decline.

The decades of economic and political turmoil that followed Independence had scourged Mexico City's poor, largely displaced the colonial aristocracy, and elevated a new elite of military officials and entrepreneurs. The Church also was deeply affected by the turbulence that swept secular society.

Threatened with the loss of many of its properties by the liberal regime that emerged in Spain in 1820, the Church threw its support behind the Independence movement led by Iturbide. As a reward, Roman Catholicism was maintained as the only legal religion in Mexico. But the Church immediately became embroiled in a dispute over patronage—the right to appoint bishops and higher clergy. Ever since Columbus's discoveries, the Spanish monarchs had been granted by the Vatican the right to name or remove Church officials in their American colonies. With separation from Spain, Church and State in Mexico each claimed to have inherited the patronage powers of the Spanish Crown. There was no quick resolution of the dispute, and negotiations were carried out for many years between the Vatican and Mexican government officials. In the meantime, the Mexican Church was unable to renovate its hierarchy. A decade after Independence, only four of ten bishops remained at their posts, and no archbishop was appointed until 1840.[64] There was also an acute shortage of priests. Many were killed during the insurrection, and large numbers returned to Spain in its aftermath.

Independence failed to resolve other major controversies involving the Church. Mexican liberals—emulating their counterparts in Spain—attacked clerical involvement in secular affairs. The clergy's near monopoly of education was questioned, particularly since all but a small minority of Mexicans remained illiterate. Liberals also advocated the appropriation of ecclesiastical properties and capital on the grounds that this wealth could be made more productive for the nation if it were in secular hands. For almost forty years, the Church largely succeeded in defending itself against these challenges. But it was reeling from severe economic problems.

Its economic decline had started with the Consolidation decree of 1804 which called for the Church to turn over to the Spanish Crown all of its loans and the properties it had accumulated from wills and other private donations. Before the decree was suspended on the eve of the Independence wars, Spain had liquidated more than one fourth of ecclesiastical holdings in Mexico. Another important source of Church income—the collection of tithes on agricultural production— had fallen sharply because of the destruction of rural properties during the insurgency, and was suspended in 1833.

But most of the Church's economic erosion was a consequence of its position as the dominant source of credit and investment capital in late colonial Mexico. The dislocations of the Independence wars and their aftermath left thousands of the Church's debtors unable to repay their loans. The haciendas and buildings used as collateral for these debts were appropriated by the Church, enhancing its status as the greatest owner of urban and rural property in Mexico. However, the clergy would undoubtedly have preferred to collect interest on its loans than to be saddled with huge holdings that generated few profits.

Thus, in the post-Independence era, the Church could be described as property rich and cash poor. Its charitable activities were severely curtailed because of lack of funds. And while it remained the chief source of credit—and certainly the cheapest provider of loans for property owners and businessmen—its dominance was being contested by the new, aggressive speculators and entrepreneurs.

The Church often found itself on the losing end of financial transactions involving this entrepreneurial elite. Because of constant budget deficits, the government repeatedly forced the Church to loan it large sums. The heaviest of these debts was incurred during the 1846–48 invasion of the country by the United States. Unable to supply funds from its own coffers, the Church raised the money by selling considerable portions of its rural and urban properties to entrepreneurs at depressed prices.

In spite of all these political and economic problems, Roman Catholicism maintained an overwhelming influence on everyday life in Mexico City. Churches, convents, and monasteries commanded the urban landscape. They anchored every plaza, large and small. Their spires rose above the tallest secular structures. No mansion or palace could match the ornate carvings of their exterior walls. No private collection could approach the artistry and wealth of the statues, paintings, and gold and silver plating that graced the interiors of the major ecclesiastical buildings.

The pealing of church bells drowned out the din of street peddlers, and brought the populace to its knees in times of panic. Guillermo Prieto, a politician of the era, recalled in his memoirs the ringing of those bells during an 1840 earthquake: "People fled their beds half-naked and screamed out their confessions in the streets. . . . They pressed their faces to the ground and raised their arms to the sky while . . . the bells tolled mournfully."[65]

Dressed in sackcloth and sandals, or in flowing robes and shovel hats, the clergymen mingled almost unnoticed with the loud throngs that swarmed through the great plazas and markets. But the sudden appearance of a mule-drawn coach transporting a priest to the deathbed of a wealthy penitent invoked instant piety. As the carriage, gaudily painted in red, blue, and yellow, warned of its approach with the tinkle of a bell, "the whole crowd were crossing themselves devoutly," observed Mrs. Calderón de la Barca. "Disputes were hushed, flirtations arrested, and to the busy hum of voices succeeded a profound silence. Only the rolling of the coach wheels and the sound of the little bell were heard. No sooner had it passed than the talkers and the criers recommenced with fresh vigor."[66]

Clergymen were an almost everyday presence in upper-class homes. R. H. Mason could not fathom why the wealthy tolerated such interference in their lives: "These insidious priests worm themselves into the most hidden secrets of families, holding private interviews with the wife, imposing the most imperious commands upon the daughters, warping and influencing the minds of sons, converting servants and dependants into spies, haunting the house in the absence of the master. . . ."[67] But with his deep anti-Catholic bias, Mason could not admit that families welcomed such priestly concern.

Middle-class households, less frequented by the clergy, often depended on devout family members to serve as religious tutors. Prieto warmly remembered his spinster aunt as the source of all religious lore for his siblings and himself. It was she who explained to them the rivalries between the Virgin of Guadalupe and the Virgin de los Remedios, how St. Catherine beheaded her own father for heresy, and how St. Rosa made feathers spring from the mouth of a chicken thief as he lied to the judge.[68] Less fondly, Prieto recalled that when he was seven years old, his grandfather dressed him in priest's vestments, placed him on a mock pulpit, and coached him to deliver a sermon during a religious festival in his neighborhood. "I began to stutter," Prieto wrote, "and then someone laughed, and I burst out crying amid the angry shouts and whistling."[69]

Foreign visitors to the capital, even the Catholics among them, were sometimes appalled at the harsh depictions of martyrdom in the paintings and statuary that were paraded through the streets on religious occasions. Thorns, arrows, spears pierced the flesh of holy figures too vividly, and the blood seemed to run excessively. But how else to convey the suffering of Christ and the saints to a populace for whom physical hardships and death were everyday occurrences?

Mrs. Calderón de la Barca was profoundly shaken after witnessing a penitential Mass at the Church of San Francisco early one morning. About one hundred and fifty men, enveloped in the ragged wool blankets that were the uniform of the poor, assembled in the dark nave, and at the command of a monk, they removed their blankets and began to whip themselves.

"Suddenly, we heard the sounds of hundreds of scourges descending upon bare flesh," wrote Mrs. Calderón.

> Before ten minutes had passed, the sound became splashing, from the blood that was flowing. . . . Now and then, but very seldom, a suppressed groan was heard, and occasionally the voice of the monk encouraging them. . . . At the end of half an hour a little bell was rung, and the voice of the monk was heard calling upon them to desist—but such was their enthusiasm that the horrible lashing continued louder and fiercer than ever. In vain he entreated them not to kill themselves; and assured them that human nature could not endure beyond a certain point. No answer but the loud sound of the scourges, which are many of them of iron, with sharp points that enter the flesh. At length, as if they were perfectly exhausted, the sound grew fainter, and little by little ceased altogether.[70]

Piety did not always mark the religious ceremonies of the poor. Louis de Bellemare, a Frenchman who resided in Mexico City during the mid-1800s, described a lower-class wake that degenerated into morbid revelry. In the cramped apartment of a vecindad lay the decomposing body of a child, while twenty mourners lost themselves in drink, dance, and cardplaying. The room reeked of smoke, liquor, food, and putrefying flesh. "The mere sight of the little corpse was heartrending amid the cries, the gambling, and the noisy conversation," wrote Bellemare. "The men and women meanwhile were laughing and singing like savages." Only when a church bell struck midnight did the guests seem to remember the reason for their assembly, and kneel to observe "the hour of the souls in Purgatory." Once the prayers were over, they returned to their amusements.[71]

Religious festivals and processions often became excuses for drunkenness, mischief, and brawls. Pageants depicting the battles between Moors and Christians were an occasion for bloody street fights among teenagers. A Church council decried the fact that "regularly during religious solemnities and particularly those of Christmas, many [poor people] meet, animated by a reprehensible joy, and above all drunkenness, to make terrible and lamentable abuses and excesses."[72] The Easter season was even worse. As soon as church services ended, the streets filled with revelers dancing in motley costumes, dousing each other with pestilent water, igniting effigies of Judas, or tying firecrackers to dogs' tails.[73]

A favorite religious holiday was Whit Sunday, in June, when rich and poor alike vented their passion for gambling. In a three-day "pilgrimage," thousands of Mexico City residents journeyed to the southern suburb of San Agustín de las Cuevas to bet their money on gamecocks, cards, and dice. Carriages, carts, horses, mules, and donkeys carried them past groves weighted down by plums and peaches. The president himself arrived in an elegant coach followed by an entourage of generals and colonels.

"San Agustín!" wrote Mrs. Calderón, who witnessed the orgy of gambling. "At the name how many hearts throb with emotion! How many hands are mechanically thrust into empty pockets! How many visions of long-vanished golden ounces flit before aching eyes! What faint crowing of wounded cocks! What tinkling of guitars and blowing of horns come upon the ear!"[74]

Gambling houses of all categories surrounded the main square of the town. For the rich, there were large, ornate parlors, with leather-cushioned chairs and mahogany tables where only gold pieces were bet. The middle class was accommodated in more plainly decorated rooms where silver was the game currency. And the poor, even the léperos, gambled copper coins under tattered awnings in the alleyways. Wealthy bettors won and lost their capital, even their haciendas and carriages. Léperos gambled away the blankets off their backs. The only religious invocations were the pleas of cardplayers, who rubbed medallions of the Virgin of Guadalupe that hung about their necks: "Ah, Holiest Mother, Mother of the Mexicans . . . throw a queen my way."

If he won the round, the gambler "devoured the medal with kisses . . . but if the Virgin turned a deaf ear to his entreaties and the stake was lost, then there was only blasphemy . . . so terrible that one had to cover one's ears."[75]

For the rich, the three-day gambling and religious fest ended with a ball al fresco on a nearby hillside. The ladies danced with their jewelry ablaze in the torchlight. And the léperos, biding patiently in the shadows until the waltzes ended, then scavenged the grass for a rich harvest of lost diamonds and pearls.[76]

Politics in Mexico City during the post-Independence era was marked by an instability and corruption unequaled in the country's history. A decline in the quality of political leadership matched the economic and social decadence of these decades. Most of the creole elite avoided politics. The poor remained disenfranchised. The new nation underwent forty-two changes in government between 1821 and 1855 as the presidency slipped from the hands of one general to another. And eventually, even they lost all confidence in their ability to rule. "Everything seems to be at odds, like the races who populate our land," said a leading general, Mariano Arista, summarizing the utter pessimism of the political class as he stepped down from the presidency toward the end of this era. "In the obstinate battle between progress and regression in the country, the ground constantly shifts under those who rule, and a perpetual state of anarchy has become the norm."[77]

To be sure, there were political ideologies and programs. The political spectrum divided broadly between conservatives—favoring a strong centralization of power in Mexico City, the preservation of the Church's privileges, a large standing army—and liberals, advocating more power sharing with the provinces, the expropriation of Church wealth, a small militia of volunteers. But there were numerous factions within these two camps. And what counted most was the personal opportunism of military officers. Among these politicians and generals, the towering figure of the era, the embodiment of its political style and substance, was Antonio López de Santa Anna.

Santa Anna was born in 1794 to a family that had emigrated from Spain to Veracruz in the early eighteenth century. He was acutely aware of the contempt that gachupínes held for creoles, particularly those born in a tropical environment like Veracruz which, according to the racial theories of the day, was supposed to quicken the degeneration of white European stock. But prejudice did not breed rebellion

in the young Santa Anna. He chose instead to advance his social status
by joining the Spanish army as a cavalry officer, and he fought almost
the entire Independence wars on the royalist side. Relatively tall, thin,
with piercing black eyes and a sallow complexion, Santa Anna early
displayed a charismatic quality of leadership over his fellow officers
and soldiers. Modeling himself after Napoleon—despite the fact that
the French ruler was a hated figure among Spaniards for his invasion
of the mother country—he wore his hair in the Bonaparte style, from
back to front, and rode only a white steed.

In 1821, in the waning days of colonial rule, Santa Anna suddenly
abandoned the royalist cause and joined Iturbide's revolt against Spain.
The transfer of allegiance was precipitated by a dispute concerning his
promotion: the vice-regal government named him a lieutenant colonel,
while Iturbide offered to promote him to full colonel and entrust him
with command of his native province of Veracruz.[78] Demonstrating
a self-interest that would mark the rest of his political life, Santa Anna
chose the rebel side.

He led several successful battles against the royalist forces. But Iturbide, recognizing in Santa Anna his own brand of extreme ambition
and penchant for self-promotion, hesitated to appoint him governor
of Veracruz after Independence was won. It was one of Iturbide's
gravest mistakes. Even when Iturbide, as Emporor Agustín I, finally
gave him the coveted governorship after a five-month delay, Santa
Anna remained his implacable enemy.

In December 1822, Santa Anna set off the first military coup attempt
of the Independence era by proclaiming a republic to replace the new
monarchy. He lost leadership of the revolt, but under the guidance
of other officers the coup overthrew and exiled Iturbide. Though promoted to full general, Santa Anna was not trusted by the new government, which sent him into exile of sorts by appointing him governor
of the distant province of Yucatán. From there he antagonized the
government by openly objecting to the execution of Iturbide, who had
returned from abroad in 1824 in an attempt to regain his throne. Santa
Anna's plea for mercy for the ex-emperor was probably heartfelt: it was
not his style to kill his political foes, and in the decades ahead he
would expect them to reciprocate.

The next significant juncture in Santa Anna's political career came
in 1829. He was named commanding general of the army against a
Spanish expeditionary force sent to Mexico to restore colonial rule.
Despite some inept military tactics and few real battles, Santa Anna
defeated the 2,700 Spanish troops, and was proclaimed "Benefactor

of the Nation" by a grateful Congress. During the next four years, he used his sizable military power to block or support several presidents as they rose and fell in the quicksand of Mexican politics.

Santa Anna reached the presidency for the first time in 1833, when sixteen of the eighteen state legislatures cast their votes for him. He was still identified with the liberal, federalist cause, which espoused a republican form of government with considerable powers for the provinces to counterbalance the traditional dominance of Mexico City. But Santa Anna was in fact not wedded to any ideology. He also displayed a boredom with everyday government administration. No sooner was he elected than he turned over actual executive functions to his vice-president and retired to his hacienda in Veracruz, where he preferred the role of ultimate political arbiter. But when the vice-president demonstrated an unexpected independence, Santa Anna drove him into exile and returned to Mexico City to direct government affairs—this time as a fervent supporter of the Church, a staunch conservative, and advocate of strong centralist rule over the provinces.

Santa Anna's first debacle came in 1836 over the issue of Texas. Mexico had encouraged Americans to move into Texas in order to develop the vast, little-inhabited province. But in the 1830s, the Mexican government became increasingly concerned that it might lose control over the territory. These fears were borne out when the American settlers declared the independence of Texas in 1835. Santa Anna quickly raised a large army and marched north. At the Battle of the Alamo, his troops killed all 183 of the Americans defending that fort, and after another engagement at Goliad, some 350 American prisoners were massacred on Santa Anna's orders.

In the weeks that followed, Santa Anna's army won a succession of battles, and the general prepared for a triumphal return to Mexico City. But in an inexplicable act of carelessness, he neglected to post sentries around his camp one night even though a large American force headed by Sam Houston was reported in the vicinity. Houston's men made a surprise attack that evening and routed the Mexican troops. Santa Anna escaped in disguise, but was taken prisoner a few days later. To obtain his release, he agreed to sign a treaty aimed at eventually granting independence to Texas. Returning to Mexico City in 1837, he was thoroughly discredited and retired from office to his Veracruz hacienda.

In 1838, war again provided Santa Anna an opportunity for political resurrection. The French blockaded Veracruz, ostensibly to collect claims against the Mexican government on behalf of French nationals.

The most outstanding of these claims was submitted by a French baker whose shop in the capital had been looted by Mexican soldiers—thus giving the conflict its name, the "Pastry War." Santa Anna was appointed commander of the Mexican troops in Veracruz, and beat back a French force that came ashore. Severely wounded in the engagement by a cannon shot, he lost his left leg.

His reputation restored, he retired once again to his estate, but continued to swing his military support behind one political faction after another. In 1841, he overthrew the government and had himself appointed president. Santa Anna's term this time was marked by his repeated looting of the treasury, lucrative contracts with entrepreneurs, and a public ostentation that surpassed even Iturbide's brief imperial rule. Theaters and statues in Mexico City were erected in his honor. He hosted elaborate state dinners and surrounded himself with a resplendently uniformed personal bodyguard of 1,200 men. The orgy of spending and self-aggrandizement reached its climax in 1842, when Santa Anna ordered that his amputated leg be transferred from a plot on his Veracruz estate and solemnly buried in Mexico City. A huge military parade escorted the urn containing his leg across the capital to the main cemetery, where it was buried with eulogies in a magnificent shrine under the gaze of the cabinet, the diplomatic corps, and other notables. It was as close as anybody had come to witnessing his own funeral, and Santa Anna was reduced to tears by the speeches, poems, and salvos to his departed limb. Only two years later, when Santa Anna marched out of the capital to put down one of the interminable military uprisings of the era, a mob stormed the cemetery, desecrated the shrine, burned the general's leg, and scattered the ashes. Santa Anna fled to exile in Havana.

But another war, this time with the United States, revived his political fortunes yet again. The Mexican government had repudiated the 1836 accord granting independence to Texas because Santa Anna had signed it under duress. And so, when the United States announced the admission of Texas into the Union in 1845, Mexico called it an annexation of its territory and declared war. From his refuge in Havana, Santa Anna played a double game: he tendered his services to the Mexican government for an end to his exile; at the same time, he offered the United States most of Mexico's territories north of the Rio Grande (virtually all of the present Southwest and California) in exchange for a payment of $30 million and Washington's aid in recovering his presidency.[79]

Santa Anna succeeded in convincing both governments. An American naval blockade was lifted to allow his ship to reach Veracruz, but after arriving in Mexico City, he took command of the army to face an American invasion force led by General Zachary Taylor in northern Mexico. Santa Anna fought Taylor's troops to a standstill, then retreated to the capital to prepare its defense against another American expeditionary army under General Winfield Scott, who had landed at Veracruz. Although the Mexican troops in the capital heavily outnumbered the invaders, Santa Anna, in a supreme act of egotism, withdrew his forces from battle after a personal dispute with another general over command of the garrison. Encountering a much-reduced Mexican force, Scott's army occupied Mexico City. The only shred of national pride plucked from the debacle was the conduct of the young cadets of Mexico's military academy who fought to the last man in defending their stronghold at Chapultepec Castle on the western outskirts of the city. Unable to find refuge with his own people, Santa Anna surrendered to the U.S. troops, and in 1848, with American aid, he exiled himself to Venezuela. Meanwhile, in a treaty ending the war, Mexico was forced to cede the northern half of its territory to the United States in exchange for a paltry $15 million.

During the next five years the country plunged into anarchy, with generals and colonels carving up fiefdoms in the provinces and refusing to recognize the authority of Mexico City. In the capital itself, troops were out of control and pillaged shops and houses at will. From Venezuela, Santa Anna sent word that he was still available to rescue the nation. Having witnessed the overthrow of five ineffectual presidents in as many years, Congress voted to make Santa Anna chief of state once again in 1853.

It was Santa Anna's eleventh presidency, and it was no better than the previous ten. He was as venal as ever, cutting deals with business cronies, indulging in endless costly ceremonies, and stealing public funds. The $10 million he split with Escandón, the entrepreneur and speculator, for turning over the Gadsden Purchase to the United States led to his final exile in 1855. As an elderly man, he was allowed back into the country in 1872, and died after four quiet years at his Veracruz hacienda.

The constant betrayals, personal rivalries, and coups of the Santa Anna era created a cynicism toward politics among Mexico City residents, rich and poor. During more than three decades, military uprisings were so common that they often excited little attention. Mrs. Calderón de la Barca captured this spirit of indifference when she wrote that three masked balls proceeded on schedule in the capital despite forecasts that a coup would occur that very night.[80] At other times, fierce battles between military factions erupted on the streets, inflicting heavy casualties among civilians and leaving just about everybody perplexed over the causes of the outbursts.

In July 1840, for example, military rebels espousing federalism seized President Anastasio Bustamante in his bed at the National Palace, and were in turn besieged by loyal troops. "The cannon are roaring now," wrote Mrs. Calderón, surveying the uprising from her bedroom window. "All along the street people are standing on the balconies, looking anxiously in the direction of the palace. . . . The state of things is very bad. Cannon planted all along the streets, and soldiers firing indiscriminately on all who pass. . . . Both parties seem to be fighting the city instead of each other."[81] For twelve days the cannonades continued, leaving hundreds of dead and wounded, and flattening scores of buildings. President Bustamante retained his office, grateful not only that the rebels were put down but also that Santa Anna, residing in his hacienda, did not oppose him this time.

"The tranquility of the sovereign people during all this period is astounding," Mrs. Calderón observed. "In what other city in the world would they not have taken part with one or other side? Shops shut, workmen out of employment, thousands of idle people subsisting heaven only knows how—yet no riot, no confusion, apparently no impatience. Groups of people collect on the streets, or stand talking before their doors, and speculate upon probabilities—but await the decision of their military chiefs as if it were a judgment from heaven from which it is both useless and impious to appeal."[82]

On a few occasions, politicians, particularly liberals, were able to ignite riots among the poor. In 1828, for example, a mob in the capital overthrew a conservative president-elect and then sacked the Parián market, famous for its luxury imports. In 1844, rioting also scuttled one of Santa Anna's attempts to establish a dictatorship. But the populace eventually demonstrated a distrust of all political factions. Liberal politicians, who claimed to be heirs of the radical populism espoused by Hidalgo and Morelos, joined with conservatives to disenfranchise the poor. Laws were passed that gave voting rights only to people earning more than 200 pesos a year. Little wonder, then, that in time the poor even failed to respond to patriotic calls in defense of the country. A liberal politician, José María Lafragua, summed up their disillusionment by contrasting the fervor of Hidalgo's hordes fighting against the Spanish Crown in 1810 and the apathy of the poor who watched American troops invade their capital in 1847: "Then . . . they were a new people whose eyes shone with liberty and all its enchantments. Today, they are a people who have been deceived a thousand times and who fear the revolutions because of the press gangs, taxes and oppressions."[83]

THIRTEEN

JUÁREZ
AND MAXIMILIAN

The final exile of Santa Anna was followed by an ideological hardening between conservatives and liberals. Their only point of agreement was that the three decades since Independence had been an unmitigated disaster. The conservatives yearned for a return to the order, stability, and economic expansion under an elite stewardship that characterized the late colonial era. So disillusioned were the conservatives by the failure in political leadership that growing numbers in their camp were willing to entertain the notion of a foreign monarch ruling over Mexico. For the liberals, Mexico was in a quagmire precisely because its rupture with its colonial past had not been more complete. They had been responsible for the armed movement—known as the Revolution of Ayutla—that overthrew Santa Anna for the last time. And their program was primarily aimed at reducing the power and influence of the Church and the military, the strongest institutions to emerge from the wreckage of the colonial era and the early Independence period. The violent confrontation between liberals and conservatives over the next dozen years brought to Mexico City two of the most unlikely leaders the country ever had: Benito Juárez, Mexico's only pure Indian president, and the Archduke Maximilian, one of the bluest bloods in Europe.

Benito Juárez has often drawn comparison with his contemporary, Abraham Lincoln. There are certain superficial parallels in their lives: the humble family backgrounds; their reputation for personal honesty and political principle; the civil wars that marked their presidencies.

But in many ways, Juárez had to overcome even greater obstacles than Lincoln faced.

Juárez was born in 1806 in the tiny, mountainous village of Guelatao in the southern province of Oaxaca. His parents were pure-blooded Zapotecs, descendants of the people who built the wondrous pyramids of Monte Albán a thousand years before. Orphaned as an infant, Juárez spent his childhood tending sheep for an uncle. At age twelve, with at best only a cursory knowledge of Spanish, he walked the forty miles to Oaxaca City, the capital of the province, intent on educating himself. He found employment as an assistant to a bookbinder, a Franciscan lay brother, who agreed to pay for his schooling if the boy aimed for a career in the clergy. Juárez attended a seminary, but eventually rejected the priesthood. Instead, he worked his way through law school, where according to his own writings, he was exposed to professors who shaped his liberal tenets.

As a lawyer, he collected fees only infrequently because his clients were poor. Many of them were involved in disputes with the clergy. In a typical case, in 1834, Juárez represented Indian villagers who refused to pay their local priest his annual parish fees, which they claimed were too high. After an ecclesiastical court ruled in his favor, the vindictive priest had Juárez arrested for allegedly inciting people against the authorities. The charge against Juárez was dropped, but only after he had spent nine days in jail. According to Juárez, this was one of many incidents that led him to oppose "religious intolerance, a State religion, and the possession by the clergy of that abundant wealth which they abused. . . ."[1]

Using his law practice as a springboard for politics, Juárez became a city councilman, state legislator, a delegate to the national Congress, and then governor of Oaxaca. He was governor in 1848, when Santa Anna, fleeing from the American occupation of Mexico City, sought refuge there. He was turned away by Juárez, who considered him a traitor for failing to defend the capital. Juárez may already have been ill-disposed toward Santa Anna from an incident twenty years before in Oaxaca when as a young waiter at the general's table he had to suffer his racial slurs. Santa Anna never did forgive Juárez for denying him asylum—that "Indian of such low degree," he called him. And when Santa Anna gained the presidency for the last time in 1853, one of his first acts was to exile Juárez.

Juárez spent his two years of exile rolling cigars in a tobacco factory in New Orleans, where he joined other Mexican liberals expelled by Santa Anna. They became the ideologues for the armed revolt aimed at replacing Santa Anna with a liberal junta. The so-called Ayutla Revolution, named after the remote mountain village where its program was conceived, triumphed in 1855. The new government marked the beginning of a period in Mexican history known as the Reform.

Juárez, who became minister of justice, played the crucial role in enforcing three controversial Reform laws that led to a confrontation between Church and State. The first of these measures, the Ley Juárez, curtailed the rights of officers and clergymen to be tried only by military and ecclesiastical courts—an anachronism dating back to the colonial era. A second law, the Ley Lerdo, ordered the Church to divest itself of its real estate other than buildings used for worship. And a third measure, the Ley Iglesias, attempted to place marriages, baptisms, and funerals within the financial reach of the poor by prohibiting the clergy from charging excessive fees for the sacraments.

In championing the Reform laws, Juárez and his liberal colleagues were not only motivated by the common injustices they had witnessed in their dealings with venal clergymen. They were convinced that the huge material holdings of the Church were the most important impediment to growth in the country, and that if ecclesiastical wealth could be transferred to the private sector, the Mexican economy would miraculously revive. The riches of the Church were as much a panacea for the liberal Reformers as the colonial silver mines had been for the advocates of Independence earlier in the century.

At the beginning of the Reform, the Church owned or administered as much as one quarter of the nation's wealth.[2] Ecclesiastical riches were openly on display to the populace. Who had not gazed with wonder upon the gold and silver ornaments on the walls and altars of church buildings, the jewel-studded chalices and crucifixes, the prelates with vestments encrusted with pearls?

But in reality, the Church's coffers were depleted in the post-Independence years by forced loans to the government, by mortgages and other credits that businessmen and landowners failed to repay, and by urban house rents that went uncollected. One key measure of the erosion of ecclesiastical wealth was the decline in clergymen. In 1850, they numbered 4,615, or about half the total reported by Humboldt at the end of the colonial era.[3] The priesthood had become a less appealing path to social and economic advancement, no doubt because incomes for the clergy had diminished, and the private donations from testaments that had sustained priests and nuns during colonial times had dried up.

Moreover, the liberals were probably mistaken in their belief that

Church properties and money were unproductive. Agricultural lands owned by the clergy were as well managed as those in private hands, and sold their produce on the open market. In fact, most ecclesiastical estates after Independence were rented to private individuals.[4] It is also difficult to fathom the liberals' complaints about the Church's role as a creditor. By charging interest rates far lower than those offered by private speculators, it acted as the nineteenth-century equivalent of a modern development bank. Even more surprising was the criticism leveled at the Church's predominant position in urban real estate. No private landlord collected lower housing rents than the Church, nor was more tolerant of impoverished tenants who failed to pay.

The liberals did not intend to bring Church properties under state control. They were champions of private enterprise, and they sought to force the sale of ecclesiastical holdings to private individuals. The government stood to benefit by charging a 5 percent transfer-of-ownership tax on all these transactions.

Although the Church was the institution most affected by the Reform laws, the liberals contended that the clergy was not being singled out. State properties deemed unnecessary for the functioning of government were also put up for sale, and an effort was made to turn communally held Indian lands over to private ownership. While the Reformers hoped that these transactions would benefit all social sectors, it soon became evident that only the more affluent Mexicans had the financial means to purchase the properties coming on the market. In Mexico City, few tenants could afford to buy their Church-owned homes, and in the countryside, ecclesiastical estates and Indian communal lands were more likely than not to end up in the hands of rich hacienda owners instead of middle-class farmers and impoverished peasants.

But even before the Reform laws could be fully tested, the choleric reaction of the clergy precipitated a civil war. The conflagration was ignited by the passage of the 1857 Constitution, which incorporated the Reform laws and permitted the practice of other religions besides Roman Catholicism. From Rome, Pope Pius IX issued an inflammatory statement depicting Mexican liberals as heretics:

> The Chamber of Deputies, among the many insults it has heaped upon our Most Holy Religion and upon its ministers, as well upon the Vicar of Christ on Earth, has proposed a new constitution containing many articles, not a few of which conflict with Divine Religion itself. . . . For the purpose of more easily corrupting manners and propagating

the detestable pest of indifferentism and tearing souls away from our
Most Holy Religion, it allows the free exercise of all cults and admits
the right of pronouncing in public every kind of thought and opinion.
. . . And so that the Faithful who reside there may know, and the
Catholic world may understand, that we energetically reprove everything the Mexican government has done against the Catholic Religion,
against its Church, its sacred ministers and pastors, and against its laws,
rights and properties, we raise our Pontifical voice in apostolic liberty
. . . to condemn, reprove, and declare null and void everything that
the civil authority has done in scorn of ecclesiastical authority and of
this Holy See. . . ."[5]

The following year, the liberal Mexican president Ignacio Co-
monfort was deposed by General Félix Zuloaga, a conservative backed
by the Church hierarchy. Juárez, whose recent appointment as chief
justice of the Supreme Court made him next in line for the presidency,
was placed under arrest. But after Zuloaga was proclaimed president
in Mexico City by the conservatives, Juárez escaped to Veracruz, where
he established a rival, liberal government and staked his own legal
claims to the nation's presidency.

The polarization between liberals and conservatives cut across all
segments of Mexican society. Accusing Juárez and his Reformists of
a godless attack on religion, the Church was able to attract support
from both rich and poor. Most military officers also sided with the
conservative cause because of the Reform's stated goal of reducing the
power and size of the armed forces. Hacienda owners and entrepreneurs
were more opportunistic. While they stood ready to profit from the
forced sale of ecclesiastical properties, many of them remained loyal
to the clergy because they were the chief beneficiaries of Church loans.
They also deeply distrusted Juárez's liberal political philosophy, much
preferring an elite authoritarian government to one that purported to
extend enfranchisement to the poor. Mexico City became a conservative stronghold even among many of the poor, at least partly because
they feared that their rents would increase if their Church-owned
homes passed into private hands.

But Juárez and his liberals also commanded a formidable following.
His supporters included people who were convinced that the Zuloaga
government was simply a continuation of the corrupt military regimes
of the past decades. Others shared the Reformist conviction that the
Church enjoyed too much political and economic power. Juárez's
reputation as a defender of his fellow Indians gave him a strong con-

stituency in the countryside. But even there, a significant minority of Indian villages backed the Church and the conservatives because they felt that their communal lands were threatened by the Reform laws.

After annulling the Reform laws, the Zuloaga government launched a military offensive against the Juaríztas. The superior equipment, training, and leadership of the conservatives gave them a string of victories during the first year of the civil war. But by holding Veracruz and other Gulf ports, the liberals were able to control the customs receipts that traditionally financed government and to receive military supplies from abroad. With the experience gained from their initial defeats, a number of able commanders emerged from the liberal ranks, and the military campaign turned in their favor.

Dissension in the conservative camp led to Zuloaga's replacement as president by General Miguel Miramón, and the war took a fiercer turn. Atrocities became frequent on both sides. Prisoners were routinely shot. After a battle for the control of Mexico City, the conservatives executed not only the wounded enemy soldiers but all the doctors who had attended them. The devastation of the countryside recalled the worst excesses of the Independence wars. "Haciendas are abandoned, ranchos deserted, and even whole villages pillaged and sacked, leaving nothing but desolation wherever the armies of the contending parties have made their tracks," wrote the American consul in Veracruz.[6]

Ironically, the conservatives began to view church holdings as the salvation of their cause, in much the same way that the liberals had. After several million pesos in Church loans proved insufficient, the government forced the sale of a significant portion of ecclesiastical properties and used the proceeds to finance the war effort. By 1860, the walls, altars, and statues of Mexico City's churches, monasteries, and convents were being stripped of their gold, silver, and gems to help cover the government's expenses. Church leaders justified these extreme measures by pointing to the increasingly radical anticlericalism of the Juárez government ensconced in Veracruz. By 1859, Juárez had decreed the nationalization of ecclesiastical property in the event of a liberal victory. The Church would no longer receive compensation for its holdings. Instead, the proceeds from their sale were destined for the Reform government as collateral to guarantee its loans from abroad.

The three-year civil war ended in 1861 with victory for the liberals and Juárez's return to Mexico City as president. Paintings and photographs of his entry into the capital all seem to capture the puritanism of the man: the austere, unsmiling Indian face that revealed no emotion except determination; the stiff-backed, square-shouldered torso fitted into a black-vested suit that gave him the air of an uncompromising judge. Juárez was in fact magnanimous with some of his opponents. After winning the presidential election in March 1861, he commuted the prison sentences of dozens of prominent conservative military officers and politicians. He faced harsh criticism from his liberal supporters because conservative rebel groups were still militarily active in the countryside, while some of their leaders, like General Miramón, had escaped abroad and continued to plot against the government.

Juárez was less lenient with the clergy. Five bishops were exiled. Religious processions were banned, and the ringing of church bells was restricted to the hours of Mass. Priests were forbidden to wear their vestments on the streets. Half of the capital's eighty-four churches were closed, because they were deemed superfluous for the spiritual needs of the populace. By early 1863, all twenty nunneries were abolished.

Of more permanent consequence was the destruction of some of the most architecturally distinguished ecclesiastical buildings in the capital. The huge monastery of San Francisco, built in the 1500s, was demolished to make way for two new streets that were supposed to ease traffic in the city's center. All that was left standing of La Merced monastery was its beautiful cloister. The San Agustín monastery was converted into the National Library. Dozens of less renowned ecclesiastical buildings were obliterated and their land sold to speculators. In later years, even liberal memoirists of the era would lament the vanished glory of the capital's religious structures and the loss of a sizable portion of its colonial architectural heritage.[7]

Nothing demonstrated the opportunism of Mexico City's entrepreneurs more than their attitude toward Church property. Although most had initially supported the conservative cause, they secretly sent bids for Church holdings to the Juárez government in Veracruz when the war appeared to be tilting in favor of the liberals. So desperate were the financial straits of the Juárez government after its victory that it was forced to sell the confiscated ecclesiastical properties as quickly and cheaply as possible. Conservative businessmen became the largest purchasers of these houses, haciendas, and churches by putting down only 20 percent in cash and covering the rest with promissory notes that were never redeemed.

Among Mexico City's entrepreneurs, Manuel Escandón was again most remarkable in displaying a talent for prospering under any regime. After being forced into exile in 1855 because of his scandalous financial dealings with Santa Anna, he was allowed back to Mexico City a few years later by the liberal government, which gave him a concession to begin building a railway from Veracruz to the capital. Escandón openly sided with the conservatives after their coup in 1859, and renegotiated his railway concession with them on better terms. He then received an even more favorable deal from the Juárez government after its civil war victory in 1861. His relations with the liberals became so strong that in July of that year a French diplomat called him "the soul of the new cabinet."[8] As a partner in a financial company, he bought into the largest mining enterprise in the country, and negotiated long-term exemption from taxes for the mine. Escandón and his brothers also invested large sums in nationalized Church properties, and took advantage of Reform laws to redeem their hacienda mortgages to the Church with very low payments.

While the liberal victory in the civil war was a financial boon for many Mexico City entrepreneurs, it left the Juárez government with crushing economic burdens. The sale of ecclesiastical properties failed to produce nearly enough revenues to cover the public deficit or the repayment of loans to foreign creditors. In July 1861, Juárez declared a two-year moratorium on Mexico's debts abroad, and thus unwittingly set the stage for another invasion.

Well before the debt crisis, the possibility of foreign intervention was mounting. In both Europe and the United States, the political and economic disorder in Mexico had encouraged widespread contempt for the country. In 1859, American diplomats in Mexico were already reporting rumors of French plans to invade and establish a colony there. U.S. intentions were hardly more honorable. To attract American loans and diplomatic support during the Mexican civil war, Juárez had been forced to dangle the possibility of ceding Baja California and Sonora to the United States. He had also considered granting overland transit rights to Americans across the Isthmus of Tehuantepec, Mexico's narrow waist connecting the Gulf-Atlantic with the Pacific Ocean. In the end, Juárez did not have to part with any territory. But influential voices in the United States continued to advocate expansion south of the border. In December 1860, for example, *The New York Times* called for the annexation of Mexico. "The Mexicans, ignorant and degraded though they are," the paper editorialized, might welcome the establishment of a U.S. protectorate in Mexico, "followed by free trade and the right of colonization . . . so that after a few years of pupilage the Mexican States would be incorporated into the Union under the same conditions as the original ones."[9] In Great Britain, the London *Saturday Review* informed its readers that Juárez and his followers were full-blooded Indians no different from "the Ojibbeways who were exhibited in London a few seasons ago," and that only a conservative victory in the civil war could "prevent the Mexican people from relapsing into the beliefs and practices of savage life."[10]

With the announcement of the debt moratorium in July 1861, Mexico's foreign creditors reacted as if the country had placed itself beyond the pale of civilization. France, Britain, and Spain prepared a joint military expedition to force the Juárez government to repay its debts. The Mexican Church and its allies encouraged the intervention, and sought to broaden their scope into a full-fledged invasion that would replace Juárez with a foreign ruler who would support their conservative program. Defeat in the civil war had led the Mexican clergy and conservatives to openly advocate monarchism as the solution to the country's ills. They had approached various royal houses in Europe hoping to find an unemployed prince who might be suitable for the throne of Mexico. And they thought they had located their candidate in Maximilian, archduke of Austria.

Viewed through the warped prism of Mexican monarchists and churchmen, the notion of Maximilian as emperor of Mexico had its merits. He was a Habsburg, a member of the same royal household as the Spanish kings who had conquered the New World. The two hundred years of Habsburg rule in the Americas had been marked by far more harmonious relations with the Roman Catholic Church than the Bourbon dynasty that succeeded to power in Spain and its colonies. In the nineteenth century, the Habsburg Empire, from its throne in Vienna, governed a crazy quilt of nationalities that extended over Austria, Hungary, and parts of present-day northern Italy, Yugoslavia, Germany, Czechoslovakia, Rumania, and Poland. To inhabit and rule yet another foreign land, even one as distant as Mexico, would be less daunting for a Habsburg than for other European monarchs accustomed to living within their national boundaries. As the Austrian viceroy of northern Italy, Maximilian, in his twenties, already had a taste for foreign rule. His appetite for a New World kingdom had been whetted by a visit he made in 1860 to Brazil, where his relative, Pedro II, was monarch. As a Habsburg, Maximilian also was on excellent terms with the Vatican, which looked to the Austrian Empire for the protection of the papal states against the ambitions of Italian nationalists.

But Maximilian's supporters among the Mexican clergy and conservatives overlooked some key traits in the archduke's personality and politics that might have led them to search elsewhere for an emperor. He grew up always aware that his older brother, Franz Joseph, was destined to become ruler of the Habsburg Empire, and the rivalry between them became increasingly acute. Maximilian embraced the liberalism of younger brothers in European households, a phenomenon common to siblings out of power. While Franz Joseph was autocratic, distant, ever conscious of protocol—in short, always displaying the behavior expected of a Habsburg emperor—Maximilian could afford to project himself as affable, benevolent, and progressive-minded to the empire's subjects. And they manifested their obvious preference for the younger brother by shouting, "Long live the Archduke Max!" as his carriage drove through the Vienna streets—an accolade rarely accorded to the less popular emperor.[11]

During his tenure as Austrian viceroy in northern Italy (1857–59), Maximilian organized relief for the victims of natural disasters, opened his purse to countless hardship cases, and helped repatriate political exiles. He invited Italian scientists, musicians, writers, and artists to his court in Monza. And he openly advocated the formation of an autonomous government for northern Italy, with its own ministry in Vienna.

Austrian conservatives were appalled by these populist gestures, which they feared would inevitably loosen the Habsburg hold over the Italian dominions. There was a personal bitterness as well among Austrian military officers who found themselves excluded from balls and other social functions at the Monza court, because Maximilian thought that the sight of their uniforms might offend his Italian guests.[12] But Maximilian's liberal behavior did nothing to appease Italian nationalists. They were not dissuaded from their goal of ridding their provinces of Austrian rule. Nor did they find the archduke's avowed progressivism in any way convincing. How liberal at heart could the man be if he delighted in all the sumptuous trappings of royalty? Every day he hosted more than a score of guests at gourmet dinners in his Monza court, with a full orchestra at their backs, waiters clad in eighteenth-century costumes, and little African pages serving coffee and deserts.

Maximilian had been viceroy for only a year when Italian rebels began to increase their activities—holding clandestine meetings, circulating anti-Habsburg literature, and occasionally attacking Austrian troops. Certain that his brother's liberalism was to blame, the Emperor

Franz Joseph ordered a return to the old policy of coercion in northern Italy. Educational reforms were suspended, Austrian currency replaced Italian money, and greater numbers of Italian youths were drafted into the occupation army. Disillusioned by both the resurgence of Italian nationalism and the Austrian hard-line reaction, Maximilian resigned as viceroy.

Maximilian's knack for antagonizing both liberals and conservatives became a portent for his rule in Mexico a few years later. His Italian experience also displayed another disturbing element in his character—a tendency to seek refuge from political crisis in aestheticism. Even before relinquishing the viceroyalty, Maximilian was spending months in Trieste supervising the construction of his white limestone castle at Miramar. It was there that he retired in 1859 with his wife Charlotte, and busied himself with gardening, landscaping, and poetry writing.

For Charlotte, the years at Miramar were difficult. As daughter of King Leopold of Belgium and grandchild of Louis Philippe of France, she felt that she was destined to share a throne. Petite and attractive if not quite beautiful, she had been courted by King Pedro of Portugal and Prince George of Saxony. Her marriage to Maximilian was a love match, with the added incentive of ruling beside him as vicereine of northern Italy, a role which she relished. In his journals, Maximilian wrote about his retirement from the viceroyalty as an opportunity to renounce "the vanities of the world, to live far removed from the deceit, the weariness and the fraud we have experienced in the last few years, content to retire to a serene and sunny climate, studying the arts and sciences and cultivating my garden."[13] In her own correspondence, Charlotte displayed no such equanimity at her sudden demotion to the life of a private, albeit aristocratic, citizen. She was bored by the few local charities that occupied her time at Miramar. And she was distressed that four years of marriage had produced no children.

Maximilian and Charlotte had settled into their Miramar castle when halfway across the world, Juárez and his liberals were making their triumphal entry into Mexico City on January 1, 1861. Disgruntled Mexican conservatives fanned across Europe attempting to gain the support of any chief of state who would listen to their proposition that Mexico was ripe for a foreign king. Three Mexican monarchists, all of them diplomats who lost their jobs when Juárez came to power, were particularly adept in pushing this scheme, and worked in close concert: José Gutiérrez de Estrada, José Hidalgo (no relation to the Mexican revolutionary priest), and Juan Almonte.

Gutiérrez de Estrada could claim credit for first suggesting Maximilian as the best candidate for the throne of Mexico. His mother-in-law, an Austrian countess, was mistress of the Maximilian and Charlotte household in northern Italy, and followed the couple to Miramar. She wrote to Gutiérrez de Estrada about the frustrations of her employers in Italy, and extolled their qualities as potential sovereigns of Mexico. The task of approaching the Austrian government fell upon Almonte, who as former Mexican minister to France was friendly with the Austrian ambassador in Paris.

But the plan would have made no progress without the approval of Napoleon III, the European ruler most in favor of foreign intervention in Mexico. It was José Hidalgo who was assigned to this delicate endeavor. Young, handsome, charming, he had befriended Napoleon's Spanish wife, Eugénie, when both of them were adolescents in Madrid. He had become one of her social intimates in Paris, and tirelessly impressed upon her the idea of Maximilian as emperor of Mexico, backed by French troops and serving the interests of France. Eugénie, in turn, repeatedly broached the subject with her husband, Napoleon, and arranged meetings between Hidalgo and the French monarch.

Napoleon III was a nephew of the great Napoleon Bonaparte, and had already embarked on an expansionist policy intent on restoring France to the glory of his famous relative's heyday. In the name of the Second French Empire, he broadened his nation's claims over Algeria, brought Indochina under colonial rule, invaded Lebanon, established French footholds along the West African coast, and helped defeat Russia in the Crimean War. But France had once enjoyed sovereignty over vast stretches of Canada and the United States. And Napoleon III was enthralled at the possibility of regaining in Mexico a New World empire for his country.

The moment appeared propitious in 1861. The United States, embroiled in its Civil War, could hardly contest an invasion of Mexico. Juárez, by suspending payments on his country's foreign debts, provided a justification for intervention. And Britain and Spain, the other main creditors, were prepared to join France in carrying out some sort of military action.

The European invasion of Mexico began in December 1861 with the landing of six thousand Spanish troops in Veracruz. A month later, seven hundred British and two thousand French soldiers also disembarked on the Mexican Gulf coast. An agreement between the three nations had called for a limited offensive aimed at recovering their debts from Mexico. But when it became obvious that Napoleon was intending to conquer the country, Britain and Spain withdrew their forces. The French army, reinforced by 4,500 troops, then prepared to march inland alone.

In the months before launching his invasion, Napoleon had already begun a search for a puppet monarch for Mexico. Eugénie and her friend Hidalgo had piqued his interest in the Archduke Maximilian, and he brought up the subject in diplomatic exchanges with Maximilian's brother, the Emperor Franz Joseph of Austria. Franz Joseph quickly agreed to the idea of placing his troublesome sibling on the throne of Mexico with French military support. But Maximilian himself was reluctant for a number of reasons.

The archduke distrusted both his brother and Napoleon. He suspected that Franz Joseph's only concern was to make him disappear from the European political and social scene. And suspicion turned to certainty when Franz Joseph insisted that Maximilian remove himself from the succession to the Habsburg throne before accepting a monarchy in Mexico. Napoleon was even less trustworthy. He had once promised Maximilian not to support Italian nationalists against the Austrian occupation of the northern provinces of their country. But when Maximilian became viceroy in Italy, Napoleon resumed his aid to the rebels. And as soon as Maximilian resigned the viceroyalty, French troops joined the nationalists to drive the Austrians out of Italy. After that sort of perfidy, what confidence could Maximilian have in Napoleon's vows to support him as emperor of Mexico?

There were other reasons for Maximilian's hesitation in accepting a New World throne. He knew nothing of Mexico, except that it was a strife-torn country that had executed a home-grown emperor (Iturbide) forty years before. He found the Mexican monarchists—Gutiérrez de Estrada, Almonte, and Hidalgo—too conservative for his tastes, and was skeptical of their assertions that their countrymen would enthusiastically accept him as king. The one meeting he had with Monsignor Antonio Labastida, the exiled archbishop of Mexico, had gone badly when Maximilian expressed little sympathy for the Mexican Church's claims to recover its nationalized properties. His doubts about the throne could be resolved, Maximilian contended, only if the Mexicans voted for him in an open plebiscite.

At first, the Mexican monarchists and Napoleon recoiled in disbelief. But then they decided that Maximilian's seemingly preposterous conditions would not impede their plans. The French conquest would proceed. Juárez would be driven from Mexico City. An election would

be arranged in the French-occupied zones that would hand the archduke his cherished mandate. What better proof could he have that
Mexico wanted him on the throne and that Napoleon's commitment
to him was steadfast? As for his rivalry with his brother, Franz Joseph,
surely Maximilian could be persuaded that the certainty of being emperor in the New World was worth giving up the remote possibility of
ever inheriting the Habsburg realms.

The French invasion of Mexico, however, was not moving
smoothly. Guerrilla snipers and yellow fever took their toll in Veracruz.
And when Napoleon's army besieged Puebla, it was routed by Juárez's
regular troops on May 5, 1862—a date that has since been enshrined
as a Mexican national holiday. But Napoleon was able to use the
Puebla defeat to his advantage. He knew all along that he would need
a far larger expeditionary force to occupy Mexico. French public opinion, which had opposed the intervention in Mexico, now clamored
for the vindication of national honor. Napoleon assembled an additional thirty thousand troops, and a year later the reinforced French
army swept aside Juárez's troops.

Juárez abandoned Mexico City on May 31, 1863, and fled to the
northern provinces. On June 10, the French occupied the capital to
a triumphal public reception organized by Mexican conservatives and
the clergy. The French commanding general, Elie Forey, was so
enthralled that he dashed off a message to the minister of war back in
Paris:

> I have just entered Mexico City at the head of the army. . . . The
> entire population of this capital welcomed us with an enthusiasm verging
> on delirium. The soldiers of France were literally crushed under the
> garlands and nosegays. . . . I attended a Te Deum with all the officers
> in the magnificent cathedral of this capital, which was filled with an
> immense crowd. Then the army, in wonderful form, paraded before
> me amid cries of Vive l'Empereur Napoleon! Vive l'Impératrice Eu-
> génie! These people are avid of order, justice and real liberty.[14]

Other French observers took a more jaundiced view of the celebrations. Captain Pierre-Henri Loizillon had entered the capital a week
before the main body of French troops, and had time to size up the
political mood of the populace. In a letter to his parents, Loizillon
readily admitted that "balconies were draped with hangings" and "windows were crowded with women, one prettier than the other." But,
he asserted, "the people were attracted by curiosity rather than enthu-

siasm. The places where we were applauded or showered with flowers were rare, and those few demonstrations had been organized by the police. . . . Nevertheless, the Commander-in-chief has taken all this for true coin, his vanity preventing him from judging things at their true value."[15]

Nobody could dispute the joy of the clergy. As soon as the French occupation began, there was a deafening peal from the capital's belfries at all hours, day after day, as if to make up for the constraint of years past. Massive religious processions, joined by French army officers, wound their way through the streets. And every Sunday, a military Mass was celebrated in the Cathedral for an entire division of French troops. Priests once again were seen on the streets wearing their vestments. Nuns returned to their convents. And a number of churches that had been shut down by the Juárez government were reopened.

Mexican conservatives were just as pleased as the clergy. General Forey appointed a thirty-five-member assembly almost entirely weighted in their favor, and also a provisional government headed by Almonte, the monarchist who worked so hard for French intervention and the eventual enthronement of Maximilian. Social life for the Mexico City elite immediately revived under the occupation. The main municipal theater was thrown open to formal balls. Once again, upper-class women could put on their Parisian gowns and jewelry. So smitten was one French colonel by their beauty that he penned the following elegy: "Supple, graceful, small, mignone, sprightly and quick-witted, with her flat complexion, her eyes like black diamonds shadowed by long lashes, her fleshy red lips disclosing teeth as white as pearls, her abundant ebony hair, the upkeep of which is one of her great cares, her opulent and delicate shape, and her arched foot, the Mexican woman might pass for one of the wonders of creation."[16]

But the goodwill between the French and their Mexican supporters began to dissolve soon enough. To the irritation of conservatives, General Forey proclaimed a program intended to reconcile them with the liberals. There was to be freedom of the press—unless, that is, a newspaper drew more than two warnings from the occupation authorities, in which case it would be closed down. The military draft would end some of its more odious practices, such as marching Indians and other impoverished conscripts to the barracks with ropes around their necks as if they were convicts. Government corruption would be severely punished. Taxes would be made more equitable and less burdensome for the poorest Mexicans. There would be religious liberty, and Church properties which had already been expropriated under the Juárez government would not be returned to the clergy.

The Church prelates were outraged by these last two decrees. When their protests to Forey went unheeded, priests took matters into their own hands. They visited houses that had once been ecclesiastical property and warned tenants not to pay rents to their landlords, since it would only be a question of time before these buildings reverted to the Church, and then tenants would be forced to pay a second time. The French counted on the passing months to cool clerical passions. But even while Napoleon's troops carried out their campaign against Juárez's forces in the provinces to make the country safe for the religious conservatives, the clergy was fighting a rearguard action against the French in Mexico City. Archbishop Labastida, who had returned to the capital from his exile, began denouncing the French as no less an enemy of the Church than Juárez. He threatened to close the Cathedral to the French army and excommunicate its officers. He relented only when a new French commander-in-chief, Achille Bazaine, warned that he would blast open the Cathedral doors with cannon.

The ill will between the French and the clergy soon infected conservative laymen. Upper-class Mexicans declined to rent their villas and mansions to French officers. By September 1863, after four months of occupying the capital, the French commander was complaining that Mexicans were ungovernable. "I assure you," he wrote Napoleon, "that I should prefer to attempt another siege of Puebla than to be here as a moderator of these people who do not want to be moderated."[17] Even the allure of Mexican upper-class women seemed to wilt for the French. The same colonel who had declared them so ravishing wrote that their "passions were entirely on the surface and that everything was sacrificed to the facade."[18]

Disillusioned by the French occupation, the Mexican clergy and conservatives placed all their hopes on the arrival of Maximilian and Charlotte. After chasing Juárez and his forces to the northernmost provinces, the French held the plebiscite demanded by Maximilian, and, to no one's surprise, it produced a heavy majority in favor of offering him the Crown of Mexico. Following intense negotiations, Maximilian and Napoleon III signed the Convention of Miramar, which called for the presence in Mexico of at least twenty thousand French troops under Maximilian's command until 1867. Their salaries and the huge French debt claims on Mexico would be paid by Maximilian's government from revenues raised among the populace. To assuage Maximilian's old distrust of the French emperor, a secret clause in the Convention included a pledge by Napoleon that "whatever should happen in Europe, France would never fail the new Mexican Empire."[19] There was still Maximilian's bitter dispute with his brother, Franz Joseph. But the archduke finally agreed to waive all claims to the Habsburg Crown in the event his brother died. Before leaving Europe for the New World, Maximilian also made it clear that Charlotte's enthusiasm to sit on a throne had helped to persuade him. "Who, in my position, in youth and health, with a devoted and energetic wife spurring me on, would do other than accept the offer?" he wrote.[20]

During the long sea voyage from Trieste to Mexico, Maximilian was in an ebullient mood, giving free rein to his fantasies of recreating a royal European atmosphere in the Mexican capital. He spent most of his time on ship putting together a manual of court etiquette, including detailed instructions for his Mexican chamberlain. A measure of his political naivete was a lengthy letter he wrote to Juárez inviting him to Mexico City to settle their differences in the best interests of the nation.

Flabbergasted by the ingenuousness of the letter, Juárez could hardly contain his sarcasm in penning his response from his redoubt in Monterrey:

"You tell me that, abandoning the succession to a throne in Europe, forsaking your family, your friends, your fortune, and what is most dear to a man, your country, you have come with your wife, Doña Carlota, to distant and unknown lands to satisfy the summons spontaneously made by a people that rest their felicity and their future in you." But what of the sacrifices of the thousands who died defending a legally constituted government from foreign invaders? And did Maximilian really believe that Mexicans had freely voted to install him as their monarch? "It is given to men, sir, to attack the rights of others, to take their property, to attempt the lives of those who defend their liberty, and to make of their virtues a crime and of their own vices a virtue," Juárez concluded. "But there is one thing which is beyond the reach of perversity, and that is the tremendous verdict of history. History will judge us."[21]

Maximilian and Charlotte arrived in Veracruz at the end of May 1864. It was not a memorable occasion for them. Their ship anchored on the wrong side of the harbor, and there were no high dignitaries to receive them. The town was hot, humid, and fetid. Flies and yellow fever mosquitoes swirled around mounds of uncollected garbage, while thousands of black vultures circled in the skies or perched on crumbling rooftops to digest their meals of rubbish. A stronghold of Mexican liberalism, Veracruz offered no festive crowds to the monarchs. By the time the royal couple boarded the train inland, Charlotte was in tears.

The railroad to Mexico City was nowhere near completion, and a short distance from Veracruz the royal party transferred to horse-drawn European carriages. But when the narrow, winding, potholed mountain roads proved impassable for these lumbering vehicles, the travelers had to board smaller, less comfortable stagecoaches. The reception in the towns grew increasingly warmer as Maximilian approached Mexico City. And entering the capital from the north in order to pay homage to the Shrine for the Virgin of Guadalupe—the preeminent symbol of religious nationalism—the monarchs received a welcome more tumultuous than the French army had experienced exactly two years before.

"All the 'Vivas' seemed to come from the heart, inspired by a genuine emotion at the sight of these young sovereigns," wrote the local French newspaper. "Even in the most isolated streets in outlying districts, far from the center, there was hardly a house which had not made some attempt at decoration—a wreath of leaves, a branch of palm, or a few brightly colored rags."[22]

But it was Juárez's assessment from his northern refuge that proved more telling in the end. "These people of Mexico are so strange," was his response to reports of the popular welcome accorded to Maximilian. "For anyone who does not know them and who is foolish, their ovations and flatteries are intoxicating, they sweep him off his feet and destroy him. . . ."[23]

At thirty-two years of age, the tall, thin Maximilian was resplendent in the full-dress uniform of a Mexican general. His flowing, muttonchop whiskers hid a weak chin, the only defect in an otherwise handsome face. Charlotte, eight years younger, wore a diamond tiara and a lace mantilla that gave her a dark Spanish look. The royal carriage slowly wended its way through the mobbed avenues to the Cathedral, where Archbishop Labastida received the couple at the doors and then presided over a coronation ceremony. From there, the royal party proceeded to the National Palace. The cheering crowds called Maximilian and Charlotte out to the balcony a score of times, while fireworks exploded throughout the night until dawn.

The celebrations were not the only cause of the royal couple's sleeplessness. The palace, unoccupied for two years, had only been cleaned perfunctorily and abounded with lice and bedbugs, finally forcing Maximilian to seek repose on a billiard table. The building's chambers, though numerous, were too cramped for the monarchs' tastes. According to Charlotte's lady-in-waiting, Countess Paula Kollonitz, "the Empress' drawing-room was exactly like a room in a European hotel."

The large Viennese retinue accompanying the monarchs was so distressed by the accommodations after years spent in the sumptuous palaces of Italy and Trieste that many of its members wished to return to Europe immediately. "They found nothing ready, and did not know where to procure anything," wrote Kollonitz. "There was no kind and sensible manager to guide and command; nothing was organized. . . . Some of them, who had come across the ocean with wives and children, did not know where to turn for absolute necessaries. They ran about, pale and disturbed, in gloomy despair. . . . Some of the Mexicans in attendance at the Palace took advantage of the complete ignorance of these poor people to defraud them, and they were in consequence in a very unhappy frame of mind."[24]

The cultural and social chasm between the Austrians and their Mexican subjects yawned wider every day. Maximilian's meticulously annotated manual of court etiquette went unread. Charlotte was surrounded by fourteen Mexican ladies-in-waiting, who stumbled over each other at every turn. The Austrians were appalled by the Mexicans' lack of punctuality. When the monarchs attended a gala performance in their honor, they arrived scrupulously on time, but found the theater empty. The Mexican elite drifted in an hour or more late.

Many of the Austrians soon reflected the racial prejudices of the French officers, who after two years in the capital showed utter contempt for the Mexicans. At a ball hosted by the French commander, General Bazaine, a number of Mexican ladies were invited without their husbands, and sisters without their brothers. "Many did not come at all," wrote Kollonitz, "And others came merely out of respect to the Imperial pair."[25] Mexicans were barred from toilet facilities used by the Europeans. And when a European lady accepted to dance a quadrille with Almonte, the highest-ranking Mexican official in the monarchy, she said her husband remarked that "he never thought he would see me partnered by a nigger."[26]

Maximilian himself was far more willing than other members of his entourage to mingle with his Mexican subjects and extol their virtues. His greatest asset as a ruler was his Viennese charm. He had made an effort to learn Spanish before coming to Mexico, and used it not only to converse with the Mexican elite but also to hear out impoverished supplicants whom he received every day at the National Palace. Touring the outskirts of the capital, he even learned to accept the hearty Mexican *abrazo* (embrace) of some of his overly exuberant subjects. Early in his reign, he wrote a letter to his younger brother expressing enthusiasm for his new realm:

> I found the country far better than I expected, the calumnies of the European press untrue, and the people far more advanced than is supposed at home. Our reception everywhere was cordial and sincere, free from all pretence and from that nauseating official servility which one very often finds in Europe on such occasions. . . . The so-called entertainments of Europe, such as evening receptions, the gossip of tea-parties, etc., etc., of hideous memory, are quite unknown here, and we shall take care not to introduce them. The Mexican's only enjoyment is to ride about his beautiful country on his fine horse and go to the theatre frequently; I too naturally treat myself to the latter.[27]

The monarchs seemed to feel that their winning personalities could overcome any adversity, even political opposition. As a gesture of goodwill to the Juaríztas, Maximilian appointed a few moderate liberals to his cabinet. But Juárez considered them no better than traitors, and conservatives also were angered. The emperor soon clashed with the Church. The clergy was irate when he declined to restore ecclesiastical properties and announced he would uphold the previous French decrees on the matter. In a meeting with the papal nuncio, Maximilian discovered that his charm was of no avail in persuading the Vatican to renounce its nationalized properties. And Charlotte was just as unsuccessful in her own lengthy interview with the Pope's envoy, who exasperated her.

"I can tell your Majesty," she wrote to Empress Eugénie in Paris,

> that nothing has given me a better idea of hell than that interview, for hell too is no more or less than a blind alley with no way out. To try to convince someone, knowing that it is love's labour lost, that one might as well be talking Greek, since one side sees things black and the other white, is a labour fit for the damned. Everything slid off the nuncio as if from polished marble. . . . Really, to assert that the country, which is steeped in hatred for the theocracy, wishes this property to be restored to the clergy, bears witness to a blindness and a stubbornness beyond compare.[28]

Maximilian and Charlotte were repeating the same political mistakes they made during their viceroyalty in Italy. As foreign usurpers of power, their natural constituency lay with those conservative elements in the local population who had helped enthrone them. Yet, in their mindless idealism, the monarchs sought to be loved and obeyed by all. The centrist balance they tried to strike left them at odds with conservatives and liberals alike.

The ultimate source of Maximilian's power, however, was Napoleon and his French troops. And here too, Maximilian deluded himself into thinking he had boundless room to maneuver. Only a few months after the Austrian arrived in Mexico, he began to receive impatient letters from the French emperor demanding that Mexico resume its debt repayments to France and foot the expenses of the occupation army. When Maximilian bridled at being treated like a puppet ruler and protested that his kingdom was too chaotic and impoverished to meet its financial obligations, Napoleon coldly reminded him that "Mexico owes her independence and her present regime to France."[29]

Maximilian reacted to his mounting political difficulties with the same sort of escapism he had demonstrated in Italy. Uncomfortable in the austere, unaesthetic National Palace, he moved to the former summer castle of the Spanish viceroys in the woody hills of Chapultepec on the western outskirts of Mexico City. Increasingly, he devoted his time to supervising the remodeling of Chapultepec Castle and its flowered terraces. With its panoramic view of the city, the valley, and mountains, Chapultepec reminded him—he said—of the spectacular vistas that unfolded from his Miramar Palace near Trieste.

Maximilian depleted a good part of his treasury on a beautification campaign for Mexico City. A broad avenue was built connecting Chapultepec Castle with the city center. Streets were realigned and bordered with trees. Gas lamps were installed in the central district, and mule-drawn streetcars made their first appearance. A National Museum was erected to place Mexico's pre-Columbian heritage on display. Fresh water supplies were improved. Garbage collection was restored. The emptying of waste water and urine from balconies was prohibited. No detail escaped Maximilian's eye: concerned for pedestrians, he ordered birdcages and potted plants to be removed from window sills.

Frustrated and bored by finances and politics, Maximilian toured the provinces surrounding the capital. He justified his prolonged absences by citing the need to become better acquainted with his realm. He was also exhilarated by the reception of the local populace, unaware as he was that they had turned out to greet him either out of curiosity or because the local authorities had insisted on their presence. Arriving in the town of Dolores on the anniversary of Hidalgo's uprising there against Spanish colonial rule, he saw no anomaly in identifying himself with the rebel priest. After repeating Hidalgo's famous cry—"Mexicans, long live Mexico!"—he evoked "the glorious word of 'independence,' which flashed like a meteor across the dark night sky and woke a nation from the sleep of centuries, lighting the way to liberty and emancipation." Such was Maximilian's self-delusion that when the crowd roared its approval, he was convinced that "the cheers were for me, not Hidalgo."[30] Later, he would repeatedly assert that Mexicans in the provinces were much gayer and loyal than those in the capital.

Only a year after their enthronement, the monarchs were complaining about their subjects in Mexico City. The sourness of the clergy had spread to other sectors. Charlotte noted that during her carriage rides through the capital the streets were silent and pedestrians ignored her. On occasion, she even had to upbraid groups of men who failed to remove their hats when she stepped out of her coach.

But much worse were the malicious rumors and gossip that were being disseminated by the clergy and conservatives about the relationship between the monarchs. Maximilian grew resentful of the widespread perception that his wife was more decisive and politically savvy than he. Eventually, he excluded Charlotte from his cabinet meetings. Tensions enveloped their private lives. They took to sleeping in separate chambers, and Maximilian was reported to have had numerous liaisons with Mexican women, who were spirited in and out of Chapultepec Castle by a side door. Seeking to evade his wife and political troubles, Maximilian began spending long stretches south of Mexico City, in Cuernavaca, where he restored the former villa of an eighteenth-century silver baron. There, Maximilian fathered his only known child, a son, from his affair with his gardener's wife. Charlotte was said to have found solace with a Belgian officer, Colonel Alfred Van der Smissen, who was her favorite at the Mexico City court and often escorted her around the capital. She was also suffering from increasingly severe bouts of depression. Her natural gaiety could suddenly give way to a distant coldness, or uncontrollable sobbing.

Far more important than the personal setbacks of Maximilian and Charlotte was the deteriorating military and political situation. The struggle in Mexico began to assume the shape of a twentieth-century guerrilla war. Juárez had been chased ever further north—first to San Luís Potosí, then to Monterrey, and finally Chihuahua on the border with the United States. Everywhere, his troops were defeated in con-

ventional, set-piece battles on open plains. But the French could do
little against Juárez's guerrillas. No sooner was a town abandoned by
the European soldiers than the Juaríztas returned to reclaim it. And
except for the immediate vicinity of the capital, roads throughout the
country were unsafe from their attacks.

Exasperated by the guerrilla activity, Maximilian declared the Juaríztas ordinary bandits subject to summary execution whenever they
were captured. Even before this decree, atrocities were being committed by both sides. But the monarch's open approval of the killing
of rebel prisoners was an act that Juárez considered unpardonable.

Events abroad were creating insoluble problems for Maximilian.
The United States was vehemently opposed to the presence of European troops on its southern border and had never recognized the
Maximilian government. With the end of the U.S. Civil War in 1865,
large quantities of American munitions were sent to the Juaríztas, and
Washington stepped up its diplomatic pressure on Napoleon to withdraw his army from Mexico. The French emperor was already under
siege at home, where public opinion had turned hostile toward his
costly intervention in the New World. He also had a worrisome military
threat in Europe with the rise of Bismarck's Prussia. By the end of
1865, Napoleon informed Maximilian that he intended to begin the
withdrawal of French troops from Mexico—notwithstanding their secret agreement signed a year before at Miramar pledging that "France
would never fail the new Mexican Empire." As viceroy in Italy, Maximilian had foolishly trusted Napoleon's promises, and now he was
again betrayed by the French ruler.

By the spring of 1866, the pressure on Maximilian to abandon
Mexico was coming from virtually all quarters—Washington, France,
his own family in Austria, and, of course, Juárez. It was Charlotte
who helped dissuade the wavering monarch from fleeing. She had
always lived in dread of abdication. Her French grandfather, Louis
Philippe, had been forced to relinquish his throne and seek exile in
Britain. Her husband and she had already surrendered rule once before—the viceroyalty in Italy. She was humiliated by the prospect of
returning to Europe with her status diminished both by the folly
of the Mexican adventure and her husband's previous renunciation of
the succession rights to the Austrian throne. "Abdication is only ex-
cusable in old men and idiots," she wrote her husband in a memorandum summarizing her arguments. "It is not permissible in a young
man of thirty-four, full of life and hope for the future, for sovereignty

is the most precious of all possessions."[31] And she vowed to go to Paris to plead Maximilian's case before Napoleon.

By this time, Charlotte's emotional instability had become notorious in the Mexico City court. Yet, in her moments of seeming clarity, her vehemence could sway Maximilian, and he gave her permission to sail to Europe. He was aware that she had little chance of convincing Napoleon to keep his troops in Mexico. But he may have wanted her away from his increasingly unsafe realm, or perhaps he wished a respite from her.

Charlotte's voyage did nothing to improve her emotional state. There was no royal farewell for her at Veracruz, and she kept to her cabin throughout the Atlantic crossing, allegedly out of fear of contracting yellow fever from the other passengers. Arriving at the French port of St. Nazaire, she found no welcoming committee from Napoleon's court, nor did any French officials receive her at the Paris train station. Napoleon sent a message to her hotel pleading illness and suggesting that she go on to Belgium where her father, King Leopold, had recently died. But Charlotte would not be put off. Without an invitation, she barged into the French court and confronted Napoleon.

At first, she argued cogently that abandoning the Mexican Empire would be a diplomatic disaster for France, and that in time Mexico's great mineral wealth would more than compensate for the costs of maintaining an army there. When logic failed, she upbraided Napoleon for breaking his promises. But he was unmoved. The Prussian threat to the east was far more serious than ignominy in Mexico. Only weeks before, on July 2, 1866, Bismarck's army had inflicted a crushing defeat on Austria at Sadowa. The balance of power in Europe had shifted against France and in Prussia's favor. Napoleon would need every soldier he had, including those in Mexico. He shed a few tears over Charlotte's plight, and then sent her away empty-handed.

From Paris, Charlotte traveled to the Vatican. Her insanity was now manifest. She had intended to plead with the Pope to use his influence on Napoleon. But when she was brought into the pontiff's presence, she broke down and accused the French emperor of plotting to kill her. All her attendants, she asserted, were Napoleon's agents, intent on poisoning her. Attempting to calm her, the Pope offered a cup of chocolate. Charlotte refused, declaring it to be poison. After more than an hour, the pontiff managed to extricate himself from the painful interview. But papal officials could not convince Charlotte to return to her hotel because she claimed she was surrounded by murderers there. The Church prelates were beside themselves. Clearly, the woman was insane, yet she was still the empress of Mexico. Finally, with great embarrassment, they agreed to allow her to become the first woman ever to spend the night in the papal palace—causing a sensation the next day in Rome.[32]

From Rome, the distraught empress was accompanied to Miramar by her Belgian family, who had been alerted by the Vatican. She ranted that even Maximilian was conspiring to kill her. Charlotte's malady was hopeless. And her personal physician wrote to Maximilian informing him that she would never return to Mexico.

At this point, the winter of 1866, Maximilian was also losing his grasp on reality. Early in his reign, he had reacted to political adversity by sheer escapism, burying himself in architectural projects and wasting time in festive tours of the provinces. Now, with his empire collapsing, he refused to flee. The news of the impending withdrawal of the French army was causing a rapid shift in loyalties among the populace of Mexico City. In political satires staged in the theaters, Maximilian and Napoleon were lustily booed, while Juárez was cheered. In the countryside, meanwhile, Juárez's armies were routing Maximilian's Mexican troops, no longer spearheaded by French soldiers.

The French commander, General Bazaine, made one last unsuccessful attempt to convince Maximilian to abdicate and return to Europe. In February 1867, the French troops evacuated Mexico City. The silence punctured by occasional jeering from bystanders on the avenues was in distinct contrast to their triumphal entry into the capital almost four years before. The military situation had deteriorated so badly that the French army had to negotiate a safe-conduct to Veracruz with Porfirio Díaz, Juárez's brilliant general, whose troops controlled the southern and eastern regions of the country. Numerous Mexican conservatives and clergymen, including Archbishop Labastida, escaped with the French to Europe.

Maximilian, meanwhile, decided to take personal command of his Mexican army. Although he had no battlefield experience, he announced he would lead them in a final clash against the Juaríztas in Querétaro, some hundred miles north of Mexico City. He was under the illusion that Querétaro was more loyal to him than the capital. But by the time Maximilian reached the provincial city, desertions had reduced his ten thousand troops to a bare sixteen hundred. They were facing an enemy army five times as large. The Juaríztas laid siege to the heavily fortified city, and almost three months later, on May 15, forced Maximilian's surrender.

Juárez ordered Maximilian to be tried by court-martial. He was to be considered a criminal, using the same standard he had decreed for Juaríztas who were captured in battle. The court found him guilty of violating Mexico's sovereignty and causing the death of thousands of Mexicans, and sentenced him to be shot.

In spite of numerous pleas for clemency from European monarchs and the U.S. government, Juárez remained adamant. He was convinced that his magnanimous pardon of his conservative opponents after the Reform War had only brought more conflict to his country. Juárez also was intent on dissuading any foreign nation from again contemplating intervention in Mexico, which had already suffered four invasions in the last four decades.

On June 19, 1867, Maximilian was executed by a firing squad. Court-martialed and shot alongside him were two of his Mexican generals: Tomás Mejía and Miguel Miramón, the same man who had once usurped the presidency from Juárez, escaped abroad, and returned to Mexico as one of the empire's more savage military officers. Months later, Maximilian's remains were shipped to Trieste, and from there transported by train to Vienna. After an imperial funeral, Maximilian was buried in the family vault.

Charlotte, meanwhile, was in seclusion at Miramar, where she was said to have given birth to a son from her liaison with Colonel Van der Smissen, the Belgian officer who was her favorite at the Mexico City court. Decades later, persistent rumors suggested that the child was General Jacques Weygand, a French officer who distinguished himself in both world wars. Weygand's family background was a mystery, but he bore a striking physical resemblance to Van der Smissen. [33]

Charlotte survived Maximilian by sixty years, dying at the age of eighty-six in 1927. Utterly deranged, she spent most of these decades in a moated castle belonging to her royal family in Belgium. One day at the beginning of every spring, she insisted on reenacting her departure with Maximilian to their New World empire. With her attendants patiently looking on, she would board a small rowboat anchored in the moat and announce: "Today we leave for Mexico."[34]

For some years, the personal tragedy of Maximilian and Charlotte colored foreign views of Juárez and his Mexico. But the former Indian shepherd was right when he wrote that he would be favored by history's judgment over the Austrian archduke. The quixotic adventure snuffed out Maximilian's life and helped to rob his wife of her sanity. For Mexico, the costs were far higher: fifty thousand killed; an already stunted economy left in total disarray; and a yearning for order over political liberties that would test a shaky electoral system in the years ahead.

Like Lincoln, Juárez was a man of law, passionately committed to strengthening political institutions, but who was best remembered as a wartime president. Unlike the American statesman, Juárez survived to face the tasks of reconstruction. He announced ambitious programs to extend public education, to attract foreign and domestic investment, and to build an extensive railway system. But no government could have revived the country so soon after its prolonged traumas.

When Juárez died in 1872 early in his fourth term, Mexico was still in the throes of political and social chaos. The countryside was plagued by peasant revolts and bandit gangs whose ranks were swelled by cashiered army troops. In Mexico City, there were more criminals, beggars, and prostitutes than ever before. Every economic sector was in disrepair. Mining output had not recovered the levels reached in colonial days. Agriculture was disrupted. The industrial revolution had hardly touched the country. The treasury was empty, and the government could not render basic public services. The nation was mired in foreign debt and its credit rating was abominable. There was no investment from abroad, and Mexicans with capital dared not risk it.

Juárez had defeated domestic autocrats and foreign monarchs. He had shattered the constituencies that bred them—the Church, the old military establishment, the conservative parties. But even among his followers, he could not quench the craving for a strong man in a nation as prostrate as Mexico. The future dictator, Porfirio Díaz, was a man of impeccable liberal Reformist credentials. He would control the country for thirty-five years, longer than any leader since the Aztec era.

FOURTEEN

THE MASTER
OF MEXICO

Porfirio Díaz looms so large in Mexican history that the era between 1876 and 1911, when he served eight times as president, is known as the Porfiriato. Women and men maturing during these decades were the first generation since the colonial period to witness no serious uprisings and no wars, no barracks revolts, and no great bloodshed in the streets. Banditry in the countryside seemed under control. In Mexico City, criminals were confined to the poor neighborhoods, and the affluent were largely spared from the beggar hordes who plagued them in earlier epochs.

"Order and Progress" was Díaz's dictum. And once his iron hand had throttled the country's notorious political and social chaos, Mexico did indeed achieve remarkable economic advances. Railroads crisscrossed the nation. New ports were built, and older ones were modernized. Electricity became a source of energy to power factories and illuminate cities. Foreign capital poured into the country, and Mexican entrepreneurs confidently invested in agriculture and industry. Mining reached unprecedented levels: the value of gold production rose from 1.5 million pesos in 1877 to over 40 million pesos at the end of the Porfiriato; the annual silver output almost quadrupled in the same period, iron, tin, copper, and lead deposits were massively exploited for the first time thanks to the low transportation costs made feasible by the railway system. Oil became a valuable new export commodity. The doubling of the volume of manufactured goods suggested that Mexico was experiencing a profound industrial revolution. Agricultural exports boomed, as huge estates devoted their resources to coffee, sugar, and tobacco. In its heyday, the Díaz regime balanced its budget, recorded heavy trade surpluses, and achieved enviable credit ratings abroad.

Díaz aimed at nothing less than the modernization of the country, and he chose Mexico City as the showplace of this effort. After decades of stagnation, the capital's population doubled during the Porfiriato, reaching almost a half million by 1910, and its surface area quintupled. For a wealthy urban elite, this was a self-assured, gilded era—the Mexican equivalent of the Belle Epoque in Paris or the Age of Privilege in Victorian London. Rich aristocrats moved into French-style mansions, finally ridding themselves of the constant sight, stench, and din of the poor who had lived so uncomfortably close to them in the old downtown neighborhoods. They had their offices in multistoried buildings constructed with the iron and reinforced concrete techniques introduced from Europe and the United States. Their opera houses and theaters drew the acclaimed performers of the Western world. Within the relatively small boundaries of the neighborhoods where the wealthy lived, worked, and amused themselves, Mexico City seemed as modern and well endowed as Paris or London, with electric streetlights and tramcars, running water and piped sewage, tree-lined boulevards and heroic statues, department stores and haute-cuisine restaurants. For the rich, the Porfiriato was the best of times. They displayed an uncanny ability to screen out whatever was poor and shabby and backward from their field of vision, or to believe that the national legacy of poverty would eventually be washed away by Porfirian economic progress.

In fact, there were more poor than ever in Mexico City and the rest of the nation. The country's population grew from 8.7 million in 1874 to 15 million in 1910. But few inhabitants shared the bounty reaped by the remarkable 350 percent rise in the gross national product during those years. More than 80 percent of Mexicans remained tied to an agrarian existence. And the concentration of land ownership, greater than any time in the country's history, transformed half the rural populace into peons, whose purchasing power at the end of the Porfiriato had sunk to the levels of 1800.[1] For urban laborers, the industrial revolution translated into fourteen- to sixteen-hour shifts, six or seven days a week, and at wages that could not begin to satisfy their food, housing, and clothing needs.

If progress was illusory for the impoverished, so was the Porfirian version of order. The poor continued to be preyed upon by urban criminals and rural bandits. They feared policemen as much as the affluent admired them. For peasants who dared rebel against the usurpation of their land and water by great estate owners, for miners and factory laborers who joined strikes, Porfirian order meant state repression.

In a sense, Don Porfirio, as most of his subjects called him, was ahead of his times. His eventual fall provoked a debate that has raged into the late twentieth century wherever authoritarian regimes as disparate as the Shah's monarchy in Iran or the recent military governments in Brazil have sought to modernize their countries by concentrating wealth in a small elite, by inviting massive infusions of foreign capital, and by creating huge economic and social gaps between cities and rural provinces. But while Don Porfirio was in power, his experiment in national development drew almost unanimous admiration in the Western world. For Tolstoy, he was the political genius of the era. Andrew Carnegie called him "the Moses and Joshua of his people . . . who guided them for the first time along the road of civilization." Teddy Roosevelt hailed him as the "greatest statesman now living."

Most surviving photographs of Porfirio Díaz portray him in elderly royal splendor. His heavy jaw angles upward to stretch the folds beneath his chin. His full set of hair is like a white brush. A walrus mustache covers his mouth. The eyes are impassive, barely flickering with life. His ample chest fairly bursts with decorations and medals bestowed upon him by foreign heads of state. There was nothing incongruous about placing the aged profiles of Don Porfirio next to similar images of Kaiser Wilhelm and the Emperor Franz Joseph. For his subjects— most of them not even born when Díaz first became president—he seemed cast in the mold of a European monarch.

Only a few of his contemporaries would have remembered the earlier photographs of the man. Barely thirty years of age, his wiry torso appears ready to uncoil before the camera's lens. The gaunt face is also taut, with sullen eyes and a wild mustache. He is already a general, according to the captions. But he could be confused with a Pancho Villa or Emiliano Zapata, country rebels who helped put an end to his regime.

Like them, Díaz had humble, provincial roots. He was a mestizo, born in Oaxaca in 1830 to a family of unsuccessful small innkeepers. Fatherless in infancy, he briefly studied for the priesthood at his mother's behest, and then switched to the law—the same paths followed by his early hero, Benito Juárez. But Díaz was not intellectually inclined, and abandoned school before receiving a degree. He became a miner and muleteer. He was also a gunman for liberal politicians in Oaxaca.

In 1855, he organized a guerrilla band against Santa Anna, and began a military career that was to last almost continuously for the next two decades. He was a fierce commander during the Reform War, fighting on the side of Juárez against the conservatives. And he was Juárez's most effective general in the war against Maximilian and the French. He inspired his soldiers to persevere while other Juarízta commanders saw their men desert. His forced marches across mountains and jungles were legendary. And his personal courage was unquestioned: he went into battle while still recovering from wounds, and made a daring escape after being taken prisoner by the French army. It was Díaz who captured Mexico City from Maximilian's forces and then welcomed Juárez back to power.

In victory, the two men became bitter political rivals. Díaz ran unsuccessfully for the presidency against Juárez in 1867 on a platform that opposed the massive demobilization of the army. In 1871, he again lost to Juárez, this time claiming to be against the reelection of a president—a principle he himself discarded later in his political career. Charging fraud at the polls, Díaz led an abortive military revolt against Juárez, and then went into hiding. He failed in a third election run at the presidency. But in 1876, his military forces overthrew the incumbent, Sebastián Lerdo de Tejada, and Díaz finally took power.

In his first term, Díaz concentrated his efforts on imposing a semblance of political order on the country. He rewarded many of the higher-ranking officers who supported his coup by appointing them as state governors and provincial political bosses. He had to cope with numerous rebellions by peasants demanding land. Even more serious were uprisings by military commanders who were disgruntled at not having been sufficiently rewarded for their loyalty to the new president. Díaz also attempted some basic economic reforms by shrinking the bloated bureaucracy and clamping down on contraband—perhaps the two greatest drains on government finances. Still adhering to his platform against reelection, he stepped down from the presidency in 1880, and was replaced by Manuel González, a trusted military colleague.

It was during the next four years, while he was out of office, that Díaz began amassing support among wealthy Mexicans, particularly in Mexico City. Initially, they were deeply suspicious of him. All his adult life, he had committed himself to the liberal, Reformist cause with its antimonarchical, anticlerical, and somewhat populist ideology. He was a rough, vulgar, and provincial man, who during many years had slept more nights in an army tent than under a roof. Before attaining the presidency, he expressed acute discomfort in Mexico City.

He was impatient with the verbose, fractious legislature, and uneasy at balls and in drawing rooms of high society.

But the aristocrats were impressed by his seeming ability to guarantee political and economic stability. And Díaz himself was eventually seduced by Mexico City and its elite circles. In 1881, a year after the death of his first wife, an unsophisticated Oaxacan like himself, he married Carmen Romero Rubio, the teenage daughter of an upper-class family in the capital. Under her guidance, the fifty-one-year-old warrior made a concerted effort to acquire a cosmopolitan air, and soon became a fixture in Mexico City's social circuit. Even his physical appearance was transformed. The unruly mop of hair turned a dignified gray. The flowing mustache was neatly clipped. He took to wearing starched collars, well-pressed suits, and, on formal occasions, tuxedo and white gloves. His dining etiquette became impeccable: no elbows on the table, nor slurping of soup, nor toothpicks in public. "In social reunions he showed himself courtly with the ladies and held conversation of good taste with the gentlemen."[2] He saved his ribald yarns and provincial slang for his military colleagues, the men who rode with him against Santa Anna, Miramón, and Maximilian.

When Díaz easily won election to a second presidential term in 1884, he had fashioned an alliance between his loyal generals and the wealthiest Mexicans. The political posts in the provinces were largely in the hands of his military officers. His cabinet in Mexico City was mainly drawn from his new aristocratic friends. He had absorbed not only their social graces but also their notions on how to set Mexico on a course of economic growth: foreign capital had to be courted to finance railways, new port facilities, mines, public utilities, and industry; rural lands had to be allotted to huge estates whose production was oriented to profitable markets abroad; labor unrest and banditry had to be subdued to create a social peace that would encourage private investment.

It was a long-range program that could not be brought to fruition in a single presidential term. But Díaz had already abandoned his qualms about reelection. He would perpetuate himself and his followers in office by a combination of military power, political cunning, and a talent for persuasion.

Brute force was a mark of his early reign. When a plot against him was discovered in Veracruz in 1879, the general who arrested the alleged conspirators queried the president on what should be done with them. "Mátalos en caliente"—"Kill them while they are still warm," was Don Porfirio's instant reply. Eight men were shot without trial, and Díaz allowed his general to release to the newspapers the telegram ordering their executions. But that was a time of disorder when Díaz sought to project himself as a merciless strongman. In later years, there would be no written proof to link him to massacres of Yaqui or Maya Indians who refused to be dislodged from their lands, or peasants who protested the loss of their water supplies to large hacienda owners, or miners and factory workers who struck for more pay and fewer hours. Many of these incidents never appeared in the newspapers except in confused versions that spoke of outnumbered police and army troops defending themselves against drunken rioters led by mysterious provocateurs.

Díaz justified his myriad arbitrary acts by wrapping them in a constitutional cloak. Thus, he insisted on regularly scheduled elections, and through intimidation and fraud he and his candidates invariably received overwhelming majorities. Courts seemed to function normally, except when judges were called upon to hand down decisions favored by the regime. An adroit mixture of bribes, threats, and unofficial censorship effectively muzzled the newspapers. Within his own political camp, Díaz practiced a classic policy of divide-and-rule: generals were constantly shifted from one command to another; politicians were made to run for office in states other than their own, or were suddenly given bureaucratic posts in order to prevent them from building an independent power base; and factions loyal to Díaz were manipulated against each other.

When operating at its best, the Díaz political machine ensured that the dictator received sole credit for the regime's successes and that his subordinates accepted full blame for failures and scandals. It was a small price for his henchmen to pay. They were rewarded with many opportunities to enrich themselves. Díaz himself was far more interested in power than wealth, and was largely untouched by the corruption charges that tainted his civilian and military supporters. He sought to project himself as the nation's ultimate arbiter. Until his final years in office, labor leaders, oppressed peasants, and dissidents of every stripe learned to fit their complaints into a well-tested formula: "If Don Porfirio only knew what his subordinates have been perpetrating . . ." And Díaz would decide whether to heed their pleas or pretend that his ministers never informed him of these complaints.

As soon as Don Porfirio began to demonstrate his mastery over politics, he turned his attention to the repression of criminals, particularly in

Mexico City and its surrounding provinces. Only political strife had tarnished Mexico's image abroad more than violent crime. The two ills had reinforced each other in the decades before Díaz came to power. The recent wars had given a large portion of the population access to weapons, and led to widespread looting by armed factions who rarely distinguished between military duty and outright banditry. After Maximilian's forces were defeated, Juárez had demobilized more than sixty thousand soldiers from the opposing armies. They were often expert shots and horsemen, long accustomed to marauding in the countryside and the capital's outskirts.

These soldiers-turned-bandits became a constant peril on the highways leading to Mexico City. Travelers making their way by stagecoach from the Veracruz port to the capital fully expected to be robbed. They could not count on protection from the driver and guard, who would halt their eight-mule team and throw down their weapons at the first sight of ruffians. At best, the travelers might hope to receive a voucher from the first gang to rob them, indicating to any subsequent bandits that the coach had already been relieved of its valuables. But this was not always an effective safe-conduct. There were occasions when stage-coach passengers were victimized repeatedly on the same journey, and arrived naked in Mexico City. The distraught travelers could not leave the station until friends or relatives brought them a new set of clothing.[3]

The fatalistic attitude of travelers on the Veracruz–Mexico City road was reflected in an account by Edward E. Dunbar, a *New York Times* reporter who made the trip in the 1860s. Before boarding his stagecoach in Veracruz, he attempted to organize a heavily armed party that might dare to resist a bandit attack. His fellow passengers found his suggestion absurdly dangerous, and informed him that "those who are obliged to travel prepare to be robbed by leaving their arms, taking little or no baggage, a few silver dollars in the pocket to purchase some degree of civility, and as little else of value about the person as possible."[4] Dunbar reluctantly accepted their advice.

Seven bandits waylaid the coach about a hundred miles east of Mexico City. As soon as the driver saw them, he stopped the vehicle and alerted his passengers that a robbery was in progress. Following the commands of the thieves, the travelers got out and lay facedown on the ground. The bandits looted the baggage, searched the lining and cushions of the coach seats, and took money and valuables from the passengers' pockets. They were expert enough to check their victims' footwear, and found two gold ounces sewn into the boots of one passenger. Dunbar was robbed of eight silver dollars, but the bandits generously agreed to give him back one dollar for his breakfast in Mexico City. The journalist noted that the holdup had taken place in full view of three haciendas, and speculated that the outlaws might even be employees of those estates. Whether or not that was the case, hacienda owners everywhere offered bandits refuge and food in exchange for immunity from robberies. It was useless to denounce the highwaymen to the army, whose own brigandage was notorious. Dunbar was told of an episode in which the passengers of a stagecoach under attack managed to barricade themselves in a village church and fight off their assailants until a contingent of army troops arrived on scene. Surprised that the soldiers were actually firing upon them, the bandits cried out: "What do you fire upon us for? We are robbers too."[5]

To combat highwaymen, Díaz used a rural police force known as the "Rurales." Juárez had first organized them, filling their ranks with bandits who accepted government amnesty. But it was only under Díaz that the Rurales gained a reputation as an effective police force. Even years after ex-criminals stopped being recruited, Díaz maintained the myth that the Rurales were bandits-turned-lawmen. It added to their romantic aura. Who was more adept at hunting down ruffians, he argued, than a former member of their ranks? And what better chance at redemption for a criminal than to work for law and order? Even the uniform of the Rurales was intended to symbolize their transformation from bandits into lawmen. They were outfitted like *charros*—dandified Mexican cowboys—just as the most famous rural outlaws had dressed, with broad-brimmed sombreros, dark bolero jackets, and tight trousers spangled with silver buttons.[6]

Supposedly incorruptible and resourceful, the Rurales were identified with the apparent decline of banditry in the Mexican countryside. In fact, the advent of railroads played a greater role in making travel more secure. Trains were less vulnerable to robbers than stagecoaches had been. The vaunted effectiveness of the Rurales was also open to doubt because of the high turnover in their ranks—40 percent deserted or were discharged for various transgressions before completing their four-year enlistments.[7] Nor were they nearly as pervasive a force as their admirers claimed them to be. At no time did their numbers rise above 2,500 men. But they were highly visible to foreign travelers and wealthy Mexicans, the people they were intended to impress most. Díaz stationed the largest Rural forces in the central provinces around Mexico City and on the capital's outskirts. Others did guard duty on trains. Garrisons of Rurales were also concentrated in zones where foreigners had invested heavily in mines, factories, and plantations.

Whatever their shortcomings, the Rurales were hailed at home and abroad as Mexico's equivalent of the Royal Canadian Mounties and the Texas Rangers. Newspapers bannered their successes, and rarely mentioned their failures. Their officers were fêted at annual banquets hosted by Díaz himself. Every parade in the capital included a large contingent of Rurales, their horses prancing to the beat of a military band.

By the end of the Porfiriato, they had won over foreign visitors who had once feared to step foot in Mexico. "The order and security that everywhere appear to reign by day and night are . . . bewildering in a country popularly supposed to be the modern fountain-head of law-lessness," wrote Charles Flandrau, an American who journeyed through parts of Mexico in the early 1900s.[8] And an English widow, Rosa King, who started her own hotel in Cuernavaca in 1910, asserted that "the reputation of the country for exotic beauty and perfect safety in traveling brought as tourists and winter vacationers people of wealth and importance in their own countries."[9]

Díaz resorted to a similarly potent mix of mythmaking and selective policing to overcome Mexico City's image as a cesspool of crime. In the fifteen years before he rose to power, the capital experienced an acute upsurge in violent delinquency. The number of convicts in the main prison more than doubled between 1862 and 1877, despite a negligible rise in the capital's population. Newspaper articles and ed-itorials frequently described the city as the most dangerous in the world. The mayor conceded that few residents dared to walk the streets at night without a gun, and one columnist asserted that the revolver had become "an indispensable article of clothing."[10]

The creation of a modern police force for Mexico City was one of Díaz's early priorities. He sought inspiration abroad, and chose as his model the French gendarmerie system. The new Mexico City police force, established in the late 1870s, was in fact called the *gendarmería*. Like the Paris policemen, they dressed in blue uniforms and wore kepis on their heads. The two forces were similar in other ways as well. They made use of secret police agents who involved themselves in political activities, and they were not subject to popular supervision. In Mexico City, the gendarmería and other police agencies were under the control of the governor of the Federal District, who was appointed by Díaz and his minister of interior. The municipal council had not the slightest influence over the police.[11]

By cutting back hours and improving salaries to match those of skilled workers or minor bureaucrats, Díaz was able to fashion a police force that attracted competent officers for the first time in Mexico City's long history of crime fighting. In earlier eras, policemen tended to be described as unreliable, with unstable family lives, prone to drunkenness, and as poverty-stricken as the delinquents they were supposed to apprehend. But by 1900, according to Julio Guerrero, a noted criminal lawyer during the Porfiriato, many of them had become stalwart middle-class citizens—marrying by church ceremonies, living in clean households in neighborhoods closer to the city center than the working-class districts, drinking only moderately, and dressing in conservative suits when off duty.[12]

Between 1880 and 1910, the gendarmería tripled in size to more than three thousand officers, a rate of expansion that far outpaced the capital's population growth. By the end of the Porfiriato, Mexico City with one gendarme for every 153 inhabitants had more than twice as many policemen per capita as Paris, London, or the major American cities.[13] Foreign visitors were awed by the apparent ubiquity of the police in the Mexican capital. "One realizes something of the number of policemen at night, when they deposit their lighted lanterns in the middle of the streets and there is until dawn a ceaseless concert of their wailing whistles," wrote Flandrau, the American traveler. "You may become as drunk as you wish in a cantina [saloon] . . . but you must walk quite steadily when you come out . . . or you will be arrested before you reel ten yards."[14]

In fact, police protection was concentrated in those neighborhoods of the capital where affluent Mexicans and foreigners were most likely to live, socialize, and carry on their business. Working-class people, inhabiting the outskirts, were left on their own to fend against crime. Thus, in spite of the vaunted gendarmería, Mexico City still had one of the highest murder rates in the world. The Federal District—encompassing the capital and its suburbs—reported 400 homicides among its half million inhabitants in 1900, compared to 840 murders in all of France with its 39 million people. "Our lowest classes are forty times more criminal than those in France," asserted a Porfirian legislator, citing those statistics.[15]

While wealthier Mexicans took pride in the seemingly higher quality of police recruits, the poor complained of frequent abuses and corruption by the gendarmes. Street peddlers had to pay extortion to police officers. Fines for drunkenness were meted out as soon as customers emerged from a saloon, and the money was pocketed by the gendarmes.

According to Guerrero, the criminal lawyer, poor people were regularly robbed at the police precinct:

> Those persons who were detained for minor crimes were asked to surrender their money and any other objects of value, and told they would be held in deposit. . . . When a prisoner was taken to his cell, the gendarme would tell him in confidence that he would either be shot trying to escape or sent to a penal colony. The prisoner would then be offered a chance for freedom in exchange for some of this clothing. The deal made, the prisoner was allowed to escape, the gendarme kept the clothes, and the precinct kept the deposit. . . .[16]

It was during the Porfiriato that systematic police corruption—eventually to become a plague in modern Mexico—was born. Gendarmes were forced to prey on the poor in order to cover kickbacks demanded from them by their higher officers. Attempting to extort money from the rich could be dangerous, except in those instances when protection money was regularly paid to gendarmes to ensure that they not hinder an illegal enterprise. Such a case was brought to light in rather dramatic fashion in 1893.

The newspaper *El Demócrata*, perhaps too eager to test the limits of public expression, denounced the existence of numerous illegal gambling houses in Mexico City owned by Manuel Romero Rubio, Díaz's father-in-law. The editors followed up their exposé by bringing charges against Romero Rubio in court. In a remarkable decision, the judge ruled that the law only prohibited gambling in general, not the cardplaying and roulette offered in Romero Rubio's establishments. *El Demócrata* and a few other newspapers ridiculed the court's verdict, pointing out how the decision could be extended to other crimes: pesos could now be counterfeited because the law prohibited only the forging of money in general; arsenic could be sold by drugstores since only poison in general was illegal; killers could demand their freedom because they had used knives, guns, and axes, which were not specifically forbidden by the laws condemning murder. And besides, the newspapers noted, now that Romero Rubio's gambling houses had been declared legal, the police should be forced to reimburse the large monthly protection fees they had collected for years from Díaz's father-in-law.[17]

Díaz was not amused by the commentaries, and responded swiftly. Several of the offending newspapers were closed and their editors jailed on charges of advocating major crimes. Other newspaper offices were ransacked by plainclothes gendarmes claiming to be ordinary patriotic citizens angered by the press attacks against the government, the police, and the president's father-in-law.

Díaz often tried to avoid such blatantly illegal repression of opponents, particularly in Mexico City where his regime was most exposed to the public glare. A notorious incident in 1897 indicated just how far he had managed to distance himself from acts of reprisal by his police.[18] In September of that year, while walking with his entourage toward the Alameda Park to deliver an Independence Day speech, Díaz was punched in the back by an apparently deranged man. The president was more stunned than hurt. The unarmed assailant, Arnulfo Arroyo, was immediately captured by soldiers and rushed to army headquarters where he was interrogated by a military judge. The investigation was interrupted by the police inspector, Edmundo Velázquez, who insisted this was a matter under civilian jurisdiction and demanded custody of Arroyo. Placed in a straitjacket and gagged, Arroyo was taken to police headquarters in the Municipal Palace, located on the capital's main plaza, and was grilled for twelve hours. Late that night, a lynch mob of gendarmes masquerading as outraged citizens and shouting "Viva Porfirio Díaz!" stormed into the police headquarters unmolested by the officers on guard. Finding Arroyo still in his straitjacket, they riddled his body with knife wounds. Only then did the police, firing in the air, disperse the assassins. The shots attracted a crowd of onlookers, some of whom were allowed into the police headquarters to satisfy their curiosity, and then were arrested on charges of murdering Arroyo.

Inspector General Velázquez, a trusted crony of Díaz, had proved himself too Machiavellian. The public probably would have shrugged if he had simply announced that the prisoner had been killed while attempting to escape. But the more elaborate plot, snaring innocent bystanders, set off a major scandal. The inspector general was arrested. A few days later, he was found dead in his cell, a gun and a note next to his corpse proclaiming his loyalty to Don Porfirio. Most newspapers accepted the official version that Velázquez had committed suicide. But a few wondered how a revolver came into his possession while he was a prisoner.

Resentment of the police among the poor and by opponents of the regime led to the romanticization of some criminals. The phenomenon had a long tradition in the countryside, where bandit leaders often covered their criminal activities with a political veneer, and were im-

mortalized in songs and folktales for their alleged personal courage or
dogged resistance to corrupt politicians. But the new criminal hero
was a different sort. Operating in an urban environment, he was a
loner, who supposedly robbed only the affluent and thumbed his nose
at the police.

The most famous of these brigands was Jesús Arriaga, better known
as Chucho el Roto (Chucho the Dandy).[19] He began as a poor mestizo
artisan in Mexico City, where he combined cabinetmaking with petty
theft. Legend had it that he became a full-time criminal only after he
fell in love and kidnapped an upper-class young woman, who refused
his offer of marriage and denounced him to the police. With a knack
for self-promotion, Chucho wrote letters to the Mexico City newspapers asserting that he never stole from the poor nor killed any of his
victims. His crimes were prolific and variform: burglarizing mansions;
holding priests for ransom by their bishops (despite his claims to be a
fervent Christian); pickpocketing wealthy parishioners during Mass;
robbing banks and company safes; and donning all sorts of disguises
to commit fraud.

When a politician offered 2,000 pesos' reward for Chucho dead or
alive, the bandit promised double the amount for anyone who brought
him the politician's head. Chucho eventually married, and professed
to have traveled to Europe to place his daughter in an upper-class
Belgian school. He had returned to Mexico, he asserted, out of patriotism, and resumed his criminal activities only to finance his daughter's education, he added. Three times he escaped from prison, thus
inflating his notoriety. By the early 1880s, his popular following had
spread beyond the poor. Famous lawyers offered to defend him free
of charge. Poets extolled him. Newspapers labeled him a "civilized
bandit" and suggested he was no worse—only more brazen—than
entrepreneurs who secretly evaded the laws to enrich themselves. One
publication facetiously nominated him for Congress.

Chucho el Roto's final capture came in 1884. He claimed he was
betrayed by his weakness for culture. He could not resist attending a
play, and was arrested in the theater when police recognized him
despite his female disguise. Though he vowed to escape again, this
time he was sent to an island prison-fortress off the coast of Veracruz.
He died there in 1885 from dysentery, according to the authorities,
although rumors circulated that he was fatally beaten by guards.

Even in death, Chucho remained an irritant to the regime. His
demise came at a time when prison reform was under serious discussion
in Mexico City. Díaz himself embarked on a highly publicized effort

to improve jail conditions. In doing so, he was responding to social currents from abroad. Prison reform had become a subject of passionate public interest in the United States and Europe. By the end of the nineteenth century, new penitentiaries, designed according to the progressive notions of the era on rehabilitation and humane treatment of convicts, were being built in European and American cities. They were considered obligatory sights for tourists visiting a foreign country.

In 1900, Mexico City inaugurated its own monument to prison reform—the Lecumbérri Penitentiary. It was hailed abroad as yet more imposing evidence of Díaz's commitment to eradicate his country's social ills. A visiting American dignitary declared it superior in some respects to the most modern penitentiaries in the United States.[20] Behind a red-brick facade designed like a European castle, Lecumbérri held more than one thousand cells in seven brightly illuminated wings. Each cell had running water and a flush toilet. Inmates, who never had access to baths outside the prison walls, were allowed hot showers daily. For most of them, Lecumbérri's meals were a distinct improvement over their usual diets. Epidemic diseases were almost nonexistent. Located in the eastern district of Mexico City, the penitentiary was easily accessible for visits by relatives. And its workshops, equipped with electrical machines, were supposed to prepare convicts for useful employment after their release.

But Lecumbérri masked the much harsher reality of prison conditions elsewhere in Mexico City and the country. Only a minority of convicts were sent to the new penitentiary. The capital's main prison continued to be the Belén jail, the same institution which began its existence in the late 1600s as a misogynist, Church-sponsored "refuge" for women. Cholera and typhoid scourged the Belén inmates. Their overcrowded, dank cells had none of the amenities offered in the modern penitentiary. Government officials were embarrassed enough by the old jail to prohibit visits there by foreigners. But any convict would have preferred Belén to internment in the San Juan de Ulúa presidium in Veracruz, where Chucho el Roto died, or the penal colony in the Valle Nacional in Oaxaca, south of Mexico City.

Imprisonment in Ulúa amounted to a death sentence for most inmates. Their dungeons were carved out of the basement walls of a colonial fortress and were regularly flooded by tides from the Gulf of Mexico. The meager food rations were served in a state of putrefaction. Beatings, yellow fever, and dysentery wiped out a majority of the prisoners.

Even more appalling was the infamous Valle Nacional where peons, political detainees, and common criminals were placed into forced labor on privately owned tobacco plantations. John Kenneth Turner, a muckraking American journalist who gained entrance into the valley in the early 1900s by posing as an agricultural investor, described it as "undoubtedly the worst slave hole in Mexico" and "probably . . . in the world." He asserted that every year fifteen thousand workers were killed by disease, malnutrition, and beatings.

"By the sixth or seventh month they begin to die off like flies at the first winter frost, and after that they're not worth keeping," the manager of the largest tobacco plantation told Turner. "The cheapest thing is to let them die; there are plenty more where they came from. . . . I have been here for more than five years and every month I see hundreds and sometimes thousands of men, women and children start over the road to the valley, but I never see them come back."[21]

Most of the victims were law-abiding, unemployed farm workers and their families, who had signed up with unscrupulous labor contractors and had no inkling that their destination was the Valle Nacional. Even as a penal colony, the valley had no apologists. The usual convict-laborer was a petty thief because the plantation owners considered violent criminals too intractable.

If political stability and the repression of crime were the main components of Porfirian "Order," then the transportation revolution was the heart of the regime's vision of "Progress." Porfirio Díaz basked in the adulation of his compatriots, especially the more affluent, for installing a railway system that finally conquered the daunting geography of Mexico. Before Díaz, there were less than four hundred miles of railroads. By 1911, more than eleven thousand miles of track had been laid, much of it spanning deep ravines and rugged terrain once considered impassable. So thoroughly was Mexico blanketed by railways that less than two thousand miles of track have been added to the network since the Díaz regime.

Before the advent of railroads, distance had constantly defeated human enterprise everywhere in the world. The French poet Paul Valéry was fond of pointing out that "Napoleon moved no faster than Julius Caesar." But in Western Europe, travelers on horseback or in coaches could still as a general rule cover about sixty miles in twenty-four hours.[22] Such a "rapid" pace was inconceivable in mountainous Mexico. Stagecoach or wagon trips over the two hundred miles separating Veracruz and Mexico City—the most important overland route in the country—took sixteen days in the dry season, and up to a month during the heavy rains. And from Mexico City, several more months were required to distribute goods to the most distant provinces.

Landscape paintings of nineteenth-century Mexico reveal the atrocious conditions of so-called highways. A road often appears as a vaguely defined strip, barely distinguishable from the hillsides it traverses. The paintings depict water-filled potholes and large stones, even boulders, that turn the route into an obstacle course. Horsemen are shown struggling to steady their mounts sunk up to the hocks in water. Carriages lurch from side to side, with their wheels stuck in mud, and so many peasants are on foot, tugging at the halter of their mules, which in turn drag unyielding carts.

The journey from the capital to Veracruz began at four in the morning in order to reach the first posting house before sunset. According to Antonio García Cubas, a nineteenth-century politician who made the trip several times, passengers were crammed together like packages and were called "cargo" by the stagecoach company manager. The vehicle set out through the cobblestone streets at reckless speed, but as soon as the capital's outskirts were reached it settled down to a tortoise pace that would be maintained for the rest of the journey.

"The horrendous state of the roads would at any instant cause your head to bang against the carriage interior and raise bumps on your face," wrote García Cubas.

> The windows had to be sealed because of the immense quantity of fine, yellowish dust from the road that dried up your tongue, blinded you and penetrated every pore in your body. You were panic-stricken whenever the heavy vehicle struck a hole or rut. At such times, the coach swayed sharply to one side obligating the passengers to immediately lean the other way as a counterweight. Often that maneuver was for naught, and the carriage overturned . . . and the passengers, if they emerged at all, suffered a broken arm, a sunken rib or a cut face.[23]

Only the desperate or foolhardy traveled in the rainy season. Every few miles, the driver ordered his passengers to get out and help push the coach through knee-deep mud. Other times, the vehicle remained mired for a day or more, until the sun dried the road enough to continue. "In view of so many calamities," observed García Cubas, mentioning also the high incidence of banditry, "it is no wonder that our forebears felt obligated to draw up their wills and make their confessions before setting out on any journey no matter how short."[24]

It is in light of such testimony that the impact of trains in Mexico can best be appreciated. The trip from Veracruz to Mexico City—a railway connection actually inaugurated before Díaz but vastly improved under his rule—was cut to less than thirteen hours. The journey between the capital and the Texas border was reduced from weeks to a few days. Of far greater consequence than passenger service was the railroads' impact on freight. The trains between Mexico City and Veracruz cut the cost per ton carried to a tenth, and total weight of cargo between the two cities rose by 500 percent only a year after the line opened.[25] Gains were even more impressive on routes between the capital and other provincial cities.

The railroad created one of the basic foundations for accelerated economic growth. The transportation costs for mining, agriculture, and industry plummeted in a matter of years. Before railways, only silver and gold justified high freight expenses; but with trains, the exploitation of distant deposits of nonprecious metals suddenly became profitable. Cattle no longer had to be herded to Mexico City, thus opening the greatest urban market to far-flung haciendas. Sugar, tobacco, and coffee were able to compete in foreign markets. With lower transportation expenses, factories achieved startling cost savings. For example, the cost of shipping a ton of cotton textile goods from Mexico City to Querétaro, about one hundred miles north, fell from $61 in 1877 to $3 in 1910.[26]

But like most of the great initiatives undertaken by the Díaz regime, the benefits of the railways were heavily skewed in favor of wealthy Mexicans and foreigners. The lines were built and owned by foreigners—mainly Americans and British—until the government bought them out in 1908. Profits from railway operations were low, ranging from 1.5 to 3.6 percent a year.[27] But the foreign owners were not primarily concerned with the return on their investment in trains. They wished to penetrate internal markets and mining regions, and cut the cost and time of transport. The Díaz government obliged them by agreeing to reduce tariffs by 50 percent on all goods destined for export and import that made use of the railways. Minerals sold abroad received railroad subsidies, while the foodstuffs produced and consumed by poorer Mexicans had to pay full freight costs. Basic necessities like corn and beans barely kept pace with the demands of the growing population, and their prices rose during the Porfiriato.

Mexican hacienda and plantation owners also received an economic windfall from the railroads. They took advantage of the lower transportation costs to raise their production of coffee, sugar, tobacco, and

other commodities destined for foreign markets. Reaching into formerly isolated provinces, the trains caused land values to soar. By
anticipating new railroad construction, the great estate owners were
able to acquire properties within easy access of future train lines and
before their prices rose. The properties were usually held by Indians
and poorer mestizos, but the wealthy landowners could count on the
support of the Díaz regime in any agrarian dispute. The government
enforced the Reform laws of the Juárez era, which called for the
conversion of communal Indian lands into properties owned by individuals. Naturally, the peasants were unable to compete with wealthy
bidders for control of these parcels. In other cases, so-called vacant
public lands were sold by the government to rich hacienda and plantation owners at cheap prices. Many of these properties were in fact
occupied for generations by Indians and mestizos, who never held
legal deeds. Thus, the railways stimulated the concentration of agrarian
landownership that was a hallmark of the Porfirian era.

The railroad boom reinforced Mexico City's hegemony over the rest
of the nation. With the capital as the terminal point for almost all rail
lines, the Díaz government was able to quickly dispatch troops by train
to quell disturbances in even the remotest provinces. The city remained
the preferential residence of the wealthy, who left bailiffs and managers
in charge of their rural estates, mines, and factories, and felt all the
more comfortable about their absentee ownership because the railways
made their properties more accessible to their occasional visits. While
trains sparked investment elsewhere in the country, Mexico City was
still the chief recipient of capital, especially money from abroad. By
1910, foreign investment totaled 3.4 billion pesos, and more than half
of it funneled into public utilities, factories, and commerce in Mexico
City.

Investors were drawn to the nation's capital not only because it
emerged as the hub of the new railway system that reached into every
major internal market. Mexico City was also the main beneficiary of
that other great technological invention of the nineteenth-century industrial revolution—electricity. Before electricity, the geographical location of factories was largely determined by the availability of
hydraulic power, that is, rivers and streams for water mills. Electrical
energy led to industrial concentration in cities. In the country's north,
for example, Monterrey emerged in the late 1800s as an important
center for industry. But the Díaz regime obtained agreements with the
foreign-owned generating companies to provide electricity to Mexico
City at half the price charged elsewhere in the country. By 1889, the

Federal District, including the capital and its outlying communities, generated more than half the nation's electricity, making the Mexico City region a stronger magnet for factories than other urban centers.[28]

Porfirio Díaz was determined to mold the capital into a city that reflected his notions of greatness and modernization. Trains and electricity alone could not have ensured this goal. But the impact of these new technological breakthroughs was magnified by other favors that the regime showered on Mexico City. Under Díaz, the capital received more than 80 percent of all government investment in infrastructure projects for the nation—the asphalting of streets, the supply of water, telegraphs, public buildings, and schools, to mention some notable examples. The most ambitious and expensive of these projects, however, was a new drainage system.

Flooding was a perennial feature of the urban landscape. Mexico City continued to rely on the drainage project engineered by Enrico Martínez in the early 1600s. But that once grandiose tunnel-and-canal system was incapable of protecting a city with seven times as many inhabitants and ten times the surface area. Every rainy season disrupted urban life for days, sometimes weeks. The waters settled into immense puddles and churned unpaved streets into bogs. Traffic came to a standstill, and sales plunged in the downtown stores. In the late nineteenth century, Mexico City was still being described as a fetid Venice, with streets that were transformed into canals by the heavy rains. "To move about the capital, we need canoes instead of carriages," commented a newspaper after a particularly serious inundation in 1886. "The downtown district has become a string of black water ponds, which . . . discharge noxious odors and force residents to walk about with handkerchiefs over their noses lest they succumb to nausea."[29]

Díaz was confident that he could solve the drainage problem. If railways and telegraphs had conquered the mountainous isolation of the country, surely modern technology could tame the waters that made life in the capital so vexing. The new drainage, built between 1886 and 1900 at a cost of $16 million, became the most monumental construction work of the Porfirian era in Mexico City.

As he had done with the railways and electric lines, Díaz entrusted the project to foreigners. The British firm of S. Pearson and Son, Ltd.—builder of the Blackwall Tunnel under the Thames and the East River Tunnel in New York—was hired as the prime contractor. Draining Mexico City, however, was a far more arduous task than either of those enterprises. After several false starts resulting from cave-ins and underpowered water pumps, the British company completed a thirty-mile canal and six-mile tunnel that disgorged the capital's excess waters and sewage into rivers flowing eastward to the Gulf of Mexico.

The ceremony inaugurating the new drainage system in March 1900 was presided over by Díaz, accompanied by his entire cabinet and the diplomatic corps. Artillery salvos, fireworks, and church bells echoed through the city. After Díaz gave the order opening the canal locks, he and his large party of dignitaries boarded a train to the northern terminus of the drainage thirty-six miles away to witness the black waters cascading out of the Valley of Mexico. The government hailed the project as "an eternal pedestal to the glory of the country . . . which will bear witness for future generations that at the end of the nineteenth century Mexico had monuments it could display with pride to the civilized countries of the Old World."[30]

But Mexico City's inundations, though less frequent and serious, did not cease. Only four months after the official inauguration of the huge drainage project, the Díaz government was embarrassed by a flood that briefly paralyzed transportation and commerce in the city center. There were other inundations before 1900 ended, and a few more the following year. In 1908, the government announced that the problem was finally resolved by dredging the beds of the northern rivers that received Mexico City's waters. But two years later, heavy rains flooded the capital yet again. The usually humorless Díaz would sometimes remark to visiting foreign dignitaries that like Canute he could always rebuke the flattery of his subordinates by showing them that the advancing waters paid no heed to his command.

For the Mexico City elite, the Porfiriato was unquestionably the golden era. Not even the splendors of aristocratic society in the late colonial period could evoke comparison to life under Don Porfirio. For all their wealth, the creole nobility of the Bourbon days had still been beholden to Spanish rule and subject to the contempt of bureaucrats born in the mother country. The new aristocrats were masters in their own nation, and had a government of which they could be proud. Steamships and telegraphy accelerated and multiplied their contacts with the Old World, and they became more cosmopolitan than rich Mexicans had ever been. They disdained the heritage of Spain—a country they viewed as being in utter decline, politically and economically weak, all too immersed in a rigid Roman Catholicism—and identified themselves instead with upper-class society in France, Britain, and Germany, where science and technology and a secular spirit seemed to herald a twentieth century of unparalleled opportunities for humankind. From these European nations, the Porfirian aristocrats of Mexico City also absorbed new ideologies—positivism and social Darwinism—to justify their monopoly of wealth and power, and to chart the evolution of Mexican society.

The origins of positivism are linked to Auguste Comte, the French philosopher, who in the first half of the nineteenth century called for a reordering of society through the application of scientific knowledge to social ills. Comte advocated a sharing of political power between what he considered the most progressive social groups—industrialists, bankers, merchants, and intellectuals. In its passage across the Atlantic to Mexico, positivism became entangled with ideas drawn from the other fashionable philosophy of the era, social Darwinism, which championed the survival of the fittest elements of society.

This ideological combination offered several obvious attractions to Díaz and his upper-class coterie. Its claims to transform Mexico through science and technology appealed to a dictator bent on modernizing his country's economic and social structure. His closest advisers even called themselves *"científicos"* ("the scientific ones"), and were precursors of the so-called technocrats who nowadays hold bureaucratic power in Mexico and other developing nations. The new philosophy was used to defend the concentration of wealth in a small minority. The economic pie had to be enlarged, the científicos argued, before it could be sliced for the benefit of the poor. Mexico's version of positivism also provided a philosophical underpinning for an authoritarian system that proclaimed the need to keep the poverty-stricken majority in harness until a distant future when it could shed its social backwardness. In this respect, the ideology of the Díaz regime was a throwback to the early colonial era, when the Church and white colonists defended their exploitation of Indian labor and property by asserting that the natives required a lengthy tutelage to raise them to European levels.

Díaz and his followers argued that they had no intention of resurrecting this discredited vision of society. Positivism, they asserted, was a profoundly secular ideology, which rejected the guidance of religious institutions. And it was identified with modern Europe, not sixteenth-century Spain. But in Porfirian Mexico the end result was the same: a moral justification for a racism that had prevailed for four hundred years.

The rich of Mexico City debated whether the Indians, whose proportions had fallen to 40 percent of the country's population by the end of the nineteenth century, could ever be lifted from their primitive social and economic state. At one extreme, Francisco Bulnes, an arch-reactionary legislator and prolific writer, contended that thousands of years of malnutrition had reduced the Indians to an intellectual and physical inferiority which they would never overcome. According to José Yves Limantour, the brilliant treasury minister and leader of the científicos, natural selection would ensure the survival of the fittest Indians and other poor. "The weak, the unprepared, those who lack the necessary tools to triumph in the evolutionary process, must perish and leave the field to the strongest," he said in a speech closing the National Scientific Congress in Mexico City in 1901.[31]

The theory became practice everywhere in the country. When Mexico City textile workers complained of fatigue because of one-hundred-hour work weeks, they were told that the schedule was designed to rid their ranks of alcoholics, laggards, and those of weaker stamina. Government policy stimulated the formation of ever greater haciendas and plantations because their produce, destined for export, was considered a more important contribution to the modernization of Mexico than the maize and bean plots of the Indians and mestizos. Those Indians like the Yaqui of Sonora who violently resisted the takeover of their properties by big land companies were deemed to be obstacles to progress, and were sent as forced laborers to the plantations of Yucatán in the southern extremity of the country. If real wages fell below subsistence levels, it was society's natural selection process at work, weeding out superfluous employees. "Nothing is just or unjust as far as remuneration is concerned," declared Bulnes. "Labor is a product like any other, such as corn, wheat, flour, and is subject to the law of supply and demand."[32]

To be sure, there were moderates among the Porfirian ideologues. Justo Sierra, the leading educator and historian of the era, maintained that cultural and social reasons, not biological ones, accounted for the lowly condition of the Indians, and that education could gradually transform them into productive, modern elements of society. In an unusually harsh critique of his científico colleagues, he raised the specter of eventual revolt among the poor: "How can you people talk of progress when even now a hundred thousand men . . . wait in ambush in the shadows of the mines, in the pallid light of the factories, along the railways; wait for the right moment to destroy the laborious advances of science, wait to destroy with arms the wealth that science has produced."[33]

But contempt for the Indians and other disadvantaged Mexicans was the prevailing view among the Porfirian elite. Andrés Molina Enríquez, an astute social commentator—whose book *The Great National Problems* has been considered the classic indictment of the Porfiriato since its publication in 1908—asserted that such contempt eventually translated into a national self-loathing: "The opinion . . . in our country is that we are a people who know less, are less able, can do less and are worth less than . . . the other nations of the earth."[34]

To reach this conclusion, Molina Enríquez had only to peruse the newspaper columns, political speeches, and pseudoscientific treatises circulating about Mexico City. One government official claimed that a Mexican mason took eleven hours to lay five hundred bricks, while an American worker could handle five thousand bricks in the same time. Carlos Díaz Dufoo, a literary critic with pretensions of economic expertise, wrote that while an English textile laborer could work six to eight looms simultaneously, a Mexican could handle only two. Bulnes asserted that the average Brazilian mulatto tended 3,868 coffee plants, compared to 1,215 plants for a Mexican peon. Using a scale of 100, a Mexican economist rated the productivity of industrial workers throughout the world. British laborers ranked highest at 100, followed by 60 to 85 for other Europeans, 50 to 80 for "Hottentots," 40 to 70 for "Zulu kaffirs," and only 25 to 40 for Mexicans.[35]

According to a growing number of Porfirian conservatives, the only solution to the nation's backwardness was to encourage foreign immigration. In 1909, a senator, Maqueo Castellanos, asserted that Mexico would be "thirty times richer, stronger and more respected" if it could exchange its darker inhabitants for a like number of immigrants of any race or country.[36] Newspapers periodically surveyed employers for their opinions on the best immigrants. In Mexico City, industrialists favored Germans; in Veracruz, plantation owners preferred blacks; and Yucatán agriculturists wanted immigrants from India. At times it seemed that immigration was a panacea for all social ills, no matter how trivial. Newspaper editorials suggested that the widespread problem of petty thievery among house servants in the capital would only end if they were replaced by Asians and Africans.

But by and large, the Porfirian upper class wanted European and American immigrants. Newspapers frequently railed against the dangers posed by nonwhite foreigners. Asians were dishonest and physically repugnant, according to *El Tiempo*, a leading conservative daily. "What can we expect from the miscegenation of an opium smoker with a pulque drinker, of a rat eater and a bean eater?" the newspaper asked its readers. A Catholic daily asserted that Asians would take over the jobs normally held by lower-class Mexican women, reducing them to prostitution. Opposition to black immigration was just as bitter. Newspapers described blacks as lazier, more vicious, and less intelligent than Mexican Indians.[37]

Considering the low number of foreigners who moved to Mexico, the immigration issue seems at first glance to have been exaggerated by the press, government, and upper-class circles. In 1910, there were still less than 120,000 foreigners living in the country, about half of them in Mexico City. By comparison, more than 33 million Europeans moved to the United States between 1820 and 1920. But in Mexico, particularly its capital, foreigners made their presence felt in proportions that far exceeded their numbers. They were most visible when they marched in phalanxes by different nationality in parades honoring Díaz. Occasionally, delegations of foreign residents in Mexico City requested audiences with Don Porfirio to entreat him to run for yet another presidential term. Foreign capital accounted for two thirds of the total invested in the country, most of it in the most modern economic sectors, like railways, finance, factories, public utilities, new mines, and plantations. For the Porfirian elite, the foreign community was a source of pride and incontrovertible evidence that Mexico was modernizing and whitening itself. As Juan Mateos, a conservative legislator, remarked in the Congress in 1890, it was a pleasure "to see that foreigners owned the banks, the credit institutions, the electric light companies, the telegraph, the railways and everything that signifies culture and progress in Mexico."[38]

Among the working class, however, there was a growing xenophobia. Americans and Europeans were their foremen in foreign-owned enterprises. Discrimination against Mexicans was particularly galling in the railways. English was the official language of the trains, thus creating a major obstacle to the training and promotion of Mexicans. Few Mexicans held administrative or supervisory jobs, or other white-collar positions like conductor. Only a third of the engineers were Mexicans. And for years, even brakemen and trainmen tended to be Americans. "It was a world dominated by foreigners, men with blond hair, white skin, blue eyes, almost all from the United States," said a Mexican who was an assistant brakeman on a line running east of the capital. "These men monopolized all the important positions. . . . A Mexican worker was a man condemned to stay on one level."[39]

Poorer, darker Mexicans were made to feel inferior to foreigners in other ways. Those who were barefoot and wore the rough white pants traditionally associated with the Indians were kept out of Mexico City's central district by the police, lest they spoil the capital's modern image for foreigners and wealthy Mexicans. At official functions, especially those attended by foreign delegates, all uniformed attendants and servants were white-skinned. At times, the Porfirian aristocrats even managed to convince themselves that Indians and darker-skinned mestizos were disappearing. In an 1898 speech to the National Preparatory School, whose student body was mostly white and upper class, the playwright Federico Gamboa asserted that while there were "still many degenerates, a poverty-stricken herd . . . lamentable and of a race which scarcely dressed its body . . . its blood is exhausted, dying out in silence without leaving anything, not even heirs to weep its demise."[40]

The wealthier residents of Mexico City certainly tried hard to cloister themselves from the "poverty-stricken herd" of Indians and mestizos. For most of the nineteenth century, rich, middle class, and poor had lived cheek-to-jowl in the capital. Though the outskirts were largely the domain of the working class, the mansions of the central district were surrounded by petit bourgeois apartments and the hovels and vecindades of the humblest inhabitants. But during the Porfiriato, there was a marked segregation of the inhabitants according to income and class that recalled the strict demarcations imposed upon the city by the conquistadores in early colonial times. The newly affluent created neighborhoods and corridors that, except for servants and other employees, were virtually free of the despised races who could remind them that they were living in Mexico, not Europe.

To trace the geography of wealth in Porfirian Mexico City, one began necessarily with the Jockey Club, the undisputed mecca of high society. Located some ten blocks west of the Zócalo, it occupied the most opulent mansion in the capital, a building with a facade of white-and-blue tiles that originally housed one of the leading families of the colonial era. Its patio, with palms, potted plants, and a large fountain, evoked the old Moorish style of southern Spain. Marble balustrades lined the balcony overlooking this airy inner garden. The rooms were adorned with floor-to-ceiling mirrors and arabesque columns.

The director of the Jockey Club was Manuel Romero Rubio, father-in-law of Porfirio Díaz, thus ensuring that members combined high standing in social and political circles. Their names—Escandón, Mier, Bulnes, Landa, Limantour, among others—appeared in the loftiest ranks of government and business. Although the club tried to cultivate

an image as a forum for literary lectures and debates on positivism and
social Darwinism, its most faithful members came to drink and gamble.
The baccarat tables opened at five every afternoon, and play continued
to the early morning hours. "Men and, alas, sometimes women . . .
will sit there all night, only rising to partake of the supper which is
provided free," wrote Mrs. Alec Tweedie, an English traveler, in 1901.
"Champagne and French cooking gratis add another inducement to
play."[41] Even the sumptuous balls at the Jockey Club could not distract
the gamblers for long. Mrs. Tweedie complained that her escort on
one such evening abandoned her to join the other men at baccarat:

"I looked around. Both sides of that drawing-room and the two
succeeding drawing-rooms were lined with women! Not a single man
was to be seen. Each male person brought a lady, deposited her on a
seat, and fled! Two hundred and fifty men congregated in the gallery
outside, whilst two hundred and fifty women sat gravely lining the
rooms inside! And what good-looking women they were, too! Such
faces, figures, jewels and dresses would have done credit to Buck-
ingham Palace!"[42]

On either side of the Jockey Club, the Escandón family—leaders
of Mexico City society since the early Independence era—occupied
two mansions. These were veritable palaces, with several inner patios,
scores of rooms, and stables for twenty to thirty horses. Each household
had forty to fifty servants. Many of them had been in the family all
their lives, as their parents before them.

But most of the capital's upper class had moved to the new neighborhoods, like Roma, Cuauhtémoc, and Juárez, that bordered Paseo
de la Reforma along its western trajectory. Maximilian had constructed
the avenue, connecting his castle at Chapultepec with the central
district, in the hopes of giving the city a modicum of Parisian ambience.
But it was only under Díaz that the Reforma was decorated with trees,
statues, and broad sidewalks to resemble the Champs-Elysées. The
new mansions were designed in the French architectural style of the
late nineteenth century, with garrets and mansard roofs that sloped
sharply—a pretentious touch in a city that never suffered a severe
snowfall.

French taste guided interior decoration as well. Parquet floors replaced native brick tiles and stone. Rooms were cluttered with velvet
draperies, marble tables and statuettes, heavy chandeliers, pianos, and
spindly chairs. On the walls, gilded mirrors alternated with full-length
portraits of somber-faced family ancestors.

It seemed as if Napoleon III's fond ambition to impose French civilization on the country had finally come to pass, at least within the confines of Mexico City's high society. Parisian cooks presided over the capital's most expensive restaurants. One of the leading aristocrats, Ignacio de la Torre y Mier, became the envy of the Jockey Club crowd when he enticed the renowned French chef Sylvain Daumont to work in his household. He placed his cook at the disposal of Don Porfirio for presidential banquets. Daumont eventually founded his own restaurant, "Sylvain," which was considered the city's gourmet establishment. Other acclaimed French restaurants, like the Maison Dorée and Fonda de Recamier, soon opened their doors. Eateries which could offer only traditional Mexican and Spanish menus learned to at least give their dishes French names. A simple vegetable soup was listed as "petite marmite"; a beef stew became "pot-au-feu"; and leg of lamb sounded tastier as "gigot d'agneau."[43]

The French mania reached into all corners of aristocratic life. Children were placed under the care of French governesses. Private schools were modeled after the lycée system. And a wealthy youth often finished his education at the Sorbonne in Paris. The cancan was the rage in the music halls. French comic opera offered season ticket holders such eminently forgettable productions as *Les cloches de Corneville* and *La fille de Madame Angot*. When the Mexican composer Gustavo Campa wrote an opera based on the life of Nezahualcóyotl, the poet-king of Texcoco, he entitled it *Le roi poète* and had the libretto published in French.[44] Bastille Day was celebrated among the capital's aristocrats with as much enthusiasm as they commemorated Mexican Independence.

Porfirio Díaz, who always vaunted his military feats against Napoleon's army, took equal pride in being identified as the patron saint of French civilization in Mexico City. Rosa King, the Englishwoman who lived in Mexico during the early 1900s, recalled the gratitude that the aristocrats felt toward Díaz in this regard. Citing the case of Pablo Escandón, a rich hacienda owner and state governor, she wrote:

> Like so many of his class, Don Pablo was more at home in Europe than in Mexico; while he loved his own country he found it a little barbarous; and the broad new boulevards, frequent parks, and magnificent public buildings that were being erected in Mexico City were a source of great satisfaction to him. "It is almost Paris!" he said. "You think it has always been like this, Señora King. But you are wrong. You cannot understand what barbarians we used to be, before Porfirio civilized us. . . . Today, we are a nation respected by other nations.

We are cosmopolitan; our young men, educated abroad, are men of the world, who are a credit to their country whilst they amuse themselves in London or Paris. We have our opera here in Mexico, and there will be brilliant gatherings when the National Theater is completed—the ladies all in their boxes, the tiaras sparkling in their hair. That will be something to see, will it not, Señora King? And all the work of Porfirio Díaz!"[45]

While francophilia reigned supreme, the British also were widely admired among the Mexico City elite. Mrs. Tweedie, who knew no Spanish, claimed she never had any problem making herself understood: "Not only is English talked by all educated men, but there is scarcely a shop of any importance in this cosmopolitan city where that language is not spoken, and the railway officials, managers, clerks and engine-drivers are all English-speaking people."[46]

She encountered numerous upper-class youths on vacation back in Mexico City from their studies at Stoneyhurst and Belmont. Their younger brothers were dressed in Jack Tar sailor uniforms, while their fathers bought their own tailored suits in London. Visiting an hacienda south of Mexico City, she was touched by the sight of Mexican aristocrats sporting black armbands in mourning for the late Queen Victoria as they played polo on English ponies. And how easy it was for her to remember her Mexican friends, she remarked, because so many of them had nicknames like Netty, Lilly, Mary, Jack, Dickie, Alec, and Patty.

The upper class maintained close ties with the clergy, but the relationship had lost much of the ardor displayed during the Reform War and the French occupation. The affluent were simply not interested in reviving the Church-State conflict that had torn the country asunder for so many years. Instead, they emulated the secular spirit in vogue among aristocrats in Paris, London, Berlin, and Vienna, where religion, while still important, had become less of an arbiter of society.

Shortly after gaining the presidency in 1876, Díaz proved conciliatory to his clerical foes as part of his campaign to secure peace and order. He permitted the clergy to amass wealth through secret contributions and even to recover lost properties through the use of trusted front men and dummy business corporations. But the Church never regained the power or riches it had enjoyed in the first half of the nineteenth century, when it was the largest urban landlord and chief source of credit for businesses. The number of clergymen also remained small. In 1910, there were only 242 priests for all of Mexico City, scarcely enough to administer the sacraments in the more populous parishes.[47] Religious instruction remained forbidden in public schools, and the relatively small number of Catholic schools confined their enrollment to middle-class or affluent students, especially girls from conservative families.

Díaz also wooed the Church through symbolic gestures. He invited Archbishop Labastida—the relentless enemy of the Reform movement and collaborator with the French occupation forces—to attend government functions, and he presided over the prelate's funeral. Despite constitutional prohibitions, religious processions were allowed in the streets of the capital under an informal agreement whereby the Church paid fines to the government for violating the law. On Independence Day, the effigy of the Virgin of Guadalupe was paraded around the city. And Díaz declined to enforce legislation forbidding priests to wear their vestments outside of church.

But clergymen were not altogether satisfied by the improvement of the Church's status under the Porfiriato. They often lamented what they perceived to be the growing spiritual decadence of Mexican society. They warned that the dearth of priests was causing Indian and poor mestizo communities to retreat toward a mixture of paganism and folkloric Catholicism. In some neighborhoods of the capital, parishioners reportedly donned Indian masks and danced in their churches. Priests were also disturbed by a tendency among the poor to believe in miraculous apparitions that were not sanctioned by the Church. Hills, trees, and boulders where images of saints and the Virgin Mary were said to have been sighted became the objects of pilgrimages and cults.

The Church occasionally denounced the spread of positivism—with its belief in human perfectability through scientific and technological progress—as a godless philosophy that contributed to the secularization of upper-class society. Among the affluent, only women seemed to attend church regularly. Men limited themselves to an occasional Mass, and allowed years to lapse between their confessions.

The Díaz household set the example. Don Porfirio himself rarely attended religious services, and was a member of a Masonic lodge that espoused positivist ideas. "In personal life and as head of my family, I am a Catholic, apostolic and Roman," he insisted. "But as chief of state, I cannot profess to any religion because the law prohibits me from doing so."[48] It was his young second wife, Carmen, who fulfilled the family's religious obligations. The Church hierarchy learned to approach her to resolve any misunderstandings with the State, to obtain semiofficial blessing for fundraising drives, and to gain government dispensation for important religious processions. A faithful churchgoer, she was accorded the place of honor during Mass at the Cathedral and the other temples she frequented. Although unable to bear children, she prevailed upon the ranking clergy to organize services at which parishioners were asked to pray that she might become pregnant. Mrs. Díaz also played a highly visible role during religious holidays. Her Christmas party was the social event of the year for the capital's aristocrats.

During the major holidays, Mexico City seemed to regain the fervor of an earlier golden era of Church supremacy. But the Catholic press and the high clergy complained that these celebrations were for the most part profane. There was little prayer and too much dancing, singing, and drinking. On November 1, the Day of the Dead, the poor flocked to the cemeteries to eat and drink pulque on the tombs of their relatives. Occasionally, they left cards, empty bottles, or cheap articles of clothing on the graves—mute testimony to a man who in life dedicated himself to gambling, drunkenness, or thievery. Middle-class Mexicans also paid their respects at the cemetery, but returned home for the banquet that climaxed the celebration. Photographs of the deceased were placed on the dining-room table, and a feast was laid out before them: pots of chicken with mole sauce, lentils, squash, limes, oranges, bananas, skulls made of candy, and bread dolls carved to resemble the dead with a powdery sugar to trace their white hair and the tears running down their cheeks.[49] After a recitation of prayers, the living relatives gorged themselves, leaving what remained of the meal on the table overnight, supposedly for the dead to consume.

Christmas festivities, running from December 16 to 24, were (and are still) called *posadas*. The term means "hostels" or "inns," and commemorates the nine-day journey by Mary and Joseph from Nazareth to Bethlehem during which they were refused lodging and finally sought refuge in a stable, where the infant Jesus was born. On each night, a posada was held in a different home. A procession of family and friends, carrying lighted candles and ivory or clay figurines of the Virgin and Joseph, would knock on the door of a room and chant Joseph's plea:

> *"In Heaven's name I beg for shelter,*
> *My wife tonight can go no further."*

The hosts would then reply:

> "No inn is this, begone from hence,
> Ye may be thieves, we trust you not."

The procession knocked at a succession of rooms until gaining admittance at the ninth door. Only the wealthiest homes could offer so many rooms. At poorer households, the supplicants simply marched back and forth from the street. Following the posadas came the breaking of *piñatas*—clay pots festooned with papier-mâché and ribbons and shaped like animals or carnival figures. In most homes, the piñatas were crammed with sweets and cheap toys, although affluent families sometimes placed hundreds of pesos in the clay pots. Blindfolded children took turns swinging a broomstick at the piñata, which dangled above them on a clothesline. When the bulbous pot was shattered, the children scrambled on the floor to claim its contents.

From December 16 to January 6—the day when the three Magi came bearing gifts for the infant Jesus—the Zócalo and all the other plazas of Mexico City were crowded with booths selling candy, sugared fruit, religious figurines, lanterns, toys, masks, and dolls. Among the most popular items were *naguales*—woolen representations of creatures from Indian mythology with four legs and a grotesque human face. They were supposed to have satanic powers and were meant to frighten mischievous children into good behavior.

The unrestrained public joy of the Christmas season contrasted with the sourness of some Church officials. "The people have become practically pagan," commented a bishop at the end of the holidays in 1900.[50] He viewed only the crowded midnight Mass of December 25 in the Cathedral as reason for religious satisfaction.

One of the great sources of disappointment for the Church was its failure to recruit middle-class men into the priesthood. The middle class expanded significantly in Mexico City under the Porfiriato. There were more shopkeepers to cater to the growing population. Accountants, lawyers, engineers, and master craftsmen found their services in demand as big business prospered. But the real cradle of the middle class was the government. By 1910, about 70 percent of the middle class was employed by the State, as bureaucrats, professionals, clerks, inspectors, military officers, and policemen. People with some education but few financial means aspired to the security of government service the way Mexicans in earlier eras had turned to the priesthood. As Bulnes, the arch-conservative legislator, remarked, middle-class people "used to live from the altar of God, and now are resolved to live from the altar of the nation."[51]

Spokesmen for the middle class saw themselves as the backbone of Porfirian Mexico. According to *El Tiempo*, the Catholic daily which drew its readership from this social sector, they constituted "the party of peace, tranquility, order and work."[52] But Don Porfirio himself apparently felt contempt for the middle class. In an interview with a foreign journalist, he dismissed them as people who aspired "to rise from bed late, to be public employees with influential godfathers, to arrive at work at any hour, to feign illness frequently and receive paid leaves, to never miss a bullfight . . . to marry young and have children in excess, to spend more than they earn, and enslave themselves to usurers to pay for their parties and social gatherings."[53]

Eager to celebrate its recent emergence from poverty, the middle class often did live beyond its means. A turn-of-the-century survey placed the income of a typical middle-class family in Mexico City at 100 pesos a month, and noted that it was spent in the following way: 25 pesos for rent, 60 pesos for food, 10 for servants, and 5 for clothing and entertainment.

For the most part, these families lived in the central district in formerly aristocratic houses that were partitioned and rented out by their owners, who had moved to more modern palatial homes off the Paseo de la Reforma toward the west. Crammed with a dozen or more families, the old downtown mansions had lost their grandeur. Their facades were perforated with new entrances and private corridors for each tenant. These passageways, leading from the street, were lined with heavy earthenware jars to store the household's water and were replenished every day by water carriers. Birdcages and flowerpots somewhat enlivened the dankness of the corridors. Inside, the decoration of the house was spare and utilitarian. Chairs and beds were made of wood and cane. Instead of a rug, mats of brightly colored, woven straw covered the stone floors. Portraits and small sculptures of saints were displayed in the living room, while crucifixes hung on the bedroom walls.

These homes had no flush toilets, and the night soil had to be placed outside early every morning for the street collectors. Tubs were also a rarity. But unlike the impoverished majority, the middle class could afford to take advantage of the thirty or so public bathhouses that existed in the city. For a few centavos, these establishments offered a tiny room with a zinc bathtub, towel, soap, and brush. While the customer bathed, a pianist in the lobby played popular melodies.[54] Few middle-class families visited the bathhouses more than once or twice a month. That still made them cleaner than bourgeois Parisians of the era, at least according to the observations of a French social commentator who affirmed that in his country most women never bathed and that only men serving in the military had occasion to do so.[55]

Almost all middle-class households had one or more servants. Maids were a sure sign that a family had risen above the threshold of poverty. But the quality of the "hired help" was a source of permanent complaint. Because servants were recent arrivals from the countryside, they allegedly required long apprenticeships to overcome their unclean habits, clumsiness, and slow work pace. They were said to rob their employers of money, clothes, and other articles almost from the day they began work. If they stayed on, they were accused of using wilier methods, such as arrangements with butchers, greengrocers, and bakers to purchase spoiled produce in exchange for kickbacks. Confronted by their employers, they were likely to respond with insolence: "If you are not happy with my services, you should find somebody better."[56] Most servants would have preferred working for upper-class households. The pay was better. So were the food and lodging. And in a mansion with ten or twenty other servants, it was easy to disappear or relax for a few hours. In a middle-class home, a maid often slept in the kitchen and ate leftovers. She was constantly under the supervision of her employers. And her salary was frequently withheld until other basic household expenses were met. Such delays could be lengthy if the family allotted some of its income to entertainment.

It was their penchant for entertainment that got most middle-class families into debt. The opera and classic repertory drew elite audiences. But music hall and comedies were the domain of the middle class. By the end of the Porfiriato, they could choose among eighteen theaters in Mexico City. The dialogue of plays had become closer to contemporary speech. Actors were less wooden, and moved more naturally, sometimes even turning their backs on the audience. And the subject matter reflected middle-class concerns: family dramas, romance, and, above all, money problems. Brief, one-act musicals called "tandas" were especially popular. Although tickets for one tanda were cheap enough, several were performed in succession, and the audience was charged each time the curtain rose.

Not even the most entertaining theater could compete with the bullfights. Sarah Bernhardt had the misfortune of scheduling her only appearance in Mexico City during the climax of the taurine season in 1887, and drew disappointing audiences. As many as twenty thousand spectators crowded into the city's five bullfighting arenas on a single Sunday afternoon. The poor sat in the cheap "bleachers" exposed to the sun, while middle-class people favored the more expensive seats in the shade. Wealthy Mexicans rarely attended the bullfights, which they considered barbaric. They did not object so much to the slaughter of the animals or injuries to the matadors but to the unruly conduct of the spectators, who tossed cushions and flaming balls of newspaper into the ring if the bulls or toreros failed to perform well, and rioted if their tickets were not reimbursed. After several such incidents, the government temporarily prohibited bullfights in the capital. But entrepreneurs quickly opened makeshift arenas just beyond Mexico City's limits, and waited for the ban to be lifted.

When their money ran out, as often happened at the end of the month, middle-class families spent their Sundays with the city's poorer inhabitants at Chapultepec Park. The Díaz government had spruced up its lawns, gardens, and woods, erected fountains, and established picnic grounds. Easily accessible from downtown by mule-drawn trams and the new electric streetcars, Chapultepec became the capital's most popular park after 1900.

Don Porfirio was convinced that he had made Mexico City a more tolerable place for all of its citizens, affluent and humble. He had favored the capital over the rest of the nation in terms of public investment, the creation of modern factories, new neighborhoods, asphalted streets, electricity, transport, schools, sewage facilities, crime prevention, urban beautification—almost every index by which the quality of life could be measured. The city enjoyed a higher income per capita than any other Mexican community, and its population was growing faster than in the rest of the country.

But for the poor, Mexico City was a devourer of human beings. With a mortality rate of forty-three people per one thousand in 1910, the Mexican capital was the most unhealthy urban center on earth. No one expected it to match the standards of Paris and London, where only six to eight out of every thousand inhabitants died each year. But even Madras, Cairo, and Istanbul had lower death rates than Mexico City. In all of Mexico, only the state of Yucatán was deadlier for its residents than the nation's capital.[57]

The median longevity in the early twentieth century was twenty-four years in Mexico City compared to forty-five years in Paris. And life was no kinder in its beginnings: one half of infants died before one year of age. Every decade, the capital exterminated the equivalent of one third of its inhabitants. But the constant flow of rural migrants—those who ceded their lands to the big haciendas or escaped from peonage—more than replenished these staggering losses.

Arriving in the city with no fixed address, they drifted from one flophouse to another. The flophouse, or *meson*, was a phenomenon of the age because policemen were less tolerant of transients who tried to bed down on the sidewalks. By 1900, one out of every six inhabitants lived in mesones. For a few centavos a night, destitute men, women, and children slept side by side amid total strangers in the windowless rooms of the cold, damp flophouses, with nothing but soiled straw mats separating them from the tamped earth floor. The water was polluted and toilet facilities were nonexistent. Every morning when the meson keeper turned out her clientele, she invariably discovered a few people too sick to stir and one or more corpses. Typhus was the greatest killer. The city's health officials found the disease in one fourth of the mesones they surveyed.[58]

Conditions were no healthier in permanent dwellings. The eastern district bordering Lake Texcoco was the largest residential zone for the poor. Lying lower than the rest of the city, it was plagued by subterranean pools of raw sewage, and during the rainy season, these black waters surfaced through patios and floors. Dysentery, typhoid, respiratory ailments, and assorted fevers quickly spread through these tenements and shacks, where each room averaged seven or more inhabitants.

Paseo de la Reforma, which spearheaded the city's westward expansion, led to the emergence of working-class neighborhoods northwest of the central district. Newspapers dubbed them instant slums, and noted that the authorities were maintaining a double standard for the wealthy and poor. Reimbursed by the government, real estate developers provided the new neighborhoods for the affluent with electricity, running water, sewage pipes, and asphalted streets graced with trees. But poorer districts received none of these amenities because the developers could expect no public subsidies. A pro-government newspaper, *El Imparcial*, described the construction of one of these new ghettos in 1902:

> An entrepreneur buys a property half-hidden between ditches and walls, badly situated, without ventilation or sewage disposal, with nothing that will ameliorate its hideous insalubrity. Within the specified perimeter, he traces dirt alleys and erects shacks cheek-to-jowl in the smallest possible space . . . and calls them private residences. . . . And here, cramped within 1,500 to 2,000 square meters, live 800 to one thousand people who do not have a single common sewer or water pipe or toilet. . . . As the wastes multiply, they poison the environment and turn the slum into a sick ward.[59]

Bathing was a rare experience for the poor. At the turn of the century, there was a ratio of one public bathhouse per fifteen thousand inhabitants in Mexico City. When a tobacco factory established free shower facilities for its employees in 1901, it was considered such an extraordinary example of entrepreneurial beneficence that the municipal health council gave the owners an award. But the poor always complained less about the dearth of water for washing than the wretched quality of water for drinking. The health council repeatedly corroborated their claims that they were consuming water which was polluted by industrial and human wastes.

The food available to working-class families was also adulterated. Bakeries sold them biscuits leavened with lead chromate, which was used instead of more costly eggs to give dough a heavier consistency. The poisonous lead residue accumulated in human tissue, eventually with fatal consequences. Milk was regularly diluted with dirty water, and then thickened with animal brains discarded by the slaughterhouses and butchers. Cat or dog meat was sold as beef. Coffee was mixed with chickpeas and bread crumbs. Lard and butter were laced with cottonseed oil.[60] The poor were aware that their food was often toxic, but they could not afford quality nutrition. According to a medical researcher who studied public health in Mexico City at the end of the Porfiriato, a working-class family of three required a minimum salary of 2 pesos daily to stave off malnutrition—"in other words, nearly three times that received by the laborers whose conditions we have been studying."[61] Most of the poor, he concluded, stood a better chance of survival if they remained in the countryside. By migrating to Mexico City, they had become firewood for the insatiable urban furnace.

FIFTEEN

REVOLUTION

As old age crept over him, Porfirio Díaz pondered his legacy and the inevitable dilemma of his succession. On both counts, he demonstrated an enormous capacity for self-delusion. Inundated by paeans from abroad and the flattering reports of his subordinates, he believed that Mexico was shedding its backwardness and was only decades away from joining the ranks of the developed nations. Lulled by social peace and political stability, he foresaw an orderly transfer of power.

By the early 1900s, Díaz ceased traveling around the country, and came to think of Mexico City—that is, its most modern and wealthy neighborhoods—as a microcosm of the nation. The mile-long drive between his mansion on Paseo de la Reforma and the National Palace on the Zócalo shaped his vision of Mexico. Automobiles, no longer a novelty in the capital, relegated animal-drawn carts to the shoulders of the road. Electric trolleys had virtually replaced mule-powered trams. A forest of telephone and electricity poles rose amid the elegant statues, monuments, tree stands, and flower beds that bordered the Reforma. The city's impoverished majority was still clad in soiled white pants, tattered black shawls, and guaraches (sandals). But on the grand boulevard, at least, the European attire of the more affluent prevailed: for men, bowler hats, English woolen suits, and laced boots; for women, long dresses trimmed with puffs and frills and draped over bodies imprisoned by corsets that pushed busts forward and buttocks out behind, necks stiffened by collars with whalebone stays, and feathered hats perched above extravagantly curled hair. Díaz allowed himself a smile of satisfaction when his numerous foreign visitors remarked that the city districts they saw compared favorably with Paris, London, and New York.

The elderly president had become equally sanguine about his nation's political prospects. And so, in an interview with an American reporter, James Creelman, in 1908, he spoke openly for the first time about the succession:

> No matter what my friends and supporters say, I retire when my presidential term of office ends, and I shall not serve again. I shall be eighty years old then. I have waited for the day when the people of the Mexican Republic should be prepared to choose and change their government at every election without danger of armed revolution and without injury to the national credit or interference with national progress. I believe that day has come. I welcome an opposition party in the Mexican Republic. If it appears, I will regard it as a blessing, not an evil. And if it can develop power, not to exploit, but to govern, I will stand by it, support it, advise it, and forget myself in the successful inauguration of complete democratic government in the country.[1]

The Creelman interview, published in *Pearson's Magazine* and reprinted in the major Mexican newspapers, was explosive. Within Díaz's own political camp, it instigated an undisguised power struggle between the científicos and the military, the two major factions which Don Porfirio had long balanced against each other. The military faction, called the "Reyistas" for their leader, General Bernardo Reyes, had a potentially greater electoral following. Reyes, a former minister of war, had been an effective governor in the northern state of Nuevo León. He espoused nationalist, somewhat populist ideas that tapped resentment in the provinces against the dominance of Mexico City and the overwhelming influence of foreign capital in the economy. The científicos, who claimed credit for the regime's economic policies, rallied around José Yves Limantour, the treasury minister. But Limantour and his colleagues were considered a Mexico City–based aristocracy and the chief propagators of European notions of social Darwinism.

Díaz himself was jolted and then angered by the unseemly haste that his supporters were displaying in their efforts to succeed him. Repudiating the Creelman interview, he decided to run for the presidency yet again. The científicos, realizing they had no chance to win an election anyway, backed Díaz. They also convinced him to create the post of vice president and choose Ramón Corral, a man of their confidence, as his running mate. Since Don Porfirio was unlikely to survive a new six-year term, Corral and the científicos stood ready to inherit Mexico. Corral, a powerful businessman and miner from the state of Sonora, where he had served as governor, was an extremely unpopular political figure, notorious for his role in sending Yaqui Indians to forced labor camps. Díaz, however, was satisfied to have as his vice president a man with no strong political following of his own. There was still the matter of General Reyes's candidacy, but Don Porfirio handily solved that problem by dispatching him on a "military study mission" to Europe, a euphemism for political exile.

Having restored mastery over his own political camp, Díaz foresaw no obstacle to his reelection. Over the last two decades, intimidation and fraud had discouraged all political opposition. His only rival in the past several presidential campaigns had been a half-mad candidate who wandered about Mexico City in a long-tailed coat and top hat forecasting earthquakes and floods. But this time, Don Porfirio seriously misjudged the temperament of his compatriots. For several years, a number of political and economic issues had been undermining the dictator. And the Creelman interview had raised expectations that a real presidential campaign would finally take place.

On the economic front, the Porfirian "miracle" was tarnished by the world financial crisis of 1907. The collapse of the international market for copper and other metals created a crisis in Mexican mining. Textiles, the most important manufacturing sector, entered a deep recession. Between 1905 and 1910, the peso lost half its purchasing power. There was serious labor unrest in these years. The 800,000 industrial workers constituted only a small percentage of employment in a country that remained overwhelmingly rural. But industry was viewed by the Porfiristas as the goal of an economically developed Mexico, and so, widespread labor discontent was troubling to the regime. Strikes by railway workers all the way from Chihuahua to Mexico City, by copper miners in Sonora, and textile employees in Veracruz and Puebla were violently repressed, resulting in scores, perhaps hundreds, of deaths. Antiforeignism was a strong element in these incidents. Europeans and Americans not only owned these enterprises, but also hired many of their compatriots and paid them twice the wages received by Mexican workers performing the same tasks. The strike by the Sonora workers at the Cananea copper mine was especially embarrassing for the Díaz regime because the American owners had been allowed to bring in Arizona Rangers to shoot down rioting Mexican employees.

Along with this economic unrest in the first decade of the twentieth century, there was a surge in political pamphlets and magazines calling for freedom of speech and press, shorter work weeks, higher wages, agrarian reform, and the end of rural peonage. Chief among these pamphleteers were the Flores Magón brothers, whose Mexico City weekly, *Regeneración*, found a readership among trade unionists and anti-Porfirian intellectuals. These dissidents hardly posed a threat to Díaz, but their writings ended the political silence that had marked the country since the 1880s.

Of more consequence to Díaz than restless industrial laborers and the small coterie of intellectual opponents was the growing disaffection of middle-class and even some wealthy Mexicans. The Porfirian regime had become a gerontocracy that shut off political and economic opportunities for all but a reduced clique of individuals who were allies of Díaz from his earliest days in power. In 1910, the state governors were virtually sclerotic. Two were over eighty years old, six were past seventy, and seventeen beyond sixty. A majority of the local political bosses, the men instrumental in maintaining stability in towns and villages, were also past their sixth decade. The army leadership was burdened with overaged generals. In the cabinet, elderly figures replaced ministers who died of old age. More than half the judges were over seventy. Octogenarians were prominent in the Chamber of Deputies. And according to one Porfirian legislator, the Senate "housed a collection of senile mummies in a state of lingering stupor."[2]

The same pattern was repeated in commerce, banking, industry, and agriculture. Patriarchs who established their enterprises in the early Díaz era grew enormously wealthy. When they died, their families inherited their fortunes, and, more important, the goodwill of Don Porfirio that enabled them to reap new business opportunities. The Terrazas-Creel clan in Chihuahua, to mention one of the most salient examples, built up an hacienda empire during the Porfiriato that exceeded the size of Belgium. And where the economy was not in the hands of Porfirian favorites, it seemed to be under the control of foreigners, who accounted for two thirds of capital investments in the country by 1910.

To become a Terrazas or Creel was of course beyond the fantasies of middle-class Mexicans. But even their more modest aspirations were being thwarted. Unless they had relatives or godfathers connected to the Porfirian elite, the new lawyers, accountants, and engineers were unable to attain lucrative employment. The bureaucracy, fountainhead for most of the middle class, was no longer expanding in the late

Porfiriato. The number of schoolteachers was growing, but their salaries were no better than unskilled workers' wages.

By holding out the prospect of his retirement in the Creelman interview, Díaz briefly raised the hopes of these varied sectors that a new, more promising era was about to begin. He then stirred their dormant resentment when he announced that he would run for office yet again. Díaz might still have been able to maintain political stability had he chosen a popular figure like General Reyes as his successor or vice president. But the selection of Corral as his running mate suggested that the closed circle of científicos would soon emerge as the rulers of Mexico and shattered any illusions of fundamental economic and political change.

The opposition to Don Porfirio's reelection coalesced around the unlikely leadership of Francisco Madero. At thirty-seven years of age, he was a physically slight man, only a few inches over five feet tall, with a balding pate and a small goatee that made him a cartoonist's delight. His oratory, delivered in halting, high-pitched cadences, was mediocre at best. He had no political experience or obvious charisma. He did not smoke or drink, and espoused vegetarianism in a country where the consumption of meat, alcohol, and tobacco was viewed as a sign of virility. A devout spiritualist, Madero claimed to be guided in moments of tribulation by the soul of one of his dead brothers. His family, based in the northern state of Coahuila, had amassed one of the largest fortunes in the country through investments in copper mines, steel mills, textile factories, wine distilleries, rubber, haciendas, and banking. Following the usual path of gilded youth, he had studied and traveled in the United States and Europe, returned to manage a family hacienda, and married a prominent debutante. As Madero himself acknowledged: "I belong by birth to the privileged class . . . neither I nor any member of my family have cause for complaint against General Díaz. . . ."[3]

In fact, Madero's relatives initially ridiculed his attempts to become president. His grandfather, the patriarch of the family and its enterprises, refused his request for a campaign contribution and likened his challenge to Don Porfirio to "the rivalry of a microbe to an elephant."[4] The elder Madero also assured his friends in the Díaz cabinet that they had nothing to fear from his grandson's quixotic campaign nor from his utopian political ideas.

Francisco Madero's political notions were spelled out in his hastily written book, *The Presidential Succession in 1910*, part of the avalanche of publications that appeared in the aftermath of the Creelman interview. He championed liberal democracy, and called for observance of constitutional laws, including freedom of press and speech, the right to vote, and guarantees for opposition parties. "Effective suffrage and no reelection" was his main slogan, reflecting his belief that the country's problems were essentially of a political nature. He offered no dramatic remedies for the profound economic and social inequities afflicting the country. While lamenting that labor wages were abysmally low, he insisted that employers should not be made to pay more than they could afford. He urged hacienda owners to conduct themselves with benevolent paternalism in their dealings with peons and other workers.

In summary, Madero was a mild reformer. He eschewed violence, and had no sympathy for revolutionary programs. He claimed to have arrived at his decision to oppose Díaz because of personal outrage over the violation of individual liberties, and his firsthand observations of injustices on his own hacienda. He was convinced that like him there were many other privileged individuals of goodwill, eager to help the country evolve economically and socially under a democratic form of government.

Madero became the opposition candidate almost by default. When General Reyes—already rejected by Díaz as his running mate—declined to mount his own challenge for the presidency and docilely accepted exile in late 1909, Madero was left as the only active campaigner. And with the election only six months away, it was probably too late for another one to emerge. For almost a year, Madero had been traveling extensively across the nation, inaugurating chapters of his Anti-Reelectionist Party, promoting his own candidacy, and supporting the gubernatorial campaigns of anti-Díaz politicians. At this time, his rallies were sparsely attended and he was ignored by the government. But the withdrawal of Reyes inflated the ranks of Madero supporters with many Reyistas. By early 1910, his campaign picked up momentum. His speeches attracted large crowds, people drawn by his liberal program or enthralled by the spectacle of a real presidential contest.

An alarmed Díaz regime moved quickly to stifle Madero's campaign. Newspapers were warned not to give him coverage. Police broke up his political gatherings. And when Madero helped one of his aides escape the grasp of the gendarmes after an abortive rally, he himself was arrested for abetting a fugitive from justice. Madero, as well as five thousand of his supporters, spent election day, June 21, 1910, in jail. Massive ballot stuffing and other irregularities then handed Díaz and Corral an overwhelming victory.

Assured of yet another mandate, Don Porfirio regained the expansive mood that had been shattered by his inopportune remarks in the Creelman interview. He expressed disappointment that so many of his compatriots had demonstrated political immaturity and ingratitude in supporting a candidate who openly repudiated the Porfirian regime. But Díaz never lost faith that he had presided over the transformation of Mexico into a modern nation. Intent on showing his country and the world just how far Mexico had progressed under his tutelage, he turned his full attention to staging a spectacular celebration in the capital throughout the month of September 1910. The excuse for the extravaganza was the one hundredth anniversary of the Independence movement against Spain, or, as cynics insisted, the commemoration of Don Porfirio's eightieth birthday.

In Mexican history, the centennial has achieved the notoriety of Maximilian's coronation, Santa Anna's homage to his amputated leg, and Motecuhzoma's orgy of sacrifices that inaugurated the temple to Huitzilopóchtli (Díaz was dubbed "Porfiriopóchtli" by his opponents). The cost of the centennial exceeded the nation's education budget for 1910. New theaters, hotels, and public buildings were inaugurated. The Statue of Independence, a gold angel on top of a soaring marble column, was installed at the western end of Paseo de la Reforma. Nearby rose the multiple columns of the Monument to the Heroic Cadets, who died defending Chapultepec Castle against the American invaders in 1847. The United States sent a statue of George Washington, and from Italy came a marble likeness of Giuseppi Garibaldi. Gala balls and banquets were staged nightly at public expense. Fireworks lit up the evening skies. The government also distributed thousands of factory-made pants to the poor, who were exhorted to wear them in place of their traditional rough white trousers, and thus impress upon foreigners that even working-class Mexicans had shed their backwardness.

But the centennial failed to shore up Don Porfirio's flagging popularity. Frederick Starr, the president of the University of Chicago, who witnessed the monthlong celebrations in Mexico City and claimed to have interviewed a thousand Mexicans of every social class, asserted that he never once heard words of praise for the ruler. "Thousands thronged to watch the passing show, yet there was no outburst of delight," he wrote. "Porfirio Díaz, brilliant with royal decorations, and distinguished guests swept by without applause."[5]

As accounts of the centennial reached the provinces—where festivities were held on a far smaller scale—resentment of Díaz mingled

with loathing for his capital. Newspapers and visitors returning from
Mexico City described the opulent gowns and dazzling jewelry of
wealthy revelers, champagne poured by the gallon, and steaks counted
in tons. In the northern city of San Luís Potosí, a youth who would
later be a historian recalled that Mexico City sounded to him like a
European capital decked out for a coronation.[6] For Luz Jiménez, an
Indian woman in the village of Milpa Alta south of the capital, her
most vivid memory of the local centennial celebration was a national
government directive ordering parents to spend their meager savings
on shoes for their children that were to be worn out of respect for Independence Day: "If the fathers and mothers did not obey, they were to be
jailed for a month or they would have to pay a large fine. . . ."[7]

Mexico City seemed to embody all that was missing in the provinces:
political power, wealth, urbanity, cosmopolitan glitter. Stories of Don
Porfirio's beneficence toward his capital were already legendary. People
of the provinces had long complained that they were subsidizing the
disproportionate share of public investment and jobs garnered by Mexico City. And provincials were convinced that they would be called
upon to foot the bill for the capital's outpouring of self-congratulation.
The centennial reinforced the natural antipathy between Mexico City
and the hinterland, a phenomenon that became increasingly significant in the months and years ahead.

The centennial ceremonies had barely ended when news reached
the capital that Madero, free on bail posted by his family, had fled the
country to Texas. Temporarily abandoning his nonviolent creed, Madero had become convinced that only an armed revolt could topple
the Díaz regime. In a document drafted with other dissidents gathered
around him in San Antonio, he declared the recent elections illegal,
claimed the provisional presidency of Mexico, and called for a national
uprising in late November 1910. The revolutionary plan offered by
Madero was essentially the same compendium of liberal ideas contained in his book on the presidential succession. But the substance
of Madero's ideology counted less than his demand for an end to the
Porfiriato. Díaz was unable to stanch the rising disaffection against his
regime, and Madero, thanks to his electoral campaign, remained the
only opposition figure of national renown.

The most glaring omission in Madero's liberal program was its failure
to address the reality of a country where the vast majority of inhabitants
lived in rural misery. As scion of a great hacienda-owning family, he

defended the inviolability of private property. During his presidential campaign, he had insisted that peasants were more concerned about political liberties than land. And the revolutionary plan which he unveiled in San Antonio contained only a single paragraph on the agrarian problem: a proposal restoring properties to peasants whose plots had been unfairly reclassified as state-owned lands and sold to big estate owners.

Terrible inequities had existed in rural Mexico for centuries. The hacienda had dominated the countryside since the 1600s, encroaching on Indian properties and reducing peasants to debt peonage. And much had happened under the Díaz regime to aggravate the mismatch between wealth and poverty. Railroads, new farm technology, and lucrative export markets spurred the expansion of great estates. In one frenzied period between 1883 and 1895, rich foreigners and Mexicans acquired seventy million acres of rural property. But the real concentration of ownership was yet to come. In 1895, 20 percent of Mexicans still possessed land; by 1910, only 2 percent could make such a claim. As the Porfiriato drew to a close, seven million Mexicans—well over half of the rural population—lived and worked on haciendas and plantations owned by an elite of 834 families and land companies.[8]

Everywhere the rural villages and their inhabitants were being deprived of their remaining communal and private plots, cut off from water supplies, and physically engulfed by the giant estates. Perhaps nowhere was this ongoing process more sharply etched and potentially explosive than in the state of Morelos just south of Mexico City. By 1908, seventeen sugar plantations and haciendas claimed a fourth of Morelos's total surface—virtually all the quality land in the state.[9] The owners, members of the Porfirian elite, lived in Mexico City. But in this case, absenteeism did not imply neglect. By the criteria of Díaz and his científico advisers, the Morelos planters were among the most progressive in the nation. They invested heavily in irrigation and the most modern sugar-refining equipment, and built railway spurs connecting their estates to the trunk lines that carried their produce into Mexico City and to the Veracruz docks. They financed research projects to develop more productive strains of sugar cane that would allow them to compete in the world market with planters from Veracruz, the Caribbean, and Hawaii where the weather provided natural advantages. And for their foremen and managers, the Morelos planters often sought out Spaniards with previous experience in the sugar estates of Cuba and the Canary Islands.

The entrance to an hacienda was marked by massive iron gates and fortresslike guard stations. Gaining admission, a visitor drove several miles, past cane fields, stables, and thatch-roofed huts where thousands of peons lived, before arriving at the central compound. There, enclosed by ten- to fifteen-foot walls, were the smokestacked sugar mill, the manor church, stores, repair shops, a clinic, housing for the managers, and the master's mansion.

The peon's world was confined by the boundaries of the hacienda. His family prayed at the estate church, and was attended by doctors employed by the owner. The average daily wage of 35 centavos—about one fifteenth the income of an agricultural worker in the United States—was the same as a century before. But the price of such staples as corn, beans, and chile had more than doubled in the same period. Unable to cover his bare necessities with his wages, a peon went deeply into debt with the *tienda de raya*, or hacienda store, which invariably charged higher prices than village shops. Marriage and funeral fees, "voluntary" contributions to fiestas, and fines for alleged transgressions increased the indebtedness—and with it, the peon's obligation to maintain his employment at the hacienda. While escape from the estate was theoretically possible, an informal agreement among hacienda owners could prevent a peon from finding other rural employment, or land him in jail for failing to repay the money he owed.

Even foreign observers who were sympathetic to the hacienda owners described the peon as no better off than a serf or slave. Mrs. Alec Tweedie, who in 1900 visited one of the largest sugar estates in Morelos, noted that the peons' quarter, a veritable "village, containing nearly three thousand souls, belongs to the hacienda." She accepted at face value her hosts' explanation that "the people pay no rent, and [as] the owners of the hacienda [we] hold the right to turn them out." And she found some merit to their contention that if the peons' wages were increased, "they would only drink away the extra money, for they have not yet learnt thrift." But she concluded that at best "hacienda life resembles that of England in time of the Barons, when feudal laws reigned," and that often the debt peonage system "renders the people little more than slaves."[10]

Another Englishwoman, Rosa King, who lived in Morelos a decade later, described the hacienda owners as "men of humane instincts, for the most part, some of them kindness itself." She lamented, however, that they were always in Mexico City, oblivious to the injustices perpetrated on their haciendas. "They thought of the land in terms of the golden stream that flowed . . . into their laps. If they had lived more at home on their haciendas they would have seen that the golden stream was tainted with the sweat and blood of their laborers. . . ."[11]

According to Mrs. King, the hacienda owners visited their estates so infrequently—once or twice a year—that such occasions were declared holidays for the peons:

> All would be waiting, the children freshly scrubbed, their mothers adorned with pitiful ribbons and ornaments hoarded for the event; there would be a fiesta with music and dancing and fireworks. The gracious lady [of the hacienda], unbelievably beautiful and glamorous, would smile on them and ask the children's names, and distribute a carload of calicoes, shoes, blankets, toys, and other things useful or pleasing. Especially she would see that there were rosaries of glass beads in every color, costing almost nothing, but . . . priceless to the recipients because they were "blessed."[12]

The workers were allowed a day or two of festivities. For the hacienda owners and their guests—brought down from Mexico City on a private train that deposited them directly at the estate—the holiday extended for a few weeks. Polo matches, horse races, and rodeos were followed by banquets and waltzes. After wearying of the country life, the hacienda masters and their entourage boarded their train back to Mexico City, and perhaps from there set out for a European vacation. "Then, as the bills began to pile up and the calls for money became urgent, the manager would tighten up on the overseers, and the overseers would drive the peons, with whips if necessary," wrote Mrs. King. "I would see the poor wretches as I drove about, their feet always bare and hardened like stones, their backs bent under burdens too heavy for a horse or mule, treated as people with hearts would not treat animals."[13]

The peons were not the only rural inhabitants being squeezed by the Morelos estate owners. Their eagerness to increase production led them constantly to expand the boundaries of their haciendas. No communal land or individual plot was safe from their thrusts. They challenged the validity of peasants' deeds, some of them dating back to colonial times, and forced them to accept paltry settlements for their properties or risk waiting years for a court decision that invariably supported the hacienda claims. Often, the estate owner not only ended up with the peasant's plot but gained another peon as well. The hacienda masters appropriated cattle that strayed onto their properties, and occupied woodlands that provided a meager livelihood for many rural inhabitants.

Almost as significant as the land conflict was the dispute over water. The years between 1905 and 1910 witnessed serious droughts throughout Mexico, and Morelos was especially hard hit. The sugar plantation owners claimed priority for waters under the control of the state and its municipalities, and denied peasants the use of springs and streams flowing through their estates. The end result was as effective as an outright land grab: the small farmers relinquished their parched, bankrupt plots and accepted peonage.

As the haciendas tightened their vise, towns and villages were literally being strangled. Cuaútla, the second-largest community in Morelos after Cuernavaca, had no room to expand its cemetery and was forced to bury its dead in villages a mile or more away. In the last decades of the nineteenth century, more than a dozen communities—some dating back before the Spanish Conquest—ceased to exist. The estates first digested their lands, and then swallowed the houses, shops, church, and any inhabitant who had not already fled or surrendered to peonage. Tequesquitengo was the most notorious example of an ancient community wiped off the face of the map. When its inhabitants came into conflict with the owner of an expanding hacienda, he diverted his irrigation water into Lake Tequesquitengo, flooding the village so thoroughly that only its church spire remained above the surface. [14]

The Morelos peasants had no allies in the courts or government. Time and again, judges ruled in favor of the big planters. There were numerous cases of small farmers who were drafted into the army and posted to distant regions because they joined suits against the encroaching haciendas. For one brief moment in 1904, the peasants of Morelos entertained the illusion that their fortunes were about to change. Díaz himself received one of their delegations and told them he supported their efforts to recover lands lost to the estates. But Don Porfirio was toying with them. Shortly after the interview, thirty-six Morelos farmers who were too vocal in their opposition to the sugar planters were sent to a forced-labor camp in southernmost Mexico. [15] Díaz feigned ignorance of the affair, and then pretended to be powerless to prevent the Supreme Court from rejecting the peasants' suit.

In 1909, the peasants and small farmers of Morelos made one final attempt to use the political system to blunt the planters' offensive. Gubernatorial elections were scheduled that year. And while voting under the Díaz regime had always been a sham, the recent assertions by Don Porfirio in the Creelman interview that Mexico was ripe for democracy had lent an aura of excitement to the Morelos campaign.

"Land and water" became the slogan of Patricio Leyva, the candidate favored by the poorer rural inhabitants, and his political rallies attracted huge, enthusiastic crowds.

Díaz's handpicked candidate, Pablo Escandón, was the perfect symbol of the Porfirian elite. He was a descendant of Manuel Escandón, the great speculator and entrepreneur of the Santa Anna and Juárez eras. The Escandón family remained a leader of high society, business, and politics under Díaz. Pablo Escandón was educated in England and France, and viewed himself as a European-style aristocrat. Tall, handsome, and snobbish, he lived in Mexico City from the lavish income of his sugar plantations in Morelos. He treated his visits to his estates mainly as country outings and opportunities to hone his skills as a horseman and polo player. In his mid-forties, with no ambitions or anxieties, he reluctantly accepted his candidacy as an act of noblesse oblige and a personal favor to Díaz, or "Porfirito," as he called him. "I told Porfirito I didn't want the appointment," he confided to his friend, Mrs. King. "Why do I have to mix in these beastly local politics?"[16]

Escandón was lustily booed during his lackluster campaign appearances. But intimidation by the police and ballot stuffing gave him a landslide victory in February 1909. He immediately embarked on a policy openly favoring the estate owners in their land and water disputes with the peasants.

Hatred of the planters turned into a generalized antagonism toward Mexico City as the seat of authoritarian politics and residence of a domineering elite. The old battle cry of the 1810 Hidalgo revolt against Spanish rule—"Death to the gachupínes!"—was frequently heard. There were relatively few gachupínes, or true Spaniards, in Morelos or the rest of the country. But the epithet now embraced anybody who was linked to the cosmopolitan capital, anybody who was white and wealthy.

At the grass-roots political level, village elders ceded their posts as municipal presidents and councilmen to younger, more radical leaders. What turned out to be the most significant of these generational shifts took place in Anenecuilco, a village of some four hundred peasant inhabitants, where a thirty-year-old mestizo, Emiliano Zapata, was elected municipal president in the late summer of 1909. Short, wiry, with an almost feline grace, Zapata was remembered by a participant in that village assembly as "a man with pants on"—someone with a reputation for not backing down.[17] His glowering eyes were his most arresting physical feature. They burn with hypnotic intensity through the sepia of seven-decade-old photographs. Compared to his neighbors, Zapata was not badly off. He had his own plot of land, some cattle, and earned additional income as a muleteer. An accomplished bronco-buster and horse trainer, he occasionally hired himself out to the rich hacienda owners. For a few months, he worked as a groom in the Mexico City stables of a sugar planter who was Don Porfirio's son-in-law. But he was ill at ease in the metropolis, and soon returned to Anenecuilco, "remarking bitterly how in the capital horses lived in stalls that would put to shame the house of any workingman in the whole state of Morelos."[18]

Within months after being elected president of Anenecuilco, Zapata had to deal with the takeover of his village's lands and water by a nearby sugar plantation. When pleas to Governor Escandón and suits filed in court produced no results, Zapata led eighty armed villagers into the disputed properties and simply reclaimed them for Anenecuilco. During the remainder of 1910, he repeated the tactic in numerous other conflicts between haciendas and villages near Cuaútla, and emerged as the effective rural authority in that part of the state. Although few people recognized it at the time, the Revolution had begun in Morelos, preceding by a few months Madero's call for revolt in the northern part of the country.

Certainly, Pablo Escandón underestimated the Zapata movement. An absentee landlord, he had become an absentee governor as well, traveling as often as he could to the capital. Political office was not going to curtail his social and cultural obligations. In Morelos, the bored governor preferred to spend his time chatting with his friend, Mrs. King, the attractive English widow who had recently moved to Cuernavaca, the state capital. At Escandón's urging, she had opened a hotel, the Bella Vista, catering to wealthy foreigners and Mexicans. And now the governor overwhelmed her with advice on how to decorate her establishment, what food to serve, what plates to use, and even what to wear to impress her guests. Her hotel was part of his reverie to somehow transform provincial Cuernavaca into an outpost of European sophistication, a little Mexico City, anything to make him forget about those barbaric Indians and peasants. "The English colony will come because you are an Englishwoman, and the Americans because they like what is new, and the Mexicans because it is the fashionable thing," he told Mrs. King. When she expressed some uneasiness over Zapata's movement and talk of Madero's uprising, Escandón assured her there was no cause for concern: "Our Porfirito with his army and his strength of character will make short work of this revolt."[19]

Escandón's confidence in Don Porfirio's military invulnerability reflected the conventional wisdom of the day. The annual parades of the army and Rurales awed everybody in Mexico City. And in the countryside, isolated instances of peasant unrest were usually quelled by rushing large units of soldiers or Rurales into a locality, thus creating the impression of an overwhelming reservoir of military manpower at the regime's disposal.

In reality, however, the army was a shadow of its old self. Díaz, who matured during the constant coups of the Santa Anna era, knew that a strong army posed the greatest potential threat to his rule. And once he had consolidated his own power, he pursued policies aimed at weakening the military. For years he had taken care to rotate his officers constantly, and to ensure their loyalty by giving them ample opportunity to embezzle. Officers exaggerated the size of their units and pocketed the salaries of nonexistent troops. They also stole money budgeted for weapons procurement. The morale of conscripts was abysmal. Many of them were drafted as punishment for petty crimes or for protesting the takeover of their lands by haciendas. By 1910, the army, though theoretically exceeding thirty thousand men, could field only fourteen thousand soldiers, most of them poorly trained, equipped, and led. And the twenty-five hundred Rurales could not compensate for this shortage in military manpower.

At first, the security forces seemed capable of coping with the armed revolt declared by Madero for late November 1910. Madero rebels in Puebla were easily gunned down. An important cache of weapons was uncovered in Mexico City and the plotters were arrested. But constant guerrilla raids soon exposed the weaknesses of the Porfirian army. There were not enough soldiers to stifle uprisings that flared in a dozen provinces. The rebels were in a particularly advantageous position in the far north of the country where they could easily smuggle weapons across the border from the United States, while the federal troops had to bring reinforcements and supplies from distant Mexico City. In January 1911, the rebels ambushed and annihilated a large army force in Chihuahua. A series of other successful battles culminated in May with the capture of a large federal garrison in Ciudad Juárez, a border city across the Rio Grande from El Paso, Texas. Within days, rebel forces overwhelmed six other key army garrisons around the country.

In Morelos, meanwhile, Zapata and his allies took the major towns and cities. The Porfirista governor, Escandón, fled to Mexico City, and then to Britain, ranting that the country was retrogressing into "true niggerdom."[20] His friend, Mrs. King, found her luxury hotel trespassed by bandoliered peasant rebels, and when she tried to eject one of them, he informed her that "these are different times . . . the peon is now the master."[21]

Don Porfirio's famed iron will melted as easily as his reputedly invincible army. He quickly dispatched a delegation to Ciudad Juárez to negotiate a treaty of surrender with Madero. Under its terms, Díaz and his vice president, Corral, resigned from office, and Francisco León de la Barra, the foreign minister, assumed the interim presidency until new elections could be staged. For the first time in thirty-five years, the shrill cries of public condemnation rang in Don Porfirio's ears. Huge crowds swirled through the Zócalo beneath the balconies of the National Palace shouting "Death to Díaz!" until a pouring rain and mounted police dispersed them with heavy casualties. The dictator had to spend his last night in the capital hidden in a friend's mansion. As dawn broke, he escaped Mexico City in a heavily armed train to Veracruz, where a ship took him into exile in Europe. "They have loosed the wild beasts—let us see now who will tame them," was Don Porfirio's parting malediction in Veracruz. He died in Paris four years later, perversely satisfied that his prophecy had been fulfilled.

He certainly knew "the wild beasts" of Mexican politics far better than Madero. Savagery had been Don Porfirio's preferred weapon while he accrued power, and he relented only as he became more secure in his rule. Madero, the apostle of democracy, was always repelled by violence. He had called for armed revolt only after peaceful methods had failed, and now that Díaz was toppled, he was anxious to declare an end to revolution.

Arriving by train from his northern redoubt, Madero basked in the usual triumphant welcome that Mexico City accorded its conquerors, whether their names were Iturbide, Santa Anna, Maximilian, Juárez, or Díaz. Paper streamers and flower garlands cascaded from balconies and rooftops. Cheers, screams, cymbals, drums, and car horns drowned out Madero's speeches, and the newest hero could barely keep his footing as admirers pressed forward to embrace him or to touch his clothing as if it had a miraculous healing quality. Leadership of the country was his for the taking. His supporters, even his opponents, expected him to grasp power no matter what terms he had negotiated with Díaz. Had not Don Porfirio violated any agreement or law that stood in his way? And had not Madero already declared himself president during his revolt against the dictatorship?

But Madero demurred. He was intent on demonstrating that a new era of democracy would succeed the Porfirian regime. And so, upholding his accord with Díaz, he turned the government over to Don Porfirio's foreign minister, De la Barra, for what proved to be a crucial six-month period while he embarked on his electoral campaign for the presidency. Madero's decision may have been nobly democratic. But it robbed all momentum from his movement, and invited the chaos that Díaz had predicted.

Resistance to Madero's brand of peaceful, democratic politics began in his own camp. Those who had joined him in the north were less a unified army than an unruly assortment of rebel battalions drawn from every social class: peons mobilized by small and moderate-sized hacienda owners, who had grown resentful of the giant land barons; peasants and temporary farm hands; students and teachers; middle-class professionals unable to secure well-paying jobs; mineworkers bitter at the Porfirian regime's harsh suppression of their strikes; criminals and beggars; and, toward the end of the revolt, thousands of federal army deserters.

Madero's leading commanders were Pascual Orozco, a muleskinner with a personal grievance against a large hacienda owner, and Francisco ("Pancho") Villa, a cattle rustler, murderer, and bandit chieftain. Both were scornful of Madero's political acumen, and especially of his military strategy. When Madero, fearing defeat, ordered them to call off their attack on Ciudad Juárez, they brazenly ignored his directive. And after that watershed victory, Orozco and Villa drew their revolvers on Madero in a dispute over back pay for their troops and political rewards for themselves. Only the entreaties of Madero's aides saved his life and temporarily restored his command over his hot-tempered generals.

Barely able to control the rebels in his stronghold in northern Mexico, Madero had even less influence over the Zapatistas in the south. Zapata represented the purest strain of the Revolution, the yearning for land by the peasantry. Elsewhere in the country, the melting pot of social classes drawn into the anti-Díaz revolt obscured the fact that the vast majority of rebel combatants were the agrarian poor. But in Morelos, the Zapatistas were peasants to the core, and would not lay down their arms until properties lost to the haciendas were restored to their villages.

This, then, was the unsettling situation which Madero faced within the movement he nominally led. He compounded his problems by underestimating the strength of Porfirian reactionaries. The dictator might be in exile, but he left behind many powerful supporters— businessmen, industrialists, hacienda owners, newspaper editors, politicians, bureaucrats, and military officers—and they were intent on sabotaging Madero even before he took office. The interim presidency of De la Barra showed signs of becoming more than a caretaker government. He appointed Porfiristas to key cabinet posts. He was backed by a Congress that was still controlled by Díaz conservatives, and he drew support from like-minded newspaper editors. Most importantly, he had at his disposal the federal army, whose officer corps was still largely intact.

While Madero occupied himself with his presidential campaign against a field of nonentities, De la Barra pursued policies aimed at weakening the revolutionary ranks. He openly backed the large estate owners in their struggle to resist peasant claims over parts of their properties. He pressured the revolutionaries to relinquish their weapons, disband their troops, and accept the federal army as the only legitimate military force. Nowhere were these initiatives more provocative than in Morelos, the stronghold of the Zapatistas.

Zapata and his followers had been wary of Madero from the beginning. They had carried on their revolt, virtually oblivious to Madero's movement in the north. Whatever they had achieved—routing the army, restoring some lost village lands, cowing the hacienda owners— was the result of their own efforts. Their horizon did not extend beyond Morelos and parts of the adjoining states. They simply wanted to be left alone to manage affairs in their own region. And they despised Mexico City as the seat of government that had always oppressed them.

Despite his skepticism, Zapata conducted himself reasonably with Madero. When Madero entered Mexico City at the head of his victorious rebel forces, Zapata traveled to the capital to meet him. Madero failed to satisfy Zapata's request for a firm commitment to restore peasant lands in Morelos. Swallowing his disappointment, Zapata nevertheless agreed to the demands of Madero and De la Barra that he demobilize most of his followers. But when it became evident that the planters were creating their own brigades, the Zapatistas refused to disband any further.

Conservative newspapers in Mexico City disseminated false reports of Zapatista uprisings in Morelos. And De la Barra, claiming that the situation was chaotic, sent a large army force to "pacify" the state.

Madero, whose presidential campaign had brought him to Morelos, witnessed these developments and began to understand why the Zapatistas distrusted the government in Mexico City. He protested to De la Barra that there were no rebel uprisings and that the federal troops, by marching directly on Zapatista headquarters, were provoking war. But De la Barra ignored Madero's entreaties, and Madero, anxious to get on with his presidential campaign in other states, made no further attempt to defuse the situation. Zapata drew the appropriate conclusion: it mattered little who was in power in Mexico City—Díaz, De la Barra, Madero—none of them could be relied upon to set things right in the countryside.

The federal army force in Morelos was led by Victoriano Huerta, one of the more brilliant and brutal generals left over from the Porfirian regime. He took up residence in Mrs. King's Bella Vista Hotel in Cuernavaca, where he drank himself into a stupor every night while waiting for Madero to leave the state so that he could proceed with his military plans. As soon as Madero departed from Morelos, Huerta dropped any pretense that his mission was one of pacification. His goal, he declared, was to annihilate the Zapatistas, and he initiated a terror campaign that included summary executions of suspected rebels and the pillaging of villages. Zapata himself barely escaped a fatal ambush. But in the end, Huerta's tactics increased the Zapatista ranks as refugees joined rebel camps hidden in the wooded hills and mountains. Setting a pattern that would endure for years, the Zapatistas operated with impunity in the Morelos countryside while the armies sent by Mexico City occupied the main urban centers.

In November 1911, Madero finally took office after easily winning the presidential campaign and a congressional majority. But his rhetoric and policies continued to reflect an aversion to radical change. He seemed determined to maintain the economic and social legacy of the Porfiriato, although under a democratic form of government. His budget for education and other social expenses barely exceeded the outlays of the Díaz regime. He failed to satisfy labor demands for higher wages and shorter hours. On the paramount issue of land reform, Madero did little more than establish a National Agrarian Commission to study the matter. The commission eventually put forth a plan to purchase some hacienda properties and distribute them to peasants, but funded the project with a meager 10 million pesos.

In his political initiatives, Madero treated the Zapatistas as if they were defeated enemies instead of revolutionary allies. The new president said he was prepared to offer amnesty to peasants who surrendered and to ensure Zapata a safe trip into exile abroad. Zapata responded by declaring himself in open rebellion and unveiling his own agrarian plan, which called for the expropriation of one third of the great hacienda lands.

At this point, Madero had no commander for the federal army forces in Morelos. He had arranged the dismissal of General Huerta because of his heavy-handed tactics against the Zapatistas. "Huerta was very, very angry and like an Indian swore revenge on Madero," wrote Mrs. King, whose ownership of the Bella Vista Hotel gave her a front-row seat in the Revolution. "I marveled at the incredible innocence of Mr. Madero, who seemed to think he could play fast and loose with men like this. He had made a foe of Zapata by just such an about-face, and now . . . he had made a foe of the more formidable Huerta."[22]

As Huerta's replacement, Madero appointed another former Porfirian general, Juvencio Robles. But Robles had no intention of abandoning Huerta's hard-line strategy against the Zapatistas. The new commander moved into Mrs. King's hotel, whose clientele by this time was almost exclusively military, and proceeded to shock his landlady by explaining his strategy for dealing with the Zapata revolt: "Why, I am trying to clean up your beautiful Morelos for you. What a nice place it will be once we get rid of the inhabitants! If they resist me, I shall hang them like earrings to the trees."[23]

These were no empty threats. Robles burned down entire villages, herded the survivors into concentration camps on the outskirts of Cuernavaca, and shipped the overflow of refugees and prisoners to labor camps and army garrisons elsewhere in the country. According to Mrs. King, who witnessed these deportations at the Cuernavaca train station, "the soldiers were hustling the poor wretches into a cattle box car, pushing them in until there was not even standing room . . . [and then] they boarded up the doors and nailed them shut."[24] Her own servant was among the prisoners, and died of suffocation like many others before the train reached its destination. General Robles's tactics were to become common practice for the federal army commanders in Morelos, reducing the state's population by more than a third before the Revolution ended.

The Morelos uprising was not the only revolt facing Madero in the year after he assumed the presidency. In the north, General Bernardo Reyes, Don Porfirio's old crony and thwarted pretender to his throne, was back from exile and calling for the overthrow of Madero. But Reyes's movement failed to gather supporters. He was arrested, and sent to prison in Mexico City. Meanwhile, in Veracruz, Don Porfirio's nephew, Félix Díaz, rallied the local army garrison in an attempt to topple the government. Madero was again able to command the loyalty of most of the army. Forced to surrender, Félix Díaz was court-martialed and condemned to death for treason. But Madero commuted his sentence to a prison term in Mexico City.

Of all the provincial revolts against Madero, however, the most threatening one was led by his former commander, Pascual Orozco, who was angered at not having been appointed governor of his native Chihuahua despite his military heroics against the Díaz regime. Orozco asserted that he was rebelling because the Madero government had not implemented a revolutionary program. But his opportunism was evident in his acceptance of financial support from the Terrazas and Creel clans, the wealthiest landowners in Chihuahua, who were wary of even the tepid reforms announced by Madero. By March 1912, Orozco had assembled an army more than six thousand strong, and began his offensive southward intent on capturing Mexico City.

His forces routed the federal battalions sent to stem his advance. With panic mounting in the government, Madero accepted the advice of his army leaders to appoint General Victoriano Huerta as commander of a new expeditionary force. Huerta had been inactive for six months, ever since his removal from the Morelos campaign against the Zapatistas, and he still resented Madero. But the general welcomed the chance to restore his professional reputation, and accepted the appointment with the proviso that this time he be given complete control over military operations until his mission was accomplished. He proceeded with great deliberation, amassing soldiers, artillery, and supplies before confronting Orozco's army in May 1912 along the Chihuahua-Durango border. Then, in two battles fought on open plains that favored his conventional forces, he crushed Orozco's rebels, pushed them back to the Texas border, and reduced them to ineffective guerrilla bands. Huerta returned to Mexico City a hero, his military and political standing vastly enhanced.

Madero himself did not emerge stronger from these victories. The focus of the threats against him merely shifted from the provinces to Mexico City. The capital had not been a hotbed of revolution even in the waning days of the Porfiriato. Labor unrest was minor compared to the provinces. There were no guerrilla bands lurking in the slums, and few instances of intellectuals or workers stealing off to the countryside to join Madero forces in the north or the Zapatistas in the south. A politician writing almost sixty years after Don Porfirio's overthrow recalled that there were so few revolutionary students in Mexico

City that "we were viewed by the majority of our colleagues as truly
'rare animals' or extraterrestrial beings, since the whole [university]
atmosphere encouraged servility and adoration of the dictator. . . ."[25]

The popular outpouring for Madero when he arrived in the capital
after Díaz's escape into exile reflected both the honest enthusiasm of
many inhabitants and the desire of many others to ingratiate themselves
with the new leader in an uncertain situation. But the metropolis never
warmed to Madero as president. His cabinet, weighted with conservatives but also including liberals, failed to command strong loyalties
in any political camp. He exposed himself to charges of nepotism by
relying heavily on a dozen of his relatives in government and Congress,
most notably his brother, Gustavo. And whatever defects Madero had,
they were magnified by the opposition newspapers, which enjoyed a
freedom unparalleled in Mexican history.

Conservative journals like *El Imparcial* and *El Diario* emerged from
the Porfiriato with a greater readership and stronger financial resources
than the newer pro-Madero press. Their attacks on the president were
merciless. Editorials denounced his agrarian policies both as a threat
to big landowners and as not radical enough to satisfy peasants. The
provincial uprisings against Madero were eagerly reported. Sensational
coverage of even minor rural conflicts evoked the image of a whole
countryside in anarchy. One leading newspaper, taking stock of the
year that followed Don Porfirio's downfall, commented: "What remains for us of the order, peace and prosperity internally, and the
credit, respect and prestige abroad which Mexico enjoyed under the
government of General Díaz?"[26] Editorials were demanding Madero's
resignation only months after he had taken office.

The opposition press also engaged in personal calumny against Madero and his family. His vegetarianism, spiritualism, his abstinence
from tobacco and alcohol, his occasional shedding of tears in public,
his childless marriage—all were offered as evidence that he was not
"macho" enough to lead the country. There were even veiled suggestions in some journals that Madero was mentally unstable. His
brother Gustavo was said to be the Svengali of the government, and
was cruelly nicknamed "Squinty" because he wore a glass eye, the
result of a childhood accident.

These relentless attacks on Madero, portraying him as indecisive,
ineffective, even ridiculous, created a sense of apathy toward his government among his supporters in Mexico City, and encouraged his
opponents to plot against him more brazenly. The focal point of their
conspiracies was the army, whose prestige had soared after its success

in dealing with the provincial revolts. Conservative politicians, businessmen, and editors repeatedly met with ranking military officers as 1912, Madero's first year in office, ended.

The formidable rollcall of Madero's enemies would not be complete without mention of Henry Lane Wilson, Washington's ambassador in Mexico City. Egotistical and autocratic, Lane Wilson was a parody of the overbearing U.S. diplomat run amok in a Latin American country's internal political affairs. The ambassador was not unhappy at the overthrow of the Porfirian regime, and initially spoke of Madero in favorable terms. But he was soon peeved at Madero for failing to seek his counsel and guidance. His assessment of the Mexican president turned even bleaker when Madero declined to grant favors to American investors. In his dispatches to Washington, Lane Wilson depicted Madero as an enemy of U.S. economic interests in Mexico, and incapable of or unwilling to protect American lives and property from the revolts in the provinces. The ambassador saw no inconsistency in peppering his reports with praise for the character and motives of anti-Madero rebel leaders like General Reyes and Félix Díaz. Lane Wilson's dispatches echoed the rumors and exaggerations printed by the opposition press, and were at variance with the less gloomy assessments of local American consular agents. The discrepancy was soon pointed out by U.S. Secretary of State Philander Knox, who was annoyed enough at Lane Wilson to cast doubts on the reliability of his reports.[27]

The reprimand left the ambassador unchastened. If Washington was not prepared to back his crusade against Madero, he would proceed on his own initiative. His residence became the tabernacle for foreigners and Mexicans with real or imaginary grievances against the government. The officers, politicians, and journalists plotting an anti-Madero coup received solace and encouragement from Lane Wilson.

By January 1913, Mexico City and even the provinces expected a coup against Madero. Mrs. King in Cuernavaca recalled that "fantastic rumors of the disloyalty of prominent men in the government itself began to reach us. . . ."[28] Madero's own attitude is difficult to fathom. He dismissed the reports as exaggerations even when they came from such reliable sources as his brother Gustavo and high-ranking officers who still supported the government. And throughout the crisis which soon unfolded, the president displayed an ingenuousness that defied belief.

The coup began on the night of February 9, 1913. Several hundred rebel troops marched to the prisons where General Bernardo Reyes and Félix Díaz were serving their sentences for their uprisings against the government. The two men were freed from their cells, and given command of the revolt. The column headed for the National Palace, which was supposed to have already fallen to other rebel forces. But the palace, located on the eastern side of the Zócalo, was still under control of loyal soldiers. And when General Reyes led a charge against the building, he was killed by a machine-gun burst.

The rebels retreated to positions in the buildings and arcades on the western end of the Zócalo and let loose a barrage against the troops holding the National Palace. The Zócalo's open plaza was already crowded with shoppers, vendors, and families en route to Mass at the Cathedral. The withering crossfire killed several hundred of these by-standers and wounded nearly a thousand more.

Madero himself was at his official residence in Chapultepec Castle. With an entourage of cabinet ministers and army officers, he rode to the city center to lead the resistance against the coup. But the intense fusillades forced him to take refuge in a photo shop near the Zócalo. After several more hours of fruitless battle, Félix Díaz and his rebels withdrew a few blocks southward and occupied the Ciudadela, an old, reddish-brown fortress that served as the main armory for the Mexico City garrison. Madero then moved into the National Palace, and, in an inexplicable lapse of judgment, named General Victoriano Huerta, his old foe, to direct operations against the rebels.

Dislodging the insurgents would have proven a difficult task even for a loyal commander. The Ciudadela's walls were thick enough to withstand the largest cannon, and its bountiful supply of guns and ammunition ensured that the rebels would not lack firepower. But Huerta had no intention of quelling the insurrection. Instead, he used the near impregnability of the fortress as an excuse to prolong the conflict in the hopes that support for Madero would eventually evap-orate. He allowed the rebels to set up their defenses on the parapets of the fortress and in the surrounding streets. He permitted a convoy carrying food to reach the Ciudadela. And one of his aides secretly met with Félix Díaz in a café a short distance from the fortress. To counter suspicions about his conduct, Huerta ordered artillery barrages against the Ciudadela, and sent a cavalry detachment of Rurales charg-ing to their death against the well-protected rebels.

When Madero learned that Huerta had sent an emissary to Díaz and had made no attempt to block food provisions from reaching the rebels, he confronted him with the reports. After first denying the allegations, Huerta conceded they were true. But he insisted that he had unsuccessfully attempted to arrange a peaceful surrender by the insurgents, and that now he would attack in earnest. Then, in a dramatic gesture to assure the president of his loyalty and determination, Huerta embraced Madero and said: "You are in the arms of General Victoriano Huerta."[29] The gullible president was appeased.

Huerta did, in fact, unleash a murderous display of firepower, which drew an equally deadly barrage from the rebels. But most victims were civilians. The events between February 9 and 18 became known as the "Decena Trágica," the Tragic Ten Days. Not since the conquistadores mounted their assault against the Aztecs had Mexico City experienced such violence and devastation. Under the indiscriminate cannonades, hundreds of buildings—offices, shops, private residences, theaters, hospitals, government agencies—crumbled and burst into flames within a radius of twenty blocks. All commerce and traffic halted. Most of the inhabitants were left without food. As casualties mounted into the thousands, the city reeked from the odor of decomposing bodies that could not be collected from the streets. During the brief intervals when the fusillades abated, soldiers and Red Cross workers hurriedly doused the corpses with gasoline and set them afire in the hopes of avoiding epidemics. "It was a spectacle difficult to forget," said a politician who was a schoolboy at the time. "When the dead were burned . . . they writhed as if they were trying to sit up."[30] Inhabitants took advantage of the lulls to scavenge for food or loot grocery shops. "People ate anything they could get their hands on," recalled a trade unionist who lived through the Decena Trágica as an adolescent. "There was not a cat left in the city, and they even ate dogs."[31]

As the battles raged, Huerta and Félix Díaz, still nominally the opposing commanders, met secretly at the home of a mutual friend to take stock of the situation. Their bloody charade was succeeding: many army officers were defecting to the conspirators or were convinced that a stalemate had developed which would end only if Madero resigned. The inhabitants of the capital were so terrified by the bombardment that they seemed likely to accept any leadership as long as peace was restored.

The conspirators were also able to count on strenuous efforts on their behalf by Lane Wilson. Only a few days after the battles erupted, the American ambassador sent a dispatch to the State Department asserting that public opinion in Mexico was "overwhelmingly in favor" of Félix Díaz.[32] He suggested that Washington empower him to threaten both Madero and the rebels with the possibility of U.S. intervention in order to force them to negotiate a settlement. Secretary of State Knox turned him down. But Lane Wilson decided to proceed on his own account. Accompanied by the German and Spanish ministers, he visited the National Palace on the fourth day of the fighting to protest against the loss of foreign lives and property. He warned Madero that unless the hostilities ceased, the American Navy would occupy Mexican ports and Marines would invade the capital to protect the foreign community.

Madero was aghast. Not only was he under fire from the rebels, but now he was being told that an American invasion was imminent. He cabled President William Taft imploring him not to make the situation worse by sending American forces. Taft, who had never authorized Lane Wilson to threaten the Mexican president, was bewildered by the note and answered back that no intervention was contemplated. But several crucial days elapsed before Madero received this reply. In the meantime, his position was further eroded because rumors spread that Washington was pressuring him to resign by threatening an invasion.

After delivering his false ultimatum to the Mexican president, Lane Wilson demanded that Madero order a cease-fire so that he and other diplomats could meet with Félix Díaz in the rebel stronghold. Madero complied, and Lane Wilson, accompanied by several European ministers, visited the Ciudadela. Díaz was delighted to receive the delegation. It gave his uprising a measure of diplomatic recognition. Whether or not he believed in the possibility of an American invasion, he was well aware that such a threat was more dangerous to Madero's political position than to his own. And the fact of the matter was that he considered Lane Wilson his ally. In his memoirs, the American ambassador noted that in the meeting at the Ciudadela, "my colleagues and I were pleased with the frankness as well as with the humane views expressed by General Díaz. . . ." By contrast, Lane Wilson summed up his earlier audience with Madero by describing the Mexican president's views as carrying "no conviction."[33]

Lane Wilson's intrigues against Madero were just starting to gather momentum. He invited the ministers of Spain, Britain, Germany, and Cuba to the U.S. Embassy. "Madero is a fool, a lunatic and should be legally declared incompetent to exercise office," the ambassador told his colleagues. He informed them that through intermediaries he had been in secret communication with General Huerta and Félix Díaz. "Madero is irremediably lost," he said. "His fall . . . depends only on an agreement which is now being negotiated between Huerta and Félix Díaz."[34] To speed up the denouement, Lane Wilson suggested that he and his colleagues select a representative among themselves to meet with Madero and ask him to step down. The diplomats chose the Spanish minister. On his own, Lane Wilson then prodded a group of conservative Mexican senators to demand the resignation of the president.

Madero rejected the representations of the senators and the diplomatic corps. Reminding them that he had been democratically elected, he vowed that he would die in office rather than resign. By now, Madero knew from Washington that there would be no American invasion. He had also discovered that Lane Wilson was behind the demands for his resignation. And so, he cabled President Taft again, this time to protest the American ambassador's efforts to subvert him.

Embarrassed by the telegram, a copy of which he received from Washington, Lane Wilson sought a retraction from Madero. It was all a misunderstanding, he wrote the Mexican president. He had not instigated his fellow diplomats, nor was their request for Madero's resignation a reflection of the official views of their governments. Rather, it was "simply friendly advice."[35] Madero, who very much needed the support of the powerful ambassador, agreed to send another cable to President Taft withdrawing his complaint against Lane Wilson. The American ambassador could have returned the favor by offering Madero another piece of "friendly advice"—namely, that he had been informed by Huerta that same day, February 17, that the president would be overthrown within twenty-four hours. But Lane Wilson said nothing to Madero. Instead, the ambassador passed the word on to his diplomatic colleagues: "Tomorrow, all will be over. . . ."[36]

Despite the careful preparations of the conspirators, the coup almost collapsed with the detention of General Huerta the next day. His secret meetings with Félix Díaz had been discovered by the president's brother, Gustavo Madero. In the predawn hours, Gustavo confronted Huerta, took his pistol from him, and led him to the president. Huerta, again protesting his undying loyalty to Madero, told him that the final assault on the Ciudadela was scheduled for that very afternoon. And Madero foolishly believed him. He ordered Gustavo to return the general his pistol, and asked Huerta to join him in a meeting with the group of conservative senators who had been demanding Madero's resignation. At Madero's prompting, Huerta repeated to the senators that the rebel stronghold would be taken in the next few hours. "Now you see?" remarked Madero. "General Huerta has his plans and is confident of good results. There is no reason for alarm."[37] What Madero did not know was that the senators and Huerta were fellow conspirators. The general and other ranking officers had met with them before to secure their support for the coup. The only "reason for alarm" as far as the senators were concerned was that Madero might replace Huerta with a loyal general. Naturally, they were relieved to discover that the president was still placing his trust in Huerta.

The coup now proceeded as scheduled. Early that afternoon of February 18, as Madero was conferring with his cabinet members, an officer barged in with a platoon and tried to place the president under detention. In the scuffle that followed, three people were shot to death, including Madero's cousin, who saved the president's life by stepping in front of him just as a soldier fired his gun. Madero fled to a patio. Believing that the rebels were a small contingent who had somehow infiltrated into the building, he sought out the commander of the palace garrison. But when Madero found him, the officer drew his gun and took him prisoner.

Huerta, meanwhile, was at a downtown restaurant eating lunch with several officials, including Gustavo Madero, who was too suspicious of the general to let him out of his sight. Huerta was called away for a telephone call. Informed that the president had been overthrown, he returned to the meal with a barely suppressed smile. After a few minutes more of table talk, Huerta drew his revolver, thanked Gustavo for returning his weapon to him, and then told him he was a prisoner.

As word of the coup's success spread, the cannonades that had laid waste to Mexico City for ten days came to an end. Dazed inhabitants emerged from their homes to search out missing relatives. Church bells pealed throughout the capital—possibly as a sign of relief that the carnage was over, or perhaps, as opponents of the clergy later charged, as evidence that the Church approved of Madero's overthrow.

There was no ambiguity about Lane Wilson's reaction. So eager was he for the coup to succeed that he prematurely cabled Washington to report that the army generals had taken power—although in fact President Madero was not arrested for another hour and a half. The American ambassador then immediately offered his embassy for a reception and conference that evening for the victors, General Huerta and Félix Díaz. At the embassy, the two chief plotters agreed that Huerta would serve as provisional president and would back Díaz as a presidential candidate in elections to be held at an unspecified date.

Outside the room where these negotiations were being held, a joyful Lane Wilson bragged about his intimate knowledge of the coup. "This is the salvation of Mexico," he told his diplomatic colleagues. "From now on there will be peace, progress and wealth. I knew that Madero would be taken prisoner for the last three days." When one of the foreign envoys expressed concern about Madero's fate, Lane Wilson chuckled: "Oh, Mr. Madero will be taken to an insane asylum, where he should have been all along." Then the American ambassador turned to greet Félix Díaz, who was emerging from the conference room. "They looked at each other intently," wrote the Cuban minister, who witnessed the scene. "It seemed as if they would devour one another, and they embraced. . . . Then, Mr. Wilson took him off to toast the coup's success with champagne."[38]

Félix Díaz departed the embassy and returned to the Ciudadela, the rebel stronghold, where Gustavo Madero was a prisoner. After Díaz and his officers condemned him to death, Gustavo was hurled into a patio where a hundred drunken soldiers punched, kicked, and beat him with staves. When he begged for his life, his tormentors responded with jeers and laughter. One of them pulled his head back by the hair and gouged out his good eye. Blind, bleeding profusely, and screaming in pain, Gustavo staggered against a wall. "Coward! Squinty! Whiner!" the troops shouted at him, as they resumed their beatings. Making him run in circles around a statue of Morelos, the hero of Independence, they stabbed at him with their bayonets. When he collapsed at the foot of the statue, someone fired a gun point-blank in his face. The others, laughing that a coup de grace was needed, riddled his body with bullets. Gustavo's corpse was then mutilated, and one soldier triumphantly extracted his glass eye as a memento. At dawn, the remains were shoved into a shallow hole dug in the patio.[39]

Ignorant of Gustavo's martyrdom, Francisco Madero and his vice-president, José María Pino Suárez, remained prisoners in a three-room suite at the National Palace. But the murder was reported on the front pages of the Mexico City newspapers on the following day, February 19, and alarm for Madero and Pino Suárez spread among foreign diplomats—with the notable exception of Lane Wilson. Led by the Cuban and Chilean ministers, the diplomats quickly negotiated an agreement between General Huerta and the two prisoners. In exchange for their resignations, Madero and Pino Suárez were to be escorted by special night train to Veracruz, where a Cuban ship would take them to exile in Europe. The deposed president and vice-president upheld their part of the bargain and signed letters of resignation. General Huerta, however, refused to free them, despite repeated representations made to him by Latin American and European diplomats in the following days.

Huerta had consulted with Lane Wilson, and apparently felt no pressure from him to safeguard the lives of Madero and Pino Suárez. This, at any rate, can be inferred from a cable sent on February 19 by Lane Wilson to Washington recounting his meeting that day with Huerta: "He asked my advice as to whether it was best to send the ex-President out of the country or to place him in a lunatic asylum. I replied that he ought to do that which was best for the country."[40]

At this point, Madero's family asked for an interview with Lane Wilson, and the ambassador reluctantly agreed to receive them the next day. According to Madero's wife, he was brusque throughout the meeting. He complained that Madero's downfall was "due to the fact that he never wanted to consult with me." His loathing for Vice-President Pino Suárez was even greater. "He is to blame for most of your husband's troubles," Mrs. Madero quoted the ambassador as saying. "That kind of man must disappear. . . ." And when Mrs. Madero asked him to intercede with Huerta to save the lives of her husband and Pino Suárez, he replied: "That is a responsibility that I do not care to undertake, either for myself, or my government."[41]

That night, however, Lane Wilson received an urgent cable from Secretary of State Knox that should have dispelled any doubts about his own government's concern for Madero. "General Huerta's consulting you as to the treatment of Madero tends to give you a certain responsibility in the matter," wrote Knox. "It moreover goes without saying that cruel treatment of the ex-President would injure the reputation of Mexican civilization, and this government earnestly hopes to hear that he has been dealt with in a manner consistent with peace and humanity." Knox added that he expected Lane Wilson to convey these sentiments to Huerta.[42]

But Lane Wilson had more important concerns than Madero's safety. He wanted to secure Washington's recognition of Huerta's provisional government. When his cables urging the State Department to take this course of action went without reply, he proceeded once again on his own, telegraphing his superiors in Washington on February 21:

In the absence of instructions and in view of the extreme urgency, I assembled the diplomatic corps relative to the recognition of the new government. My colleagues agreed that recognition of the new government was imperative, to enable it to impose its authority and establish order. I shall accordingly unite with my colleagues, believing I am interpreting the desires of the Department. . . . I am sending a circular

telegram to all consuls instructing them to do all possible to bring about
a general acceptance of the Provisional Government.[43]

But Washington withheld recognition of the Huerta government,
as did virtually all foreign countries. Contrary to Lane Wilson's assertions, other foreign emissaries in Mexico City were focusing their
efforts on saving the lives of Madero and Pino Suárez rather than
pressing their government for early recognition of the new regime.

During the four days that Madero and Pino Suárez remained prisoners in the National Palace, Huerta, Díaz, and the other military
leaders of the coup debated their fate. In the end, they were convinced
that Madero in exile would attempt to regain the presidency. After all,
he had succeeded spectacularly against much greater odds in overthrowing the Porfirian regime with a movement that he led from his
refuge in Texas. Long-term incarceration for Madero and Pino Suárez
was just as problematical. Sooner or later, pressure for their release
would mount in Mexico and abroad. And neither Madero nor Pino
Suárez was likely to retire quietly to their haciendas, the way so many
deposed leaders had done during the unstable era of Santa Anna.

They would have to be assassinated, but a cover story was needed,
good enough for partisans of the new regime to be able to defend.

At about ten-thirty on the night of February 22, a colonel aroused
Madero and Pino Suárez from their beds and told them they were
being transferred to Lecumbérri, Porfirio Díaz's model penitentiary.
Two automobiles rolled up to the National Palace. Madero was placed
in the first, alongside army and Rural personnel led by a Major Francisco Cárdenas. In the second car, Pino Suárez rode with a similar
escort. After a drive that lasted only a few minutes, the vehicles stopped
behind the penitentiary, whose lights were extinguished, plunging the
street into darkness.

"Get out, you cunt!" Major Cárdenas screamed at President Madero.
As Madero took a few tentative steps, Cárdenas leveled his revolver
and shot him twice in the back of the head. Pino Suárez, who had
been dragged out of his car at the same moment, saw Madero fall
dead, but had time only to turn his head. He was shot three times in
the face. As he writhed on the ground, Cárdenas walked over to him
and said to the other assassins: "This son of a whore is still moving—
shoot him some more." The soldiers fired ten more bullets into the
vice-president's body. Then Cárdenas ordered both automobiles to be
raked by machine-gun fire, as if they had been targets of an ambush.[44]

The following day, the Huerta government announced that the

convoy transferring the deposed president and vice-president to the penitentiary had been attacked, apparently by Madero partisans, and the prisoners shot while trying to escape. Hardly anyone believed this account. In cables to their governments, most diplomats expressed extreme skepticism. Here again, Lane Wilson was an important exception. On February 24, two days after the murders, he telegraphed the State Department: "I am disposed to accept the Government's version of the affair and consider it a closed incident."[45] His cable drew a riposte a few days later from Knox, who stated that neither Washington nor the American public gave credence to the official explanation of the murders.

Lane Wilson lingered as ambassador in Mexico for almost five more months, strenuously defending the Huerta government and urging Washington to grant it official recognition. Woodrow Wilson, who succeeded Taft as president in March 1913, was even less disposed than his predecessor to recognize the Huerta regime. In July, the American ambassador was permanently recalled from Mexico City, and a few months later retired to private life. But his role in Madero's downfall continued to haunt him as books and articles appeared on the subject. Years later, Lane Wilson still pronounced himself perplexed that people had made such a fuss over his failure to intervene on behalf of Madero. After all, the ambassador noted, Madero "had resigned the office of President and at the time of his death was a simple Mexican citizen in no wise entitled . . . to the diplomatic intervention of any foreign government."[46]

Lane Wilson's assertion that Madero's death was a "closed incident" quickly proved to be one of the worst diplomatic assessments ever received by the State Department. The assassination, in fact, signaled the start of the most violent stage of the Mexican Revolution, which would end only seven years later with more than one million people dead. Initially, the upheaval pitted Huerta against insurgents who believed he was attempting to return the country to a Porfirian status quo. But as the struggle lengthened and grew more confusing, factionalism and sheer opportunism counted more than ideology. Revolutionary commanders and their followers repeatedly shifted to whichever camp gained temporary ascendancy. War became a national way of life as nomadic hordes of combatants, often accompanied by their families, survived by marauding through the countryside.

Sometimes scourged by famine and scarred by battle, and always swelled by refugees, Mexico City lived with a siege mentality. Many of its inhabitants viewed the Revolution as a maelstrom of peasant rabble sweeping out of the hinterlands and threatening to devastate their city. The capital's allegiance to any leader was conditioned by the fear that he might be replaced by more despotic forces.

It was in this spirit that Mexico City extended a tenuous loyalty to Victoriano Huerta. Whatever sense of revulsion they may have felt over the murders of Madero and Pino Suárez, most residents were too numbed by the bloodshed of the Tragic Ten Days and too uncertain about the alternatives to Huerta's rule to consider actively opposing him. Huerta did not delude himself into believing that he commanded a greater public following than his predecessor. He knew that his support depended on whether he proved more decisive and more able than Madero to impose order on the country.

Huerta was above all an army man. Born to an Indian woman and mestizo peasant in a village of Jalisco, northwest of Mexico City, Huerta was only fifteen years old when he embarked on his military career. A general leading a convoy through Huerta's village took on the adolescent as his personal secretary, and later rewarded him by arranging his entry into the Military College in Mexico City. After graduation in 1876, Huerta served as an officer throughout the Porfirian regime, distinguishing himself both at desk jobs and in the field. He was brutal in putting down guerrilla revolts by Yaqui Indians in northern Mexico and the Maya in Yucatán during the late years of the Porfiriato. And it was because of this reputation that he was sent to Morelos to battle the Zapatistas in the months between Díaz's downfall and Madero's assumption of office. Unlike the majority of the Porfirista officer corps, he was considered an able commander, unafraid of combat, and untainted by widespread corruption and graft.

Huerta was fifty-nine years old when he became provisional president in February 1913. Of medium height, compact build, bald, and with a brush mustache, he wore tinted glasses to protect his chronically diseased eyes, which along with a leering smile, gave him a sinister look. But as Madero and his aides discovered to their great misfortune, Huerta could draw upon considerable reserves of charm and wile to disarm his prey. He courted his military staff assiduously in long drinking bouts. Even as president, he was more likely to be found discharging his executive duties in the cafés and bars of Mexico City than in the National Palace.

Within days after taking office, Huerta extracted pledges of support from virtually all the state governors, who were intimidated by his evident mastery over the federal army. The notable exception was Venustiano Carranza, governor of Madero's home state of Coahuila and an ardent supporter of the slain president. Carranza called for a revolt against Huerta, and was able to rally forces led by Pancho Villa in Chihuahua and Alvaro Obregón in Sonora. These were the same three states that provided the core of Madero's support when he embarked on his crusade against Díaz. Nothing had occurred in the two years since Don Porfirio's overthrow to defuse their rebelliousness. And again, proximity to the porous U.S. border gave revolutionaries in these states easy access to weapons.

Meanwhile, in Morelos to the south, the government still had to contend with Zapata. It made little difference to the Zapatistas whether Madero or Huerta held power. They would continue to battle against Mexico City until their village lands were restored. They were also skeptical of Carranza's commitment to agrarian reform, and never entered into an alliance with the revolutionaries of the north.

To combat these insurrections, Huerta ordered a military mobilization unprecedented in the nation's history. By the end of 1913, the federal forces had quadrupled to almost 200,000 troops. Mexico City and its surrounding countryside—where the government was most firmly in control—suffered most from the army's enormous manpower demands. A relentless draft system kidnapped males between the ages of fifteen and forty off the streets and sent them to the barracks and into battle without even a farewell to their families. In a single day, up to one thousand men were conscripted as they emerged from saloons, movie theaters, or bullfight rings.[47] Even workers with government cards deferring them from military service were herded into the draft patrol wagons. The dragnet was especially active at night, and as soon as darkness approached the beggars and ambulatory peddlers scurried for shelter. Men who had to run errands went into the streets carrying infants in their arms, hoping that the patrols would let them pass unmolested. But the ruse often failed; the man was conscripted and the child was sent to a police station to await the mother's arrival. "The dragnet . . . became so frenzied," wrote a Mexico City resident who lived through the era, "that not even hunchbacks or invalids were exempted. As Huerta's partisans used to say: if they are not good enough to kill, then they are good enough to be killed."[48]

Factory workers and shop clerks were required to participate in martial drills on Sundays. Students wore military uniforms to their classes, and even elementary schoolchildren paraded through the streets with mock weapons under an escort of teachers. The police were reorganized into army battalions. The railway stations of Mexico City became military embarkation points. With trains, motor vehicles, and even pack animals commandeered by the army, the capital returned to the ancient system of human carriers to help meet its demands for food and other essential civilian goods.

Huerta initially had the support of considerable portions of Mexico City society. The loyalty of businessmen, industrialists, and estate owners was to be expected since their main concern was to preserve their enterprises and restore order in the country. But Huerta was surprisingly successful in wooing industrial workers. Not only did he adopt the mild reforms of Madero, but he pushed for new labor legislation and championed trade unions in an effort to keep them out of the revolutionary camp. University and secondary schools also offered unexpected backing for the regime. "Among the students there were great demonstrations of adhesion and outbursts of applause for the usurper, Huerta," recalled a politician enrolled in the university in 1913 when the regime took power. The tiny minority of Madero supporters, like himself, were "viewed with . . . contempt" by the majority of the student body and expelled from classes by pro-Huerta militants.[49]

The ecclesiastical hierarchy wholeheartedly supported Huerta. The ringing of bells after the overthrow of Madero had already fed suspicions that the Church favored Huerta's coup. The clergy followed up this demonstration by parading effigies of the Virgin Mary throughout the capital and organizing pilgrimages to express gratitude for the restoration of peace after the devastating Tragic Ten Days. And when the insurrections against Huerta broke out in the provinces, the prelates issued a pastoral letter warning Catholics that it was sinful to rebel against the "legitimate government."[50]

Huerta also used political terror to assure his power. By the end of 1913, Mexico City's jails were crowded with people suspected of disloyalty to the regime. Dissident students, workers, army officers, and politicians were murdered. When the Senate protested the assassination of one of its members, Huerta dissolved both houses of Congress and arrested a majority of the legislators. He then reneged on his agreement to support the presidential aspirations of Félix Díaz, his co-conspirator against Madero. Although presidential elections were held in October 1913, they were so blatantly rigged in Huerta's favor and the turnout was so low that he decided to have them declared null and void. He simply remained in office as dictator.

Huerta's position in Mexico City was secure enough, but in the countryside his regime was under growing threat. Vowing to crush the Zapatistas in the south, Huerta assured the sugar planters of Morelos that "the government is going . . . to depopulate the state, and will send to your haciendas other workers" from different parts of the country.[51] General Robles, already notorious for his cruelty under the Madero government, was sent back into Morelos, where he resumed with even greater vigor his campaign to burn villages, execute Zapatista suspects, resettle inhabitants on the outskirts of the larger towns, and deport thousands of men to army battalions on the northern front. But by now, many Morelos peasants had learned to cope with these tactics. At the first sign of approaching federal troops they moved to the Zapatista hideouts, and if the army destroyed their villages, they joined up with the guerrillas. According to Mrs. King, who stayed in Cuernavaca still trying to maintain her hotel, "the Zapatistas were not an army; they were a people in arms." The government's repression had "turned the Zapatistas into fighting demons," she asserted. "The women cooled and reloaded the guns and scoured the country for food for the men, and old people and young children endured the hardships of their lot without complaint."[52]

Zapata went on a major offensive. His guerrillas blew up trains, killing hundreds of soldiers; overran garrisons, taking huge stores of guns and ammunitions; and laid siege to the major urban centers. Even the outskirts of Cuernavaca, the state capital, were attacked. "Zapata raided to the very edge of the town," wrote Mrs. King. "We were safe in the Bella Vista only because it was located in the very heart of the town."[53]

Far more threatening than Zapata were the rebel forces led by Carranza, Villa, and Obregón in the north. These were large, well-supplied armies, and almost from the start, they managed impressive victories against Huerta's troops. In May 1913, Carranza announced that any federal soldiers taken in battle would be executed. Besides raising the atrocity level of the war, it led to large-scale desertions among Huerta's troops, many of whom were poorly motivated and still in shock from the conscription dragnet.

Combatants were not the only victims of brutality in the northern campaigns. Villages, towns, and cities were pillaged by soldiers and insurrectionists alike. The mere presence of a battalion in a small community exhausted its food supplies in a few days, leaving the inhabitants on the verge of starvation. Pancho Villa had a particularly fearsome reputation for terrorizing civilians considered unsympathetic to the insurrection. A man of mercurial temperament, he was capable of ordering the execution of scores of noncombatants on a whim. He was especially prejudiced against the small Chinese community of farmers, businessmen, and shopkeepers, and murdered hundreds of them simply for racial reasons. He was also the most rabid clerophobe among the revolutionary leaders.

"I believe in God, but not in religion," Villa told an American journalist. "I have recognized the priests as hypocrites ever since, when I was twenty, I took part in a drunken orgy with a priest and two women he had ruined. They are all frauds—the priests and their cloth. . . . I shall do what I can to take the Church out of politics and to open the eyes of the people to the tricks of the thieving priests."[54]

Although the worst reports of Villa's atrocities against the clergy—allegations of nuns raped and priests murdered—may have been fabricated by Huerta propagandists, it is certain that as his rebels moved southward, the Church suffered attacks and plunder rarely before experienced in Mexican history. Priests were held hostage, and often beaten, until the faithful in their communities raised enough money for ransom. Churches and the homes of prelates were ransacked. Nuns were expelled from their convents, which were then turned into public brothels.[55]

By the spring of 1914, the war had clearly turned against Huerta. The economy was in acute crisis, as harvests went uncollected, mines and factories ceased to function, and the treasury ran bare. Huerta also faced mounting troubles with Washington. Lane Wilson, his stalwart supporter, was recalled. The emissaries who replaced him were sending back reports that painted a bleak picture of instability, corruption, economic chaos, and military weakness. Huerta himself was portrayed as a hopeless alcoholic. Once lionized by the American and European community in the capital, Huerta, according to a U.S. diplomat's wife, now spent his time "closeted with the only 'foreigners' he considered really worth knowing—Hennessy and Martell."[56]

The murder of Madero and the dictatorial style of Huerta aroused the moral indignation of President Wilson, who considered it his special mission to spread democracy through Latin America even at the risk of meddling in Mexico's internal affairs. Wilson encouraged the smuggling of American weapons to the northern revolutionaries. When this failed to bring down the Huerta regime as speedily as he hoped, he searched for an excuse for direct U.S. military intervention.

The opportunity arose in April 1914. A U.S. Navy vessel cruising off the Mexican Gulf coast port of Tampico sent ashore a landing party in search of fuel. Tampico had been under siege by the revolutionaries, and when the American sailors entered a restricted dock area, they were immediately arrested by a Mexican army patrol. Although the sailors were released within an hour, the American naval commander demanded that the Mexicans demonstrate their contrition by raising an American flag over the shore and according it a twenty-one-gun salute. Huerta's government denied the request. As tension mounted, Washington was informed that a German vessel, carrying arms smuggled out of the United States for the use of Huerta's army, was about to dock at Veracruz. With a logic that escaped most Mexicans, Wilson concluded that the two incidents were enough to merit intervention. On April 21, a U.S. Marine force occupied Veracruz, inflicting hundreds of casualties on Mexican soldiers and civilians.

The invasion detonated an explosion of anti-Americanism throughout the country. In Mexico City, mobs looted American-owned stores and demolished the statue of George Washington that had been sent as a gift during the centennial celebrations in 1910. United States flags were burned, and American tourists were accosted on the streets of the capital. Most of the revolutionary leaders also protested the American occupation of Veracruz. But they refused Huerta's call for a joint crusade against the Yankee invaders.

Huerta decided to pull back part of his army from the civil war fronts and at least make a show of defying the Americans. The revolutionaries took advantage of the weakened federal forces. After a series of quick engagements, they laid siege to the key northern city of Zacatecas, where in late June, Villa's columns routed the federal army, killing thousands of Huerta's troops.

Recognizing the hopelessness of his situation, Huerta resigned in July 1914, and boarded a ship into exile, first to Cuba and then to Spain. He traveled to the United States a year later, but his attempts to organize a movement of his partisans landed him in several Texas jails. Alcoholism had seriously impaired his health, and he died of liver cirrhosis while still under detention in Texas in January 1916.

With the overthrow of Huerta, the common enemy, the revolutionary movement abandoned any semblance of unity. The four leaders—Carranza, Obregón, Villa, and Zapata—each had their own armies and agendas. Only Zapata remained ideologically consistent. He wanted an extensive agrarian reform program to be quickly implemented, beginning with the return of village lands to his followers in Morelos. But he had never aspired to become president, and his movement, localized mainly in his state, could only exercise a peripheral role in what became a national struggle for power between the northern revolutionaries.

Among the northerners, Venustiano Carranza was first among equals, by virtue of his early leadership in the uprising against Huerta and his ability to play Villa and Obregón against each other. At fifty-four years of age, Carranza was the oldest of the revolutionary commanders, the most politically experienced, and easily the most intellectual, with a solid grasp of history, economics, and current events. Over six feet tall, with flowing white whiskers, he projected the image of a tough grandfather, as comfortable leading his cavalry on campaign as he was haranguing crowds from a balcony. Before the Revolution, Carranza was a moderately wealthy hacienda owner in Coahuila and a grudging supporter of Porfirio Díaz. When Don Porfirio maneuvered to deprive him of the state governorship in the elections of 1909, Carranza cast his lot with Madero. And after Díaz was overthrown, Madero appointed him governor of Coahuila.

While Carranza criticized Madero for being too cautious—"The revolution that compromises commits suicide," he told him[57]—his own ideology scarcely labeled him a radical. He was no impassioned advocate of land reform or trade union causes. A classic nineteenth-century liberal, he held up Benito Juárez as his ideal, and emphasized political freedoms rather than economic and social issues. His speeches lamenting poverty, berating the rich, and denouncing the weighty role of U.S. investments in Mexico did, nonetheless, establish his reputation as a populist and nationalist.

Even before Huerta was defeated, Carranza considered Pancho Villa the bane of his political ambitions. Villa was simply incapable of following directives he disagreed with, and at times his insubordination drove Carranza into frenzy. A burly six-footer with a florid complexion and a full mustache, Villa was the epitome of the bandit-turned-rebel. Born in 1878 to a family of sharecroppers from a small village in the northern state of Durango, Villa became a petty thief as a teenager and fled the Rurales into neighboring Chihuahua. He was said to have joined the Madero revolt because he likened his own persecution by the legal authorities to the Díaz regime's oppression of the downtrodden. As a revolutionary, Villa continued to partially finance himself and his army by cattle rustling and payroll robberies. His feral sense of politics combined personal vendetta with a crude vision of social justice that could be summed up as stealing from the rich to favor the poor. By Villa's definition, the poor included first of all his followers, whom he rewarded with shares of plunder and parcels of land from haciendas taken in war. Villa was a brawler, womanizer, and rapist. So volatile were his moods that he could gun down a man he had warmly embraced a moment before. Only his strict abstinence from liquor marred his macho image. His men were an accurate reflection of their leader: cowboys, bandits, army deserters, peons, railroad workers, and drifters with no strong bonds to their native lands or communities and no firm ideological convictions. They adored Villa for his buccaneer charisma, the loot he showered upon them, and his courage in personally leading them into battle. His military strategy was almost always the lightning-quick cavalry charge that struck panic in enemy lines. It worked because Villa convinced his men that they were invincible. By the time Huerta fled the country, Villa had the most powerful, well-equipped, and motivated revolutionary army in Mexico, and he was openly challenging Carranza's leadership of the rebel movement.

To hold Villa partially in check, Carranza needed a strong ally, and he found him in Alvaro Obregón, who recruited his own army mainly from his native state of Sonora. Obregón was a self-taught military genius. His astounding visual memory enabled him to size up a potential battlefield at a glance and months later position his forces to take full advantage of the terrain. He studied opposing commanders so thoroughly that he could predict their tactics. Obregón was also a consummate political organizer and negotiator. A witty, spellbinding raconteur, he could cool the passions of antagonists and bring them into agreement. He distrusted ideologues and considered himself a pragmatic liberal, supportive of moderate political freedoms and mild versions of agrarian reform and trade unionism.

Obregón was born in 1880, one of eighteen children of middle-class hacienda owners. He was a sturdy six-footer, handsome and white-skinned. With little formal education, he plied numerous trades before he was thirty: mechanic, schoolteacher, traveling shoe salesman, hacienda foreman. An inveterate tinkerer, he invented a machine to plant chickpeas, and sold it to enough farmers to purchase a four-hundred-acre spread for himself. Obregón joined the Revolution later than Carranza and Villa. He sat on the sidelines during Madero's struggle against Díaz. But running as a Madero supporter in 1912, he was elected municipal president of his small town. Since political power was already a function of military might, he used his post to recruit a modest armed force. By the time Madero fell, Obregón's gunmen had swelled to an army, giving their leader military preeminence in Sonora for the fight against the Huerta regime.

Obregón allied himself with Carranza because both men feared and despised Villa. When Villa's forces crushed Huerta's troops in Zacatecas and were only a train ride away from Mexico City, Carranza ordered coal supplies withheld from Villa, enabling Obregón's army to reach Mexico City first, on August 15, 1914.

The night before the arrival of Obregón's troops, there was panic in the capital among supporters of the fallen Huerta regime. Thousands of federal soldiers and their families, hundreds of nuns and priests, as well as uncounted bureaucrats and businessmen fled by train, car, wagon, horse, and on foot toward Veracruz, preferring to take their chances with the U.S. Marines occupying that port rather than face the northern revolutionary forces.

Obregón, who considered Mexico City a stronghold of reaction, was unmoved by the huge crowds lining the avenues to greet his army. He immediately placed the capital under martial law, and proclaimed the death penalty for anyone disturbing public order. He then made his way to the cemetery where Madero was buried and paid homage to the slain president. There, he lashed out at what he called the cowardice of the city's population for failing to defend Madero.

"It was inexcusable for you men to have abstained from taking up arms," said Obregón to the chastened crowd. Turning to a woman who was known as a Madero partisan in Mexico City even under the Huerta regime, he delivered another rebuke to the capital's male inhabitants: "Since I know how to admire valor, I cede my gun to this lady, the only person among you worthy of possessing it."[58]

The arrival of Venustiano Carranza cut short plans of reprisals against the capital. As commander-in-chief of the northern revolutionary forces, Carranza now claimed political leadership of the nation, and he had greater preoccupations than punishing suspected Huerta supporters in Mexico City. He still had to negotiate an end to the American occupation of Veracruz. This was only accomplished three months later, in November 1914, after he made public guarantees to President Wilson that the pro-Huerta refugees in that port would not be harmed. Of even more concern to Carranza was the growing threat posed by Pancho Villa, who was furious at having been prevented from occupying Mexico City.

Carranza convoked a convention to discuss grievances between the various revolutionary factions and to determine who would be provisional president of Mexico until elections could be scheduled. The convention was held in October in the town of Aguascalientes, considered neutral ground between Villa's forces to the north and Carranza's army in Mexico City. Obregón represented himself and Carranza, who expected that the Aguascalientes gathering would at the very least support his claims to national leadership. But in a stunning development, an alliance was worked out at the convention between the followers of Villa and Zapata, who had enough votes to elect General Eulálio Gutiérrez, a political nonentity under their control, as provisional president of the country. Angered by this outcome, Carranza ordered his delegates to withdraw from the convention. The forces of Villa and Zapata then converged on Mexico City from the north and south, while Carranza and Obregón hastily retreated with their armies to Veracruz. The third civil war of the Mexican Revolution had begun.

As the Villistas and Zapatistas approached Mexico City, the newspapers—which dubbed Zapata "the Attila of the south" and Villa "the centaur of the north"—prepared the inhabitants for any eventuality. The Villistas were reputed to be merciless rapists, murderers, and looters, while the Zapatistas were said to be barbaric Indians who practiced Aztec rites of human sacrifice. Stores, restaurants, factories, even police stations closed their doors. Automobiles, trams, and pedestrians deserted the streets. Only the chimes of the public clocks broke the silence.

Zapata's troops were the first to enter the city, in late November 1914. They were not tight columns of marching soldiers dressed in flashy uniforms and led by military bands. Instead, they paraded in the same way they fought: straggling in small guerrilla bands, wearing broad-brimmed straw hats, guaraches, rough white trousers and shirts, with bandoliers across their chests, machetes hanging from their waists, and guns of every vintage and caliber in their arms. It was impossible to distinguish officers from soldiers, and the women combatants could be made out only by the braids that cascaded down from under their huge hats. The cavalry rode emaciated horses and even burros. They carried a few flags and large banners of the Virgin of Guadalupe, like Hidalgo's peasant hordes in the Independence revolt a century before. Their only musical instrument was the cow horn, which sounded chillingly like a jaguar's roar.[59]

During the first few days, the Zapatistas seemed anything but tigers. Ragged and hungry, they timidly begged for food at homes, stores, and restaurants. The capital's residents, in obvious relief, responded generously. Most of the several thousand Zapatistas and their families camped out in the Zócalo and other plazas, where they cooked, slept, and unashamedly carried out their natural necessities in full public view. The only alarming incident occurred when a fire engine hurtled down a main street one night. The Zapatistas, never having seen such a strange apparatus, let loose a fusillade that killed a dozen firemen.[60]

Zapata himself arrived in Mexico City on the second day of the occupation and was greeted at the train station by his supporters firing their weapons in the air. Suffering from as much cultural shock as his followers, Zapata spent the night in a cheap hotel and returned to Morelos the next day, muttering that the metropolis was unfit for human habitation.

In early December, Villa and his forces marched into the capital from the north. They were a much larger army, better equipped and uniformed than the Zapatistas. Initially, they also behaved well enough to soothe the population. The Zapatistas and Villistas vaunted their war exploits in posters plastered on the downtown walls, and fraternized in the plazas and saloons while waiting for a summit between their leaders.

The meeting took place in the southern suburb of Xochimilco, because Zapata abhorred the congested downtown district. By all accounts, neither Villa nor Zapata was comfortable with each other and little was accomplished during their brief conference. An uneasy silence was broken when Villa denounced Carranza and his followers as middle-class revolutionaries, "who have always slept on soft pillows," and Zapata called Carranza "a son of a bitch."[61] The next hour was spent trading insults about Carranza and Obregón. Otherwise, about all they could agree upon was that General Gutiérrez, the figurehead they had chosen as provisional president, would remain in office for the time being while their forces braced for the expected counteroffensive by the Carranza and Obregón armies. Zapata and most of his troops then returned to their base in Morelos, while Villa remained for a few more weeks in Mexico City determined to engage in his own violent brand of revelry before returning to the battlefield.

The initial moderation displayed by the Villistas and Zapatistas occupying the capital soon vanished. With no police to contend with, many of the revolutionaries began to rob, rape, murder, and kidnap for ransom. They executed hundreds of residents accused of being supporters of Díaz, Huerta, or Carranza. Several cabinet ministers went into hiding when they learned that Villa or Zapata gunmen questioned their revolutionary credentials.

Villa set a reprehensible example for his followers. In a particularly notorious incident, he paid a visit to the luxurious Hotel Palacio, took a liking to the attractive receptionist, and announced he would return for her later in the day. The woman reported the incident to the hotel owner, Mrs. Fares, a French national, who sent the frightened receptionist home and temporarily took her place behind the desk. Villa returned to the hotel and demanded the whereabouts of the receptionist. Informed by Mrs. Fares that she had been sent away, Villa told the hotel owner: "In that case, you'll do." When Mrs. Fares tried to resist, she was beaten unconscious by Villa's henchmen and dragged to his headquarters. She was released later that day only after Villa, tiring of her, responded to the frantic pleas of the French consul.[62]

General Gutiérrez was unable to control the revolutionaries. "Every day there have been attempts against life and property, gross violations even in people's homes, to the extent that fear and alarm have spread throughout society," asserted the provisional president of the nation. "With shame and indignation I have had to be a helpless spectator of all these infamies. . . ." Not only did Gutiérrez's entreaties go unheeded, but he himself was threatened by Villa, who, gun in hand, called him a coward for refusing to execute some members of his government accused of being "counterrevolutionary traitors."[63]

In late January 1915, Carranza and Obregón, having strengthened their armies, marched back into Mexico City. As the Villistas and Zapatistas fell back, they engaged in one last orgy of looting, and destroyed the pumping station that supplied the capital with most of its fresh water. Their figurehead president, General Gutiérrez, also fled to the provinces and into political oblivion.

For Mexico City, 1915 proved to be the worst year of the Revolution. Snipers terrorized residents. Fighting in the countryside disrupted harvest shipments and created acute shortages of staples. People scavenged garbage, begged for food, and slaughtered any pet that could be captured. Women—some of them barely in puberty, others old enough to be grandmothers—prostituted themselves for a meal of bread. Hospitals, insane asylums, and orphanages emptied their wards because their kitchens were bare. At dawn, death wagons circulated the streets to retrieve the unidentified bodies of people who had starved, and carried the corpses to the main cemetery for incineration.[64]

Middle-class people were reduced to peddling firewood, homemade cigarettes, and spoiled food products at makeshift stands in the capital's slums. "Among the many persons of previous good social, political and economic standing that I saw in this grievous condition . . . was a lawyer who for several years had occupied an important post in General Díaz's judicial system," recalled a memoirist of the era. "Wearing an old, beaten derby and covered with a greasy butcher's apron, he was selling what he boasted to be calves' tripe, although to judge from its thinness and repugnant aspect it seemed more like dogs' guts."[65]

Factories and stores shut down because of the chaotic currency situation. Every revolutionary faction had printed its own paper money, without any reserves to back the bills. And the Carrancistas, Villistas, and Zapatistas refused to recognize each other's denominations. Since Carranza's provisional government prevailed in Mexico City during most of 1915, its paper money became legal tender, especially after merchants were threatened with prison if they failed to accept it. But with little currency to back the printed money, prices bolted upward.

Carranza and Obregón launched reprisals against people considered to be political enemies. The bureaucracy was purged of employees who were denounced as Díaz and Huerta sympathizers. Obregón summoned all the priests of the capital to the National Palace and told them that they would be held hostage until the Church contributed 500,000 pesos to the war effort against Villa and Zapata. Claiming their treasury was empty, the ecclesiastical authorities declined to pay. The ransom idea was eventually discarded, and the clergymen were released upon payment of bribes as low as 5 pesos per priest. By the end of 1915, almost every priest, bishop, and nun had fled the country.[66] In Mexico City, the churches they left behind were ransacked and used as offices and assembly halls for labor leaders who proclaimed themselves socialists.

Carranza, despite his distrust of radical trade unionists, allowed a coalition of left-wing unions to occupy the aristocratic Jockey Club as the headquarters of their "Casa del Obrero Mundial" ("House of the World Worker"). Until 1915, the trade union movement had remained largely aloof from the warring revolutionary factions, claiming that none of them championed labor. But now, the radical trade unionists associated with the Casa del Obrero offered their support to Carranza, and helped organize the so-called Red Battalions of urban workers to fight against Villa and Zapata. It was schisms like these, pitting industrial laborers against peasant guerrillas, that robbed the Revolution of any ideological consistency.

The military strategy of Carranza and Obregón was to ignore Zapata's guerrillas in the south and concentrate their forces against the more dangerous Villa in the north. Obregón embarked on the campaign in

March 1915 with eleven thousand troops, less than half the number of Villa's forces. Good strategy would have dictated that Villa draw Obregón as far away as possible from his base in Mexico City to make it more difficult to reinforce and supply his troops. But Obregón, counting on his opponent's impatience and pride, lured Villa into a confrontation at Celaya, barely one hundred miles northwest of the capital and almost seven hundred miles south of Villa's own base in Chihuahua. At Celaya, Obregón surrounded his forces with barbed-wire entrenchments and backed them with artillery and machine guns. When Villa's cavalrymen carried out their usual reckless charge, they were slaughtered by a barrage of cannon and bullets or entangled on the wire fences. Never before defeated in battle, Villa was incredulous at his setback. He stubbornly mounted another frontal cavalry assault a few days later, with the same disastrous results. The two battles of Celaya, in April 1915, became known as the most famous military engagement of the Revolution. Four thousand Villistas were killed and another six thousand were taken prisoner. Obregón lost less than one hundred and fifty troops.

Although bloodied, Villa's army was by no means destroyed. In May and June 1915, a monthlong battle was fought in nearby León, and ended in another victory for Obregón's forces. The fighting almost proved fatal for Obregón. An artillery shell blew off his right arm, and only quick medical attention saved him from bleeding to death. Years later, the limb was enshrined in a monument to Obregón in Mexico City. With macabre humor, Obregón would joke that his well-known penchant for money was responsible for the recovery of the arm: one of his aides supposedly wandered through the corpse-strewn terrain around León holding out a gold coin, and when a severed hand and arm leaped up and grabbed it, he knew he had found Obregón's limb.[67]

By late summer of 1915, Obregón's campaign had given Carranza a commanding military and political position in the country, and in October, President Wilson extended diplomatic recognition to his regime. Furious at the gesture, Villa tried to provoke American military intervention in Mexico in the hope of undermining Carranza. In March 1916, the Villistas crossed the U.S. border and attacked Columbus, New Mexico, killing eighteen Americans. President Wilson responded by dispatching a punitive expedition into Mexico led by General John J. Pershing. Villa easily evaded the six thousand American troops, whose presence in the country caused acute embarrassment to the Carranza government until their withdrawal in January

1917. But Villa was unable to improve his military situation, and spent the next three years engaged in ineffectual guerrilla activities mainly in his Chihuahua stronghold.

In the south, meanwhile, the Zapatistas had taken advantage of the Carranza regime's singleminded war effort against Villa. By early 1915, Zapata's forces controlled the entire countryside and the main towns of Morelos, and laid siege to Cuernavaca. The beleaguered federal garrison and thousands of their civilian supporters evacuated the city one night and attempted to reach Mexico City by horse and on foot. Most of the refugees were gunned down in repeated attacks by the guerrillas. Among the survivors was the redoubtable Mrs. King, who finally abandoned her ill-fated Bella Vista Hotel and reached Mexico City after harrowing episodes that saw her slide down a precipice, dodge bullets, and collapse several times from hunger and thirst. "Out of the eight thousand who had started from Cuernavaca, only two thousand were left," she wrote. "All our artillery was lost, all provisions gone; we ourselves were torn, wounded, and starved, no longer caring much what they did to us."[68]

For the Zapatista peasants, 1915 was the only year of sweet respite in the Revolution. With no army forces to oppose them, they launched a utopian agrarian reform in the state. The great haciendas were partitioned and their lands returned to the villages either as communal property or individual plots. A few sugar mills were put back into operation under the control of the guerrillas, and their profits were funneled into the Zapatista war chest. A crude armaments factory refurbished old rifles and refilled spent cartridges. Victory celebrations were held in the plazas of the larger towns, which were overrun by former peons who had rarely ventured beyond the confines of their haciendas.

The Zapatistas' unreal secession from Mexico City's rule lasted only until Carranza and Obregón defeated Villa's forces. By April 1916, the Carrancista army was back in Morelos led by General Pablo González. In early May, his troops captured Cuernavaca, and resumed their scorched-earth campaign, destroying villages, deporting their inhabitants, and hanging guerrilla suspects by the hundreds.

Mrs. King also slipped back into the state, anxious to discover the fate of her hotel. She found it a shambles, with pigs and chickens inhabiting the few rooms that had not been demolished by fire and shelling. Her own servants had turned Zapatista. As she listened to them, Mrs. King claimed for the first time to understand the peasant leader's hold over his native state:

It was, I sensed, the essence of their trust in Zapata that he stayed so close to the soil . . . eschewing honors and wealth and sleeping always away from the towns . . . like a holy person dedicated to the service of his people. . . . And then I caught the rhythm of their feeling, and understood that to them la revolución was . . . the long continuous movement of resistance, like a rolling wave, that had swelled against Cortés and his conquistadores, and the greedy Aztec war lords before them. . . . It was the struggle of these people for a birthright, to develop in their own way, in spite of strangers [from Mexico City] who came greedily to skim the cream, and, ignorantly, to make the people over.

In her own mind, there was a place for her and her hotel even in a Morelos ruled by Zapata. Gazing again upon the wreckage of the Bella Vista, she decided it "looked like the cheerful, promising disorder about a house in the building. . . . I thought, with wonder, 'I can make it come true. I can bring masons and carpenters and set them to work, and when they see me building, then the others will come back and build, too.' " She hastened to share her reverie with the Carrancista commander, General González, but he thought the eccentric Englishwoman had finally gone mad.

"This is no time to talk of reconstruction, Señora King!" shouted the general. "The work of destruction is not yet completed. Will you not comprehend, señora—I am about to destroy what still remains of Cuernavaca!" The war effort against the Zapatistas had begun by rooting them out of the countryside, stamping out their villages, and herding them into the towns. And with the failure of those tactics to end the rebellion, it was deemed necessary to demolish even the state capital.

"But our homes! Our property!" cried Mrs. King.

"Oh, señora!" retorted the angry general. "That is past. That is all over. . . ."[69]

As the dangers posed by Zapata and Villa receded, Carranza came under increasing pressure from his own supporters to promulgate a new Constitution that would take into account the transformations in the country over the last six years of revolutionary upheaval. He agreed to the proposal mainly because he wanted to legitimize his own rule. In December 1916, a Constitutional Congress was convened in Querétaro to consider a draft submitted by Carranza. Much to his annoyance, however, the delegates amended it into a more radical document.

Anticlericalism was the most glaring aspect of the Constitution that emerged from the Querétaro Congress in 1917. All education was to be secular and universal. No foreign priests were allowed in the country, and local legislatures could set a limit on the number of clergymen within their state boundaries. The Church was banned from participating in political activities. Marriage was declared a civil ceremony.

Another key article provided for an eight-hour workday, a minimum wage, and the right to organize trade unions that could call strikes and bargain collectively. Perhaps the most radical feature of the Constitution concerned the issue of land. All properties seized illegally from the peasantry during the Porfiriato were to be restored. The state was given the right to impose on private property any limitations considered to be in the public interest—a deliberately ambiguous provision that opened the door to further agrarian reform. And foreigners were allowed to hold land only if they agreed to consider themselves as having no more rights over their property than Mexicans, and bound themselves not to invoke the protection of their governments.

There were two, not necessarily contradictory, explanations for the radical articles contained in the 1917 Constitution. First, many delegates felt that only a document that called for far-reaching social reforms could justify the enormous bloodletting and material destruction in the country and elevate the Revolution to a higher plane than the naked power struggle between various factions and their leaders. Ironically, a second explanation was the emerging power struggle between Carranza and Obregón, now that their common enemies, Villa and Zapata, appeared less threatening. Obregón, no radical himself, swung his support behind the left-wing majority of delegates who pushed through the 1917 Constitution. As a result, in the public mind he was identified with the historic document far more than Carranza. Obregón was not yet willing to challenge Carranza for the presidency. But he was positioning himself as Carranza's successor and broadening his political base.

Carranza was elected president virtually unopposed in March 1917 and assumed office in May. Setting a standard that would be followed by other presidents, he interpreted the Constitution as a statement of future intentions, not a practical guide for governing. In the three years of his presidency, Carranza distributed to the peasantry only 450,000 acres of land, somewhat less than one-half percent of the agrarian property in the country. He did not hesitate to use the army to break labor strikes. Less than one tenth of a percent of his government's budget was funneled into the school system, making irrelevant the constitutional provision on universal, secular education. And public expenditures for all social programs were even lower than during the Porfiriato.

As president, Carranza did enjoy considerable public support in Mexico City. His campaigns to impose order, restore essential services, and improve what he called "public morality" were welcomed in the war-weary, chaotic, and vice-ridden capital. Policemen replaced guerrillas and army troops on the city streets, and terrorism declined sharply. Electricity, telephones, and telegraph service began to function normally. Fresh water flowed again. Bullfighting—which Carranza considered a pagan spectacle catering to base instincts—was banned. Gambling was driven underground. Bars and saloons had their hours severely restricted. In brief outbursts of populism, Carranza distributed free food to the poor and suspended rent payments by slum dwellers. He also enhanced his reputation as a nationalist by increasing the oil and mining taxes paid by foreigners.

By late 1919, the Revolution seemed distant indeed from Mexico City, particularly for its middle-class and affluent residents. Mrs. King described high society life as "very gay: a constant round of parties, and war-time balls and benefits of all kinds."[70] Hotels, theaters, and luxury stores reopened. Arthur Rubinstein gave piano recitals, and Anna Pavlova led a ballet troupe. Spectators flocked to the cinemas to view the latest Chaplin films.[71]

But Mexico City was an oasis. Outside the capital, Carranza's claims to have brought the Revolution to a close seemed premature as long as Villa and Zapata remained active. Of the two, Zapata was the most irritating. His obstinate calls for agrarian reform had become the dogma of the Revolution, embodied in the 1917 Constitution and part of the rhetoric which Carranza himself reluctantly uttered for public consumption. The entire thrust of Carranza's military offensive in Morelos was aimed at capturing or killing Zapata. By early 1919, almost 40 percent of the state's inhabitants were dead, forcibly deported, or living as refugees elsewhere in the country. In villages, towns, and cities, only half-demolished buildings rose above the rubble and weed. But neither the torture and execution of Zapata partisans nor the bounties offered by the Mexico City government had led to the capture of the peasant leader. Repeated claims of Zapata's death were quickly belied by his raids on isolated army outposts, plantations, and trains throughout Morelos, and sometimes even in the adjoining states of Mexico and Puebla.

In desperation, Carranza and his army commander in Morelos,

General González, schemed to lure Zapata into an ambush. Zapata was led to believe that a Carrancista officer, Colonel Jesús Guajardo, would defect to the guerrilla cause with his entire regiment and much-needed guns and ammunition. Such desertions were common enough during the long struggle in Morelos, and Guajardo demonstrated his good faith to Zapata by executing several Zapatista turncoats at the peasant leader's request. On April 10, 1919, Zapata, accompanied by a small guerrilla escort, rode into an abandoned hacienda where Guajardo and his men were supposed to negotiate the terms of their defection. A guerrilla who was part of the escort later gave the following account:

> Ten of us followed [Zapata] just as he ordered. . . . The rest of the people stayed [outside the walls] under the trees, confidently resting in the shade with their carbines stacked. Having formed ranks, [Guajardo's] guard looked ready to do him the honors. Three times the bugle sounded the honor call; and as the last note died away, as the general-in-chief reached the threshold of the door . . . at point blank, without giving him time even to draw his pistols, the soldiers who were presenting arms fired two volleys, and our unforgettable General Zapata fell never to rise again.[72]

With Zapata's death, the guerrilla movement in Morelos fragmented and finally disappeared in 1920. Years later, a close aide of Zapata came forward with a strongbox said to contain the slain peasant leader's "legacy." The legacy turned out to be the ancient land titles of the village of Anenecuilco, entrusted to Zapata when he was elected municipal president of his native community in 1909. He had been obsessed with the possibility that the documents might be lost or destroyed during the war, and had shifted them from one hiding place to another in the hope that eventually a government in Mexico City would guarantee their legitimacy. "I'm bound to die someday," he would say, "but my pueblo's papers stand to be guaranteed."[73]

The Revolution ended for Pancho Villa a year after Zapata was killed, although the circumstances were entirely different. In return for laying down his arms, the government gave Villa a 26,000-acre hacienda in Chihuahua. Never a sincere advocate of land reform, Villa hired gunmen to fight off peasants—some of them his former soldiers—who encroached on the edges of his huge domain. One hot summer day in 1923, when he was returning from a rendezvous with one of his mistresses, his car was raked with gunfire. Villa and several companions were killed in the ambush. Some reports suggested Villa was murdered by government agents because he threatened to resume his revolutionary career. Others said he was the victim of a personal vendetta, or a plot by peasants coveting his estate. In any case, after Villa's death, his land was partitioned among his poorer neighbors.

Inevitably, the final chapter of Mexico's decade-long holocaust pitted the last two revolutionary leaders, Carranza and Obregón, against each other. Alvaro Obregón had retired from government service in 1917. His military victories and his identification with the new Constitution had greatly enhanced his prestige. And the Revolution had helped make him a wealthy man. His chickpea farm in Sonora employed 1,500 workers. His business acumen and government contacts landed him lucrative deals to supply railway ties for the nationalized train lines. An impressive import-export company on the U.S. border added to his personal fortune.

Obregón fully expected to succeed Carranza in the presidential election scheduled for 1920. And in preparation for that campaign, he had expanded his already large political base by courting every major group disaffected with Carranza: cashiered army officers and soldiers who failed to receive land or financial benefits for their military service; trade unionists angered by Carranza's efforts to bring the labor movement to heel once he had established military control over the country; and even the Zapatistas, who never forgave Carranza for the murder of their leader.

Carranza had announced that he would retire from politics after the 1920 election, which he promised would be an open campaign. But as the contest drew near, he could not stomach the notion of losing power, especially to Obregón, his longtime rival and erstwhile ally. Carranza resolved instead to impose his own servile candidate—Ignacio Bonillas, the ambassador to Washington and a man with no political following—and continue to govern Mexico behind the scenes. When Obregón persisted in campaigning for the presidency and was on the verge of winning the 1920 election, Carranza had him arrested and brought to Mexico City to face trumped-up charges of plotting against the government.

Obregón escaped thanks to his extraordinary network of supporters. Railway workers disguised him as a train engineer and hid him on the outskirts of Mexico City, where Zapatista guerrillas then took him to a more secure refuge in Morelos. In Sonora, meanwhile, his military allies launched an armed movement on his behalf. Within two weeks, virtually the entire army rallied behind Obregón, and the country fell under his control.

In May 1920, Carranza decided to transfer his government to Veracruz and rebuild a military force there strong enough to resist Obregón. The flight from Mexico City was ill-starred from the beginning. Carranza and his entire government—ministers, bureaucrats, even secretaries and clerks—crowded into a twenty-one-car train, with voluminous archives and the treasury's hoard of gold. Many of the troops Carranza had expected to accompany him defected even before the journey began. Soon after the train left the capital, pro-Obregón workers rammed a locomotive against it, causing a delay of several hours. Torn-up railway tracks accounted for further setbacks. Desperate to convince himself and his subordinates that he still had public backing, Carranza drew crowds to his train at several stops by handing out gold coins from the treasury to passersby.

Further acts of sabotage along the tracks forced Carranza and his entourage to abandon their train in the mountains of Puebla and continue their escape on horseback. Hoping to buy the loyalty of his dwindling military escort, Carranza ordered that the troops be paid with fistfuls of gold coins from the treasury.

"So many people had access to that money," a young officer who accompanied Carranza recalled many years later. "They filled their sacks with gold only to discover that it was the worst possible thing they could have done because . . . their horses were too loaded down to continue. And so they tried to rid themselves of the gold giving it to anybody in their path. . . . It really is true what they tell you as a child and you never believe—that money is worth nothing. It truly is worthless compared to saving your life!"[74]

Pursued by Obregón's troops, Carranza and his followers hid in the mountains of Puebla. They accepted the protection of a military unit, whose commander, Rodolfo Herrero, was secretly an agent of Obregón. And in the early morning hours of May 21, 1920, Carranza was shot to death in his tent by Herrero and his soldiers. The fact that Obregón later declined to punish Herrero strengthened suspicions that Obregón was responsible for Carranza's murder, or had even ordered it.

In September 1920, Alvaro Obregón was elected president, finally bringing an end to the Mexican Revolution. The upheaval had witnessed the overthrow and exile of Porfirio Díaz by Madero; the assassination of Madero following his betrayal by Huerta; Huerta's overthrow by the combined forces of Carranza, Obregón, Villa, and Zapata; the defeat of Villa by Obregón; the slaying of Zapata on Carranza's orders; and the killing of Carranza by Obregón's supporters.

At a political level, the Revolution was an allegory of treachery. In terms of human lives and material losses, it was a catastrophe unparalleled since the Conquest. At least one million, and possibly more than two million, Mexicans perished. With corn harvests plunging to one tenth the national needs, perhaps even more people died from starvation and disease than were killed in battles or civilian massacres. The gross national product in 1920 was only a fraction of its level a decade earlier. Little wonder that Obregón, the ultimate political victor, set aside the revolutionary rhetoric of social justice and instead likened the upheaval to a near-fatal national illness requiring a lengthy convalescence. "We are going to show the world either that we are capable of reconstructing the country we have half destroyed," he said a few days after his election, "or that we are only able to destroy and not to reconstruct the country of the future."[75]

The Revolution has left Mexican historians perplexed about its aims, motives, accomplishments, and savagery. And the literary world has not had much more success in interpreting the prolonged cataclysm. The poet-essayist Octavio Paz called the Revolution a "death-feast"— "a prodigious fiesta in which the Mexican, drunk with his own self, is aware at last, in mortal embrace, of his fellow Mexican."[76] The novelist Mariano Azuela offered the much simpler image of a great rebellion that gathered a momentum beyond the control and comprehension of its participants. In his masterpiece *The Underdogs*, the main character, a peasant rebel, is asked by his wife why he continues to fight with no goal or end in sight. He responds by flicking a rock down the side of a canyon: "Look at that stone, how it keeps on going. . . ."[77]

SIXTEEN

REVOLUTIONARY ART, CAUTIOUS POLITICS

As president, Alvaro Obregón faced a conundrum: How to convince his compatriots that a profound revolution had taken place even though he was unable to offer them immediate material satisfaction. Agrarian reform, the creation of urban industrial jobs with decent salaries, improvements in health care and housing, all remained distant goals. In the meantime, inculcating a new nationalism and sense of pride in the Revolution would have to substitute for action.

Obregón's secretary of education, José Vasconcelos, launched an ambitious campaign, under the slogan "Forging the Fatherland," to construct a thousand rural schools, encourage popular crafts and trades, and subsidize Mexican music, dance, theater, and literature. But what was most distinctive about this nationalistic campaign was the drafting of art into the service of politics.

Mexico had a long, though lapsed, tradition of mural painting. The Aztecs had used this art form on their temples and palaces to convey a version of history that justified their rise to supremacy, and to instruct their subjects on the social and religious precepts that governed their empire. During the colonial era, church murals unfurled the Christian vision to the Indians, holding out the possibility of eternal salvation after brief lives of misery, submission, hardship, and disease. Vasconcelos proposed to cover the walls of Mexico City's public buildings with murals that would communicate to a largely illiterate citizenry the Revolution's vision of a troubled history and hopeful future.

Among the scores of Mexican painters who enthusiastically took up Vasconcelos's offer, none understood the alchemy of art and politics better than Diego Rivera. His talents and his flair for controversy transformed him into one of the luminaries of postrevolutionary Mexico City. For many Mexicans, his murals and canvases are still a *Baedeker* of their country's past and present.

Diego Rivera was born in the silver-mining center of Guanajuato in 1886, the only surviving child of a middle-class couple. His father was a petty bureaucrat and rural school inspector, who considered himself a freethinker and espoused mildly anticlerical views. His mother played the traditional family role of faithful Catholic. Although predominantly of European stock, Diego—always eager to project himself as the prototypical Mexican—claimed a cosmic racial ancestry of white, Indian, and African blood.

He demonstrated an aptitude for drawing at an early age, and was enrolled in Mexico City's prestigious San Carlos Academy of Fine Arts shortly after his family moved to the capital in the 1890s. The Porfirian era was aesthetically sterile, relying heavily on outdated European models. Grandiose neo-Renaissance and neoclassical styles prevailed in the design of mansions, public buildings, and theaters. At San Carlos Academy, the instructors steadfastly ignored the already decades-old Impressionist movement, and served up to their students warmed-over versions of David, Goya, and early-nineteenth-century Spanish and French landscape painting.

It was outside the Academy that Rivera found the popular folklore that was to inspire his art: the pottery and blankets woven with Indian designs; the ribald murals on the walls of the pulque taverns; the votive paintings in churches; and the cartoonlike sketches that illustrated Mexican ballads and political broadsheets. The most renowned illustrator of the period was José Guadalupe Posada, whose engraving shop, located near San Carlos Academy, was a daily haunt for Rivera and other students. Posada's fierce drawings of corrupt politicians, bloated aristocrats, emaciated beggars, and dancing skeletons filtered into Rivera's works decades later.

Like the best of Mexico's youthful artists, Diego aspired to advance his career in Europe. His father arranged a government stipend that enabled him to study and paint in Spain and later in France. Rivera left Mexico in 1907, and except for a brief visit in 1910, he stayed in Europe until 1921. Perhaps feeling somewhat guilty over having remained safely abroad throughout the entire Revolution, he posed as a political exile among his fellow artists in Paris. He asserted, rather improbably, that he had witnessed the massacre of striking textile workers at Orizaba (Veracruz) in 1906, and was then forced to seek asylum in Europe. The incident, one of the most serious outbursts of prerevolutionary unrest in the late Porfiriato, left scores of workers dead. But it is doubtful that the factory area, sealed off by government troops for weeks during the crisis, could have been visited by Rivera. And his graphic descriptions of the massacre sounded suspiciously like the more famous "Bloody Sunday" of the failed 1905 Revolution in Moscow, when saber-wielding czarist troops slaughtered hundreds of demonstrators. Rivera also claimed to have planned to assassinate Porfirio Díaz in 1910 when he returned briefly to Mexico City to exhibit his paintings during the centennial celebration. According to the artist, he intended to offer the dictator a gift-wrapped bomb, but abandoned the attempt when Díaz's wife presided over the exhibition instead of her husband.

Fabrications always seeped into Rivera's conversational repertoire. His chief biographer, Bertram Wolfe, was so flustered by his subject's propensity to embellish the truth that he wrote a second biography of Rivera in part to correct the "disinformation" he had unwittingly recorded in a first version published twenty-four years earlier. "Diego counted on his listener's politeness as much as his credulity," wrote Wolfe, casting Rivera's mythomania in the most favorable light. "Who could be so discourteous, who so foolish and dully matter-of-fact, as to disbelieve such attractive, exciting, baroquely designed, richly detailed, marvelously verisimilar yet preposterous stories, told while the painter smiled and snorted, his bulging eyes fastened directly upon one's own?"[1]

In Paris, Rivera was a fixture in a Bohemian society that included Picasso, Braque, Gris, Apollinaire, Max Jacob, Jean Cocteau, and a lesser constellation of artists, writers, political exiles, and hangers-on. They warmly accepted this character so outlandish in speech and physical appearance. Over six feet tall and three hundred pounds, with protuberant, froglike eyes, wide mouth, scraggly beard, and paint-stained clothes, Rivera prided himself in being "attractively ugly" and never lacked female companionship. No one denied his considerable artistic talents. His paintings, mostly in the Cubist style, sold well enough to support him even through the depressed market of World War I. "If he had remained among us," a Cubist poet and art critic remarked years later, "Rivera would have occupied an honorable place in the Paris school."[2] But Diego aspired to greater recognition and an artistic style of his own. Neither seemed attainable in the shadow of such giants as Picasso and Matisse.

Historical and political influences were shaping Rivera's restless aesthetic vision. During an extensive visit to Italy, he furiously sketched

the frescoes of antiquity and the Renaissance. Their monumentality
and didacticism awoke in him a yearning to resurrect a lost style of
painting that could appeal to a much broader and more popular audience than the canvases hanging in galleries and salons of the
bourgeoisie. The Bolshevik Revolution also had an enormous impact
on him. In Paris, some of his closest friends were Russian Marxist
émigrés who returned to their country to write and paint for the glory
of the proletariat during those early, heady days after Lenin's triumph.
The Russian Revolution gave a new aura to Mexico's upheaval. For
all its obvious differences with the Soviet experience, the Mexican
Revolution offered certain superficial similarities: the overthrow of an
imperious ruler and a landowning and industrial elite ensconced in a
glittering capital; a strong anticlerical current; a radical rhetoric that
championed the downtrodden and held out the promise of land to
peasants and a living income for urban workers.

Nostalgia for his homeland undoubtedly colored Rivera's assessment
of the Revolution. He would not allow his vision to be dimmed by
the factionalism, opportunism, corruption, brutality, and betrayal that
had prolonged the upheaval for a decade. "An artist with my revolutionary point of view could find in Mexico . . . a place to work and
to grow," he asserted in his autobiography. [3] And so, abandoning Paris
and the European Cubist mainstream, he accepted the Obregón government's invitation to return to Mexico City to paint murals exalting
the Revolution.

Arriving in Veracruz after his transatlantic voyage in 1921, a
homesick Rivera could barely contain his enthusiasm. It seemed to
him that everything and everybody had been benevolently touched by
the Revolution. He even claimed to discern a new dignity in the white-
clad workers with broad-brimmed sombreros who struggled to unload
his baggage on the dock. And how he warmed to the revolutionary art
tasks ahead:

> It was as if I was reborn; reborn into a new world. All the colors I
> saw seemed sublime; they were clearer, richer, better, more filled with
> light. The black tones had a depth which they never attained in Europe.
> I was in the very center of a world . . . where colors and forms existed
> in absolute purity. In each and every thing I saw a potential master-
> piece—the masses of people, the marketplaces, the fiestas, the battalions
> on the march, the laborers in the workshops and fields—in each splendid
> face, in each luminous child. Everything was revealed to me. I was

convinced that even if I lived a hundred lifetimes I would never exhaust the storehouse of buoyant beauty.[4]

Rivera was not the first artist to confuse beauty with truth. The reality of Mexico in 1921 was a country prostrated by war and governed by hard-eyed survivors who were not seduced by their own revolutionary rhetoric. The laborers whom Rivera saw working idyllically in the fields were mostly landless peons; the workshop employees still toiled for eighty-hour weeks at wages that could not ensure their livelihoods; the "luminous" children were the fortunate 50 percent who did not succumb to infant mortality.

As president, Alvaro Obregón displayed his battlefield caution in grappling with the nation's inequities. He was committed to the concept of organized labor for the betterment of the working class; but he would tolerate only a trade union movement that neither challenged his government nor its economic policies. Thus, he favored the Regional Confederation of Mexican Labor, better known by its acronym, CROM. In the four years of Obregón's presidency, the CROM's membership rose from 50,000 to 1.2 million. But it remained an officialist union whose leadership readily accommodated itself to government manipulation, establishing a tradition that has continued to the present era. Neither the government nor the CROM brooked independent trade unions. The CROM stifled strikes that might prove irritating to Obregón. In most cases, affiliation with the powerful union improved neither the livelihood nor working conditions of laborers. The union did, however, prove bountiful for its leaders. In return for labor peace, they extorted money from enterprises, and also enriched themselves from union dues and their administration of state-owned companies. Luís Morones, the founder of the CROM, reputedly became one of the wealthiest figures in Mexico, with vast urban real estate holdings, a fleet of cars, and a princely wardrobe.

The rural poor fared even worse than urban laborers. Obregón had little confidence in the abilities of peasants, and believed that the revitalization of agriculture had to be led by the large estates. "The great majority of our poor," he told an assembly of hacienda owners, "have no inkling of what thrift is; they can gather a harvest but not save for another." And he rebuked the framers of the generous land reform plan in the 1917 Constitution for being "totally destitute of a practical sense and agricultural knowledge."[5] During his administration, land remained concentrated in a few hands. Even in Morelos, where the Zapatistas had carried out the Revolution's bitterest struggle for agrarian reform, the big sugar planters reclaimed their properties. Their chief complaint was the reduced labor force, cut almost in half by wartime casualties, deportations, and the exodus of refugees.[6] Throughout the country, hacienda owners resorted to a variety of maneuvers to retain their lands: filing injunctions in courts to endlessly delay government decrees ordering the break-up of large estates; bribing agrarian reform officials; subdividing their properties on paper among family members and trusted employees, while in fact retaining ownership for themselves; and when all else failed, recruiting armed bands to intimidate peasants legitimately demanding plots. By the time Obregón left office in 1924, only three million acres—about 3.5 percent of the agrarian land in the country—had been distributed to the poor.

One of the underlying issues of the Revolution had been the struggle of the provinces against the dominance of Mexico City. But the political and economic gap between the capital and the hinterland yawned wider than ever during the 1920s. The Revolution had wrought most of its casualties and property damages in the countryside. And the provinces were victimized more than Mexico City by the post–World War I depression that crushed the prices of metals and agrarian exports. Little wonder then that in the years following the Revolution, there was a massive influx of rural poor into the capital. By 1925, Mexico City surpassed a million inhabitants, doubling its population of fifteen years before. Many of the newcomers survived as beggars, porters, messengers, clerks, factory workers, and as servants for the remnants of Porfirian upper- and middle-class society and a new postrevolutionary elite.

The new elite of bureaucrats and politicians consisted mostly of small-town lawyers, teachers, and rebel commanders who quickly shed their provincial animosity toward Mexico City. By installing themselves in the capital, they claimed to be able to better serve their local constituencies and at the same time gain a broader perspective on the battered nation's problems. But the fact was that in the economic stagnation of the postrevolutionary years, public office offered the surest path to financial advancement. Beginning in the Obregón era, the bureaucracy, centered in Mexico City, expanded to satisfy the frantic search for public employment by the revolutionaries, their relatives, friends, and supporters.

Illicit income, rather than meager official salaries, made bureaucratic sinecures irresistible. The favoritism and corruption that had plagued Porfirian Mexico continued to fluorish during and after the

Revolution. In his brief tenure, Madero was accused of allowing his family to secure lucrative government contracts. Carranza rewarded his supporters with land seized from his opponents, and he liberally bribed his officers to ensure their loyalty. "How sad," commented Obregón during his presidential campaign in 1920, "to see the most distinguished men, civilians and soldiers, turn the revolutionary movement into a butt of ridicule and devote heart and soul to the pursuit of the almighty peso."[7] Once in office, however, he took a more cynical view of corruption, bragging that no Mexican general could "withstand a cannonball of fifty thousand pesos."[8] He lured at least five hundred generals to Mexico City and placed them on the government payroll in useless or fictitious posts that gave them ample opportunity to indulge in graft. Obregón conceded they were "men who refuse to live by their labor, who . . . offer up incense to those on their way to power." But to leave them in the provinces in command of their armies was to invite large-scale banditry. By bringing the bandits to the capital, Obregón joked, he was rendering them harmless.[9]

For the new elite, Mexico City was a twentieth-century cornucopia of running water, electricity, sewage facilities, refrigerated food, telephones, phonographs, and automobiles. Two thirds of the country's 55,000 motor vehicles in 1925 were on the capital's streets—and the largest limousines were reserved for the ranking bureaucrats and generals, their wives, and mistresses. They moved into spacious villas and mansions along Paseo de la Reforma and its adjoining neighborhoods. "When I first knew them, they lived in such modest apartments in the humblest zones of the capital," remarked a revolutionary returning to Mexico City after a few years of exile. "But, that's life!"[10] Lip service to populist, revolutionary ideals led the elite to shun schools run by the Church or foreigners. But public education was considered of such poor quality that they enrolled their children in a private academy, the Colegio Mexicano.

"All the new aristocracy attended this school: sons of generals, of nouveaux riches, of distinguished plunderers of the national budget," recalled a former student a half century later.

But the marvelous thing was when the directors, diligent in their desire to pass as revolutionaries and friends of the people, brought two [Zapotecan] Indian boys from Oaxaca to study in their school. . . . They always seated them, dressed in gaudy fashion, on the proscenium, where they had to endure the fulsome phrases of official speakers: "You, the mother race, will be rehabilitated . . ." and ad nauseam. . . . [But] the two Zapotecans again became servants as soon as the invited guests had departed, and worked out their expenses cleaning even toilets. The two boys were the directors' best servants: they were paid nothing and served as a political snare. And long live the Revolution![11]

The unrevolutionary conduct of the new political class that governed the country was too blatant to be overlooked even by ardent converts like Diego Rivera and his fellow artists. Their reaction was a mixture of self-interest and idealism. They did not enjoy the option of private patronage, and besides, these artists had proclaimed the decadence of easel-painting because it was rarely displayed outside the confines of wealthy residences. For all its defects, the government was the sole source of their livelihood, and, from their point of view, a patron of greater moral standing than any private collector because it sought to expose the populace to art. "The painter who does not feel attuned to the aspirations of the masses—this man may not produce a work of permanent worth," asserted Rivera. "Not so the man who paints walls, palaces, public buildings. Art cut off from practical aims is not art."[12]

If the government was unwilling to enforce a radical political program, then the muralists insisted with unvarnished naivete, they themselves would emerge as the vanguard of the Revolution. Artists have often been proclaimed the conscience of their society, but rarely has this encomium been taken so literally as in Mexico City during the 1920s. The muralists would depict the socialist country which they hoped Mexico would become. In speech and writing, they would urge revolutionary action to overcome national injustices. And they would band together with their plasterers, stonecutters, glaziers, cement pourers, carpenters, and apprentices to set an example of how a classless system could be fashioned in the workplace.

To promote their ideology, the artists created the Syndicate of Revolutionary Painters, Sculptors, and Engravers in 1922, selecting Diego Rivera as its president. One of the Syndicate's lofty aims was "to destroy all egocentrism, replacing it by disciplined group work."[13] The nature of mural, particularly fresco, painting encouraged this sort of utopian camaraderie. In the fresco technique, watercolors were painted on freshly laid plaster that had not yet dried. As Rivera pointed out, it demanded close cooperation between the artist and dozens of assistants at every stage, from the manufacture of the basic materials to the final brushstrokes.

The plaster was made of lime and marble dust (sand, though cheaper, did not absorb the paint as well as ground marble). The lime had to be free of salt and organic matter, which could ruin the watercolors, and it had to be burned by wood, instead of coal, whose sulfur impurities could alter the pigments. The same care was taken in making the watercolor paints. These pigments—selected by Rivera—were ground by his assistants on marble slabs and combined with distilled water to form a paste.

Workers applied two layers of plaster on the wall. Then Rivera mounted the scaffold and with charcoal sticks traced the outlines of his mural from sketches he had drawn in his studio. His assistants, using knives, would carefully etch Rivera's charcoal marks so that the mural's outlines could be visible under the final, thin coat of plaster. While this third layer of plaster was still wet, Rivera again climbed the scaffold and did his painting, applying the pigments with brushes moistened in distilled water devoid of impurities. He had to paint swiftly and continuously for hours at a stretch because if the plaster dried, the pigments would peel off. During his breaks for meals or sleep, his assistants covered a new section of the wall with a final coat of plaster, and alerted him as soon as the wet layer was ready. There were numerous occasions when Rivera, dissatisfied with a whole day's labor, would order his helpers to wash off the whole offending section of the mural and apply fresh plaster so that he could rework the design the following day.[14]

In organizing their Syndicate, Rivera and his fellow artists wanted to exalt the role of their skilled assistants, and to negotiate collectively for the salaries and job security of all who worked on murals. The problem, however, was that the Syndicate, unlike other labor unions, had no bargaining power. "The one-man market for our mural wares was [Secretary of Education] José Vasconcelos," wrote one of the Syndicate painters, "and he was not impressed."[15] Before unceremoniously dismissing a delegation of artists and craftsmen sent to apprise him of the Syndicate's existence, Vasconcelos informed them that he intended to contract painters individually for each mural and to let them deal with the salaries and jobs of their assistants. The revolutionary artists found themselves in the unwanted position of being bosses, much like the heads of any traditional small enterprise.

The fact that the painters were unable to eradicate the class structure even in their own working environment only made them more vociferous on the subject of revolution. Their Syndicate published the most radical broadsheet in Mexico City. Called *El Machete*, its masthead was a huge peasant knife with the motto:

> *The machete serves to cut the cane,*
> *To open paths in shadowed woods,*
> *To decapitate serpents, to cut down weeds,*
> *And to humble the pride of the impious rich.* [16]

Its contents included treatises on communism, denunciations of labor conditions, art manifestos, and the verses of radical poets. But its price and stilted language made *El Machete* inaccessible to the peasants and urban workers who were its intended audience, and the publication survived only from subsidies contributed by the more successful artists, especially Rivera.

Rivera and his colleagues were also among the earliest members of the Mexican Communist Party, whose executive committee included himself and two other artists, David Alfaro Siqueiros and Xavier Guerrero. They developed a fetish for guns, and formed platoons of armed muralists and craftsmen who stood ready, they said, to defend the Obregón government against counterrevolutionaries. Rivera took to mounting his scaffolds with a cartridge belt wrapped around his ample waist and a large revolver dangling in its holster. Even his friends ridiculed his claim to be as adept with a pistol as a brush.

As part of their revolutionary theatrics, the artists engaged in endless ideological discussion. Their debates in studios, homes, and cafés ran into the morning hours, with Rivera standing somewhere between the extreme viewpoints of David Alfaro Siqueiros and José Clemente Orozco. The mercurial, bombastic Siqueiros insisted that artists should abandon their elitism by encouraging the poor and untutored to express their aesthetic impulses, and by employing modern industrial materials—paint guns, air brushes, and poured concrete—that proved their commitment to the proletarian world. Impatient and undisciplined, Siqueiros became notorious for failing to complete his murals, and running off on sudden revolutionary impulse to recruit members for provincial cells of the Communist Party, organize workers in distant mines, or attend political conferences around the country.

Orozco, on the other hand, was a loner, deeply skeptical of the trendy nationalism, populism, and Marxism of his fellow artists. To Siqueiros's insistence that anybody was capable of creating art, he retorted: "Blessed are the idiots and cretins, for masterpieces of painting shall issue from their hands!" Was it any different, he demanded, from handing violins to "deaf men or suckling babes, taco vendors, lottery-ticket sellers, or bus drivers" and expecting them "without more ado to make music like Beethoven's?" [17] Orozco was equally scathing about the pretensions of his colleagues—for the most part, Mexico City–bred and middle-class—to replace traditional artisans as the aesthetic representatives of the rural poor: "Painting for the people? But the people make their own art; they need no help."[18]

The artists aimed to be as provocative in their lifestyle as in their politics. With an adequate income from their government benefactors, they could afford to thumb their noses at the conventional mores of the aristocrats and clergy who had been the art patrons of earlier eras. Mexico City had never before witnessed the Bohemian society they created. They drew sketches on the walls and tablecloths of their favorite restaurants and cafés as payment for bills that mounted over weeks and months. They consumed enchiladas and pulque instead of European cuisine and wines; they danced the jarabe and sandunga rather than waltzes; shunned the established theaters in favor of crude street plays performed under tents; and praised pre-Columbian Indian idols—hitherto considered barbaric junk—as more worthy of collection than Old World paintings and sculptures. Affluent youths, rebelling against their parents' conservatism, flocked to the artists' hangouts, joined their parties, and occasionally spent a night in jail, assuming the blame for an unpaid restaurant bill or the streetlamps shot out by a pistol-wielding Rivera or Siqueiros.

A greater source of outrage for some well-to-do families was the attraction their daughters felt for these Bohemian artists. Despite their strict Catholic upbringing, a number of young, affluent women became part of the muralists' entourage. They dressed in proletarian work shirts, or borrowed shawls and cotton skirts from their maids. They peppered their conversation with Marxist phrases and the scatological slang of the poor. They drank tequila and belted out mariachi songs. They posed as models for the artists, and inevitably became their mistresses, sometimes their wives.

Rivera himself was the greatest of womanizers. But what irked conventional society more than his conquests was his passive style of seduction, so unlike the aggressive, macho philandering held up as the norm. Women gathered at the foot of his murals, hoping he would take notice from his perch on the scaffold and perhaps address them when he descended for a lunch break or rest. American debutantes, on vacation in Mexico City, appeared uninvited at his studio, eager to brag on their return home that they had posed for the great painter, enjoyed a brief fling with him, or simply listened to his wondrous stories.

Among Diego's many fabrications, none titillated them more than his claims to have once been a cannibal. According to Rivera, he indulged in the practice as a young art student in Mexico City. He had heard that a fur trader had improved the quality of his pelts by feeding his animals the meat of their own species. Diego suggested to his colleagues in anatomy class that perhaps they might discover similarly unexpected benefits from consuming human flesh.

"Those of us who embarked on the experiment sought cadavers in the city morgue," explained Rivera. "We chose only corpses of people who had died violently—instead of those who succumbed to illness or old age. After prolonging this cannibal diet for two months, all of us enjoyed better health. . . . I found that I preferred the legs and breasts of the female of the species . . . and best of all, women's brains vinaigrette. . . . I have never again eaten human flesh; not out of scruples, but rather because society takes a dim view of this custom."[19]

Mexican upper-class males—brought up to believe that ardent entreaties and serenades, an athletic physique, and sartorial splendor were prerequisites of amorous conquest—viewed Rivera with a mixture of loathing and envy. They could not fathom the appeal of a disheveled, obese painter who dubbed himself a frog prince and spouted macabre tales. And Rivera seemed to them just as unorthodox in his more serious relationships with women.

His first marriage, to Guadalupe (Lupe) Marín, started off blissfully enough. A tall, long-limbed, dark beauty from a middle-class provincial family, Lupe was one of Rivera's models, and posed as an idealized version of womanhood in his earliest murals. But Diego's numerous affairs eventually took their toll. He made no attempt to hide them from Lupe. During parties and dinners, she often reacted to his provocations with angry outbursts that inevitably found their way into Mexico City's newspapers. Rivera reveled in the scandalous accounts that pictured him passively parrying Lupe's windmill blows, standing by helplessly as she ripped apart his drawings or tore at a rival's hair, and gagging when she fed him a stew sprinkled with shards from his prized Aztec idols.

The image of women fighting over their lovers was deeply imbedded in his psyche. He claimed that when he was only six years old, one of his fondest ambitions was to become the object of affection of the volatile prostitutes who offered themselves to the miners of Guanajuato, his provincial birthplace. "These women frequently became embroiled in murderous quarrels among themselves which left them with scars running from ear to lip," said Rivera, with his usual blend of fact and fantasy. "But until the day I die, I will never forget them.

I became their favorite, and they were my love."[20] Diego had often praised Lupe as a wild animal. But as the marriage became more turbulent, the sexual allusion gave way to his more fearsome descriptions of her "animal teeth" and "eagle talons,"[21] capable of inflicting scars as livid as those by his beloved childhood prostitutes. A second marriage, to the artist Frida Kahlo, repeated the same pattern of publicly exposed tumult. Rivera encouraged a friendship, tinged with rivalry, between Frida and Lupe, and among his mistresses. He enjoyed overhearing them discuss their experiences with him, his merits and his foibles.

Unfaithful husbands were no novelty in Mexico City society. What made Rivera's conduct unusual enough to serve as grist for newspaper columns and social gossip was his willingness to appear just as much a victim as his wives or mistresses. A macho was not expected to tolerate public humiliation by "his" women, no matter how much he had wronged them.

Rivera played out his psychodrama with women in his art. So many of them made their way into his murals and canvases. Indeed, Diego often excused his infidelities as an inevitable facet of his artistic temperament: How could he not be smitten by the women he immortalized in painting, especially when they offered themselves so willingly? In his murals, women achieved the dignity he often failed to accord them in life. In his evocations of Aztec society, they were not subservient to males, not even to the fierce warriors. In the Conquest, they were far more radiant than the Spaniards. In the Revolution, they looked as heroically determined as their rebel husbands. And the few times that Rivera in his paintings juxtaposed himself with women, they were the more overwhelming presence—most notably, in his last great mural in which a motherly Frida Kahlo draped her hand gently over the shoulder of a tubby, childlike rendition of the artist.

With the passage of decades, the political and personal theatrics of Rivera and his colleagues have become incidental to their artistic legacy. But they help explain the controversy that greeted the muralist movement in Mexico City during the 1920s. The artists had achieved notoriety even before they completed their first wall paintings. They relished their role as lightning rods against the Revolution's many conservative opponents, who found it easier to attack the artists and their highly politicized murals than to directly confront the government.

The first murals dramatically appeared on the walls of the National Preparatory School in the central district of Mexico City. The building, dated 1740, had been erected as a Jesuit school in a Baroque colonial style, but using the reddish *tezontle* volcanic stone favored by the Aztecs. Beyond its massive doors were three open patios, each lined with a triple tier of arcades. The architecture offered numerous walls divided by bays and was ideally suited for murals. Orozco was assigned to paint three tiers of corridor walls off the main stairway. Siqueiros chose a more remote series of bays leading off a small patio. A half dozen other muralists worked the remaining corridors. And Rivera was given the largest space: almost a thousand square feet of wall under an arched ceiling in the school's amphitheater.

By Diego's own admission, this mural, completed in early 1923, was not one of his best. Its theme was the creation of Mexico's races, and he used monumental figures to represent Indian, Spaniard, African, and mestizo. Other human figures stood as metaphors for wisdom, poetry, music, dance, tragedy, comedy, passion, and tradition. The murals of Siqueiros and Orozco were considerably more provocative. Using flamboyant red pigments and fearsome characters, Siqueiros appeared to have designed a satanic den, although he insisted he was painting angels. One of Orozco's panels, called "Youth," portrayed gossiping schoolgirls with hair ribbons and textbooks, seemingly unaware of gigantic naked men who romped overhead. In another Orozco panel, "The New Redemption," a beardless Christ puts a torch to his cross after chopping it down with an ax he still holds in his right hand.

Even while the Preparatory School murals were in progress, they incited a furor. The students—most of them from the affluent, pre-revolutionary classes—were conservative in their politics and cultural tastes. They signed petitions denouncing the murals as travesties of art that were defacing their school buildings. Passersby shouted insults to the artists as they worked on their scaffolds, and accosted them when they descended. The Preparatory became a daily beat for journalists, who reported the confrontations and then added sarcastic commentaries of their own. Rivera was caricatured and parodied on stage. Newspapers denounced his Indian figures as grotesque, "apocalyptic monsters," and charged that his depictions of naked women had no place in a school built by Jesuits.

Rivera, at least, was able to carry on his work by locking himself and his assistants in the amphitheater. The other muralists, working on scaffolds in the corridors and patios, tried to ignore the catcalls, but could not escape the hail of paper wads and stones that became a daily ordeal. When they resumed work in the mornings, they often found their murals defaced by posters, chewing gum, spittle, and graffiti. To protect themselves against the assaults and vandalism, the artists erected screens and barricades. At one point, students announced their intention to tar and feather the painters. The muralists, backed by gunmen, repulsed their tormentors by firing in the air and screaming "Long live the Revolution!" But on another occasion, Orozco and Siqueiros were expelled from the Preparatory by a determined student mob, who then damaged their murals with clubs, knives, and tar.

Later in 1923, the artists moved on to a more secure working environment, the Ministry of Public Education. It was in the huge patio of this building that Rivera began the first of his great works, a series of 124 frescoes that made the Mexican muralist movement renowned in the world. Covering a corridor space three stories high and three city blocks long, the task occupied most of his next four years. The project, a historical and contemporary evocation of Mexicans through their work and popular festivals, was divided into a Court of Labor and a Court of Fiestas.

In the Labor murals, obese landlords, with greedy faces and thumbs tucked in cartridge belts, weigh bags of grain offered by their peons. Silver miners descend a shaft with wooden beams strapped to their backs—like Christ bearing the cross—and reemerge exhausted, to be subjected to a humiliating search by their overseers. The power of the murals lies less in the revolutionary dogma tinged with Marxism than in the choreography of the laborers. They dance rhythmically through their toils, in a subtle refusal to succumb to the dehumanizing tasks imposed on them.

In his other panels, grouped under the Court of Fiestas, Diego portrayed Indians invoking the hunting deity in a Deer Dance, peasants giving thanks for the corn harvest, urban and rural poor gathering on the Day of the Dead, worshippers performing folklore dances in a church, peons celebrating the distribution of land, and workers parading on May Day. The implicit message of these murals was that Mexicans did not need the clergy to attain spiritual gratification. They preserved pre-Conquest beliefs, they mixed pagan and Christian ritual without the intercession of priests, and eventually, they embraced the secular religion of class struggle.

Conservative critics attacked the Education Ministry frescoes as antiaesthetic, Marxist defamations of Mexican history and Catholicism. Rivera and his fellow artists did not deny their radical, antireligious intent. For them, Vasconcelos's slogan of "Forging the Fatherland" meant a struggle between the Church and a nationalistic, revolutionary government for the allegiance of the Mexican people. They were using art to explain and propagate the new gospel. The murals, in Orozco's words, were "really painted bibles . . . [for the] many people who can't read."[22]

The virulent press campaign and street protests gave the muralists an exaggerated view of their political significance. The public passion stirred by their art convinced them that they were leading the revolutionary cause against a seawall of conservative resistance. But before 1923 ended, the muralist controversy was relegated to a sideshow as the country neared a full-blown political crisis over the crucial question of who would succeed President Obregón when his term came to a close.

Obregón believed that he had struck a balance between revolutionary rhetoric and pragmatic compromise during his first three years in office. A limited agrarian reform program had maintained the expectations of the rural poor without threatening most of the big landowners. Urban workers were being recruited into the trade union movement, even if it was controlled by the corruption-ridden CROM. So many revolutionary generals had been put on the government payroll that Obregón hoped the army would tolerate deep cuts in its budget and manpower. He was confident enough about his nationalist credentials to negotiate a treaty with Washington that extended U.S. diplomatic recognition to his government in exchange for guarantees that American oil companies in Mexico would not be expropriated. He even felt optimistic that his ecclesiastical opponents had been mollified. True, there were Catholics who would never forgive the anticlericalism he displayed during the Revolution. And he made no apologies for the militantly secular campaign of the muralists in Mexico City, or for the thousands of government teachers who were seeking to woo the rural poor away from the traditional influence of the curates. But he had reopened churches, allowed most clergymen to return from exile, and tolerated religious schools, despite articles in the 1917 Constitution declaring them illegal.

Thus, Obregón was confident he could arrange a peaceful presidential succession. His choice was his trusted fellow Sonoran and secretary of interior, Plutarco Calles. But Calles was unacceptable to conservatives and Catholic leaders who considered him more radical than Obregón. This hard-core opposition was joined by an unlikely assortment of disgruntled factions: military officers who failed to benefit from the spoils of the postrevolutionary era; left-wing trade unions resentful of the hegemony of the officialist CROM; nationalists who accused Obregón of bowing to U.S. oil interests. These motley antagonists rallied behind Adolfo de la Huerta, a former cabinet minister in the Obregón government, and precipitated a civil war in late 1923 and early 1924. It was a bloody struggle that claimed about seven thousand lives. But with most military units loyal to him and an ample supply of weapons from the United States, Obregón put down the De la Huerta rebellion. And when he relinquished power to Calles in 1924, it was the first time in forty years that a Mexican president had been replaced without being assassinated or overthrown.

The muralist movement was an indirect casualty of the De la Huerta rebellion. A steep increase in the military budget reduced other government expenditures, and the painters fought among themselves for shares of the dwindling public subsidies. The artists' Syndicate collapsed. Some muralists found work elsewhere in Mexico; others swallowed their antibourgeois distaste for easel-painting and accepted commissions for portraits of the revolutionary elite, their wives, mistresses, and children. Eventually, only Diego Rivera would survive this shakeout.

None of his colleagues could begrudge Diego his talent; only Orozco consistently matched his level of artistry. But the other muralists felt victimized by Rivera's extraordinary self-promotion. Journalists grew tired of Siqueiros's ranting political monologues and Orozco's moody introspection. Rivera, on the other hand, was always "good copy." He mesmerized interviewers with discourses enlivened by humor, politics, braggadocio, and outrageous fantasy. Reporters returned to their offices with astonishing accounts of how Rivera had discovered a tequila-based solvent that would revolutionize painting; how the artist had secretly joined Zapata in a furtive visit to Mexico a dozen years before; how he personally mediated the ideological dispute between Lenin and Trotsky; and how pre-Columbian idols that had recently come into his possession proved the existence of Mexican civilization before the ancient Egyptians and Mesopotamians.

The press nicknamed the other artists "Dieguitos" ("Little Diegos"), as if they were acolytes or mere imitators of the master. "Though the murals were separate enterprises governed by distinct contracts," wrote a fellow artist, "people took it for granted that all the works were Diego Rivera's."[23] European art critics, dazzled by the Mexican muralist movement, also focused almost exclusively on Rivera. He spoke French, was worldly, and knew many of them from his long sojourn in Europe. He was articulate in explaining to them his break with Cubism, his need to develop a native style, and the brave new world he was trying to convey. Their articles, praising him as the foremost artist in the Americas, were reprinted in Mexican journals. And soon his local detractors, not wishing to appear as philistines in the eyes of foreigners, were reluctantly conceding that Rivera's art might have some merit—a reassessment they were unwilling to extend to the other muralists.

Rivera was also more adroit than his colleagues in accommodating himself to the political shifts that followed the transition from Obregón to Calles. Education Secretary Vasconcelos, the patron saint of the muralists, was forced out. The new secretary, José Puig Casauranc, a political rival of Vasconcelos, was ill-disposed to the muralist projects that were identified with his predecessor. Before his appointment, Puig sided with critics who demanded that the Calles government whitewash the paintings from the walls of public buildings. Most of the muralists understandably supported Vasconcelos, who clashed with Puig in a bitter series of articles in the local press. But Rivera wooed the new education secretary, escorted him through the buildings where frescoes were in progress, and insisted to him that the paintings were a national heritage, not simply the personal legacy of Vasconcelos.

Puig emerged from these tours a convert. "All things considered, we are not empowered to pass judgment," he told an entourage of journalists. "We must let future generations give a final judgment." Later, in the privacy of his car, he added, "Rivera is the philosopher of the brush."[24] Puig became even more enthusiastic about Rivera some months later when the artist depicted Vasconcelos in a fresco at the Education Ministry as a dwarf comically straddling a white elephant and dipping his pen in a spittoon. "A sad ending for an alliance which had begun so hopefully," remarked one of Rivera's biographers. "Without Vasconcelos, Rivera would never have had the chance to paint frescoes on public walls; without the great fresco renaissance, Vasconcelos would have won less renown."[25] Opportunism, deviousness? Disloyalty, cunning? The artist would have to grade himself.

For the remainder of the decade, Rivera monopolized the muralist movement. He spent fifteen-hour days on his frescoes, often working himself into exhaustion. Several times, he fell asleep in the midst of painting and toppled off his scaffold, once even fracturing his skull. Between 1924 and 1929, he completed hundreds of panels in the Education Ministry, the National Palace and the Health Ministry in Mexico City, at the Agricultural School of Chapingo a few miles northeast of the capital, and in the former palace of Cortés in Cuernavaca. Eventually, his murals would cover two and a half miles of wall space.

Critics who later accused Rivera of being an official propagandist missed the point: it was Diego who imposed his vision of Mexico on his government patrons rather than the reverse. The fables spun out on his murals became orthodox history, the raw material of textbooks and classroom lectures for future generations of public school youngsters. He evoked pre-Columbian Indian civilization as a lost paradise. In his frescoes, tribes live in harmony, reap bountiful harvests, hunt a profusion of wildlife, weave, paint, and sculpt, congregate in bustling markets, use native technology to erect pyramids and harness rivers, and carry out their religious rituals without human sacrifice or cannibalism.

The idyll is shattered by the Conquest. Indian faces lose their appealing, individual features and become blank, dehumanized masks, as the natives are herded into anonymous slave battalions by their Spanish masters. The Spaniards' own faces are contorted by anger and hatred, and the ugliest visage belongs to Cortés, portrayed as a syphilitic hunchback. Even the landscape recoils from the foreign invasion: rivers splay out of their beds, mines gouge the velvety earth, pristine woods turn into swampy jungles, fields become patches of stunted corn plants.

Under Rivera's brush, the Revolution buried its contradictions. It was fought, in Diego's murals, to resurrect the lost Indian heritage and to restore dignity and land to the native race. Zapata, the apostle of agrarian reform, emerges as the central figure of the uprising. There is little in these panels that hints at the ferocious rivalries between the revolutionary leaders. Zapata, Madero, Villa, Carranza, and Obregón are all given their due as national heroes. Peasants and urban laborers achieve a mythical unity in revolt. And the future evoked by the artist is a Marxist vision of Mexican workers, dressed like Russian proletarians, in full command of giant industrial machinery, with the radiant faces of Marx and Lenin looming above like saintly apparitions.

President Calles, no Marxist himself, enjoyed the outrage that Rivera's murals elicited from conservatives. He applauded the artist's efforts to portray the rebel commanders bound together in a national crusade, though Calles, as an Obregón partisan, loathed Carranza, Villa, and Zapata. But what stirred the president's sympathy most in Rivera's frescoes was their relentless anticlericalism: porcine friars, smiling with undisguised avarice, accept the tribute of their Indian wards; priests hold wooden crosses aloft as brigades of native laborers are driven forward by Spanish overseers; and clergymen preach salvation to shivering, ragged Indians.

Hatred of the Church was the dominating obsession in Plutarco Calles's adult life. Born out of wedlock in the northern state of Sonora in 1877, he became a schoolteacher before he was twenty years old, but was fired for drinking heavily and using profane language to denounce the clergy. He drifted through a succession of jobs—bartender, hotel manager, and farmer—before finding his true vocation as a revolutionary. Following Madero's assassination in 1913, Calles joined Carranza's rebel army and served under Obregón, rising to the rank of general and then governor of Sonora. A reformed alcoholic, he considered liquor salesmen and priests as equal evils, and persecuted both during his governorship.

Tall, burly, with a craggy, unsmiling face, Calles was an imposing, authoritarian figure as president. While his mentor, Obregón, was jovial, gregarious, and diplomatic, Calles was sullen, ruthless toward real or imagined enemies, and suspicious of all but a few political associates. Determined to prove himself more revolutionary than Obregón, he distributed twice as much land to the peasants as his predecessor, and embraced the trade union movement with more conviction. But it was in his relations with the Church that Calles became every bit as radical as his opponents had feared. Under his presidency, Obregón's conciliatory policies were jettisoned, and the state reduced the Church's activities until there seemed to be no place for the clergy at all.

Calles fired the opening shot of his anti-Catholic campaign in Mexico City in February 1925, less than two months after he assumed office. Mass at La Soledad church in a working-class district was disrupted by one hundred armed men. They ejected the priest and sacristans, and proclaimed the building the property of the "Mexican Catholic Church"—a previously unknown sect that asserted independence from the Vatican. The following day, two men dressed as priests appeared at La Soledad and attempted to conduct services on behalf of the new sect. They were attacked by parishioners, and in a riot that spilled into the streets, many were injured and one person was killed by mounted police. Press stories suggested that the incident was instigated by Calles himself. The thugs who initially occupied the church were identified as policemen and CROM trade unionists. The two men posing as priests for the "Mexican Catholic Church" turned out to be lapsed clergymen—one of them had resigned his ministry to fight in the Revolution a decade earlier, and the other was expelled for living openly with a woman. The Calles government, obviously sympathetic to the schismatics, deplored their violent methods but promised them their own house of worship. Three weeks later, Calles ordered that La Soledad be closed and that the building be turned into a public library. Meanwhile, the schismatics were given the use of another abandoned church.

The incident was an attempt by Calles to create an alternative Church beholden to the government. La Soledad had been singled out because of its location in a poor neighborhood where trade union enrollment was high and popular support for the president was believed strong. The violent resistance of the parishioners took Calles by surprise, but only convinced him to focus his anti-Catholic campaign outside the capital for the time being. In the months that followed, several state governments announced limits on the number of local priests. The state of Tabasco, on the Gulf coast, virtually ended church services by insisting that only clergymen who were married and over forty years old could perform religious functions.[26] And in several states, parochial schools were closed in sudden compliance with the 1917 Constitution.

By early 1926, Mexico City again became the chief target of the offensive. One of the least observed articles of the Constitution specified that churches built after 1917 were government property, and that their priests would have to seek the state's approval to keep them open. The Calles administration decided to enforce this law, and chose one of the newer churches, the Sagrada Familia, as a test case. In February 1926, the church, located in an affluent parish of the capital, was closed down by government agents, and its priests were arrested on charges of using the building for worship without the state's permission. Even before the clergymen were led away, several thousand angry women parishioners gathered in front of the Sagrada Familia. They were hosed down by a brigade of firemen, but regrouped for a protest march on government offices. This time the police opened fire, killing two women and wounding another score.

In the months ahead, clashes between Catholics and policemen became commonplace in the streets of Mexico City. Meanwhile, violence in provincial cities claimed dozens of casualties. The Catholic hierarchy warned that unless the anti-Church provisions of the Constitution were repealed, all religious liberty would end. Calles lashed back with some of his most intemperate language. The clergy had been a blight on Mexico since the country gained independence, he told a convention of the CROM, and he was prepared to bring them to heel, "without regard to the sacristans' grimaces or the farts of monks."[27]

In July, his government published a decree ordering the enforcement of all the anticlerical provisions of the Constitution, and adding even more drastic restrictions: all parochial schools would cease to function; foreign clergymen were forbidden any religious activity; monasteries and nunneries were to close; no political parties were permitted to have ties with any religious creed; and all Church buildings were declared state property.

With the approval of Pope Pius XI, the Mexican prelates responded on July 24, 1926. Because of the "impossibility of practicing our sacred ministry under this decree," they wrote in a pastoral letter, "we order that after July 31 . . . all religious services requiring the intervention of priests shall be suspended in all churches of the country."[28] Faithful Catholics were asked to withdraw their children from the public schools, and to join an economic boycott against all goods and services, except those necessary for daily subsistence.

In the last week of July, the imminent closure of churches led to an outpouring of religious fervor unmatched since the early colonial era. From dawn to late evening, churches were crammed with worshippers and penitents anxious to hear Mass and make their last confessions, as if the Apocalypse were upon them. In Mexico City, parents cradling their unbaptized infants formed long lines outside the Cathedral. Up to two thousand baptisms were performed daily by exhausted priests at the church. Other clergymen herded thousands of youngsters through confirmation rites. Hundreds of religious weddings were held in the capital as couples living in free union or married in civil ceremonies sought Church sanction. Pilgrims congregated in unprecedented numbers at the Basilica of the Virgin of Guadalupe, the holiest shrine for poor Mexicans.[29]

The Church strike lasted for three years, but after the initial hysteria, its impact was tempered by the fact that most Mexicans had always carried on their religious life with minimal intercession of the clergy. There had never been enough priests to minister to the population. In villages and cities, the faithful attended churches whether or not a vicar was present, or prayed at home before the tiny altar of their favorite saint. The Church-State conflict that had continuously flared during the century between the Independence wars and the Revolution had produced relatively few atheists, but it shaped a country in which many people could simultaneously claim to be religious and anti-clerical.

The economic boycott called by the Church hierarchy also was relatively ineffectual against the Calles government. The majority of people could never afford to buy anything beyond basic necessities anyway, and thus carried on as usual. The more affluent Mexicans resumed their spending when it became obvious that the Church-State confrontation would be indefinitely prolonged.

But by raising political tensions, the Church strike helped provoke a violent revolt against the Calles government. The *"Viva Cristo Rey"* ("Long live Christ the King") movement erupted in rural areas of a half-dozen states in August 1926, and at its peak, commanded twenty-five thousand armed adherents. Affluent and middle-class conservatives were prominent as officers, while most combatants were landless peasants, impatient with the progress of agrarian reform. Even though prelates denied any ties to the rebel bands, the movement obviously had the sympathy of the Church hierarchy and attracted numerous Catholic laymen and local curates into its ranks. The "Cristeros"—as the insurgents called themselves—never seriously threatened to topple Calles. But with highly motivated troops adept at guerrilla tactics, their revolt lasted three years and claimed almost eight thousand lives.

The conflict resurrected the brutal tactics of the Revolution. Prisoners on both sides were killed. Priests made no effort to interfere in the execution of captured federal soldiers, except to offer them last confessions. Numerous clergymen were murdered by government troops. Among the most frequent civilian victims of the Cristeros were public school teachers, who were accused of being enemies of the Church. Perhaps the worst single massacre occurred in April 1927, when Cristero guerrillas attacked a Mexico City train bound for Guadalajara. After overwhelming the armed escort, the rebels set the train on fire and killed more than one hundred civilian passengers.

Mexico City was spared large-scale battles, but there were almost daily fights in the streets between youth gangs of government supporters and Catholic militants. Churches were stoned and vandalized by adolescents, even schoolchildren, encouraged and protected by the police. Terrorist bands—some with links to the Cristeros, others operating as independent cells of laymen and clergy—hurled bombs at government buildings and assassinated public officials.

Former President Obregón became one of their targets. For the Cristeros and their more fanatic sympathizers, his conciliatory policies toward the Church had not redeemed his anticlerical excesses during the Revolution. They also held him responsible for the repression of the Church because he had chosen his protégé, Calles, as his successor. No matter what misgivings Obregón had about Calles's handling of the religious issue, he publicly supported him. In return, Calles was backing Obregón's quest for another presidential term in 1928.

The first attempt against Obregón came in November 1927. Obregón was being chauffeured in his Cadillac from his Mexico City residence to a bullfight when another car pulled alongside. Its occupants opened fire and lobbed several bombs at the ex-president and his bodyguards, but failed to kill anyone. Obregón emerged from the incident with only minor facial wounds and his reputation as a charmed survivor intact. After a wild car chase through the downtown streets, Obregón's escort succeeded in capturing two of the terrorists when their vehicle crashed. A police investigation linked them to Humberto Pro Suárez, the leader of a militant lay Catholic association, and his brother, Father Miguel Pro Suárez, a Jesuit whose activities included charitable aid for the widows and orphans of Cristeros killed in combat.[30]

According to the police chief in charge of the inquest, President Calles read the dossier and commented: "So there is proof of the guilt of these individuals, and of the priest, who was the mastermind behind it. Here, it was General Obregón. Tomorrow it will be me. . . . Give the necessary orders and have them all shot."[31] And the following morning, Father Pro Suárez, Humberto Pro Suárez, and the two terrorists were executed by a firing squad in the courtyard of police headquarters.

The Pro Suárez brothers were among the most highly respected of the Catholic militants, and their execution only made their radical sympathizers more determined to carry out another attempt on Obregón's life. A twenty-six-year-old artist, José de León Toral, decided to undertake the mission.[32]

Toral was in some ways typical of the middle-class recruits to the Catholic rebel cause. Born and educated in the north, he moved to Mexico City as an adolescent, married, began a family, and earned a modest income as a portrait painter and art teacher. He was deeply alienated by the social and political atmosphere of the capital. Generals and politicians spouted revolutionary slogans while flaunting their illicit wealth. Left-wing labor leaders, living in sumptuous apartments off Paseo de la Reforma and riding in limousines, proclaimed the dawn of a godless, socialist era. Meanwhile, ambitious provincial youths like

Toral, with no contacts to ease their way into secure employment, drifted from one ill-paying job to another.

Toral was appalled by the artists' community he had once sought to join. He loathed the muralists' Bohemian lifestyle, their scandalous romantic affairs and political theatrics. But it was their art that most sickened him: vile, ill-drawn figures that distorted the human face and body; allegories that deliberately misrepresented history and contemporary reality; sacrilegious attacks on the Church; exercises in sheer propaganda for their government patrons. Toral was among the protestors who raged at the murals that covered the public buildings of the capital. Rivera, Siqueiros, Orozco deserved the opprobrium of an honest painter like himself, who had spent years learning to render portraits and landscapes as faithful as photographs. Even the caricatures he occasionally sold to conservative journals were almost as lifelike as their subjects.

In the Gomorrah that Mexico City had become for him, Toral found solace in religion. He attended Mass daily, and joined Catholic sports and meditation groups. But these havens came under siege by the Calles government. Toral, believing that good Catholics should not kill, wanted no part of the Cristeros or the other armed bands. Instead, he became a member of the association headed by Humberto Pro Suárez, who professed to support the Catholic cause by peaceful means. Toral had known the Pro Suárez brothers as far back as 1920, and became their devoted friend. He was shaken not only by their execution but because they seemed, in fact, to have conspired to assassinate Obregón despite their reputation for nonviolence.

Some weeks after the deaths of the Pro Suárez brothers, Toral came under the influence of a charismatic nun, María Concepción Acevedo, better known as "Madre Conchita." She had been in charge of a convent in a southern suburb of Mexico City until it was closed down during the government campaign against the Church. The thirty-seven-year-old Madre Conchita then became a Catholic militant. She turned her home into a clandestine chapel and meeting place for fervent young Catholics, who regarded her as their spiritual adviser and even a saint. Madre Conchita spoke to her followers in parables and biblical allusions which they interpreted as signs of approval for terrorist acts. Some of those who sought her guidance became bomb makers and snipers. Others offered themselves as spies for the Cristeros, or accompanied Madre Conchita in her visits to Catholic prisoners and their families.

Toral confided in Madre Conchita his desire to become a martyr. And when he asked her whether God would wish to see the persecutors of the Church struck down, she referred him to the Old Testament book of Judith, who seduced and then slew the commanding general of the Israelites' enemies. Toral studied the biblical passage, and decided that Madre Conchita had given him the answer: it was his divine mission to kill Obregón. Toral had briefly considered an attempt against Calles, but Obregón seemed a more appropriate target because he had won the recent presidential election and was preparing once again to take charge of the government.

In July 1928, Obregón was in Mexico City to celebrate his electoral victory with banquets, rallies, and parades. Toral, armed with a pistol borrowed from a friend, stalked him for several days, but the crowds prevented him from getting close to the revolutionary hero. On July 17, however, Obregón, against the advice of some of his security men, decided to attend a luncheon in his honor at a restaurant in San Angel, a southern district of the capital. The president-elect teased his aides that they were nervous only because the restaurant was called "La Bombilla" ("The Little Bomb").

The banquet, held in a partially open-air patio, was festive, and Obregón's companions were soon put at ease by the food, drink, and mariachi music. Some of them later remembered seeing Toral circulate from one table to another. He carried a large pad and was drawing caricatures of various guests, who congratulated him for sketching them so accurately. He seemed such an unthreatening presence, with his handsome, angelic face and thin, frail body. Toral made his way to the head table, and positioned himself next to the guest of honor.

Obregón smiled approvingly as the artist displayed a sketch he had made of him. And then, as the president-elect glanced across the table and was about to make a comment to one of his followers, Toral whipped out the pistol from his jacket and fired five shots into Obregón's head. Killed instantly, Obregón fell facedown on the table and then slumped to the floor.

In a fury, bodyguards and guests rushed forward to tear the assassin to pieces. Toral, seemingly in a trance, offered no resistance as the blows and curses rained upon him. A congressman had the presence of mind to scream at Obregón's security chief not to allow Toral to be killed since he might be part of a wider conspiracy. The security chief, firing shots in the air, managed to rescue the assassin, whose face had already been beaten almost beyond recognition.

As word of the assassination spread, paranoia overwhelmed Obregón's followers. Many of them were prepared to believe that Calles himself was behind the murder in order to maintain himself in power. Obregón's corpse was taken to his residence, and when Calles arrived there to pay his respects, he was confronted by an ugly mob mixing accusations with demands for justice.

From Obregón's home, Calles and his entourage drove to police headquarters where they found the atmosphere just as strained. Obregón's bodyguards, fearing Toral might be killed by the police to prevent him from revealing official collusion in the assassination, were demanding to share custody of the prisoner.

Calles himself interrogated Toral. The prisoner refused to reveal his identity and had no papers on him. He did, however, respond to Calles's question on why he had killed Obregón and not Calles. In order to destroy a building, said Toral, it was best to attack its foundations. "We feel that you are the house and General Obregón the foundation," he added.[33] Calles then left police headquarters and announced to the press that the assassin was a Catholic terrorist linked to the clergy. But Obregón's men remained suspicious and told journalists that they did not yet share Calles's opinion.

Despite being tortured by the police throughout the night of July 17, Toral refused to disclose anything about himself. However, police detectives, investigating a laundry mark on the prisoner's clothes, traced his residence and family within hours. The next day, the investigators brought Toral's wife and parents to police headquarters. Faced with the threat that they would be tortured too, Toral made a full confession, and that evening personally led the police to Madre Conchita's house. Opening her door, the nun was startled by Toral's bloody, battered face. He begged forgiveness for implicating her. Madre Conchita warmly embraced him, and then insisted to the police that only Toral and she were involved in killing Obregón.

The Church condemned the assassination and denied any complicity by the ecclesiastic leadership. "We point out in defense of the rest of the religious Mexicans," said a bishop, "that it is public knowledge that [Madre Conchita's] brain is not normal and that, unfortunately, in her family there have been some mental abnormalities."[34]

In November 1928, Toral and Madre Conchita were brought to trial. The small courtroom in San Angel, not far from the restaurant where the murder had taken place, was jammed with Obregón partisans who cursed Toral as a Judas and screamed "Death to the whore Concha!" Toral was sentenced to death and executed. Madre Conchita also received the death sentence, but it was later commuted to twenty years in prison.

After the assassination of Obregón, Calles lost his stomach for continued confrontation with the Church. Using the mediation of American Catholic officials and U.S. Ambassador Dwight Morrow, he reached an agreement with the Mexican high clergy that led to an end of the Cristero revolt and the Church strike in 1929. Publicly, Calles appeared to have conceded little to his clerical opponents—allowing exiled clergymen to return and permitting religious instruction within the confines of churches. More important, though, were his private assurances that the government would cease its ideological campaign against Catholics.

A new conservatism pervaded the entire spectrum of government policies. After 1928, agrarian reform slowed. The education drive carried out by zealous public school teachers in rural areas was curtailed. Trade union recruitment slowed, and labor leaders abandoned their left-wing rhetoric. The tiny Mexican Communist Party became a target of the government. Its leaders were jailed, and its members and sympathizers were beaten by Fascist thugs, called Gold Shirts, who claimed allegiance to Calles.

The rumors linking him to Obregón's assassination forced Calles to renounce any further presidential ambitions after his term ended in later 1928, but he continued to control politics during the next five years. So obvious was his power that he was popularly known as the "Jefe Máximo," or "Supreme Chief." He handpicked the three presidents who followed him into office, and when one of them, Pascual Ortíz Rubio, had the temerity to question the Jefe Máximo's policies, Calles arranged his ouster without even bothering to inform him. Ortíz Rubio had to read the newspapers to discover that he was no longer president. He then made it official by meekly signing a resignation letter drafted by a Calles aide.

Calles's lasting contribution to Mexico was his creation of a broadly based political party. The Partido Nacional Revolucionario (PNR) absorbed factions of left, center, and right, military officers, bureaucrats, peasant, and trade union officials, and virtually every elected politician. Though its name changed, the party is the same one that has governed the country since Calles organized it in 1929.

The conservative shift in politics did not favor Diego Rivera. His revolutionary art no longer pleased Calles. Government funding and public walls for his murals vanished. But these setbacks in Mexico City barely fazed Rivera. Already eyeing a new, grander stage for his blend of political drama and art, he moved to the United States in 1930 and remained there for most of the next three years.

In Detroit, Henry Ford offered Rivera the courtyard of the Institute of Art to paint murals on industry and labor. The $25,000 commission was far greater than any he had received in Mexico—and Rivera was delighted with the irony of being invited to the hub of capitalist industry by a Yankee "robber baron" to evoke his vision of private enterprise. The twenty-seven panels Rivera completed in 1933 celebrate the working spirit of laborers, scientists, and technicians as they hammer steel, brandish welding torches, pirouette along assembly lines, hover over test tubes, and sketch automobile designs. As in the Mexican murals, tedium is overcome by the choreography of labor, and men emerge as masters of their enormous machines, which are more sensuous than intimidating under Rivera's brush.

Although the Detroit panels were almost devoid of the strident ideology of his Mexican paintings, Rivera could not resist a few controversial touches. In one panel, a physician is vaccinating a child in the arms of a nurse crowned by a halo. In the foreground, a horse, a cow, and a sheep—the sources of serum—add to the illusion of a modern-day nativity scene in which science has replaced religion. Another panel shows a huge cash register shaped like a church. And a third section of the mural seems to update the temptation of St. Anthony: a factory manager wrestles with his accounts despite the constant distraction of the exposed legs of the women working around him.

Rivera's political reputation had preceded him. Even before the murals were completed, Detroit's conservatives, led by clergymen, were attacking Ford for commissioning works by a "well-known Communist." And when the paintings were unveiled, these critics excoriated the panels, which were alleged to be sacrilegious. Trade unionists, however, supported Rivera, and provided a daily cordon of protection for the museum and its murals. The controversy helped make Diego's paintings the most attended cultural event in Depression-ridden Detroit. Two years later, officials of the art institute wrote to Rivera that his murals were still attracting enormous crowds.

From Detroit, the artist traveled in 1933 to New York, where he had been commissioned by the Rockefellers to paint a mural in the lobby of the new RCA Building. The theme selected by John D. Rockefeller, Jr., and his son, Nelson, was "Man at the Crossroads Looking with Hope and High Vision to the Choosing of a New and Better Future." But Rivera was determined to create a far more politically radical work than his Detroit panels. In his view, the worsening

Depression precluded a cheerful painting. He was also under attack from his former Communist comrades. They had expelled him from the party in 1929 after an arcane doctrinal dispute, and were roasting him in their publications for accepting a commission from those paragons of capitalist evil, the Rockefellers, whom he had caricatured in his Mexican frescoes. Diego, who still considered himself a Communist, resolved to paint a Marxist-Leninist mural. And ideology aside, he relished the prospect of another stirring public dispute over his art.

Rivera made no attempt to disguise most of his plans for the RCA project. Nelson Rockefeller approved the sketches submitted by the artist, who reproduced them with few changes in his mural. At the center of the fresco was a blond worker in overalls. The apprehension of his face belied his firm grip on an instrument panel, which unleashed the powers of modern science and technology to probe the microscopic world and survey the heavens. On one side of the mural was the legacy of injustice: police routing jobless protestors outside a nightclub crowded with affluent revelers; and in the panel above, a battlefield scene of bayonet-wielding troops with gas masks. The other side of the fresco was Rivera's evocation of a hopeful future: the proletariat marching under red flags in a May Day demonstration; and beneath this panel, women competing in an athletic meet.

Rivera sensed the uneasiness of his patrons, but he was saving his most controversial thrust. In the sketches that the Rockefellers approved, he had depicted a labor leader with a blurred face grasping the outstretched hands of a soldier, peasant, and worker. This was to become the central scene in the side of the mural devoted to a hopeful future vision for humanity. But as the sketch evolved into fresco, the anonymous labor leader took on the unmistakable features of Lenin.

Nelson Rockefeller warned Rivera that his mural would be unacceptable unless the portrait of Lenin was changed back into "the face of some unknown man."[35] When Diego refused, security guards removed the scaffold, covered the fresco with canvas, and barred Rivera and his assistants from the premises. The affair quickly escalated into the biggest cause célèbre in New York's art history. Trade unionists, artists, leftists, and other Rivera sympathizers gathered at the entrance of the RCA Building for a huge demonstration, which was broken up by the police. Diego's half-fanciful account of this clash reads like war correspondence:

> [The] streets surrounding the center were patrolled by mounted policemen and the upper air was filled with the roar of planes flying

around the skyscraper. . . . The proletariat reacted rapidly. Half an hour after we had evacuated the fort, a demonstration composed of the most belligerent section of the city's workers arrived before the scene of battle. At once the mounted police made a show of their heroic and incomparable prowess, charging upon the demonstrators and injuring the back of a seven-year-old girl with a brutal blow of a club. Thus was won the glorious victory of Capital against the portrait of Lenin in the Battle of Rockefeller Center. . . ."[36]

For weeks, demonstrators continued to picket the RCA Building demanding the mural be preserved and unveiled. Anti-Communist hecklers called for its destruction. The Rockefellers waited several months until the street protests dwindled before imposing their own solution. Then at midnight on February 9, 1934, workers under their orders entered the building and smashed the fresco into fragments.

The grotesque climax did nothing to diminish the personal tour de force of Rivera's American sojourn. No artist had ever stirred such violent public passions in the United States. He had demonstrated that New York was as vulnerable as Mexico City to his explosive concoction of art and revolutionary antics. The controversy of Rockefeller Center also elevated Rivera's fortunes at home. He was already back in Mexico City when news of the mural's destruction was disclosed, and the Mexican government quickly responded by inviting him to reproduce the fresco on the walls of the Bellas Artes Palace in the capital.

Rivera returned to Mexico City at a time when Calles's dictatorial powers were beginning to wane. The Supreme Chief of Mexican politics was under intense criticism from his former revolutionary colleagues for his conservatism, the rampant corruption in government and the labor movement, and an economic stagnation that was in large measure attributable to the worldwide Depression. Calles was also beset by an assortment of maladies, and spent much of his time interned in clinics or recuperating in his several rural estates. The three puppets he had chosen to serve out the slain Obregón's presidential term had been ineffectual. With a new election scheduled in 1934, Calles desperately needed a candidate who could appear to be independent, relatively honest, and somewhat left-wing, yet still amenable to his manipulation. He settled upon Lázaro Cárdenas, his protégé since the Revolution, and thus inadvertently chose the man

who would become Mexico's greatest president in the twentieth
century.

Cárdenas was born in 1895 in a small town of Michoacán, west of
Mexico City. His father was a weaver, a purveyor of folk medicine,
and eventually, owner of a billiard hall. Under his father's prodding,
Cárdenas completed the six years of elementary schooling that was
available in his community, and then apprenticed himself to the local
tax collector. When the Revolution erupted, Cárdenas, still a teenager,
enlisted in a rebel band, and soon led a force of several hundred men.
Chased out of Michoacán by Huerta's federal troops, he and his followers made their way north to Sonora, where they joined Obregón
and Calles, his leading general. Cárdenas's battlefield successes and
quiet demeanor made him a favorite of Calles, who promoted him to
the rank of general shortly after his twenty-first birthday. After the
Revolution, he remained in the army and campaigned against the De
la Huerta rebels and the Cristeros. Calles rewarded this prolonged
military service by supporting Cárdenas's bid to become governor of
Michoacán in 1928.

Cárdenas became a formidable governor. While the Calles administration in the late 1920s was miring itself in conservatism, he pressed
ahead with agrarian reform and the construction of rural schools in
Michoacán. He opened his offices to peasants, urban workers, and
plaintiffs of every sort, and traveled constantly across the state, even
into the most remote backwaters, to meet with his poorest constituents.
By 1933, Cárdenas had a national reputation as a hardworking,
independent-minded, and left-wing politician. Calles, however, still
remembered him as the youthful general who never crossed him, and
believed Cárdenas's sense of loyalty to him outweighed his other
attributes.

But almost as soon as he made him his presidential candidate, Calles
began to have doubts about Cárdenas. Although his election was a
foregone conclusion, Cárdenas insisted on campaigning all over Mexico. His numerous speeches promising to revive agrarian reform, improve industrial wages, and increase social expenditures seemed to
rebuke the policies of the Calles era.

A few days after his election in July 1934, Cárdenas paid a courtesy
visit to Calles at his plantation south of Mexico City. Calles was
determined to use the occasion to demonstrate that he remained the
Supreme Chief of Mexican politics. He was in the midst of a card
game with several generals when an aide informed him of the president-
elect's arrival. "Tell him to wait until I finish playing," barked Calles

in a voice loud enough to carry into the next room where Cárdenas was seated.[37] The president-elect also noticed that the army commanders declined to leave the card table to welcome him. When Calles finally emerged to greet Cárdenas, he joked that as usual his generals had let him win his poker hand.

Cárdenas seemed intimidated by this none too subtle message, and in the first six months of his presidency he avoided a confrontation with Calles. But he continued to enhance the populist image he had created for himself during the electoral campaign. He moved the presidential living quarters from Chapultepec Castle to a less ostentatious residence called "Los Pinos." He eliminated much of the ceremony surrounding the chief executive's office, including the sartorial honor guards and the bugle rolls that announced the president's arrival. European cuisine and wines disappeared at official functions. And guests emulated the president by donning business suits instead of tuxedos.

What most characterized the Cárdenas style, however, was his insatiable desire for personal contact with the poor. Businessmen, politicians, and diplomats learned to endure long waits in the president's crowded antechamber at the National Palace while Cárdenas closeted himself for hours with delegations of peasants and workers, listening to their complaints, and promising solutions within the restraints of the budget and political realities. A man of medium height and build, with a dark mestizo face, and stiff bearing—partly the result of a battlefield wound—he held his emotions rigidly in check and spoke so softly that his audiences strained to listen.

He was the first Mexican president to attempt to narrow the political chasm between Mexico City and the provinces. He spent one third of his term away from the capital, logging 55,000 miles by airplane, train, car, coastal vessel, and horse. Journalists who accompanied him evoked a country unknown to most residents of Mexico City: virgin coasts and sparsely settled deserts; thick forests and labyrinthine mountain ranges; hot valleys of tobacco and sugar plantations; fertile plateaus where corn and wheat abounded; and a mosaic of Indian languages and customs that had survived four centuries of turmoil.

The constant travels and meetings with his humblest constituents broadened Cárdenas's popular following but did little to convince political observers that he was a strong, decisive figure. Meanwhile, Calles, already peeved by the president's failure to consult him more regularly, waited to exploit any signs that Cárdenas was turning out to be a weak leader.

The first significant test of Cárdenas's mettle was a flare-up of the religious issue, magnified all the more because it took place in Mexico City. Cárdenas, who had little sympathy for the Church, brought into his cabinet Tomás Garrido Canabal, the most rabidly anti-Catholic politician in the country. As governor of Tabasco, Garrido had at one point rid his state of virtually all priests, and even encouraged his constituents to destroy the clay figurines of saints that most of them kept in household altars. A collector of fine livestock, he dubbed his prized steed bull "the Bishop" and his largest donkey "the Pope." The two animals invariably led the parades that inaugurated state agricultural fairs, and Garrido's men would exhort spectators to take off their hats to the Pope and the Bishop when they sauntered by.[38]

In the Cárdenas cabinet, Garrido served as secretary of agriculture, but devoted himself to provoking the Catholic faithful. He staffed his offices with hundreds of left-wing thugs, called Red Shirts, most of them from Tabasco where they were notorious for harassing churchgoers. In Mexico City, Garrido organized "Red Saturday Nights" at the Bellas Artes Palace where speakers denounced the Church. On one occasion, an orator defied God to prove his existence by bringing down the building's dome on the audience. Conservative newspapers gleefully reported that scores of Red Shirts fled the premises as soon as the speaker issued his challenge.[39]

On Sunday morning, December 30, 1934—not long after Cárdenas assumed office—Garrido's Red Shirts converged outside a church in Coyoacán, a suburb of the capital, and began intimidating worshippers. In the melee that erupted, the Red Shirts gunned down several Catholics and then took refuge in the police station, which was soon besieged by an angry mob. One Red Shirt, who arrived late at the scene apparently ignorant of what had transpired, was captured by the mob and beaten to death. On New Year's Day, twenty thousand Catholics marched in the funeral procession for the slain Coyoacán worshippers, while Garrido and his Red Shirts held a raucous burial ceremony for their own martyr.

Cárdenas sent a wreath to the Red Shirt's funeral, but also irritated Garrido by ordering the arrest of forty of his followers implicated in the Coyoacán shootings. In the months that followed, the governors of a dozen states, interpreting the president's ambiguous gestures as a signal to renew the antireligious crusade, closed churches and expelled priests from their territories. Cárdenas finally removed Garrido from his cabinet in 1935, but it took another year before tensions eased between Church and government.

Calles, who had experienced his own worst political moments in battles with Catholic militants, was delighted to watch from the sidelines as Cárdenas suffered through the controversy. He chose instead to attack the president on the other great issue of his first six months in office—his handling of labor unrest. Calles had turned against the trade union movement as he grew more conservative. In 1928, his last year as president, he allowed only seven strikes. And in the next five years, the number of labor strikes was rarely higher.

Cárdenas, however, was anxious to rebuild the trade unions in return for their political backing. He made no effort to contain labor unrest, and by the end of 1935, an unprecedented 642 strikes shook the country. Calles spoke out when a strike by telephone workers in May 1935 disrupted communications in the capital for a month and slashed the profits of the Mexican Telephone and Telegraph Company (a subsidiary of AT&T) in which Calles had a large block of shares.[40] He denounced the labor unrest for "risking the economic life of the nation," and a few weeks later warned that unless the strikes ended, Cárdenas might suffer the same fate as Pascual Ortíz Rubio—the puppet president whom Calles had driven from office.

Calles seemed to be holding the winning poker hand. Business associations and leading politicians from the government party, the PNR, sent congratulatory messages to the Supreme Chief. And the silence of the army generals was widely interpreted as a sign of their continuing acquiescence to Calles.

But Cárdenas was waiting for his own support to manifest itself. The trade unions backed him with stinging denunciations of Calles. Younger military officers, who had been discreetly courted by Cárdenas with pay raises and increased benefits during the preceding months, also signaled their loyalty to the president.

When Cárdenas finally responded on June 13, 1935, to Calles's remarks, he was anything but contrite. The strikes, he said, were creating a necessary balance between laborers and their employers. He had no desire to hobble private capital, he added, but it was common knowledge that most industrial workers were not even being paid the minimum wage. "I have complete confidence [that] the labor and peasant organizations of the country . . . will know how to behave themselves with the self-control and patriotism which are demanded by the legitimate interest which they represent," declared the president, hinting that he expected the labor strife to subside shortly.[41]

A few days later, Cárdenas forced the resignation of Calles sympathizers among his ministers and formed a new cabinet staffed ex-

clusively with his own supporters. Calles had to concede that his bluff
had been called. He issued a brief statement announcing his retirement
from politics and promised to confine himself to his haciendas. Less
than a year later, however, he was implicated in a conspiracy involving
several generals to overthrow the government. Rousted out of bed at
midnight in his hacienda near Cuernavaca by loyal army officers,
Calles was told that Cárdenas had ordered him into exile. With a copy
of Hitler's *Mein Kampf* under his arm, the former Supreme Chief
boarded a plane to Texas on April 11, 1936. "I was expelled from
Mexico for fighting Communism," he told reporters in Dallas. "God
willing, things will change, and I will be able to return to my country."[42]

With Calles's departure, Cárdenas accelerated his reform program.
The charges of communism leveled against him had no substance,
but he did come closer than any other president to matching the
Revolution's rhetoric with action. By the end of his term in 1940, he
had distributed almost fifty million acres to the peasants—more than
twice as much as his predecessors. Almost one third of Mexicans
received land. Most of the property was not parceled out to individuals,
but rather to communal "ejidos." The ejido system—with roots in
both pre-Conquest Mexico and medieval Spain—allowed families to
make use of lands that were held in common by their village. Decades
later, the ejidos became unproductive and unprofitable. But during
the Cárdenas era, they were a social and political success, ending the
agricultural monopoly exercised by the traditional hacienda system.

Cárdenas also displaced the CROM with the more militant Confederation of Mexican Workers (CTM, by its acronym). Born in 1936,
the CTM was initially less corrupt than the CROM, and its membership surpassed one million laborers within two years. Although the
union did manage to push through wage increases, most workers'
incomes still lagged behind the levels specified by government surveys
as adequate to support their families. The undisputed leader of the
CTM was Vicente Lombardo Toledano, an avowed Marxist. But the
trade union movement remained firmly under state control, and in
fact became a wing of the government party, or the Partido Revolucionario Mexicano (PRM), as it was renamed by Cárdenas.

Cárdenas had used the trade unions to consolidate his position
against Calles. He continued to rely on the labor movement to reduce
the power of private industry and to thrust the government into the
role of arbiter for Mexico's economy.[43] Nowhere was this strategy more

evident than in his confrontation with foreign oil companies—the most dramatic episode of his presidency.

As recently as 1925, Mexico produced one fourth of the world's oil, or 165,514,700 barrels a year, almost all of it owned by American and European petroleum companies. But a decade later, annual output had fallen to only forty million barrels. The foreign companies had uncovered important reserves elsewhere in the world, and had no need to develop new deposits in Mexico as older wells dried up. With the sharp plunge in government revenues from oil exports, Cárdenas was probably considering the nationalization of the petroleum industry, but it was an altercation between the foreign companies and their Mexican laborers that set the stage for a government takeover of the oil fields.

Demanding higher wages and better working conditions, the oil laborers went on strike in 1936. Cárdenas ordered an industrial arbitration board to settle the dispute. The board ruled that workers' wages be increased by a third and that their pensions and other benefits be improved. The companies appealed to the Mexican Supreme Court, but then refused to obey the court's decision upholding the ruling of the arbitration board.

The arrogance of the foreign oil companies grew out of their experience in Mexico over the previous two decades. They had survived the Revolution without serious losses. They had humbled the great Obregón in 1923, forcing him to guarantee their operations in exchange for diplomatic recognition of his government by Washington. They were left alone by Calles even at the peak of his radicalism. And thus, they were confident that in the end Cárdenas would also buckle, and engineer a solution in their favor.

But Cárdenas instead accused the foreign companies of flouting Mexican sovereignty by their refusal to obey the Supreme Court, and he signed a decree nationalizing their holdings on March 18, 1938. Such outright expropriation was unprecedented in Latin America. It aroused a nationalistic fervor that had not been witnessed since the American occupation of Veracruz in 1913. Huge celebrations erupted in Mexico City. Even the Church hierarchy backed the nationalizations. And when the foreign oil companies cut off export markets for Mexico's petroleum, further reducing government revenues, Mexicans rich and poor responded generously to fundraising drives to keep the state solvent. "Politicians whose sources of illicit income Cárdenas cut off pledged their aid," wrote one historian of the era. "Wealthy exrevolutionists wrote fat checks. Government workers turned back part of their pay. Fashionable women stripped off earrings, necklaces, even wedding rings and threw them into collection urns. Peasant women straggled into the city carrying live chickens as their donation."[44]

With three invasions of Mexico by U.S. troops in the previous eighty years, the possibility of another American military intervention seemed real. In Washington, the oil lobby was pressing for a show of force against the "Communist" regime in Mexico. But President Franklin D. Roosevelt, who had initiated his "Good Neighbor" policy, was inclined toward a negotiated settlement. The issue was turned over to a binational commission, which ruled that the American oil companies should receive $24 million plus interest payments for the loss of their Mexican properties—a far lower total than they were demanding.

The oil expropriations marked the climax of Cárdenas's nationalist and left-wing programs. In the last two years of his term, agrarian reform and social expenditures slowed, and labor militancy declined. The president made an effort to assuage wealthy Mexicans who had all but halted their investments out of fear that the country was tilting too far left. Economic setbacks also dictated a more cautious policy. For all the euphoria over the expropriations, the state-run company that now monopolized the petroleum industry had failed to increase production, and oil revenues continued to decline. National debt rose and the peso was devalued. Inflation staggered the country, with food prices alone rising by 50 percent between 1935 and 1940.

But this lackluster performance did not dim the accomplishments of the earlier Cárdenas years. Before Cárdenas, the Mexican Revolution might have been dismissed as a pointless sacrificial orgy. His presidency at least lent substance to claims that the upheaval had led to reforms benefiting millions of the rural and urban poor.

The nationalism and populism fostered by the Cárdenas government had an enormous impact on Mexico City society and culture. Radio, the phenomenon of the age, enraptured its listeners with dramas and comedies about peasants and recent rural migrants to the city. Broadcasts were dominated by music from the countryside—boisterous mariachi bands, "corridos" or ballads celebrating revolutionaries and bandit-rebels, and plaintive songs of unrequited love and tragic romantic triangles. Cantínflas began a stage and movie career that earned him a reputation as the Mexican Chaplin. Like the Hollywood master, he was riotously effective at deflating the rich and pompous, the staid and conventional. Any recent poor migrant to the metropolis could recognize in Cantínflas the disheveled, unshaven hustler whose schemes for enrichment go comically awry. And for middle-class Mexicans, he was the clown of the dispossessed, who allowed them to transform their apprehensions of the burgeoning urban poor into laughter. Novels about the Revolution and its aftermath in the countryside found a wider audience in the 1930s. But they could not match the drawing power of the nascent movie industry. The most popular cinema evoked an idealized version of rural life: honest, hardworking peasants rescued from land-grabbing hacienda owners by an upright *charro* (cowboy), who sings as well as he shoots. For many residents of the capital, the country portrayed in these folk films became "the real Mexico."

Given the richness and variety of Mexico City's culture during the 1930s, Diego Rivera and the other great muralists could not possibly equal their impact of a decade earlier. Radio and cinema were far better able to convey revolutionary ideals to a broader public. And so, despite the fact that Rivera returned to a Mexico that had become more congenial to his own political notions, he found it impossible to regain the unique stature he had enjoyed in the 1920s. He completed the reproduction of his shattered RCA fresco. He also did further work on the panels he had begun years before in the National Palace, and tried to ingratiate himself with Cárdenas by including in these murals some scathing portraits of Calles and his cronies. But during the remainder of Cárdenas's term, the government offered him no more wall space.

Forced to turn to the private art market which he abhorred, Rivera became known as a painter of the wealthy. He turned out a succession of oils, watercolors, and drawings for the growing bourgeoisie that was moving into new neighborhoods north and south of Chapultepec Park. In 1936, he was finally given the opportunity to paint another mural— but for a private patron. Alberto Pani, a former Obregón official turned wealthy entrepreneur, was building the Hotel Reforma to accommodate American tourists, and he commissioned Rivera to paint four panels in the banquet hall.

Murals always awoke in Rivera an urge to be controversial, and he surrendered to the old temptation once again. Since the space he was offered in the hotel was to be used for dancing and dining, he painted a series of carnivalesque scenes. On one end of the hall were panels evoking idyllic folk festivals from the Mexican past. The other paintings were more savage caricatures: American scholars strut about with donkey ears; other Yankees grab sacks of gold and leave behind a plucked chicken that represents Mexico; a Mexican general with a piggish face waltzes with Miss Mexico and reaches a hand behind her to rob fruit from a basket strapped to her back; and Mexican politicians, clearly recognizable despite their animal masks, gorge themselves and join the dancing.

Pani did not complain while the murals were in progress, but as soon as Rivera completed his work, the hotel owner and his two brothers personally took up brushes to alter the offensive scenes. Rivera rushed over to the hotel and brandished two pistols under Pani's nose. The police were called, and Diego was arrested. In a courtroom crowded with Rivera aficionados, a judge awarded him 2,000 pesos in damages for the defacement of his art and allowed him to restore the paintings. But Pani had the panels removed, and eventually sold them to a private dealer, who warehoused them for more than twenty years.

The Hotel Reforma incident revived Rivera's appetite for political theatrics, but there were few venues open to him. Artists had been chased off center stage by the Calles and Cárdenas governments. And in 1929, Diego had been expelled from the small Communist party, still the vehicle for most artists who wished to affirm their revolutionary commitment. Rivera decided to return to the political arena as a supporter of Leon Trotsky. In Europe and the United States, the conflict between Stalinists and Trotskyites may have riveted intellectuals, but it was no more than a sideshow for the public at large. In Mexico City, where intellectual circles were far more reduced, the dispute had even less political impact—that is, until Rivera joined the battle.

At first, Rivera confined himself to debates with his former muralist colleague, David Alfaro Siqueiros, a vociferous Stalinist who returned from the Spanish Civil War with the rank of colonel in the Republican Army. In public assemblies and magazine articles, they excoriated each other's ideological position, and argued over which of them had morally debased himself more by accepting private art commissions. But the dispute took a quantum leap when Rivera invited Trostky to Mexico City in 1936.

Hounded by Stalin and expelled from the Soviet Union, Trotsky had spent seven years in exile, first in Turkey, then France, and finally Norway, always unable to gain permanent asylum because his hosts feared reprisals from the Russians. Upon hearing that the Norwegian government was about to order Trotsky to pack his bags once again, Rivera appealed to Cárdenas. The president was intent upon establishing Mexico City as an asylum for foreign political refugees. He had already invited thousands of Spanish Republicans fleeing Franco's forces. And he granted Rivera's request with the understanding that Trotsky not meddle in Mexican politics.

Trotsky and his wife arrived in the port of Tampico in January 1937, and traveled in a well-guarded train provided for them by Cárdenas to Mexico City, where they were welcomed by Rivera and as many Trotskyites as he could round up. Diego offered them a house he owned in Coyoacán, and the Trotskys lived there for the next three years without paying rent.

Rivera was overjoyed to be in the political limelight once again. His name was on the front pages of the Mexico City newspapers every day, and foreign correspondents arrived from all over the world to interview his house guest. The publicity became a windfall between April and September 1937, when Trotsky convened an international commission at the Coyoacán residence to examine evidence used against him at the Moscow trials that led to his expulsion from the Communist party. The American philosopher and educator John Dewey served as chairman of the commission, which included six Americans, two Germans, a Frenchman, an Italian, and a Mexican. After numerous sessions, the commission pronounced Trotsky innocent of all charges leveled against him, and issued instead a lengthy indictment of Stalin for perverting the lofty aims of the Russian Revolution.

For about a year, Rivera and Trotsky got along famously. Only Rivera seemed capable of distracting the older, cerebral revolutionary from his disciplined schedule of book and letter writing. They would spend hours discussing politics, or riding horses in the nearby countryside. Despite his formal, Old World demeanor, Trotsky was intensely interested in the opposite sex, and he was delighted to learn that around Rivera there were always opportunities to meet women.

Eventually, however, the friendship between artist and revolutionary cooled. Rivera tired of Trotsky's rigidly ideological approach to politics. And according to Rivera's biographer, Diego "drove the old man into such a towering rage by outrageous inventions of 'facts' and doctrines in the field of politics that the argument ended with Trotsky and his wife packing their bags and leaving their goods on the sidewalk until they could find a new refuge."[45] The break may also have been hastened by Rivera's discovery that his wife, Frida Kahlo, had a brief affair with Trotsky.

Relations between Rivera and Trotsky deteriorated to the point that the artist came under suspicion when the first attempt was made against the Russian's life. Early in the morning of May 23, 1940, twenty armed men led by Siqueiros, the fervent Stalinist, surrounded Trotsky's residence and disarmed his police bodyguards. They then machine-gunned the house for almost twenty minutes. Trotsky and his wife survived the barrage by huddling under their bed. The assassins fled with a hostage, Robert Shelton Harte, a young American disciple of Trotsky who was a house guest, and they left his bullet-riddled corpse in a patch of woods on the city's outskirts. Siqueiros was jailed, but later released because no witnesses would testify against him. Rivera was also briefly under police investigation.

The second attempt against Trotsky's life took place a few months later. Ramón Mercader, a Spanish Stalinist who passed himself off as a Belgian Trotskyite with the alias of Jacque Mornard, used his affair with Trotsky's secretary to gain access to the old man. On the afternoon of August 20, 1940, Mercader-Mornard arrived at the Trotsky home with a request that the Russian read over some political tracts he was preparing to publish. As Trotsky leaned over the material, Mercader-Mornard struck him on the head with an ice ax. Trotsky bellowed in pain, struggled to his feet, and managed to fight off the assassin, who fled the house and was later arrested. Trotsky lapsed into a coma and died at midnight, August 21.

At the time of the assassination, Rivera was in San Francisco working on a mural. He joined in the denunciations of Stalin for the killing of Trotsky. But years later, as part of the price for being readmitted into the Mexican Communist Party, Diego claimed rather improbably that he had lured Trotsky to Mexico City in 1937 with the intention all along of having him assassinated.

By his very presence in the country, Trotsky had helped Mexico to maintain its revolutionary aura. But at the time of his murder, the Cárdenas presidency was nearing an end. In the conservative political era that was getting under way, economic development would take precedence over ideological struggle.

SEVENTEEN

THE
GOLDEN DECADES

The transformation of Mexico City during the thirty years that followed the Cárdenas presidency was in its own way as dramatic as the changes wrought by the Porfiriato at the turn of the century. These were the golden decades (1940–70) when the Mexican capital enjoyed world renown as a pulsating, modern metropolis that managed to preserve rich remnants of its colonial and Indian heritage. Factories, commerce, and service jobs sucked in hordes of rural migrants who swelled Mexico City's population from 1.5 million inhabitants in 1940 to 8.5 million in 1970. The prodigious expansion of urban slums would become a much-lamented phenomenon in later years. But, meanwhile, the city's eclectic architecture elicited the admiration of residents and foreign visitors alike. Glass and steel skyscrapers vaulted up along Avenida Juárez, on the edge of the colonial core, and along Paseo de la Reforma, the Parisian-style boulevard lined with trees, gardens, and heroic statuary. Porfirian mansions still graced the side streets of these arteries, and an older Spanish legacy of palaces and churches survived around the Zócalo.

Many of the wealthier residents retreated to the semirustic neighborhoods on the southern outskirts, where industrial fumes and traffic exhaust had not yet poisoned the crystalline skies nor obscured the snow-wreathed volcanoes and purple mountains encircling the Valley of Mexico. In communities like San Angel, Mixcoac, and Coyoacán, nostalgia could be indulged without forgoing the amenities of modern life. Asphalt dissolved into cobblestone streets where the clip-clop of horseshoes and the squeak of peddlers' carts were as familiar as the rumble of automobile tires. As they had for centuries, artisans and vendors, each with their patented musical ditty or whistle, hawked their wares from house to house: woolen rugs and serapes with brightly woven Indian designs; parrots, parakeets, and exotic songbirds; honeycakes, preserves, and gelatins; charcoal-singed corn-on-the-cob sprinkled with cheese; slices of succulent jícama and radish smeared with lemon juice and chile. Sprawled over leafy plazas a short walk from most residences were the Indian marketplaces offering a cornucopia of vegetables, fruit, flowers, tortillas hot off the griddle, live chickens, and freshly laid eggs. Wandering past the stalls, servants and housewives feigned indifference to the chorus of entreaties and rhymed sales pitches. After an inevitable haggle over prices and a seemingly pained surrender by the vendors, the purchases were stuffed into dyed hemp bags and the shoppers continued on their way.

These vestiges of a slower-paced traditional life, however, were being overwhelmed by Americanization. Luxury hotels catered to armies of visitors from the United States who were first drawn south in large numbers during World War II when Europe became inaccessible. The tourist trade emerged as the largest industry in Mexico, and spearheaded an American economic and cultural invasion. Ciudad Satélite, on the northwest outskirts of Mexico City, grew into a huge, middle-class suburb of cookie-mold houses patterned after postwar communities in southern California and Long Island. Throughout the capital, fast-food outlets serving hamburgers, hot dogs, and pizza vied with taco stands. Baseball crowds rivaled those at bullfights and soccer matches. Supermarkets stocked their shelves with Kellogg's Rice Krispies, Campbell's soups, Coca-Cola, Heinz catsup, and Van Camp's Boston baked beans. Neon signs flashed a lexicon of U.S. corporate names: Ford, General Motors, Chrysler, Zenith, General Electric. Blue jeans became the uniform of the younger generation, rich and poor. A hit parade of rock 'n' roll competed with Mexican "corridos" on the radio. *Ozzie and Harriet*, *Leave It to Beaver*, *Mannix*, *Dragnet*, *The Lone Ranger*, and many other American television series had a loyal following. Hollywood relegated Mexican films to the more decrepit movie houses. Even Christmas became Americanized: in department stores, adoring youngsters sat on the lap of a red-coated, white-bearded Santa Claus; at home, stockings were hung over the fireplace, and gifts were piled under fir trees festooned with pulsing lights and cotton snow fluffs. Only the more tradition-bound families continued to stage posadas, the Nativity processions commemorating the nine-day journey by Mary and Joseph from Nazareth to Bethlehem.

This architectural, economic, and cultural metamorphosis of Mex-

ico City was presaged by an eventful shift in political power. The
provincial revolutionary generals ceded the government to an urban
middle-class elite. Flocking to the metropolis for law degrees which
became their passports into the high bureaucracy, this new generation
of politicians made the city their permanent residence, the locus of
their entire careers, and the prism that refracted their vision of the rest
of the country.

Revolutionary slogans continued to exalt the ideals of land for the
rural dispossessed, living wages for the proletariat, and a determinant
voice for the state in economic affairs. But the rhetoric masked a
growing alliance between politicians and Mexico City–based entrepreneurs, who shared the conviction that wealth had to be amassed
before it could be distributed. And so, Mexico embarked on an era of
unbalanced growth. Explosive urbanization, particularly in Mexico
City, contrasted with the torpor of the countryside. Rampant consum-
erism among the more affluent classes co-existed with social neglect
of the disadvantaged majority. Corruption greased the wheels of commerce and industry, but also diverted potential benefits for the poor.
Peasant and labor organizations were effectively excluded from poli-
cymaking and the upper rungs of politics. Still, the nation did achieve
a record enviable in Latin America for prolonged economic expansion
under a stable, civilian government with a democratic facade.

The dominant political personality of this era, the man credited
most for its dynamism and its excesses, was Miguel Alemán, president
of Mexico from 1946 to 1952. Historians have tended to portray Cárdenas and Alemán as mirror opposites on the ideological spectrum.
Cárdenas is identified with the populist, left-wing aspirations of the
postrevolutionary years: the distribution of wealth in land and higher
wages; the establishment of the state's hegemony over natural resources
and basic industries; the desire to court the poorest Mexicans; the
attempt to make the seat of political authority in Mexico City seem
less distant and aloof to the provinces. Alemán, on the other hand, is
commonly viewed as the force behind more conservative trends: the
encouragement of private investment, both domestic and foreign; the
repression of trade union militance; a hell-bent drive toward industrialization; the reemergence of a cosmopolitan, upper-crust Mexico
City society, unafraid to flaunt its riches.

Photographs have etched the contrasts between the two men deep
in the memory of Mexicans who lived through both epochs. For every
shot of the rumpled, stocky Cárdenas riding his horse through mountain trails to a forgotten Indian village, there is a picture of the svelte

Alemán effortlessly driving a golf ball past a gallery of well-heeled admirers.

Here is Cárdenas surrounded by peasants, clad in sandals and rough-cotton tunics and pants, thanking him for their land titles; a grim-faced Cárdenas announcing to a raucous crowd assembled below his presidential balcony that he has expropriated the American oil companies; a patient Cárdenas hearing out a delegation of factory workers in his office.

While Alemán often recorded his reunions with the rural and urban poor, his pictorial archives also include vignettes that would have been inconceivable for a Mexican chief of state just a decade before: a beaming Alemán flanked by socialites in mink stoles at the Bellas Artes Palace; a proud Alemán welcoming the first president of the United States (Harry S Truman) to set foot in Mexico City; a jocular Alemán inaugurating a luxury hotel in Acapulco.

What separated the two men as much as ideology was their very different paths to the presidency. Cárdenas, like Obregón and Calles before him, was a member of the old revolutionary guard. His battle-field exploits catapulted him into politics. Alemán, the first president not to have participated in the Revolution, established a tradition of civilian hegemony. He created a blueprint for success in politics that is still followed by aspirants to the upper reaches of government.

Alemán was born in the small Veracuz town of Sayula in 1903. His father, a storeowner, joined the Madero uprising against Porfirio Díaz, later fought against Victoriano Huerta, and eventually achieved the rank of brigadier general. He was rewarded by the new revolutionary government with loans and commercial opportunities that enabled him to become a businessman of considerable magnitude in Veracruz, and he was elected to Congress. Like many of his fellow officers who had achieved at least middle-class status, the father did not view the military as an honorable career for his son. The revolutionary colonels and generals were not heir to a praetorian tradition. On the contrary, they had shattered the regular armed forces of the Porfiriato and forged a new army from a motley assortment of rebel bands. Once the fighting ended, many of them resigned their commissions to pursue politics and business careers. They prodded their sons to enroll at the National University in Mexico City and take up liberal professions that could launch them into politics.

Even before the Revolution came to a close, Alemán's father sent him to the capital to study at the National Preparatory School, the usual prerequisite for admission into the National University. The youthful Alemán founded *Eureka*, a journal extolling the Revolution, which was distributed by the Obregón government to secondary schools throughout the country. He then went on to the National University's Law School, which was emerging in the 1920s as a greenhouse of future politicians.

Many of Alemán's professors were high-level politicians who taught at the university on a part-time basis. They often arranged government jobs for their student protégés after graduation, and integrated them into their political factions. Neophyte politicians who rose through the bureaucracy surrounded themselves with former classmates, promoting them and, in return, expecting their support.

The friendships Alemán made at the Law School proved crucial almost as soon as he graduated. His father, back in Veracruz, joined a minor armed revolt against the Calles government in 1928, and committed suicide rather than surrender to the federal troops. Only the intercession of Miguel Alemán's university professors—some of them ranking bureaucrats in the Calles administration—prevented him from being blacklisted from government employment. Alemán then erased any doubts about his loyalty by agreeing in 1933 to head a pro-Calles political club in Veracruz, where his late father was still revered.

The young Alemán displayed an uncanny ability—a hallmark of his entire life—to further his political and business interests simultaneously. He accepted a succession of government posts in agriculture, justice, and labor affairs, while maintaining a private law practice and managing the Veracruz business ventures he inherited from his father. He also demonstrated talents for swimming with the prevailing ideological currents and making himself indispensable to more senior politicians.

Alemán came to the attention of President Cárdenas by securing compensation for miners and industrial workers in numerous legal cases. With Cárdenas's support, he became senator, and then governor of Veracruz in 1936 after the incumbent was assassinated. Despite his later reputation as one of the most conservative political leaders in postrevolutionary Mexico, Alemán was known as a liberal governor. He set aside half of his state's budget for public education, encouraged land reform, and raised workers' salaries. In 1938, he backed Cárdenas's decision to expropriate oil companies in Veracruz, and organized a national conference of governors in support of the measure. He further endeared himself to Cárdenas a few months later when the president faced the only serious military insurrection of his term in office—an uprising by General Saturnino Cedillo in the northern state of San

Luís Potosí. Alemán again united his fellow governors behind Cárdenas, and helped convince wavering army commanders to remain loyal to the government. Virtually abandoned by his military colleagues, Cedillo was defeated and killed.

Because of Alemán's reputation as an indefatigable organizer, he became campaign manager for the next president, General Manuel Avila Camacho. Elected in 1940, Avila Camacho made Alemán his interior secretary and cabinet chief.

Among the least radical of the rebel commanders to emerge from the 1910–20 upheaval, Avila Camacho smothered the inflammatory issues left over from the early postrevolutionary years. Asked about his attitude toward the Church, he dismayed left-wing ideologues by declaring during his electoral campaign: "I am a believer." And with that simple statement, he brought an end to official anticlericalism. Once in power, he replaced the Marxist leader of the labor movement, Vicente Lombardo Toledano, with the far more conservative Fidel Velázquez, and ordered the Education Ministry to purge socialist ideology from the public school curriculum. Land distribution lost its priority and fell to one fourth the level of the Cárdenas years. Instead, the Avila Camacho government concentrated on promoting private industry. The sudden interest in factories was not so much a new strategy for economic development as it was a response to the outbreak of World War II, which forced Mexico to rely on domestic industry to replace imported goods.

The war also brought about dramatically improved ties with the United States. The oil dispute of the Cárdenas years was forgotten as American military plants eagerly purchased all the minerals and other raw materials Mexico could provide. Mexican workers were hired to harvest crops across the border because the American labor force had been depleted by the draft. And as further evidence of the close wartime relationship, Mexico assigned a small air force contingent—Squadron 201—to General Douglas MacArthur's command in the Philippines in early 1945.

The Avila Camacho presidency marked the transition toward civilian leadership of the nation. Army commanders shared the public consensus that their dominant role in politics was no longer necessary. And after Avila Camacho removed the military as an official wing of the government party in 1940, it was clear that his successor would be a civilian. As the strong man of the cabinet, Alemán became the official candidate in the 1946 election.

Once installed in the presidency, Alemán reduced the military's political influence even further: the armed forces' share of the government budget fell below 10 percent, the lowest level since the Porfiriato. (It continued to decline to 2 percent by the 1960s, a niggling proportion in comparison to other Latin American countries.) Army commanders began to be rotated frequently to prevent them from establishing local power bases. Their units were given limited supplies of fuel and ammunition to inhibit any prospect of rebellion. Military life, with its low salaries, benefits, and social status, became so unappealing that the officer corps was able to attract only lower-middle-class Mexicans.

Under Alemán, the National University—and especially its law school—replaced the old revolutionary guard as the most important recruiter of high-level politicians and bureaucrats. Of the 107 men who held senior posts in Alemán's government, 40 were in the law school at the same time he was, either as students or professors.[1] A partial list of his former schoolmates included his attorney general, the mayor of Mexico City, several governors, the director general of the National Railroads, and the cabinet secretaries for treasury, public works, industry and commerce, labor, and public education.

Alemán's use of his university contacts as a reservoir of political talent established a pattern for subsequent administrations. Between 1946 and 1971, two thirds of all cabinet ministers were graduates of UNAM, as the National University was popularly called.[2] Most of them were from the Law School, which became known as the "cradle of politicians." Students may have been born in states as far-flung as Veracruz, Chihuahua, and Yucatán, but arriving in Mexico City as teenagers to enroll first at the National Preparatory and then UNAM, they came to exhibit a startling degree of homogeneity. As one political scientist recently wrote: "The majority of successful politicians have lived in the same place during their adolescent years, have gone to school in the same environment, have had many of the same teachers, have read the same textbooks, have had many of the same friends, and have simultaneously begun their careers in the same agencies. . . ."[3]

Once a politician embarked on his career, he was loathe to quit Mexico City for fear of distancing himself from the center of power. Even if he hoped to become a deputy, senator, or governor, he spent most of his time campaigning in the public ministries of the capital instead of courting his local constituents. The process was vividly described by Braulio Maldonado, a former classmate of Alemán's who rose to governor of his native state of Baja California:

The aspiring candidate must join the battle early; he must mobilize friends and political influence; he must become a determined "antesalero" [a person who frequents the antechambers of government officials] and wait hour after hour, day after day, in the hopes of being received by functionaries, high and low. He must suffer countless humiliations; yet he must smile and be courteous to everybody from the doorman to the boss. . . .

The aspirant must also ensure that his name figure in the "political dossier" alongside the other hopefuls, with ample and precise information about his background: where he was born, who his parents were, whether they were revolutionaries or reactionaries, what party faction he joined, who his political godfathers are and what interest they have taken in his "case." Such information comes to resemble nothing so much as a criminal record in a police file. . . .

It is also of utmost importance that the president know the aspirant, or be his friend or relative. . . . By the time [the aspirant] is about to be designated as candidate, he has given the shirt off his back, he has made promises of all sorts, and lost all dignity. He has been mercilessly importuned by hundreds of politicians, labor bosses, peasant leaders and mercenary journalists. He has had to portray himself as a "revolutionary" without peer. He has already committed himself to disburse the public budget, even his own salary, before beginning his term of office.

Only after suffering through this calvary does the aspirant receive the president's blessing. From then on, things become exceedingly easy, for the battle has been won, and victory secured in the government antechambers. Now the trade unions, the peasant organization, and the party declare him the Official Candidate, and he becomes the man of the hour, a person of talent, of impeccable honesty and revolutionary merit.[4]

Alemán was astute enough to realize that a government of lawyers drawn from his alma mater and promoted by the rituals described above had even less of an appearance of political legitimacy than the old military guard who had ruled by virtue of their battlefield victories during the Revolution. And so, with great fanfare, he reorganized the official party in 1946, and renamed it the Institutional Revolutionary Party, or PRI, as it is still known today. In theory, the PRI was supposed to provide a voice for peasant, worker, and middle-class sectors in formulating broad government policy; ensuring that the Revolution's ideals survived; and designating official candidates for all elective posts ranging from the presidency down to municipal councils. The overwhelming organizational and financial resources of the PRI—besides its popular support—guaranteed that a majority of its candidates would be elected over politicians from the small opposition parties. And the government could always resort to fraud in districts where political opponents showed unexpected strength at the polls.

The PRI was also useful in providing a large pool of loyalists to staff lower levels of the government bureaucracy. It could be counted upon to stage demonstrations by peasants or workers in support of agrarian and industrial labor programs unveiled by the government. The party's local political bosses, called caciques, were adept at turning out the vote on election day, and were rewarded with sinecures in municipal councils, state legislatures, and, occasionally, the National Congress.

But the PRI did not alter the elitist, authoritarian nature of the government. Although the bulk of the party's membership was rural and working class, no labor or peasant leader was ever appointed to the cabinet. Alemán picked his candidates for governor without consulting the PRI, despite frequent protests from local leaders of the party. Most of the highest-ranking government officials never bothered to toil in party politics, nor did they waste their time serving on the PRI's executive committee. Without an effective voice in selecting the men who ran the government, the PRI was helpless to influence administration policies.

This was certainly the case in economic affairs. For advice in this domain, Alemán looked outside the PRI to the business community. Commercial farming, industry, and mining ventures had led the surge in national income between 1940 and 1945, and Alemán was determined to nourish the boom by encouraging the private sector.

In agriculture, he favored larger, private holdings over the communally owned ejidos so strongly pushed during the Cárdenas era. Credit policies benefited wealthier farmers. Most of the major irrigation projects were located in the less populous northwest states where large commercial farms held sway. The maximum legal limits on the size of private farms were raised, and violations of these limits were overlooked. Productivity, rather than land reform, was the focus of the government's agrarian program.

Industry, however, was the star performer of the Alemán years. Entrepreneurs, through their newly created chambers of industry, lobbied hard to convince government officials and the press that only the rapid creation of factories could conquer underdevelopment. Foreign investment was once again courted, but it was not allowed to reach the proportions of Don Porfirio's heyday when money from abroad accounted for as much as two thirds of all investment. Instead, Alemán fostered a more nationalist economic policy under which 90 percent of investment was financed by domestic savings.[5] To nurture new industries under Mexican ownership, the government erected barriers against foreign goods that threatened to compete with local manufactures. Tax rates on business were among the lowest in Latin America. And new enterprises were granted exemptions from payments of major taxes for periods of up to ten years.

More controversial was Alemán's support for business demands that labor costs be held down. He manipulated the Mexican labor movement with a skill honed by long personal involvement in its affairs. In the dozen years before he reached the presidency, Alemán built strong ties with conservative trade union leaders. As interior minister under Avila Camacho, he compiled extensive dossiers on all labor officials. And as president, he backed more moderate and amenable trade unionists in their struggle against radicals. His government steered labor disputes into the courts where judges were encouraged to hand down decisions that favored management. And he did not hesitate to use the police and army to break strikes.

But the crucial factor in keeping industrial wages low was the availability of an almost bottomless reservoir of rural laborers. Huge numbers of landless, unemployed workers moved to the cities, especially the capital. Their mood was more despairing than militant, and they readily accepted factory, construction, and service jobs at incomes that often fell short of the minimum levels decreed by law.

With low labor costs, a light tax burden, and protection against foreign competitors, businesses quickly accumulated profits and invested them in new industrial ventures. Almost all these new factories were encouraged to locate in large urban centers, particularly Mexico City. Since the days of the Porfiriato, the capital had emerged as the most favorable site for industrial development. By the 1940s, the city boasted the largest consumer market in the country, the most numerous labor force, the biggest concentration of entrepreneurial and managerial talent, the banks and government agencies upon which business depended for credit and permits, and an advanced urban infrastructure—public transportation, sewage facilities, running water, electricity, and telephone networks. Between the Alemán era and the mid-1960s, this infrastructure was vastly improved by government programs that funneled five times as much money for public works into Mexico City as the total spent in all other municipalities combined. During the Alemán years, the capital was also the hub of a national transportation network that had been modernized by new airports, a refurbishing of the railway system, and a fourfold extension of asphalted highways.

In making Mexico City such a magnet for industry, Alemán pioneered a model of economic growth that was soon emulated throughout the developing world. By placing most new factories in a few large cities, a backward, rural nation was able to accelerate its economic expansion. From 1946 through 1970, Mexico's gross domestic product grew by more than 6 percent annually, propelled by Mexico City's own economy that was rising by 12 percent a year. The capital's performance as an economic locomotive was even more impressive when measured in industrial terms. In 1940, there were 56,314 factories in the country, of which 4,920 were located in Mexico City. By 1950, near the end of Alemán's term, the capital had 12,704 of the 63,544 factories nationwide. And in 1970, Mexico City—with more than one fourth of the country's 118,993 factories—accounted for almost half the nation's industrial output.[6]

While the so-called Mexican economic miracle launched by the Alemán government clearly benefited industrialists and businessmen more than any other group, relations between politicians and these entrepreneurs were often marked by ambiguity, tension, even animosity. There were some glaring exceptions to this pattern, beginning with Alemán himself. He and several of his cabinet ministers were linked socially and as business partners to a coterie of wealthy industrialists and financiers during and after their years in government. But by and large, the Alemán era failed to end the separation between political and economic elites that had grown out of the Revolution.

Politicians usually advanced their early careers with the aid of fathers or older relatives who distinguished themselves in the Revolution and achieved at least middle-class status in its aftermath. Entrepreneurs emerged most frequently from affluent or middle-class families who were sympathizers of the Porfiriato, staunch Catholics, or descendants of foreigners—that is, groups who were viewed with suspicion by the postrevolutionary political class. Given their family backgrounds, entrepreneurs were reluctant or unable to enter politics. If they studied at UNAM, they steered clear of the Law School because of its reputation as an incubator of politicians. And after graduation, few businessmen sought or were offered even temporary employment in the government bureaucracy or in state-run companies.

Politicians found the entrepreneurial world just as inbred and ex-
clusionary. Before the 1960s, family businesses dominated private enterprise in Mexico.[7] An outsider could rarely aspire to rise above the
status of employee. Even if he were motivated primarily by financial
gain, a young man lucky enough to have the right political connections
was more likely to seek personal enrichment in government than to
consider a career as an executive in a private enterprise that offered
him no hope of ownership or a top management position. And besides,
there was nothing to prevent a successful politician from amassing
illicit wealth in office and embarking on a business venture of his own
after retiring from public service.

Corruption was ingrained in government since colonial times. Officials of the Spanish Crown stole Indian tribute and became partners
of miners, merchants, and hacienda owners whose activities they were
supposed to regulate. In the nineteenth century, Santa Anna and his
associates plundered the public treasury and even ceded national territory for personal gain. During the Porfiriato, the high bureaucracy
was staffed by wealthy Mexicans who believed the principal aim of
government was to ensure their further accumulation of riches. And
after the Revolution, the military victors considered graft their spoils
of war.

What made corruption such a notable phenomenon beginning in
the Alemán era was the fact that the economic boom created so many
more opportunities for the enrichment of government officials. They
extracted huge bribes from private contractors who were hired to help
erect irrigation dams, hydroelectric projects, airports, harbors, and
public buildings. Illicit payments were imposed on businessmen seeking to import raw materials and manufactured goods. A host of public
officials had to be suborned before ground could be broken for the
new apartment buildings and factories that mushroomed across Mexico
City, and further bribes were needed to hold off government inspectors
while construction proceeded. Kickbacks on government purchases of
goods and services from the private sector lined the pockets of many
officials. And the least imaginative offenders embezzled public money
under their control.

Years after leaving office, Ramón Beteta, the treasury secretary under
Alemán, complained about the public perception that politicians simply stole the funds entrusted to them. While not denying that self-
enrichment in government was commonplace, he insisted that it was
accomplished by more sophisticated means:

I don't understand how people can believe that the treasury minister or the president of the republic or some other minister can say on any given day: "Send one-half of those budget appropriations to my home. . . ."

There is no need to do it in that way, which is, let's say, the crassest means of taking advantage [of one's position]. There are so many ways by which a functionary can enrich himself, and they are not strictly speaking illegal, although they are not ethical either. Consider, for example, the public official who knows that a new highway is about to open, or knows the contractor who will build or supervise it. Together they can conspire to purchase, either directly or through intermediaries, the properties along this highway and thus make a killing. . . . A public official has innumerable ways of wringing advantages from his position without necessarily being corrupt in the sense of holding his hand out for money. . . .[8]

In Mexico City, real estate transactions were among the most lucrative sources of income for politicians. According to Beteta, President Alemán made a fortune by purchasing a large hacienda on the northwestern outskirts of the capital and then subdividing it into residential plots when that zone became Ciudad Satélite, the most populous middle-class suburb.[9] This was a case involving private land. More frequently, however, politicians who speculated in real estate were dealing with communal property. In the three decades that followed Alemán's election, about half of Mexico City's expansion occurred through the expropriation of ejidos, whose peasants were compensated at prices far below market value. The ejidos were supposedly protected by agrarian reform legislation. But influential politicians could circumvent the law and make enormous profits by delivering these parcels to developers who then blanketed them with factories and residences for middle- and upper-class Mexicans.[10]

Rapid economic growth was not the only reason for the rising levels of official corruption. The political system that evolved under Alemán was also to blame. Politicians and their entourages began their careers early, advanced through a quick succession of bureaucratic posts, and then were forced into retirement by middle age in order to make way for a younger elite. Successful politicians felt under intense pressure to take advantage of their brief tenures in the upper bureaucracy to enrich themselves and their protégés as quickly as possible. Their attitude, in the words of one scholar, was "you better take what you can while you're there."[11]

Corruption fueled the contempt that most entrepreneurs harbored for politicians. According to surveys taken among businessmen in the 1950s and 1960s, only army generals and trade union leaders were regarded with less esteem than politicians.[12] Not that businessmen were virtuous in their own conduct: they engaged in tax evasion on a massive scale; paid off union representatives in their factories to ensure labor peace; and bribed public officials to skirt regulations, acquire import licenses, and obtain contracts with government agencies. But entrepreneurs convinced themselves that these practices were rooted in official corruption and that businesses were forced to follow suit.

Viewing themselves as the most productive members of society, businessmen felt that their contributions to the Mexican economic miracle did not receive enough official acclaim. They considered the government's revolutionary rhetoric—extolling the rural and urban poor—as an exercise in hypocrisy. Politicians, on the other hand, saw little reason for businessmen to complain about a government that protected them from foreign competitors, allowed them to keep the bulk of their profits, and held the labor force at bay.

The low opinion which entrepreneurs had of politicians spilled over into their private lives. Both elites may have lived cheek-to-jowl in posh Mexico City neighborhoods like Lómas de Chapultepec, Coyoacán, and San Angel, but they rarely mingled socially. For businessmen, the politicians were parvenus. Their palatial homes were often the largest residences on the block. Outer walls and iron fences only partially obscured their garish architectural hodgepodge of Spanish colonial and postwar European styles, with facades displaying brick or volcanic stone on one side and a stucco finish on the other. Politicians always seemed to own too many cars, and their chauffeurs looked suspiciously like bodyguards. Their daughters were said to be vulgar, loud, and overdressed. They spent too much money and still left too many bills unpaid. They were alleged to treat their servants despotically, and to be so uncouth that they flirted with the mariachis hired for their parties. Politicians' sons were reputed to be even worse. They bragged about their fathers' influence and wealth. And they drag-raced their hotrods and motorcycles around the block, defying neighbors to press complaints. Modest behavior and social graces were certainly not the norm among the offspring of the entrepreneurial elite either, but their parents remained convinced that children of politicians were incomparably more boorish. Not surprisingly, there were few instances of intermarriage between sons and daughters of politicians and entrepreneurs.

While marital alliances and close friendships were rare among ranking public officials and businessmen, the two groups did find a common social ground when it came to their choice of mistresses. They both favored women from the world of entertainment—singers, stage actresses, television vedettes, film starlets, and beauty contestants. The affluent macho, always inclined to distinguish between the virtuous mother of his children and the impure object of his sexual desires, clearly placed women entertainers in the second category. They were seductive, often charismatic, petulant, less encumbered by conventional morality. Their celebrity status was an added incentive for men who craved the admiration and envy of their peers. And there was an assumption among politicians and businessmen that careers in entertainment had prepared these women for relationships that traded sexual favors for economic rewards and professional advancement.

A mistress of the elite was often on a career path that had its parallels in the political world. Usually from a middle-class background, she got started young, displayed loyalty while a relationship lasted, ensured that each successive attachment was with a higher-ranking person than the previous one, and prepared for early retirement by amassing a fortune. By these criteria, the most successful courtesan of the era was Irma Serrano, whose memoirs detailed her meteoric rise as a mistress to politicians, tycoons, and eventually a president.[13]

Her parents owned a moderate-sized hacienda carved out of the jungles in the southern state of Chiapas, near the Guatemala border. As a child, Irma chafed at the monotony of farm tasks, school lessons taught by rote, dreary catechism classes and Sunday Mass, social gatherings that dissolved in drunken stupor, and the constant discomfort of the chastity belt that she and other provincial girls were forced to wear (*Knotted Underwear* is the title of her autobiography). In her case, rebellion was streaked with violence. As an eight-year-old, she clubbed her stepfather in his sleep—retaliating for a spanking earlier that day—and sent him to the hospital with a fractured skull. Irritated at being forced to attend a church service, she set her mother's braids on fire with a votary candle. And when the priest and his acolytes appeared at her home to exorcise the devil who had evidently taken possession of her soul, she drove them off with bites, kicks, punches, and curses, the likes of which they had never heard.

The opportunity to escape Chiapas came unexpectedly in 1955 when Irma was barely a teenager. Her cousin was chosen to represent the state in a beauty contest held in Acapulco, and Irma was allowed to accompany her to the beach resort. The contest was little more than an excuse for Mexico City movie moguls, entrepreneurs, and politicians to recruit naive, eager teenagers as mistresses and party girls. The highlight of the social rounds was a visit by all the contestants to the sumptuous offices of Fernando Casas Alemán, a distant relative and crony of former President Alemán. He had been Alemán's professor in the UNAM Law School, then rose to governor and senator for Veracruz, and was appointed mayor of Mexico City by Alemán. He was Alemán's personal choice to succeed him as president, but was rejected because of charges that he had been excessively corrupt in running the capital. As a consolation, Casas Alemán had been named ambassador to Italy and Greece by the new president, Adolfo Ruíz Cortines (1952–58). Though he accepted the appointments, he spent most of his time commuting between Mexico City and Acapulco, where he was reputed to be Alemán's business associate in lucrative tourism ventures.

Tall, rugged, and handsome, with wavy hair streaked gray, the fifty-year-old Casas Alemán had a wife and children in Mexico City. He evidently preferred very young mistresses. When the beauty contestants crowded into his Acapulco office, he ignored them, and fixed his gaze on the thirteen-year-old Irma, who resembled a prepubescent Rita Hayworth in her blue, pleated dress and ankle socks.

"He sat me on his lap and I smelled his strong perfume," recalled Irma. "I was enchanted to be next to such an important man, so sure of himself. . . . He hugged me and I felt the warmth of his hands."[14]

Irma and her cousin returned to Chiapas. Casas Alemán followed a few weeks later, allegedly to promote tourism in that backward state and renew his contacts with local politicians. "When it came time for his departure, instead of saying goodbye, he simply led me into his plane and would not allow me to get off," Irma wrote. "I guess you could say he kidnapped me. But I was overjoyed to abandon a world that did not attract me in the least for a man I adored."[15]

The affair lasted four years, with Irma playing the multiple roles of Pygmalion, nymphette, and sophisticate. Casas Alemán installed her in a mansion on the southern outskirts of Mexico City, provided a chauffeured car, and enrolled her in literature courses at UNAM.

On occasion, he treated her like a child. At bedtime, she recounted, he delighted in pretending she was Little Red Riding Hood and he the seductive Big Bad Wolf. On her birthdays, he dressed her in bobbysox and took her to Alameda Park to buy dozens of balloons. At other times, though, he demanded a sophistication beyond her years. Clad in haute-couture gowns, she accompanied Casas Alemán through a whirl of cocktails and banquets for film producers, industrial tycoons, and politicians. Having tutored her in politics and business, he expected her to report back in detail any snatches of information she collected during these social occasions.

When Casas Alemán commissioned Diego Rivera to paint a nude portrait of fifteen-year-old Irma, it was a sure sign that she had been elevated to the status of elite courtesan. In old age, Diego was as contradictory as ever. He had become the society artist par excellence, the darling of upper-class matrons who lavished him daily with cakes, expensive clothing accessories, and other gifts in the hope that he would agree to paint them or their family members. But Diego had also returned to the Stalinist fold with the fervor of a born-again Christian. When his wife, Frida Kahlo, died in 1954, he stirred a political scandal by having her bier draped with the Communist party banner instead of the Mexican flag as she lay in state during a government-sponsored ceremony at the Bellas Artes Palace.

Even his own fatal illness became an occasion for propaganda. Suffering from cancer of the penis, he journeyed to Moscow for radiation therapy, and pronounced himself cured thanks to the miracles of Soviet medicine. But the symptoms of the disease reappeared (he would die of cancer in 1957, just short of his seventy-first birthday), and added some bizarre twists to his already offbeat conversational repertoire, particularly on the subject of sex. Irma recalled that as she posed for her portrait, he would gently run his hand over her body and comment: "A woman's skin is the most extraordinary thing. The world should be ruled by women because men are so filthy, hairy and physically repulsive. . . . In reality, I am like a woman: my bone structure and broad hips are quite feminine. I have always hoped to weld myself to someone who considered me as much a woman as herself."[16]

When she related these conversations to Fernando Casas Alemán, he was outraged. Declaring Rivera an unhealthy influence on a young girl, he ordered the artist to speedily finish the portrait. "That was when Fernando began to cloister me," Irma complained. "He wanted me to remain pure so that he could continue to mold me as he pleased."[17] The headstrong traits of her childhood surfaced again. She felt "asphyxiated" by the schedule he so carefully orchestrated for her—university studies, music lessons, hunting trips, long sojourns in Acapulco. And she was infuriated by his occasional infidelities. Surprising him in a tryst, she cut off the braids of her rival and slashed Casas Alemán's face so severely that "it took him a month to fully recuperate."[18] There was a brief reconciliation between Irma and Fernando. But the longstanding affair finally ended because, according to her, she declined to bear his child and arranged for an abortion without previously informing him.

Irma maintained that she refused to touch the fortune Fernando left her as a parting gift, and instead launched herself with some effort as a singer. During her years as Casas Alemán's mistress, she had met many people in the entertainment industry, and was given opportunities to audition. She appeared on television variety shows with Cuco Sánchez, a famous singer of Mexican ballads and country music. He complained that her voice was abominable, and refused to perform alongside her. Viewers mailed her "a stream of protests and insults." But it was the opinion of her producer that mattered most, and for reasons left unclear in her memoirs, he made her the lead singer in thirty-two broadcasts. A recording contract followed, and then tours throughout Mexico.

Though her voice improved, it was probably her stage personality that transformed Irma Serrano into one of the most popular female singers in Mexico during the early 1960s. Her lithe figure had become voluptuous, and she showed it off with short, tight-fitting "country girl" outfits. Her brawls with rival entertainers became grist for gossip columns. Audiences were drawn to Irma's performances by her feistiness. They relished her acid exchanges with rowdy spectators and the irascibility she displayed toward her mariachi accompanists. On one notorious occasion when she felt a musician was not playing his best, she interrupted her performance, walked across the stage, and splintered his guitar on his head—"It hung around his neck like a tie," she recalled. *La Tigresa* ("The Tigress"), her adoring fans began to call her. And she made up her eyes with grotesquely large strokes to project a wildcat aura.

Not every man could be expected to find her seductive, perhaps least of all Gustavo Díaz Ordaz, president of Mexico (1964–70) and a politician noted for his austere image. Irma had first met him at one of the many parties she attended with Casas Alemán. He was short, dark-skinned, buck-toothed, with eyes distorted by thick-lensed glasses. His rigid posture, conservatively tailored suit, and the strained formality of his speech gave him the air of a martinet. And although Irma found him intelligent and blessed with a sense of humor, she was frank to admit that she initially dismissed him as "Mr. Nobody."

But the next time she encountered him he was the government party's presidential candidate, and the mantle of power had miraculously transformed him into an Adonis. By chance, his limousine pulled up next to hers at a traffic light during a downpour. Smiles were exchanged across closed car windows. Díaz Ordaz gestured with his hands that they have a cup of coffee. And Irma signaled that he follow her back to her Lómas residence. "I discovered that he was a lot more attractive than I remembered him," she wrote. Besides, she admitted, "from that rainy day onwards, my ambitions knew no bounds: I was going to conquer the most powerful man in the country."[19]

Being the mistress of the chief of state had certain inconveniences. Díaz Ordaz cherished his reputation for personal propriety. Of all the postrevolutionary presidents, he was considered the most Catholic, even breaking tradition by accompanying his daughter to her religious wedding ceremony. (He did, however, uphold the principle of Church-State separation by waiting in the courtyard while the nuptials were performed.) The newspapers, always so accommodating to a reigning president, never published articles that might have suggested he had time for any affairs but those of state. There were no photographs of Díaz Ordaz waltzing across a ballroom or teeing off at a golf tournament. The message of his publicity shots was that being president was all business and no fun—just ribbon-cutting ceremonies, unsmiling speeches, working reunions with ministers and regional politicians, formal presentation of credentials by new ambassadors.

"With this type of lover," lamented Irma, "one doesn't enjoy the privilege of going to a movie or theater hanging from his arm. I considered myself lucky to get him to watch television with me. Mostly, we would just climb into bed and take advantage of the little time he had available."[20]

While the public at large was not privy to the relationship, it was not kept secret from those people who could advance Irma's career. She could pick from a lucrative assortment of television, film, stage, and recording contracts. The president's inner circle, so like a royal court, fawned over Irma as if they believed that one word from her could raise their standing with the monarch or place their political fortunes in jeopardy. Among these elite politicians, none treated her with more obsequiousness than Luís Echeverría Alvarez, secretary of interior and heir apparent to the president.

With malicious delight, she put his servility to the test at every opportunity. When Echeverría arrived at her residence to escort President Díaz Ordaz back to a government meeting, she would remark to her lover that his shoes were undone, knowing full well that Echeverría would hasten to tie the laces before Díaz Ordaz could bend down to do it himself. And when Echeverría brought her baskets of fresh fruit as a token of his esteem, she demanded that he peel her oranges. According to Irma, it was Echeverría's responsibility to ensure that she received the material rewards owed her as the president's mistress. But his efforts did not earn her gratitude.

"He obtained for me the permits to import . . . a variety of raw materials whose importation was normally prohibited," she wrote. "Since I have a good head for business, I knew how to take advantage of these favors and quickly turn a profit. My coffers overflowed with riches."[21]

Irma soon owned two clothing plants in Puebla, a textile loom in Toluca, a shoe factory, three brick-manufacturing facilities, and various holdings of choice real estate. She constructed a Mexico City mansion in a jarring architectural style that indulged both her Hollywood fantasies and a newfound nostalgia for the hacienda life she had left behind. The rustic veranda and balcony were framed by thick, castlelike turrets. A swimming pool was flanked by stone horses. And in the garden, amid the hibiscus and jacaranda trees, lurked statues of lecherous devils and pious saints. Her bedroom was cluttered with wild animal skins and furs, dolls, and statuettes of Disney characters. Posing in her circular bed with its canopy rigged like a glittering shell, she imagined herself as the goddess in Botticelli's *Birth of Venus*.

Her romance with President Díaz Ordaz lasted until 1969, some eighteen months short of the end of his term. According to Irma, his wife grew increasingly incensed by the affair, and gave orders that La Tigresa's film and record contracts be canceled. When Irma protested to Díaz Ordaz that her entertainment career was being sabotaged, he declined to interfere, claiming it was beneath the dignity of his office. In a rage, Irma plotted an elaborate revenge on the president and his wife.

On Mrs. Díaz Ordaz's birthday, Irma dressed herself in her "country girl" costume, hired a band of mariachis, and set off in the morning hours to the presidential residence at Los Pinos. A mariachi serenade was a traditional birthday offering, and the famous Tigresa had no trouble convincing the security guards that her services had been contracted by the president himself as a surprise for his wife. The mansion was already crowded with high-level politicians, their wives, and other notables when Irma planted herself beneath the main balcony and let loose a ribald song she had composed for the occasion:

> *I spent my time with a married man*
> *But that's all over now. . . .*
> *His wife caught on and gunned him down,*
> *How I escaped I'll never know.*
> *My friends ask me:*
> *"Irma, why did it come to pass?"*
> *Well, just when we were engaged in sin*
> *It was our bad luck the old lady barged in.*
> *I spent my time with a married man*
> *Because I loved him so,*
> *But that's all over now*
> *And I'll never let it happen again.*[22]

A pall of shocked silence descended over the guests. Summoning up what remained of his dignity, President Díaz Ordaz walked over to Irma. A forced smile broke across his face. Giving no hint of their involvement, he pretended only to recognize her as the famous entertainer who had come to pay homage to the First Lady.

> "Thank you very much, señora," he said to me. I punched him with all my might. His glasses went flying. The mariachis stopped playing. Not a sound for a few seconds, and then the "click, click" of the rifles and machine guns being readied to defend the monarch. The guards had me in their gunsights, and my hair stood on end. . . . [But Díaz Ordaz] signaled the soldiers not to shoot and to lower their weapons. He then put his hand over the eye which had been injured by my blow.[23]

Irma and her entourage were allowed to leave the residential grounds. Once outside the gate, the mariachis, who had not suspected her intent, were shaking in fright and anger. She assuaged them with a generous tip, then returned to her mansion on the southern outskirts of Mexico City to "await the funereal consequences."

She had prepared for her act of vengeance by liquidating most of her holdings and sending the money abroad, certain that if she survived, she would at the very least be forced into exile. But in the days and weeks that followed the incident, no police or soldiers appeared at her door.

Eventually, she was able to contact Díaz Ordaz, who asked only that she not publicize their affair or the dramatic confrontation. Her career as a political courtesan, of course, came to an end. Surprisingly, however, she continued to receive choice acting roles and record contracts. For a time, she was also romantically linked with several wealthy entrepreneurs, who were intrigued at the thought of having as a mistress the tigress who could not even be tamed by the president. They soon tired of her, and newspaper stories suggested that she was involved with gangsters. More than notoriety, it was middle age that finally pushed Irma off center stage. But looking back on her conquests, she struck a Mae West pose: "I've never had to ask anything from men— they just took it upon themselves to be so generous."[24]

In her more reflective moments, Irma Serrano congratulated herself for having displayed the good sense to move early in life to Mexico City. Like her, most members of her charmed circle of politicians and entrepreneurs had taken up residence in the metropolis while they were still young and found their fortunes there. Mexico City was a beacon for the ambitious poor as well. Between 1940 and 1970, more than four million people left their homes in the countryside to establish themselves in the capital. They were part of a massive migration that transformed Mexico into a nation with an urbanized majority as early as 1960.

The migrants were expelled from the countryside by prolonged droughts, the inability of ejidos to sustain families, the mechanization of private farms, and the rise of population resulting from health care improvements that cut mortality rates of infants and adults. Taken together, these factors led to a spectacular 74 percent increase in the number of landless agrarian workers between 1940 and 1960.[25]

Besides being pushed out of agriculture, the migrants were pulled toward Mexico City by the communications revolution—radio, films, and newspapers reaching into the most isolated rural zones—that evoked an advanced, remunerative, and exciting way of life as an alternative to the static poverty of the countryside. This vision was both a reality and a mirage. By 1960, the average family income in the capital exceeded by 185 percent the average for the nation as a whole.[26] Jobs were more plentiful, and there was a greater possibility for wives and children to supplement the earnings of male heads of households. The metropolis also offered more access to running water, electricity, cooking fuel, medical clinics, schools, movies, sports events, and other entertainment. But these advantages were vitiated by economic inequalities that were greater in Mexico City than in the rest of the country. In 1960, the wealthiest 10 percent of the capital's population received 40 percent of all income, with the top 3 percent alone claiming 21 percent of income. Between 1940 and 1950, the cost-of-living index for working-class families in Mexico City tripled, while real wages fell by as much as one third.[27]

The deficiencies of life in the metropolis began with housing. In the 1940s and 1950s, most migrants settled first in the old downtown tenements abandoned generations before by the middle class. Over a third of the population dwelled in these "vecindades," many of them constructed during the Porfiriato. In *The Children of Sánchez*, the classic study of Mexico City's poor during the 1950s, Oscar Lewis evoked a typical vecindad.[28] It was located in Tepito, a tough neighborhood a ten-minute walk north of the Zócalo. This warren of rutted streets and dusty alleys enclosed small factories and warehouses, tiny shops, public baths, run-down cinemas, overcrowded schools, foul-smelling saloons and pulquerías, wooden stands selling soups and tacos, and the open-air thieves' market where stolen and used goods could be purchased at a bargain. Once the lair of the underworld, Tepito was now populated mainly by artisans, vendors, factory laborers, unskilled workers, waiters, office clerks, messengers, and porters. The average income per capita was somewhat less than $20 a month.

Casa Grande, the vecindad described by Lewis, sprawled over an entire square block and housed seven hundred people in its two-story tenements. The two narrow entrances to the vecindad's alleyway were guarded by ceramic statues of the Virgin Mary and high gates which were locked at night. Residents returning home in the late evening had to pay the janitor a small toll to have the gates unlocked. In the daytime, Casa Grande's four courtyards were alive with dogs, cats, and caged songbirds, and an assortment of farm animals—turkeys, chickens, pigs, goats—that were slaughtered on festive occasions. Children played in these courtyards to avoid the heavily trafficked streets. Women used the public faucets to wash their laundry, which was then hung on clotheslines that crisscrossed the tenements. Vendors wandered through until the late afternoon when teenagers took charge of these enclosures for their soccer games. At night, the men played card games over upturned wooden boxes. And on Sunday evenings, the courtyards were reserved for outdoor dances.

A family of up to a dozen members crowded into each windowless one-room dwelling, aired only by the door opening onto a courtyard or the alleyway. Parents and favored children claimed the bed, while the rest spread themselves out on straw mats. With so many people in a single room, it was almost impossible to get a night of uninterrupted sleep. Someone was always returning late from work or play, and shuffling between prostrate bodies to prepare a meal before bedding down. The disruptions were repeated in the hours before dawn by those family members whose jobs began early. Odors were overpowering and inescapable: from the tiny toilet only half-closeted near the doorway; from the exposed kitchen area; from the animals in the courtyards. In these cramped dwellings, tempers flared and family violence easily erupted. Sexual tensions mounted, and incest between half brothers and sisters, fathers and stepdaughters was not uncommon. There was no privacy in Casa Grande, not even in its public bathhouse, where women were constantly being spied upon by male children and adults.

In the mid-1950s, monthly rent for a one-room apartment in Casa Grande was under $4. The basic diet consisted of coffee, tortillas, beans, and chile, supplemented by meat perhaps once a week. Recent arrivals from the countryside still used tortillas to scoop up their food; more "citified" residents relied on spoons. The possessions of the poor were meager. Besides the bed and mats, furniture consisted of a table and several wooden chairs, and a large dresser shared by the entire family. Clothes were worn a week or more before being laundered. Half the residents used gas stoves, serviced by tanks in the courtyard. The rest depended on kerosene ranges, or charcoal braziers—the mainstay of the peasant kitchen. A measure of Casa Grande's relative affluence compared to nearby tenements was the presence of modern luxury items: almost 80 percent of tenants had radios, more than half sported wristwatches, and 20 percent owned televisions.[29]

In this pre-subway era, the poor relied entirely on buses and trolleys for public transportation. Children and teenagers, eager to save fares, clung precariously to back bumpers and rear windows of these vehicles. Bicycles, the sole form of private transport, were the urban burros. Overloaded with packages reaching up to six feet high, they were balanced and pushed along by owners on foot. Their handlebars were decorated with multicolored plastic lace, perhaps even a foxtail, and fleece-lined pads were fitted on the crossbars to carry sweethearts or wives.

Free unions prevailed over legal marriages in the urban tenements, more so than in the countryside. From a man's perspective, there were greater opportunities in the metropolis to meet women, and less social and moral pressure to marry or remain attached to one spouse. Men also pleaded poverty to justify free unions.

"If one begins to examine what a marriage comes to, a poor man realizes he doesn't have enough money for a wedding," explained Manuel Sánchez, a resident of Casa Grande.

> Then he decides to live this way, without it, see? He just takes the woman, the way I did Paula. Besides, a poor man has nothing to leave his children so there is no need to protect them legally. If I had a million pesos, or a house, or a bank account or some material goods, I would have a civil marriage right away to legalize my children as my legitimate heirs. But people in my class have nothing. . . . And the majority of women here don't expect weddings; even they believe that the sweetheart leads a better life than the wife. What usually happens is that the woman goes with the man and it isn't until after a honeymoon of about six months that she begins to protest and wants him to marry her. But that is just the conventionalism of women. They want to tie a man up in chains![30]

None of the women interviewed by Lewis in Casa Grande agreed with these sentiments. They entered free unions as the only opportunity to escape the oppressive, tense atmosphere of a crowded one-room dwelling for a tenement space of their own. But they preferred a legal marriage, especially one sanctioned by the Church.

"To enter [a church] on my father's arm, in my white dress, and to go up to the altar with him, where the one who was going to give me his name would be waiting for me"—this was the fantasy of Manuel's sister, Consuelo, who nevertheless agreed to live out of wedlock.[31]

Despite the infrequency of church weddings and low attendance at Mass, religion played an essential role in the lives of the urban poor. They relied on the clergy mainly for baptisms and funerals—and even then, a corpse might not be entrusted to a priest until it had lain for a night suspended in a coffin above a tray of vinegar and onions which absorbed the evil spirit that had caused death. They prayed, or at least genuflected, daily before the tiny altar of their favorite saint or of the Virgin Mary in a corner of their apartment. If a family member failed to return home at the end of the day, they placed the image of St. Anthony upside down until the missing relative reappeared, or all hope was abandoned.

The religious fervor of Mexico City's poor was most evident in their pilgrimages. They journeyed once every few years to Chalma, some forty miles southwest of the capital, to pay homage to the "Black Lord," the Christ with the dark skin of an Indian. The final two or three miles to Chalma were taken on foot. The more penitent worshippers—and those grateful for miraculous responses to prayers offered in previous visits—insisted on completing this last segment on their knees, and arrived soiled and bloodied at the altar. The crowds were even larger at the Basílica for the Virgin of Guadalupe, on the northern outskirts of Mexico City. On the greatest occasion, December 12, close to a million of the poor gathered at this hillside altar to commemorate the day in 1531 when a tawny Virgin Mary appeared before a newly converted Indian. The faithful rarely paid heed to the priests offering up Mass or the sacraments. They wanted no intermediaries between themselves and this most Mexican Virgin Mary, the traditional protector of the poor. Passing before her statue, they brushed their hands on the folds of her robe, or rubbed their faces and bodies against the effigy. Those who had been wondrously cured left behind silver images of their healed parts—a leg, a hand, a heart. [32]

While the urban poor could on occasion reveal a boundless faith in religion, their expectations from the temporal world were set much lower. For them, the only thing miraculous about the Mexican economic miracle was finding employment that enabled them to survive. There were never enough jobs in industry, commerce, or services to meet their demands. And the huge pool of labor created by successive waves of new migrants to Mexico City ensured that salaries would remain inadequate.

Jesús Sánchez, the patriarch of the family profiled by Lewis, earned only a dollar a day after thirty years as a food buyer for a lower-middle-class restaurant. He was grateful that his boss allowed him to increase his salary by working seven days a week and all holidays. But he still had to supplement his income by selling lottery tickets and performing an assortment of odd jobs between his busiest hours at the restaurant. His sons, despite enjoying the elementary schooling he lacked, were unable to secure better employment. Their efforts to peddle second-hand wares in the street markets were foiled by the police, who demanded incessant bribes that amounted to confiscatory taxes. And their attempts to seek factory jobs were thwarted by corrupt union officials who demanded unaffordable and illegal payments for the union card that was often a prerequisite for industrial employment.

To become a union member was to join the working-class elite. By 1960, less than 12 percent of Mexico's peasants and urban laborers were enrolled in unions. The government, exercising control over organized labor, had no interest in fomenting a large trade union movement that might become a political rival or threaten economic growth by pressing for higher salaries. Thus, the vast majority of the poor had no organized means to make political or economic demands.

Well aware that there were limits beyond which their unions would not be allowed to grow, labor leaders were more beholden to the government than to their rank and file. The labor ministry could appoint or remove union chiefs, sanction or prohibit strikes, let stand or veto wage settlements. The sort of labor leader favored by the regime was pliable without seeming subservient, astute enough not to allow dissent in his union to become a nuisance that required government action, and deft at exaggerating the gains he negotiated for his rank and file.

Unions, management, government, and press collaborated in charades to impress upon the public that an independent, militant, yet responsible labor leadership was defending the working class without wrecking the nation's economic and political stability. The ritual began with a labor leader putting forth demands for salary raises and more fringe benefits. Management would claim that the demands were unreasonable. A brief strike might ensue with the discreet consent of the labor ministry. And after a settlement, newspapers would trumpet victory for the union. However, the fact that real wages tended to fall behind inflation throughout most of the 1940s and 1950s suggested that many of these victories were illusory.

The system encouraged corruption in the trade union movement. Labor leaders were secretly on the government payroll. They received kickbacks from management to forgo strikes or cut them short and to accept lower wage settlements for their rank and file. They also extracted bribes from workers in exchange for union membership. And they gained the loyalty of subordinates by sharing these proceeds and allowing them leeway to collect illicit payments on their own. Labor leaders also enforced their control over their unions by subverting laws aimed at protecting workers. For example, relying on legislation intended to achieve a union shop, they could expel dissidents from their ranks and then insist that management fire these individuals because they were no longer union members. At other times, labor leaders advised management to transfer dissidents to subsidiaries far away from Mexico City. The mere threat of such a dislocation was usually enough to convince rebellious workers to resign from both the union and their jobs.

During the late 1950s, however, labor corruption became a national scandal when the railroad workers' union, racked by internal revolt, exploded in the most serious strike of the era.[33] This crisis was all the more embarrassing for the government because the railroads were state-owned, and their history was intimately bound to revolutionary folklore and the economic growth of the country.

Under Porfirio Díaz, the national railway network was mostly owned by foreign investors and operated mainly for their benefit by under-charging freight costs for their raw materials and finished goods. Be-cause foreign employees were favored in terms of wages and promotions, Mexican railroad workers were among the earliest converts to the Revolution. In the dizzying shifts in revolutionary leadership, they were fortunate to have sided with the ultimate victor, Alvaro Obregón.

During the postrevolutionary period, the railroad workers were praised as models of the new proletariat, and earned salaries that were high by working-class standards. No one begrudged them these re-wards. They labored hard to rebuild the network shattered by the long years of civil war, and to keep in service an inventory of antiquated rolling stock. In the late 1930s, President Cárdenas nationalized the train lines that were still in private hands, and turned over management of the entire system to the railroad workers' union. It was during these Cárdenas years that the union achieved its greatest prestige and independence.

With operational costs of the railways rising sharply, President Avila Camacho ended the experiment in workers' management and turned over administration of the trains to a newly created public corporation in 1940. Shortly after coming to power, Miguel Alemán resolved to bring the union itself under government control. To accomplish this aim, he used tactics that would be repeated often against independent labor leaders during his presidency. He swung his support behind a conservative, pro-government faction in the railroad union led by a flamboyant labor official named Jesús Díaz de León. With the backing of policemen and soldiers disguised as trade unionists, Díaz de León and his followers physically expelled the incumbent leadership from union headquarters in Mexico City in October 1948. Newspapers bannered charges by Díaz de León that the deposed officials had permitted Communist infiltration and embezzled union funds. Rank-and-file opponents of Díaz de León were forced out of their jobs, and replaced by new workers beholden to him.

As head of the railroad workers, Díaz de León became a wealthy man. He was said to own a large dairy farm on the outskirts of Mexico

City that sold milk to government agencies at inflated prices. He was also an avid participant in rodeos and horse-breeding shows, where he appeared in extravagant cowboy costumes that earned him the sobriquet "El Charro."[34] The term, first associated with Díaz de León, became slang for a corrupt labor leader.

During his tenure, the railroad union was a creature of the government. The train system incurred heavy financial losses for the state because of large capital expenditures and a policy of subsidizing fares for the public and freight costs for private enterprise. But no one could accuse Díaz de León and the charro leaders who succeeded him of adding to this economic burden by fighting for the livelihood of the 100,000 members of the union. According to a report issued in 1958 by a committee of union dissidents meeting in Mexico City, railroad workers had suffered a 40 percent loss in their purchasing power over the previous decade.

The leader of this left-wing dissident faction was Demetrio Vallejo, a former Communist Party member. Since 1954, he and his followers had been campaigning against both the union leadership and the state-owned railroad corporation to improve workers' salaries. The struggle had been bitter and violent. When the dissidents provoked slowdowns in train service, they were reviled in the press. Some of their supporters were transferred or dismissed. Both left-wing and conservative workers had been injured or killed in internecine brawls.

But by 1958, Vallejo and his faction were clearly in ascendancy. They followed up the Mexico City report on income erosion with a demand for an immediate raise of $28 a month. The charro officials, who still held the union's top posts, were torn between an internal revolt and pressure from the government to keep wages down. As usual, they opted for the government side, and recommended a monthly increase of only $16. Moreover, the charros agreed to a request by the railroad management that it be granted sixty days to consider the salary demand. This grace period would allow Mexico's presidential elections, scheduled for July 4, 1958, to proceed without any labor controversy.

But Vallejo, sensing that the government would be especially vulnerable in the days before the elections, called for a work slowdown on June 26. This escalated two days later into a full-scale strike that paralyzed the train system. To counter press allegations that only a subversive minority was behind the strike, Vallejo also organized massive demonstrations by railroad workers in Mexico City and Guadalajara on June 28.

At this point, President Adolfo Ruíz Cortines was forced to intervene. He decreed a $17 monthly increase—well short of Vallejo's demands— but, more important, he allowed the union to hold internal elections in August. The dissidents easily won the vote, and Vallejo was installed as secretary-general. An uneasy truce prevailed until December, when Adolfo López Mateos took office as Mexico's new president.

Seeking to create a public image distinct from his dour, more conservative predecessor, López Mateos had campaigned as a pro-labor, left-wing politician. His government would be "of the extreme left . . . within the Constitution," as he put it.[35] These convictions were quickly tested by Vallejo. In negotiations with management of the main railway line, Vallejo insisted that the government's offer of a $17 monthly raise be supplemented by housing allowances for train employees. Such benefits, he pointed out, were guaranteed by the Constitution and recent labor legislation. The package Vallejo was seeking would be worth close to the $28 monthly increase he had initially proposed in May 1958. Unless the government managers of the railroads agreed to these demands, he warned, a strike would be called in late February 1959.

As the deadline approached, the government used the newspapers to state its case against the union. Vallejo was accused of being a Communist agent in the pay of foreigners. Acts of subversion were alleged to be taking place on the train lines. And the press claimed that a pro-government faction was quickly gaining strength in the union.

The strike began on February 25, and paralyzed Ferrocarriles Nacionales, the main railroad line. When government agreed to the union's demands the following day, Vallejo appeared to have scored a complete victory. But the settlement turned out to be only the first act in an unfolding drama. The train system was organized into thirteen different lines, each with its own labor contract that had to be negotiated separately. When Vallejo tried to impose the Ferrocarriles Nacionales settlement on the other lines, he was rebuffed by the government. The newspapers, which had hailed the government for its alleged generosity in granting workers' demands at Ferrocarriles Nacionales, portrayed Vallejo as an ingrate whose excessive demands were aimed at precipitating a confrontation between organized labor and the state.

Vallejo then made a fateful miscalculation. In an attempt to force the López Mateos government to extend the new contract to all railroad lines, he called for a work stoppage on March 25. This was only a few days before the start of Easter Week, when Mexicans en masse boarded cars, buses, and trains to flee the hot, dry cities for the seashore and countryside. Apparently, Vallejo reasoned that government would cave in to his demands rather than risk the ire of millions of frustrated travelers. But the barrage of anti-Vallejo stories in the press—and the prospect of a spoiled vacation—had in fact turned public opinion against the union's position.

As soon as the strike began in the early morning of March 25, the government moved swiftly to safeguard the Easter holiday—and break the union. Soldiers took command of all train stations and replaced union telegraphers. Police and army troops searched out strikers in their homes and forced them back to work at gunpoint. Other thousands of workers were imprisoned, including Vallejo and his chief aides. The attorney general insisted that the union leaders were part of a conspiracy aimed at bringing down the government. Vallejo was alleged to have received money from the Russian Embassy, and two Soviet diplomats, who had supposedly been his paymasters, were expelled from Mexico.

Train service was almost normal throughout the holiday. And by the time vacationers returned to Mexico City, all of the railroad union leaders had been replaced by pro-government officials. In the months that followed, most of the jailed workers were released. Vallejo and his top aides, however, were bound over for trial.

With the railroad crisis behind him so early in his term, President López Mateos set about restoring his left-wing image. He maintained diplomatic relations with Fidel Castro's government despite pressure from Washington. He seemed to revive the agrarian reform program that languished after the Cárdenas era (in fact, barely a quarter of the 28.7 million acres officially expropriated by the López Mateos government were ever distributed to peasants).[36] And he pushed through a profit-sharing plan which eventually raised the salaries of many workers by 5 percent or more a year.

Once López Mateos felt confident that he had established a progressive record, he turned to the unfinished business of his first few months in office. Demetrio Vallejo and the other left-wing railroad union leaders who had remained in jail for four years were finally brought to trial in 1963. Vallejo and his chief aide were convicted under the antisubversion law and condemned to sixteen years in prison—a longer sentence than murderers usually receive in Mexico. Twenty-three other union officials were also found guilty and given harsh jail terms.

There was a clear message in this denouement: Any gains that accrued to the working class were a reflection of the regime's benevolence, and not the result of victories wrested by independent unions in confrontations with the government.

As the 1960s drew to a close, Mexican leaders had reason to congratulate themselves. The civilian regime born in the Alemán era was working smoothly. Every six years, the political elite regenerated itself, choosing with little friction or controversy a presidential candidate who invariably won a landslide election. Every governor and big city mayor belonged to the government party, which also enjoyed overwhelming majorities in Congress. The trade union movement and the national peasant association were large and visible enough to claim to speak for the country's urban and rural laborers. Yet these working-class organizations remained loyal to the government, supporting its vision of cooperation between capital and labor, and willing to help crush dissenters in the factories and countryside.

The mass media could be counted upon to project a sense of well-being and prosperity. There was little need for the government to exercise heavy-handed censorship. Beholden to the state for licenses and advertising revenues, radio and television executives subscribed to the views expressed by President Díaz Ordaz in a 1965 speech: "Before broadcasting a news item, before emitting a comment, before transmitting a program, think first and always whether it . . . helps to promote harmony among Mexicans or to exacerbate their differences and resentments."[37]

Newspapers and magazines depended on the government for low-priced newsprint and for at least two thirds of their advertising income. Journalists and editors received monthly stipends from public officials and private entrepreneurs in return for favorable coverage. Not surprisingly, front-page stories trumpeted government announcements and future public projects while incidents of labor strife were relegated to small articles next to the crime pages. Accounts of the president and his policies bordered on adulation, and most of the political elite enjoyed a similar immunity from press criticism. Lack of credibility among the readership, however, was a constant problem. A scholar investigating public attitudes toward the press in the 1960s encountered widespread cynicism, perhaps summed up most succinctly by one informant who said: "If I read something in the paper I must think to myself, 'Why am I being told this particular lie today?' "[38]

The postwar era did produce intellectual writing that profoundly questioned official optimism about the country's ability to grapple with social injustice. In his masterpiece *The Labyrinth of Solitude*, the poet-essayist Octavio Paz indelibly described a people still unable to heal the wounds ripped open by conquest and colonialism, civil war and revolution, wealth and poverty. In *The Death of Artemio Cruz* and *Where the Air Is Clear*, the novelist Carlos Fuentes spun riveting tales of provincial revolutionary commanders seduced by the riches and cosmopolitan enchantments of Mexico City. But the high illiteracy rates and the public's low purchasing power necessarily limited the audience of all authors. Unable to live from the income of their works, they were beholden to the government for bureaucratic, diplomatic, and university posts. As a result, even the most honest and critical intellectuals could be made to feel that they were less an irritant than a blessing for a government eager to demonstrate its tolerance of dissent.

The pride of government leaders in their adroit political management of the nation was matched by their buoyant feelings about the economy. Growth had continued without interruption since the 1940s. Inflation remained low. By 1968, the peso had resisted devaluation for fifteen years. Foreign investment was pouring into the country. Economists abroad were often unstinting in their praise for the Mexican model of urban industrialization. And Mexico City was a showcase for the developing world: a seemingly modern metropolis that preserved its autochthonous character, a city of new factories and artisan workshops, European-style boulevards and colonial cobblestone streets, supermarkets and Indian marketplaces, department stores and ambulatory vendors.

There was an almost palpable need in official circles to celebrate these many successes. And it was in this spirit that the government looked forward to hosting the 1968 Olympics in Mexico City. It was the first time the august Games were being held in a developing nation, and it provided an occasion to display the Mexican economic miracle to the world. Cultural events were to be as important a part of the agenda as sports competition, thus giving Mexican artists the opportunity to collect the honors that would elude Mexican athletes in the stiff contests for medals. With a budget of $175 million, the government provided impressive facilities for the hordes of foreign athletes, trainers, artists, and journalists. These outlays were considered a long-term investment as well. The Olympics would surely stimulate more tourism in the years ahead, and the facilities built for the Games would be used later for housing and public recreation.

The last time an extravaganza on this scale had been staged in Mexico City was in 1910, when Porfirio Díaz commemorated the hundredth anniversary of Mexico's Independence wars. Don Porfirio had been motivated by the same impulses that guided the Olympic organizers: a genuine pride in the nation's skewed economic progress and imperfect political system; a desire to announce to the world that Mexico was fast emerging from the throes of underdevelopment; and the conviction that Mexico City offered a futuristic glimpse of where modernization was leading the rest of the country.

To the Díaz Ordaz government, the notion that there were any parallels between the 1968 Olympics and the infamous 1910 centennial was absurd and malicious. The moral legitimacy of every government since 1920 rested on the premise that the Revolution had overturned the unjust political, social, and economic system created by Don Porfirio. According to government officials, only a perverse, unpatriotic minority could equate the blemishes of the modern regime with the dark age of the Porfiriato.

As 1968 unfolded, however, one significant minority—left-wing university students in Mexico City—was increasingly willing to make such a connection. Before large audiences of their peers, student leaders were asserting that the PRI was the new Porfiriato, that the Mexican economic miracle was a hoax, and that the lavish outlays for the Olympics would be far better spent on programs to aid the majority of citizens mired in poverty.

From the government's vantage point, the students were engaging in a tasteless display of ingratitude. The Mexican miracle had certainly benefited them. The expanding economy had swelled the ranks of affluent and middle-class Mexicans who accounted for the bulk of university enrollment. While tuition was free at state institutions, students needed considerable financial resources to cover living expenses and remain outside the job market until their early twenties. Yet by 1968, enrollment in Mexican universities nationwide reached 350,000, a sevenfold increase since the beginning of the Alemán era.

UNAM remained the centerpiece of the state's higher education system. Alemán had moved it to a sparkling new campus ten miles south of the capital's center. The so-called University City that opened in 1954 was an architectural wonder. Spread over three square miles, its buildings had outer walls adorned with murals by Rivera, Siqueiros, and other artists. Just as dramatic was UNAM's rising enrollment, which climbed from about 22,000 students in 1946 to almost 85,000 by 1968.

UNAM had maintained its reputation as the cradle of politicians. Throughout the fifties and sixties, about half of all cabinet ministers taught there, and recruited thousands of students into the government bureaucracy.[39] Students joined various campus factions of the PRI, which turned university disputes into plebiscites that tested the popularity of potential candidates for the nation's presidency.[40]

But the PRI was by no means the only vehicle for UNAM activism. The campus was plastered with manifestos of Leninists, Trotskyists, Castroists, Maoists, and New Leftists. Internal issues, such as curricula content, enrollment policies, faculty appointments, and bus fares mobilized large groups of students. In 1966, during a huge student strike—called partly in response to attempts by the UNAM administration to limit rising enrollment—the rector was held hostage and forced to resign. But more disturbing to the government was a growing tendency among student activists to involve themselves in issues off campus and to forge ties with militants at other universities and even preparatory schools.

Students were joining demonstrations in support of strikes by independent unions. Demetrio Vallejo, the jailed railway workers' leader, became an icon on campuses, and his release was demanded at every leftist rally. Charges of electoral fraud in the northern states stirred protests at UNAM and the Politécnico, the other major state university in Mexico City. Campus activists were also influenced by events abroad. In the first half of 1968, that watershed year of youthful uprisings around the world, militant students were paralyzing universities in the United States and seemed on the verge of toppling the government in France.

But no matter what the causes of the mounting protest movement, no matter how keenly Mexican students resented political corruption and authoritarianism, 1968 would have evolved very differently had the Olympic Games not been scheduled in Mexico City. The government was extremely concerned that the Games proceed without any embarrassing disruptions. And student activists, well aware of this discomfort, believed that an unparalleled opportunity was at hand to press any outstanding demands upon the government. Perhaps never again in their university years would political authority be so vulnerable to dissent. It did not seem to have occurred to them that this same sense of weakness might provoke the government to respond with abnormal violence.

The chain of events that unleashed an explosive confrontation between university militants and the government began with a minor incident on July 22, 1968. A street fight erupted between students from a private preparatory school and several public vocational institutes in the central district of Mexico City. The causes of the fracas were inane: teenage rivalries over "turf"; the traditional resentment that public vocational students harbored against more affluent private school pupils; and the restlessness of the youngsters as their school term drew to a close. But in the previous weeks, similar brawls had led to vandalism against neighborhood shops, and this time the local merchants called upon the police to intervene. When the intramural fighting resumed the next day, July 23, the mayor overreacted and sent out two hundred *"granaderos,"* a paramilitary force notorious for its harsh methods of riot control.

The sight of the granaderos seemed to unite the battling students, who began to taunt the policemen and then stoned them. The granaderos responded by firing tear gas and liberally clubbing students. When some of the youths fled into a nearby vocational school, the police invaded the building and pummeled every student in sight, even those who had not been involved in the street melee.

The brutality of the police drew a strong reaction in the universities, particularly at the Politécnico, which recruited most of its students from vocational schools like the one attacked by the granaderos. Thousands of Politécnico students staged a protest march on July 26 in downtown Mexico City. By coincidence, that day, leftist students, mainly from UNAM, were holding a rally in the same general vicinity to commemorate the fifteenth anniversary of Fidel Castro's initial uprising in Cuba. The two groups joined and began to march toward the National Palace. They were intercepted by a huge force of granaderos. The students dispersed through the side streets and engaged in hit-and-run skirmishes with the police throughout the night. By dawn, the central district was a shambles. Buses were overturned and charred by Molotov cocktails. Windows were shattered and stores looted. Tear gas and smoke saturated the air. Scores of students and granaderos had been injured, and hundreds of rioters were under arrest.

The government chose to portray the clash as a conspiracy aimed at embarrassing the nation as the Olympics approached. On the night of July 26, while the student-granadero battles were still raging, policemen broke into the Mexican Communist Party headquarters, where they arrested several party officials, ransacked the premises, destroyed files, and confiscated propaganda. The next day, government spokesmen asserted that the raid had uncovered evidence of Communist leadership of the downtown riot. In the weeks ahead, the argument that Communist and foreign agitators were undermining public order would become a constant refrain in government pronouncements and press coverage.

Student activists, meanwhile, responded by convoking an assembly at the Politécnico on July 28. They called for a strike in Mexico City universities, preparatory and vocational schools unless the government agreed immediately to release all students arrested during the riot, indemnify injured students and the families of those who allegedly had been killed by the police, dissolve the granadero forces, and abolish the antisubversion law that had been used to prosecute Demetrio Vallejo and other dissidents.

The government's reaction was to close down all public schools in the capital. On the night of July 29, student rioting flared again in the downtown streets near the Zócalo, the capital's main plaza, and this time army soldiers joined the granaderos. After smashing barricades of overturned buses, the soldiers assaulted schools where students sought refuge. In the most notorious incident, the troops used a bazooka to blast open the massive Baroque wooden doors of the original National Preparatory School—the same institution where Rivera, Siqueiros, and Orozco had launched the muralist movement in the 1920s. By the early morning hours of July 30, more than one thousand six hundred students were under arrest and close to one hundred were hospitalized.

The government denied that the army had used a bazooka, and asserted that whatever damage was done to the old preparatory was the result of Molotov cocktails hurled by subversives. Most newspapers printed only this official version. But reports of the "bazukazo" quickly spread through the city by word of mouth. Besides further galvanizing the students, the incident began turning important sectors of the public against the government for its excessive display of force.

On August 1, the rector of UNAM led eighty thousand students in a peaceful demonstration aimed at protesting the invasion of the schools by army and police. The march, which began on the southern outskirts of the capital, ended well short of the downtown district in an effort to avoid provoking the government.

That same day, President Díaz Ordaz, who had tried to remain aloof from the growing conflict (he was, in fact, on a political tour in Guadalajara), spoke out for the first time. "A hand is stretched out," he declared, striking a conciliatory pose. "Mexicans will say whether the hand will find a response. I have been deeply grieved by these deplorable and shameful events. Let us not further accentuate our differences. . . ."[41]

The president, however, did not follow up his remarks with any offer for a government meeting with student spokesmen to discuss their grievances. And the image of his "outstretched hand" became a subject of ridicule for demonstrators whose placards asserted that "The outstretched hand has a pistol in it," "The outstretched arm wears a swastika," and "The dead cannot shake the outstretched hand."[42]

These slogans and others far more insulting to Díaz Ordaz were carried on picket signs or shouted out in chorus by 150,000 demonstrators who joined a march from the Politécnico to the Zócalo on August 13. In a country were a ruling president is treated with the reverence accorded to a deity, the rhetoric was shockingly sacrilegious. Plainclothesmen monitoring the march rushed to public phones to report the remarks to their superiors. Spectators lining the demonstration route turned to each other in disbelief.[43] Newspaper and television coverage, focusing on the personal attacks against the president, suggested that the protestors had placed themselves beyond the pale of civilization.

But the ranks of dissidents swelled with working-class youths—many of them not affiliated with preparatories or universities—and the demonstration routes drew larger crowds of spectators fascinated by such unprecedented disrespect for political authority. On August 27, the largest protest took place. About 400,000 demonstrators—most but by no means all of them students—wound their way from Chapultepec Park, up Paseo de la Reforma and Juárez Avenue, and into the Zócalo, where in front of the National Palace they chanted for the president to appear before them: "Come out on the balcony, loudmouth!"

The next day, still euphoric over the unexpectedly massive turnout, student leaders demanded that Díaz Ordaz engage them in a "public dialogue" to be held in the Zócalo and televised nationally on September 1. This was the date when he was scheduled to deliver the traditional state of the union address. It was an act of provocation to suggest that the speech be shelved in favor of a freewheeling debate in which the president would surely be drowned out by a chorus of catcalls. A spokesman for the National Strike Council—formed by militant students from one hundred fifty schools to steer the protest movement—insisted that the proposal for an open dialogue was intended "to end the corrupt practice of smoke-filled rooms or little groups, where the give and take excludes the masses from any participation."[44]

Suddenly, the protest movement had escalated from a few specific demands to a general repudiation of the government's authoritarian style. It was a challenge that not even the most moderate member of the political elite could accept. The PRI, the national trade union and peasant organizations, indeed the entire political system operated on the premise that decisions were made at the summit and ratified—not discussed or contested—by assemblies of the rank and file who were deemed to represent the various sectors of Mexican society. And from the viewpoint of any government partisan, it was intolerable even to entertain the suggestion that the president—standing at the very pinnacle of the regime—be exposed to a humiliating confrontation with youthful dissidents, who were not affiliated with any officially sponsored groups and did not recognize the established rules of political conduct.

The state of the union address proceeded without disruption on September 1. As expected, Díaz Ordaz took a hard line toward the student movement. He offered the possibility of negotiations with the dissidents. But such a dialogue would be held in closed session, over an agenda chosen by the government, and would not necessarily involve him as a direct participant. With the Olympics only six weeks away, he warned that further protests would not be tolerated and that any resistance would be met by "all the elements that the people have placed in our hands." Appealing to government partisans for a show of support, he expressed confidence that the "small group" of student radicals would meet "a widespread and indignant repudiation by millions of Mexicans."[45]

In the following days, newspapers echoed the president's tough stance. Unions and peasant organizations excoriated the students as foreign-led subversives. The Senate authorized the president to use the armed forces "in defense of the internal and external security of Mexico."[46] But the massive outpouring of popular support that Díaz Ordaz had invoked was nowhere in evidence. The few government-sponsored rallies could not turn out more than two or three thousand state employees, civilian-clad policemen, and bewildered peasants trucked in from the outskirts of the capital.

These demonstrations were dwarfed by yet another protest march in mid-September that gathered 250,000 people. As proof of their resolve to avoid any confrontation with security forces, the dissidents walked to the Zócalo in utter silence, except for the sounds of their footsteps and the rustle of their placards and clothing.[47] But this impressive display of discipline only angered the government further.

On September 18, the army occupied UNAM. It was the first time security forces had set foot in the university since it was granted autonomy to run its internal affairs in 1929. More than a thousand students were arrested, and troops did not leave the campus until the end of the month, after vandalizing classrooms, offices, and laboratories. The occupation sparked street battles in the downtown area that resulted in the deaths of several protestors. And on September 24, the army occupied the Politécnico after some further skirmishes with students there.

The government's increasingly tough tactics seemed to be sapping the momentum from the protest movement. The security forces, which now included raw army recruits, were losing their self-control and inflicting greater casualties. Thousands of students had been arrested, and many of them were held incommunicado, without any notification to their families on their whereabouts, and even without official acknowledgment of their detention. The occupation of the UNAM and Politécnico campuses by security forces had also seriously disrupted the ability of student militants to convoke large gatherings of their followers.

But as September drew to a close, dwindling bands of student activists were making use of an alternative site for their assemblies—the open square of a public-housing project known as the Plaza of the Three Cultures, which was located conveniently close to the Zócalo and the occupied Politécnico. The plaza's name alludes to the presence there of architectural structures from the Aztec, Spanish colonial, and contemporary eras. The modern epoch looms most prominent. Apartment towers, rising thirteen stories and higher, house thousands of tenants drawn mainly from the middle class: teachers, other professionals earning moderate incomes, and government employees. Representing colonial times is the restored sixteenth-century Santiago Tlatelolco church. And pre-Columbian civilization is rendered homage by traces of masonry and carvings that formed part of Tlatelolco, where the Aztecs made their last stand against the conquistadores.

On October 2, 1968, the Plaza of the Three Cultures became the site of another last stand—this one pitting government forces against the protest movement. With the official opening of the Olympic Games only ten days away, President Díaz Ordaz resolved to end the crisis by any means. He delegated two ranking politicians to open negotiations with student representatives of the National Strike Council that morning at the UNAM campus, whose occupation by the army had been lifted two days before. Much to the government's annoyance, however, other student militants had drawn a crowd in the late afternoon at the Plaza of the Three Cultures, with the intention of organizing a march to the Politécnico to demand the evacuation of troops from that campus.

Judged by the mammoth demonstrations in previous weeks, this rally was a failure. Estimates of crowd size varied from five thousand to ten thousand people—most of them students, but also parents and children who resided in the adjoining apartment towers. Because of the small turnout and the presence of so many soldiers and policemen on the plaza's periphery, student leaders announced that the march to the Politécnico was being called off. Instead, there was a round of rather tame speeches that drew perfunctory applause.

The crowd was already beginning to ebb at 6:00 P.M. when a helicopter circling over the plaza dropped two green flares. Suddenly, on the ground, a heavy volley of gunfire erupted.[48] The government would later claim that snipers perched on the apartment roofs initiated the violence by shooting at security forces. But many other witnesses, including survivors, foreign reporters, and television crews, gave convincing testimony of a well-planned massacre. While soldiers shot their way into the plaza, other troops and policemen—dressed in civilian clothes but identifiable by the white glove on their left hand—began firing on the crowd from within the square. Students, parents, and children were indiscriminately gunned down. With armored vehicles and security forces blocking escape routes, the panic-stricken crowd dashed back and forth from one end of the plaza to another, unable to evade the murderous barrages. Attempts to surrender were met by gunfire, and even those people who prostrated themselves on the ground were raked by bullets. Heavy volleys continued without interruption for an hour, and there was intermittent shooting until early morning.

Ambulances were permitted on the scene at 11:00 P.M., only after most of the dead and wounded had been removed by military vehicles, which also drove off with more than two thousand prisoners. Police were stationed at hospitals to prevent relatives from inquiring about victims, and to evacuate the bodies of those who died under medical care. Prisoners who were being held in military camps asserted they saw large bonfires at these installations and smelled the burning of corpses.

It was impossible to determine accurately just how many people died at the Plaza of the Three Cultures—a tragedy that has become known as the Tlatelolco Massacre. The government insisted that the death toll was no higher than forty-nine persons, and did not permit any independent investigation of casualties. Newspapers and television stations made no attempt to probe the massacre, and paid little attention to the claims of relatives of missing persons. But the estimate of several hundred dead—put forth by student leaders—has come to be generally accepted as more plausible than the government's figures.

The Tlatelolco Massacre brought an abrupt end to the 1968 protest movement. Caught off balance by the rapid surge of discontent in the previous three months, the government now recovered control of the political situation. On October 3, just a day after the mass killings, the Chamber of Deputies passed a resolution characterizing all events that transpired since July as "a subversive action . . . perpetrated by foreign elements."[49] The press began emphasizing stories about the upcoming Olympic Games. Business groups, trade unions, and rural associations supported the government's contention that the country, already shamed by the violence, could not afford to be further embarrassed in the world's eyes by fumbling the Olympiad.

The Games, in fact, proceeded smoothly and were widely judged a success. Sports arenas rocked with avid fans, and cultural events were also heavily attended. There were few complaints from athletes or tourists about accommodations. And many foreign visitors undoubtedly interpreted the violent outbursts of the previous weeks as simply another manifestation of the youthful protests which shook the world that year in places as far-flung as New York, Chicago, Paris, Prague, and Tokyo. Few spectators from abroad even saw any irony in the traditional ceremony that closed the Olympics—the release of thousands of doves, signaling hopes for peace.

But the Olympics proved to be only a brief palliative for the trauma of Tlatelolco. Though the protest movement was crushed, it had precipitated the gravest political crisis since the early postrevolutionary period. "At the very moment in which the Mexican government was receiving international recognition for forty years of political stability and economic progress, a swash of blood dispelled the official optimism and caused every citizen to doubt the meaning of that progress," noted Octavio Paz.[50]

The fact that this skepticism ran deepest among educated middle-class Mexicans was a particular source of discomfort to the government. They had purportedly been the greatest beneficiaries of the economic boom since the Alemán years. The era had begun with the recruitment of middle-class university graduates into the upper rungs of the government bureaucracy. And it was now ending with a rupture between the regime and the university that had been the wellspring of the political elite.

EIGHTEEN

MEGALOPOLIS

In the generation since 1968, Mexico City has turned into an urban planner's nightmare. Political, social, economic, and ecological forces have conspired to make the capital increasingly unmanageable, over-populated, unproductive, and insalubrious. With twenty million peo-ple, Mexico City has become a true megalopolis, the greatest urban concentration in history. It sprawls over 950 square miles, about three times the area of New York City. More than three million motor vehicles slow traffic to the pace of the horse-and-buggy era. Every day, automobile exhaust and industrial fumes spew 12,000 tons of pollutants into the atmosphere, provoking uncounted thousands of premature deaths and thickening the once azure skies to a yellow-gray opacity that veils both distant mountains and nearby skyscrapers. The ground can be as deadly as the air: ten thousand lives and hundreds of buildings were claimed by the monster earthquake of 1985, largely because the downtown area rests upon the gelatinous residue of the dried-up Aztec lake that magnifies the effects of any temblor.

Office and apartment towers, shopping malls, freeways, middle-class residential projects, and gigantic squatter settlements of the poor have obliterated most of what was identifiably "Mexican" in the urban landscape. Traces of the Indian heritage are preserved only in the museums. Architectural remnants of the colonial past are confined to a few blocks in the center and tiny cul-de-sacs in outlying neighbor-hoods. Long known as a city that encouraged walkers, the capital has become daunting for people who try to get about on foot. They must persevere through a gauntlet of cars illegally parked across sidewalks, traffic lights designed for sprinters, a maze of pedestrian overpasses that test even youthful stamina, and noise levels that often reach 90 decibels—the equivalent of standing next to a jackhammer.

Supergrowth has robbed Mexico City of economic logic. From 1940 to 1970, its powerful industrial muscles tugged the rest of the country forward. As the twentieth century comes to a close, however, the Mexican capital is being borne on the unsteady shoulders of the hinterland. Because of monumental government subsidies for public transportation, food, health facilities, education, fuel, water, and other essential services, Mexico City is absorbing more from the nation's economy and contributing less. The political elite has discovered that it was far easier to stimulate the growth of the city than to bring it under control; easier to encourage industrial concentration than the dispersal of factories; easier to attract rural migrants than to expel them back to the provinces; easier to build and centralize a huge federal bureaucracy than to reduce and scatter it across the country.

Even an able leadership would be hard pressed to grapple with these awesome problems. But the precarious condition of Mexico City has been exacerbated by the ineptitude of the political elite that has guided the nation since the crisis of 1968. Whatever else could be said about the Tlatelolco Massacre, it was a clearly recognizable watershed in Mexico's modern history, a dividing line to a new era. The protest movement ripped away the benevolent mask of authoritarianism and drew attention to the foundation of poverty upon which the economic miracle was built. The assumed benefits of rapid urbanization were also severely questioned. After all, the protests had erupted in Mexico City, the nation's urban showcase. Although the unrest had been largely confined to middle-class students, surely next time there would be a heightened risk that a conflict might pull the capital's working-class majority into the fray. Thus, there was a widespread public expectation that dramatic changes were in store under the president who followed Díaz Ordaz.

The successor was Luís Echeverría. Born in 1922 to middle-class parents in Mexico City, Echeverría in many ways typified the evolution of the political elite since the Alemán era. As a teenager, he had already decided upon a career in government, enrolling first in the National Preparatory School, and then going on to UNAM's Law School. Upon graduation, he carefully chose his political mentor, General Rodolfo Sánchez Taboada, a revolutionary war commander who was well placed in the government. From 1946 to 1954, he gripped tightly to Sánchez Taboada's coattails as the general moved through a series of high bureaucratic posts. Echeverría also allied himself to a strong political family by marrying the daughter of the governor of Jalisco. He earned a reputation for loyalty and diligence at the ministries of the Navy, Public Education and, finally, Interior, where he was Díaz Ordaz's chief assistant. As president, Díaz Ordaz made Echeverría his interior minister and heir apparent.

When Echeverría became president in 1970, he had never held any previous elective office. This would also be the case for his three immediate successors, José López Portillo, Miguel de la Madrid, and Carlos Salinas de Gortari. Bureaucratic skills and the ability to deal with small, powerful factions had become the most important criteria for political advancement. Elections and the manipulation of large groups were left to lower-echelon politicians who had risen up the ranks of the official party, the PRI, rather than through UNAM and the government bureaucracy.

President Echeverría quickly sought to distance himself from his predecessor and create his own political style and program. Gone was any trace of the servility that Irma Serrano had observed in him as cabinet minister. He had, after all, been elevated to the status of a demigod. Now, when he spoke, his bald pate, stern face, and slightly shaded glasses tilted upward over the heads of his audience of mere mortals, as if he were fixated on a distant, mystical vision. That vision was left-wing and populist, in the mold of Lázaro Cárdenas, whom Echeverría claimed to emulate. Like Cárdenas, he journeyed indefatigably throughout the country, promising peasants and industrial workers a more equitable share of the national wealth, and vowing to increase the state's role in the economy. He began to sport leather jackets or the tieless "guayabera" shirts favored by more modest Mexicans in the tropical zones, and soon most of his entourage dressed the same way.[1] To their annoyance, wives of the politicians were asked to appear at state dinners in Mexican folk costumes instead of their usual haute-couture gowns.

Echeverría was especially intent on wooing back the university students and intellectuals who, after the events of 1968, had become the group most visibly disaffected with the regime. It was not an easy task for the new president. They were extremely skeptical of Echeverría's efforts to disassociate himself from Díaz Ordaz. As Díaz Ordaz's minister of interior, he could hardly escape direct responsibility for the Tlatelolco Massacre. Throughout the government's confrontation with the protest movement, he had showed no qualms about the harsh repression of demonstrators.

An incident in June 1971 aggravated student hostility toward Echeverría. When left-wing youths marched through downtown Mexico City—the first public protest since 1968—in support of university autonomy and the release of political prisoners, they were attacked by a right-wing group called the *Halcones* (Hawks). Wielding staves and guns, the assailants killed at least eleven persons. Police not only declined to interfere, but offered the *Halcones* their walkie-talkies to better coordinate the attacks, and then allowed them to escape. Echeverría disclaimed responsibility. His aides protested that he was the victim of a plot by conservative PRI officials to embarrass him and thwart his attempts to move leftward. But even after Echeverría fired his attorney general, Mexico City's mayor and police chief, most of the public remained convinced that the *Halcones* incident took place with his knowledge or approval.

To a surprising extent, however, Echeverría did eventually succeed in gaining the support of the intellectual community. His speeches began to appropriate the leftist rhetoric used by dissenters during the 1968 crisis and its aftermath. He led Mexico into the Third World camp, and championed the cause of developing countries in their economic dealings with industrialized nations. He spoke out against the growing power of multinational corporations, and often disagreed with Washington, particularly over hemispheric affairs. He strengthened Mexico's economic, political, and cultural ties with Castro's Cuba. He was a supporter of Salvador Allende, and when the Chilean president died during the 1973 military coup, he broke relations with the new right-wing government in Chile and welcomed thousands of political refugees from that country into Mexico City. Under Echeverría, the Mexican capital became the foremost haven for left-wing Latin American exiles.

Ideology alone did not seduce Mexican intellectuals. Even more important were the employment and financial inducements that Echeverría dangled before them. After releasing the protestors jailed during the 1968 crisis, he offered many of them jobs in government. It was the beginning of a spectacular expansion of the bureaucracy that continued through the administration of Echeverría's successor, López Portillo. Between 1970 and 1982, the two presidents added 1.2 million people to the federal government rolls, a rate of increase that outpaced the country's demographic growth by six to one. The state universities, which remained the chief source of recruitment for the bureaucracy, doubled their enrollment during the Echeverría administration. By the mid-1980s, UNAM alone had 350,000 students, four times as many as in 1968.

The salaries of university professors increased sharply, as did the
number of state scholarships for travel and postgraduate study abroad.
Academic researchers, especially in economics and social sciences,
received a windfall of government grants. Publishing houses, magazines, and newspapers proliferated with the aid of government subsidies. According to Alan Riding, the *New York Times* correspondent,
by the early 1980s affluence and social status had transformed intellectuals into a privileged class who "lived better in Mexico than in the
United States or Western Europe, moving in circles of influence at
home and frequently traveling abroad."[2]

In every society and era, intellectuals have always expressed frus-
tration at reaching a broad audience. What changed in Mexico after
1970 was that many of them simply stopped trying. Unable to sell
their "high-brow" journals and "serious" tomes at newsstands and
bookstores, intellectuals instead targeted politicians as their audience,
sending them hundreds of samples of their writings. And politicians
were flattered by these attentions. To be known as a patron of intellectuals, to include them in social affairs, to incorporate them into
one's entourage added luster to an ambitious politician. When he
traveled abroad, Echeverría was accompanied by hundreds of scholars,
writers, and artists. And soon, the mayor of Mexico City, the governor
of the state of Mexico, and other politicians were also touring their
constituencies with intellectuals at their side.

It would be wrong to suggest that intellectuals had become mere
government acolytes or publicists. Within limits, they were expected
to be controversial, to provoke debates, to hold critical views. This was
particularly true on the subject of foreign affairs. Many intellectuals
were far more outspoken than the government in their criticism of the
United States and their sympathies for Cuba, the Viet Cong, and the
PLO. On domestic issues, books and journalistic articles have appeared
since the 1970s excoriating capitalism, social injustices, corruption,
and undemocratic politics. But attacks on a president still in office
were rarely permitted. When the leading newspaper, *Excelsior*, became
too critical of his administration, Echeverría engineered an internal
revolt that ousted its chief editors in 1976. Few journalists came to
the defense of their deposed colleagues. Once Echeverría's term was
over, however, he was as vilified in the press as his predecessor, Díaz
Ordaz, had been after he stepped down. López Portillo endured even
more vitriolic exposés in newspapers, magazines, and books following
his retirement in 1982.

Literature offered intellectuals the most uncensored forum to dissect their society. For novelists who first emerged in the 1970s, the Revolution and its decadent aftermath seem a distant history, so irrelevant to contemporary Mexico that they merit no mention. The subjects that most preoccupy these writers—social alienation in Mexico City and the political disillusionment that followed the violent repression of the 1968 protest movement—cast the government in an extremely negative light. This new writing has at times been criticized as too narcissistic, too focused on the middle class, and too indifferent to the great social themes, such as poverty, violent upheaval, and corruption, that attracted a previous literary generation. But in their defense, these contemporary novelists argue that their experience is urban and middle class.

One of the most acclaimed of the recent urban novels is *The Princess of the Iron Palace* (the Iron Palace is a large department store in Mexico City) by Gustavo Sainz. The book is a recitation of a middle-class girl's memories, sometimes appalling, sometimes ridiculous, often banal, of adolescence in the capital. Her boyfriends are manic-depressives, drug pushers, pimps, and brawlers. Sex is passionless and casual—light-years away from the drama and sensuality of lovemaking evoked in Mexican novels of an earlier generation. This "princess" is incapable of emotional attachments. When a former lover phones up to pour out his suicidal impulses, her mind drifts. She stares at the rain lashing her window and is somehow reminded of another boyfriend. The princess herself is just as much a victim of insensitivity. She absentmindedly takes a near-fatal dose of barbiturates, while her parents—transfixed by a television soap opera in their living room—are completely oblivious to their daughter's plight in the bedroom a few steps away.

There is no warmth or beauty in the Mexico City that Sainz describes. Cars crash in the traffic-clogged streets, and thieves run off with the hubcaps. Nightclubs are sinister: the brass bands grate on the nerves, the waiters are rude, the food provokes nausea, the patrons are junkies and prostitutes. There is little respite from the city's abrasions for these urban creatures. The princess and her friends drive to Cuernavaca every Sunday, only to gulp down a few Bloody Marys before returning to the capital by sundown.

The homosexual novel, certainly a daring innovation in a country that coined the concept of machismo, is another example of the new urban literature. Luís Zapata's *The Vampire of the Roma Neighborhood* is set mainly in the capital's most fashionable retail, nightclub, and restaurant district. The protagonist is a male prostitute for whom sex is even more monotonous and affectionless than it was for Sainz's princess. The Mexico City he inhabits is one where heterosexuals can be simply ignored. They are as irrelevant to his existence as the street signs, traffic lights, and automobiles that serve as urban props for the novel.

Shadows of Silence by Arturo Azuela (grandson of Mariano Azuela, the leading novelist of the Revolution) is the most celebrated novel to emerge from the 1968 crisis. Depicting young intellectuals as a beleaguered caste, Azuela traces the lives of a close-knit circle of friends—several journalists, a novelist, an actress, an aspiring politician, a book editor—in post-1968 Mexico City. They are marginal people in many senses. In their thirties and forties, they are still single or survivors of broken marriages, incapable of sustaining their romantic attachments for long. Despite their intellectual pretensions, they spend the better part of their lives dancing, smoking, drinking, or conversing until daybreak. Their acts of courage are ephemeral: writing polemical books that most Mexicans cannot afford to buy; publishing occasional articles on graft or the wholesale destruction of Mexico City neighborhoods by unscrupulous real estate operators; serving brief stints in jail after being arrested in antigovernment protests.

These intellectuals could never be mistaken for revolutionaries. None of them even contemplates an act of political violence. They are puny Quixotes tilting verbally at a government windmill. They measure their political commitment in terms of how long they can resist the various temptations to sell out—by joining self-censored newspapers, securing tenure in state universities, or accepting lucrative posts in government. The appeal of Azuela's characters is their commitment to one another. To outsiders they show a cynical and bitter face. But within the confines of their coterie, they are able to applaud their meager accomplishments, share in their mythomania, to humor and chide themselves, offer solace whenever tragedy overtakes one of them, and wallow together in nostalgia and apathy.

While the urban literature of the post-1968 period has the virtue of being more unfettered in its treatment of controversial subjects than newspapers, magazines, and nonfiction books, it suffers like the rest of the printed media from an inability to reach out to a broad enough public. Mass communication in contemporary Mexico is the province of radio and television, and the government has shown little tolerance of dissent in broadcasting. Even privately owned stations submit their programs to government examiners. Commercial television, which draws far more viewers than state-owned channels, offers mainly a blend of dubbed American sitcoms and Mexican soap operas on the travails of the wealthy.

The courting of intellectuals ranks as the government's most successful policy of the last twenty years. With few exceptions, intellectuals have become stronger allies of the regime than they were before the Tlatelolco Massacre. They have little impact on the shaping of official policies, but at least they are allowed to roam through the corridors of bureaucratic power, speak out more freely on politics than they could a generation ago, and lay claim to social prominence and economic security. Intellectuals have become indistinguishable from the political elite with whom they share a common social background, educational formation, and residence in Mexico City. They are in fact more comfortable with politicians than with any other group, including businessmen, professionals, organized labor, and the clergy. And in spite of their claims to an acute social conscience, they are far more absorbed by political gossip, factional rivalries within the PRI, and the inner workings of the bureaucracy than they are by social realities in Mexico City's teeming slums or in the provinces.

Perhaps the ultimate measure of the intellectuals' renewed allegiance to the government has been their attitude toward the minor guerrilla factions that sprouted in Mexico after 1968. These armed groups attracted few recruits or sympathizers from the Mexican intellectual establishment, in contrast to other Latin American countries during the 1970s. Nor did the Mexican government face serious criticism from the intellectual community for its routine use of torture and assassination in quelling the guerrillas. Between 1971 and 1978, more than four hundred people "disappeared," and not all of these presumed victims of the security forces were armed rebels.[3]

Whatever criticism the government received for its handling of the guerrilla movement came mainly from the business community, which was the chief target of these gunmen. To entrepreneurs, Echeverría's leftist rhetoric had encouraged an environment that spawned terrorism. After the assassination of the leading Monterrey industrialist, Eugenio Garza Sada, during a kidnap attempt in 1973, some businessmen even accused the government of complicity with the guerrillas. And the following year, when Echeverría's father-in-law briefly disappeared in a suspicious incident, there were many businessmen willing to believe rumors that the president had somehow engineered the alleged guerrilla kidnapping to gain public sympathy.

Relations between government and business continued to deteriorate after the small guerrilla factions were virtually crushed. Even during the golden decades of private enterprise that began with Alemán, the enterpreneurial and political elites viewed each other with considerable suspicion and disdain. The chasm between the two groups now widened because of the government's growing involvement in economic affairs.

The seventies and early eighties were a time of increasing economic intervention by the state throughout the Third World. In Latin America, governments as disparate as Salvador Allende's Marxist coalition in Chile, the right-wing Peronists in Argentina, and the military regime in Brazil were investing heavily in manufacturing, mining, and commerce, and tightening their control over financial institutions. The state was willing to take more long-term risks than private companies, interested as they were in immediate profits. Only governments were able to raise the large amounts of investment capital to create new enterprises that could compete against huge multinational corporations. The state was also more concerned than the private sector in ensuring employment for the vast number of young adults entering the job market.

In Mexico, this new orthodoxy sweeping the Third World was given added impetus by the government's desire to mold a progressive image for itself after the Tlatelolco Massacre. Besides wooing intellectuals through jobs, money, and left-wing rhetoric, Echeverría adopted their argument that the Mexican economic miracle had benefited the business elite without satisfying the basic needs of the poor. Under his administration, taxes on corporate profits and personal incomes rose sharply. So did public spending in education, housing, and agriculture. Government industries like oil, electricity, and iron and steel doubled their production. The number of state-owned corporations mushroomed from 86 to 740.[4] Meanwhile, the economy grew at an annual average rate of 5.6 percent, only slightly below the levels reached during the previous three decades.

These shifts in economic policy embittered businessmen. For them, the crisis of 1968 was the result of the politicians' mishandling of the protest movement, and the government was about to compound its errors by economic mismanagement. Before 1970, most businesses had financed their expansion through their own profits. Now that higher taxes had reduced these profits, entrepreneurs turned to the banks for credit. But they discovered that they were competing with the government, which needed ever larger loans to foot the bill for its huge spending programs. When these loans proved insufficient, the government simply printed additional currency. Between 1970 and

1976, the money supply expanded by almost 20 percent annually, and the federal deficit soared by 600 percent. Inflation rose by 22 percent a year, pricing Mexican goods out of foreign markets and tripling the balance-of-payments deficit.[5] Shortly before Echeverría left office in 1976, the peso was devalued by more than 50 percent, bringing to a close twenty-two years of stable currency.

Business confidence was shattered. Billions of dollars fled across the border into American real estate, banks, stocks, and bonds. Dismayed by the bloated enrollment and political activism in UNAM and other state universities, affluent families placed their children in private institutions. Among Mexico City's entrepreneurial elite, the conventional wisdom was that the government was infested with Marxist ideologues trained at UNAM and the Politécnico.

In fact, the left-wing intellectuals recruited by Echeverría represented a minority of the state university graduates and dropouts who flocked to the expanding federal bureaucracy. Most of the new government employees were no different from those of the previous generation, only far more numerous. Their desire for political and economic advancement superseded any ideological convictions. And despite Echeverría's insistence that his government represented a radical break from past regimes, the rules for getting ahead in the bureaucracy remained the same.

A scholar researching one of the key bureaucratic agencies in Echeverría's government, CONASUPO, which operates stores offering food, clothing, medicine, and other essential goods to the poor at subsidized prices, found that personal loyalty between superiors and subordinates was still the most important qualification for employment and promotion.[6] Of the seventy-eight middle- and high-level bureaucrats she interviewed, only twelve worked in CONASUPO prior to the Echeverría government. The turnover had nothing to do with shifts in policy or ideology, but rather was a consequence of the massive bureaucratic exodus that accompanies the presidential succession every six years. Only eight of these seventy-eight individuals had secured employment by their own efforts. All the rest had landed their jobs through friendships cemented in childhood, at the university, and during work in other government agencies. About a third of the new job holders had been recommended to CONASUPO by their benefactors in the official party hierarchy or in other government agencies. The majority, however, were members of already existing *"equipos"* or teams, each led by a rising politician who had recruited his followers in UNAM or during an earlier bureaucratic assignment.

CONASUPO was considered a politically important agency during the Echeverría years because of its efforts to distribute greater benefits to the low-income population. Between 1970 and 1976, its budget quadrupled and its staff more than doubled to 8,300 people. But few of the ranking bureaucrats came to CONASUPO with any special expertise, strong social convictions, or desire to stay at the agency for more than a few years. A political career in Mexico City did not function that way. One had to be prepared to follow the team leader through a succession of unrelated bureaucratic assignments, each higher than the previous post.

The most prominent team leader at CONASUPO was the agency's director, Jorge de la Vega Domínguez, and as the 1976 presidential succession neared, the members of his equipo were excited by the prospects of his promotion in the new administration. "If he becomes a minister," commented one of them, "then his entire [equipo] will follow him and we'll all have positions in the Ministry."[7] And when De la Vega Domínguez was eventually appointed trade minister, he did indeed bring his equipo in tow.

While the 1976 presidential succession led to the usual massive turnover in the bureaucracy, it was also marked by greater tensions than at any time in the previous forty years. Echeverría confounded politicians and the public by picking a dark horse, his finance minister José López Portillo, as the next president. He had been Echeverría's close friend since childhood. They studied together in grammar school, at the National Preparatory, in UNAM's Law School, and in Chile on a political science scholarship. López Portillo, like Echeverría, had never run for an elective post before the presidential campaign. He exemplified the technocrats who now dominated the political elite. After a dozen years as law professor at UNAM, he ascended through a variety of bureaucratic agencies. But his two years as finance minister—a post not previously considered a springboard to the highest office—did not make him the likeliest presidential candidate. And there were widespread suspicions that López Portillo might be too weak politically to shed his image as Echeverría's protégé even after assuming the presidency.

These suspicions were fed by Echeverría's obstinate behavior during his last months in office. While López Portillo campaigned throughout the country—a strenuous ritual undertaken by all PRI presidential candidates no matter how little opposition they face—Echeverría refused to play the role of lame duck. In speeches filled with invective, he charged that the private sector was plotting against his government with the help of foreign agents. Through frequent and dramatic press conferences, he continuously upstaged López Portillo. At the very least, Echeverría seemed to be staking his claims to exercise power behind the scenes after his presidency ended. But there were also darker, wilder insinuations that he was scheming to remain in office.

On August 11, 1976, a car driving a sister of López Portillo through the streets of Mexico City was attacked by unidentified terrorists. She was unscathed, but one of her bodyguards was fatally shot and several others wounded. It was rumored that the intended victim was López Portillo himself. In the weeks that followed, a number of ranking politicians and their family members were said to be targeted for assassination.

But the most persistent rumor—a subject of heated discussion in the streets, cafés, clubs, and offices of Mexico City—was that Echeverría was trying to foment a military coup to maintain himself in power. In retrospect, the notion was implausible: there had not been a military uprising in almost four decades, nor was there any indication that the army was abandoning its low political profile. Yet a wide spectrum of public opinion was prepared to believe that Echeverría, by creating an atmosphere of crisis, was paving the way for military intervention.

He blamed antipatriotic speculators for the devaluation of the peso that his government announced on August 31. And when the currency continued its downward float over the next two months, he escalated his attacks against the business community. With coup rumors at their peak in November, the country was shaken by the news that peasants had invaded rich farmlands in the northern state of Sonora. Echeverría expropriated almost 250,000 acres of these properties and turned them over to peasant cooperatives. In protest, more than twenty thousand private landowners in the northern states announced a farm strike. They were joined by thousands of businessmen and merchants who carried out brief work stoppages in provincial cities elsewhere in the country. Meanwhile, peasants in the states of Durango and Jalisco staged further land takeovers, hoping that Echeverría would also back their claims. The month closed with a rash of nighttime bombings of office buildings in Mexico City. Nobody claimed credit for the explosions, which caused considerable damage but no fatalities.

Talk of a military coup ended only with the inauguration of López Portillo on December 1, 1976. The new president also made it apparent that he was not going to be manipulated by his predecessor. With Echeverría seated only a few feet away after having handed over the presidential sash, López Portillo pointedly announced to the politicians and foreign dignitaries assembled in Mexico City's National Auditorium that he would not share the powers of his office with anybody. The rest of his inaugural speech amounted to a repudiation of Echeverría's style and policies. He was conciliatory toward the business community, upholding their "legitimate expectations." While vowing to make every effort to aid the poor, he avoided militant rhetoric. Instead of confrontation and radical change, he stressed the need for cooperation and patience to cope with the nation's economic crisis and badly frayed political nerves.

Echeverría left the presidency virtually bereft of a political following. His huge public spending programs aimed at benefiting the poorest Mexicans were eroded by inflation. Corruption had reached the highest levels since the days of Alemán. And most politicians were furious at his conduct during his last months in office, which had rattled a political system that had run so smoothly for decades.

López Portillo's cabinet included almost no officials identified with his predecessor. Within months, Echeverrístas were rooted out of even middle-level bureaucratic posts. A few noteworthy supporters of the former president were indicted on corruption charges, probably to warn their patron against any attempt to reassert his influence. Echeverría himself was sent out of the country, as ambassador to UNESCO in Paris and later as envoy to Australia. He would be allowed to return to Mexico City only in 1980, when López Portillo was more than halfway through his term.

Besides benefiting from widespread antipathy toward his predecessor, López Portillo displayed personal attributes that immediately gained him a large popular following. He was affable, good-humored, and quick to smile. He cultivated the image of a scholar-athlete, who spent early mornings practicing javelin throws and late evenings poring over literary tracts in his library. Businessmen, emerging from reunions with the president, spoke of a revival of confidence in the private sector. Foreign creditors applauded his apparent commitment to dampen inflation and meet heavy debt payments abroad. Trade union officials agreed to endure a period of belt-tightening. With this large reservoir of goodwill, López Portillo was able to navigate unscathed through the economic austerity that marked his first year in office.

The nation's willingness to tolerate a drop in living standards during 1977 seemed rewarded when enormous petroleum deposits were discovered on the Gulf coast the following year. Coming at a time of sharply rising oil prices, the new finds promised another Mexican economic miracle. Between 1978 and 1981, the gross domestic product grew by 8 percent annually. Mexican companies reported record profits and investments. Government spending far exceeded the levels of the Echeverría years. Industry, both private and state-owned, was especially promoted to ensure continued prosperity in a distant future when oil reserves would be depleted. But the countryside also received massive revenues to bolster a lag in food production. Intoxicated by the soaring price of oil, the government borrowed abroad against future revenues, and encouraged the private sector to follow suit. Despite the mounting balance-of-payments deficit and inflation, the peso held steady, permitting even middle-class Mexicans to enjoy luxury imports and foreign vacations.

The economic reverie ended just as suddenly as it began. Oil prices collapsed in 1981, causing a fall in government revenues. Interest rates abroad rose sharply, and a world recession reduced demand for Mexican petroleum and gas. Anticipating another devaluation of the peso, capital flowed across the American border by the tens of billions of dollars—amounts that far exceeded the levels of Echeverría's waning days in office. By August 1982, the government was no longer able to service its foreign debt, which had grown by $60 billion in the six years of López Portillo's presidency. The battered peso plunged to less than one hundredth of a dollar, and showed no sign of stabilizing. Inflation was out of control. The greatest economic surge in modern Mexican history had turned into the worst economic crisis in six decades.

Attempting to salvage his reputation in history, López Portillo announced a "revolutionary" takeover of Mexico's banks by the government in his last state of the union address on September 1, 1982. The move, he asserted, was intended to punish the private banking system for permitting the hemorrhage of capital to foreign havens. His aides likened the measure to Cárdenas's nationalization of the oil industry in 1938. It was not the first time a beleaguered president had sought refuge in Cárdenas's shadow: only six years before, Echeverría compared the land expropriations that closed his own discredited term to the watershed agrarian reform program of Cárdenas. But few contemporary Mexicans would place López Portillo and Echeverría in such hallowed company. Their combined presidencies (1970–82) have become popularly known as the *"Docena Trágica,"* or the "Tragic Twelve Years"—an allusion to the Tragic Ten Days that devastated Mexico City when the first revolutionary president, Francisco Madero, was overthrown in 1913.

López Portillo finished his presidency in even greater disgrace than his predecessor. He took up residence in Rome for a few years to escape the withering criticism from middle-class and affluent Mexicans. Their anger was heightened by the sense of deception they felt in a political leader who had raised and then betrayed their expectations. They had been seduced by his warm personality and political style, so different from Echeverría's scowling demeanor and militant rhetoric. And yet in the end, López Portillo's stewardship of the economy was more damaging. Not that the private sector had displayed greater responsibility than his government. Businesses, large and small, had borrowed and spent beyond their means during the brief boom of 1977–81, and in the aftermath some of the largest private corporations were as insolvent as the government.

From the viewpoint of the business community, however, the chief underlying cause of the crisis was the spectacular economic imbalance that had been created between public and private sectors. When Echeverría left office in 1976, the government's share of the gross domestic product had almost doubled, to about 25 percent. At the end of López Portillo's term, 70 percent of the nation's economy was in the hands of the state. Some 1.5 million bureaucrats, ensconced in 3,500 buildings of the capital, were managing enterprises that ranged from petrochemical production and steel manufacturing to supermarkets and parking lots. Their accounting methods were shoddy and sealed from public scrutiny. Their criteria for hiring combined a concern for ameliorating urban unemployment with an even stronger desire to reward political loyalty. They displayed a cavalier disregard for productivity and profitability. Yet, in the wake of the bank nationalizations, these bloated state enterprises received the bulk of available loans while cash-strapped private companies went empty-handed.

The relative merit of state versus private management of the economy was not an issue that troubled most Mexicans. Excessive corruption in government, on the other hand, provoked an angry and widespread public reaction. The country had long tolerated the practice of illicit enrichment in public office. Mexicans, affluent and poor, accepted the inevitability of paying bribes to police, government inspectors, and minor bureaucrats to obtain official permits, facilitate business transactions, or avoid traffic summonses. A cynical humor pervaded popular comments on the alleged venality of politicians. Alemán, for example, was often defended as someone "who stole a lot, but also did a lot." When López Portillo attempted to stir the citizenry with the refrain, *"La solución somos todos"* ("The solution lies within us all"), it echoed back to him from the public as "*La corrupción somos todos*" ("Corruption lies within us all"). "The Revolution did him justice" is the way many Mexicans describe a functionary whose sumptuous lifestyle belies his modest official salary.

But as the dimensions of the economic crisis became apparent toward the end of the López Portillo regime, the public mood turned bitter. There was a willingness to believe that the country's economic troubles were linked to the rapacity of the political elite. "Why did they have to steal so much?" was the common lament of cab driver, waiter, and businessman. On the walls of Mexico City's buildings, the PRI's name was altered to read *Partido del Robo Institucionalizado* (Party of Institutionalized Robbery, instead of Party of the Institutionalized Revolution). It was easy to believe that multibillion-dollar public projects were launched by the government solely to allow officials to embezzle a portion of the huge funding.

What made any accusation seem credible was the brazen display of wealth and nepotism by the highest politicians. As his term drew to a close, López Portillo built a five-mansion retreat atop a pristine hillside on the northwestern outskirts of Mexico City. With swimming pools, tennis courts, stables, and star-gazing observatory, the lavish estate was viewed as evidence that the president's fortune could be measured in billions of dollars. He appointed a half dozen of his family members to ranking bureaucratic posts. But it was his well-publicized generosity toward his mistress, Rosa Luz Alegría, that became a symbol of the era's political decadence.

A dozen years before, Irma ("La Tigresa") Serrano had grudgingly endured the drawbacks of an affair with the chief of state: furtive liaisons with Díaz Ordaz between his cabinet meetings; dull evenings at home, away from the social and political limelight; and a sense of powerlessness against the jealous wrath of the president's wife. Miss Alegría, on the other hand, found her horizons much less restricted. Mexico City's upper class had become more openly tolerant of extramarital affairs, and women were making a place for themselves in the macho world of Mexican politics. And so, Miss Alegría was able to combine the careers of political courtesan and elite politician. A graduate of UNAM, she launched herself into the federal bureaucracy, aided by her marriage to one of Echeverría's sons. Such was the incestuousness of the political class that, upon her divorce, she became mistress to Echeverría's protégé and finance minister, López Portillo. As president, he appointed Miss Alegría minister of tourism, one of the choicest cabinet posts. He also bought her a two-million-dollar mansion in

Acapulco, and when his wife, in a fit of pique, appropriated the house, López Portillo purchased Miss Alegría another villa.

Allegations of illegal enrichment in office tarnished other ranking politicians of the López Portillo regime. Carlos Hank González, the mayor of Mexico City, who amassed a business fortune during his impressive political career, was embarrassed by revelations that he had purchased a million-dollar mansion in New Canaan, Connecticut. Jorge Díaz Serrano was convicted and sentenced to ten years in prison for a $34 million kickback scheme while he headed Pemex, the state-owned oil company. But the most notorious case of all involved the former police chief of Mexico City, Arturo ("El Negro") Durazo, whose misconduct in office became the subject of the greatest best seller in the nation's history. [8]

Like so many others who achieved power and fortune in government service, Arturo Durazo owed his political destiny to a friendship during his student days—in his case, with José López Portillo, the future president of Mexico. They were the unlikeliest of pals: the taller, handsome, fair-skinned López Portillo, son of an upper-middle-class family of literary and political renown, was articulate, intellectually inclined, and socially graceful; the short, swarthy (thus the nickname "El Negro") Durazo, poverty-stricken and of uncertain parentage, was an apathetic student, a brawler, and member of a juvenile street gang. Durazo, playing the role of bodyguard, shielded his friend from the tougher elements at the Benito Juárez School where they both studied, accompanied him on nighttime adventures through the city's more tawdry districts, and chaperoned López Portillo's sisters to dance halls where adolescent girls risked being accosted by drunken machos. In return, López Portillo ghost-wrote Durazo's term papers, supplied him with answers to exams, and often brought him home for dinner which the slum kid gulped down with a ravenous zest that astonished his hosts.

Among Mexican politicians, a friendship made in childhood or adolescence can lie dormant for many years and then be rekindled when it proves useful. Still, the paths taken by these two youths after their school days were so divergent that the renewal of their relationship decades later was startling. López Portillo followed the conventional trajectory of an elite politician through the UNAM Law School and the federal bureaucracy. Durazo, on the other hand, became a body-guard and chauffeur for Manuel Prieto, the capital's most notorious gangster. When Prieto drew a long prison sentence, Durazo, suddenly out of a job, became a clerk for the postal service and then with a bank. His meager salary forced him to share a tiny apartment with a friend. Unable to afford a wardrobe, the two men regularly exchanged suits so that they would not have to appear at work every day in the same clothes. After a few years, Durazo's longstanding application to the transit police department was accepted. The official income of traffic cops was low, but they could expect to supplement their earnings through bribes.

Over the next three decades, his assignments in various police agencies brought him in contact with drug traffic, contraband, and alleged political subversion. When Fidel Castro and Che Guevara sought refuge in Mexico City during the mid-1950s before their successful revolutionary offensive in Cuba, they were briefly detained and interrogated by Durazo. According to his aide, José González, many years later Durazo bragged that he had tortured the two famous rebels with electric shocks and repeated water submersion. "You should have seen it," Durazo allegedly told González. "The bastards' eyes were about to explode and the wax oozed out of their ears."[9]

Durazo's career took a providential turn in 1976 when López Portillo became the presidential candidate of the government party and appointed his old friend as his chief of personal security during the electoral campaign: forty years later, El Negro was again playing bodyguard to his former school chum. López Portillo then rewarded Durazo by making him police chief of Mexico City. The appointment briefly outraged the public because Durazo was already under grand jury indictment in the United States on charges of drug trafficking.

The Mexico City police had an unsavory reputation long before Durazo assumed command. It was an organization that weeded out honest cops from the very moment they were recruited. Rookies had to buy their uniforms, service revolvers, even their badges from their superiors. A policeman was expected to extort bribes from motorists, petty criminals, and merchants. His ranking officers had their own estimates of how much income each beat was likely to generate, and demanded a percentage of the take. The rare policeman who declined to collect bribes was assumed to be cheating his superiors and was quickly dismissed from the force. The more ambitious and dishonest officers paid their commanders for choice assignments: as motorcycle cops who could chase after potentially wealthy drivers; as flatfoots in commercial districts where merchants slipped them money to overlook infractions by delivery vehicles and sidewalk displays; and as car patrolmen on the highways leading into the city where trucks were regularly "fined" for alleged mechanical deficiencies.

The image of the police department was also tarnished by its treatment of suspects. Guilty or innocent, they were often tortured into confessions, particularly if they were poor and without influence. "If you are assaulted by a criminal," goes one popular saying in the capital, "don't shout for help because you risk attracting the police." So deep is the contempt of the populace for their cops that during the Independence Day parade through Mexico City's central district, the large contingent of police motorcycles and patrol cars pass review by assembled dignitaries with their sirens screaming in order to drown out the jeers of spectators.

Within months after Durazo became police chief, however, residents of the capital were expressing something akin to nostalgia for his predecessors. Using his friendship with the president, Durazo brought the police budget completely under his control by replacing the city officials in charge of investigating his agency's expenditures with his own trusted henchmen. He assigned relatives and notorious criminals to key posts in the police department. Almost a century before, Porfirio Díaz had recruited bandits into his police force with the rationale that their delinquent past made them more resourceful in tracking down ruffians. Durazo, however, was not interested in repentant sinners. If the police department was to become a more proficient racketeering empire, the expertise of criminals was needed. Thus, drug traffickers were placed in charge of narcotics control; the leader of a large ring of car thieves joined the bureau of missing vehicles; a kidnapper was made responsible for investigating extortion plots against industrialists and other wealthy businessmen; smugglers oversaw the drive against contraband. [10]

José González, who was Durazo's chief bodyguard and later wrote the best-selling exposé of his boss, described himself as typical of the aides recruited by Mexico City's police chief. He had known El Negro in early adolescence, and as policemen their paths crossed again several times. A self-admitted professional gunman, González estimated that he had slain more than fifty people, including several bystanders caught up in the Tlatelolco Massacre. "I killed on orders from people like [President] Gustavo Díaz Ordaz, [Mexico City's mayor] Alfonso Corona del Rosal and many others," he wrote, expressing his gratitude to them for ensuring that these murders were wiped clean from his police blotter. [11] According to González, it was his reputation as a cold-blooded killer and expert shot that landed him his job with Durazo.

With high-level collaborators like these, Durazo's police department soon became indistinguishable from a crime syndicate. Every illicit activity had a more lucrative wrinkle. Drivers discovered that their vehicles were being towed away by the police with intolerable frequency, and that they were required to pay higher bribes to recover them from police parking lots. Almost all car owners were forced to make under-the-table payments to have their license plates renewed. Merchants, particularly wholesale food distributors, protested that fees imposed on them by the police for alleged infractions reached exorbitant levels.

Police involvement in narcotics trafficking became more scandalous than ever. Cocaine shipments that fell into the hands of agents during the course of raids or investigations were distributed among a dozen ranking officers who, after cutting the drugs to a fraction of their original purity, sold them to the rest of the police personnel. They, in turn, peddled the cocaine in the streets or kept it for their own use. According to González, a majority of the police agents involved in the drug trade were heavy abusers of cocaine. "In the very corridors of the [police headquarters] building, some officers were so brazen that they would come up to me and say: 'Hey boss, how about a snort?' "[12]

The high command also organized and protected gangs who robbed banks and company rolls, and then shared their loot. Such bands were usually recruited among South American gunmen who had been brought into the country illegally. With no criminal records in Mexico, they baffled unsuspecting police detectives called in to investigate their robberies. The existence of these gangs became public knowledge when fourteen badly decomposed bodies were recovered from the Tula River near Mexico City in 1982. Durazo told the press that the victims were foreign subversives who were shot in a dispute with their confederates. But this official version failed to hold up when one of the dead was identified as a Mexican taxi driver by his relatives, who said that he had been hired by "Colombian tourists." According to González, the thirteen Colombians and their Mexican companion had been tortured by police agents into surrendering the booty from their robberies, and then massacred.[13]

During his reign as Mexico City's police chief, Durazo constructed an enormous house—equipped with horse and dog racing tracks, discotheque, gambling casino, swimming pools, and artificial lakes— some fourteen miles south of Mexico City, off the highway to Cuernavaca. Known as the "Cabaña de Ajusco," it was built in alpine style by 650 policemen, who were paid out of his department's budget. The cost soared because the Cabaña had to be connected to distant water sources and electricity lines. On weekends, Durazo staged parties at the house for as many as three hundred guests, including President López Portillo, cabinet ministers, the mayor of Mexico City, police cronies, and famous entertainers. A platoon of policemen were drafted as kitchen help, butlers, and servants. On an island off a Pacific beach resort, Durazo also built himself a villa, which was dubbed the "Parthenon of Zihuatanejo" for its neoclassical columns, marble statues, and pool-sized baths.

Durazo's daily journey from his suburban mansion to police headquarters was a spectacle that both dazzled and unnerved scores of thousands of other commuters. The road to Cuernavaca was closed to all vehicles for up to a half-hour while the police chief's heavily armed convoy of motorcycle cops and patrol cars sped along the highway. From the city's outskirts to the downtown headquarters, every intersection was blocked by policemen until the convoy drove by. Police sharpshooters were stationed on pedestrian overpasses and on the roofs of the buildings surrounding the headquarters. The same security arrangements were reactivated for Durazo's return home in the evening, or when he traveled to an appointment elsewhere in the capital. According to his chief bodyguard, Durazo lived in constant fear of assassination. A few times a week, he would cancel his usual itinerary on short notice and instead order a helicopter to transport him to his offices because, as he told his aides, he wanted "to befuddle the enemy." Even in the tight security of police headquarters, Durazo was so wary that he went to the toilet under escort. In the expensive restaurants he frequented almost daily, he positioned himself at a table with his back to the wall and was flanked by armed guards. If he decided that nearby patrons looked suspicious, he ordered his aides to remove them from the restaurant.[14]

His favorite son, nicknamed "Yoyo," shared some of his unpleasant traits. He arrived at his exclusive private school—a parochial institution favored by the political elite—in a bulletproof car with bodyguards. In such company, the heavyset, ill-tempered teenager could afford to play the bully. On one occasion, Yoyo used the butt of a machine gun borrowed from one of his bodyguards to smash the windows of a faculty member's automobile while the professor cowered inside the vehicle. "I just trashed a teacher's car 'cause the bastard failed one of my buddies," Yoyo explained over the phone to González, who was usually the first to be informed of his antics. "So if he comes whining to dad, don't let him pass."[15]

Durazo, however, did receive the aggrieved professor, bought him a new car, and made a generous contribution to the school. And he used his money and influence to hush up other scandalous incidents involving Yoyo: like the two separate occasions when the youngster, racing his automobile through the capital, ran over a cyclist and an elderly woman; or the time he and his bodyguards beat up a pilot, who took exception to Yoyo's lewd remarks to his wife (the Acapulco-bound flight was delayed for several hours while Yoyo and his entourage were escorted off the plane, and airline officials located a replacement for the battered pilot who was rushed to the hospital); or that afternoon when Yoyo had his police escort block traffic on a Mexico City freeway so that he could impress his girlfriend with his acrobatic handling of a motorcycle.[16]

Near the end of his term in 1982, Durazo realized that his notoriety might make him an inviting target for a new administration. And so, he begged López Portillo to arrange a seat for him in the Senate, which would grant him a measure of immunity from criminal prosecution. But his old friend, citing previous commitments to other politicians, turned him down.

Miguel de la Madrid became the next president, after running on a platform of anticorruption. Yet in the six years of his administration (1982–88), his heralded "moralization" campaign showed few dramatic results. Several hundred policemen were cashiered for extortion and other transgressions. Some of these former cops were later suspected of robberies during a crime wave that swept Mexico City in the mid-1980s. On occasion, the government announced the suspension or dismissal of scores of minor civil servants accused of demanding bribes from the public. But among major figures, only Durazo and Díaz Serrano, the former head of Pemex, were eventually arrested. And it became apparent that by drawing out legal proceedings against them over five years, the government was hoping to forestall public demands for a wider dragnet against other important officials suspected of large-scale corruption.

Durazo was able to flee abroad before orders were issued for his arrest. He was reported to have moved about Europe, Canada, and the Caribbean before finally being extradited from the United States to Mexico City in 1986. His two sumptuous residences were confiscated by the government, which opened his Ajusco estate to the public as a "museum of corruption." But Durazo was still a figure of considerable power. Of the fifty police department witnesses who originally gave depositions against him, all but one—his former chief bodyguard, González—recanted their testimonies. Some of them acknowledged that they were threatened with the loss of their jobs. González himself asserted that he was once beaten up and his wife was assaulted on three different occasions by unidentified thugs. By 1987, Durazo faced only the reduced charges of illegal possession of arms and extortion.

Díaz Serrano, the former chief of the state petroleum company, remained in Mexico even though the De la Madrid government was building its embezzlement case against him. Elected to the Senate in 1982, he relied on his seat to protect him from prosecution. But in June 1983, his fellow senators voted to waive his immunity, and a few weeks later he was indicted and jailed. For the next four years, he was one of the more privileged inmates in Mexico City's prison system. In interviews with the news media, Díaz Serrano described his regimen of tennis and television viewing, unrestricted conjugal and family visits three days a week, and the tidy condition in which his chambers were kept by prisoners on his payroll. Díaz Serrano insisted that he was a scapegoat, but was astute enough not to make any accusations against specific politicians. And from the government's viewpoint, the publicity he was generating from prison was helping to preserve the illusion of a still vigorous anticorruption campaign.

It was already obvious, however, that the political elite would not tolerate a wholesale purge of its ranks on the grounds of illicit enrichment in office. Any attempt to prosecute López Portillo, for example, was out of the question. De la Madrid was not the least inclined to attack López Portillo, who had selected him as president from among a half-dozen more prominent candidates.

De la Madrid was the ultimate technocrat, even among elite politicians who had come to prize bureaucratic expertise over electoral experience. Born to a prominent family in the Pacific coast state of Colima, he had lived since childhood in Mexico City. Following the requisite stint in UNAM's Law School, he received a master's degree in public administration from Harvard University. His career in government was devoted to financial affairs: adviser to the Bank of Mexico; subdirector of finances for Pemex; various ranking posts in the treasury ministry; and minister of planning and budget under López Portillo.

Just short of his forty-eighth year when he assumed the presidency, De la Madrid was of medium stature, thin, handsome, with graying hair about his temples, and an unruffled mien—a Mexican casting director's image of a corporate CEO or bank director. Facing an economic crisis that would endure throughout his term, he set about to restore a semblance of balance between public and private sectors. He curbed government spending, slashed subsidies for a range of basic services and commodities, boosted exports (mainly from the private sector) by allowing the peso to steadily devalue, and sold or shut down more than half the 1,155 government-owned companies. At the very least, the contraction of the state's economic role was a relatively effective way to reduce official corruption: with fewer enterprises and smaller budgets under their control, bureaucrats and politicians had less opportunities to enrich themselves in office.

But even after six years, De la Madrid could claim few economic successes. The nation was plagued by annual inflation rates of over 150 percent. The economy either stagnated or grew only marginally during his term. Unemployment rose, and real wages fell by 50 percent compared to 1982. De la Madrid became the target of a growing public disenchantment rarely displayed toward an incumbent Mexican president. When he inaugurated the 1986 world soccer championship in the capital, his words were drowned out by jeers and whistles from many of the 100,000 spectators. Perhaps his most visible economic achievement was the rise in Mexico's international reserve account to a hefty $15 billion by late 1987, enabling the country to continue servicing a foreign debt of over $100 billion. But De la Madrid was determined to ensure that his economic policies remain in place, and thus picked as his successor Carlos Salinas de Gortari, his budget minister and the government official most closely identified with enforcing his austerity program.

A key assumption of De la Madrid's administration was that the postwar Mexican economic miracle could be revived once government spending was brought under control and the private sector regained its enthusiasm to invest. But the economic growth of the golden decades (1940–70) was largely powered by big-city industrialization, a model that no longer seemed viable in the late 1980s.

The logic behind urban industrialization was that cities offered "economies of scale" conducive to the rapid growth of enterprises: a pool of skilled labor and managerial talent; a concentration of investment capital; a large market for industrial and consumer products; transportation and communication facilities; and a geographic compactness that made for a more efficient use of energy, water, and sewage networks.

The urban demographic explosion, however, has wiped out all these economies of scale. In 1940, Mexico was a rural country, with 70 percent of its population living in villages of less than twenty-five hundred inhabitants. By 1982, fifty-five million Mexicans, out of a total population of seventy-seven million, were urban dwellers. Gua-dalajara (five million people) and Monterrey (three million) have be-come true metropolises. Still, they are dwarfed by Mexico City, where almost a quarter of the nation's inhabitants resided in 1988.

To keep the capital functioning, the government has allocated it more than half the total budget earmarked for municipalities. As re-cently as 1986, heavy government subsidies enabled commuters to pay only one third of a penny for a ride on Mexico City's seventy-five-mile-long subway system, while a bus fare in smaller cities cost five to eight times as much. Because of its depleting natural aquifers, Mexico City increasingly depends on water pumped from intermon-tane valleys scores of miles away; the cost of supplying a gallon of water to the capital is ten times as much as for a city like Tampico on the Gulf coast. Since Mexico City lies in a closed basin, its sewage must be pumped out at great expense. Asphalting and road maintenance, the construction of additional subway lines, the building of schools, the extension of electricity and telephone grids, new water and sewage pipelines, and the salaries of the mammoth bureaucracy—all claim additional portions of the government budget. And public subsidies ensure that basic food items like beans, tortillas, vegetables, and milk sell more cheaply in Mexico City than in the countryside that produces them.

But the government is no longer getting a reasonable return from these enormous investments in the megalopolis. Between 1970 and 1980, federal spending in Mexico City far exceeded the worth of its entire existing industrial plant, according to a leading Mexican econ-omist.[17] In 1985, figures released by the Ministry of Urban Devel-opment and Ecology showed that the city's contribution to the gross domestic product had slipped to 37 percent from about 45 percent at the end of the 1970s.[18] Moreover, in recent years, government spend-ing in the capital has surpassed the tax revenues it collects there.

Put another way, the cost of supporting Mexico City is exceeding its contribution in goods and services. The Mexican model of rapid growth through concentrating industry in the largest cities—pioneered here four decades ago and copied throughout the developing world—is floundering. And no new economic master plan has emerged to replace it.

One of the most vexing problems facing Mexican urban planners and economists is the fact that Mexico City has expanded far beyond its traditional administrative boundaries. The capital was once con-tained within the limits of the Federal District created in 1824, shortly after Independence. But in recent decades, Mexico City has sprawled into the surrounding state of Mexico, which now accounts for almost 45 percent of the metropolitan zone's inhabitants. While the Federal District is ruled by a mayor appointed by the president, the state of Mexico is headed by an elected governor. The interests of these two powerful politicians are often in conflict: the mayor sees his mandate as limiting the growth of population and factories; the governor measures his accomplishment in terms of his successful efforts to attract more industry into his state, no matter what additional burdens this places on the megalopolis and the federal government which foots most of its bills.

De la Madrid made the capital's disproportionate claim on the federal budget a cornerstone of his presidential campaign. "When I travel in the interior of Mexico and come across communities where there is no water, no sewage facilities, no schools, no trucks or buses, I am asked why the government provides such important subsidies to the inhabitants of Mexico City," he remarked. "I cannot come up with an adequate response."[19]

De la Madrid adopted a slow-growth strategy for Mexico City that included tax incentives to move businesses elsewhere, reduction of subsidies for essential services, and promotion of birth control. But with an economic crisis enveloping the nation during the 1980s, these initiatives did not have much effect.

"At this moment, ninety percent of bank funds have been set aside by the government for its own needs," Francisco Calderón, head of a group called the Businessmen's Coordinating Council, said in 1985. "The little financing that is available for the private sector is being used to keep businesses running, not to set up new factories outside Mexico City." Nor did he envision industries rushing to relocate outside the capital even when the financial crunch eases. "The provinces don't yet have the infrastructure—roads, electricity, sewage, schools—that can support large enterprises," he explained. "It's not at all like moving a factory from Detroit to a small community in Tennessee."[20]

Old firms that have been in Mexico City for years exhibit no desire to leave. "Even with the traffic mess in the city, we are still ideally situated to sell to our retailers," said the chief executive of Puritan, S.A., a shirt and sweater manufacturer that has been operating in the capital since 1931. Besides, most of his six hundred employees would resist transferring to the provinces. "I can't say I would blame anyone who refused to move to places like Zacatecas or Sonora," he added. "I have young children. What sort of education, culture, friends could they expect out there? I'm not prepared to make these sorts of sacrifices."[21]

New firms also find reasons to choose Mexico City. Apple de México, a subsidiary of the California computer company, opened a factory in the capital in 1984. After studying provincial sites, it decided that quality control dictated proximity to suppliers, all of which are near Mexico City, said an Apple vice-president.[22]

The size and power of the federal bureaucracy continues to draw firms to the capital. "To try to get a price increase for products, or an import license, or anything that requires government permission, a businessman must come to Mexico City if he wants quick action," said Alfredo Sandoval González, president of Coparmex, an association of employers.[23]

In 1984, the De la Madrid government announced that fifty minor agencies and state companies would be transferred elsewhere as the beginning of a long-term project to decentralize the bureaucracy. But the larger state enterprises have actually increased their presence in the capital. In recent years, Pemex, the national petroleum company, inaugurated its fifty-two-story flagship building downtown. And after being nationalized, Banamex, one of the largest banks, rescinded plans made when it was private to move its headquarters to Querétaro, one hundred miles northwest.

The government has shown some determination in slashing subsidies of essential services in Mexico City as part of an effort to make the capital less attractive to new migrants. Subway and bus fares have risen, as have the prices of basic food items. But fears of a backlash among the urban poor—already scourged by an economic crisis that has caused their real wages to fall and unemployment to swell—have prevented the government from making deeper cuts in public spending. And as a result, Mexico City continues to offer even its destitute residents more and cheaper amenities than the provinces.

Public officials point hopefully to the recent success of birth control programs as evidence that the megalopolis's growth is slowing down. From a 3.5 percent annual population increase in 1970, the nationwide rate fell to 2.2 percent in 1985. The decline was steeper for Mexico City. For people already living in the capital, there was a natural growth rate—births minus deaths—of less than 2 percent in 1986. Unfortunately, the city's total population continued to rise by more than 4 percent because rural migrants were still arriving at a rate of one thousand a day.

It is not necessary to travel far from Mexico City to discover the causes of this massive provincial exodus. In the state of Morelos, just south of the capital, hundreds of people make the move every day, hoping to repeat the relative success of individuals like Roberto Jara, a peasant–turned–factory worker.[24] Jara, born in 1955, is a native of Villa de Ayala, a small Morelos community steeped in revolutionary lore and the ideals of agrarian reform. It was there that Emiliano Zapata unfurled his Plan de Ayala in 1911 calling for the distribution of land to Mexico's peasants. Jara's maternal grandfather rode with the hero, and was, until recently, a guide at the Zapata Museum, a concrete building encasing the remains of the rebel's adobe home in the village of Anenecuilco, a few miles south of Villa de Ayala.

During Roberto Jara's childhood, the slaughter and devastation of the revolutionary years were kept alive for him by the tales of his elderly relatives, schoolteachers, and government-sponsored parades and public speeches. In the nearby village and ejido, called Hospital, Jara and his boyhood friends came across the archaeology of the Porfirian era: the charred walls of an hacienda mansion, and the broken tracks of the narrow-gauge railway that transported the great landowner between his sugar-cane estate and Mexico City.

Decades of peace in Morelos had transformed the people, the economy, even the landscape. Only an hour's drive from Mexico City, the state had become dotted with spas, country retreats, and tourist hotels. Automotive and metallurgical industries were implanted in Cuernavaca. Small towns like Jojutla and Cuaútla grew into major urban centers, with three and four times as many inhabitants as in the 1920s. Many peasants also benefited from the boom. The old haciendas were parceled into ejidos. With credits from the government-owned Ejido Bank, irrigation facilities, fertilizers, tractors, and new crop strains, productivity surged. Better diets and more access to health facilities cut mortality rates.

Eventually, however, the ancient mismatch between people and resources reasserted itself. There was not enough land to accommodate a new, far more populous generation of peasants. Some of these rural youths were fortunate to find employment in nearby factories, commercial establishments, and hotels. Others spent part of the year as temporary farm workers in the United States. But most were drawn to Mexico City, the great lodestone for half the rural migrants who abandoned the Mexican countryside during the postwar decades.

Roberto Jara was a stocky, moon-faced fifteen-year-old when he decided to move to Mexico City in 1970. He was the youngest of five children. After his father died, the eldest son inherited the ejidal plot and encouraged his siblings to find a livelihood elsewhere. Roberto needed little prodding. Two cousins, who had migrated to the capital, returned periodically to Villa de Ayala and beguiled him with tales of money, women, and big city adventures. They barely mentioned the noise, pollution, and tenements where a dozen people slept side by side in windowless rooms.

The cousins were *"albañiles,"* unskilled construction workers, and arranged a job for Roberto with the labor contractor who employed them to build houses in wealthy neighborhoods like Coyoacán, San Angelín, and Pedregal. One of his cousins also invited him to stay temporarily in his vecindad in Tepito, the former thieves' quarter near the Zócalo. Roberto did not get along with his cousin's wife, however, who complained there was barely enough space in their single-room apartment for her two children, her husband, and herself. So Roberto bedded down at the building sites where he worked, returning to Tepito only during those weeks between the end of one construction assignment and the beginning of another.

Within three years of arriving in Mexico City, Roberto had a family of his own. He met his common-law wife, Hortensia, at a construction site in Coyoacán where she sold tacos and soft drinks to the work crews. When she became pregnant, they moved into a one-room tenement Roberto had rented in his cousin's vecindad. Through another relative, Roberto also found a steadier, higher-paying job as a mixer in a cement factory in Azcapozalco, a grimy industrial district in northern Mexico City. And from his fellow factory workers, he got the idea to take up residence in Ciudad Nezahualcóyotl, the huge slum ten miles east of downtown Mexico City.

"Neza"—as residents call it—is the largest of the working-class settlements that have mushroomed mainly beyond the eastern and northern outskirts of the capital. As recently as 1957, it had only ten thousand people. Yet when Jara moved there in 1974, Neza had added a startling one million inhabitants. And with more than three million residents in 1987, it had become the fourth most populous city in the nation. More than half of the inhabitants were refugees from the teeming downtown slums of the capital. The rest had migrated directly from rural zones.

It is easy to see why the poor found living space in Ciudad Nezahualcóyotl. Neza is an ecological wasteland spurned by middle-class and affluent Mexicans. Sprawling over the partially dried bed of Lake Texcoco, its earth is so saline that hardly a tree or shrub grows in the community. And because it is located at the very bottom of the Valley of Mexico, Neza becomes a natural tub during the wet season. The rains accumulate in stagnant pools, mix with raw sewage, and seep into wells, polluting the drinking water.

An overpowering smell of organic waste saturates the air. Some of it emanates from the shrinking remains of Lake Texcoco, which receives piped sewage from Mexico City. There is also the stench from the enormous open-air garbage dump that creates a no-man's-land between the lake and the eastern periphery of the slum. In the dry season, dust and fecal particles swirl up in the winds, spreading airborne gastrointestinal diseases.

Many of the migrants settling in Neza during the 1960s were forced to pay developers who claimed to have title over the land. But in subsequent years, new arrivals insisted that the entire zone belonged to the state because it occupied land that had once lain below Lake Texcoco. Squatting became the most usual way to take possession of property. Developers and corrupt municipal officials sent the police to dislodge the invaders. But by the early 1970s, President Echeverría, taking a more benign and populist view, sided with the squatters. The government expropriated the disputed properties and sold them to occupants at prices well below market value, with payment terms stretched over five to ten years.

Roberto Jara was a beneficiary of this new policy. Arriving in Neza in 1974, he squatted on a plot of land close to the garbage dump, and erected a shack from corrugated tin, wood, and carton. He "hijacked" electricity by stringing a wire from his home to the closest utility pole. Every day, Hortensia used a public faucet down the block to fill buckets that supplied the household with water for washing and drinking. As soon as the state government "regularized" Jara's title to his property, he built a sturdier two-room house with cinder blocks bought at a discount from a government agency. In 1977, the Jaras' dwelling was legally connected to the municipal electricity grid and water system. By then, he had convinced his two cousins to move to Neza, a few blocks from his home on adjoining lots which he had claimed for them. "I wanted to show my gratitude for all they had done for me," said Jara. "If it had not been for them, I would still be a peon back in Villa de Ayala."

In the dozen years since Jara settled there, Neza has gained a solidity that often confounds an outsider's preconceptions of what a Third World shantytown should look like. The stench of sewage and rubbish is still inescapable. In the newer outlying districts, flimsy shacks still rise along dusty, unpaved roads where mangy dogs rummage through garbage heaps. But slightly older neighborhoods have two-room cinder-block houses built by their residents in the mold of Jara's home, with television antennae sprouting from their roofs. Their streets are as-phalted and relatively clean. On the larger avenues, there are stores of every sort, although they do not sell the luxury or higher-quality goods available in downtown Mexico City and the shopping malls of its affluent districts. At the government-run CONASUPO stores, food and other basic necessities can be purchased at subsidized prices. An outdoor market, running along the avenue that marks the boundary between Neza and the capital, serves as a permanent bazaar for the community's underground economy. Unlicensed peddlers sell used clothes, motor vehicle parts, fresh and cooked foods, household goods (new, used, or stolen), candies, razor blades, and every variety of hardware. Barbers shave and shear their customers while they sit on wooden chairs in full view of passing cars and strollers. Back inside Neza proper, young men and children battle over scuffed balls on dusty soccer fields. At night, spectators of all ages jam into theaters that screen mostly kung-fu movies and insipid Mexican melodramas about loyal servants helping their wealthy employers survive a family crisis. Even more popular is the local sports palace—one of the few buildings higher than two stories—where masked wrestlers heave each other across a wilting canvas ring.

On workdays, most residents rise before dawn. Jara is out of the house by 6:00 A.M. He catches a bus that drops him in front of the subway station on the outskirts of Neza, boards the packed train to Azcapozalco, and emerging there, takes another bus to his factory—altogether a ninety-minute journey that still costs less than a nickel, thanks to the heavily government-subsidized transportation system. His factory job pays about twice the official minimum wage, ranking Jara near the top of Neza's thoroughly proletarian hierarchy. Urban in-dustrialization may have been the magnet that drew rural migrants to Mexico City, but most of them had to settle for marginal, nonfactory occupations. In Neza, less than a quarter of adult males are industrial workers. It is far more usual to be a construction laborer, a street peddler, or a messenger or porter for offices and stores in the capital.

Among women, the most common professions are domestic ser-vants, seamstresses, and vendors of tacos and sandwiches. Children under ten years old are sent into the streets of the capital to hawk gum and candy, wipe the windshields of cars stalled by traffic lights, or to openly beg. Jara's wife, Hortensia, works at home as a seamstress earning somewhat less than a third of her husband's salary. Two of her children are in the local elementary school and have not been required to contribute to the household income. The oldest son, a teenager, is apprenticed to an electrician.

Jara is bitter over the inflation of recent years, which has cut deeply into his purchasing power. "We used to have meat as often as we wanted," he says. "Now, once, twice a week, and only chicken. Otherwise, it's tortillas and beans, beans and tortillas. New clothes, a new bed—forget it." For him, the causes of the persistent economic crisis are clear: "Those politicians who can't stop stealing, union leaders who won't fight for their people, patrones [employers] who send their money out of the country."

But whatever the deficiencies of life in Ciudad Nezahualcóyotl, Roberto prefers it to the countryside he left behind. He barely disguises his contempt for peasants who "lack the courage" to move to the city. "They have no ambition," he says. "Even the ones who have land are lazy. Give them a few pesos, and they drink pulque and chase after women. They resent people who work hard—they try to pull them down."

Hortensia chides him about his own drinking bouts and infidelities. She is thinner, darker, and less ebullient than her husband, and, with creases on her face and gaps between her teeth, she looks almost ten years older than he. Occasionally, she visits relatives in her native Veracruz town of Tierra Blanca, and once lingered there with her children for several months when Roberto took up with a younger woman. She has fantasies of buying a small mango and papaya orchard in Veracruz and retiring there someday with her husband. "But in the city, the children have more opportunities," she concedes. "If we took them to Tierra Blanca, they would only be back here a few years later looking for jobs."

The sudden appearance of so many migrants in Mexico City and other urban centers has made it necessary for the political elite to find strong local leaders who can act as liaisons between the government and these mushrooming communities. Most often, these local bosses, called caciques, emerge at the very moment a new slum is born. They are leaders of the squatters who invade an uninhabited strip of land on the urban periphery. To draw the attention of the public authorities, they initially display an irksome militance—banners with antigovernment slogans, noisy demonstrations, even a willingness to clash with the police. But once the government concedes recognition to a cacique, he becomes an unconditional supporter of the PRI. It is a pretty straight deal, really: the municipal authorities grant legal deeds to the squatters, and slowly extend basic services like running water, electricity, sewage canals, garbage disposal to the new community, and, in return, expect the cacique to deliver the vote; the cacique convinces his followers that he was instrumental in obtaining these benefits, and expects the municipal authorities to allow him great leeway in maintaining his local political hegemony and extracting personal financial gains from his community.

The most notorious and powerful of Mexico City's slum caciques in recent years was Rafael Gutiérrez Moreno, the so-called garbage czar.[25] Until his death in 1987, Gutiérrez was the boss of thousands of *"pepenadores,"* the scavengers who live and toil in the huge refuse dumps on the capital's periphery. Through intimidation and persuasion, he gouged a fortune from this caste of virtual "untouchables," and molded them into a voting bloc that elected him to Congress. His many detractors portrayed Gutiérrez as a gangster who preyed on his constituents and thwarted efforts to sanitize Mexico City's garbage disposal system. According to his defenders, he preserved the livelihood of some of the most destitute residents of the megalopolis, and demonstrated that the PRI could extend its political control even into the most abandoned, dispossessed sectors of urban society.

Pollution, poverty, and politics wind together like a single strand in Mexico City's garbage industry. Most of the 5 million tons of refuse collected in the capital in 1987 were delivered to compacting plants or incinerators. But about 1.5 million tons a year are handled by the lowly pepenadores, who sift through mammoth dump sites for the food, glass, metal, plastic, paper, fabric, and wood wastes that are sold for reprocessing in factories. This primitive recycling of garbage, often carried out illegally by small businesses that are unsupervised by the municipal authorities, poses serious health hazards to the population at large. Discarded livestock fodder from these dumps is transformed into vegetable lard; rotted fruit wastes end up flavoring soft drinks; decayed animal corpses are ground into sausage meat; car grease is reprocessed into cooking oils; and bones are pulverized into soup concentrates.[26] The garbage, in its unprocessed form, is even deadlier for the pepenadores. The wastes pollute their water and air, spreading gastrointestinal and respiratory ailments that reduce their life expectancy far below the city's norm. And for their eight- to ten-hour workdays, the pepenadores earn less than the legal minimum wage.

Gutiérrez himself was a product of this environment. He spent his childhood as a pepenador at Santa Cruz Meyehualco, a garbage dump on the eastern outskirts of Mexico City, where he was born in 1942.

As a teenager, he was ambitious and lucky enough to escape the refuse heaps and become a sanitation truck driver, the next rung up the labor hierarchy of the garbage industry. In his early twenties, he had figured out the shadowy links between trade union affairs, municipal government, and party politics. By 1965, he was elected president of the union representing Mexico City's pepenadores. He also held several minor posts in the PRI, mainly involving tasks as a bodyguard. Even more important, he had found his political godfather in Benjamín Carpio, head of the city's sanitation department, who acted as a go-between for Gutiérrez and his future wife. (As usual in Mexican politics, personal ties helped cement a political relationship.)

In the early 1960s, the pepenadores of Santa Cruz Meyehualco, which had become the city's largest dump, organized a cooperative to bypass intermediaries and sell their sifted garbage directly to businesses that recycled it. Carpio, the municipal sanitation chief, was earning a considerable income as an intermediary in the garbage trade and vehemently opposed the cooperative. He found a willing ally in Gutiérrez, who in the guise of union organizer purported to be acting against the cooperative in the true interests of the pepenadores. In the prolonged conflict that ensued, the sanitation department withheld garbage from Santa Cruz Meyehualco, fights broke out between supporters of the cooperative and those who backed Gutiérrez, and a few pepenadores were killed. By 1965, the cooperative disintegrated, and the bulk of income from the resale of the dump's refuse was going to Carpio and Gutiérrez. To further reward Gutiérrez for his loyalty, Carpio agreed to give him absolute control over Santa Cruz Meyehualco.

In the next two decades, an avalanche of garbage flowed into Santa Cruz. After being thoroughly scavenged, the refuse piled up in three hundred-foot mounds, foul-smelling and smoky from the natural combustion of the decomposing wastes at their bottom. The dump site expanded until it covered all but a tenth of the community's land. Despite the cramped residential space, the local population doubled, roughly keeping pace with Mexico City's demographic increase. Rural migrants, wanted criminals, and Santa Cruz's own elevated birth rate swelled the numbers of pepenadores to about five thousand. And Gutiérrez—"Rafael," as everyone in the dump called him—dictated their lives.

He unquestionably had a benevolent side, although he was quick to claim credit for any favors bestowed on his people. Thus, when the municipal government constructed seven hundred homes for the pepenadores of Santa Cruz, Rafael decided which families would occupy them. And he earned the gratitude of the new homeowners by arranging to have them pay part of their mortgages with garbage instead of cash. He sponsored local soccer teams, supplied the uniforms, and built four playing fields, which he named the Rafael Sports Center. He constructed a church and a large cross overlooking the dump site. He personally handed out gifts to all youngsters on Children's Day, and to their parents on Mother's Day and Father's Day. Once a year, he organized a pilgrimage to the shrine of the Virgin of Guadalupe on the northern outskirts of the capital. And every January, he hired buses to transport virtually all five thousand pepenadores to Acapulco, where they received free accommodations and meals for a week. He also claimed to instill in his people a sense of pride and class-consciousness by festooning Santa Cruz with catchy painted slogans, like "We pepenadores are also Mexicans," and "Land for the peasants who till it, garbage for the pepenadores who sift it."

But no amount of charity or demagoguery could obscure the misery that Gutiérrez helped perpetuate among the garbage scavengers. According to estimates in 1979, he and his henchmen syphoned off more than half the income made by the pepenadores of Santa Cruz Meyehualco. Put another way: while the average pepenador collected less than $3 daily, Gutiérrez and his aides raked in more than $15,000 a day.[27]

All refuse that entered and left Santa Cruz was under Gutiérrez's control. Every morning, sanitation trucks lumbered through the dump site's sole gate under the watch of armed guards. After the garbage was unloaded, the pepenadores sifted out the valued wastes, collected them in sacks, and delivered them to Gutiérrez's foremen. The foremen weighed the refuse on scales that automatically subtracted 10 kilos from each load, allegedly on account of extraneous material and dirt mixed in with the recyclable rubbish.[28] After being baled, the sifted garbage was trucked to businesses under contract to Gutiérrez. The pepenadores were not allowed to sell their pickings to anybody except the cacique and his assistants, and were prohibited from leaving the dump with rubbish in their possession. To reduce discontent, Gutiérrez occasionally rotated rights to the choicer garbage—for example, aluminum and tin refuse that commanded higher prices—among the pepenadores, who vied with each other to be known as Rafael's men of confidence.

Only once, during the early 1970s, did Gutiérrez encounter a challenge to his stranglehold over Santa Cruz Meyehualco. A small faction of pepenadores led by José Velázquez tried to contest his management of the dump. But the dissidents disbanded after Velázquez died in what police said was an automobile accident. Some of his followers claimed that when his corpse was removed from the car wreckage, there was a bullet wound in his neck. Gutiérrez was generous to the widow Velázquez, allowing her to collect a portion of the incomes of the three hundred pepenadores who supported her husband.[29]

Gutiérrez constantly sought to strengthen his political clout in the government and the PRI. When his godfather, Carpio, lost his post as head of the city's sanitation department in 1966, Gutiérrez had to seek alliances with numerous other politicians. He ingratiated himself with them by turning out his pepenadores for political rallies of every sort. He dressed his men as peasants or factory workers or in their own pepenador uniforms, and trucked them by the hundreds to May Day parades, demonstrations on patriotic holidays, and to the airport to welcome visiting foreign dignitaries or the nation's president returning from a trip abroad. In 1972, Gutiérrez finally found an impressive political benefactor, Carlos Sansores Pérez. After completing his term as governor of the southern state of Campeche, Sansores Pérez became the PRI's legislative candidate for the Mexico City electoral district that included Santa Cruz Meyehualco. Gutiérrez joined his campaign, contributing large funds and, of course, the votes of his pepenadores.

By 1979, Gutiérrez himself had become politically prominent enough to run as his district's "alternate" legislator (a largely superfluous post created by the government to reward a rising politician, allowing him to automatically replace an incumbent legislator who is forced to step down because of illness or a new political assignment). At the convention in the National Auditorium where the PRI formally unveiled its legislative candidates that year, Gutiérrez both fascinated and appalled his political colleagues and journalists. Dark glasses, an enormous scar along the right side of his jaw, and the glitzy, powder-blue suit draped over his short, barrel-chested frame gave him the classic aura of a gangster. Six armed bodyguards made him seem even more sinister. When his name was called out by the master of ceremonies, the floor erupted with chants of "Rafael! Rafael!" from hundreds of pepenadores. As soon as the assembly ended, Gutiérrez took out a fat roll of pesos from his money belt, gave it to one of his aides, and, within earshot of journalists and other politicians, instructed him: "Take this for the press and tell them who it came from, huh? Photos, articles, I want everything."[30] When the election results a few months later announced the usual PRI landslide, Gutiérrez had his "alternate" seat in Congress.

For a brief moment in the early 1980s, Gutiérrez's fortunes seemed about to decline. Santa Cruz Meyehualco was so immersed in garbage that another dump site had to be found. And because Gutiérrez's power was linked to geography, it appeared likely that a new venue would erode his political and financial clout. But when Santa Cruz closed down in 1982, he arranged to have most of his pepenadores transferred to Santa Catarina, the new dump further east, where he continued to reign as garbage czar. Press reports suggested that he had previously bought much of the land in Santa Catarina and made a spectacular profit by selling it to the government before the dump opened there.

By the mid-1980s, Gutiérrez, still in his forties, had lived a rags-to-riches story that was hardly ever supposed to occur in Mexico. In a system that increasingly ignored "mass politics" in favor of bureaucratic expertise, he had fashioned one of the strongest grass-roots followings, and among the sort of constituents whom political analysts claimed to be beyond the reach of the PRI. He had become a considerable power broker in the official party and municipal government, courted by elite politicians who were embarrassed to socialize with him but anxious to tap his extravagant bankroll and solid bloc of votes.

The dark fable ended abruptly in 1987. A pepenador, who claimed his wife had been raped by Gutiérrez, fatally shot him. Assassinations of politicians usually fan rumors of Machiavellian plots, but Gutiérrez was so notorious for his uncontrolled sexual appetite that no other version surfaced in the press or political circles. And soon after his death, women who announced they were his common-law wives and scores of his alleged children and grandchildren filed claims to his fortune, which reputedly reached tens of millions of dollars.

Whatever their moral deficiencies, caciques like Rafael Gutiérrez have played a crucial stabilizing role in Mexico City and elsewhere in the country. They have been buffers between a burgeoning underclass and the political elite. In this respect, caciques are comparable to trade union leaders, with whom they often act in concert. While trade union leaders exercise power over workers in their places of employment, it is the caciques who wield influence in the communities where laborers and their families reside. Moreover, with only a third of Mexican workers enrolled in unions, the caciques are able to claim political leadership over vast numbers of the urban poor who are untouched by the labor movement.

As the 1980s unfolded, the government continued to demonstrate its political acumen in coping with the possibility of social unrest in Mexico City's shantytowns. But the megalopolis was being tested on a more unexpected front: its potential devastation by natural and man-made environmental accidents.

The first great ecological disaster of the decade took place in Tlalnepantla, an industrial and slum district eight miles northwest of the capital. Tlalnepantla was so sparsely populated in the 1950s that it was selected by Pemex as the site of a major gas storage plant. The area attracted hordes of squatters. They were well aware of the plant's dangers, but they hoped to benefit from the transportation, electricity, and water grids that were put in place to service the installation. By the early 1980s, several hundred thousand people lived within a two-mile radius of the Pemex plant, and similarly dense populations surrounded a score of other gas storage depots elsewhere on Mexico City's outskirts.

At 5:42 A.M. on November 19, 1984, a truck parked in the Tlalnepantla plant exploded. Within seconds, four huge tanks holding more than 1.5 million gallons of liquefied gas erupted. Balls of flame shot up into the air, raining fiery debris on the shantytown. More than five hundred inhabitants perished, most of them so badly burned that they could not be identified. About five thousand people were injured, and a hundred thousand were evacuated. Sixty-six acres had been razed.

Tlalnepantla, however, was virtually forgotten only ten months later when the worst earthquake in the nation's history struck the capital.

The cataclysm originated about two hundred fifty miles west of Mexico City beneath the floor of the Pacific Ocean. The earth's crust there is composed of several tectonic plates—twenty to one hundred and forty miles thick—straddling a molten mantle that causes them to creep forward an average length of half a finger every year. The most important of these tectonic formations are the Cocos plate, pushing northeastward below the Pacific floor, and the North American plate, thrusting westward from the Mexican landmass. The oceanic plate slides under the continental plate until friction between the two halts their motion. Eventually, however, the stress builds until huge masses of subterranean rock fracture explosively.

In the early morning hours of September 19, 1985, a section of the Cocos plate overcame the resistance of the North American plate and burst forward by more than ten feet. This earthquake, measuring 8.1 on the Richter scale of 10, unleashed shock waves that were felt as far away as Houston, about eleven hundred miles from the epicenter. Coastal towns in Michoacán and Jalisco, only fifty miles from the quake's origin, were relatively resistant to the tremors because their solid rock, geological foundations diminished the shaking of buildings on the surface. But the quake was devastating for Mexico City. The muddy sediments of the Aztec lakes under its central district reacted like a bowl of gelatin that magnified and multiplied the vibrations of the shock waves.

That Thursday had begun propitiously in the capital. Radio announcers, with their incongruous early morning cheer, remarked that the usual shroud of yellow-gray smog had lifted, and the crisp, azure skies offered clear views of Popocatépetl and Iztaccíhuatl, the legendary snow-capped volcanoes. It was shortly after 7:00 A.M., and the rush hour was in full progress for the working-class population. Clothing factories in the city center had started up their sewing machines. Bleary-eyed laborers squeezed into buses en route to the northern industrial districts. Subways were packed with secretaries, clerks, and messengers who initiated office activity. Public schools, functioning in two daily shifts because of crowded enrollment, had opened their doors to the morning session of students.

The intense tremors began at 7:19 A.M., and continued for almost three full minutes. With their voices and images shaking, television newscasters informed viewers what was already apparent to them—and then abruptly went off the air. In the downtown neighborhoods, electricity was cut and faucets ran dry as underground water mains and copper cables snapped. Throughout much of the capital, telephones went dead. The streets undulated like a rolling sea, bucking motor vehicles until their engines stalled. Subway riders were plunged into claustrophobic darkness and continuously heaved against each other. Commuters fortunate enough to be caught waiting in the stations scurried up to the surface. There they found an urban landscape that seemed under intense bombardment. Buildings swayed and buckled, showering pedestrians with brick and mortar, crumbling upon their foundations or exploding in fireballs. Thousands of people lay buried in their ruins. Those who escaped the entombment gave miraculous accounts of their survival.

Eduardo Vázquez, an architect, had spent Wednesday evening alone at his apartment in a small, multistory building in the Zona

Rosa, the city's poshest restaurant and boutique district.[31] Jolted awake by the tremors, he scrambled out of bed and sought shelter in the open doorway of his room—the usual precaution taken by the capital's residents during the many minor earthquakes they have experienced. But he quickly realized this was no ordinary temblor. "The movement was so strong that the room lost its right angles, lost its geometric contours," he recalled. The ceiling burst, the floor partially collapsed, and glass, brick, wooden beams, and objects of every sort hurtled about the room as Vázquez covered his head with his arms.

"And then, I don't know if everything went dark or if I had just shut my eyes," he continued. "I plunged through the darkness and expected something to crush my head. Objects fell all around me, and something pinned my back and twisted my face down. Suddenly there was absolute silence. I opened my eyes, and my first reaction was the enormous horror of being buried alive."

His next sensation was the acute pain along his back. He failed in a first attempt to extricate himself from the rubble. For several minutes he shouted for help. The only response was the screaming of a woman, the neighbor in the apartment above, who was also trapped. "Since my right arm is free, I begin to move the blocks and staves that are crushing my legs," he said. "With great patience, I lift one stone after another until my right leg is freed, and then I do the same with my left leg. How marvelous it is to be able to move them." Using his legs and right arm as levers, he pulled himself from under the ruins pressing against his back. "As I turn over, I realize the ceiling is now only a meter above me." Half-naked, he crawled to a hole in the wall where sunlight was streaming into the room. Squirming through the aperture, he fell headfirst into the courtyard, got to his feet, and limped to the street. On the sidewalk, he found a neighbor, bleeding profusely and sobbing that his wife was dead. She was not the only victim: of the fifty residents in the building, no more than ten survived.

About twenty blocks away, on the edge of Alameda Park, closer to the historic center, Hector Sen Flores, a Veracruz congressman, was staying at the Regis, a former luxury hotel that had been demoted several notches in recent decades.[32] The night before, Sen Flores had asked the hotel manager to transfer him to an interior room away from the noisy traffic of Avenida Juárez, the main artery that leads downtown. The move saved the congressman's life.

He was up by 6:00 A.M. on Thursday because he was scheduled to join other members of a legislative committee at a working breakfast.

He had already bathed, shaved, and dressed when one of his assistants arrived at the room shortly after 7:15 A.M. to accompany him to the reunion.

"As soon as the earthquake began, we braced ourselves in the doorway," said Sen Flores. "We quickly perceived that the situation was a lot more serious than that, and we ran out to the corridor, and literally bounced from side to side until we reached the stairwell which was jammed with other fleeing guests. In moments of real anxiety like this, you stop thinking. There isn't even time to consider how scared you are. You only feel the instinct of survival that tells you to get out any way you can."

Gas fumes, smoke, and dust enveloped the hotel guests, and they could barely see or breathe as they groped down the shaking steps. Below the second floor, the stairway had caved in. "But there was a light from a huge crack in the building, and we ran down the corridor and jumped [from the second floor] to the street," said the congressman. From the sidewalk, he saw that the front of the building, including the room he had initially reserved, had collapsed entirely. Moments later, a gas explosion pulverized the rest of the hotel.

A few blocks further downtown, the Diplomático, the Versailles, the Romano, the De Carlo, and several other venerable hotels built during the 1940s for the postwar wave of foreign tourists were also in shambles, their employees and guests crushed under stone and twisted steel girders. On Avenida Juárez, several hundred students were entombed in the wreckage of their public secondary school. Less than a hundred yards away, the Navy Ministry building sagged like an accordion, and officers in shredded, bloodied uniforms frantically pulled their wounded and dead colleagues from the rubble.

The locus of greatest mayhem was the Tlatelolco public housing project, site of the 1968 massacre of antigovernment demonstrators. A fourth of its 103 buildings—home to lower-income and middle-class families—were severely damaged. "My seven-year-old daughter and I were rushing through breakfast before I took her to school on my way to work," said a government employee, who lived with his family in a fourth-floor apartment of one of the buildings. "All of a sudden the shaking began. Trying to calm my daughter, I shouted for my wife to join us. We embraced tightly. Only by pretending to protect them could I control my terror. Things fell all around us and the windows shattered. After what seemed an eternity, the trembling stopped. We were alive. I said to my wife: 'Let's get out of here before it begins again!' She turned her head slowly to the window. 'Oh my

God, look!' she said. 'The people in the Nuevo León building!' And we saw that massive cement structure collapsing like a castle of cards."

María Gutiérrez, a housewife living on the sixth floor of the Nuevo León, had just dropped her teenage daughter at school and was driving her car into the building's parking lot. Her three youngest children and her mother-in-law had stayed behind in the apartment. "As I got out of the car, I could see my home, everybody's homes, the entire building being ripped apart. Walls, windows, everything crumbled. And I could not get there. My three little kids were inside. . . ."[33]

There were about three thousand residents in the block-long, thirteen-story Nuevo León, and almost half of them were trapped, dead or alive. As soon as the temblor ceased, hundreds of people from the adjoining buildings began a desperate search through the ruins for survivors. "There was so much dust that we had to cover our faces with handkerchiefs, and bystanders were shouting that there would be an explosion because of all the gas in the air," said Tito Montalbán, a nineteen-year-old Politécnico student. "But the screams and cries from the people buried under the rubble were too much to bear. We just kept digging until our hands bled without giving a thought about whether we would be blown up."[34]

Ambulances arrived within minutes. Unable to handle all the victims, their drivers begged the owners of private cars and pickup trucks to help transport the injured. The closest major hospitals were at the National Medical Center. With twenty-five buildings, it was the biggest facility of its kind in Latin America, and experienced in dealing with large-scale catastrophes. (It was there that most of the victims of the Tlalnepantla gas explosion were treated.) But the ambulances had to be waved back: the earthquake had devastated the medical complex too. Virtually all its buildings were damaged, among them the General Hospital, and the separate structures specializing in traumatology, pediatrics, oncology, and gynecology and obstetrics ceased to function. The Cardiology Hospital, pride of national medicine, had collapsed, killing seventy physicians, nurses, and other employees. Throughout the medical center, several hundred patients were fatally crushed or smothered, and more than three thousand had to be evacuated.

"When we ran out of litters, we used bedsheets to carry them out," said a doctor at one of the hospitals. "We just lay the patients on the pavement, and attended them there. I kept screaming to the hospital workers not to go back into the building because the stairwells were so unsteady that they shook with every step. But they wouldn't listen. They just kept going back for more patients."[35]

Almost as soon as the ground stopped trembling, the political aftershocks began. Throughout the capital, ordinary Mexicans railed against their government for its ineptitude during the emergency. On paper, at least, a well-conceived plan existed in the Interior and Defense ministries to rapidly mobilize security forces and other government personnel in the event of a massive earthquake. Several thousand troops and policemen were, in fact, rushed to zones of greatest damage. But most of them merely cordoned off the sites, instead of plunging ahead with excavation and rescue work. When government workers finally began digging out the victims, it was apparent that their picks and shovels were woefully inadequate. Private construction companies sent bulldozers into the worst-hit neighborhoods, but the government, anxious to project a nationalist image of self-reliance, declined relief offers from abroad during the thirty-six hours that followed the quake. Foreign equipment and expert personnel were eventually welcomed, though the crucial time lost probably doomed many victims who suffocated or bled to death before they could be reached under the rubble.

The vaunted organizational talents of the PRI were nowhere in evidence. The party's labor and agrarian wings, which on numerous occasions had convoked hundreds of thousands of trade unionists and peasants for political rallies, failed to mobilize anybody to aid the earthquake victims. Nor did the caciques play any visible role. Instead, the volunteers who converged on the disaster sites were citizens reacting spontaneously to the emergency. They came from slums, middle-class projects, and wealthy neighborhoods, private and state universities, public and parochial schools. Forming themselves into brigades, they shoveled and clawed for survivors under the mass of concrete and steel. Small, wiry men, known as *topos* (moles), burrowed through narrow tunnels and crevices to rescue the injured and retrieve the dead. Thousands of other volunteers dispensed medicine, food, drinking water, clothes, and tents.

The size and fervor of the volunteer effort surprised many of those involved, who had never thought of themselves as civic-spirited. They responded despite government entreaties that the public remain at home or at least avoid visiting the disaster zones. And they suspected that the government was wary of a citizens' movement which it did not control. Suspicion turned to anger when public officials seemed intent on downplaying the scope of the tragedy.

Only thirty-six hours after the great temblor, a second, lesser earthquake struck the city. Government leaders dismissed its effects as negligible, but at least a score of buildings were brought down by the new quake. It was also lethal for uncounted numbers of survivors still entombed in the ruins of hundreds of structures knocked down earlier. Throughout the crisis, Mayor Ramón Aguirre and other officials released casualty and property damage figures that were consistently lower—far lower—than the estimates reported by journalists and relief workers. Their intention may have been to dampen panic and despair, and to counteract exaggerated accounts in the foreign press that pictured a city wiped off the face of the map. (In fact, most of the earthquake damage was confined to a thirteen-square-mile zone, less than 2 percent of the megalopolis's surface area.)

But for many citizens, especially those living in the devastated neighborhoods, the government appeared to be engaged in a perverse effort to belittle their losses. As a result, the authorities were not given enough credit for some of their solid successes in handling the emergency: food shortages were averted; epidemics were forestalled; electricity, running water, and telephone service were restored in the affected zones within days; and most of the city continued to function even in the immediate aftermath of the cataclysm.

President De la Madrid was also stung by the public backlash against the government. He had come to office in 1982 determined to avoid the histrionics and populism of his predecessors, and establish a low-key image of a sober, cautious executive. It was a style of leadership better suited for an economic crisis than a natural disaster. After inspecting the downtown district by helicopter the day of the first quake, he announced prematurely that "we are ready to return to normality." To his credit, De la Madrid was willing the very next day, September 20, to adopt a more compassionate and self-critical stance. "The truth is that in the face of an earthquake of this magnitude, we did not count on sufficient elements to confront the catastrophe with speed and efficiency," he conceded in the most emotional speech of his career. He also acknowledged the "extraordinary solidarity" of the brigades of volunteers who upstaged the government's lead-footed relief efforts. He then toured dozens of demolished neighborhoods, where he was greeted warmly by appreciative survivors.

Such a welcome was not extended to other officials. Quake victims, lodged in tent camps, spurned offers by municipal aides to move to government-run refugee centers, and, in some cases, chased them away. When a delegation of politicians' wives, clad in elegant dresses and baubles, toured a wrecked neighborhood, they were heckled by homeless survivors demanding to know why the government had not yet sent food and tents. With bodyguards holding the angry crowd at bay, the wives scrambled back into their vehicles and sped away.

Police and soldiers were special targets of public ire. In the ruins of the downtown building occupied by the attorney general's office, rescue workers found the corpses of prisoners bearing signs of torture. When the attorney general blamed the injuries on the earthquake, he was contradicted by several prisoners who survived the quake and described being repeatedly subjected to electric shocks, beatings, and cigarette burns by their police interrogators. In Tepito and Morelos, poor neighborhoods devastated by the temblor, residents reported that police looted their abandoned, shattered homes. In nearby Garibaldi Square, where hundreds of mariachis entertained tourists with traditional Mexican ballads, police were accused of stealing guitars, trumpets, and valuables from the ruins of the musicians' apartment building. At several temporary refuge sites, private donors bearing clothes, blankets, and food for the disaster victims were so suspicious of the security forces that they insisted on personally distributing the offerings to the needy. There were numerous complaints from people who were forced to pay bribes to claim the corpses of their relatives from temporary morgues. Bribes enabled clothing manufacturers to cross police cordons and rescue their inventory, machinery, and strongboxes from their wrecked downtown factories—in some cases, even before their injured and dead employees had been dug out of the ruins.

The fact that a large percentage of the buildings destroyed in the quake were constructed and maintained by the government also became a source of controversy. Months before the catastrophe, residents at the Tlatelolco public housing complex had protested the government's failure to shore up the weakening foundations of their buildings. Some architects and civil engineers asserted that the National Medical Center was structurally unsound because corrupt bureaucratic officials had allowed contractors to flout government regulations designed to make the buildings more resistant to earthquakes. Many of the downtown clothing factories which were toppled or heavily damaged showed gross violations of building codes that would have rendered them unsafe even if the temblor had never occurred.

However, the height of structures may have been as important as government venality in determining their fate. A majority of the 855 buildings that were partially or totally destroyed were between six and seventeen stories high.[36] The earthquake's shock waves produced a pendular motion in all buildings. But in the case of a tall skyscraper—

like the Torre Latinoamericana—the shock waves that rattled its structure oscillated faster than it took the building to complete a full pendular movement. Before the skyscraper finished swaying to one side, a new shock wave hit its foundation, forcing the building to sway back in the opposite direction. The total lateral movement thus decreased, and this lessened the stress on the connections between support beams and floors. Buildings under eighteen stories, however, vibrated and swayed roughly in tandem with the movement of the earth below them until they toppled or were seriously damaged.

Many of the wounds of the 1985 earthquake have scarred over. Most of the seventy thousand people made homeless have been accommodated in new or repaired housing with the aid of the government. A large number of these residences have been built on 625 acres of downtown real estate expropriated by the government in the temblor's aftermath. Some of this acreage, particularly vacant lots formerly held by private speculators, has been reserved for small parks and open areas.

Predictions that the government would be politically vulnerable in the wake of the cataclysm have not come to pass. The small parties of left and right were unable to claim the loyalty of potential dissidents. The youthful volunteers who spent sleepless days and nights excavating the ruins for victims and generously aiding the survivors returned to home, school, and work. Only the passage of years will tell if they will look back on these experiences as a social or political awakening that changed the course of their lives. In the meantime, the regime has continued to display enormous resourcefulness in taming and coopting its critics. They have been invited to voice their opinions in government-subsidized publications, on state-owned television, and at conferences organized by public officials. Perhaps the most insistent political proposal to emerge from these forums has been a call for the election of the mayor of Mexico City, instead of his appointment by the president. It is a concession that the government could easily tolerate, for there is no reason to believe that an elected mayor would be anybody but a PRI candidate and loyal member of the political elite.

The widespread discussions and debates about the earthquake's long-term impact have at the very least heightened public consciousness that Mexico City lives on an ecological abyss—vulnerable not only to another killer temblor but also to catastrophes brought on by water shortages and worsening pollution.

The treatises and statements churned out by scholars, politicians, and professionals have focused a great deal of attention on ways of improving the deplorable quality of the city's air. They envision a gradually evolving set of circumstances that might lessen the threat of a fatal smog: cleaner fuel and emission controls for motor vehicles and factories; the dispersal of "dirty" industries to outlying regions as older manufacturing installations shut down in the capital; and an unbearable combination of traffic congestion and insufficient parking facilities that forces even middle-class commuters to abandon their automobiles for mass transit. But Mexico City will remain a victim of its topography. The 7,500-foot altitude reduces the level of oxygen by almost a third. As a result, motor vehicles produce twice the carbon monoxide and hydrocarbon emissions they would at sea level. The surrounding volcanic range traps the noxious fumes, stifles the flow of cleansing air currents, and spreads a permanent mantle of pollution. Breathing the air is like smoking two packs of cigarettes a day, according to recent environmental studies.

The specter of massive water shortages is very real in the not too distant future. Mexico City is drawing 1 billion gallons of water per day from its underground aquifers—twice the rate of their natural replenishment. To meet current needs, the capital is already being supplied an additional 700 million gallons a day from western lakes and rivers. An elaborate system of canals, pipelines, and pumps is being built to tap water supplies lying more than a hundred miles away and thousands of feet lower than the megalopolis. The scale of these projects and the distances they cover have never before been attempted anywhere. The cost has not been calculated because the peso is so unstable in terms of the world's major currencies. Theoretically, these gigantic schemes will bring in an extra 200 million gallons per day by the end of the century. Unfortunately, by then the city's needs will have grown still greater, to an extra 700 million gallons a day.

The government's hydraulic experts hope this projected shortfall will be met through conservation efforts. Repairing the underground pipe network will recover part of the 20 percent of water supply lost because of massive leaks. The recycling of water from factories offers other possibilities. Middle-class and affluent residents may eventually prove amenable to pleas for less wastage of water. But among the poor majority, there is little margin for additional conservation. Several million slum dwellers still have no running water in their homes and depend on public faucets. If anything, their per capita consumption seems likely to increase once their households become connected to the municipal water grid.

Virtually all solutions offered for the ecological dilemmas facing Mexico City are based on demographic projections that are optimistic. Government urbanologists still base estimates on a National Population Program published in 1982 that set a goal of 23.4 million inhabitants for metropolitan Mexico City by the year 2000. But in 1988, there were already twenty million residents, so a figure of over thirty million seems more likely by the dawn of the next century.

Recent legislation in the United States aimed at controlling illegal immigration will probably ensure a more bloated population for the megalopolis. Since the 1940s, one out of three Mexicans who left the countryside headed at least temporarily across the U.S. border. If the frontier does indeed prove to be impermeable, Mexico City and the other great urban centers will be the only alternative destinations for these migrants.

For all its problems, Mexico City continues to draw the rural destitute. A current (1987) employment rate of 12 percent and under-employment levels that may be twice as high would seem to be discouraging. But even if they are reduced to becoming bootblacks, street peddlers, and beggars, these agrarian refugees still feel they stand a better chance of surviving here than in the countryside.

And sometimes, if the people don't come to Mexico City, Mexico City goes to them. The community of Cuauhtitlán, for example, existed for centuries in rural torpor twenty miles from the capital's center. Once considered the epitome of provincial backwardness— "Outside Mexico City every place is Cuauhtitlán," is an old saying— the town has recently become a flourishing industrial district and officially the northernmost limit of metropolitan Mexico City.

Cuauhtitlán has bequeathed to the modern inhabitants of Mexico City some of the bleakest annals from the ancient Indians, including the legend of the Fifth Sun, as the Aztecs called their last epoch.

"It is also known as the Sun of Movement," stated the *Annals of Cuauhtitlán*, "and as the elders tell us, it will bring the shaking of the earth, and there will be famine, and thus we shall perish."[37]

But the Aztecs tempered such fatalism with a cyclical view of history that is still embraced by residents of the Mexican capital in the present era of urban overdevelopment. Throughout its existence, the city has been scourged by war, social upheaval, plague, flood, earthquake. Yet the city has always reemerged, sometimes diminished by its ordeals, and sometimes catapulted to greater splendor.

BIBLIOGRAPHY

Adams, Robert McC. *The Evolution of Urban Society: Early Mesopotamia and Prehistoric Mexico*. Chicago: Aldine, 1966.

Aguirre Beltrán, Gonzalo. "The Slave Trade in Mexico," *Hispanic American Historical Review*, 24, 1944, pp. 412–431.

———. *La población negra de México, 1519–1810*. Mexico: Ediciones Fuente Cultural, 1946.

———. *Medicina y magia: El proceso de aculturación en la estructura colonial*. Mexico, 1963.

Aiton, Arthur. *Antonio de Mendoza, First Viceroy of New Spain*. Durham, N.C.: Duke University Press, 1927.

Ajofrín, Francisco de. *Diario del viaje que . . . hizo a la América septentrional en el siglo XVIII*. 2 vols. Mexico: Archivo Documental Español, 1958.

Alamán, Lucas. *Historia de Méjico*. 5 vols. Mexico, 1942.

Alberro, Solange B. de, ed. "Proceso y causa criminal contra Diego de la Cruz," *Boletín del Archivo General de la Nación*, tercera serie: tomo II, numero 4 (6), octobre–diciembre 1978, pp. 8–17.

———. "Negros y mulatos en los documentos inquisitoriales: Rechazo e integración," in Elsa Cecilia Frost, et al., eds. *Labor and Laborers Through Mexican History*. Tucson, Ariz.: University of Arizona Press, 1979. Mexico: El Colegio de México, 1977.

Altman, Ida, and Lockhart, James, eds. *Provinces of Early Mexico: Variants of Spanish American Regional Evolution*. Los Angeles: UCLA Latin American Center Publication, 1976.

Anales de Cuauhtitlán, noticias históricas de México. Mexico: Impr. de I. Escalante, 1885.

Anderson, Arthur J. O., et al., eds. *Beyond the Codices: The Nahua View of Colonial Mexico*. Berkeley: University of California Press, 1976.

Anderson, Rodney D. *Outcasts in Their Own Land: Mexican Industrial Workers, 1906–1911.* DeKalb, Ill.: Northern Illinois University Press, 1976.

Anna, Timothy E. *The Fall of the Royal Government in Mexico City.* Lincoln, Nebr.: University of Nebraska Press, 1978.

Archer, Christon I. "To Serve the King: Military Recruitment in Late Colonial Mexico," *Hispanic American Historical Review,* 55, May 1975, pp. 226–250.

————. *The Army in Bourbon Mexico, 1760–1810.* Albuquerque, N.M.: University of New Mexico Press, 1977.

Arens, W. *The Man-eating Myth: Anthropology and Anthropophagy.* New York: Oxford University Press, 1979.

Arizpe, Lourdes. *Migración, etnicismo y cambio económico (un estudio sobre migrantes campesinos a la Ciudad de México).* Mexico: El Colegio de México, 1978.

Arnold, Linda Jo. "Social, Economic, and Political Status in the Mexico City Central Bureaucracy, 1808–1822," in Elsa Cecilia Frost, et al., eds. *Labor and Laborers Through Mexican History.* Tucson, Ariz.: University of Arizona Press, 1979.

————. *Bureaucracy and Bureaucrats in Mexico City, 1742–1835.* Ph.D. Diss. Austin, Tex.: University of Texas, 1982.

Arrom, Silvia Marina. *The Women of Mexico City, 1790–1857.* Stanford: Stanford University Press, 1985.

Ashburn, P. M. *The Ranks of Death: A Medical History of the Conquest of America.* New York: Coward-McCann, 1947.

Ashby, Joe C. *Organized Labor and the Mexican Revolution Under Cárdenas.* Chapel Hill, N.C.: University of North Carolina Press, 1967.

Ayala Anguiano, Armando: *México en crisis.* Mexico: Ediciones Oceano, 1982.

Azuela, Mariano. *The Underdogs,* trans. by E. Munguía, Jr. New York: New American Library, Signet Classic, 1962.

Bailey, David C. *Viva Cristo Rey: The Cristero Rebellion and the Church-State Conflict in Mexico.* Austin, Tex.: University of Texas Press, 1974.

Bakewell, Peter J. *Silver Mining and Society in Colonial Mexico: Zacatecas, 1546–1700.* Cambridge: Cambridge University Press, 1971.

————. "Zacatecas: An Economic and Social Outline of a Silver Mining District, 1547–1700," in Ida Altman and James Lockhart, eds., *Provinces of Early Mexico.* Los Angeles: University of California Press, 1976.

Barlow, R. H. "The Extent of the Empire of the Culhua Mexica," *Ibero-Americana,* 28. Berkeley: University of California Press, 1949.

Bazant, Jan. *Alienation of Church Wealth in Mexico, 1856–1875.* Cambridge: Cambridge University Press, 1971.

Beals, Carleton. *Porfirio Díaz: Dictator of Mexico.* Philadelphia: J. B. Lippincott, 1932.

Bellemare, Louis de (pseud. for Gabriel Ferry). *Vagabond Life in Mexico*. New York: Harper & Brothers, 1856.

Benítez, Fernando. *The Century After Cortés*, trans. by Joan MacLean. Chicago: Chicago University Press, 1965.

———. *Lázaro Cárdenas y la Revolución mexicana*. 3 vols. Mexico: Fondo de Cultura, 1977–78.

———. *La Ciudad de México, 1325–1982*. 3 vols. Mexico: Salvat, 1981.

———. *Los demonios en el convento: Sexo y religión en la Nueva España*. Mexico: Ediciones Era, 1985.

Benson, Nettie Lee. *La disputación provincial y el federalismo mexicano*. Mexico, 1955.

Berdan, Frances M. *Trade, Tribute and Market in the Aztec Empire*. Ph.D. Diss. Austin, Tex.: University of Texas, 1975.

Berlin, Heinrich, ed. *Anales de Tlatelolco*. Mexico: José Porrúa e hijos, 1948.

Bierhorst, John. *Cantares Mexicanos: Songs of the Aztecs*. Stanford: Stanford University Press, 1985.

Bisbal Siller, María Teresa. *Los novelistas y la Ciudad de México (1810–1910)*. Mexico: Ediciones Botas, 1963.

Blanton, Richard E., et al. *Ancient Mesoamerica: A Comparison of Change in Three Regions*. New York: Cambridge University Press, 1982.

Bobb, Bernard E. *The Viceregency of Antonio María Bucareli in New Spain, 1771–1779*. Austin, Tex.: University of Texas Press, 1962.

Borah, Woodrow W. "New Spain's Century of Depression," *Ibero-Americana*, 35. Berkeley: University of California Press, 1951.

———. *Justice by Insurance: The General Indian Court of Colonial Mexico and the Legal Aides of the Half-Real*. Berkeley: University of California Press, 1983.

———, and Cook, Sherburne. "The Aboriginal Population of Central Mexico on the Eve of the Spanish Conquest," *Ibero-Americana*, 45. Berkeley: University of California Press, 1963.

Boserup, Ester. *The Conditions of Agricultural Growth: The Economies of Agrarian Change Under Population Pressure*. Chicago: Aldine, 1965.

Bowser, Frederick P. "The Free Person of Color in Mexico City and Lima: Manumission and Opportunity, 1580–1650," in Stanley L. Engenman and Eugene D. Genovese, eds., *Race and Slavery in the Western Hemisphere*. Princeton: Princeton University Press, 1975.

Boyer, Richard E. *La gran inundación: Vida y sociedad en la Ciudad de México (1629–1638)*. Mexico: Sep Setentas, 1975.

———. "Mexico City as Metropolis: Transition of a Colonial Economy in the Seventeenth Century," *Hispanic American Historical Review*, 57, 1977, pp. 455–478.

———. "La Ciudad de Mexico en 1628. La visión de Juan Gómez de Trasmonte," *Historia Mexicana*, 29 (115), enero-marzo 1980, pp. 447–471.

Brading, D. A. *Miners and Merchants in Bourbon Mexico, 1763–1810.* Cambridge: Cambridge University Press, 1971.

———. "The Haciendas as an Investment," in Robert G. Keith, ed., *Haciendas and Plantations in Latin American History.* New York: Holmes & Meier, 1977.

Brandenburg, Frank. *The Making of Modern Mexico.* Englewood Cliffs, N.J.: Prentice-Hall, 1964.

Braudel, Fernand. *The Mediterranean and the Mediterranean World in the Age of Philip II,* trans. by Siân Reynolds. 2 vols. New York: Harper Colophon Books, 1976.

———. *The Structure of Everyday Life: The Limits of the Possible,* trans. by Siân Reynolds. New York: Harper & Row, 1981.

———. *The Wheels of Commerce,* trans. by Siân Reynolds. New York: Harper & Row, 1982.

———. *The Perspective of the World,* trans. by Siân Reynolds. New York: Harper & Row, 1984.

Bray, Warwick. "The City-State in Central Mexico at the Time of the Spanish Conquest," *Journal of Latin American Studies,* 4 (2), 1972, pp. 161–185.

Brennan, Ellen M. "Contradictions in Mexico's National Spatial Policy," *Regional Development Dialogue,* 4 (2), Autumn 1983, pp. 21–41.

Brenner, Anita. *Idols Behind Altars: The Story of the Mexican Spirit.* Boston: Beacon Press, 1970.

Brooks, Francis Joseph. *Parish and Cofradía in Eighteenth-Century Mexico.* Ph.D. Diss. Princeton University, 1976.

Bullock, W. *Six Months' Residence and Travels in Mexico.* London: John Murray, 1824.

Burke, Michael E. "The University of Mexico and the Revolution, 1910–1940." *The Americas,* 34 (2), October 1977, pp. 252–273.

Calderón de la Barca, Frances Erskine. *Life in Mexico During a Residence of Two Years in That Country.* Garden City, N.Y.: Doubleday, 1966.

Calnek, Edward E. "The Organization of Urban Food Supply Systems: The Case of Tenochtitlán," in Jorge E. Hardoy and Richard P. Schaedel, eds., *Las ciudades de América Latina y sus áreas de influencia a través de la historia.* Buenos Aires: S.I.A.P., 1975.

———. "The Internal Structure of Tenochtitlán," in Eric Wolf, ed., *The Valley of Mexico.* Albuquerque, N.M.: University of New Mexico Press, 1976.

Camara Barbachano, Fernando. "El mestizaje en México," *Revista de Indias,* 24 (95–96), 1964, pp. 27–83.

Camp, Roderic Ai. "Education and Political Recruitment in Mexico: The Alemán Generation," *Journal of Interamerican Studies and World Affairs.* 18 (3), August 1976, pp. 295–321.

———. *Mexico's Leaders: Their Education and Recruitment.* Tucson, Ariz.: University of Arizona Press, 1980.

———. *Intellectuals and the State in Twentieth-Century Mexico*. Austin, Tex.: University of Texas Press, 1985.

Cardoso, Ciro F. S., ed. *Formación y desarrollo de la burguesía en México, siglo XIX*. Mexico: Siglo Veintiuno, 1978.

Carrasco, Pedro, and Monjarás Ruíz, Jesús, eds. *Colección de documentos sobre Coyoacán*. 2 vols. Mexico: CIS-INAH, 1976–78.

Casas, Fray Bartolomé de las. *Brevísima relación de la destrucción de las Indias occidentales*. London: Shulze and Dean, 1812.

Case, Alden Buell. *Thirty Years with the Mexicans: In Peace and Revolution*. New York: Fleming H. Revell Co., 1917.

Castillo Berthier, Hector F. *La sociedad de la basura: Caciquismo en la Ciudad de México*. Mexico: UNAM, 1983.

Castillo Negrete, Emilio de. *México en el siglo XIX*. 26 vols. Mexico: Las Escalerillas, 1875–92.

Cervantes de Salazar, Francisco. *Crónica de la Nueva España*. Madrid, 1914.

———. *Life in the City of Mexico in New Spain*, trans. by M. L. Barrett Shepard. Austin, Tex.: University of Texas Press, 1953.

Charlot, Jean. *The Mexican Mural Renaissance, 1920–1925*. New Haven: Yale University Press, 1967.

Chavez Orozco, Luís, ed. *Documentos para la historia económica de México*. 12 vols. Mexico: Secretaría de la Economía Nacional, 1933–39.

Chevalier, François. *Land and Society in Colonial Mexico: The Great Hacienda*, trans. by Alvian Eustis; edited, with a foreword, by Lesley Byrd Simpson. Berkeley: University of California Press, 1963.

Chiaramonte, José Carlos. "En torno a la recuperación demográfica y la depresión económica novohispana durante el siglo XVII," *Historia Mexicana*, 30 (120), avril–junio 1981, pp. 561–604.

Clark, Marjorie Ruth. *Organized Labor in Mexico*. Chapel Hill, N.C.: University of North Carolina Press, 1934.

Cline, Howard. *Mexico: Revolution to Evolution, 1940–1960*. New York: Oxford University Press, 1962.

Cline, Sue Louise. *Culhuacán, 1522–1599: An Investigation Through Mexican Indian Testaments*. Ph.D. Diss. Los Angeles: UCLA, 1981.

Coatsworth, John H. "Obstacles to Economic Growth in Nineteenth-Century Mexico," *The American Historical Review*, 83 (1), February 1978, pp. 80–100.

———. *Growth Against Development: The Economic Impact of Railroads in Porfirian Mexico*. DeKalb, Ill.: Northern Illinois University Press, 1981.

Códex Ramírez. Relación del origen de los indios que habitan esta Nueva España según sus historias. Mexico: Editorial Leyenda, 1944.

Colección de documentos inéditos relativos al descubrimiento, conquista y organización de las antiguas posesiones españolas de América y oceania. 14 vols. Madrid, 1927–32.

Collis, Maurice. *Cortes and Montezuma*. London: Faber and Faber, 1954.

Cook, Pauline, ed. and trans. *The Pathless Grove: Sonnets by Juana Inés de la Cruz*. Prairie City, Ill.: Decker Press, 1950.

Cook, Sherburne. "Human Sacrifice and Warfare as Factors in the Demography of Pre-Colonial Mexico," *Human Biology*, 18, 1946, pp. 81–102.

Cooper, Donald B. *Epidemic Disease in Mexico City, 1761–1813*. Austin, Tex.: University of Texas Press, 1965.

Cornelius, Wayne A. *Politics and the Migrant Poor in Mexico City*. Stanford: Stanford University Press, 1975.

Cortés, Hernán. *Letters from Mexico*, trans. by A. R. Pagden. New York: Grossman Publishers, 1971.

Corti, Egon. *Maximilian and Charlotte of Mexico*. 2 vols. New York: Alfred A. Knopf, 1928.

Coruña, Martín Jesús de la. *Relación de los indios de la provincia de Mechuacán*. Madrid: Aguilar, 1956.

Cosio Villegas, Daniel, ed. *Historia Moderna de México*. 5 vols. Mexico: Editorial Hermes, 1955–60.

―――. *El estílo personal de gobernar*. Mexico: Joaquín Mortiz, 1974.

―――. *La sucesión presidencial*. Mexico: Joaquín Mortiz, 1976.

Costeloe, Michael P. *Church Wealth in Mexico, 1800–1856*. Cambridge: Cambridge University Press, 1967.

―――. *Church and State in Independent Mexico: A Study of the Patronage Debate, 1821–1857*. London: Royal Historical Society, 1978.

Creelman, James. *Díaz: Master of Mexico*. New York: Appleton, 1976.

Cronon, William. *Changes in the Land: Indians, Colonists and Ecology of New England*. New York: Hill and Wang, 1983.

Crosby, Alfred W., Jr. *The Columbian Exchange: Biological and Cultural Consequences of 1492*. Westport, Conn.: Greenwood Press, 1973.

Cruz, Sor Juana Inés de la. *Carta atenagórica. Respuesta a Sor Filotea*, edited by E. Abreu Gómez. Mexico, 1934.

Cuevas, Mariano P., ed. *Documentos inéditos del siglo XVI para la historia de México*. 3 vols. Mexico: Editorial Porrúa, 1975.

Cumberland, Charles C. *The Mexican Revolution*. Austin, Tex.: University of Texas Press, 1952.

―――. *Mexico: The Struggle for Modernity*. New York: Oxford University Press, 1968.

Cummins, J. S., ed. *The Travels and Controversies of Friar Domingo Fernández Navarrete, 1618–1686*. Cambridge: Hakluyt Society Publications, 1962.

Davidson, David M. "Negro Slave Control and Resistance in Colonial Mexico, 1519–1650," *Hispanic American Historical Review*, 46 (2), August 1966, pp. 235–253.

De Fuentes, Patricia, ed. *The Conquistadores: First-Person Accounts of the Conquest of Mexico*. New York: Orion Press, 1963.

Denevan, William, ed. *The Native Population of the Americas*. Madison, Wis.: University of Wisconsin, 1976.

Derossi, Flavia. *The Mexican Entrepreneur*. Paris: OECD, 1971.

Díaz del Castillo, Bernal. *The Discovery and Conquest of Mexico, 1517–1521*, trans. by A. P. Maudslay; introduction by Irving A. Leonard. New York: Grove Press, 1956 (published by arrangement with Farrar, Straus and Cudahy).

————. *Historia verdadera de la conquista de la Nueva España*. 2 vols. Mexico: Editorial Porrúa, 1955.

Díaz y de Ovando, Clementina. "La Ciudad de México en 1904," *Historia Mexicana*. 24, julio–septiembre 1974, pp. 122–144.

DiTella, Torcuato S. "The Dangerous Classes in Early Nineteenth-Century Mexico," *Journal of Latin American Studies*, 5 (1), May 1973, pp. 79–105.

Dorantes de Carranza, Baltasar. *Sumaria relación de las cosas de la Nueva España, con noticia individual de los descendientes legítimos de los conquistadores y primeros pobladores*. Mexico, 1902.

Dulles, John W. *Yesterday in Mexico*. Austin, Tex.: University of Texas Press, 1961.

Dunbar, Edward. *The Mexican Papers*. New York: J.A.H. Hasbrouck & Co., 1860–61.

Durán, Diego de. *Historia de las Indias de Nueva España*. 2 vols. Mexico: Editorial Porrúa, 1967.

Durand, José. *La transformación social del conquistador*. 2 vols. Mexico, 1953.

Dusenberry, William H. "The Regulation of Meat Supply in Sixteenth-Century Mexico City," *Hispanic American Historical Review*, 28 (1), 1948, pp. 38–52.

————. *The Mexican Mesta: The Administration of Ranching in Colonial Mexico*. Urbana, Ill.: University of Illinois Press, 1963.

Elliott, J. H. *Imperial Spain, 1469–1716*. New York: St. Martin's Press, 1963.

Elton, J. F. *With the French in Mexico*. Philadelphia: J. B. Lippincott, 1867.

Eckstein, Susan. *The Poverty of Revolution: The State and the Urban Poor in Mexico*. Princeton: Princeton University Press, 1977.

Farriss, Nancy M. *Crown and Clergy in Colonial Mexico, 1759–1821: The Crisis of Ecclesiastical Privilege*. London: Athlone Press, 1968.

Feijoo, Rosa. "El tumulto de 1624," *Historia Mexicana*, 14, 1964, pp. 42–70.

————. "El tumulto de 1692," *Historia Mexicana*, 14, 1965, pp. 656–679.

Fernández, Justino, ed. "Códice del tecpan de Tlatelolco," *Investigaciones históricas*, I, no. 3, 1939, pp. 243–264.

Fernández del Castillo, Francisco. *Apuntes para la historia de San Angel y sus alrededores*. Mexico: Museo Nacional de Arqueología, Historia y Etnología, 1913.

Fitzgerald, E.V.K. *Public Sector Investment Planning for Developing Countries*. London: Macmillan, 1978.

Flandrau, Charles M. *Viva Mexico*. New York: D. Appleton & Co., 1908.

Flores Caballero, Romeo. *Counterrevolution, 1804–1838*. Lincoln, Nebr.: University of Nebraska Press, 1974.

Florescano, Enrique. *Precios de maíz y crisis agrícolas en México, 1707–1810*. Mexico: Colegio de México, 1969.

———. "El problema agrario de los últimos años del virreinato, 1800–1821," *Historia Mexicana*, 20 (4), avril–junio 1971, pp. 477–510.

Frank, Andre Gunder. *Mexican Agriculture, 1521–1630: The Transformation of the Mode of Production*. Cambridge: Cambridge University Press, 1979.

Frost, Elsa Cecilia, et al., eds. *Labor and Laborers Through Mexican History*. Mexico: Colegio de México, 1977; Tucson, Ariz.: University of Arizona Press, 1979.

Gage, Thomas. *Thomas Gage's Travels in the New World*, edited by J. Eric S. Thompson. Norman, Okla.: University of Oklahoma Press, 1958.

García, Genaro. *Leona Vicario, heroína insurgente*. Mexico: Edición Inovación, 1979.

García Cubas, Antonio. *El libro de mis recuerdos*. Mexico: Impr. A. García Cubas, 1904.

García Icazbalceta, Joaquín., ed. *Nueva colección de documentos para la historia de México*. 5 vols. Mexico, 1886–92.

Gardiner, C. Harvey. *Naval Power in the Conquest of Mexico*. Austin, Tex.: University of Texas Press, 1956.

———. *Martín López: Conquistador Citizen of Mexico*. Lexington, Ky.: University of Kentucky Press, 1958.

Garza, Gustavo. *El proceso de industrialización en la Ciudad de México, 1821–1970*. Mexico: Colegio de México, 1985.

———, and Schteingart, Martha. "Mexico City: The Emerging Megalopolis," in Wayne A. Cornelius and Robert V. Kemper, eds., *Metropolitan Latin America: The Challenge and Response*. Latin American Urban Research, Vol. 6. Beverly Hills: Sage Publications, 1978.

Gibson, Charles. *The Aztecs Under Spanish Rule*. Stanford: Stanford University Press, 1964.

———. "Rotation of Alcaldes in the Indian Cabildo of Mexico City," *Hispanic American Historical Review*, 33, 1953, pp. 212–222.

———. "The Aztec Aristocracy in Colonial Mexico," *Comparative Studies in Society and History*, 2 (2), January 1960, pp. 169–196.

Gómez de Cervantes, Gonzalo. *La vida económica y social de Nueva España al finalizar el siglo XVI*. Mexico, 1944.

González Casanova, Pablo. *Democracy in Mexico*. New York: Oxford University Press, 1970.

González G., José. *Lo negro del Negro Durazo*. Mexico: Editorial Posada, 1983.

González Obregón, Luís, ed. *Carlos, cacique de Texcoco: Proceso inquisitorial*. Mexico: Biblioteca Enciclopédica del Estado de Mexico, 1980.

———. *Los precursores de la Independencia mexicana en el siglo XVI*. Mexico: Librería de la Vda. de C. Bouret, 1906.

———. *La vida de México en 1810*. Mexico: Editorial Stylo, 1943.

Graham, John A., ed. *Ancient Mesoamerica*. Palo Alto, Calif.: Peek Publications, 1981.

Greenleaf, Richard E. *Zumárraga and the Mexican Inquisition, 1536–1543*. Washington, D.C.: Academy of American Franciscan History, 1961.

———. "The Obraje in the Late Mexican Colony," *The Americas*, 23, 1967, pp. 227–250.

———. *The Mexican Inquisition of the Sixteenth Century*. Albuquerque, N.M.: University of New Mexico Press, 1969.

Gillmor, Frances. *Flute of the Smoking Mirror: A Portrait of Nezahualcóyotl, Poet-King of the Aztecs*. Albuquerque, N.M.: University of New Mexico, 1949.

Grindle, Merilee. "Patrons and Clients in the Bureaucracy: Career Networks in Mexico," *Latin American Research Review*, 12 (1), 1977, pp. 37–66.

Gruening, Ernest. *Mexico and Its Heritage*. New York: Century, 1928.

Guerrero, Julio. *La génesis del crimen en México, estudio de psiquiatría social*. Mexico: Librería de la Vda. de C. Bouret, 1901.

Guijo, Gregorio M. de. *Diario, 1648–1664*. 2 vols. Mexico, 1953.

Gutiérrez Dávila, Julián. *Vida y virtudes del padre Domingo Pérez de Barcia*. Madrid, 1720.

Guzmán, Martín Luís. *El águila y la serpiente*. Mexico: Editorial Anahuac, 1941.

Hall, Linda B. *Alvaro Obregón: Power and Revolution in Mexico, 1911–1920*. College Station, Tex.: Texas A&M University Press, 1981.

Hamill, Hugh M., Jr. *The Hidalgo Revolt*. Gainesville, Fla.: University of Florida Press, 1966.

Hamilton, Earl J. *American Treasure and Price Revolution in Spain*. Cambridge, Mass.: Harvard University Press, 1934.

Hamnett, Brian. "The Appropriation of Mexican Church Wealth by the Spanish Bourbon Government," *Journal of Latin American Studies*, 1 (2), November 1969, pp. 85–113.

———. *Política y comercio en el sur de Mexico, 1750–1821*. Mexico, 1976.

Handbook of Middle American Indians. Austin, Tex.: University of Texas Press, 1964.

Hansen, Roger D. *The Politics of Development in Mexico*. Baltimore: Johns Hopkins University Press, 1971.

Harner, Michael. "The Ecological Basis for Aztec Sacrifice," *American Ethnologist*, 4, 1977, pp. 117–135.

Harris, Marvin. *Cannibals and Kings: The Origins of Cultures.* New York: Vintage/Random House, 1978.

Harrison, John P. "Henry Lane Wilson, el trágico de la decena," *Historia Mexicana*, 6, 1957, pp. 374–405.

Haslip, Joan. *Imperial Adventurer: Emperor Maximilian of Mexico.* London: Weidenfeld and Nicolson, 1971.

Hawks, Henry. "A Relation of the Commodities of Nova Hispania, and the Manners of the Inhabitants," in Richard Hakluyt, *Voyages.* 8 vols. London: Everyman, 1962.

Herrera, Hayden. *Frida, a Biography of Frida Kahlo.* New York: Harper & Row, 1983.

Hoberman, Louisa. "Bureaucracy and Disaster: Mexico City and the Flood of 1629," *Journal of Latin American Studies*, 6 (2), November 1974, pp. 211–230.

———. "Merchants in Seventeenth-Century Mexico City: A Preliminary Portrait," *Hispanic American Historical Review*, 57, 1977, pp. 479–503.

Humboldt, Alexander von. *Political Essay on the Kingdom of New Spain.* 2 vols. New York: Riley, 1811.

Iduarte, Andrés. *Niño: Child of the Mexican Revolution*, trans. and adapted by James F. Shearer. New York: Praeger, 1971.

"Información del Señor de Coyoacán," *Anales del Museo Nacional de México*, epoca 4, Vol. 5, 1927.

Instrucciones que los virreyes de Nueva España dejaron a sus sucesores. 2 vols. Mexico, 1873.

Israel, Jonathan I. *Race, Class, and Politics in Colonial Mexico, 1610–1670.* London: Oxford University Press, 1975.

———. "Mexico and the 'General Crisis' of the Seventeenth Century," *Past and Present*, 63, May 1974, pp. 33–57.

Ixtlilxochítl, Fernando de Alva. *Obras Históricas.* 2 vols. Mexico, 1891–92.

———. *Historia Chichimeca: Nezahualcóyotl, 1402–1472.* Mexico: Biblioteca Enciclopédica del Estado de México, 1977.

Jiménez, Luz. *Life and Death in Milpa Alta: A Nahuatl Chronicle of Díaz and Zapata*, trans. and edited by Fernando Horcasitas. Norman, Okla.: University of Oklahoma Press, 1972.

Johnson, William Weber. *Heroic Mexico.* San Diego: Harcourt Brace Jovanovich, 1984.

Jones, Oakah L., Jr. *Santa Anna.* New York: Twayne Publishers, 1968.

Juzgado de Toral y la Madre Conchita. Stenographic text. 2 vols. Mexico: Archivo General de la Nación.

Kagan, Samuel. "The Labor of Prisoners in the Obrajes of Coyoacán, 1660–1693," in Elsa Cecilia Frost, et al., eds., *Labor and Laborers Through Mexican History.* Tucson, Ariz.: University of Arizona Press, 1979.

Keen, Benjamin. *The Aztec Image in Western Thought.* New Brunswick, N.J.: Rutgers University Press, 1971.

Kemper, Robert V. *Migration and Adaptation of Tzinzuntzan Peasants in Mexico City*. Ph.D. Diss. Berkeley: University of California, 1971.

Kicza, John E. *Colonial Entrepreneurs: Families and Business in Bourbon Mexico City*. Albuquerque, N.M.: University of New Mexico Press, 1983.

————. "The Pulque Trade of Late Colonial Mexico City," *The Americas*, 37 (2), October 1980, pp. 193–221.

King, Rosa Eleanor. *Tempest Over Mexico*. Boston: Little, Brown, 1935.

Knowlton, Robert J. *Church Property and the Mexican Reform, 1856–1910*. DeKalb, Ill.: Northern Illinois University Press, 1976.

Kollonitz, Countess Paula. *The Court of Mexico*. London: Saunders, Otley and Co., 1868.

Kubler, George. *Mexican Architecture in the Sixteenth Century*. 2 vols. New Haven: Yale University Press, 1948.

Ladd, Doris M. *The Mexican Nobility at Independence, 1780–1826*. Austin, Tex.: University of Texas Press, 1976.

Lafaye, Jacques. *Quetzalcóatl and Guadalupe: The Formation of Mexican National Consciousness, 1531–1813*. Chicago: University of Chicago Press, 1976.

Lattimore, Owen. *Inner Asian Frontiers of China*. New York: American Geographical Society, 1940.

León-Portilla, Miguel. *Visión de los vencidos: Relaciones indígenas de la conquista*. Mexico: UNAM, 1959.

————. *El reverso de la Conquista*. Mexico: Editorial Joaquín Mortíz, 1964.

Leonard, Irving A. *Don Carlos de Sigüenza y Góngora: A Mexican Savant of the Seventeenth Century*. Berkeley: University of California Press, 1929.

————. *Baroque Times in Old Mexico*. Ann Arbor, Mich.: University of Michigan Press, 1959.

————. *Books of the Brave*. New York: Gordian Press, 1964.

Levy, Daniel. *University and Government in Mexico: Autonomy in an Authoritarian Regime*. New York: Praeger, 1980.

Lewis, Leslie Kay. *Colonial Texcoco: A Province in the Valley of Mexico, 1570–1630*. Ph.D. Diss. Los Angeles: UCLA, 1978.

Lewis, Oscar. *The Children Of Sanchez*. New York: Random House, 1961.

Liebman, Seymour B. *The Jews in New Spain*. Coral Gables, Fla.: University of Miami Press, 1970.

Lira, Andrés. *Comunidades indígenas frente a la Ciudad de México*. Mexico: El Colegio de México, 1983.

Liss, Peggy K. *Mexico Under Spain, 1521–1556: Society and the Origins of Nationality*. Chicago: University of Chicago Press, 1975.

Litvak King, Jaime. *Cihuatlán y Tepecoalinco: Provincias tributarias de México en el siglo XVI*. Mexico: UNAM, 1971.

Lizardi, José Joaquín Fernández de. *El periquillo sarniento*. 3 vols. Mexico: Editorial Porrúa, 1949.

————. *Don Catrín de la Fachenda*. Mexico: Ediciones Porrúa, 1959.

Lockhart, James M., and Otte, Enrique, eds. *Letters and People of the Spanish Indies, Sixteenth Century*. New York: Cambridge University Press, 1976.

Lombardo de Ruíz, Sonia, ed. *Antología de textos sobre la Ciudad de México en el período de la Ilustración (1788–92)*. Mexico: INAH—Colección Científica, no. 113.

Lomnitz, Larissa Adler. *Como sobreviven los marginados*. Mexico: Siglo Vientiuno, 1975.

López, de Gómara, Francisco. *Cortés: The Life of the Conquistador by His Secretary*, trans. by Lesley B. Simpson. Berkeley: University of California Press, 1964.

Lynch, John. *The Spanish American Revolutions, 1808–1826*. New York: Norton, 1973.

Mabry, Donald. *The Mexican University and the State: Student Conflicts, UNAM Students, 1910–1971*. College Station, Tex.: Texas A&M University Press, 1982.

Macedo, Miguel S. *Mi barrio, segunda mitad del siglo XIX*. Mexico: Editorial "Cultura," 1930.

MacLachlan, Colin M., and Rodríguez O., Jaime E. *The Forging of the Cosmic Race*. Berkeley: University of California Press, 1980.

McNeill, William H. *Plagues and Peoples*. Garden City, N.Y.: Anchor Press/Doubleday, 1976.

MacNeish, Richard S. "The Origins of New World Civilization," in *Readings from Scientific American. Cities: Their Origin, Growth and Human Impact*. San Francisco: W. H. Freeman and Co., 1954–73.

Madariaga, Salvador de. *Hernán Cortés, Conqueror of Mexico*. New York: Macmillan, 1941.

———. *The Fall of the Spanish American Empire*. London: Hollis & Carter, 1947.

Madero, Francisco I. *La sucesión presidencial en 1910*. San Pedro, Coahuila, 1908.

Maldonado, Braulio. *Baja California: Comentarios políticos*. Mexico: Costa Amic, 1960.

Maldonado R., Calixto. *Los asesinatos de los Señores Madero y Pino Suárez*. Mexico, 1922.

Márquez Sterling, Manuel. *Los últimos días del Presidente Madero*. Havana: Impr. El Siglo XX, 1917.

Martin, Norman F. *Los vagabundos en la Nueva España, siglo XVI*. Mexico, 1957.

Martínez, Enrico. *Reportorio de los tiempos*. Mexico: S.E.P., 1948.

Martínez, José Luís. *Nezahualcóyotl: Vida y obra*. Mexico: Fondo de Cultural Económica, 1972.

Mason, R. H. *Pictures of Life in Mexico*. 2 vols. London: Smith, Elder, 1851.

Mathes, Valerie. "Enrico Martínez of New Spain," *The Americas*, 33, 1976, pp. 62–77.

Mathes, W. M. "To Save a City: The Desagüe of Mexico-Huehuetoca, 1607," *The Americas*, 26, April 1970.

Mayer, Brantz. *Mexico As It Was and Is*. New York: J. Winchester, 1844.

Maza, Francisco de la. *Enrico Martínez: Cosmógrafo e impresor de Nueva España*. Mexico, 1943.

Memoria de las obras del sistema de drenaje profundo del Distrito Federal. 3 vols. Departamento del Distrito Federal. Mexico: UNAM, 1975.

Mendieta, Jerónimo de. *Historia Eclesiástica Indiana*. Madrid: Ediciones Atlas, 1973.

Mendizábal, Miguel Othón de. *Obras completas*. 6 vols. Mexico: Talleres Gráficos de la Nación, 1946–47.

Meyer, Michael C. *Huerta: A Political Portrait*. Lincoln, Nebr.: University of Nebraska Press, 1972.

———, and Sherman, William L. *The Course of Mexican History*. New York: Oxford University Press, 1979.

Millon, René. "Teotihuacán," in *Readings from Scientific American. Cities: Their Origin, Growth and Human Impact*. San Francisco: W. H. Freeman and Co. 1954–73.

Millon, Robert Paul. *Mexican Marxist: Vicente Lombardo Toledano*. Chapel Hill, N.C.: University of North Carolina Press, 1966.

Miranda, José. *El tributo indígena en la Nueva España durante el siglo XVI*. Mexico, 1952.

Molina Enríquez, Andrés. *Los grandes problemas nacionales*. Mexico: A. Carranza e hijos, 1909.

Morales, María Dolores. "Estructura urbana y distribución de la propiedad en la Ciudad de México en 1813," *Historia Mexicana*, 25, 1970, pp. 363–402.

Moreno Toscano, Alejandra, ed. "Ciudad de México: Ensayo de construcción de una historia," Mexico: INAH—*Colección Científica*, no. 61, 1978.

Mosk, Sanford A. *Industrial Revolution in Mexico*. Berkeley: University of California Press, 1950.

Motolinía, Fray Toribio de Benavente. *Libro de las cosas de la Nueva España*. Mexico: UNAM, 1971.

———. *Memoriales*. Mexico: UNAM, 1971.

Mumford, Lewis. *The City in History: Its Origins, Its Transformations, and Its Prospects*. New York: Harcourt, Brace & World, 1961.

Muriel de la Torre, Josefina. *Conventos de monjas en la Nueva España*. Mexico, 1946.

———. *Los recogimientos de mujeres*. Mexico: UNAM, 1974.

Navarrete, Alfredo. *Alto a la contrarrevolución*. Mexico: Editorial Libros de Mexico, 1971.

Novo, Salvador. *La vida en México en el período presidencial de Lázaro Cárdenas*. Mexico, 1965.

———. *La vida en México en el período presidencial de Miguel Alemán*. Mexico, 1967.

———. *Cocina Mexicana: historia gastronómica de la Ciudad de Mexico*. Mexico: Editorial Porrúa, 1967.

———. *Historia y leyenda de Coyoacán*. Mexico: Editorial Novaro, 1971.

Oldman, O., et al. *Financing Urban Development in Mexico City*. Cambridge, Mass.: Harvard University Press, 1967.

Orozco, José Clemente. *Autobiografía*. Mexico: Ediciones Era, 1970.

O'Shaughnessy, Edith. *A Diplomat's Wife in Mexico*. New York: Harper & Brothers, 1916.

Padden, R. C. *The Hummingbird and the Hawk: Conquest and Sovereignty in the Valley of Mexico, 1503–1541*. Columbus, Ohio: Ohio State University Press, 1967.

Palerm, Angel. *Obras hidráulicas prehispánicas en el sistema lacustre del Valle de México*. Mexico: INAH, 1973.

Palmer, Colin A. *Slaves of the White God: Blacks in Mexico*. Cambridge: Cambridge University Press, 1976.

———. "Religion and Magic in Mexican Slave Society, 1570–1650," in Stanley L. Engeman and Eugene D. Genovese, eds., *Race and Slavery in the Western Hemisphere*. Princeton: Princeton University Press, 1975.

Pani, Alberto. *Hygiene in Mexico: A Study of Sanitation and Educational Problems*. New York: G. P. Putnam and Sons, 1917.

Parry, J. H. *The Spanish Seaborne Empire*. New York: Alfred A. Knopf, 1966.

Parsons, Jeffrey R. "The Role of Chinampa Agriculture in the Food Supply of Aztec Tenochtitlán," in Charles E. Cleland, ed., *Cultural Change and Continuity*. New York: Academic Press, 1976.

Paso y Troncoso, Francisco del, ed. *Epistolario de Nueva España, 1505–1818*. 16 vols. Mexico: Antigua Librería Robredo, 1939–42.

Payno, Manuel. *Los bandidos de Río Frío*. 5 vols. Mexico: Editorial Porrúa, 1945.

Paz, Octavio. *The Labyrinth of Solitude*, trans. by L. Kemp. New York: Grove Press, 1961.

———. *The Other Mexico: Critique of the Pyramid*, trans. by L. Kemp. New York: Grove Press, 1972.

Pérez López, Enrique, et al. *Mexico's Recent Economic Growth: The Mexican View*. Austin, Tex.: University of Texas Press, 1967.

Phelan, John L. *The Millennial Kingdom of the Franciscans in the New World*. Berkeley: University of California Press, 1956.

———. *The Kingdom of Quito in the Seventeenth Century*. Madison, Wis.: University of Wisconsin Press, 1967.

Pike, Ruth. *Enterprise and Adventure: The Genoese in Seville and the Opening of the New World*. Ithaca, N.Y.: Cornell University Press, 1966.

Poinsett, Joel R. *Notes on Mexico, Made in the Autumn of 1822 by a Citizen of the United States.* Philadelphia: H. C. Carey, 1824.

Pomar, Juan Bautista. *Relación de Texcoco.* Mexico: Biblioteca Enciclopédica del Estado de México, 1975.

Ponce, Alonso. *Relación breve y verdadera de algunas cosas que sucedieron al padre Fray Alonso Ponce en las provincias de Nueva España.* Madrid, 1873.

Poniatowska, Elena. *La noche de Tlatelolco.* Mexico: Ediciones Era, 1971.

Portes, Alejandro, and Walton, John. *Urban Latin America.* Austin, Tex.: University of Texas, 1976.

Potash, Robert A. *Mexican Government and Industrial Development in the Early Republic.* Amherst, Mass., 1983.

Prieto, Guillermo. *Memorias de mis tiempos, 1828 a 1853.* Mexico: Editorial José M. Cajica, 1970.

Prieto Laurens, Jorge. *Cincuenta años de política mexicana, memorias políticas.* Mexico, 1968.

"Proceso inquisitorial del cacique de Texcoco," in *Publicaciones del Archivo General de la Nación,* Vol. 1. Mexico: AGN, 1910.

"Procesos de indios idólatras y hechiceros," in *Publicaciones del Archivo General de la Nación,* Vol. 3. Mexico: AGN, 1912.

Quirk, Robert E. *The Mexican Revolution and the Catholic Church, 1910–1929.* Bloomington, Ind.: Indiana University Press, 1973.

Raat, William D. "Los intelectuales, el positivismo y la cuestión indígena," *Historia Mexicana,* 20, 1971, pp. 412–427.

———. "Ideas and Society in Don Porfirio's Mexico," *The Americas,* 30, 1973, pp. 32–53.

Ramírez, Ramón. *El movimiento estudiantíl de México: Julio–diciembre de 1968.* 2 vols. Mexico: Ediciones Era, 1969.

Ramírez Plancarte, Francisco. *La Ciudad de México durante la revolución constitucionalista.* Mexico: Impresiones Unidas, 1940.

Ramos, Samuel. *Profile of Man and Culture in Mexico.* Austin, Tex.: University of Texas Press, 1962.

Reed, Alma. *Orozco.* New York: Oxford University Press, 1956.

Reed, John. *Insurgent Mexico.* New York: Simon and Schuster, 1969.

Reynolds, Clark W. *The Mexican Economy: Twentieth Century Structure and Growth.* New Haven: Yale University Press, 1970.

Ricard, Robert. *The Spiritual Conquest of Mexico.* Berkeley: University of California Press, 1966.

Richmond, Douglas W. *Venustiano Carranza's Nationalist Struggle, 1893–1920.* Lincoln, Nebr.: University of Nebraska Press, 1983.

Riding, Alan. *Distant Neighbors: A Portrait of the Mexicans.* New York: Alfred A. Knopf, 1985.

Riley, James D. "The Wealth of the Jesuits in Mexico, 1670–1767," *The Americas,* 33, 1976, pp. 226–266.

Rivera, Diego. *Mi arte, mi vida*. With Gladys March. Mexico: Editorial Herrero, 1963.

Robertson, William S. *Iturbide of Mexico*. Durham, N.C.: Duke University Press, 1952.

Robleto, Hernán. *Obregón, Toral y la Madre Conchita*. Mexico: Ediciones Botas, 1935.

Roeder, Ralph. *Juárez and His Mexico*. 2 vols. New York: Viking, 1947.

Rohlfes, Lawrence John. *Police and Penal Correction in Mexico City, 1876–1911: A Study of Order and Progress in Porfirian Mexico*. Ph.D. Diss. New Orleans: Tulane University, 1983.

Ross, Stanley R. *Francisco I. Madero, Apostle of Mexican Democracy*. New York: Columbia University Press, 1955.

Ruíz, Ramón Eduardo. *The Great Rebellion: Mexico, 1905–1924*. New York: Norton, 1980.

Rutherford, John David. *Mexican Society During the Revolution*. Oxford: Clarendon Press, 1971.

Sahagún, Fray Bernardino de. *Historia General de las Cosas de Nueva España*. 10 vols. Mexico: Editorial Robredo, 1938.

Salazar, Rosendo. *Pugnas de la Gleba*. 2 vols. Mexico, 1923.

Sanchez-Albornoz, Nicolas. *The Population of Latin America*. Berkeley: University of California Press, 1974.

Sanders, William T., Parsons, Jeffrey R., and Santley, Robert S. *The Basin of Mexico: Ecological Processes in the Evolution of a Civilization*. New York: Academic Press, 1979.

Sanders, William T., and Price, Barbara J. *Mesoamerica: The Evolution of a Civilization*. New York: Random House, 1968.

Sarabia Viejo, María J. *Don Luís de Velasco, virrey de Nueva España, 1550–1564*. Mexico, 1978.

Sauer, Carl O. *Agricultural Origins and Dispersals*. New York: American Geographical Society, 1952.

Scardaville, Michael Charles. *Crime and the Urban Poor: Mexico City in the Late Colonial Period*. Ph.D. Diss. Gainesville, Fla.: University of Florida, 1977.

Schurz, William L. *The Manila Galleon*. New York: E. P. Dutton, 1939.

Seed, Patricia Pauline. *Parents versus Children: Marriage Oppositions in Colonial Mexico, 1610–1779*. Ph.D. Diss. University of Wisconsin/Madison, 1980.

———. "Social Dimensions of Race: Mexico City, 1753," *Hispanic American Historical Review*, 62 (4), November 1982, pp. 569–606.

Serrano, Irma, and Robledo, Elisa. *A calzón amarrado*. Mexico: Grupo Editorial Sayrols, 1984.

Shafer, Robert J. *Mexican Business Organizations: History and Analysis*. Syracuse, N.Y.: Syracuse University Press, 1973.

Shaw, Frederick John, Jr. *Poverty and Politics in Mexico City, 1824–1854.* Ph.D. Diss., Gainesville, Fla.: University of Florida, 1975.

Sigüenza y Góngora, Carlos de. *Alboroto y motín de México del 8 de junio de 1692.* Mexico: Talleres gráficos del Museo Nacional de Antropología, Historia y Etnografía, 1932.

Silva Herzog, Jesús. *Una vida en la vida de México.* Mexico, 1972.

Simpson, Lesley B. *The Encomienda in New Spain.* Berkeley: University of California Press, 1950.

———. "Exploitation of Land in Central Mexico in the Sixteenth Century," *Ibero-Americana,* 36. Berkeley: University of California Press, 1956.

———. *Many Mexicos.* Berkeley: University of California Press, 1966.

Slicher van Bath, B. H. *The Agrarian History of Western Europe, A.D. 500–1850.* New York: St. Martin's Press, 1963.

Smith, Peter H. *Labyrinths of Power.* Princeton: Princeton University Press, 1979.

Solorzano y Pereyra, Juan de. *Política Indiana.* 5 vols. Madrid, 1930.

Sommers, Joseph. *After the Storm.* Albuquerque, N.M.: University of New Mexico Press, 1968.

Sotomayor, Arturo. *México, donde nací: Biografía de una ciudad.* Mexico: Librería M. Porrúa, 1968.

Soustelle, Jacques. *The Daily Life of the Aztecs on the Eve of the Spanish Conquest.* Stanford: Stanford University Press, 1970.

Spell, Jefferson Rea. *The Life and Works of José Joaquín Fernández de Lizardi.* Philadelphia: University of Pennsylvania, 1931.

———. "The Historical and Social Background of El Periquillo Sarniento," *Hispanic American Historical Review,* 36 (4), November 1956, pp. 447–470.

Starr, Frederick. *Mexico and the United States.* Chicago: Bible House, 1914.

Stevens, Evelyn P. *Protest and Response in Mexico.* Cambridge: MIT Press, 1974.

Suárez de Peralta, Juan. *La conjuración de Martín Cortés y otros temas.* Mexico: UNAM, 1945.

Sweet, David G., and Nash, Gary B., eds. *Struggle and Survival in Colonial America.* Berkeley: University of California Press, 1981.

Tannenbaum, Frank. *Peace by Revolution: An Interpretation of Mexico.* New York: Columbia University Press, 1932.

———. *Mexico: The Struggle for Peace and Bread.* New York: Alfred A. Knopf, 1950.

Taracena, Alfonso. *Madero: Vida del hombre y el político.* Mexico: Ediciones Botas, 1937.

Taylor, William B. *Drinking, Homicide, and Rebellion in Colonial Mexican Villages.* Stanford: Stanford University Press, 1979.

TePaske, Jan J., and Klein, Herbert S. "The Seventeenth-Century Crisis in

New Spain: Myth or Reality," *Past & Present*, 90, February 1981, pp. 116–135.

Tezozomoc, Hernando Alvarado. *Crónica Mexicayótl*, in *Anales del Museo de Arqueología, Historia y Etnografía*, epoca 4, Vol. 5, 1927.

———. *Crónica Mexicana*. Mexico: Editorial Leyenda, 1944.

Thompson, Waddy. *Recollections of Mexico*. New York: Wiley & Putnam, 1846.

Timmons, William H. *Morelos of Mexico: Priest, Soldier, Statesman*. El Paso, Tex.: Texas Western College Press, 1963.

Todorov, Tzvetan. *The Conquest of America*, trans. by Richard Howard. New York: Harper & Row, 1984.

Topete, Jesús. *Terror en el riel de El Charro a Vallejo*. Mexico: Editorial Cosmonauta, 1961.

Torquemada, Juan de. *Monarquía Indiana*. 3 vols. Seville, 1723.

Townsend, William Cameron. *Lázaro Cárdenas, Mexican Democrat*. Ann Arbor, Mich.: O. Wahr Publishing Co., 1952.

Turner, John Kenneth. *Barbarous Mexico*. Chicago: Charles H. Kerr and Co., 1911.

Tutino, John M. *Creole Mexico: Spanish Elites, Haciendas, and Indian Towns, 1750–1810*. Ph.D. Diss. Austin, Tex.: University of Texas, 1976.

———. "Hacienda Social Relations in Mexico: The Chalco Region in the Era of Independence," *Hispanic American Historical Review*, 55 (3), August 1975, pp. 496–528.

———. "Power, Class, and Family: Men and Women in the Mexican Elite, 1750–1810," *The Americas*, 39 (3), January 1983, pp. 359–381.

Tweedie, Ethel Brilliana. *Mexico As I Saw It*. London: Hurst & Blackett, 1901.

Unikel, Luís, et al. *El desarrollo urbano de México: Diagnóstico e implicaciones futuras*. Mexico: El Colegio de México, 1976.

Urías Hermosillo, Margarita. "Manuel Escandón: De las diligencias al ferrocarril, 1833–1862," in Ciro F. S. Cardoso, ed., *Formacíon y desarrollo de la burguesía en Mexico, siglo XIX*. Mexico: Siglo Veintiuno, 1978.

Vaillant, George C. *Aztecs of Mexico*. Garden City, N.Y.: Doubleday, 1953.

Van Young, Eric J. *Hacienda and Market in Eighteenth-Century Mexico*. Berkeley: University of California Press, 1981.

Vanderwood, Paul J. *Disorder and Progress: Bandits, Police, and Mexican Development*. Lincoln, Nebr.: University of Nebraska Press, 1981.

Vasconcelos, José. *A Mexican Ulysses: An Autobiography*, trans. by William Rex Crawford. Bloomington, Ind.: Indiana University Press, 1963.

Vélez-Ibañez, Carlos G. *Rituals of Marginality: Politics, Process, and Cultural Change in Urban Central Mexico, 1969–1974*. Los Angeles: University of California Press, 1983.

Vernon, Raymond. *The Dilemma of Mexico's Development*. Cambridge, Mass.: Harvard University Press, 1963.

Villarroel, Hipólito. *México por dentro y fuera bajo el gobierno de los virreyes*. Mexico: Impr. C. Alejandro Valdés, 1831.

"Visita a los obrajes de paños en la jurisdicción de Coyoacán, 1660," *Boletín del Archivo General de la Nación*, Vol. XI (1), enero-marzo 1940, pp. 33–116.

Walsh, Thomas, ed. *Hispanic Anthology: Poems Translated from the Spanish by English and North American Poets*. New York and London: G. P. Putnam's Sons, 1920.

Ward, H. G. *Mexico in 1827*. 2 vols. London: H. Colburn, 1828.

Wilkie, James W., and Wilkie, Edna Monzón de. *México visto en el siglo XX: Entrevistas de historia oral*. Mexico: Instituto Mexicano de Investigaciones Económicas, 1969.

Wilson, Henry Lane. *Diplomatic Episodes in Mexico, Belgium and Chile*. Garden City, N.Y.: Doubleday, Page, 1927.

Wise, George S. *El México de Alemán*. Mexico: Editorial Atlante, 1952.

Wittfogel, Karl A. *Oriental Despotism*. New Haven: Yale University Press, 1957.

Wolf, Eric R. *Sons of the Shaking Earth*. Chicago: University of Chicago Press, 1959.

————, ed. *The Valley of Mexico*. Albuquerque, N.M.: University of New Mexico Press, 1976.

Wolfe, Bertram D. *The Fabulous Life of Diego Rivera*. New York: Stein and Day, 1963.

Womack, John, Jr. *Zapata and the Mexican Revolution*. New York: Vintage, 1970.

Zavala, Silvio. *La encomienda indiana*. Madrid, 1935.

————, ed. *Tributos y servicios personales de indios para Hernán Cortés y su familia*. Mexico: Archivo General de la Nación, 1984.

Zorita, Alonso de. *The Brief and Summary Relation of the Lords of New Spain*, trans. by Benjamin Keen. New Brunswick, N.J.: Rutgers University Press, 1963.

NOTES

ONE
THE VALLEY AND ITS FIRST INHABITANTS

1. William T. Sanders, Jeffrey R. Parsons, and Robert S. Santley, *The Basin of Mexico*, p. 89.
2. Marvin Harris, *Cannibals and Kings*, pp. 36–39.
3. Richard S. MacNeish, *Handbook of Middle American Indians*, Vol. 1, p. 425.
4. The following account is drawn from René Millon, "Teotihuacán," pp. 82–92.
5. The most important advocate of this theory of the "hydraulic society" is Karl A. Wittfogel, in his book *Oriental Despotism*.
6. Sanders, Parsons, and Santley, pp. 286–287.
7. Ibid., p. 344.
8. Owen Lattimore, *Inner Asian Frontiers of China*.
9. Sanders, Parsons, and Santley, pp. 183–184.

TWO
THE CANNIBAL EMPIRE

1. The royal historian Cuauhcóatl, speaking to the Aztec king Motecuhzoma I, quoted in Diego de Durán, *Historia de las Indias de Nueva España*, Vol. II, pp. 216–217.
2. Bernardino de Sahagún, *Historia General de las Cosas de Nueva España*, Book X, chapter 29, pp. 142–143.
3. Quoted in the *Codex Ramírez. Relación del origen de los indios que habitan esta Nueva España según sus historias*, p. 62.
4. Sahagún, Book VI, chapter 14, pp. 103–104.
5. See R. C. Padden, *The Hummingbird and the Hawk*, pp. 22–23.
6. Durán, Vol. II, chapter 12, p. 106.
7. Ibid., p. 111.
8. Ibid., p. 117.
9. Ibid., p. 118.
10. Hernando Alvarado Tezozomoc, *Crónica Mexicana*, chapter XIX, p. 75.
11. Durán, Vol. II, chapter 15, p. 128.
12. Ibid., p. 129.
13. Sahagún, Book VI, chapter 14, p. 106.
14. Hernán Cortés, *Letters from Mexico*, pp. 103–104.

15. Edward Calnek, "The Internal Structure of Tenochtitlán."

16. Juan de Torquemada, *Monarquía Indiana*, Vol. I, Book II, chapter 47, p. 157.

17. Durán, Vol. II, chapter 16, p. 136.

18. Sahagún, Book IX, chapter 14, p. 383.

19. Durán, Vol. II, chapter 16, p. 143.

20. Ibid., Vol. II, chapter 17, p. 146.

21. Padden, pp. 32–34.

22. Estimates by Sherburne Cook, "Human Sacrifice and Warfare as Factors in the Demography of Pre-Colonial Mexico."

23. Durán, Vol. II, chapter 36, p. 278.

24. Ibid., Vol. II, chapter 20, p. 175.

25. Fernando de Alva Ixtlilxochítl, *Obras Históricas*, Vol. II, chapter 41.

26. Durán, Vol. II, chapter 29, pp. 236–237.

27. Padden, p. 41.

28. Durán, Vol. II, chapter 40, p. 311.

29. Ibid., Vol. II, chapter 41, pp. 315–316.

30. Ibid., Vol. II, chapter 44, p. 344.

31. Tezozomoc cites the lower figure, while Durán and Ixtlilxochítl use the higher total.

32. Durán, Vol. II, chapter 40, p. 310.

33. Ibid., Vol. II, chapter 44, p. 345.

34. Tezozomoc, p. 333.

35. Ixtlilxochítl, Vol. II, chapter 60, p. 274.

36. Tezozomoc, p. 384.

THREE

MOTECUHZOMA

1. *Codex Ramírez*, p. 94.

2. Ibid., p. 97.

3. Ixtlilxochítl, Vol. II, p. 310.

4. Durán, Vol. II, p. 404.

5. *Codex Ramírez*, pp. 97–98.

6. Durán, Vol. II, chapter 53, p. 407.

7. Ibid., p. 406.

8. Ibid., p. 407.

9. Sanders, Parsons, and Santley, p. 163.

10. *Anales de Cuauhtitlán*, pp. 30, 49–50.

11. Francisco del Paso y Troncoso, *Epistolario de Nueva España*, Vol. 4, p. 169.

12. Jeffrey R. Parsons, "The Role of Chinampa Agriculture in the Food Supply of Aztec Tenochitlán."

13. Sahagún, Book II, chapter 20, p. 121.

14. Ibid., Book IV, chapters 1–38.

15. See especially W. Arens, *The Man-eating Myth: Anthropology and Anthropophagy*, which assails accounts of cannibalism in Mexico and elsewhere.

16. See especially Michael Harner, "The Ecological Basis for Aztec Sacrifice," and Marvin Harris, *Cannibals and Kings*.

17. Sahagún, Book IX, chapter 10, pp. 370–371.

18. Ibid., Book IX, chapters 10–14.

19. Ibid., Book II.

20. Ibid., Book II, chapter 21, p. 124.

21. Cited from the *Matrícula de Tributos* in Frances M. Berdan, *Trade, Tribute and Market in the Aztec Empire*.

22. Durán, Vol. II, chapter 53, p. 407.

23. Ibid., Vol. II, chapter 54, p. 416.

24. Ibid., Vol. II, chapter 54, p. 421.

25. Ibid., Vol. II, chapter 57, p. 434.

26. Ixtlilxochítl, Vol. II, chapter 71, pp. 301–311.

27. Durán, Vol. II, chapter 59, p. 449.

28. Ibid., Vol. II, chapter 62, p. 466.

29. *Codex Ramírez*, p. 101.

30. Ixtlilxochítl, Vol. II, chapter 72, p. 313.

31. Durán, Vol. II, chapter 61, p. 459.

32. Ibid., Vol. II, chapter 61, p. 460.

33. Ibid., Vol. II, chapter 61, p. 461.

34. Sahagún's Indian informants, quoted in Miguel León-Portilla, ed., *El reverso de la Conquista*, p. 29.

35. Durán, Vol. II, chapter 62, p. 469.

36. León-Portilla, ed., pp. 29–32.

37. Ixtlilxochítl, Vol. II, chapter 74, p. 324.

38. Ibid., chapter 75, p. 328.

39. Durán, Vol. II, chapter 65, p. 483.

40. Ibid., Vol. II, chapter 66, p. 490.

41. Ibid., Vol. II, chapter 66, p. 490.

42. Ibid., Vol. II, chapter 66, p. 491.

43. Ibid., Vol. II, chapter 69, p. 506.

44. Ibid., Vol. II, chapter 69, p. 507.

45. Ibid., Vol. II, chapter 69, p. 508.

46. Ibid., Vol. II, chapter 70, p. 516.

FOUR
THE SPANISH BACKGROUND

1. On Aztec cosmology, see Jacques Soustelle, *The Daily Life of the Aztecs on the Eve of the Spanish Conquest*, pp. 95–119, and George C. Vaillant, *Aztecs of Mexico*, pp. 169–184.

2. Quoted in Fernand Braudel, *The Structures of Everyday Life*, p. 335.

3. B. H. Slicher van Bath, *The Agrarian History of Western Europe*, A.D. *500–1850*, p. 24.

4. Probably the best exposition of this thesis is contained in William H. McNeill, *Plagues and Peoples*.

5. J. H. Elliott, *Imperial Spain, 1469–1716*, p. 34.

6. Irving A. Leonard, *Books of the Brave*, p. 6.

7. Elliott, p. 99.

8. Fernand Braudel, *The Wheels of Commerce*, p. 405.

9. Bartolomé de las Casas, *Brevísima relación de la destrucción de las Indias occidentales*, p. 20.

10. Ibid., p. 14.

11. Leonard, *Books of the Brave*, pp. 25–26.

12. Quoted in Salvador de Madariaga, *Hernán Cortés, Conqueror of Mexico*, p. 32.

13. Francisco Cervantes de Salazar, *Crónica de la Nueva España*, Book II, p. 98.

14. Las Casas, p. 34.

15. Bernal Díaz del Castillo, *The Discovery and Conquest of Mexico 1517–1521*, p. 32.

16. Díaz del Castillo, p. 3.

FIVE
CONQUEST

1. Sahagún, Book XII, chapter 4, pp. 139–140.

2. Ibid., Book XII, chapter 5, p. 141.

3. Quoted in Francisco López de Gomara, *Cortés: The Life of the Conqueror by His Secretary*, p. 58.

4. Sahagún, Book XII, chapter 7, pp. 144–145.

5. Díaz del Castillo, p. 74.

6. Sahagún, Book XII, chapter 9, p. 148.

7. Ibid., p. 148.

8. Ixtlilxochítl, Vol. II, chapter 80, pp. 347–348.

9. Díaz del Castillo, p. 87.

10. Ibid., p. 90.

11. Ibid., p. 92.

12. Ibid., p. 116.

13. Ibid., p. 130.

14. Ibid., p. 131.

15. Hernán Cortés, *Letters from Mexico*, pp. 67–68.

16. Cortés, p. 75.

17. Ibid., p. 73.

18. Díaz del Castillo, p. 179.

19. Sahagún, Book XII, chapter 11, p. 47.

20. Díaz del Castillo, pp. 182–183.

21. Ibid., p. 187.

22. Ibid., pp. 190–191.

23. Ibid., p. 208.

24. Cortés, p. 86.

25. Ibid.

26. Díaz del Castillo, p. 206.

27. Cortés, p. 103.

28. Díaz del Castillo, pp. 219–220.

29. Ibid., p. 220.

30. Ibid., p. 226.

31. Ibid., p. 230.

32. Ibid., p. 232.

33. Ibid., p. 236.

34. Ibid., p. 300.

35. Braudel, *The Structures of Everyday Life*, p. 79.

36. Sahagún, Book XII, chapter 29, p. 85.

37. Martín Jesús de la Coruña, *Relación de los indios de la provincia de Mechuacán*, Vol. III, pp. 20–22.

38. Díaz del Castillo, p. 416.

39. Quoted in Miguel León-Portilla, *The Broken Spears: The Aztec Account of the Conquest of Mexico*, pp. 107–109.

40. Díaz del Castillo, p. 449.

SIX

BIRTH OF THE SPANISH CITY

1. Bernál Díaz del Castillo, *Historia verdadera de la conquista de la Nueva España*, Vol. II, p. 66.

2. Ibid., Vol. II, p. 72.

3. Ibid., Vol. II, p. 73.

4. See, for example, the "Matrícula de Tributos" in Frances M. Berdan, *Trade, Tribute and Market in the Aztec Empire*.

5. Díaz del Castillo, Vol. II, p. 75.

6. Toribio de Benavente Motolinía, *Memoriales*, p. 29.

7. Justino Fernández, ed., "Códice del tecpan de Tlatelolco."

8. Cortés, *Letters*, p. 323.

9. Ibid., p. 321.

10. Ibid., p. 158.

11. Elliott, *Imperial Spain*, pp. 141–149.

12. Cortés, pp. 279–280, 336–337.

13. Díaz del Castillo, Vol. II, p. 98.

14. Madariaga, *Hernán Cortés*, p. 417.

15. Cortés, p. 275.

16. Ibid., p. 310.

17. Ibid., p. 333.

18. John L. Phelan, *The Millennial Kingdom of the Franciscans in the New World*, pp. 24–25.

19. Ibid., p. 29.

20. Cortés, *Letters*, pp. 327–328.

21. Díaz del Castillo, Vol. II, p. 264.

22. Diego Hurtado de Mendoza, *De la guerra de Granada*, quoted in Fernand Braudel, *The Mediterranean and the Mediterranean World in the Age of Philip II*, pp. 681–682.

23. Díaz del Castillo, Vol. II, p. 87.

24. James M. Lockhart and Enrique Otte, eds., *Letters and People of the Spanish Indies, Sixteenth Century*, p. 198.

25. Ibid., pp. 199, 201.

26. Ibid., p. 202.

27. Arthur Aiton, *Antonio de Mendoza, First Viceroy of New Spain*, p. 34.

28. Madariaga, *Cortés*, p. 471.

29. Díaz del Castillo, Vol. II, pp. 356–370.

30. See Joaquín García Icazbalceta, ed., *Nueva colección de documentos para la historia de México*, Vol. I, p. 45.

31. Norman F. Martin, *Los vagabundos en la Nueva España, siglo XVI*, p. 7.

32. Richard E. Greenleaf, *Zumárraga and the Mexican Inquisition, 1536–1543*, pp. 113–114.

33. Ibid., pp. 117–121.

34. Ibid., p. 117.

35. C. Harvey Gardiner, *Martín López: Conquistador Citizen of Mexico*.

36. Quoted in Lesley B. Simpson, *The Encomienda in New Spain*, p. 7.

37. Quoted in Icazbalceta, ed., *Colección de documentos . . .* , Vol. I, p. 471.

38. Martin, p. 37.

SEVEN

THE INDIANS UNDER SPANISH RULE

1. For the higher figure, see Woodrow Borah and Sherburne Cook, "The Aboriginal Population of Central Mexico on the Eve of the Spanish Conquest." For the lower estimate, see William T. Sanders, Jeffrey R. Parsons, and Robert Santley, *The Basin of Mexico: Ecological Processes in the Evolution of a Civilization.*

2. Charles Gibson, *The Aztecs Under Spanish Rule*, pp. 448–449.

3. Alfred W. Crosby, Jr., *The Columbian Exchange*, pp. 124–125.

4. Ibid., p. 158.

5. Ibid., p. 66.

6. Ibid., pp. 73–74.

7. François Chevalier, *Land and Society in Colonial Mexico*, p. 85.

8. Quoted in Lesley B. Simpson, "Exploitation of Land in Central Mexico in the Sixteenth Century," pp. 2–3.

9. Ibid., p. 4.

10. Chevalier, p. 93.

11. *Colección de documentos inéditos relativos al descubrimiento, conquista y organización de las antiguas posesiones españolas de América y Oceania.* Vol. VI, pp. 511–512.

12. Chevalier, pp. 100–101.

13. Ibid., p. 92.

14. Ibid., p. 93.

15. Robert Ricard, *The Spiritual Conquest of Mexico*, p. 91.

16. Motolinía, *Memoriales*, p. 122.

17. Ibid., p. 91.

18. Phelan, p. 47.

19. Fernando Benítez, *The Century After Cortés*, p. 21.

20. Motolinía, p. 21.

21. Quoted in Francisco del Paso y Troncoso, ed., *Epistolario de Nueva España*, *1505–1818*, Vol. IV, p. 232.

22. From the *Annals of the Cakchiquels*, quoted in Crosby, p. 58.

23. Motolinía, p. 21.

24. Jerónimo de Mendieta, *Historia Eclesiástica Indiana*, Vol. V, chapter 36, p. 100.

25. William Cronon, *Changes in the Land: Indians, Colonists and Ecology of New England*, p. 90.

26. Quoted in Simpson, *The Encomienda*, p. 100.

27. Ibid., p. 149.

28. Ibid.

29. Quoted in Lesley B. Simpson, *Many Mexicos*, p. 87.

30. Quoted in Benítez, pp. 82–83.

31. Gonzalo Aguirre Beltrán, "The Slave Trade in Mexico," p. 414.

32. Ibid., p. 413.
33. Leslie Kay Lewis, *Colonial Texcoco: A Province in the Valley of Mexico, 1570–1630*, pp. 13–14.
34. Chevalier, p. 249.
35. Quoted in Paso y Troncoso, ed., *Epistolario . . .* , Vol. IV, pp. 169–170.
36. George Kubler, *Mexican Architecture in the Sixteenth Century*, Vol. II, p. 417.
37. Alonso de Zorita, *The Brief and Summary Relation of the Lords of New Spain*, p. 227.
38. Gibson, pp. 124–125.
39. Simpson, *Many Mexicos*, pp. 87–88.
40. Gibson, p. 277.
41. Ibid., p. 126.
42. Ibid., p. 283.
43. Quoted in Lewis Hanke, "The Contribution of Bishop Zumárraga to Mexican Culture," *The Americas*, 5 (1948), pp. 276–277.
44. Quoted in Tzvetan Todorov, *The Conquest of America*, p. 151.
45. Quoted in Crosby, p. 11.
46. Aiton, p. 94.
47. Quoted in Ricard, p. 150.
48. Gibson, pp. 400–401.
49. Ricard, p. 98.
50. Ibid., p. 272.
51. Motolinía, pp. 34–35.
52. Ricard, p. 226.
53. Quoted in Benítez, p. 82.
54. Viceroy Luis de Velasco II to his successor, the Count of Monterrey, in *Instrucciones que los virreyes de Nueva España dejaron a sus sucesores*, Vol. I.
55. "Proceso inquisitorial del cacique de Texcoco," Archivo General de la Nación, *Publicaciones*, 1, p. 2.
56. Ibid., p. 3.
57. Ibid., p. 6.
58. Ibid., p. 38.
59. Ibid.
60. Ibid., pp. 32–35.
61. Ibid., pp. 53–54.
62. Ibid., p. 37.
63. Ibid., p. 43.
64. Salvador Novo, *Historia y leyenda de Coyoacán*, p. 151.
65. Francisco Fernández del Castillo, *Apuntes para la historia de San Angel y sus alrededores*, pp. 29–30.
66. Ibid., pp. 23–24.

67. Archivo General de la Nación, *Ramo Tierras*, Vol. 1735, exp. 2.

68. Pedro Carrasco and Jesús Monjarás Ruíz, eds., *Colección de documentos sobre Coyoacán*, Vol. I, p. 234.

69. Ibid., p. 84.

70. Ibid., p. 201.

71. Gibson, p. 335.

72. Fernández del Castillo, p. 26.

73. Novo, p. 157.

74. Carrasco and Monjarás Ruíz, eds., pp. 93–94.

75. Fernández del Castillo, p. 29.

76. Archivo General de la Nación, *Ramo Tierras*, Vol. 1735, exp. 2.

77. Quoted in Arthur J. O. Anderson, et al., eds., *Beyond the Codices: The Nahua View of Colonial Mexico*, p. 224.

78. Silvio Zavala, ed., *Tributos y servicios personales de indios para Hernán Cortés y su familia*, pp. 215–216, 223.

79. Ibid., p. 213.

80. Carrasco and Monjarás Ruíz, eds., pp. 88–90.

81. Ibid., p. 91.

82. Ibid., p. 234.

83. Ibid., p. 11.

84. Gibson, p. 159.

85. Ibid.

86. Archivo General de la Nación, *Ramo Vínculos*, Vol. 242, exp. 1.

87. Gibson, p. 160.

EIGHT
CITY OF SILVER

1. Francisco Cervantes de Salazar, *Life in the City of Mexico in New Spain*.

2. Ibid., p. 43.

3. Zorita, *Life and Labor in Ancient Mexico*, pp. 118–119.

4. Cervantes de Salazar, p. 48.

5. Ibid., p. 27.

6. Ibid., p. 33.

7. Ibid., p. 75.

8. Ibid., p. 59.

9. Braudel, *Structures of Everyday Life*, pp. 466–467.

10. Earl Hamilton, *American Treasure and Price Revolution in Spain*, p. 43.

11. Peter J. Bakewell, "Zacatecas: An Economic and Social Outline of a Silver Mining District, 1547–1700," p. 203.

12. Elliott, *Imperial Spain*, p. 176.

13. William L. Schurz, *The Manila Galleon*, p. 15.

14. Quoted in ibid., p. 255.

15. Quoted in ibid., p. 267.

16. Ibid., p. 265.

17. Braudel, *The Mediterranean* . . . , pp. 141–144.

18. J. H. Parry, *The Spanish Seaborne Empire*, p. 121.

19. Miguel de Cervantes Saavedra, *Novelas Ejemplares*, Vol. II (Madrid: Editorial Marín, 1944), p. 88.

20. Hamilton, p. 202.

21. Ruth Pike, *Enterprise and Adventure: The Genoese in Seville and the Opening of the New World*, p. 9.

22. Quoted in Elliott, p. 183.

23. Juan Suárez de Peralta, *La conjuración de Martín Cortés y otros temas*, p. 10.

24. Suárez de Peralta, p. 5.

25. Ibid., p. 12.

26. Ibid., p. 17.

NINE
THE FORGOTTEN CENTURY

1. Lesley B. Simpson, in his foreword to François Chevalier, *Land and Society in Colonial Mexico: The Great Hacienda*, p. iii.

2. Woodrow W. Borah, "New Spain's Century of Depression."

3. Quoted in Chevalier, p. 8.

4. Díaz del Castillo, *The Discovery and Conquest of Mexico*, p. 191.

5. Gibson, p. 305.

6. Alonso Ponce, *Relación breve y verdadera de algunas cosas que sucedieron al padre Fray Alonso Ponce en las provincias de Nueva España*, Vol. I, p. 177.

7. Thomas Gage, *Thomas Gage's Travels in the New World*, edited by J. Eric S. Thompson, p. 74.

8. Juan de Torquemada, *Monarquía Indiana*, Vol. I, p. 308.

9. Enrico Martínez, *Reportorio de los tiempos*, p. 180.

10. Louisa Hoberman, "Bureaucracy and Disaster: Mexico City and the Flood of 1629," p. 212.

11. Alexander von Humboldt, *Political Essay on the Kingdom of New Spain*, Vol. II, p. 95.

12. Quoted in Hoberman, p. 213.

13. Quoted in ibid., p. 214.

14. Richard E. Boyer, *La gran inundación: Vida y sociedad en la Ciudad de México (1629–1638)*, p. 34.

15. Hamilton, p. 34.

16. Gibson, p. 326.

17. Chevalier, p. 215.

18. "Visita a los obrajes de paños en la jurisdicción de Coyoacán, 1660," pp. 33–116.

19. Quoted in Samuel Kagan, "The Labor of Prisoners in the Obrajes of Coyoacán, 1660–1693," p. 211.

20. Jonathan I. Israel, *Race, Class, and Politics in Colonial Mexico, 1610–1670*, pp. 182–183.

21. William B. Taylor, *Drinking, Homicide, and Rebellion in Colonial Mexican Villages*, p. 68.

22. Quoted in ibid., p. 191.

23. Braudel, *The Structures of Everyday Life*, p. 248.

24. Taylor, pp. 104–105.

25. Ibid., p. 37.

26. Gibson, pp. 91–92.

27. Gonzalo Aguirre Beltrán, *La población negra de México, 1519–1810*, p. 221.

28. Gonzalo Aguirre Beltrán, "The Slave Trade in Mexico," p. 428.

29. Quoted in Colin A. Palmer, *Slaves of the White God: Blacks in Mexico*, p. 45.

30. Gage, p. 73.

31. Quoted in Palmer, p. 42.

32. Quoted in Israel, p. 74.

33. Quoted in Aguirre Beltrán, "The Slave Trade . . . ," p. 427.

34. Gage, pp. 68–69.

35. See Gonzalo Aguirre Beltrán, *Medicina y magia*, pp. 362–416.

36. Case cited in Solange B. de Alberro, "Negros y mulatos en los documentos inquisitoriales," pp. 142–143.

37. Solange B. de Alberro, ed., "Proceso y causa criminal contra Diego de la Cruz," pp. 8–17.

38. Gregorio M. de Guijo, *Diario, 1648–1664*, Vol. I, pp. 38–47.

39. Quoted by Manuel Romero de Terreros in his prologue to Guijo, Vol. I, p. viii.

40. Alberro, ed., "Proceso y causa . . . ," p. 10.

41. Ibid., p. 11.

42. Ibid., p. 15.

43. Aguirre Beltrán, *La población negra de México*, p. 221.

44. Padden, *The Hummingbird and the Hawk*, p. 232.

45. Gonzalo Gómez de Cervantes, *La vida económica y social de Nueva España al finalizar el siglo XVI*, p. 98.

46. Israel, p. 65.

47. Ibid., p. 66.

48. Frederick P. Bowser, "The Free Person of Color in Mexico City and Lima: Manumission and Opportunity, 1580–1650," p. 346.

49. Palmer, p. 60.

50. Patricia Seed, *Parents versus Children: Marriage Oppositions in Colonial Mexico, 1610–1779*, pp. 78–79.

51. Ibid., pp. 80–81.

52. Elliott, *Imperial Spain*, p. 216.

53. Israel, p. 93.

54. Quoted in John L. Phelan, *The Kingdom of Quito in the Seventeenth Century*, p. 266.

55. Quoted in Irving A. Leonard, *Don Carlos de Sigüenza y Góngora: A Mexican Savant of the Seventeenth Century*, pp. 62–63.

56. Gage, pp. 67–68.

57. Quoted in Israel, p. 36.

58. The intertwining stories of Aguiar y Seixas, Barcia, Arellano y Sosa, and Pedroza are drawn from Fernando Benítez, *Los demonios en el convento: Sexo y religión en la Nueva España*, and Julián Gutiérrez Dávila, *Vida y virtudes del Padre Domingo Pérez de Barcia*.

59. Benítez, *Los demonios . . .* , p. 119.

60. Ibid., p. 149.

61. Ibid., p. 148.

62. Ibid., p. 40.

63. Translation by Peter H. Goldsmith, in Thomas Walsh, ed., *Hispanic Anthology: Poems Translated from the Spanish by English and North American Poets*, p. 359.

64. Translation by Pauline Cook, in Cook, ed. and trans., *The Pathless Grove: Sonnets by Juana Inés de la Cruz*.

65. Quoted in Benítez, *Los demonios . . .* , p. 168.

66. Ibid., p. 169.

67. Translation by Pauline Cook, op. cit., p. 25.

68. Translation by Robert Graves, in *Encounter*, no. 3, December 1953, quoted in Irving A. Leonard, *Baroque Times in Old Mexico*, p. 189.

69. Sor Juana Inés de la Cruz, *Carta atenagórica. Respuesta a Sor Filotea*, edited by E. Abreu Gómez, p. 47.

70. Leonard, *Baroque Times . . .* , p. 191.

71. Israel, p. 85.

72. Ibid., p. 267.

73. Gage, p. 78.

74. Quoted in Israel, p. 152.

75. The following account is based mainly on Irving A. Leonard's translation of the "Letter of Don Carlos de Sigüenza y Góngora to Admiral Pez Recounting the Incidents of the Corn Riot in Mexico City, June 8, 1692," in Leonard, *Don Carlos de Sigüenza y Góngora*, pp. 210–277.

76. Ibid., pp. 219–220.

77. Ibid., p. 221.

78. Ibid., p. 223.

79. Ibid., p. 232.

80. *Carta de un religioso sobre la rebelión de los indios mexicanos de 1692* (Mexico: Editorial Vargas Rea., 1951), pp. 48–49.

81. "Letter of Don Carlos . . . ," p. 246.

82. Ibid., p. 256.

83. Rosa Feijoo, "El tumulto de 1692," p. 670.

84. Ibid., p. 672.

TEN

THE BOURBON ERA

1. *Instrucciones que los virreyes de Nueva España dejaron a sus sucesores*, p. 258.

2. D. A. Brading, *Miners and Merchants in Bourbon Mexico, 1763–1810*, p. 97.

3. Quoted in Schurz, *The Manila Galleon*, p. 364.

4. J. H. Parry, *The Spanish Seaborne Empire*, p. 317.

5. John E. Kicza, *Colonial Entrepreneurs: Families and Business in Bourbon Mexico City*, p. 64.

6. Ibid., pp. 77–85.

7. Ibid., pp. 71–72.

8. Michael C. Meyer and William L. Sherman, *The Course of Mexican History*, pp. 254–255.

9. Brading, pp. 183–184.

10. Ibid., p. 312.

11. Kicza, pp. 88–89.

12. Humboldt, *Political Essay on the Kingdom of New Spain*, Vol. I, p. 170.

13. Brading, p. 184.

14. Doris M. Ladd, *The Mexican Nobility at Independence, 1780–1826*, p. 32.

15. See especially Chevalier, *Land and Society in Colonial Mexico*, p. 311, and Brading, *Miners and Merchants in Bourbon Mexico*, p. 219.

16. See especially John M. Tutino, *Creole Mexico*, Eric J. Van Young, *Hacienda and Market in Eighteenth-Century Mexico*, and John E. Kicza, *Colonial Entrepreneurs*.

17. John M. Tutino, "Power, Class, and Family: Men and Women in the Mexican Elite, 1750–1810," p. 363.

18. Ibid., p. 361.

19. Enrique Florescano, *Precios de maíz y crisis agrícolas en México, 1708–1810*, pp. 95, 105–109.

20. Tutino, *Creole Mexico*, p. 127.

21. Ibid.

22. Florescano, p. 191.
23. Kicza, p. 24.
24. Ladd, pp. 49–50.
25. "Discurso sobre la policía de México, 1788," attributed to Baltasar Ladrón de Guevara, in Sonia Lombardo de Ruíz, ed., *Antología de textos sobre la Ciudad de México en el período de la Ilustración (1788–1792),* p. 22.
26. Tutino, *Creole Mexico,* p. 137.
27. Humboldt, Vol. I, p. 168.
28. Kicza, p. 16.
29. Quoted in Brading, p. 310.
30. Humboldt, Vol. II, pp. 26–27.
31. Timothy E. Anna, *The Fall of the Royal Government in Mexico City,* p. 16.
32. Ladd, p. 32.
33. Ibid., p. 68.
34. Tutino, *Creole Mexico,* p. 220.
35. Ladd, p. 56.
36. Lucas Alamán, *Historia de Méjico,* Vol. I, p. 8.
37. Ibid., Vol. I, p. 11.
38. Tutino, "Power, Class and Family . . . ," p. 367.
39. Ibid., p. 368.
40. Ibid., pp. 368–369.
41. Tutino, *Creole Mexico,* p. 86.
42. Tutino, "Power, Class and Family . . . ," pp. 373–374.
43. Ibid., p. 376.
44. Ibid.
45. Brian Hamnett, "The Appropriation of Mexican Church Wealth by the Spanish Bourbon Court," p. 87.
46. Quoted in Francis Joseph Brooks, *Parish and Cofradía in Eighteenth-Century Mexico,* pp. 26–27.
47. Seed, *Parents versus Children . . . ,* p. 133.
48. Bernard E. Bobb, *The Viceregency of Antonio María Bucareli in New Spain, 1771–1779,* pp. 54–55.
49. José Joaquín Fernández de Lizardi, *El periquillo sarniento,* Vol. I, p. 158.
50. Ladd, p. 41.
51. Quoted in Brading, p. 35.
52. Kicza, p. 94.
53. Humboldt, Vol. I, p. 176.
54. Francisco de Ajofrín, *Diario del viaje que . . . hizo a la América septentrional en el siglo XVIII,* Vol. I, p. 90.
55. Michael Charles Scardaville, *Crime and the Urban Poor: Mexico City in the Late Colonial Period,* p. viii.

56. Quoted in Fernando Benítez, *La Ciudad de México, 1325–1982,* Vol. II, p. 12.

57. Humboldt, Vol. I, p. 185.

58. Donald B. Cooper, *Epidemic Disease in Mexico City, 1761–1813,* p. 24.

59. Ibid., p. 28.

60. Lombardo de Ruíz, ed., *Antología de textos . . . ,* p. 63.

61. Hipólito Villarroel, *México por dentro y fuera bajo el gobierno de los virreyes,* p. 70.

62. Ibid., p. 110.

63. Brading, p. 14.

64. Augustín Cue Canovas, *Historia social y económica de México (1521–1854),* p. 134.

65. Villarroel, pp. 107–108.

66. Scardaville, p. 48.

67. Lizardi, *El periquillo sarniento,* Vol. II, pp. 268–269.

68. Scardaville, p. 72.

69. Anna, p. 24.

70. Florescano, p. 139.

71. Humboldt, Vol. I, p. 91.

72. Quoted in Florescano, p. 175.

73. Cooper, pp. 72–75.

74. Florescano, p. 163.

75. Cooper, p. 59.

76. Ibid., p. 73.

77. Ibid., p. 50.

78. Ibid., p. 80.

79. Humboldt, Vol. I, p. 112.

80. Lombardo de Ruíz, ed., *Antología de textos . . . ,* p. 47.

81. Scardaville, pp. 209–211.

82. Kicza, p. 128.

83. Scardaville, p. 226.

84. Villarroel, p. 116.

85. Scardaville, p. ix.

86. Ibid., p. 61.

87. Ibid., p. x.

88. Ibid., p. 248.

89. Lombardo de Ruíz, ed., *Antología de textos . . . ,* p. 70.

90. Quoted in Bobb, p. 93.

91. Christon I. Archer, *The Army in Bourbon Mexico, 1760–1810,* p. 225.

92. María Dolores Morales, "Estructura urbana y distribución de la propiedad en la Ciudad de México en 1813," pp. 363–402.

93. Kicza, p. 101.

94. Quoted in Archer, p. 191.
95. Lizardi, Vol. I, pp. 71–72.
96. Scardaville, pp. 96–101.

ELEVEN
INDEPENDENCE

1. Hamnett, "The Appropriation of Mexican Church Wealth by the Spanish Bourbon Court," p. 85.
2. Romeo Flores Caballero, *Counterrevolution, 1804–1838*, pp. 26–27.
3. Ibid., p. 31.
4. Hamnett, p. 96.
5. Alamán, Vol. V, p. 905.
6. Anna, p. 54.
7. Nancy M. Farriss, *Crown and Clergy in Colonial Mexico, 1759–1821*, p. 198.
8. Hugh M. Hamill, Jr., *The Hidalgo Revolt*, p. 65.
9. Ibid., pp. 69, 78.
10. Ibid., pp. 74–75.
11. Brading, p. 341.
12. Alamán, Vol. I, p. 354.
13. Ibid., Vol. I, pp. 433, 435.
14. Christon I. Archer, "To Serve the King: Military Recruitment in Late Colonial Mexico," pp. 226–250.
15. Quoted in Alamán, Vol. II, p. 210.
16. Quoted in Hamill, p. 149.
17. Quoted in Alamán, Vol. II, Appendix, pp. 22–23.
18. Quoted in Anna, p. 65.
19. Quoted in Lesley B. Simpson, *Many Mexicos*, pp. 216–217.
20. William H. Timmons, *Morelos of Mexico*, p. 21.
21. Timmons, pp. 50–51.
22. Quoted in John Lynch, *The Spanish American Revolutions, 1808–1826*, p. 316.
23. Luís González Obregón, *La vida de México en 1810*, pp. 129–130.
24. Anna, p. 157.
25. Ibid., p. 170.
26. Cooper, p. 158.
27. Quoted in ibid., p. 164.
28. All cases are cited in Anna, pp. 91–93.
29. Genaro García, *Leona Vicario, heroína insurgente*, p. 14.
30. Ibid., p. 60.
31. Ibid., p. 71.

32. Quoted in Ladd, p. 121.
33. William S. Robertson, *Iturbide of Mexico*, p. 34.
34. Alamán, Vol. V, p. 56.
35. Robertson, p. 49.
36. Ibid., p. 77.
37. Ibid., p. 173.

TWELVE
A NATION BETRAYED

1. Guillermo Prieto, *Memorias de mis tiempos, 1828 a 1853*, pp. 183–184.
2. R. H. Mason, *Pictures of Life in Mexico*, Vol. I, p. 14.
3. Miguel S. Macedo, *Mi barrio, segunda mitad del siglo XIX*, p. 25.
4. Prieto, p. 55.
5. Antonio García Cubas, *El libro de mis recuerdos*, pp. 202–206.
6. Frances Erskine Calderón de la Barca, *Life in Mexico During a Residence of Two Years in That Country*, pp. 109–110.
7. García Cubas, pp. 238–239.
8. Ibid., p. 219.
9. Frederick John Shaw, Jr., *Poverty and Politics in Mexico City, 1824–1854*, p. 97.
10. Ibid.
11. Prieto, pp. 323–324.
12. Calderón de la Barca, p. 168.
13. Brantz Mayer, *Mexico As It Was and Is*, p. 41.
14. Calderón de la Barca, p. 369.
15. Ibid., p. 106.
16. Mason, Vol. I, pp. 61–62.
17. Shaw, p. iv.
18. John H. Coatsworth, "Obstacles to Economic Growth in Nineteenth-Century Mexico," p. 82.
19. Shaw, p. 168.
20. Prieto, p. 104.
21. Shaw, p. 158.
22. Ibid., p. 193.
23. Calderón de la Barca, p. 131.
24. Shaw, p. 189.
25. Waddy Thompson, *Recollections of Mexico*, p. 173.
26. Mayer, pp. 268–269.
27. Calderón de la Barca, p. 168–169.
28. Mason, Vol. I, pp. 12–13.
29. Ibid., Vol. I, pp. 43–45.

30. Shaw, p. 295.

31. María Teresa Bisbal Siller, *Los novelistas y la Ciudad de México (1810–1910)*, p. 96.

32. Manuel Payno, *Los bandidos de Río Frío*, Vol. I, pp. 30–43.

33. Ibid., Vol. I, pp. 119–131.

34. Andrés Lira, *Comunidades indígenas frente a la Ciudad de México*, p. 78.

35. Ibid., pp. 139–140.

36. Quoted in ibid., pp. 147–148.

37. Ibid., p. 154.

38. Calderón de la Barca, p. 125.

39. H. G. Ward, *Mexico in 1827*, Vol. II, p. 57.

40. Meyer and Sherman, *The Course of Mexican History*, p. 304.

41. Calderón de la Barca, p. 470.

42. Shaw, pp. 26–27.

43. Ladd, pp. 139, 140, 142.

44. John Tutino, "Hacienda Social Relations in Mexico: The Chalco Region in the Era of Independence," p. 508.

45. Calderón de la Barca, p. 108.

46. Ibid., p. 145.

47. Ibid., p. 423.

48. Ibid., p. 767.

49. Flores Caballero, p. 120.

50. Calderón de la Barca, pp. 176–177.

51. Ibid., p. 133.

52. Ibid., p. 132.

53. García Cubas, p. 241.

54. José Joaquín Fernández de Lizardi, *Don Catrín de la Fachenda*, p. 66.

55. Mason, Vol. I, pp. 95–96.

56. Calderón de la Barca, p. 156.

57. Ibid., p. 287.

58. Ibid., p. 114.

59. This account of Guerrero as a Chalco hacienda owner is drawn from Tutino, "Hacienda Social Relations . . ."

60. Ibid., pp. 511–512.

61. The best account of Manuel Escandón is found in Margarita Urías Hermosillo, "Manuel Escandón: de las diligencias al ferrocarril, 1833–1862," pp. 25–56, in Ciro F. S. Cardoso, ed., *Formación y desarrollo de la burguesía en México, siglo XIX*.

62. Quoted in Urías Hermosillo, pp. 45–46.

63. Coatsworth, "Obstacles to Economic Growth . . . ," p. 82.

64. Michael P. Costeloe, *Church Wealth in Mexico, 1800–1856*, p. 4.

65. Prieto, p. 268.

66. Calderón de la Barca, p. 202.

67. Mason, Vol. I, p. 80.

68. Prieto, pp. 59–61.

69. Ibid., p. 52.

70. Calderón de la Barca, pp. 336–337.

71. Louis de Bellemare (pseudonym for Gabriel Ferry), *Vagabond Life in Mexico*, pp. 34–38.

72. Shaw, p. 256.

73. Ibid., pp. 255–266.

74. Calderón de la Barca, p. 268.

75. Prieto, pp. 340–341.

76. Calderón de la Barca, p. 273.

77. Quoted in Lira, pp. 191–192.

78. Oakah L. Jones, Jr., *Santa Anna*, pp. 27–28.

79. Ibid., pp. 100–102.

80. Calderón de la Barca, p. 177.

81. Ibid., pp. 295, 298, 300.

82. Ibid., p. 314.

83. Quoted in Shaw, p. 349.

THIRTEEN
JUÁREZ AND MAXIMILIAN

1. Quoted in Ralph Roeder, *Juárez and His Mexico*, Vol. I, p. 57.

2. Jan Bazant, *Alienation of Church Wealth in Mexico, 1856–1875*, p. 13.

3. Ibid., p. 7.

4. Coatsworth, "Obstacles to Economic Growth . . . ," p. 90.

5. Quoted in Simpson, *Many Mexicos*, pp. 274–275.

6. Quoted in Robert J. Knowlton, *Church Property and the Mexican Reform, 1856–1910*, p. 71.

7. See, for example, García Cubas, pp. 1–136.

8. Quoted in Bazant, p. 187.

9. Quoted in Roeder, Vol. I, p. 367.

10. Ibid., Vol. I, p. 235.

11. Joan Haslip, *Imperial Adventurer: Emperor Maximilian of Mexico*, p. 122.

12. Ibid., p. 111.

13. Quoted in ibid., p. 125.

14. Quoted in Roeder, Vol. II, pp. 512–513.

15. Quoted in ibid., p. 513.

16. Quoted in ibid., p. 524.

17. Quoted in ibid., p. 531.

18. Ibid., p. 524.

19. Quoted in Haslip, p. 212.

20. Quoted in ibid., p. 162.

21. Roeder, Vol. II, pp. 565–567.

22. Quoted in Haslip, p. 251.

23. Quoted in Roeder, Vol. II, p. 605.

24. Countess Paula Kollonitz, *The Court of Mexico*, pp. 140–142.

25. Ibid., p. 204.

26. Quoted in Haslip, p. 259.

27. Quoted in Egon Corti, *Maximilian and Charlotte of Mexico*, Vol. II, pp. 452–453.

28. Quoted in ibid., Vol. II, pp. 452–453.

29. Ibid., Vol. II, p. 902.

30. Quoted in Haslip, p. 273.

31. Quoted in ibid., p. 376.

32. Corti, Vol. II, pp. 706–711.

33. Haslip, pp. 506–507.

34. Ibid., p. 505.

FOURTEEN

THE MASTER OF MEXICO

1. Paul J. Vanderwood, *Disorder and Progress: Bandits, Police, and Mexican Development*, p. 79.

2. Carleton Beals, *Porfirio Díaz: Dictator of Mexico*, p. 252.

3. García Cubas, p. 201.

4. Edward Dunbar, *The Mexican Papers*, pp. 110–111.

5. Ibid., p. 114.

6. Vanderwood, p. 53.

7. Ibid., pp. 107–108.

8. Charles M. Flandrau, *Viva Mexico*, p. 270.

9. Rosa Eleanor King, *Tempest Over Mexico*, p. 24.

10. Lawrence John Rohlfes, *Police and Penal Correction in Mexico City, 1876–1911: A Study of Order and Progress in Porfirian Mexico*, p. 141.

11. Ibid., p. 25.

12. Julio Guerrero, *La génesis del crimen en México, estudio de psiquiatría social*, p. 172.

13. Rohlfes, pp. 77–78.

14. Flandrau, p. 221.

15. Moisés González Navarro, *El Porfiriato: la vida social*, p. 451, in Daniel Cosío Villegas, ed., *Historia Moderna de México*.

16. Guerrero, p. 381.

17. Beals, p. 315.

17. Beals, p. 315.

18. Rohlfes, pp. 59–62.

19. Vanderwood, pp. 96–98.

20. Rohlfes, p. 327.

21. John Kenneth Turner, *Barbarous Mexico*, p. 67.

22. Braudel, *The Structures of Everyday Life*, p. 424.

23. García Cubas, pp. 197–202.

24. Ibid., p. 202.

25. Gustavo Garza, *El proceso de industrialización en la Ciudad de México, 1821–1970*, pp. 107–108.

26. Rodney D. Anderson, *Outcasts in Their Own Land: Mexican Industrial Workers, 1906–1911*, p. 20.

27. Garza, p.114.

28. Ibid., pp. 120–122.

29. *El Tiempo*, Oct. 21, 1886.

30. *Memoria de las obras del sistema de drenaje profundo del Distrito Federal*, Vol. II, p. 187.

31. Quoted in William D. Raat, "Los intelectuales, el positivismo y la cuestión indigena," p. 419.

32. Quoted in Anderson, p. 37.

33. Quoted in Raat, p. 423.

34. Andrés Molina Enríquez, *Los grandes problemas nacionales*, p. 315.

35. González Navarro, p. 151.

36. Ibid., pp. 150–151.

37. Ibid., pp. 168–173.

38. Quoted in ibid., p. 157.

39. Anderson, p. 236.

40. Quoted in Beals, p. 323.

41. Ethel Brilliana (Mrs. Alec) Tweedie, *Mexico As I Saw It*, p. 237.

42. Ibid., pp. 239–240.

43. Salvador Novo, *Cocina mexicana: Historia gastronómica de la Ciudad de México*, pp. 125–129.

44. Meyer and Sherman, pp. 473–474.

45. King, pp. 34–35.

46. Tweedie, p. 146.

47. González Navarro, p. 486.

48. Ibid., p. 480.

49. Arturo Sotomayor, *México, donde nací: Biografía de una ciudad*, p. 8.

50. *El Tiempo*, Jan. 7, 1900.

51. Quoted in González Navarro, p. 358.

52. *El Tiempo*, April 17, 1906.

53. Quoted in González Navarro, p. 389.

54. Benítez, *La Ciudad de México*, Vol. II, p. 301.

55. Eugen Weber, *France, Fin de Siècle* (Cambridge: Harvard University Press, 1986), p. 60.

56. González Navarro, p. 391.

57. Alberto Pani, *Hygiene in Mexico: A Study of Sanitation and Educational Problems*, pp. 3–7.

58. González Navarro, p. 100.

59. Quoted in Alejandra Moreno Toscano, ed., *Ciudad de México: Ensayo de construcción de una historia*, p. 200.

60. González Navarro, pp. 94–95.

61. Pani, p. 56.

FIFTEEN

REVOLUTION

1. *Pearson's Magazine*, XIX (3), March 1908, p. 242.

2. Quoted in Ramón Eduardo Ruíz, *The Great Rebellion: Mexico 1905–1924*, p. 27.

3. Francisco I. Madero, *La sucesión presidencial en 1910*, p. 23.

4. Stanley R. Ross, *Francisco I. Madero, Apostle of Mexican Democracy*, p. 86.

5. Frederick Starr, *Mexico and the United States*, pp. 289–290.

6. Jesús Silva Herzog, *Una vida en la vida de México*.

7. Luz Jiménez, *Life and Death in Milpa Alta*, trans. and edited by Fernando Horcasitas, p. 111.

8. Ross, p. 31.

9. John Womack, Jr., *Zapata and the Mexican Revolution*, p. 49.

10. Tweedie, pp. 338–341.

11. King, p. 37.

12. Ibid., pp. 37–38.

13. Ibid., p. 39.

14. Womack, p. 45.

15. Ibid., p. 51.

16. King, p. 35.

17. Womack, p. 9.

18. Ibid., p. 7.

19. King, p. 4.

20. Womack, p. 142.

21. King, p. 67.

22. Ibid., p. 87.

23. Ibid., p. 93.

24. Ibid., p. 90.

25. Jorge Prieto Laurens, *Cincuenta años de política mexicana, memorias políticas*, p. 17.

26. Quoted in Ross, p. 233.

27. Ibid., p. 239.

28. King, p. 106.

29. Benítez, *La Ciudad de México*, Vol. III, p. 26.

30. Quoted in Wilkie, James W., and Edna Monzón de Wilkie, eds., *México visto en el siglo XX: Entrevistas de historia oral*, p. 26.

31. Ibid., p. 240.

32. Ross, p. 293.

33. Henry Lane Wilson, *Diplomatic Episodes in Mexico, Belgium and Chile*, pp. 257–258.

34. Manuel Márquez Sterling, *Los últimos días del Presidente Madero*, pp. 415–416.

35. Wilson, pp. 266–267.

36. Márquez Sterling, p. 448.

37. Quoted in Ross, p. 307.

38. Márquez Sterling, pp. 471–477.

39. From an account provided by one of the participants, quoted in Alfonso Taracena, *Madero: Vida del hombre y del político*, pp. 597–600.

40. Quoted in Ernest Gruening, *Mexico and Its Heritage*, p. 569.

41. Ibid., p. 571.

42. Ibid., p. 569.

43. Quoted in ibid., p. 570.

44. Testimony from the chauffeurs, in Calixto Maldonado R., *Los asesinatos de los Señores Madero y Pino Suárez*, pp. 10–12.

45. Quoted in Gruening, p. 573.

46. Wilson, p. 286.

47. Michael C. Meyer, *Huerta: A Political Portrait*, pp. 99–100.

48. Francisco Ramírez Plancarte, *La Ciudad de México durante la revolución constitucionalista*, p. 53.

49. Prieto Laurens, p. 22.

50. Robert E. Quirk, *The Mexican Revolution and the Catholic Church, 1910–1929*, p. 38.

51. Womack, p. 165.

52. King, pp. 93–94.

53. Ibid., p. 228.

54. Quoted in Quirk, pp. 42–43.

55. Ibid., pp. 51–56.

56. Edith O'Shaughnessy, *A Diplomat's Wife in Mexico*, p. 48.

57. Douglas W. Richmond, *Venustiano Carranza's Nationalist Struggle 1893–1920*, p. 25.

58. Quoted in Ramírez Plancarte, pp. 65–66.

59. Ibid., pp. 241–251.

60. Womack, p. 219.

61. Ibid., p. 221.

62. Ramírez Plancarte, pp. 291–292.

63. Ibid., p. 297.

64. Ibid., pp. 366–367, 423–427, 539–540.

65. Ibid., p. 398.

66. Quirk, pp. 75–77.

67. Linda B. Hall, *Alvaro Obregón: Power and Revolution in Mexico, 1911–1920*, pp. 134–135.

68. King, pp. 245–246.

69. Ibid., pp. 294–298.

70. Ibid., p. 307.

71. Richmond, p. 170.

72. Quoted in Womack, p. 326.

73. Ibid., p. 372.

74. Ramón Beteta, quoted in Wilkie and Wilkie, eds., p. 3.

75. Quoted in Hall, p. 247.

76. Octavio Paz, *The Labyrinth of Solitude*, trans. by L. Kemp, p. 149.

77. Mariano Azuela, *The Underdogs*, trans. by E. Munguía, Jr., p. 147.

SIXTEEN

REVOLUTIONARY ART, CAUTIOUS POLITICS

1. Bertram D. Wolfe, *The Fabulous Life of Diego Rivera*, p. 8.

2. Quoted in ibid., p. 107.

3. Diego Rivera, *Mi arte, mi vida*, p. 97.

4. Ibid., p. 97.

5. Ruíz, pp. 314, 181.

6. Womack, p. 354.

7. Quoted in Ruíz, pp. 377–378.

8. Ibid., p. 171.

9. William Weber Johnson, *Heroic Mexico*, p. 366.

10. Prieto Laurens, p. 158.

11. Andrés Iduarte, *Niño, Child of the Mexican Revolution*, trans. and adapted by James F. Shearer, pp. 119, 121–122.

12. Quoted in Jean Charlot, *The Mexican Mural Renaissance, 1920–1925*, pp. 133–134.

13. Quoted in ibid., p. 243.

14. Rivera, pp. 107–108.

15. Charlot, p. 244.

16. Wolfe, p. 153.

17. José Clemente Orozco, *Autobiografía*, pp. 77–78.

18. Quoted in Charlot, p. 222.

19. Rivera, p. 38.
20. Ibid., pp. 26–27.
21. Hayden Herrera, *Frida, A Biography of Frida Kahlo*, p. 85.
22. Alma Reed, *Orozco*, p. 9.
23. Charlot, p. 152.
24. Quoted in ibid., p. 301.
25. Wolfe, p. 211.
26. David C. Bailey, *Viva Cristo Rey: The Cristero Rebellion and the Church-State Conflict in Mexico*, p. 61.
27. Quirk, p. 155.
28. Quoted in ibid., p. 173.
29. Ibid., pp. 174–175.
30. Bailey, pp. 167–168.
31. Quoted in ibid., p. 169.
32. Toral's story is drawn mainly from *El juzgado de Toral y la Madre Conchita*, stenographic text, 2 vols., Archivo General de la Nación. Also, John W. Dulles, *Yesterday in Mexico*, and Hernán Robleto, *Obregón, Toral y la Madre Conchita*.
33. Quoted in Dulles, p. 371.
34. Quoted in ibid., p. 376.
35. Wolfe, p. 325.
36. Quoted in ibid., pp. 328–329.
37. Fernando Benítez, *Lázaro Cárdenas y la Revolución mexicana*, Vol. II, pp. 245–246.
38. William C. Townsend, *Lázaro Cárdenas, Mexican Democrat*, pp. 103–104.
39. Ibid., p. 104.
40. Joe C. Ashby, *Organized Labor and the Mexican Revolution Under Cárdenas*, p. 25.
41. Quoted in ibid., p. 27.
42. Benítez, *Lázaro Cárdenas . . .*, Vol. III, p. 46.
43. Frank Tannenbaum, *Mexico: The Struggle for Peace and Bread*, p. 114.
44. Johnson, p. 420.
45. Wolfe, p. 7.

SEVENTEEN

THE GOLDEN DECADES

1. Roderic Ai Camp, "Education and Political Recruitment in Mexico: The Alemán Generation," p. 302.
2. Peter H. Smith, *Labyrinths of Power*, p. 130.

3. Roderic Ai Camp, *Intellectuals and the State in Twentieth-Century Mexico*, pp. 20–21.

4. Braulio Maldonado, *Baja California: Comentarios políticos*, pp. 14–15.

5. Roger D. Hansen, *The Politics of Development in Mexico*, p. 42.

6. Garza, p. 142.

7. Flavia Derossi, *The Mexican Entrepreneur*, p. 101.

8. Quoted in Wilkie and Wilkie, eds., p. 67.

9. Ibid., p. 69.

10. Gustavo Garza and Martha Schteingart, "Mexico City: The Emerging Megalopolis," pp. 72–73.

11. Smith, p. 164.

12. Derossi, pp. 182–186.

13. Irma Serrano and Elisa Robledo, *A calzón amarrado*.

14. Ibid., p. 98.

15. Ibid., p. 101.

16. Ibid., pp. 107–108.

17. Ibid., p. 108.

18. Ibid., p. 110.

19. Ibid., p. 138.

20. Ibid., p. 139.

21. Ibid., p. 183–184.

22. Ibid., pp. 149–150, loosely translated by the author.

23. Ibid., p. 151.

24. Ibid., p. 249.

25. Wayne A. Cornelius, *Politics and the Migrant Poor in Mexico City*, p. 17.

26. O. Oldman, et al., *Financing Urban Development in Mexico City*, p. 21.

27. Hansen, pp. 72–73.

28. Oscar Lewis, *The Children of Sánchez*.

29. Ibid., pp. xvi–xvii.

30. Ibid., pp. 58–59.

31. Ibid., p. 267.

32. Quirk, p. 4.

33. The account that follows is drawn from Evelyn P. Stevens, *Protest and Response in Mexico*, and Jesús Topete, *Terror en el riel de El Charro a Vallejo*.

34. Stevens, p. 105.

35. Quoted in Smith, p. 263.

36. Alan Riding, *Distant Neighbors: A Portrait of the Mexicans*, p. 184.

37. Quoted in Stevens, p. 55.

38. Quoted in ibid., p. 32.

39. Roderic Ai Camp, *Mexico's Leaders: Their Education and Recruitment*, p. 168.

40. Stevens, pp. 188–189.

41. Quoted in ibid., p. 203.

42. Ibid., p. 204.

43. Witnessed by the author.

44. Quoted in Stevens, p. 220.

45. Ibid., p. 224.

46. Ibid., p. 228.

47. Donald Mabry, *The Mexican University and the State: Student Conflicts, UNAM Students, 1910–1971*, p. 261.

48. The following description is drawn from Stevens; Mabry; Elena Poniatowska, *La noche de Tlatelolco*; and Ramón Ramírez, *El movimiento estudiantíl de México: Julio–diciembre de 1968*.

49. Stevens, p. 238.

50. Octovio Paz, *The Other Mexico: Critique of the Pyramid*, trans. by L. Kemp, pp. 12–13.

EIGHTEEN
MEGALOPOLIS

1. Camp, *Intellectuals and the State* . . . , p. 18.

2. Riding, p. 300.

3. Ibid., p. 103.

4. Smith, p. 281.

5. Ibid.

6. Merilee Grindle, "Patrons and Clients in the Bureaucracy: Career Networks in Mexico."

7. Ibid., p. 52.

8. José González G., *Lo negro del Negro Durazo*.

9. Ibid., p. 46.

10. Ibid., pp. 190–193.

11. Ibid., p. 17.

12. Ibid., pp. 124, 212–213.

13. Ibid., pp. 204–210.

14. Ibid., pp. 131–137.

15. Ibid., p. 183.

16. Ibid., pp. 185–187.

17. Gustavo Garza in interview with author, September 1985.

18. *Wall Street Journal*, Oct. 4, 1985, p. 8.

19. Quoted in ibid.

20. Francisco Calderón in interview with author, September 1985.

21. Ibid.

22. Ibid.

23. Alfredo Sandoval González in interview with author, September 1985.

24. Based on interviews conducted by author between 1984 and 1987.

25. The following portrait of Gutiérrez and his garbage empire is drawn largely from Hector F. Castillo Berthier, *La sociedad de la basura: Caciquismo en la Ciudad de México.*

26. Ibid., p. 9.

27. Ibid., p. 135.

28. Ibid., p. 64.

29. Ibid., p. 88.

30. Ibid., p. 89.

31. His account was reported in *Uno más uno,* and reproduced in a summary report on the earthquake published by that newspaper under the title *19 de septiembre* (Mexico: Editorial Uno, 1985).

32. His account is taken from the newspaper *El Universal,* Sept. 24, 1985.

33. Fernando Marti, et al., *El Temblor* (Mexico: Almanaque de México, 1985), pp. 29–30.

34. Interview with the author, September 1985.

35. *19 de septiembre,* p. 46.

36. See "Engineering Aspects of the September 19, 1985, Mexico Earthquake," Washington, D.C.: National Bureau of Standards, U.S. Department of Commerce, 1987.

37. *Anales de Cuauhtitlán,* p. 10.

INDEX

U

ABOUT THE AUTHOR

JONATHAN KANDELL grew up in Mexico City and is attuned to the language, culture, history, and geography about which he writes in this book. He covered Latin America for five years for *The New York Times*, and for his reporting of every type of story he won the Maria Moors Cabot Award. He was also the recipient of the Edward R. Murrow Fellowship awarded by the Council on Foreign Relations. His previous book was *Passage Through El Dorado*. He now resides in New York City and is assistant foreign editor of *The Wall Street Journal*.